BARRON'S

AP

WORLD HISTORY

3RD EDITION

John McCannon, Ph.D.
Department of History
University of Saskatchewan
Saskatoon, Saskatchewan, Canada

BARRON'S

ABOUT THE AUTHOR

John McCannon earned a Ph.D. in history from the University of Chicago in 1994. He has taught Russian history, modern European history, and world history at several universities in the United States and Canada, and he has worked as an Advanced Placement faculty consultant for the College Board. He is the author of *Red Arctic: Polar Exploration and The Myth of the North in the Soviet Union, 1932–1939*. Professor McCannon is now a faculty member in the Department of History at the University of Saskatchewan; he also serves as editor-in-chief of the *Canadian Journal of History*.

ABOUT THE CONTRIBUTOR

Pamela Jordan received a Ph.D. in political science from the University of Toronto in 1997. In addition to her academic background, she has worked as a news writer for Facts on File News Services, Inc., and as executive director of a non-governmental organization affiliated with the United Nations. Dr. Jordan is a faculty member in the Department of History at the University of Saskatchewan, as well as the author of *Defending Rights in Russia: Lawyers, the State, and Legal Reform in the Post-Soviet Era*.

ACKNOWLEDGMENTS

This book is dedicated to Pamela Jordan, a co-author in every sense of the word. Without her formidable research skills, her invaluable written contributions to the manuscript, and her sharp editorial eye, this book could never have come into being.

Both the author and contributor would like to thank David Rodman and Anna Damaskos, whose editorial supervision made the preparation of this manuscript a smooth and easy process. We are also grateful to Bill Kuchler for art direction, to Debby Becak for production assistance, and to the anonymous reviewers of this manuscript for their insightful and encouraging comments.

All inquiries should be addressed to:
Barron's Educational Series, Inc.
250 Wireless Boulevard
Hauppauge, New York 11788
www.barronseduc.com

ISBN-13 (book only): 978-0-7641-3822-5
ISBN-10 (book only): 0-7641-3822-7

ISBN-13 (book w/CD-ROM): 978-0-7641-9403-0
ISBN-10 (book w/CD-ROM): 0-7641-9403-8

International Standard Serial Number: 1937-8874

PRINTED IN THE UNITED STATES OF AMERICA

9 8 7 6 5 4 3 2 1

Contents

UNIT SIX: THE TWENTIETH CENTURY AND CONTEMPORARY WORLD CULTURES (1914–PRESENT)

UNIT ONE

INTRODUCTION

How to Use This Book

TO TEACHERS AND STUDENTS

This book can be a useful supplement to classwork and study materials. For readers who are not taking—or have never taken—a course in world history, this volume can serve as an independent study aid. Ideally, however, this book will be used in conjunction with an actual academic course in world history, or by students who have taken such a course and are attempting to review.

Unit One offers strategies that students may find useful in approaching the various types of questions they will encounter on the Advanced Placement Examination in World History. These include multiple-choice questions, the document-based essay question, the change-over-time essay question, and the comparative essay question.

Units Two through Six contain review chapters. Each unit is dedicated to one of the major historical periods covered by the exam. There are five to eight chapters within each unit. Each chapter deals with a major geographical area or historical topic. Every chapter is followed by a set of 10 multiple-choice questions; these will allow students to review material immediately after having read it. Each unit is preceded by a historical overview. A major review section, consisting of 20 multiple-choice questions and four essay questions, follows each of these five units.

TO THE TEACHER

The review chapters contained within this book can be used as supplements to summarize or reinforce particular teaching units and classroom or homework assignments. Unit overviews and chapter introductions assist students in looking at historical events from a broad perspective. The unit overviews also strive to place historical events and developments in the comparative context that the World History exam emphasizes. The multiple-choice questions at the end of each chapter and each unit focus the learning.

The sample examinations in Unit Seven can be used near the end of the academic year as a culmination of a world history course. The sample exams also serve as good practice for the actual Advanced Placement exam.

Unit One should be covered with students at the beginning of a world history course and then at several points afterward. The sooner students are familiar with the structure of the Advanced Placement Examination in World History, as well as the examination's procedures, the more comfortable they will be with the exam process itself.

TO THE STUDENT

This book can be used as an independent review device, whether or not you are taking an Advanced Placement course in world history. Even for those who have never taken an academic or Advanced Placement course in world history, this book can prove helpful. It is optimal, however, if you are using this book while taking a course in world history, or if you have taken a world history course in the past and are using this book as a refresher.

It is best to use this book over a long period of time, rather than trying to cram at the last minute. You will want to absorb information and ideas slowly and thoroughly.

At the beginning, read Unit One, on the structure of the Advanced Placement exam and the types of questions asked by it. To do well on the Advanced Placement exam, it is crucial to know the procedure and follow directions closely. The sooner you acquaint yourself with the rules and procedures, the more natural they will feel when you take the actual test.

Also pay special attention to unit overviews and chapter introductions. These will help you to see world history from a "big picture" perspective. They place trends and facts in a comparative context. Your ability to compare and contrast different eras and parts of the world will be tested extensively by the Advanced Placement exam.

SUGGESTED TIMELINES

How you use this book will largely depend on how much time you have to prepare. The more time, the better. Three possible timelines are provided; adapt as necessary to your own situation and abilities.

7-DAY TIMELINE

With such limited time, it is best to concentrate on test-taking methods and big-picture issues.

Day 1: Read Sections B through G of Unit One carefully. Take one of the model exams in Unit Seven to get a sense of how ready you are.

Day 2: Read Unit Two. Read ALL the overviews for Units Two through Six.

Day 3: Read Unit Three. Again, read all the unit overviews.

Day 4: Read Unit Four. Read all unit overviews.

Day 5: Read Unit Five. Read all unit overviews.

Day 6: Read Unit Six. Read all unit overviews.

Day 7: Review Unit One. Take the second model exam in Unit Seven.

4-WEEK TIMELINE

Having roughly a month to prepare will allow you some time to examine topics in depth, in addition to focusing on essentials.

Week 1: Read Sections B through G of Unit One to get a sense of how the AP exam works. Move on to study Unit Two.

Week 2: Study Units Three and Four.

Week 3: Study Units Five and Six.

Week 4: Take the model exams in Unit Seven. Review Unit One about the exam itself, as well as the overviews for Units Two through Six.

SCHOOL-YEAR (9-MONTH) TIMELINE

This is the ideal scenario. Here, you are likely using this book as a supplement to a world history course. If so, you should probably proceed at the same pace and in the same order as your teacher and classmates. Otherwise, the following will give you a good grounding.

Month 1: Read Unit One. Study Unit Two.

Month 2: Review Unit Two. Study Unit Three.

Month 3: Review Unit Three. Study Unit Four.

Month 4: Review Unit Four. Study Unit Five.

Month 5: Review Unit Five. Study Unit Six.

Month 6: Review Unit Six. Take the model exams in Unit Seven. Assess your strengths and weaknesses.

Month 7: Skim Units Two through Six, focusing on weak points. Use the unit overviews to help you think about comparisons.

Month 8: Continue reviewing the unit overviews. Reread Unit One carefully.

Month 9: Review as needed. Skim unit overviews and Unit One a final time.

GENERAL NOTES

Dates are given according to the standard Western calendar, with one exception. The abbreviations B.C.E. ("before common era") and C.E. ("common era") are used, rather than the traditional B.C. ("before Christ") and A.D. (*anno domini,* or "year of our Lord"). This usage shows more respect to those world cultures whose traditions are not based on Christianity. It should be noted that the Western calendar is only one of many systems used for measuring time. According to the Hebrew calendar, for example, year 1 is the equivalent of 3760 B.C.E. Year 1 of the Muslim calendar, by contrast, is 622 C.E.

Dates with no designation—those that appear simply as numerals—are assumed to be C.E.

Names and terms from a variety of languages are used throughout this book. Many, such as Russian, Chinese, Arabic, Japanese, and Hebrew, use different alphabets, rather than the Latin script used by English speakers. There is no single way of transliterating, or converting, one alphabet to another.

When referring to people or terms transliterated from non-Latin scripts, this book will try to use versions that are both linguistically accurate and easily recognizable. Students should be aware that there are several variants of certain well-known names and terms. For example, Genghis Khan versus Chinggis Khan (or Jenghiz Khan), Mao Tse-tung versus Mao Zedong, Mohammed versus Muhammad, or Sundiata versus Son-Jara. Students may encounter some or all of these different versions in different textbooks and readings.

The Advanced Placement Examination in World History: An Overview

FORMAT

The Advanced Placement exam lasts a total of 3 hours and 5 minutes.

Students are allowed 55 minutes in order to complete 70 multiple-choice questions.

For the completion of the free-response, or essay, section of the examination, 130 minutes are allotted. This section of the test consists of the following types of questions:

- *Document-based question (DBQ):* Roughly 50 minutes, including a mandatory period of 10 minutes to read and select documents.
- *Change-over-time essay question (COT):* Roughly 40 minutes, devoted to a thematic essay touching on at least two of the time periods covered in the exam.
- *Comparative essay question:* Roughly 40 minutes given to a question focusing on broad issues and dealing with at least two societies.

The free-response portion of the exam begins with a 10-minute document-reading period. During this time, students may make notes on the document sheets, but they are not be allowed to work on actual essays. Once the document-reading period is over, for each of the essay questions, it is recommended that students spend 5 or so minutes planning their answers.

GRADING

Grades for the Advanced Placement Examination in World History are calculated as follows:

- The 70 multiple-choice questions: one half of the total raw score (60 out of 120 possible points).
- The 3 free-response questions: one half of the total raw score. Each essay receives a grade of 0 (the worst) to 9 (the best). A complex formula converts

the total of 0 to 27 to a raw score of 0 to 60. This is added to the raw multiple-choice score, for a total of 0 to 120.

Another calculation converts the 0–120 raw score to a standard score of 1 through 5. This is the number students will see at the end. The higher the number, the better. Scores can be interpreted as follows:

5: Extremely well qualified. Accepted by the majority of colleges and universities for some kind of academic credit or benefit. Earned by roughly 10 percent of the students.

4: Well qualified. Accepted by many colleges and universities for some kind of academic credit or benefit. Earned by roughly 18 percent of students.

3: Qualified. Accepted by many colleges and universities for some kind of academic credit or benefit, but often of a limited nature. Earned by roughly 30 percent of students.

2: Possibly qualified. Accepted by a few colleges and universities for credit or benefit, generally quite limited. Earned by roughly 24 percent of students.

1: No recommendation. Not accepted anywhere. Earned by roughly 18 percent of students.

Universities and colleges have different policies regarding Advanced Placement exams. Students should contact the school of their choice to determine what benefit, if any, a particular score will give them.

TIME FRAME

The Advanced Placement Examination in World History focuses on global developments between 8000 B.C.E. and the present. The percentage of questions pertaining to each era is approximately as follows:

- Foundations period (prehistory to 600 C.E.): 19–20 percent of questions
- 600 to 1450: 22 percent of questions
- 1450 to 1750: 19–20 percent of questions
- 1750 to 1914: 19–20 percent of questions
- 1914 to the present: 19–20 percent of questions

THEMES

By its nature, the Advanced Placement World History exam is extremely broad in scope. It seeks to test students not merely on their ability to memorize information but on their critical and interpretive skills, as well as their ability to examine and analyze historical issues from a "big-picture" perspective. Both multiple-choice and free-response questions will emphasize social, economic, and cultural trends; issues of gender and ethnic identity; interrelationships and exchanges among various civilizations; and the ability to compare different historical eras and societies.

Topics such as battles, the lives of monarchs and political leaders, and the careers of individual "great figures" will receive some coverage, but less than on traditional history exams. It will be necessary to place such events, lives, and careers in their broader political, economic, cultural, and social contexts.

A note about coverage of European and United States history: One of the declared purposes of the AP world history course is to focus more attention on areas of the world other than Europe and North America. No more than 30 percent of the questions (multiple-choice or free-response) will cover topics in European history. The United States will be included only as part of topics that are global or comparative in nature, such as colonization, foreign affairs, and the globalization of trade and culture. There will be no coverage of the internal politics of the United States.

The six overarching themes outlined formally by the Advanced Placement world history course are as follows. These themes are intended to assist students in focusing their study efforts in a way that enables them to analyze broad trends and make insightful comparisons across time and place.

- The impact of interaction among major societies. Interaction can take many forms, including trade, war, and diplomacy.
- The relationship of change and continuity within periods of world history, as well as between different historical periods.
- The impact of technology and demography on people and the environment. Such issues might touch on population growth and decline, disease, manufacturing, migrations, agriculture, and weaponry.
- Systems of social organization and gender structure. Who has power and status? What is the place of minority populations? How are women and men treated by various societies and at different times?
- Intellectual and cultural developments and interactions among and within societies. How do art, literature, ideas, and religions affect societies and individuals?
- Changes over time in the functions and structures of states. This includes discussion of various types of political organization, principally the nation-state.

HABITS OF MIND

One of the declared purposes of the Advanced Placement world history course is to develop "habits of mind" or skills. Being aware of these will help students anticipate what they will be expected to do on the actual exam. The "habits of mind" are as follows:

- The construction and evaluation of arguments.
- The analysis of documents, data, and primary material.
- The assessment of continuity and change over time.
- The analysis of differing interpretations, biases, and perspectives.
- The perception and understanding of global patterns across geographic space and over time.
- The ability to compare different societies and their reactions to global processes.
- A sensitivity to the common denominators and differences that unite and divide human communities, and awareness of the historical context of ideas, beliefs, and values.

Multiple-Choice Question Strategies

The Advanced Placement Examination in World History will require you to answer 70 multiple-choice questions. Each question will have five answer choices. Your goal is to pick the one answer that BEST responds to the question.

You will be given 55 minutes to complete this section of the test.

Multiple-choice questions will cover political-diplomatic topics, economic and social topics, and intellectual and cultural topics. The percentage of questions devoted to each historical period will be roughly the same as that described in Unit One, Section B (foundations period, 19–20 percent; 600–1450, 22 percent; 1450–1750, 19–20 percent; 1750–1914, 19–20 percent; 1914–present, 19–20 percent).

As a general rule, you must answer 50 percent of the multiple-choice questions correctly in order to qualify for an overall score of 3 ("qualified"). This assumes that you complete the free-response (essay) portions of the exam acceptably. You receive a point for each correct answer. If you answer a question incorrectly, you lose one fourth of a point. If you skip a question altogether, leaving it blank, you lose no points, but you gain nothing, either.

TIPS FOR THE MULTIPLE-CHOICE QUESTIONS

There are a number of guidelines to keep in mind when taking the multiple-choice section of the Advanced Placement exam. They are as follows:

- *Remember that you are looking for the BEST answer to the question.* Read the question carefully. On occasion, there may seem to be more than one acceptable answer. If so, is the question calling for the "most important"? Or "most influential"? Or some other qualifying factor? For example, a question asking you to choose the IMMEDIATE cause of World War I might give you a choice among "the assassination of the Archduke Francis Ferdinand," "the Anglo-German naval race," and "competition over colonies in Africa." All three factors helped cause World War I. But because the question asks for the most immediate cause, the BEST answer is "the assassination of Archduke Francis Ferdinand." The other two responses deal with long-term causes.
- *Be aware that some questions include the answers "none of the above" and "all of the above."* If either is one of the responses, you must evaluate all the others carefully. "None of the above" prevents you from making vague guesses. "All of the above" keeps you from settling for the most obviously correct answer. If you can determine that a second answer is also correct, then you are fairly safe in assuming that "all of the above" is the right response (although you should check the other two answers as well).
- *Do not make too many wild guesses.* Remember that you are penalized one-fourth of a point for every incorrect answer, but nothing for a question left blank. You may lose more points due to wrong answers than you gain by blind guessing.

- *Do not leave too many questions blank.* This statement may seem like a contradiction of the previous point, but you must also remember that not answering a question means giving up the opportunity to gain points. A good rule of thumb is that if you can narrow the number of likely answers to two, you should pick one of them, even if you are not sure.

- *Read the question and all 5 answer choices twice.* Skim once for a general sense, then read again for details. Questions asking what is NOT true (and, similarly, "except" questions) reverse the normal logic by giving four "correct" answers and one that is "incorrect" but actually the right choice. Careful reading will help you keep this straight.

- *Start by eliminating obviously incorrect answers.* This step will help you focus your attention on the two or three possibly correct answers. If you eliminate any answers at all, and one of the responses is "all of the above," then you have really eliminated two answers, because "all of the above" obviously cannot be correct if one of the other responses is wrong.

- *Beware of statements and answers containing the words* always *and* never. Such absolute statements are almost always incorrect (note the use of the word *almost* here). You should feel secure in eliminating such answers right away. Look for answers that contain the phrases *frequently, most often, generally*, and so on.

- *Trust your intuition—up to a point.* Most teachers and exam-preparation specialists say that your first choice is generally the correct one. If you have read the question and the answers carefully, you should probably stick with your first choice, unless you have a specific, concrete reason for changing your mind. On the other hand, this rule of thumb should not be used as an excuse for lazy reading or sloppy thinking. Do not make your first choice until you have read and thought about the question and answers carefully.

TYPES OF MULTIPLE-CHOICE QUESTIONS

There are many types of multiple-choice questions, each of which attempts to test a different skill or "habit of mind." A list of the major types would include the following:

- Identification
- Analytical
- Quotation-based
- Image interpretation
- Map-based
- Graph and chart identification

Identification Questions

Identification questions test your mastery of information and command of facts. Some are quite simple: You either know the fact the question is based on, or you do not. Who did what? Which religion or philosophy does a certain principle belong to? What happened when? Other identification questions are more complicated, with some analysis mixed in.

Of the multiple-choice questions offered on the Advanced Placement exam, about 35 to 40 percent are likely to be of the identification type.

1. Which Chinese emperor cemented the Qing dynasty's position by issuing effective laws and using Confucianism to increase respect for political authority?

   (A) Yuan Shikai
   (B) Kangxi
   (C) Hong Xiuquan
   (D) Sun Yat-sen
   (E) Yongle

2. This city became one of West Africa's greatest centers of trade and Islamic scholarship from the thirteenth to the fifteenth centuries.

   (A) Timbuktu
   (B) Zimbabwe
   (C) Mogadishu
   (D) Zanzibar
   (E) Mombasa

3. Which of the following would best fit in with the beliefs of a practicing Buddhist?

   (A) Justice should be based on the principle of an eye for an eye, a tooth for a tooth.
   (B) Each individual should place trust in a personal savior in order to ensure a place in heaven.
   (C) At the end of the world, God will judge all sinners and condemn them to eternal torment.
   (D) Yogic discipline and mastery of the body helps to improve the quality of one's spirit.
   (E) People are born and reborn into lives of suffering but can escape this cycle by attaining enlightenment.

ANSWERS: 1. **B** 2. **A** 3. **E**

The first two questions are pure identification. They require only that you know a specific fact. The third question is more analytical, in that you must think about the basic tenets of Buddhism. It still boils down to a slightly complicated way of asking you to pick one correct "fact."

Analytical Questions

Analytical questions are more complicated than identification questions. Rather than simply testing your factual knowledge, they require you to think about historical relationships, to understand cause and effect, to place events and developments in proper chronological order, and to ponder more abstract points.

Approximately 20 to 25 percent of the multiple-choice section of the examination is made up of analytical questions.

1. Which of the following is NOT true of most human societies during the Stone Age?

   (A) Despite limitations on their technological aptitude, Stone Age humans designed many innovative and clever tools.
   (B) Biological differences between men and women gave rise to a gender division of labor in most Stone Age societies.
   (C) Human beings tended to be more aggressive during the Stone Age than during later periods in history.
   (D) Human beings settled North and South America later than they did Africa, Asia, and Europe.
   (E) Human societies developed complex forms of tribal organization, religious ritual, and oral traditions during the Stone Age.

2. Which of the following can be attributed to World War II?

   I. In many Western nations, such as Great Britain and the United States, women received the vote shortly after the war.
   II. Late in the war, the United States took the lead in creating an international system of rules and agencies to foster free trade after the war.
   III. The war dramatically reduced Europe's global influence, making it difficult for nations such as Great Britain and France to retain control over their empires.
   IV. The war concentrated strategic might and economic power in the hands of the United States and the Soviet Union, which were now superpowers.

   (A) I, II, and III
   (B) II and III
   (C) I, III, and IV
   (D) II, III, and IV
   (E) all of the above

3. Which of the following lists is in the correct chronological order?

(A) the calling of the Estates General, the storming of the Bastille, the execution of Louis XVI, the Declaration of the Rights of Man and the Citizen

(B) the calling of the Estates General, the storming of the Bastille, the Declaration of the Rights of Man and the Citizen, the execution of Louis XVI

(C) the storming of the Bastille, the calling of the Estates General, the Declaration of the Rights of Man and the Citizen, the execution of Louis XVI

(D) the Declaration of the Rights of Man and the Citizen, the storming of the Bastille, the execution of Louis XVI, the calling of the Estates General

(E) none of the above

ANSWERS: 1. **C**   2. **D**   3. **B**

Quotation-Based Questions

This type of question is comparatively rare. Only 10 percent or less of multiple-choice questions will be of this sort. You will be required to read a short quotation about an event, person, or phenomenon. You will then choose which answer best relates to the quotation.

1. "A fierce conqueror, he is often perceived in the West as a vicious barbarian. But while this warlord and his horseback warriors were, in the beginning, primitive, they proved surprisingly capable, by means of cultural borrowing, of developing a legal system, bureaucracy, and communications system suitable for governing vast stretches of Eurasia for decades."

The individual referred to in this quotation is

(A) Xerxes I.
(B) Genghis Khan.
(C) Mehmet II.
(D) Oda Nobunaga.
(E) Abbas the Great.

ANSWER: 1. **B**

Image Interpretation

A few questions will ask you to identify or interpret images. These may include paintings, cartoons, photographs, architectural works, or other artworks. You may be asked to determine the message or purpose of the image, or you may be required to identify the artist who created it, the movement it belongs to, or the civilization it comes from.

Less than 10 percent of multiple-choice questions will be of this type.

1. The sculpture pictured is most likely

   (A) a personal likeness commissioned by a wealthy patron.
   (B) an example of Asian influence on Western art.
   (C) an experiment in modernist abstraction.
   (D) a ritual object with religious significance crafted in Africa.
   (E) an artistic protest against the dehumanizing effects on women caused by male domination.

ANSWER: 1. D

Map-Based Questions

Some questions will require you to use map-reading skills. Map-related questions typically fall into two categories. One will ask you to identify what the map depicts. The other will ask you to analyze the map and draw conclusions from the information contained on it.

In either case, map questions require fairly basic skills and general knowledge. They present an excellent chance to gain points.

Less than 10 percent of multiple-choice questions will be map-based.

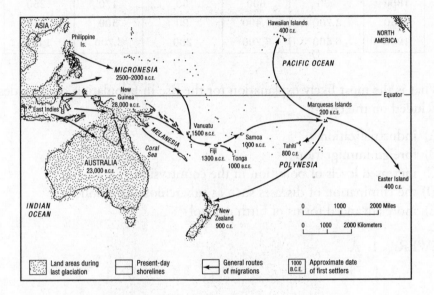

1. What historical development does the map depict?

   (A) the expansion of Chinese trade routes
   (B) James Cook's voyages of discovery
   (C) Japan's military assault on the South Pacific
   (D) Thor Heyerdahl's *Kon-Tiki* expedition
   (E) the migration of Polynesian peoples throughout the Pacific

ANSWER: 1. **E**

Graph and Chart Interpretation

A number of questions will make use of graphs and charts. The information needed to answer the question is generally contained within the chart or graph.

Less than 10 percent of questions will be of this type.

Year	Cities (Pop. in thousands)				
	London	Paris	Antwerp	Berlin	Moscow
1800	960	600	60	170	250
1850	2,700	1,400	90	500	360
1900	6,500	3,700	280	2,700	1,000

1. What is the most likely explanation for the rise in population of the cities included on the chart?

    (A) industrialization
    (B) foreign immigration
    (C) increased levels of pollution in the countryside
    (D) the elimination of diseases such as tuberculosis and polio
    (E) more advanced forms of birth control

ANSWER: 1. **A**

Free-Response (Essay) Questions: General Tips

The free-response section of the Advanced Placement Examination in World History lasts 130 minutes. During this time, you will be required to write three essays: a document-based question (DBQ), a change-over-time (COT) question, and a comparative essay.

Once the 10-minute document-reading period is over, you can write the essays in whichever order you like. The essay you SHOULD write first is the DBQ. For one thing, the documents will be fresh in your mind. Also, the DBQ is the most complicated essay you will write, and it will be good to have it out of the way first. This section outlines general tips for successful essay writing.

APPROACHING THE ESSAYS

Unlike the multiple-choice questions, which are graded by machine, the written portions of AP examinations are evaluated by hand. To mark the written portions of the examinations given in each subject area, several hundred high-school teachers and university professors gather in June, generally on a college campus, for about a week.

In that time, an AP reader is likely to mark several hundred essays. He or she is careful and well-trained. Still, because your reader will be looking over so many essays in such a short time, it is up to you to make sure the quality of your work stands out.

Each of your essays will receive a score of 1 through 9 (later, these numbers are plugged into a complicated formula to determine your overall free-response score). In each case, the AP grader will check to see if your essay meets five or six elementary requirements (the *basic core*); you can earn up to 7 points this way. If you fulfill ALL the requirements of the basic core, the grader will check your essay against a list of advanced criteria (the *expanded core*). If your essay measures up well against the expanded core, you can earn an additional 1 or 2 points.

The requirements for fulfilling the basic core and moving on to the expanded core are different for each essay. However, one thing is the same for all three: you CANNOT earn ANY of the expanded-core points unless you earn ALL the basic-core points. Think of this as opening a gate with five or six locks. Until you open them all, you cannot go any farther. The happy news is that, if you do a good job on each part of the basic core, you will already be doing some of the things necessary to score well on the expanded core.

One way to impress your reader is to follow some basic dos and don'ts. By keeping these guidelines in mind, you will make it easier for your reader to appreciate your work—and more likely that he or she will assign you a high score.

- *Develop a thesis and state it clearly*. You must make an argument or draw a concrete conclusion, and you must let your reader know you are doing it. No matter how good the rest of your essay is, you will lose many points if you fail to do so. See the section immediately below for more details.
- *Read the directions and follow them closely*. You are writing three different types of essays, each with its own set of rules. Advanced Placement readers are trained to judge your work based on how well you follow those rules. Even if your essay is beautifully written, it will lose points if you do not follow the directions.
- *Look at the question's key verb*. Answer the question on that basis. Questions will ask you to *defend* or *refute* (argue for or against); *assess the validity of* (judge the truth of); *evaluate* (determine the worth of, discuss advantages and disadvantages); *describe*, *discuss*, or *detail* (tell about, consider points of view); *outline* (list); *explain* (offer reasons for, make clear); *analyze* or *examine* (look at in detail, consider relationships, take into account cause and effect); and *compare* and *contrast* (show differences and similarities).
- *Write neatly and clearly*. Your reader will be marking hundreds of essays, and he or she will not grade generously if he or she has to struggle to understand what you are saying. Guidelines state that "substance takes precedence over neatness," but neatness helps the reader appreciate the substance more fully.
- *Divide your essay into paragraphs*. Paragraphs should be clearly indented. Correct and effective use of paragraphs shows the reader that you know how to think and write in an organized fashion.

- *Give an answer of an appropriate length.* There is no hard-and-fast rule as to how long your essay should be. Length may depend on how large your hand-writing is. Also, quantity does not always mean quality. A good argument can be made concisely, and a bad essay can ramble on for pages. However, an essay less than two pages long will be regarded with suspicion. Assuming your hand-writing is of average size, a MINIMUM length to aim for is two FULL pages. Three, even four, pages is optimal.
- *If you have time, reread your essay.* If necessary, revise it. Cross out mistakes or awkward phrasings. If new information or a good idea occurs to you, add it. Make corrections neatly.

Organization is just as important as any of the points discussed above. Your essay should have an introduction, and it should include an explicitly stated thesis. Your essay should be divided into paragraphs. Make sure your reader can tell where your paragraphs begin and end (indent clearly and/or skip a line between paragraphs).

Paragraphs should correspond with specific points or arguments you wish to make. These should serve to back up or prove your thesis. You should have at least three main points, although there can be more. If you have time, write a conclusion to sum up your arguments or make some general remarks about the topic you have just written about.

GENERAL TIPS FOR WRITING THESIS PARAGRAPHS

To get a high score—a 7 or above—on your essays, you must begin each of your answers with an effective thesis paragraph, containing a clear, effective thesis statement.

A good thesis is the first thing your grader will look for. According to the AP guidelines, your essay must have "an acceptable thesis" in order to meet the standards of the *basic core*. To get through the gateway to the *expanded core*, your essay has to start off with "a clear, analytical, and comprehensive thesis." In other words, without an effective thesis, your maximum possible score will be 6 or 7 out of 9.

In addition, a well-written thesis paragraph strengthens the whole essay. It creates a good first impression and shows the reader that you understand the question. It demonstrates your ability to analyze a complex issue and construct an argument (meaning a logical assertion, NOT a quarrelsome or aggressive rant) about it. It allows you to display some general historical knowledge. You can get a lot done—and earn some key points—with just this one paragraph.

Each type of question calls for a slightly different approach to the thesis paragraph. No matter what, though, you want to do the following things, all of which are interrelated:

- Begin with a restatement of the question. This step gets you started, and it keeps you focused on the subject at hand.
- Refer to the principal elements contained in the question. Who or what is this question about? What regions and/or time periods are you being asked about? What sort of relationships (between cultures, events, social classes, etc.) are being stressed?

- Pay attention to the question's key verb. As noted, this is how you determine what the question is asking you to do. Your thesis paragraph should tell the reader right away that you have figured this out.
- Show up front that you are aware of the bigger picture. Most questions are designed to get you to talk about a larger historical issue: sometimes a standard debate or interpretive point, sometimes an important phenomenon or historical pattern.
- Be balanced. Stories and debates have more than one side. More than one reasonable argument can be made about an issue. Events and phenomena generally have more than one cause. Acknowledge this fact, even if you favor a particular side argument or explanation.
- Give some hint about what the rest of the essay will cover. Preview what your main points will be—but do it briefly.
- Provide a clear transition to the next paragraph. Your reader should know when it is time to move on. (Even something as simple as clearly indenting will make your essay appear better organized.)

Here's one example of how a thesis paragraph might be constructed. The following question combines the characteristics of the change-over-time and comparative essays; with some adjustment, it could appear as either:

3. Choose one of the following regions. Compare and contrast Europe's colonial and imperial relationship with it, first during the fifteenth and sixteenth centuries and then during the nineteenth century.

Central and South America
South and East Asia
Africa

POSSIBLE THESIS PARAGRAPH

Although certain things remained constant over the centuries, the character of Europe's relationship with South and East Asia changed considerably between the 1400s–1500s and the 1800s.

[In one sentence, the question has been restated. Most of the question's principal elements—Europe, South and East Asia, and the time periods—have been mentioned. The key verbs ("compare and contrast") are not mentioned explicitly, but they are implied by the phrases "remained constant" and "changed considerably." This is already an "acceptable" thesis (although, by itself, not a very sophisticated one), because it makes a clear assertion and shows some scholarly judgment.]

During both eras, Europeans traveled to Asia to seek profit, spread Christianity, and expand their global power. In the nineteenth century, however, a newer group of nations—England and France, for example, as opposed to Spain and Portugal—held sway. Religious activity was carried out by Protestants as well as Catholics, and it was reinforced by a clearer sense of racial superiority, reflected in the doctrine of "social Darwinism."

[These sentences (1) continue what the key verbs ("compare and contrast") say to do; (2) preview some of the things the essay is likely to talk about in more depth; and (3) show that the author has a big-picture grasp of the historical context. The concept of social Darwinism could have been introduced later, but it does not hurt to get credit now for mentioning it—and it can be brought up again.]

Perhaps most important, European colonial efforts in nineteenth-century Asia met with greater success than before. Many historians refer to the "new imperialism" of the late 1800s, recognizing how overwhelming military, economic, and technological superiority gave European empire builders advantages that had not existed earlier. When one compares and contrasts the European imperial experience in Asia during the 1400s–1500s with that of the 1800s, it appears that the differences outweigh the similarities.

[Here, the essay highlights an important difference (the greater degree of European power in the 1800s). It strengthens the thesis by suggesting that change is greater than continuity. It introduces a major historiographical concept—the "new imperialism"—and, while this concept could have been mentioned later, it is a good way of demonstrating historical knowledge and an appreciation of the big picture. As with social Darwinism, it can be discussed again later. The last sentence does three important things. It tells the reader what to expect in the rest of the essay. It formally mentions that the essay will be about comparing and contrasting. Finally, it restates the thesis and adds extra punch to it by taking a definite position.]

Ideally, this paragraph would be followed by at least three main points and then a conclusion, for a MINIMUM of two full pages. As you study the answers to sample essay questions in the rest of this book, take some time to look at how the thesis paragraphs are written. They are constructed according to the same principles as this one.

Document-Based Question Strategies

A total of 50 minutes will be alloted for the DBQ. The first 10 minutes will be devoted to reading the documents. You will not be allowed to write your essay during this time. After the document-reading period, you will be given 40 minutes to complete your essay.

The DBQ should be the first essay you write (although you can choose differently). The DBQ is also the essay with the most elaborate rules. It is extremely important for you to be familiar with the procedure.

APPROACHING THE DOCUMENT-BASED QUESTION (DBQ)

You will be provided with anywhere from four to ten documents. Most of them will be traditional written documents: excerpts from books, memoirs, and essays; transcriptions of speeches or radio and television addresses; government papers; and so on. Sometimes song lyrics, poetry, or popular-culture material may be included. Occasionally, you will see a painting, cartoon, or some type of map or chart. The authors or speakers may or may not be famous.

The purpose of the DBQ is to assess your ability to evaluate and comment on primary documents. Therefore, you must not only write a good essay with a clear thesis but actively incorporate all, or all but one, of the documents. You must also comment on at least one OTHER type of document, NOT included, that might shed light on the question.

Following is the official AP scoring guide for the DBQ.

Generic Scoring Guide for AP World History Document-Based Question

Basic Core	Points	Expanded Core	Points
1. Has an acceptable thesis.	1	Expands beyond the basic core of 1–7 points. A student must earn **7** points in this core area before earning points in the expanded-core area.	0–2
2. Comprehends the documents' basic meaning. (One document may be misinterpreted.)	1	**Examples:**	
3. Thesis is supported by evidence from all documents or all but one. (Supported by all but two documents.)	2	• Has an analytical, clear, comprehensive thesis. • Demonstrates careful and insightful analysis.	
4. Analyzes bias or point of view in two or more documents.	1	• Makes convincing use of documents as evidence.	
5. Analyzes documents by clustering them in two or three ways.	1	• Discusses bias or point of view in most or all documents. • Compares, groups, and synthesizes the documents in additional ways.	
6. Identifies one type of additional document and explains why it is needed.	1	• Employs useful external historical content. • Identifies and explains the need for two or more additional document types.	
Subtotal	**7**	**Subtotal**	**2**
		TOTAL	**9**

A few of the items on the scoring guide deserve additional attention because they must be done in specific ways to avoid losing points.

Using and analyzing documents, and adding "outside" content. As the directions state, use all the documents or all but one (better to use them all if possible). "Careful and insightful analysis" will follow if you group the documents effectively, discuss point of view well, and present interesting comparisons and contrasts. Demonstrating external knowledge—by providing information about the author of a document or a document's historical context—is a good way to earn expanded-core points, and it can be done in combination with attribution.

Attribution. You are allowed to refer to documents simply by number (e.g., "Document 1," "# 5," or "doc. 3"). However, it is better to identify the author and title. This leads more naturally to providing information about the author and/or text—a good way of bringing in "outside" historical knowledge.

Point of view. Simply attributing the documents is not sufficient. You must also comment on point of view. What is the bias or perspective of the author, speaker, or artist? The point of view may be clear from the speaker's or writer's nationality, ethnicity, gender, social class, religion, or political affiliation. If the speaker or writer is famous, his or her point of view may be easy to describe. If he or she is not well known, you will have to read the document closely to determine its point of view. For partial credit, you must analyze the point of view of two or three documents. For full credit, especially if there are fewer than five or six documents, you must do this for all or most of the documents.

Grouping documents. One of the skills you MUST demonstrate is an ability to group documents into useful and meaningful categories. Can the documents be grouped by national origin (generally a weak approach)? By chronology? From a class perspective? According to a political philosophy or outlook? By purpose? By gender? According to cultural attitudes? There is no single right way to group. However, your groupings must make sense, and the DBQ will be designed in such a way that some methods of grouping will be more appropriate than others. Also, the NUMBER of groups is typically two or (generally more prefereable) three. More may be too complicated or, with a small set of documents, not feasible.

Identifying additional documents. The DBQ asks you to demonstrate your historical judgment by commenting on what is missing from the picture presented to you. If you could have OTHER documents provided to you, what types would you find useful in answering your question? And why would you choose them? This must be done at least once. Doing it more than once is a way to earn expanded-core points.

Thesis. Don't forget your thesis. Most often, your thesis will determine the way you group your documents. Conveniently, each category of document—especially if you have three or four categories—can be used as a main point in the body of your essay.

SAMPLE QUESTION

1. In the modern world, major political and social changes have been brought about by different means: national liberation, revolution, reformism, and parliamentary action. Using the documents presented below, discuss the various methods of political and social transformation that they call for or advocate. Be sure to explain the need for at least one additional type of document.

DOCUMENT 1

Source: Vladimir Lenin, Russian revolutionary leader and head of the Soviet state, *What Is to Be Done?* (1902).

A small, compact core of the most reliable, experienced, and hardened workers, with responsible representatives in the principal districts and connected by all the rules of strict secrecy with the organization of revolutionaries, can . . . perform all the functions of a trade union organization.

I assert: 1) that no revolutionary movement can endure without a stable organization of leaders that maintains continuity . . . 3) that such an organization must consist chiefly of people professionally engaged in revolutionary activity; 4) that in an autocratic state, the more we confine the membership of such an organization to people who are professionally engaged in revolutionary activity and have been professionally trained in the art of combatting the political police, the more difficult it will be to wipe out such an organization. . . .

Only a gross failure to understand Marxism . . . could prompt the opinion that the rise of a mass, spontaneous working-class movement relieves us of the duty of creating a good organization of revolutionaries. On the contrary, this movement imposes this duty upon us, because the spontaneous struggle of the proletariat will not become its genuine "class struggle" until this struggle is led by a strong organization of revolutionaries.

DOCUMENT 2

Source: Gamal Abdel Nasser, Arab nationalist and president of Egypt, "The Philosophy of the Revolution" (1959).

As I often sit in my study and think quietly of this subject, I ask myself: "What is our positive role in this troubled world, and where is the scene in which we can play that role?"

Can we ignore that there is a Muslim world to which we are tied by bonds which are not only forged by religious faith, but also tightened by the facts of history? . . . It is not in vain that our country lies to the southwest of Asia, close to the Arab world, whose life is intermingled with ours. . . . It is not in vain that Islamic civilization and Islamic heritage, which the Mongols ravaged in their conquest of the old Islamic capitals, retreated and found refuge in Egypt, where they found shelter and safety as a result of the counterattack with which Egypt repelled the invasion of these Tartars at Ein Galout.

All these are fundamental facts, whose roots lie deeply in our life. Whatever we do, we cannot forget them or run away from them.

DOCUMENT 3

Source: Mikhail Bakunin, nineteenth-century anarchist, "Principles of Revolution" (1869).

We recognize no other activity but the work of extermination, but we admit that the forms in which this activity will show itself will be extremely varied—poison, the knife, the rope, etc. In this struggle, revolution sanctifies everything alike.

DOCUMENT 4

Source: Kwame Nkrumah, leader of Ghana's independence movement, "The African Personality," speech delivered to a conference of independent African states (April 13, 1958).

Africa is the last remaining stronghold of colonialism. Unlike Asia, there are on the continent of Africa more dependent territories than independent sovereign nations. Therefore we, the free independent states of Africa, have a responsibility to hasten the total liberation of Africa . . .

We, the delegates of this conference, in promoting our foreign relations, must endeavor to seek the friendship of all and the enmity of none. We must stand for international peace and security, in conformity with the United Nations charter.

This will enable us to assert our own African personality and to develop our own ways of life, our own customs, traditions, and cultures. . . .

If we can as independent African states show by our own efforts that we can settle our own problems in Africa, then we shall be setting an example to others. . . . For this reason it may be necessary for this conference to examine the possibility of setting up some sort of machinery to maintain the links we shall forge here and to implement the decisions we shall reach. . . .

Today we are one. . . . An injury to one is an injury to all of us. From this conference must go out a new message: "Hands off Africa! Africa must be free!"

DOCUMENT 5

Source: Gloria Steinem, American feminist, "Far from the Opposite Shore" (1978).

Even the late suffragists, the ones who are most often labeled reformers because of their concentration on the vote, used radical tactics. Yes, they lobbied politely, sometimes, and took tea with their friends in Congress, but they also picketed the White House and engaged in the civil disobedience that those same congressmen abhorred. . . .

Chaining themselves to the White House fence, going to jail, declaring a hunger strike, being cruelly force-fed: those events are now famous. But the range of tactics [also] included humor, theatrics, passive resistance, [and] persuasion.

DOCUMENT 6

Source: Mao Tse-tung, leader of the Chinese Communist Party, "The Peasant Movement in Hunan" (1926).

In a very short time, . . . several hundred million peasants will rise like a mighty storm. . . . There are three alternatives. To march at their head and lead them? To trail behind them, gesticulating and criticizing? Or to stand in their way and oppose them?

Every revolutionary comrade should know that the national revolution requires a great change in the countryside. The Revolution of 1911 did not bring about this change, hence its failure. This change is now taking place, and it is an important factor for the completion of the revolution. Every revolutionary comrade must support it, or he will be taking the stand of counterrevolution.

DOCUMENT 7

Source: Henry David Thoreau, American philosopher and activist, *On the Duty of Civil Disobedience* (1848).

How does it become a man to behave toward this American government today? I answer that he cannot without disgrace be associated with it. I cannot for an instant recognize that political organization as *my* government which is the *slave's* government also.

All men recognize the right of revolution; that is, the right to refuse allegiance to and to resist the government, when its tyranny or its inefficiency are great and unendurable . . . those who call themselves abolitionists should at once effectually withdraw their support, both in person and property, from the government of Massachusetts. . . . Under a government which imprisons any unjustly, the true place for a just man is also a prison. . . . A minority is powerless while it conforms to the majority . . . but it is irresistible when it clogs by its whole weight.

DOCUMENT 8

Source: Mohandas K. Gandhi, member of the Indian National Congress and leader of the Indian independence movement, letter to Russian novelist Leo Tolstoy (1909).

These Indians [living in South Africa] have for several years labored under various legal disabilities. The prejudice against color and in some respect against Asiatics is intense in that colony. . . . The climax was reached three years ago, with a law which I and many others considered to be degrading and calculated to unman those to whom it was applicable. I felt that submission to a law of this nature was inconsistent with the spirit of true religion. I and some of my friends were and still are firm believers in the doctrine of non-resistance to evil. The result has been that nearly one-half of the Indian population [of Transvaal], that was unable to stand the heat of the struggle, to suffer the hardships of imprisonment, have withdrawn from the Transvaal rather than submit to a law which they have considered degrading. Of the other half, nearly 2,500 have for conscience's sake allowed themselves to be imprisoned, some as many as five times. . . . The struggle still continues, and one does not know when the end will come. This, however, some of us at least have seen most clearly, that passive resistance will and can succeed where brute force must fail.

Sample Answer

Many times throughout history, legal, within-the-system means of political and social change have failed to bring about desired results. On such occasions, there are frequently calls for radical or drastic forms of transformation. As the documents discussed in this essay demonstrate, these include national liberation, revolution, and civil disobedience. As a rule, when any of these courses of action—as opposed to reform or gradual change—is seen as necessary, it is a sign that the existing system has failed in some fundamental way.

[The thesis paragraph correctly identifies the nature of the documents and tells the reader how they will be categorized. A simple but acceptable thesis results from the grouping of the documents into three categories of political and social change. The last sentence adds an insightful observation—even a secondary thesis—about how radical forms of change tend to be caused by general social or political failure.]

Documents 2 (Nasser's "The Philosophy of the Revolution") and 4 (Nkrumah's "The African Personality") have to do with the wave of decolonization that swept Africa and Asia after World War II. Like Sukarno in Indonesia, Nasser, president of Egypt, was one of several charismatic, modernizing strongmen who led successful national liberation movements, then encouraged the so-called Third World to assert its global power and defy the West. Nkrumah came to power in Ghana, the first British colony in sub-Saharan Africa to gain freedom. Both appeal not just to their own people but to larger cultural units: the Muslim world in Nasser's case, all of Africa in Nkrumah's. Both are politicians, and this is a way to boost their international influence (but it also reflects the fact that national boundaries in Africa and the Mideast had been artificially imposed by Western colonizers). Such appeals stirred up pride, but they had their limits. Nasser's pan-Arab nationalism did not catch on, and his patriotic appeal at home has to be balanced against his authoritarianism. Nkrumah's pan-Africanism was too unrealistic to succeed in a region plagued by such extreme ethnic and linguistic diversity.

[Two documents are grouped here. They are attributed by number, title, and author. There is a good deal of historical context about postwar decolonization, including an outside reference to a similar political leader. The documents are not just listed; their political purpose is discussed, as is the question of whether the ideals they express were met. Point of view—that of politicians trying to increase their stature—is touched on. So far, there has been no discussion of what other documents might be helpful. (One possibility would have been to suggest diaries, newspaper editorials, or other materials to indicate whether or not ordinary people found pan-Arabism or pan-Africanism appealing.) Another option to be aware of: Document 8 (Gandhi) could have been included here, but this essay uses it differently. There will generally be more than one "right" way to group documents.]

Revolutions inspired by radical ideologies are a hallmark of modern history, as shown by Documents 3 (Bakunin's "Principles of Revolution"), 1 (Lenin's *What Is to Be Done?*), and 6 (Mao's "The Peasant Movement in Hunan"). Bakunin, founder of the anarchist movement, is the most extreme: in declaring that "revolution sanctifies everything alike," he restates the age-old argument that the ends justify the means. Lenin, leader of the Soviet Union, subscribes to the same idea in *What Is to Be Done?*, written while he was still a young Marxist, plotting to overthrow the tsar. Lenin discourages working-class democracy on the grounds that absolute secrecy is necessary for revolution to succeed. This stance can be explained partly by Lenin's point of view: he was leader of an illegal party in a repressive country with a powerful secret police. Unfortunately, Lenin's antidemocratic approach was one of many things that later turned the USSR, a state founded on utopian ideals, into a rigid dictatorship. In #6, Mao, years before communist victory in China, appears to be more committed to open mass movements as he describes the revolutionary power of the peasantry (an unusual position for a Marxist, because Marxism puts more stress on the industrial working class). After coming to power, however, Mao proved just as much a dictator as Lenin and Stalin did in the USSR. All three documents propose that the potential benefits of revolution are worth any price, but they say nothing about actual costs. For the sake of balance, it would be useful to have statistics or first-hand accounts related to the mass arrests, persecutions, and famines that resulted from revolution in Soviet Russia and Maoist China.

[This paragraph provides a second effective grouping, dealing with revolution. Transition from the previous paragraph is clear, and the attribution of documents remains explicit. Historical information is included for the sake of context. Detailed point of view is provided in Lenin's case. (Also, a reader might give point-of-view credit for mentioning the unorthodoxy of Mao's Marxist views.) This paragraph fulfills the basic core by making a suggestion about additional documents that might prove useful.]

Another way to bring about change is nonviolent resistance. The American thinker Henry David Thoreau argues in *On the Duty of Civil Disobedience* (#7) that even democratic governments can do wrong. An idealist philosopher who was angry about the Mexican-American War and slavery, Thoreau asks whether a good person acting in a good cause is justified in violating his or her country's laws. His answer is "yes." In her essay "Far from the Opposite Shore" (#5), American feminist Gloria Steinem describes how nineteenth-century suffragettes used civil disobedience, not just lawful reform, to fight for the vote. (Steinem seems to be encouraging similar action in her own day, and the fact that she is writing about history to a modern audience for political purposes should be noted.) Perhaps the most admired advocate of civil disobedience is Gandhi, spiritual father of India's freedom movement. In a 1909 letter (#8) to Russia author Leo Tolstoy—also known for his activism and pacifism—Gandhi explains his strategy of passive resistance in South Africa, where Indians, like blacks, were racially discriminated against. Later, Gandhi's method of *satyagraha*, which combined Hindu faith with nonviolent political action, was an effective tool in persuading the British to grant India its independence. As effective as civil disobedience has been, however, it works only under certain circumstances. Gandhi's confident assertion that "passive resistance will and can succeed where brute force must fail" applies only in liberal or democratic societies, where the use of brute force is seen as embarrassing or shameful. It is hard to imagine civil disobedience bringing about change in a truly dictatorial regime such as Hitler's, Stalin's, or Mao's.

[A third and final grouping appears in this paragraph. Attribution is complete, and Steinem's point of view is noted. So are Thoreau's and Gandhi's, to a lesser extent. (Many readers would assign an expanded-core point to this essay for analyzing the point of view of "all or most" of the documents.) Much historical information is provided, as well as an evaluation of civil disobedience as a political strategy.]

None of the documents discuss what is perhaps the fairest and most desirable means of social and political change: the proper functioning of democratic government. Also, while the documents provide examples of one extremist form of change, communist revolution, they do not mention fascism, another common form of extremism. Memoirs or newspaper reports demonstrating fascist excess and the effective operation of democracy would have been useful.

[This brief conclusion caps off the essay, even though time is running out. It also raises a general analytical point about democratic change. Most important, it earns an expanded-core point by making a second suggestion about potentially useful documents.]

Change-Over-Time Essay Question Strategies

Another type of essay the World History exam will ask you to write is the change-over-time (COT) question. The goal of this exercise is to test your ability to trace a broad trend or development over a long period of time. Topics may include cultural interchange, global trade, the movements and migrations of peoples, the role of minorities in a given society, the status of women, environmental issues, biological developments, changes in technology, artistic and cultural attitudes, and scientific innovations.

The COT lends itself to a topical approach. In order to follow how a particular issue changed or stayed the same through long periods of time, consult the overviews that appear at the beginning of Units Two through Six. These overviews attempt to track "big-picture" issues as they played out over different eras.

Moreover, as you read through the material covered in Units Two through Six, try to keep in mind how long-term trends develop, not just within geographical areas but across borders.

APPROACHING THE CHANGE-OVER-TIME ESSAY

As with all essays, follow the General Tips provided earlier in this unit.

It is recommended that you take 40 minutes to complete the COT. Spend 5 or so minutes (no more than 10) looking over the question, thinking about it, then organizing and outlining your thoughts.

The COT will request that you analyze the evolution of a trend or phenomenon over a long period of time. You will be asked to focus on a particular nation or geographical region, although you may be given a choice. On the next page is the official AP scoring guide for the COT.

The requirements for the COT are more straightforward than those for the DBQ. Aside from following the general essay-writing tips, concentrate on showing that you understand what changed, and how. Start by establishing a baseline: what were things like at the beginning of the period you have been assigned? What changed? How and why did it change? What were things like at the end of the period in question? What differences did those changes make? What, if anything, remained the same?

Generic Scoring Guide for AP World History Change-Over-Time Essay

Basic Core		Expanded Core	
	Points		**Points**
1. Thesis deals acceptably with the global issues and time period(s) in question.	1	Goes beyond the basic core of 1–7 points. A score of **7** must be earned before a student can gain expanded-core points.	0–2
2. Deals with all parts of the question, though not necessarily evenly or completely.	2	Examples:	
(Deals with most parts of the question.)	(1)	• Has a clear, analytical, and comprehensive thesis.	
3. Backs up the thesis with appropriate historical evidence.	2	• Deals with all aspects of the question: global issues, chronology, causation, change, continuity, content.	
(Partially backs up thesis with appropriate historical evidence.)	(1)	• Deals with all parts of the question evenly.	
		• Gives ample historical evidence to back up thesis.	
4. Uses historical context to illustrate continuity and/or change over time.	1	• Creatively links topic to relevant ideas, events, and trends.	
5. Analyzes the process of change and/or continuity.	1		
Subtotal	**7**	**Subtotal**	**2**
TOTAL 9			

One easy way to create a change-over-time thesis is to focus on the cause(s) and/or effect(s) of the change(s) you are writing about. Another is to discuss whether change outweighed continuity or vice versa. Either way, discuss both for the sake of balance.

SAMPLE QUESTION

2. Choose one of the following regions. Discuss the changes and continuities in how women were treated—socially, economically, and politically—between 1000 C.E. and 1750 C.E. If a woman's social class factored into the way she was treated, discuss that in your answer.

the Middle East
India
China and Japan
sub-Saharan Africa

Sample Answer

In most times and places, women have occupied a secondary status in society, whether because of gender division of labor, cultural and religious bias, or simple sexism. However, the type of discrimination a woman experienced, and how bad it was, varied greatly, depending on where and when she lived, as well as what social class she was from. Neither China nor Japan between 1000 and 1750 is an exception. In both places, women remained subservient to men. Of course, there were changes, but in both cases, they tended to go from bad to worse.

[This introduction refers to all key elements in the question. It tells the reader what region the essay will focus on. It recognizes that change and continuity are both relevant. Most important, it clearly states a complex thesis by discussing the secondary status of women generally and asserting that, both in the case of China and Japan, the situation of women worsened over time.]

Around 1000 C.E., women in Song China and Heian Japan enjoyed some rights and privileges, although their situation was still secondary. As in many societies, they could own and inherit property, and they could have informal influence where the management of households was concerned. Women of the upper classes could exercise indirect power through their husbands or personal connections at the imperial court. Japanese women were luckier in this regard: the Heian aristocracy placed a great emphasis on cultural brilliance, and the literary achievements of women like Lady Murasaki, author of *The Tale of Genji*, gained them some prestige. Also, Confucianism, which did nothing to improve the status of women, was not yet as prevalent as it was in China, where it had been part of tradition for centuries. One woman, Wu Zhao, had actually ruled China as empress, but hers was an extremely rare case that says little about the lives of most women there.

[This paragraph establishes a baseline by describing the situation as it was at the beginning of the time period in question. It provides much outside historical knowledge. It shows analytical awareness by noting that generalizing from one unusual case (Wu Zhao's) is risky.]

In China, conditions worsened for women mainly because of religious and cultural reasons. Since the 400s B.C.E., Confucianism, with its strict sense of hierarchy, had done much to lower the status of Chinese women, but its influence had waxed and waned over time. Starting in the 600s C.E., though, Confucianism revived more permanently in the form of Neo-Confucianism. The Song, Yuan, and Ming dynasties were increasingly drawn to Neo-Confucian dictates, and the place of women lessened as a result. Brides' families now paid dowries to the groom; earlier, it had been the other way around. This change in custom made it expensive to marry off daughters, and families came to want girl children less. The most infamous means of subjugating women was foot binding. Tiny feet were considered to be more attractive, but observing this fashion had the effect of crippling women's feet and turning them into little more than beautiful objects. Foot binding gradually gained in popularity, spreading from the upper classes downard. It was widely practiced by 1200 and continued till the 1900s.

[This paragraph discusses change in China. It identifies a primary agent of change and provides a good deal of concrete historical information.]

Political events were more important in changing the role of women in Japan. The transition from the culturally refined Heian regime to the feudal shogunates in the late 1100s led to a steep decline in the status of women. During the first shogunates and the period of disunity of the 1400s and 1500s, prestige belonged to the samurai class, and their warrior ethic left little room for the accomplishments or abilities of women. Also, unlike European chivalry, which at least required knights to respect and cherish women (however condescending this was), the Japanese code of Bushido did nothing to encourage samurai to treat women well. Things got even worse as Japan reunited in the late 1500s and early 1600s. Society became tremendously stratified, and under the Tokugawa shoguns who completed the unification, women were required to obey their husbands without question—and if they did not, they could be put to death.

[Like the previous paragraph, this one discusses change, this time in Japan. It identifies the principal reason for change and provides concrete details and information.]

It should be noted that all these changes were less pronounced among the lower classes, as was often the case in most societies. In China, lower-class families were less likely than upper-class families to follow Confucian rules closely. Foot binding was for the aristocracy: A peasant woman with bound feet would be useless for farm or household work. In Japan, samurai ideals were irrelevant to the lives of people farther down in society. Even among the lower classes, though, the question of who paid dowries for marriage was important, and in both countries, regardless of class, the overall desirability of girl children decreased. (This is still a cultural problem today in much of Asia, especially in China.) During the premodern era, female infanticide was not uncommon.

[This supplemental paragraph addresses the question of social class, talking about likenesses AND differences. Links with the present ("still a cultural problem today") are a way of earning expanded-core points.]

To sum up, the condition of women tended to worsen, both in China and Japan, between 1000 and 1750. The increased role of Neo-Confucian beliefs was mainly responsible for change in China, while the rise of warrior government was the primary cause in Japan. Feminism and equal rights took a long time to come to both countries—not until late in the twentieth century—and one could argue that the influence of this traditional sexism is still felt today.

[This short conclusion recaps the thesis and its main points. It gives a sense of what followed the historical period in question and also comments on the present (one way to get an expanded-core point).]

Comparative Essay Question Strategies

Yet another exercise you will complete on the World History exam is the comparative essay. As its name suggests, this essay will ask you to compare and contrast the ways different societies deal with major issues and phenomena. These may include technological innovation; the social and economic impact of warfare; the treatment of minorities and women; the evolution of political systems; international trade and economic exchange; and systems of labor organization.

The organizers of the AP World History course consider the comparative approach especially important. The overviews preceding Units Two through Six provide lists of issues that lend themselves well to comparative questions. Read them carefully. In addition, as you study the material covered in Units Two through Six, think about broad patterns and see if you can come up with examples of major developments that most, if not all, societies undergo as they evolve historically.

APPROACHING THE COMPARATIVE ESSAY

As with all essays, follow the General Tips provided.

You should devote 40 minutes to complete the comparative essay. Spend 5 or so minutes (no more than 10) looking over the question, thinking about it, then organizing and outlining your thoughts.

The comparative essay will require you to compare and contrast how at least two (perhaps more) civilizations or nations have undergone or responded to a historical event or experience. Be sure to give equal weight to both (or all) civilizations or nations specified in the question. Also be sure to balance similarities and differences, although you may decide that one is more important than the other.

The official AP scoring guide for the comparative essay is on the next page.

Because the central task of the comparative essay is so heavily focused on comparison, rather than a specific theme, developing a strong thesis for a comparative essay may appear difficult. The question, or the way you want to answer it, may not lend itself to a clear-cut theme or argument. In that event, you can still create a thesis by stating that, in the case you are discussing, the likenesses outweigh the differences. Or, the differences may seem more important than the likenesses. You may argue that likenesses and differences are equally balanced. This is not the most sophisticated approach, but it will fulfill the requirement.

SAMPLE QUESTION

3. Compare and contrast the degree to which TWO of the following regions modernized between the end of the First World War and the beginning of the Second World War.

South Asia
Latin America
the Middle East
Russia

Generic Scoring Guide for AP World History Comparative Essay

Basic Core (Competence)	Points
1. Opens with acceptable thesis. (Compares the issues or themes specified.)	1
2. Deals with all parts of the question, perhaps not evenly or thoroughly.	2
(Deals with most parts of question.)	(1)
3. Backs up thesis with appropriate historical evidence.	2
(Partly backs up thesis with appropriate historical evidence.)	(1)
4. Provides one or two relevant, direct comparisons between or among societies.	1
5. Analyzes one or more reasons for a difference or similarity discussed in a direct comparison.	1
Subtotal	**7**

Expanded Core (Excellence)	Points
Goes beyond the basic core of 1–6 points. The basic core score of **7** must be earned before a student can gain expanded core points.	0–2
Examples:	
• Opens with an analytical, clear, comprehensive thesis.	
• Deals with all relevant parts of the question: comparisons, chronology, causation, connections, themes, interactions, content.	
• Gives ample historical evidence to back up thesis.	
• Demonstrates ability to link comparisons to larger global context.	
• Demonstrates ability to show similarities as well as differences.	
• Draws direct comparisons consistently between or among societies.	
Subtotal	**2**

TOTAL 9

Sample Answer

The two decades that followed World War I brought immense changes to most parts of the globe. Among the regions affected were the Middle East and Latin America, each of which modernized during the 1920s and 1930s. Both had several things in common, such as relative backwardness, heavy influence from outside powers, and not much success with representative government. However, there were also key differences that, arguably, outweigh the similarities: Latin American states were already more modern and more independent, traditional Islam was more an obstacle to change than Catholicism, and events like WWI and the Depression affected both areas differently.

[This introductory paragraph addresses the question's key elements and identifies the regions to be compared. It acknowledges that there are similarities and differences, and it tackles the basic core by starting the process of comparison right away. It lays out a thesis about modernization in both regions, then strengthens the thesis by proposing that differences may outweigh similarities.]

Prior to WWI, the Middle East was backward in comparison to the West, and it was dominated by outside powers. Egypt was under British control, and Persia, while technically free, was divided into British and Russian spheres of influence. The one major independent state, the Ottoman Empire, was in decline and widely known as the "sick man of Europe." The Ottomans attempted some changes, the Tanzimat reforms, in the nineteenth century, and there was some social modernization and industrialization—but not enough to prevent the Young Turks from taking over in 1908 and attempting even faster change. Unfortunately for the Ottomans, the Young Turks sided with the Germans in WWI. Therefore, more so than Latin America, the Middle East was directly involved in the war. The Ottomans were among the losers, and their empire was broken up.

[This paragraph sets the stage by describing the existing state of modernization in the Middle East before and during World War I. This essay is about comparing two processes of change, so a starting point has to be established in both cases. One comparative note—the Middle East's greater involvement in World War I—has already been included.]

At first, the end of WWI brought greater foreign domination to the Middle East. Egypt and Persia remained under British influence. Arabs, who had rebelled against Ottoman rule and sided with the Allies, hoping to gain a united, independent Arab state, were disappointed. The English and French imposed a mandate system over Arab regions such as Iraq, Syria, Lebanon, Jordan, and Palestine. These were not technically colonies, but they were dominated by the French and British. (Britain's Balfour Declaration, which guaranteed a Jewish homeland in Palestine, also alienated the Arabs.) In 1932, Ibn Said created the state of Saudi Arabia, but it remained very traditionalist. Economic modernization came only after the discovery of oil in 1938, and even then, it benefitted only the Saudi elite and foreign investors.

Real modernization in the Middle East occurred in Turkey and Persia, in both cases as a result of bold action by strong-willed and authoritarian leaders. In 1923, Mustafa Kemal took over the Turkish government and renamed himself Ataturk ("father of all Turks"). In 1925, Reza Khan Pahlavi rose to power in Persia, threw out the British, and crowned himself shah. Both were Westernizers who industrialized their economies and encouraged Western ideas and education (Ataturk even gave women the vote). Both saw Islam as a backward force standing in the way of change, and both sought to reduce, even eliminate, Islam's role in law and politics. Middle Eastern modernization took place only in a handful of countries, and it was imposed from above.

[These two paragraphs describe where and how modernization in the Middle East occurred. Good historical detail is provided, and several examples are analyzed in order to demonstrate a general pattern.]

Like the Middle East, Latin America before and during WWI was relatively backward and heavily influenced by outside powers, especially the United States. On the other hand, most nations in Latin America had been free since the early 1800s, thanks to the Latin American wars of independence, and foreign domination was economic, not directly colonial. There was also more industrialization in Latin America—although most Latin American economies were based on the exploitation of one or two commodities, such as an agricultural crop (coffee or bananas) or a natural resource (copper, fertilizer, or steel), and foreign investors had great control over those economies. One more difference is that Latin American nations had almost no direct involvement with WWI.

[Just as the second paragraph did for the Middle East, this paragraph establishes a starting point for Latin America. It also continues the process of comparing the Middle East with Latin America directly.]

After WWI, American economic influence over Latin America increased, because countries like Britain and France were in such bad economic shape that they pulled out many of their investments. During the 1920s, the U.S. backed up its business interests with political pressure and military force. This course of action lessened only when President Franklin Roosevelt started his Good Neighbor Policy. By that point, though, the Great Depression had begun, and because Latin American economies were so dependent on U.S. investment, the Depression hurt Latin America badly and slowed down modernization. (The Middle East was much less affected by the Depression, another important difference.)

Industrialization and modernization took place in Latin America during the 1920s and 1930s but not, as in the Middle East, because of one ruler's will. Instead, the economic interests of a larger elite—and foreign investors—stimulated growth. Dictatorial governments, some mild (like Mexico's PRI party), and some severe, were common. This authoritarianism grew worse in the 1930s, largely because of economic stress caused by the Depression, partly because of the influence of European fascism. A military government seized control of Argentina in 1930, and that same year, the right-wing dictator Vargas took power in Brazil and created one of the continent's most brutal regimes.

[These two paragraphs describe change in Latin America during the 1920s and 1930s. They provide concrete details but also discuss general trends. There are direct comparisons to the Middle East.]

During the interwar period, both Latin America and the Middle East modernized and industrialized despite lingering backwardness from the 1800s, outside interference, and, on the whole, undemocratic government. Latin America started from a more advanced position, however, with politically independent countries and partially industrialized economies and societies. In the Middle East, modernization was rarer and, when it happened, was pushed through by westernizing politicians opposed to Muslim traditionalism.

[This conclusion restates key similarities and differences. It is somewhat rough and rushed, but when time is running out, it is more important to get points across than to worry about style.]

UNIT TWO

FOUNDATIONS OF WORLD CIVILIZATION (ca. 8000 B.C.E.–600 C.E.)

Unit Overview

GENERAL REMARKS

This unit is so wide-ranging in terms of time and geography that it is difficult to encapsulate in a brief overview. The purpose of this unit is to provide an understanding of the foundations of world civilization.

Humanlike, or hominid, creatures emerged on earth approximately 3 to 4 million years ago. Modern humans (*Homo sapiens sapiens*) developed sometime between 100,000 and 250,000 years ago. According to most scholars, humanity's birthplace was Africa. From there, humans spread to the rest of the globe, starting around 100,000 years ago.

The period from approximately 5,000 or 6,000 years ago to 2.5 million years ago is referred to as the Stone Age. During this time, human communities took shape, but remained at a relatively primitive state of development, socially and technologically. After around 10,000 years ago, however, thanks to the phenomenon generally known as the Neolithic revolution, human societies gradually became more advanced. Various peoples learned how to domesticate plants and animals. They developed what are generally considered to be the basic attributes of civilized society. They practiced agriculture, invented systems of recordkeeping (especially writing), and made metal (rather than stone) tools. They developed complex forms of social and political organization, and sophisticated modes of economic exchange.

The earliest "civilized" societies appeared between 4,000 and 5,500 years ago, or between 3500 and 2000 B.C.E. All four were born along the banks of major river systems. They were

- The Sumerian-Babylonian civilization of Mesopotamia (the Tigris and Euphrates rivers)
- Egypt (the Nile River)
- The Indus valley civilization (the Indus River)
- Early China (the Yellow River, or Huang Ho)

Also among the world's oldest civilizations were the Olmec, who arose in Central America around 1200 B.C.E., and the Chavin, who appeared in the Andes Mountains after 900 B.C.E.

Quickly, other developed societies appeared throughout the world. By 600 C.E., civilizations had emerged in Asia, Europe, North Africa, sub-Saharan Africa, North America, and Central and South America. Many were connected by trade, warfare, and other forms of interaction. Most of the major religions of the world had been born by 600 C.E. (Islam is the key exception).

BROAD TRENDS

Global Power and International Relations

- Early on, the most advanced civilizations were to be found in the Middle East (especially the river valleys of Egypt and Mesopotamia) and China.
- As time passed, other developed societies emerged. Especially powerful and sophisticated was the Mediterranean world (particularly Greece and Rome).
- Cultures in North and South America were physically and culturally isolated from the rest of the continents.
- The peoples of Europe, North Africa, the Middle East, South Asia, and East Asia were linked, directly or indirectly, by war, conquest, trade, travel, and cultural and religious exchange.
- By 600 C.E., several civilizations were among the world's most powerful and advanced, especially China, Persia, and Byzantium. Europe was slowly recovering from the collapse of Rome in the late 400s.

Political Developments

- With the development of agriculture during the Neolithic revolution, advanced forms of political organization began to appear.
- Most governments were monarchies (rule by a single leader) or oligarchies (rule by a small elite). Representative forms of government, such as republics and democracies, were very rare.
- Decentralized civilizations were often governed by confederations of independent city-states (such as Greece) or feudal systems (such as Europe after the fall of Rome).
- Many civilizations, by means of military conquest, built empires. Among the largest and longest lasting were Assyria's, Persia's, Rome's, and China's.

Economic and Environmental Developments

- Until the development of agriculture during the Neolithic revolution, systems of economic exchange remained quite primitive. Most prehistoric cultures, mainly hunting and gathering societies, lived at subsistence (they gathered or grew only enough food to feed themselves) and possessed few goods. There was little specialization of labor. Trade tended to be limited, and based on simple barter.
- The development of agriculture allowed the accumulation of food surpluses, which enabled some members of society to make a living by means other than growing food. The result was specialization of labor.
- Specialization of labor led to social stratification and the emergence of socioeconomic classes (upper-class aristocracies, middle-class merchants and artisans, lower-class urban dwellers and peasants).

- The switch from nomadic life to sedentary, or settled, life led people to develop the concept of private property.
- Resource consumption and resource extraction increased, causing human societies to have a greater (and often negative) impact on the environment.
- As settled civilizations encountered each other, they traded. Trade became one of the most important forms of interaction between civilizations. Trade networks tended to follow waterways, for ease of transport. Trade routes were especially wide-ranging in Eurasia, connecting civilizations in Europe with those as far away as East Asia.
- Systems of currency (particularly coinage) were devised.

Cultural Developments

- Even during the Stone Age, human beings expressed themselves artistically, by means of painting and music.
- Prehistoric societies buried their dead, worshipped gods, and practiced religious rituals.
- Writing and other forms of recordkeeping emerged in most civilized societies, starting around 3000 B.C.E.
- Systematic scientific observation, experimentation, and thought emerged, especially in China, the Middle East, and the Mediterranean world.
- The world's major religions were born (except for Islam).

Gender Issues

- The ability of humans to mate when and with whom they chose gave rise to family units during the prehistoric era.
- Basic physical differences between the sexes led to a gender division of labor in most Stone Age societies.
- The emergence of agriculture deepened the gender division of labor. In most agricultural and settled societies, gender division gave rise to gender inequality.
- Organized religions often reinforced this sense of inequality.
- In most societies up to 600 C.E., women were relegated to a secondary, subservient role. The degree of subservience depended on the society. In some cultures, women had at least some rights (divorce, inheritance, and ownership of property, for example). They might also exercise certain forms of influence within their societies or, at least, their families. In other cultures, women had almost no rights or influence. Whatever the case, in almost no society were women granted a status equal to that of men.

QUESTIONS AND COMPARISONS TO CONSIDER

- What roles do geography, climate, and environment play in shaping human societies? How have different societies affected their environments?
- How do human societies develop into civilizations? What does it mean to be "civilized"?

- How do agricultural and urban societies compare with pastoral and nomadic ones?
- What is the importance of cultural interaction and diffusion versus that of independent innovation in changing societies technologically, scientifically, or culturally?
- Compare how different religious and philosophical traditions have determined how societies organize themselves, justify class systems and hierarchies, and treat women.
- Examine and compare various forms of social inequality (slavery, caste systems, patriarchy, gender inequality) in different cultures.
- How have different societies organized themselves economically? What role did trade play? Be able to describe the features of at least one interregional trading system (for example, the Indian Ocean trade network or the overland route linking the Mediterranean and Middle East with East Asia).
- What are "classical" civilizations? What does that concept mean? Be able to compare major civilizations—such as India, China, Greece, or Rome—during their classical phases.
- How and why do empires and major civilizations decline or collapse? Good comparisons might include Egypt versus Mesopotamia or the Roman Empire versus Han China. More generally, why did imperial collapse prove more devastating in western Europe than it did farther to the east?
- What roles did large-scale migrations play in various parts of the world during this period? Consider the passage of Asiatic peoples to the Americas over the Bering land bridge, the Pacific-wide migration of the Polynesians, the Bantu migrations throughout Africa, and the movement of Eurasian nomads into Roman and Chinese territory.

Geography, Environment, and Humanity

CHAPTER 1

> - Major continents and regions
> - Major oceans, seas, and rivers
> - Water transport versus overland travel
> - Environmental impact
> - Resource extraction and consumption
> - Agriculture

One of the key forces shaping any human society is its physical environment. A basic knowledge of the earth's major geographical features is indispensable for any understanding of world history. There are also certain patterns where human interaction with the environment is concerned.

GEOGRAPHIC ORIENTATION

While the earth is approximately 5 to 6 billion years old, the present configuration of the continents dates back to less than 60 million years ago. Scientists speculate that, originally, all the earth's landmasses were clustered into a single supercontinent called **Pangaea**. Over time, geological forces separated Pangaea into smaller bodies of land, which eventually became today's continents and major islands.

Antarctica, covering the south polar region, has no native human population. Australia, the world's smallest continent, is home to what is probably the earth's oldest surviving ethnic group (the Aborigines) but remained largely isolated for most of its history. The thousands of islands sprinkled throughout the Pacific Ocean form no continent but are often referred to, along with Australia, as **Oceania**.

Africa is considered by most scholars to be the birthplace of humanity. The northern third of Africa is home to the world's largest desert, the **Sahara**. (The AP World History course prefers the following terms to describe African subregions: North Africa, West Africa, East Africa, Central Africa, and Southern Africa.) **Asia** is by far the largest and most populous continent on earth, ranging from the Middle East (also called the Near East) to the Indian subcontinent and, farther to the east, China and Japan. The island chains that make up the nations of Indonesia, Malaysia, and the Philippines are also considered to be part of Asia. Thanks to its size, Asia contains the world's most diverse mix of climates, geographical features, ethnicities, languages, and cultures. (In addition to the Middle

> **NOTE**
>
> There are seven continents (Africa, Antarctica, Asia, Australia, Europe, North America, and South America) and four oceans (Arctic, Atlantic, Indian, and Pacific). Several seas—including the **Caribbean** Sea, the **Mediterranean** Sea, the Red Sea, the Arabian Sea, and the seas of Japan, East China, and South China—are important as well.

East and Siberia, the continent contains three distinct regions: South Asia, Southeast Asia, and East Asia.) **Europe**, a relatively small continent with a large population, is resource-rich and, on the whole, mild and temperate in climate. Europe is physically joined to Asia, and the two continents are often referred to together as **Eurasia**. From humanity's earliest days, there was constant interaction among the populations of all three continents.

North and **South America** were originally settled by nomadic peoples from Asia, crossing a land bridge that existed only temporarily. Until the late 1400s C.E., the Americas developed in almost complete isolation from the other three major continents. Abundant in resources and, in most parts, agriculturally fertile, the Americas became home to many advanced cultures. Contact with European societies changed the Americas dramatically. From 1492 C.E. onward, cross-oceanic transportation, trade, and communication turned the Atlantic basin into a gigantic cauldron of economic, cultural, religious, ethnic, political, and military interaction.

HUMANITY AND THE ENVIRONMENT

Human societies and their physical environments mutually influence each other. Geography is not the only, or even the most important factor, that shapes a society, but it can play a crucial role.

Human beings have lived and created societies in all but the most inhospitable environments on earth. As a general rule, though, preindustrial societies—the only type in existence until the 1700s C.E.—tended to thrive and develop into advanced civilizations if one or more of the following preconditions existed: the climate was not extremely hot, cold, dry, or wet; a suitable amount of arable, fertile land, preferably flat, was available; a reliable source of water was present; and topography (the shape of the land) permitted reasonably easy movement. Access to a river or a seacoast or both, for the sake of transport (and food supply), was helpful. The presence of one or more desirable natural resources was a bonus, as was proximity to one or more trade routes, whether overland or by water. Not all these conditions have to prevail; think of the monsoons of India (extreme weather) or the terraced fields of the Andean civilizations (little or no flat land for agriculture). However, a society is unlikely to develop without at least some of these advantages. To some degree or another, human societies are compelled to adapt to their geographical setting; in many ways, environment does shape society.

One especially important geographic reality during the long preindustrial era has to do with oceans, seas, and rivers. For centuries, water transport remained much easier, cheaper, and more efficient than overland travel. Throughout history, lakes and river systems have been vital to the birth, growth, and continued viability of human societies. Rivers served as sources of food (fish) and drinkable water. They stimulated the invention of agriculture and the emergence of cities. They made possible the large-scale movement of passengers and freight, encouraged trade and travel, and linked communities with each other.

Likewise, oceans and seas not only provided food and other resources, but also enabled the transfer of people, goods, ideas, technology, religious beliefs, and cultural practices. For civilizations without the scientific knowledge and technological ability to cross them, large bodies of water were formidable barriers. (The first known transatlantic voyage, that of Leif Eriksson, did not take place until the eleventh century C.E., and the Pacific is thought not to have been crossed until Ferdinand Magellan's circumnavigation of the globe in 1519–1522.) However, even early and less-advanced societies were generally capable of coastline navigation. Once oceans and seas became fully navigable, they offered societies with access to them an effective means by which to communicate, trade, fight, and otherwise interact. The **Atlantic**, **Indian**, and **Pacific** oceans, as well as the seas listed above, have been particularly important in this respect. Major river systems include the **Nile**, the Congo, the **Tigris** and **Euphrates**, the **Indus**, the Ganges, the **Huang Ho (Yellow)**, the **Yangzi** (Yangtze), the Volga, the **Danube**, the Rhine, the **Mississippi-Missouri**, and the **Amazon**.

The larger and more advanced the society, the greater its level of **resource consumption** and **resource extraction**. Even less advanced modes of economic production influence the environment: the gathering of nuts, berries, and other foodstuffs; the grazing of herds; and the creation of simple tools all involve resource consumption. Also, although it is common to think of this only as a modern problem, all societies, even early and less-advanced ones, produced **waste** and **pollution**.

As societies developed, they became more able to shape their environment. Practices such as **forest clearing**, **irrigation**, and **agriculture** increased humanity's impact, or "ecological footprint," on the land. The same is true for **mining**, as well as engineering projects such as swamp dredging, dam building, canal digging, and so on. Even in the preindustrial era and surprisingly early in the historical record, advanced societies were capable of such accomplishments—and thus capable of affecting their environments, just as their environments affected them. (From the late 1700s onward, industrialization vastly heightened humanity's ability to affect and control the environment, though not always for the better.)

> **NOTE**
>
> If the environment helps to influence the development of human societies, the development of human societies, in return, has a profound environmental impact.

QUICK REVIEW

1. What continent is home to the people considered to be earth's oldest surviving ethnic group?

   (A) North America
   (B) Asia
   (C) Australia
   (D) Europe
   (E) None of the above.

2. The largest and most populous continent is

   (A) North America.
   (B) Asia.
   (C) Europe.
   (D) South America.
   (E) Antarctica.

3. The populations of which three continents were able to interact and trade with relative ease since humanity's earliest days?

   (A) Africa, Asia, and Europe
   (B) Africa, Asia, and Australia
   (C) North America, South America, and Asia
   (D) North America, South America, and Europe
   (E) Europe, Africa, and North America

4. A geographic determinist would most likely believe which of the following?

   (A) Topography and climate have little or no effect on the course of a society's development.
   (B) Societies cannot survive in harsh environments such as deserts and mountains.
   (C) Human societies influence their environments far more than they are influenced by them.
   (D) Geographic conditions play a key role, if not the most important role, in shaping human societies.
   (E) None of the above.

5. Which of the following is LEAST likely to encourage the growth of an advanced civilization?

   (A) the presence of a nearby river
   (B) surroundings dominated by steep, landlocked mountains
   (C) temperate climatic conditions
   (D) proximity to a lakeshore or seacoast
   (E) rich deposits of precious metals in the neighboring hills

6. Why are rivers considered so important to the development of the first civilizations?

   (A) They discouraged ocean travel.
   (B) They encouraged both the growth of agriculture and urban areas.
   (C) They retarded the invention of agriculture.
   (D) They slowed down the emergence of cities.
   (E) They were really not very important to the development of early civilizations.

7. The benefits of having access to an oceanic coastline include

   (A) food resources, especially in the form of fish.
   (B) the ability to move passengers and freight more easily than by overland transport.
   (C) the increased likelihood of being able to participate in regional or even global trade networks.
   (D) all of the above
   (E) none of the above

8. The sea most responsible for encouraging trade, cultural interaction, and general movement between southern Europe, North Africa, and the Middle East is

   (A) the Mediterranean.
   (B) the Caribbean.
   (C) the Red Sea.
   (D) the Arabian Sea.
   (E) none of the above

9. Deforestation and swamp draining are examples of

    (A) ancient humanity's innate sensitivity to environmental issues.
    (B) the practices of herding societies.
    (C) projects that allowed societies to shape their environment.
    (D) large-scale efforts that ancient societies were not capable of.
    (E) none of the above

10. Which of the following is an example of resource extraction?

    (A) the sowing of crop seed
    (B) building a dam
    (C) the planting of trees
    (D) mining for iron ore
    (E) digging a canal

Answers

1. **(C)** The Aborigines of Australia are thought to have originated at least 40,000 years ago.

2. **(B)** This is a matter of simple factual knowledge.

3. **(A)** Because of the continents' close proximity to each other, the populations of Africa, Asia, and Europe were able to move relatively freely across them. Until the fifteenth century C.E., North and South America remained isolated from the other continents.

4. **(D)** The school of geographical determinism, once quite prevalent, argued that geographical and environmental factors played the most important role in how human societies developed.

5. **(B)** Although communities can overcome them, topographical and climatic extremes tend to discourage social development, and the lack of a source of water does the same.

6. **(B)** From earliest times, rivers have been great facilitators of social development, movement, trade, and interaction. They make agricultural production more feasible.

7. **(D)** The importance of water transport, both oceanic and riverine, in the preindustrial world cannot be stressed enough. Also, oceans, like lakes and rivers, provide food.

8. **(A)** The Mediterranean is one of the most important bodies of water in the history of many European, African, and Middle Eastern cultures.

9. **(A)** Even ancient societies were able to exercise a great deal of control over their environments.

10. **(D)** Resource extraction—one way human societies affect their environments—involves gathering, harvesting, or otherwise taking material commodities for one's own use.

Building Blocks of Civilization

CHAPTER 2

- Prehistory
- Civilization
- Hominid development and the "Out of Africa" thesis
- The Stone Age (Paleolithic and Neolithic)
- Hunter-gatherer societies
- Gender division of labor and gender inequality
- The Neolithic revolution
- Pastoralism and herding societies
- Agriculture
- Urbanization and the role of cities
- Specialization of labor
- Metallurgy
- The Bronze Age
- Writing and systems of recordkeeping

Hominid, or humanlike, life has existed on earth for 3 million to 4 million years. Humans and their immediate ancestors appeared 100,000 to 200,000 years ago and have gathered themselves into social groups for almost as long. The history of human civilization, however, stretches back only a little more than 5,000 years. The vast expanse of time that precedes the birth of civilized societies is called **prehistory**. During this long prehistoric period, human beings evolved into their present biological form. It was also then that human populations developed the technological, cultural, political, and economic features that characterize civilized societies.

Much of the knowledge historians have of the prehistoric period comes from the work of other types of scholars, including paleontologists (who study the physical remains and fossils of animals and plants), anthropologists (who study the physical, social, and cultural characteristics of human beings), and archaeologists (who study the objects and buildings left behind by humans). These scientists constantly make new discoveries and form new theories. Therefore, the ways in which historians understand the prehistoric age often change.

What distinguishes a civilization from less advanced forms of society (those often referred to as primitive or barbaric)? Webster's Dictionary defines civilization as "social organization of a high order, marked by advancements in the arts and sciences." Four features are commonly associated with the development of civilization:

- An economic system able to make available basic goods and services
- A form of political organization capable of governing, creating social institutions, enforcing laws, and protecting people from outside threats
- A moral code, generally in the form of a shared religion
- An intellectual tradition that typically includes a written language and encourages the pursuit of knowledge, science, and the arts

EARLY HUMANS AND THE STONE AGE

The earliest hominids, or humanlike creatures, emerged in southern and east Africa around 3 to 4 million years ago. They were part of the zoological order called primates, which includes apes and monkeys. Between 2 and 3 million years ago, humanity's immediate ancestors, the early members of the genus *Homo*, appeared, also in Africa. Later versions of genus *Homo* made basic stone and wooden tools and clothed themselves in skins and furs.

At some point between 100,000 and 200,000 years ago, true humans (*Homo sapiens*, meaning "wise human") appeared. The best-known of *Homo sapiens*'s early variants are the Neanderthal and Cro-Magnon. Modern humans, known as *Homo sapiens sapiens,* may have lived as early as 200,000 years ago. How or whether *Homo sapiens sapiens* interacted with Neanderthals or Cro-Magnons is unknown. What seems more certain is that *Homo sapiens sapiens*, like all other hominids, emerged in Africa and then migrated outward. This theory is informally referred to as the "**Out of Africa" thesis**. (An opposing model, the multiregional thesis, proposes that modern humans, descending from earlier hominid groups that had already left Africa, appeared simultaneously throughout the world. However, this theory is held by a minority of scholars.) *Homo sapiens sapiens* continued the pattern of worldwide hominid movement, spreading first to Asia and Europe and then to Australia, the Arctic, and the Americas.

Hominid prehistory has traditionally been divided into eras based on levels of technological capability. Early humans made tools out of many materials, such as wood, bone, and animal skins. The most important (and the most numerous today, because they have survived best over time) were made of stone. Consequently, the first period of hominid prehistory is known as the **Stone Age**, which lasted roughly from 2.5 million years ago to 5,000 or 6,000 years ago. The Stone Age is typically subdivided into the Paleolithic ("Old Stone Age," ending approximately 12,000 years ago, and overlapping with the Great, or Pleistocene, Ice Age), the Mesolithic ("Middle Stone Age," a transitional period lasting from about 12,000 years ago to 10,000 years ago), and the **Neolithic** ("New Stone Age," beginning around 8000 B.C.E.).

NOTE

Tool use during the Stone Age was intended to provide shelter, protection, clothing, and food.

Humans moved out of natural dwellings (such as caves and canyons) and learned to build tents, huts, and, with time, wooden and stone structures that demanded advanced carpentry and construction skills. They used fire for light and heat. At what point organized warfare began to be practiced is unknown, but Stone Age humans had to protect themselves against dangers of many sorts. The first weapons included rocks and clubs.

The greatest concern of Stone Age humans was ensuring a steady and plentiful food supply. Clothing was important as well. Most tools were designed to serve these needs. Multipurpose devices such as knives and axes were especially useful. Spears, bows and arrows, fishhooks, and harpoons were used for hunting and fishing. There were wooden implements to dig roots from the ground, as well as mats and baskets to carry nuts, berries, and other foodstuffs. Clay pots were used for cooking as early as 12,500 years ago. The earliest clothes were made from furs or animal hides. As time passed, humans also began to use plant fibers. By 26,000 years ago, at least some Stone Age peoples were weaving cloth and even dyeing it to add color.

NOTE

Certain tools meant for hunting and food preparation, such as the knife, spear, ax, and bow and arrow, could also be used in combat.

Almost universally, early Stone Age social groups sustained themselves by **hunting and gathering** (also referred to as foraging). Rather than produce food themselves, hunter-gatherer societies lived off the resources they could take directly from the land, including birds and animals. They fished lakes, rivers, and seashores. They gathered nuts, berries, and roots. If and when these resources grew scarce, hunter-gatherers moved on to another area.

Primitive by later standards, the hunter-gatherer societies of the Stone Age had their own social and cultural complexities. The political and cultural organization of clans and tribes could be quite sophisticated. Some historians speculate that the coordination and teamwork necessary to hunt large creatures helped to develop effective means of waging war.

Stone Age humans worshipped deities and practiced a variety of religious rituals. They buried their dead, made sacrifices to gods and spirits, and performed ceremonies. Prehistoric humans also expressed themselves by means of art and music.

A final social feature to note is the **gender division of labor.** Because of basic physical differences, various food-gathering tasks and everyday activities tended to be assigned by sex. Men, who were on average stronger and larger, hunted, made war, and performed heavy labor. Women, for the most part smaller and weaker, gathered nuts, berries, and plants; prepared food; maintained the home; and tended children. Some historians theorize that, during the Stone Age, division of labor did not necessarily mean that men's roles were seen as superior to those of women (although this assumption remains open to debate). Whatever the case, the division of labor by gender continued long after the Stone Age and eventually gave rise to a long-standing **gender inequality** that most commonly favored men and greatly disadvantaged women. Regrettably, traces of this inequality are still found today, in even the most advanced societies, despite technological advances that have made the genders' differences in physical strength much less important.

> **NOTE**
>
> Social organization during the Stone Age was based on the family unit, which took shape during this time. Extended families tended to cluster together, forming clans bound by ties of kinship as well as larger groups such as bands and tribes.

> **NOTE**
>
> Most hunter-gatherer societies were mobile, or nomadic. Until the Neolithic era, this foraging mode of existence was the dominant form of social organization. It survived into and even after the Neolithic.

> **NOTE**
>
> The oldest cave paintings discovered to this date are 32,000 years old. The first known musical instruments are flutes from 30,000 years ago.

NEOLITHIC REVOLUTION: PASTORALISM AND AGRICULTURE

The Neolithic Revolution

The end of the Great (Pleistocene) Ice Age, around 10,000 to 12,000 years ago, gradually brought about milder conditions, warmer temperatures, and higher ocean levels. These and other climate changes profoundly altered the lives of Stone Age people. Human population increased rapidly. It is estimated that fewer than 2 million humans were alive during the ice age. There were at least 10 million by 5000 B.C.E. By 1000 B.C.E., the human population had reached somewhere between 50 million and 100 million.

Just as important as population growth (and a major cause of it) was a key transformation in how human societies provided themselves with food. Although activities such as hunting and gathering did not cease, different groups in various parts of the world, starting around 12,000 years ago, began to produce their own food.

The Practice of Agriculture, ca. 8000 B.C.E.
During the transition from the Paleolithic Era to the Neolithic, communities in the Middle East and northern China began to practice agriculture systematically.

This lifestyle depended on a new skill: the domestication of animals and plants. This skill gave birth to the practices of pastoralism and agriculture. Both allowed humans to manipulate their environment to a greater degree than ever before.

The tremendous importance of pastoralism and agriculture has made it traditional for historians to refer to their emergence as the **Neolithic revolution**. Recently, some scholars have questioned the validity of this label on the grounds that the "revolution" took place over a long period of time and that, in some parts of the world, the changes began in the Mesolithic period. However, whether one considers them revolutionary or gradual, the changes were immense.

> **NOTE**
>
> Because it required great effort and organization, agriculture encouraged closer social ties and the formation of long-lasting settlements. The permanence and stability associated with agriculture proved crucial in making early societies fully civilized.

Pastoralism and Herding Societies

Pastoralism resulted from humankind's **domestication of animals**. The first to be tamed was the dog, which, early in the Stone Age, provided many societies with companionship, security, and help in hunting. The goat was also domesticated early on for meat and milk.

The Neolithic era saw the full-scale domestication of many more animals. Horses, water buffalo, oxen, and (in the Americas) llamas provided transport and labor. For groups already involved in agriculture, animal droppings were useful as fertilizer. Many animals, particularly sheep, were raised for wool or hides, in order to make clothing. Most important, animals provided a steady source of food. Sheep, goats, cattle, pigs, and poultry yielded meat, milk, eggs, and other edible products.

Pastoralism affected early social development primarily in two ways. Groups that domesticated animals, but not plants, became **herding societies**. Because livestock consumed great quantities of grass or other fodder, herders had to migrate constantly, generally according to the pattern of the seasons. This wandering made it less likely for herding groups to develop quickly into civilized societies. Other pastoral societies began to mix animal husbandry with the domestication of plants. This combination of pastoralism and agriculture became a powerful engine driving forward many social advancements, leading to the emergence of the first civilizations.

> **NOTE**
>
> Like hunter-gatherer societies, herding societies tended to be nomadic.

Agriculture

The cultivation of plants, or **agriculture**, began in many parts of the world about 10,000 years ago. In the Middle East, wheat and barley cultivation began approximately around 8000 B.C.E. From there, it spread to the Balkans (6500 B.C.E.), the Nile valley (6000 B.C.E.), other parts of northeast Africa (5500 B.C.E.), and continental Europe (4000 B.C.E.). Central Africa developed its own agricultural tradition, growing crops such as plantains, bananas, and yams. Likewise, the peoples of North and South America, isolated from the other continents, learned agriculture on their own. Their early crops were maize (corn), beans, and squash. Millet and barley were grown in India as early as 7000 B.C.E. Probably independently, the people of northern China were growing millet by 6000 B.C.E. Rice cultivation began in Southeast Asia around 5000 B.C.E. and seems to have spread from there to southern China.

After the initial emergence of agriculture in separate parts of the world, cultural diffusion played a greater role. As more societies began to domesticate plants, certain techniques were borrowed and handed on. Seeds and crops were exchanged as well.

The most primitive forms of agriculture included migratory farming and slash-and-burn farming. The former consisted of farming in a single area for a brief time and then moving on when the soil was exhausted. The latter involved burning down forest land to clear a space for cultivation. For a time, ashes from the trees kept the soil fertile. When the soil wore out, the people farming it moved on and started the cycle elsewhere. Later, a more sophisticated technique, shifting (or swidden) agriculture, avoided using up all the soil's nutrients. Rather than cultivating all the fields in a given region, farmers planted in some fields, left others fallow (that is, unfarmed), then switched on a regular basis. Other innovations, such as fertilizing, irrigation, and mixing crop types, were also helpful.

As the Neolithic era continued, more societies began to combine agriculture with the domestication of animals. They also began to raise a variety of crops, including grains (such as wheat and barley), rice (especially in Asia), peas, beans, corn (particularly, if not only, in the Americas), and roots (such as potatoes and yams). Near the end of the Neolithic, the fermentation of alcoholic beverages, beginning with beer, had been discovered in the Middle East.

FROM STONE AGE TO CIVILIZATION: EARLY CITIES, METALLURGY, AND WRITING

Transition to Civilized Societies

More elaborate types of social organization took root throughout the Neolithic era. Agriculture required an increased commitment to a single region and caused social groups to give up nomadic life.

There was a corresponding increase in the complexity of religious practices. Rituals became more complicated. Stone Age peoples worshipped a greater variety of deities, in addition to forces of nature and the spirits of departed ancestors. They also built permanent sites of worship, including shrines, temples, and megaliths (large standing stones, such as those used at Stonehenge).

NOTE

Whether the concept of agriculture arose in one place and then spread through a process of cultural diffusion or originated and was adopted independently by many peoples at the same time is a matter of debate. The prevailing theory combines both views.

NOTE

The majority of scholars agree that women, already responsible for food collection in most Stone Age cultures, played a key part in stimulating the transition from hunting and gathering to agriculture.

NOTE

As noted before, these practices—all of which involved the diversion of water or the reshaping of the land—greatly increased the impact of human societies on the environment.

NOTE

When groups stopped wandering, they gathered into villages and communities with strong social ties and clear-cut rules of government and politics.

Cities and the Specialization of Labor

In some places, the increased social sophistication of the Neolithic era led to the emergence of a key ingredient in the development of early civilizations: the city. Cities offer protection and defense for large numbers of people. They serve as points of trade and economic activity. They enable the exchange of ideas, information, religious beliefs, and cultural values. Cities also permit people with different skills and talents to gather in a single area, allowing specialization of labor, an important feature of civilized societies. Artisans and craftspeople joined agricultural laborers in increasingly diverse social groups. The first cities date to 8000 to 7000 B.C.E. They include Jericho, on the west bank of the Jordan River, and Çatal Hüyük, in what is today Turkey. An urban center, Danpo, also appeared in China, approximately 5000 to 4000 B.C.E.

NOTE

Rare during most of the Neolithic era, cities became common after 4000 to 3000 B.C.E.

New Tools and the Bronze Age

All during the Neolithic, technological aptitude improved. Tools invented during the Paleolithic—axes, knives, bows and arrows, for example—became more refined. Newer devices, such as plows, needles, baskets, hoes, shovels, chisels, and saws, appeared. Peoples in the Middle East invented the wheel. Many groups taught themselves the multipurpose craft of pottery. The plow extended the areas of land under cultivation and increased the productivity of a society's labor force. The result was surplus production, and such surpluses gave rise to the specialization of labor described previously, as well as the stratification of society.

By the middle of the Neolithic, many societies were on the brink of discovering how to use new substances: metals. As a tool-making material, metal is much stronger and more versatile than stone. However, metallurgy (the science of extracting and refining metal from raw ore) and metalworking (the craft of shaping refined metal into tools) are highly advanced skills that took thousands of years to discover and perfect.

NOTE

Small objects and jewelry of relatively soft metals—gold, silver, lead, copper—date back as early as 6400 B.C.E. Not until harder metals could be produced affordably and in large quantities did societies start to make tools out of metal and thus move out of the Stone Age.

Large-scale metallurgy first began in the Middle East and China, sometime between 4000 B.C.E. and 3000 B.C.E. In both areas, toolmakers hit upon the idea of mixing copper and tin to create a harder alloy, bronze. Bronze tools were greatly superior to stone implements in terms of quality and adaptability, and eventually replaced them. The Neolithic era ended, and the Bronze Age (ca. 3500–1200 B.C.E.) began. Around 1200 B.C.E., with the development of iron, a metal of even greater strength and usefulness, the Bronze Age came to a close.

A final innovation that almost always accompanies the emergence of civilization is writing. During the Stone Age (and, in the case of some groups, even afterward), societies relied on the spoken word to preserve their knowledge and cultural heritage. Although many ancient societies developed rich oral traditions, it was the written word that enabled them to keep records, pass on learning, and transfer information more effectively than before. Perhaps the earliest form of writing was developed in the ancient Middle East, by the Sumerians, between 3500 and 3000 B.C.E. A handful of cultures, including the Incas, reached a civilized state without the benefit of writing, but this happened rarely.

NOTE

By capturing poems, stories, and folktales in permanent form, writing gave birth to literary traditions. The skill of writing allowed societies to leave behind detailed historical accounts of themselves.

QUICK REVIEW

1. Paleontologists

   (A) study the physical, cultural, and social characteristics of humans.
   (B) study the physical remains and fossils of animals and plants.
   (C) study the objects and buildings created by humans.
   (D) study astronomy.
   (E) study ancient urban centers.

2. Surplus production

   (A) is caused by poor cultivation methods.
   (B) prevents specialization of labor.
   (C) gives rise to the specialization of labor and stratification of society.
   (D) can never occur in modern societies.
   (E) none of the above

3. The term *Stone Age* is used to describe the earliest period of hominid prehistory because

   (A) stone was the only material early humans used to make tools.
   (B) the first humans lived primarily in elaborate dwellings built of stone.
   (C) of early humanity's tools, those made of stone were not only important but survived in large enough numbers for archaeologists to study.
   (D) early humans worshipped idols carved out of stone.
   (E) the first humans made their homes in stone caves.

4. Hunting and gathering societies were marked by

   I. widespread specialization of labor.
   II. a subsistence lifestyle.
   III. limited trade.
   IV. little specialization of labor.

   (A) I and III
   (B) II and IV
   (C) I, II, and III
   (D) II, III, and IV
   (E) IV only

5. The "Out of Africa" thesis

   (A) argues that the human species appeared throughout the world at the same time.
   (B) proposes that the human species emerged in Africa.
   (C) submits that only the Neanderthal emerged in Africa.
   (D) argues that crops were first cultivated in Africa.
   (E) proposes that only the most primitive human behavior originated in Africa.

6. Which of the following would NOT be associated with the "Neolithic revolution"?

   (A) the discovery of techniques to refine steel
   (B) the domestication of many types of animal
   (C) the widespread adoption of agriculture
   (D) the emergence of the first cities
   (E) rapid population growth

7. How did pastoralism affect early social development?

   (A) Herding societies tended to settle on particular lands, and thus civilization emerged relatively quickly.
   (B) Pastoralism led to the adoption of a monotheistic approach to religion.
   (C) No pastoral societies mixed animal husbandry with the domestication of plants.
   (D) Herding societies tended to migrate frequently, and thus civilization took longer to emerge.
   (E) Pastoral societies tended to be led by women.

8. How were women generally treated in Stone Age societies?

   (A) Most Stone Age societies revered women and placed them in positions of superiority.
   (B) Equal treatment and lack of gender differentiation was the norm.
   (C) Although gender division of labor was not as pronounced as it would later become, there was still gender inequity.
   (D) The majority of Stone Age societies were matrilineal and have been proven to have respected women's equality.
   (E) none of the above

9. Which of the following is the least advanced agricultural technique?

   (A) slash-and-burn
   (B) shifting
   (C) irrigation
   (D) fertilizing
   (E) mixing crop types

10. What development marked the end of the Bronze Age?

   (A) the first use of tools
   (B) the use of iron
   (C) the beginning of agriculture
   (D) the invention of the wheel
   (E) the adoption of the earliest form of writing

Answers

1. **(B)** Paleontologists, like archaeologists and anthropologists, are among the scholars whose scientific work assists historians in understanding prehistory.

2. **(C)** If a society regularly produces surplus food, certain individuals are free to use their time to develop high levels of expertise (or specialize) in other skills and work at them full-time.

3. **(C)** The early ages of human prehistory are categorized by the most advanced material people used to make tools. While Stone Age societies made important tools out of stone, they used other materials (wood, bone, etc.) as well.

4. **(D)** Hunting-and-gathering societies tend to be the most primitive in terms of organization and labor specialization. They rarely accumulate surpluses, and most individuals were generalists in terms of other skills.

5. **(B)** The overwhelming majority of scholars believe, on the basis of paleontological evidence, that human beings and their immediate ancestors originated in Africa.

6. **(A)** Pastoralism and agriculture were the great innovations of the Neolithic era. The earliest cities appeared as well. Metallurgy of any type was not widespread until the Bronze Age, and the ability to produce steel (which is even more advanced than iron) was a long time in coming.

7. **(D)** Herding societies are generally forced to be nomadic in order to graze their animals year-round. Nomadism tends to slow down or stall the development of civilized society.

8. **(C)** Physical differences caused some degree of gender inequity from the beginning, and at almost no time have women enjoyed complete equality, even in the modern era.

9. **(A)** Clearing a field by burning was the first and easiest way to begin agricultural production. The other techniques described in the question were developed later.

10. **(B)** Bronze gave way to iron, a stronger and more easily worked metal. Tool use, agriculture, the wheel, and writing all preceded or existed during the Bronze Age.

Major Societies, Kingdoms, and Empires to 600 C.E.

CHAPTER 3

- The river valley civilizations
- Hammurabi's law code
- Alphabets (including cuneiform and hieroglyphics)
- The *Gilgamesh Epic* and the Egyptian *Book of the Dead*
- The role of cities
- Classical Greece and Hellenic culture
- The Roman Republic and Empire

- Qin and Han China
- The mandate of heaven
- Mauryan and Gupta India
- The Indian caste system
- Migrations
- Europe's medieval period
- The Bantu
- Nubia and Ghana
- The Olmec
- The Anasazi

Although the AP World History exam places most of its weight on the period of history following 600 C.E., it requires some knowledge of the major civilizations that existed before that time. Of particular interest are the cultural, political, economic, and intellectual legacies that these older societies left behind to the newer ones that replaced them.

This chapter provides an overview of the principal states, kingdoms, and empires of the world before 600 C.E. It begins with the four earliest civilizations. It then focuses on various regions of the globe, highlighting the key characteristics and achievements of societies in those places.

THE RIVER VALLEY CIVILIZATIONS

Mesopotamian Societies

From around 3500 to 2000 B.C.E., river systems in the Middle East, India, and China gave birth to the world's first four civilizations. One of the two oldest—if not the oldest—was the Sumerian-Babylonian civilization that arose in the region of **Mesopotamia** (a Greek term meaning "land between the waters"). The rivers that gave life to this so-called Fertile Crescent were the Tigris and Euphrates. Settlement began in this area as early as 8000 B.C.E., and large-scale agriculture was practiced by 5000 B.C.E. Between 3500 and 2350 B.C.E., the first true civilization in Mesopotamia was begun by the **Sumerians**. As time passed, a variety of other local groups, especially the Babylonians (1900–1600 B.C.E.), achieved political dominance. Still, the language, culture, and religious traditions of the Sumerians influenced the peoples of Mesopotamia for centuries to come.

The Ancient Middle East, ca. 1200 B.C.E.

Note the importance of bodies of water in giving birth to ancient civilizations. The Fertile Crescent, between the Tigris and Euphrates rivers, encouraged the formation of advanced societies in Mesopotamia. The Nile did the same in Egypt. The Mediterranean Sea was crucial for the movement of people and trade goods.

The Mesopotamians built many cities (including **Babylon**) and created a society governed by a small ruling class of priests and a kinglike figure known as the *lugal* (literally, "big man"). Mesopotamia was not always politically centralized; at times, individual city-states enjoyed relative antonomy.

In the Western tradition, if not worldwide, the Sumerians were the first to develop a written language. Around 3300 B.C.E., they created a script called **cuneiform**, in which wedge-shaped characters were pressed into clay tablets with a small stick. Sometime before 2000 B.C.E., one of the world's oldest literary works, the *Gilgamesh* epic—which tells the story of a king's quest to achieve immortality—appeared in Sumeria. One of the world's first law codes was designed in Mesopotamia, by the Babylonian king Hammurabi (1792–1750 B.C.E.). Although **Hammurabi's law code** was very harsh (death and mutilation were common punishments) and favored the upper classes, the idea that a systematic, consistent set of regulations, rather than the arbitrary will of a ruler, should govern society was an important innovation.

The peoples of Mesopotamia were skilled builders and craftspeople. Using clay, they erected dozens of large cities and, to honor their many gods and goddesses, large, pyramid-like temples called **ziggurats**. They built canals and dams. They were accomplished at pottery and metalworking (bronze working began here around 3000 B.C.E.). Skilled astronomers, the Sumerians and Babylonians developed a high level of mathematical knowledge, originating the **base-60 number system** that is still used today to measure time and navigational calculations. The peoples of Mesopotamia were great traders, and their economic network extended throughout the Middle East, as well as North Africa and the Indian Ocean.

Egypt

The other early civilization of the Middle East appeared in Egypt, on the banks of the Nile. Surrounded by desert, Egypt depended for survival on the Nile's waters. Agricultural settlements began to emerge along the Nile as early as 5500 B.C.E.

The history of Egypt as a civilization is considered to have begun in 3100 B.C.E., when the king Menes united Upper (southern) and Lower (northern) Egypt. The political history of ancient Egypt is traditionally divided into several long periods. During the Early Dynastic (ca. 3100–2575 B.C.E.) and Old Kingdom (2575–2134 B.C.E.) periods, the basic features of Egyptian society and politics took shape. Civil war tore Egypt apart during the First Intermediate Period (ca. 2134–2040 B.C.E.), but a more powerful and culturally dynamic Middle Kingdom arose around 2040 B.C.E. The Middle Kingdom lasted until approximately 1640 B.C.E., when outside invaders called the Hyksos conquered it and ushered in a Second Intermediate Period (ca. 1640–1532 B.C.E.). Rebelling against Hyksos rule around 1532 B.C.E., the Egyptians formed a New Kingdom that lasted until 1070 B.C.E. Under vigorous leaders, especially Rameses II (ca. 1304–1237 B.C.E.), New Kingdom Egypt conquered a great deal of territory in northern Africa and the Middle East. Eventually, the grandeur of the New Kingdom collapsed, due to internal disorder and foreign invasions. By the 900s B.C.E., most of Egypt had lost its independence.

Although Egyptian women were secondary to men in terms of power and status, they enjoyed certain privileges. Women managed household finances and the education of children. They had the right to divorce their husbands and could receive alimony. They could own property. Some women managed businesses, and upper-class women could become priestesses. One queen, Hatshepsut, became pharaoh of Egypt in her own right.

The Egyptians had an elaborate religion and worshipped many gods and goddesses. The chief deity was Re, the sun god. What happened to the soul after death and how to reach a happy afterlife were the subjects of the Egyptians' most important religious text, the **Egyptian Book of the Dead**. Concern about life after death gave rise to mummification (the art of preserving bodies after death) and the building of gigantic tombs (including the famous **pyramids**, which provided resting places for pharaohs after they died).

The cultural and scientific attainments of the Egyptians were many. Around 3100 B.C.E., they developed a written script made up of pictorial characters called **hieroglyphics**. Using the fiber of reeds called **papyrus**, they invented the craft of papermaking. The Egyptians were skilled engineers and architects. From the beginning, they knew how to irrigate their fields, extending the reach of the Nile's waters far from the river valley itself. They began to construct pyramids around 2630 B.C.E., and their other buildings and monuments were impressive. The Egyptians were talented makers of bronze tools and weapons. They possessed a great knowledge of medicine, mathematics, and astronomy.

> **NOTE**
>
> Even more so than the Mesopotamians, the Egyptians developed a centralized society that was presided over by a monarch and a small caste of priests. The monarch, or pharaoh, was considered the living incarnation of the sun god. Although their society was less urban than that of the Mesopotamians and although they did not trade as widely, the Egyptians still erected many cities and built up a sizable economic network—particularly during the Middle and New Kingdoms.

> **NOTE**
>
> The Egyptians devised the **365-day calendar** that, with only minor modifications, is still in use today.

The Indus Valley Civilization

Farther to the east was a third civilization, which grew up on the coast of the Arabian Sea and farther inland, in what is today Pakistan and northwestern India. This was the Indus River civilization, and it arose around 2600 B.C.E. Although the people of the Indus River had a written language, it has never been deciphered by modern scholars. As a result, much about the Indus River civilization remains unclear, especially their origins, their religious beliefs, their culture, and the reasons for their decline and disappearance.

What is known is that the Indus River civilization was quite large (about the size of present-day France) and heavily urbanized. The Indus River people built several hundred cities, the largest of which, **Harappa** and **Mohenjo-Daro**, had populations of perhaps 100,000 apiece (these are the modern names, since the original names are unknown). Because the design of most of these cities is virtually identical, it is thought that the Indus River society was unified and highly centralized. The Indus River civilization produced metal tools and objects of high quality, as well as precious stones. It traded not only with its neighbors, but far beyond its borders, perhaps even with the peoples of Mesopotamia.

The Indus River civilization lasted until approximately 1900 B.C.E. How it met its end is a matter of debate. It used to be thought that invasion by outside enemies, the Aryans, destroyed the Indus River society. However, a majority of scientists now believe that environmental factors—most likely the drying up of local rivers or the erosion of soil—led to the downfall.

Early China and the Yellow River

The fourth river valley civilization emerged in China, along the Yellow River (or Huang Ho). The western reaches of China border on desert, and much of China's center is hilly or mountainous. This makes the two east–west rivers, the Yellow and the Yangtze, exceptionally important in supporting agriculture, allowing movement between communities, and fostering social and political unity. Around 8000 B.C.E., small agricultural societies formed along the Yellow River. The Chinese grew wheat, millet, and, later, rice, a high-yield crop that required an immense amount of cooperative labor. By 2000 B.C.E., the Chinese had discovered the science of bronze working.

Most of China's long history as a civilization, from the 1700s B.C.E. to 1911 C.E., is measured in dynasties, or successions of emperors. Myth and tradition speak of a dynasty called the Xia arising around 2000 B.C.E., but most scholars consider it not to have existed. Therefore, the first historically verifiable dynasty—and the bedrock of Chinese civilization—is the **Shang Dynasty**, which emerged on the banks of the Yellow River around 1750 B.C.E. and ruled a gradually growing state until 1027 B.C.E. Led by a warrior aristocracy, the Shang fought its northern and western neighbors (whom it considered to be barbarians) and expanded its boundaries by conquest.

The Shang traded extensively, its economic network stretching perhaps as far as the Middle East. Principal commodities included jade, ivory, and silk (on which the Chinese enjoyed an unbroken monopoly for over a thousand years). The Chinese system of writing, pictograms, originated with the Shang. So did two of the most important aspects of Chinese religion: fortune-telling and ancestor worship (a tradition that reinforced a strong sense of patriarchalism). The Shang also considered themselves to be at the center of the world. This idea gave rise to a sense of superiority and the long-standing tradition of thinking of China as the "Middle Kingdom."

The second, and longest-lasting, dynasty was the Zhou (Chou), founded when King Wu rebelled against the Shang and overthrew it in 1027 B.C.E. The Zhou lasted until 221 B.C.E., although it was in serious decline long before that, from around 800 B.C.E. The internal collapse and civil wars that plagued the Zhou are reflected in the name given to the last phase of the dynasty's history: the "Warring States" period (480–221 B.C.E.).

The Zhou preserved the knowledge of the Shang but added innovations of its own. Around 600 B.C.E., the Chinese learned how to make iron tools and weapons. Political sophistication increased: a central principle of the Zhou was the **Mandate of Heaven**, the idea that, as long as a leader governed wisely and fairly, he could claim a divine right to rule. Key religious and philosophical traditions, such as Confucianism and Daoism, emerged during these years (see Chapter 5).

THE CELTS

Their lack of a written tradition, as well as the fact that they never united politically, has led most scholars to consider the Celts noncivilized. However, the Celts are widely regarded as the first ethnic group to establish a widespread presence in Europe. They are believed to have emerged somewhere in central Europe, north of the Danube, thousands of years ago. After 500 B.C.E., the Celts began to migrate west, spreading throughout Europe. Their legacy is strongest in northwestern France, parts of Spain, and the British Isles (particularly Ireland, Scotland, and Wales).

> **NOTE**
>
> Although they never formed an actual state, the Celts developed a society based on close-knit tribal groups.

Although they had no written language, the Celts had a rich oral tradition, which survives in the form of myths, songs, and folktales. The Celts were highly skilled at crafts, especially metalworking. They worshipped a variety of gods and goddesses, developing a sophisticated form of religion whose priests were known as druids.

THE ANCIENT MIDDLE EAST

From approximately 1500 B.C.E. onward, the ancient Middle East witnessed the rise and fall of a number of important civilizations besides the Egyptians and the peoples of Mesopotamia. Many of them made noteworthy contributions. Although they did not invent the science of ironworking, the Hittites, who appeared in Mesopotamia around 1700 B.C.E. and dominated the region in the 1200s B.C.E., were very likely the first group to make systematic use of iron weapons.

Even more powerful were the Assyrians, who created the world's first true empire—a large state created by the conquest of one's neighbors—from 911 to 612 B.C.E. Armed with iron weapons and making use of the new skill of cavalry (horseback) warfare, the Assyrians took over most of the Middle East, including Mesopotamia and Egypt. They held their empire together by means of a deliberate policy of ruthlessness and cruelty. Assyrian rule over the Middle East was ended by a new conqueror, the Chaldeans, or Neo-Babylonians, who controlled the region from 626 to 539 B.C.E. Their most famous ruler was Nebuchadnezzar (ca. 605–562 B.C.E.), renowned for building the Hanging Gardens of Babylon.

The last group to dominate the Middle East politically before Alexander the Great (discussed below) was the Persians (550–331 B.C.E.), who, in a short time, created one of the largest empires in world history. The Persians' first ruler, Cyrus the Great, conquered present-day Iran in 550 B.C.E. By the end of the reign of the third emperor, Darius the Great (522–486 B.C.E.), the empire stretched from Turkey and Libya to the borderlands of India, measuring more than 2 million square miles, the largest empire seen in the world to that date. The Persians governed with the help of an advanced postal system, an excellent network of roads, a single currency, and a flexible form of government, in which around twenty local officials called satraps ruled in the name of the emperor. The official religion of the Persians was Zoroastrianism (see Chapter 5), but they remained relatively tolerant of other faiths. The Persians would fight several wars with their Greek neighbors to the west during the 500s and 400s B.C.E. In 331 B.C.E., Persia fell to the Macedonian conqueror Alexander the Great.

Other notable peoples of the ancient Middle East include the Hebrews (later known as Israelites and Jews). Sometime after 2000 B.C.E., this tribe, under the leadership of Abraham, became the first in the world to practice **monotheism** (worship of only one god). The Hebrews were politically weak during most of their history. They were enslaved by the Egyptians (ca. 1400–1200 B.C.E.), conquered by the Assyrians (in 721 B.C.E.), and taken over by the Neo-Babylonians (ca. 587–539 B.C.E.). Nevertheless, the religious and cultural legacy of the Hebrews, in the form of the Judeo-Christian tradition, has shaped world history in countless ways.

By about 1100 B.C.E., the **Phoenicians** had settled on the eastern coast of the Mediterranean, in what is today Syria and Lebanon. From their great cities of Tyre and Sidon, the Phoenicians developed an advanced economy based on the export of timber (particularly cedar) and highly valued purple dye made from shellfish. The Phoenicians were skilled traders and sailors, and they established many colonies along the coast of North Africa. One of these, Carthage, became one of the ancient world's great cities and a serious rival to Rome (discussed subsequently). Around 1400 B.C.E., the Phoenicians devised the world's first true **alphabet**: a system of writing in which the signs represent sounds, rather than pictures. These twenty-two letters made writing and reading much easier. They were adapted by the Greeks, then (in modified form) by the Romans. The Latin script devised by the Romans now serves as the alphabet for most modern Western languages, including English. In this way, the cultural legacy of the Phoenicians persists. A last Middle Eastern people, the **Lydians** (ca. 600–500 B.C.E.) are reputed to have invented metal **coinage** as a practical and portable form of currency.

GREECE AND ROME

Over the course of many centuries, the ancient Greeks and Romans lay the political and intellectual foundations of Western culture. Both of these Mediterranean civilizations played a central role in shaping the history of Europe, the Middle East, North Africa, and, in a sense, the entire world.

Early Greek History

The earliest civilizations in what became the Greek world were the Aegean civilizations (ca. 2000–1150 B.C.E.), centered on the island of Crete (the Minoan culture) and the Greek mainland (the Mycenaean civilization). Both were trading societies, and the Mycenaeans also grew wealthy through conquest (they are best known for fighting the Trojan War, ca. 1250 B.C.E.). Around 1200 B.C.E., Greek-speaking tribes invaded the southeastern tip of Europe, as well as the nearby islands. Over time, these tribes joined together into a single culture, the **Greeks** (or, as they called themselves, **Hellenes**). These years of gradual cultural union are known as the Greek Dark Ages (1150–800 B.C.E.). Although a common language and religion emerged during this period, political and social development remained at a relatively low level.

Greek City-States

More advancement characterized the archaic period (ca. 800–500 B.C.E.). Rugged, mountainous terrain and the fact that so many of the Greeks lived on islands prevented them from creating a single nation. Instead they formed dozens of independent—and typically competing—city-states (urban centers that controlled the immediate regions surrounding them).

NOTE

It is from the Greek word for **city-state,** *polis,* that the word "politics" comes.

Key city-states included Corinth and Thebes, but even more important were Sparta and Athens. Sparta was a rigid, slave-holding dictatorship that created the Greek world's most effective and most feared army. Athens became a culturally and politically advanced city that gained wealth through trade and power thanks to its naval strength.

The Greek city-states governed themselves in a variety of ways, but most were oligarchies, in which a narrow elite made up of rich, powerful families ruled. Slavery was common in all Greek city-states, but it was most prevalent in Sparta. Greek women were treated as social and political inferiors. Ancient Greece's most significant political innovation came from the city of Athens. This was **democracy**, or rule by the people. Democratic government began in Athens in 508 B.C.E. It reached its peak under the leadership of the statesman **Pericles** (ca. 461–429 B.C.E.). As in other Greek city-states, women and slaves were excluded from Athenian political life and did not have the right to vote. Even with these restrictions, however, Athens had the most representative government in the entire ancient world.

The Classical Period and the Age of Alexander the Great

During the classical period (ca. 500–338 B.C.E.), the Greeks fought two major wars with the Persians, in 492–490 B.C.E. and 480–479 B.C.E. In both cases, the Persians attempted to invade Greece only to be driven back, thanks to Spartan and Athenian leadership. Afterward, competition between Sparta and Athens for dominance over the Greek world led to a devastating civil conflict known as the **Peloponnesian War** (431–404 B.C.E.). Although Sparta and its allies won the war, the conflict left all of Greece's city-states weakened. That weakness opened Greece first to Persian influence, then, in 338 B.C.E., to conquest by its neighbor to the north, Macedonia (a region whose people were related to the Greeks but not as politically or socially advanced).

It was from this Greek-Macedonian kingdom that the ancient world's most skilled general, **Alexander the Great** (356–323 B.C.E.), launched one of the most successful military campaigns of all time. Alexander crossed into Asia, took over the Persian Empire, and conquered territory all the way to the borderlands of India. Before dying at the age of thirty-three—of exhaustion, alcoholism, and fever—he had led a large army on a journey of more than 20,000 miles, lasting almost 3,600 days. An important effect of Alexander's conquest was to preserve Greek culture and spread it throughout a vast portion of Eurasia and northern Africa. Under Alexander, the Egyptian city of Alexandria, with its Great Library, became one of the Mediterranean world's great centers of trade, learning, and culture.

Hellenic (Greek) Culture

The cultural accomplishments of ancient Greece are too numerous to describe in a short space. The Greeks' general cultural outlook is known as Hellenism (after the Greeks' name for Greece, Hellas). Although the polytheistic Greeks worshipped a number of gods, Hellenism tended to be more worldly and rational than other ancient cultural traditions. Science was extremely important. From the 600s to the 300s B.C.E., Greek thinkers (influenced somewhat by learning from Egypt) outlined many of the basic laws of geometry, physics, mathematics, and astronomy.

The celebration of life and the experience of being human (as opposed to fear of the gods and fixation on the afterlife) was a hallmark of Hellenic culture. Starting with the poet Homer (ca. 850–800 B.C.E.), who composed the *Iliad* and the *Odyssey*, and ending with the classical playwrights Aeschylus, Sophocles, and Euripides (all during the 500s and 400s B.C.E.), Greek writers created the Western world's first literary masterpieces. Western thought rests on the intellectual foundation established by the philosophers Socrates (470–399 B.C.E.), Plato (428–347 B.C.E.), and Aristotle (384–322 B.C.E.). Aristotle's writings on logic, observation, and experimentation set into place a mode of scientific inquiry that influenced the Middle East and the Western world for centuries, and remains at the heart of the modern scientific method. Greek sculpture and architecture are still considered to be among the world's finest. In countless ways, ancient Greece can be considered the wellspring of much of Western culture.

Early Roman History

As the Greeks faded politically, a new power emerged in Mediterranean Europe, the city of Rome, traditionally considered to have been founded in 753 B.C.E. From their homeland on the Italian peninsula, the **Romans** gradually spread outward to dominate the Mediterranean world and the regions bordering it, creating one of the largest and longest-lasting empires in history. For several centuries, Rome was governed by a monarchy. It was also controlled for some time by foreign overlords, the Etruscans. In 509 B.C.E., the Romans rebelled against the monarchy (and the Etruscans), forming a new government called the **Roman Republic** (509–31 B.C.E.).

The Roman Republic

During the republican period, Roman society experienced tensions between the lower (**plebeian**) and upper (**patrician**) classes. Through a long process of compromise and negotiation, the plebeians gained greater, but never complete, social and political equality. The most important governing body was the Senate, dominated by the patrician class. Executive power rested with two consuls, elected every year (but not in a completely democratic fashion). It was during the republican period that Rome began to expand into a Mediterranean power. By 270 B.C.E., the Romans had conquered almost the entire Italian peninsula. From 264 to 146 B.C.E., Rome fought three bitter campaigns, collectively called the **Punic Wars**, against the powerful city of Carthage, a Phoenician colony on the North African coast. Rome's victory in the Punic Wars made it the strongest state in the western Mediterranean, with a large amount of new territory in Europe, the Mediterranean islands, and North Africa. From 214 to 169 B.C.E., the Romans turned east, absorbing Greece, the Balkans, and parts of what is today Turkey. From that point forward, the Romans would take over even more territory, moving steadily to the east (into Asia and Egypt) and north (into Europe).

The Collapse of the Roman Republic

Such rapid territorial expansion caused a number of political, economic, and social crises throughout the first century B.C.E. In particular, small farmers (the closest Rome had to a middle class) began to go bankrupt, thanks to falling grain prices and the increased use of slave labor by larger landowners. Poverty worsened, and many of the urban poor joined violent mobs (which were often manipulated by unscrupulous politicians) or sold their votes to the highest bidder.

Rome was shaken by a series of civil wars from 91 to 30 B.C.E. During this period, the republican form of government to fail, and political power began to fall into the hands of a single ruler. The most famous of the late republican politicians was Julius Caesar, who assumed dictatorial powers during Rome's second civil war (49–45 B.C.E.). Although Caesar seems to have wanted to use his powers to benefit Rome, he was assassinated in 44 B.C.E. by those opposed to his growing strength. More war followed, until the republic came to an end in 31 B.C.E.

The Roman Empire

A new regime, the **Roman Empire**, remained in place for approximately five centuries, from 31 B.C.E. to Rome's downfall in 476 C.E. The first emperor was Julius Caesar's grandnephew and adopted son, Octavian, who renamed himself Caesar Augustus (30 B.C.E.–14 C.E.). Augustus restored order, revived Roman strength and wealth, and, despite the fact that he gained even more dictatorial power than Julius Caesar, enjoyed a long reign as a respected ruler. Over time, the emperor's powers grew, and his position became more despotic. During the first two and a half centuries C.E., Rome's economic and military might increased. Its huge territory extended from Spain in the west to Asia Minor in the east, from northern Africa in the south to the British Isles in the north.

From the early 200s C.E. onward, Rome found itself in crisis. During the 300s C.E., the eastern half of the empire broke away. It formally separated in 395 C.E., evolving into the Byzantine Empire. Overextension of military and political strength made it difficult to govern what remained of the western empire. The army gained a large degree of control over the imperial government. The economy experienced severe downturns. Perhaps worst of all, migrating waves of Asiatic and Germanic barbarians attacked Roman lands from the east and the north for more than four centuries. By the 400s C.E., the heartland of the empire lay open to barbarian invasion. The city of Rome itself was sacked by Gothic tribes in 410 C.E. Another wave of Goths took over the city completely in 476 C.E., the year when Rome and the entire western empire are considered to have fallen.

> **NOTE**
>
> Despite occasional episodes of political violence, Rome experienced a period of power, prosperity, and peace from the reign of Augustus to the 200s C.E. known as the *pax Romana* ("Roman peace"), which proved to be Rome's golden age.

> **NOTE**
>
> Roman imperial policy was to respect the cultural and religious practices of subject peoples, as long as they obeyed Roman law and authority.

Roman Society

Roman society was sharply divided into citizens and noncitizens, who were subject peoples with no civil rights. Within the Roman citizenry, the primary social distinction was between upper-class patricians and lower-class plebeians. As time passed, however, Roman social divisions became less rigid. Wealth, as much as one's ancestry or birth, determined one's place.

As in ancient Greece (and most ancient societies), slavery was widely practiced. Roman social and economic functions depended heavily on slave labor, and occasional slave revolts (such as that of Spartacus in the 70s B.C.E.) periodically disturbed the order of things.

The role of women in Roman society changed over time. During the republican period, Roman society was strictly patriarchal. The family head (**paterfamilias**), always male, had almost absolute power over his wife and children. By the late republican period and early empire, this tradition was breaking down somewhat. Although males remained dominant and women could not vote, women gained more freedom to divorce, more economic rights, and greater influence over family financial affairs.

Rome's Cultural Legacy

For the Western world, the cultural heritage of Rome is incalculable. To begin with, the Romans, who were great admirers of Greek culture (to the point of adapting most of the Greeks' gods), preserved for generations to come the Hellenic philosophy, literature, and scientific learning of ancient Greece.

The Romans were master builders and engineers. Many of the roads, **aqueducts**, fortifications, cities, and buildings they constructed were of use to the people who came after them for many centuries (in cases, up to the present).

The ideal of Roman imperial unity was a political concept that kings and emperors in a disunified Europe would attempt to live up to during the medieval period. Roman political thinking guided the formation of many of Europe's nations. Roman law remains one of the keystones of Western legal thought. Finally, it was at the eastern edge of the Roman Empire that the religion of Christianity was born, during the first century C.E. By making Christianity legal (313 C.E.), and then making it the empire's official faith (380 C.E.), the Romans ensured that the new religion would remain a major intellectual, cultural, and even political force, centuries after the empire itself had faded away.

> **NOTE**
>
> The concept of "innocent until proven guilty" derives from Roman law as codified in the **Twelve Tables**.

CHINA THROUGH THE HAN AND SUI DYNASTIES

From the 200s B.C.E. to 600 C.E., a united and steadily growing China was ruled by three major imperial dynasties. These were the Qin, or Ch'in (221–206 B.C.E.); the Han (206 B.C.E.–220 C.E.); and the Sui (589–618 C.E.).

The Qin Dynasty

Although short-lived, the Qin dynasty was important because of its principal ruler, **Shi Huangdi**, whose name means "first emperor." Shi Huangdi turned the Qin state—which many historians believe gave the country its name, China—into a dictatorial, tightly centralized nation. He standardized weights and measures and modernized the Chinese army by introducing iron weapons, crossbows, and cavalry warfare. Shi Huangdi used forced labor to build thousands of miles of roads, as well as the first of the structures that collectively came to be known as the **Great Wall of China**. Many of the political institutions that the Qin handed down to later dynasties—among them the concept of a strong emperor, the emphasis on legalism, and the importance of a large **bureaucracy**—became basic features of the Chinese state.

The Great Wall of China.
The so-called Great Wall was in actuality a network of many walls. Construction began as early as the 200s B.C.E., under the emperor Shi Huangdi, and took centuries. Thousands of the workers, many of them prisoners forced to labor on the walls, died. As impressive a feat of engineering as the Great Wall is, it failed in its main purpose of defending China from attack. Note the state of disrepair depicted in this engraving.

The Han Dynasty

The Qin state survived the death of Shi Huangdi by only four years. Then, in 206 B.C.E., rebellion brought to power a new dynasty, one of China's strongest and longest lasting. This Han Dynasty, building on the foundations of Shi Huangdi's Qin state, created a mighty, efficiently governed empire. Especially under the emperor Wu Ti (140–87 B.C.E.), Han armies expanded hundreds of miles to the west, north, and south, absorbing all of Inner China, much of Outer China, parts of Southeast Asia (including northern Vietnam), portions of Korea and Manchuria, and inner Mongolia. Where they did not take over directly, they established a tributary system, exacting payment from neighboring states.

Like the Qin before them, Han rulers put into place an effective administration, postal service, and tax-collecting system. They built roads, defensive fortifications (enlarging the Great Wall), and canals to link the country's major rivers. During most of the Han dynasty, the economy was strong, spurred by improved agricultural techniques and China's monopoly on silk production. By 200 C.E., however, the Han state was in decline. A downturn in agricultural production and an overall economic slump sapped its strength, as did governmental corruption and weak leadership. Outside invaders, bandits, and rebels on the frontiers made it difficult for the Han to protect their borders. In 220 C.E., the Han dynasty collapsed. It has become increasingly common for historians to draw parallels between the Han and Roman empires, which existed at roughly the same time and became large and powerful by similar combinations of conquest and effective administration. Over the next three and a half centuries, several minor dynasties rose and fell, while China itself was mired in a state of chaos and anarchy. Not until 589 C.E. did a strong dynasty, the Sui (589–618), reestablish order.

CENTRAL ASIA

Although it did not give rise to settled civilizations until comparatively late, Central Asia was the birthplace of enough important nomadic groups that it deserves mention. The grasslands and deserts of Central Asia and Mongolia were home to many herding societies. They lived highly mobile lifestyles and were adept at horsemanship and cavalry warfare.

Many cultures that originated here migrated thousands of miles to other parts of Eurasia and had a great impact on the development of civilizations and the movement of peoples in Europe and Asia. Central Asia may be the birthplace of the Indo-European linguistic and cultural group, although this question has not been proven conclusively. Certainly many of the ethnic groups belonging to the Indo-European tradition came from Central Asia, including the Aryas (or Aryans), who invaded India in approximately 1500 B.C.E., and perhaps the Persians. Many Turkic peoples, among them the Scythians, Tatars (Tartars), Seljuks, and Ottomans, trace their origins to Central Asia. Others from Central Asia who affected the course of early history were the Huns (who helped bring an end to China's Han dynasty, India's Gupta Empire, and the Roman Empire), the Magyars (ancestors of the modern Hungarians), and the Mongols (see Chapter 10), who, during the thirteenth and fourteenth centuries, carved out one of the world's largest empires ever.

EARLY JAPAN

Origins of the Japanese State

The origins of civilization on the Japanese islands remain cloudy. Communities gathered together during the Stone Age. As early as the 300s and 200s B.C.E., larger societies were appearing, but the mountainous terrain of the home islands kept settlements relatively isolated. Although Shinto tradition traces the ancestry of the Japanese imperial family back to the 600s B.C.E., there is no evidence of an organized Japanese government before the 300s or 400s C.E.

> **NOTE**
>
> It was from China (and through Korea) that, in 522, **Buddhism** arrived in Japan. Nara became famous throughout Asia as a center of Buddhist scholarship.

The Nara State

The first imperial state was ruled by the Yamato family, starting in the 300s or 400s C.E. The Shinto religion—which remained important even after the arrival of new faiths like Buddhism—legitimated the emperors, declaring them descendants of the sun goddess. The Yamato initially ruled from Nara, which, until the late 700s, served as Japan's capital. During the Nara period (ca. 300–794 C.E.), the foundations of the Japanese nation were laid. Japan also came into contact with Korea and China. The Chinese had a tremendous influence on the development of Japanese art, architecture, literature, and religion.

CLASSICAL INDIA

The Aryan Invasion

To what degree the Indus River valley civilization, which existed until approximately 1900 B.C.E., can be considered "Indian" is unclear. Therefore, the true foundations of

Indian culture remain unknown. Conventionally, Indian history is said to have begun around 1500 B.C.E., when northern India was invaded by a nomadic group known as the Aryans (also called the Aryas). Originally from Persia and Central Asia, the Aryans are considered to be among the earliest of the Indo-Europeans, one of the principal linguistic and ethnic groups of Eurasia. (Famously and tragically, Adolf Hitler and the Nazis had, centuries later, misinterpreted the concept of the "Aryan" race to justify their genocidal racial policies.) The light-skinned Aryans conquered the darker-skinned natives of India (collectively known as the Dravidians), expanding from north to south. At first, the Aryans established a warrior aristocracy and enslaved the Dravidians. Over time, Aryan and Dravidian elements blended to form a culture that was truly Indian. However, it should be noted that, even today, India is home to dozens of ethnicities, languages, and traditions.

The Aryan-Dravidian fusion gave to India several of its characteristic features. One was an elite language, Sanskrit, for religious, literary, and intellectual purposes. Another was a religious tradition, the Vedic and early Hindu faiths, that would shape India for centuries to come. In addition, a caste system emerged, dividing society into specific social classes. Over time, the Indian caste system grew increasingly complex, with new groups and subgroups. People were born into their castes, and their descendants remained in the same caste permanently. Movement from one caste to another was almost impossible, and the system led to social rigidity and stratification that persisted into modern times.

> **NOTE**
>
> The original castes included, from top to bottom, priests (brahmins), warriors and political rulers (kshatriyas), commoners (vaishyas), servants and peasants (shudras), and "untouchables."

The Mauryan Empire

India is large and diverse enough that, during the ancient and classical periods of its history, it was rarely unified as a single state. The first rulers to bring most of India together politically were the Mauryas, who created an empire lasting from 324 to 184 B.C.E. Mauryan India was characterized by a strong military and an extensive trade network, which stretched all the way to Mesopotamia and the eastern parts of the Roman Empire. A key good was cotton.

The best known of the Mauryan emperors was Ashoka (269–232 B.C.E.). A great warrior as a youth, Ashoka became sickened by war after one of his greatest victories. He converted to Buddhism and became an advocate of peace and tolerance. He spread those ideals throughout India by means of his Rock and Pillar Acts. He encouraged trade with China, especially for its silk, and opened trade routes to the north. Ashoka was admired for his justice and wisdom, and he remains famous for his efforts to create harmony between Buddhists, Hindus, and the followers of India's other religions.

The Gupta Empire

In 184 B.C.E., the Mauryan Empire collapsed, because of attacks by outside enemies. For the next five hundred years, India reverted to a state of political disunity. Not until 320 C.E. did another large empire rise up: the Gupta Empire, which lasted until 550 C.E. and controlled most of northern and central India. The Gupta Empire was smaller and less centralized than the Mauryan, but it thrived culturally and economically. Although the Gupta rulers were Hindu, they practiced religious toleration. Gupta India traded with China, Southeast Asia, and even the eastern Mediterranean. Gupta scholars created the **decimal system** used today (the misnamed "Arabic numerals"), along with the concepts of *pi* and **zero**.

Like the Mauryans before them, the Gupta emperors fell as a result of outside pressure, especially from Hun attacks on the northwestern frontier. From then until after 1000 C.E., India would remain decentralized. Then, Muslim invaders would begin to move into the subcontinent, doing much to shape Indian politics and culture after 1000 C.E.

BYZANTIUM

When the Roman Empire split in two in 395 C.E., the eastern half flourished, even after the western empire fell in 476. It was known as Byzantium, after the original name of its capital, better known as **Constantinople**. The unique position of Constantinople, between the Black and Mediterranean seas, the crossroads of Europe and Asia, made it a city of remarkable economic and military importance for a millennium and a half. The **Byzantine Empire** played a crucial role in providing commercial and cultural connections among the Europeans, the peoples of the Middle East, and Asia. It also served as a preserver of Christianity in eastern Europe and the Middle East.

NOTE

Byzantium was a glorious center of art and culture, blending Greek and Roman elements.

Under the emperor **Justinian**, who reigned during the 500s C.E., Constantinople underwent a breathtaking architectural renovation. It was during this time that the Church of Hagia Sophia was built. Now an Islamic mosque, it remains one of the ancient world's finest monuments. The famous form of religious art known as the icon originated in Byzantium and spread throughout medieval Europe, the Middle East, and eastern Europe (especially Russia). Justinian was also responsible for the **Corpus Juris Civilis** (*Body of Civil Law*), a codification of all existing Roman laws. It became (and remains) a key foundation of most European and western legal systems.

The territorial might of the Byzantine Empire reached its peak in the 500s C.E., under Justinian, who succeeded in recapturing many of the lands controlled by the western Roman Empire before its fall. From the 600s onward, the Byzantine Empire gradually lost territory in northern Africa and the Middle East, because of the rapid expansion of Islam (discussed in the next unit). Until the 1400s C.E., though, Byzantium remained a strong regional power, both in Europe and Asia.

EARLY MEDIEVAL EUROPE

The Concept of "Middle Ages"

NOTE

The first 500 years, or early medieval period, is commonly called the Dark Ages, although most historians consider this label to be inaccurate and judgmental.

After the fall of the western Roman Empire, Europe entered a state of relative backwardness. In the west, the centralizing institutions of Roman rule had been rotted out by economic decay and political corruption, then shattered by the incursion of Germanic and Asiatic barbarians. This collapse began Europe's long **medieval period**, also known as the **Middle Ages** (the term *medieval* comes from the Latin translation of this phrase). Europe's Middle Ages lasted approximately from 500 to 1500 C.E.

Barbarian Invasions

During the early medieval period, Europe continued to undergo numerous invasions by **barbarian tribes** from the north and east. This **great age of migrations** was one of the principal forces shaping European culture during these years. Most of these people were **Germanic** (Saxons, Angles, Goths) or **Asiatic** (Huns, Magyars) in origin. A number of them, especially the former, settled permanently in European lands. The kingdoms they formed tended to be unsophisticated and short-lived. Nonetheless, as the barbarian tribes of the medieval era became less nomadic and more settled, they helped form Europe's emerging (but still decentralized) nations.

BANTU AFRICA, NUBIA, AND GHANA

The incredible linguistic and ethnic diversity of Africa, especially the sub-Saharan portions, makes it difficult to generalize broadly about early societies and civilizations there.

The Bantu

The one language-based group that most resembles a common cultural source in sub-Saharan Africa is the **Bantu**. Bantu-speaking peoples emerged in the Niger River basin of west central Africa. Around 1000 B.C.E., they began to migrate throughout the continent. By 1000 C.E., their descendants had spread to the southern and eastern ends of Africa.

It is inaccurate to say that the Bantu provided Africa with a single cultural heritage. It can be argued, though, that, of the many peoples of sub-Saharan Africa, the Bantu played the greatest role in shaping the region's cultural, ethnic, and linguistic character. They transformed an area that had earlier been sparsely populated by groups of hunter-gatherers to one that was more densely populated and dominated by farming communities. All Bantu-speaking groups of southern and eastern Africa—including the Swazi, Sotho, Tswana, Shona, Ndebele, Venda, Xhosa, and Zulu—came to depend on the ownership of cattle as the foundation of their economic and political systems.

> **TIP**
>
> It is believed that Bantu-speaking tribes spread the knowledge of agriculture and ironworking to many parts of eastern and southern Africa.

Nubia and Ghana

Not counting Egypt, the first major civilizations in Africa appeared in Nubia and Ghana. The former is a thousand-mile region south of Egypt that links sub-Saharan Africa with the Mediterranean coast. With the Nile running through it, **Nubia** became an important corridor for trade between north and south. A particularly valuable commodity was gold. Nubia was settled around 3000 B.C.E. More advanced societies appeared about 2300 B.C.E., and a powerful kingdom known as Kush emerged in approximately 1750 B.C.E. For 500 years, the Egyptian New Kingdom dominated Nubia, but its control gradually faded.

A new Nubian kingdom rose during the 700s B.C.E. From the fourth century B.C.E. to the fourth century C.E., that kingdom was centered at the prosperous city of **Meroë**, south of Egypt. Meroë, surrounded by grasslands and, on three sides, by rivers, could support agriculture and livestock grazing. It also contained large deposits of iron ore and the scale of iron production in Nubia was once large. Meroë collapsed in the second century C.E., as a result of changing trade patterns in the Red Sea and environmental factors, especially the erosion of topsoil, caused by heavy deforestation.

Far to the west, on the Atlantic coast, was **Ghana**. The first major sub-Saharan kingdom, this "land of gold" dates back to the 500s C.E. Part of the **trans-Saharan trade network** that extended throughout the Sahara, Ghana grew during the next 500 years, expanding throughout northwestern Africa.

EARLY CULTURES IN THE AMERICAS

Mexico and Central America

Advanced civilizations began to appear in the Americas after 1200 B.C.E. The oldest and most sophisticated were in Mexico and Central America (also known as Mesoamerica), where a succession of cultures, each influencing the ones that followed it, emerged. The first major society in the Americas was that of the Olmecs (ca. 1200–400 B.C.E.). Located in east-central Mexico, on the coast of the Gulf of Mexico, the Olmecs created what is considered to be the "mother civilization" of Central America. Although their written language remains a mystery to modern scholars, it is clear that the art (consisting mainly of large heads carved from stone), monumental architecture, and religion of the Olmecs had an impact on the peoples that came after them. One interesting comparative point is that, unlike other early civilizations—such as Mesopotamia, Egypt, Shang China, and the Indus culture—the Olmec arose without the benefit of a nearby major river system.

The next major society in the region was centered on the vast city of Teotihuacán, founded approximately 150 to 100 B.C.E., near modern-day Mexico City. With a population greater than 200,000, Teotihuacán was one of the world's largest cities at the time. It existed until 750 C.E. By that point, it had been eclipsed, perhaps taken over, by one of the most complex societies of the ancient Americas, the Maya, who flourished from 250 to 900 C.E. (On the Maya, see Chapter 12.)

Andean Societies In South America

In the northwestern portion of South America, several civilizations rose up in the peaks and valleys of the Andes. Recent archaeological discoveries indicate that the first city in the Americas, Caral, was probably founded along the Supe River, in central Peru, around 2600 B.C.E. Most Andean cultures were skilled at weaving, pottery, and metalworking. It is thought that in the Americas, metallurgy originated here, then spread northward. Andean cultures formed heavily urban, class-stratified societies. Their most important domesticated animal was the llama. The oldest of these societies was the Chavin (ca. 850–250 B.C.E.). Like the Olmec civilization, Andean societies created advanced cultures without growing up on the banks of a major river.

The South American plains gave rise to nomadic herders. The rain forests of the Amazon basin were home to innumerable tribes. However, in neither area did settled civilizations of the complexity found in the Andes appear before 1000 C.E.

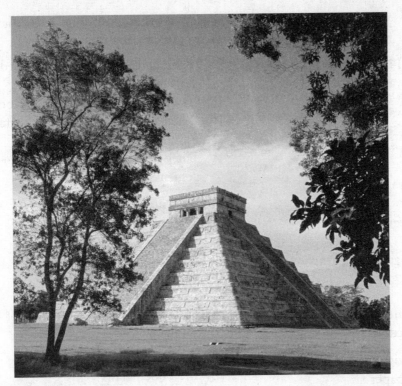

Mayan Pyramid of Chichén Itzá.
The Maya founded the city of Chichén Itzá around 250 C.E. It remains a treasure trove of archaeo-logical evidence about how the Maya lived. The pyramid was constructed in approximately 1100 C.E. For more, see Chapter 12.

North American Cultures

To North America, advanced social structures came comparatively late. A number of tribes began to form in the forests of the eastern part of the continent. The first was the Adena (ca. 500 B.C.E.–100 C.E.), fol-lowed by the Hopewell (100–400 C.E.) and Missis-sippian (700–1500 C.E.) cultures. All three spread out along the Ohio and Mississippi river valleys. Their most famous legacy is a variety of giant earth mounds, built for ceremonial and religious purposes.

Sometime in the first millennium C.E., a civiliza-tion in North America's desert Southwest reached its peak. This was the Anasazi (a Navajo word meaning "ancient ones," because the original name is lost). Small settlements date to 400 C.E., but the Anasazi may have appeared years before that, and the exact date of their origins remains unknown. The Anasazi—and the Native Americans of the Southwest who followed them—are famous for their elaborate cliff dwellings, made of clay and rock, perched hundreds of feet above the floors of the canyons and desert below.

MONUMENTAL ARCHITECTURE

The modern world takes large-scale architectural projects for granted. Ancient peoples were capable of equally grand feats of construction, such as the ziggurats, Stonehenge, the Great Wall of China, the Parthenon, the Colosseum, and the pyramids of Egypt and Mesoamerica. Monumental architecture required an enormous expenditure of resources and labor, which was often forced or provided by slaves. Why did societies make such mammoth investments? Motivations include religion (burial or the perfor-mance of rituals), defense, entertainment, and the public display of political power. Over time, com-merce became important as well.

QUICK REVIEW

1. One of the philosophical innovations of Hammurabi's law code was that

   (A) the ruler's will is to be followed at all costs.
   (B) the upper classes are to have the most rights.
   (C) the lower classes were to have special privileges.
   (D) a consistent set of regulations should govern society.
   (E) anyone who spoke against the king would be executed.

2. Which of the following are the Egyptians thought to have originated?

   (A) the construction of ziggurats
   (B) the manufacture of paper
   (C) the numerical concept of zero
   (D) the secret of silk production
   (E) none of the above

3. What do many researchers now think brought about the fall of the Indus River society?

   (A) fighting between the Hindus and Sikhs
   (B) outside invasions from Mesopotamia
   (C) environmental factors
   (D) population growth
   (E) all of the above

4. Why was the Zhou dynasty in China so long-lived?

   (A) It innovated technology and increased China's political sophistication by obligating the leader to rule fairly.
   (B) Its leaders were ruthless.
   (C) It did not have to contend with the conflicting dictates of Confucianism.
   (D) It prevented average people from acquiring weapons.
   (E) It actually was very short-lived.

5. What factors account for the Assyrians' success in creating their empire?

   I. They had a large army that used horseback warfare.
   II. They made and used iron weapons.
   III. Their leaders ruled with deliberate ruthlessness.
   IV. They treated their subject peoples with leniency.

   (A) I, II, and III
   (B) I, II, and IV
   (C) I and III only
   (D) II and IV only
   (E) all of the above

6. Which people developed the world's first true alphabet?

   (A) the Lydians
   (B) the Phoenicians
   (C) the Hebrews
   (D) the Persians
   (E) the Egyptians

7. In Greek society, women were treated as

   (A) equals to men, especially when it came to voting.
   (B) gods.
   (C) inferior to men in both social and political affairs.
   (D) slaves in every household.
   (E) none of the above

8. Which of the following was NOT one of Rome's cultural legacies?

   (A) The Romans preserved Hellenic philosophy.
   (B) The Romans built roads and fortifications that have lasted for centuries.
   (C) The Romans adopted the Islamic religion as the official faith of the empire.
   (D) The Romans made Christianity the official faith of the empire.
   (E) The Romans adopted a legal code still in some use today.

9. Which of the following is an accurate statement about the Indian caste system?

    (A) Its top stratum was the untouchables.
    (B) Its top stratum was the Sikhs.
    (C) People enjoyed social mobility.
    (D) All Aryans were in the untouchable caste.
    (E) There was virtually no social mobility.

10. Which of the cities below is correctly matched with its civilization?

    (A) Meröe—Nubia
    (B) Mohenjo Daro—Persia
    (C) Alexandria—Gupta India
    (D) Sparta—Han China
    (E) Teotihuacán—the Incas

Answers

1. **(D)** The notion that society and law were to operate according to something other than the will of the ruler did not naturally occur in early societies.

2. **(B)** The Egyptians made paper from the fiber of papyrus reeds. Ziggurats were built in Mesapotamia, mathematicians in India elaborated the concept of zero, and silk production began in China.

3. **(C)** It used to be thought that the Aryan invasions of 1500 B.C.E. destroyed the Indus culture, but most scholars now believe that soil erosion or the drying up of rivers caused its decline.

4. **(A)** The Mandate of Heaven, which required the emperor to treat his people well if they obeyed, originated with the Zhou and became one of the most powerful political concepts in China.

5. **(A)** Advanced technology and military effectiveness helped the Assyrians to build their great empire. They maintained it by means of unusual brutality.

6. **(B)** Unlike hieroglyphs and cuneiform, an alphabet uses symbols to represent sounds, not concepts. The Phoenician alphabet, the first, was adopted and modified by the Greeks and Romans.

7. **(C)** One of the ironies of ancient Greek culture is that, while the Greeks originated democracy as a form of government, they treated women as inferiors. Even in Sparta, where women had more rights than most, they were not equal.

8. **(C)** Islam did not emerge until a century and a half after the fall of Rome.

9. **(E)** India's caste system, justified by Hindu doctrine, was extremely rigid.

10. **(A)** This is a matter of factual knowledge. Meröe was a great trading center in West Africa.

CHAPTER 4

Social Structure and Cross-Cultural Connections

- Cultural diffusion versus independent innovation
- Class structures
- Specialization of labor
- Social stratification and hierarchy versus social mobility
- Monarchies, oligarchies, and feudalism
- Noble/aristocratic classes

- Republics and democracies
- The nation-state
- Slavery and serfdom
- Warfare
- Trade (water transport versus overland caravan routes)
- Religious interchange and missionaries
- Migrations

To generalize about civilizations around the globe—and throughout history—is difficult, if not impossible. Human communities are diverse, and each possesses unique characteristics. Nonetheless, most have certain broad features in common. This chapter will discuss some of those features, focusing on various ways that cultures have tended to organize themselves politically, socially, and economically.

This chapter will also show how societies interacted, especially in the early eras of world history. Cross-cultural interaction can take place in a number of ways, all of which bring civilizations into closer contact with each other, with both positive and negative consequences. By 600 C.E., many civilizations had begun to interact with other groups, in some cases over considerable distances. Sometimes encounters were peaceful, often they were not.

Many things about individual societies—what they knew, how they lived, the material possessions they had available to them, whether or not they survived at all—were deeply affected by how they met and dealt with other civilizations. One of the most common forms of social, cultural, technological, and economic change is diffusion: the spread of inventions, foods, trade goods, concepts, and practices from one people to another. Determining to what degree a given society's basic features are shaped by cultural diffusion or independent innovation is one of the most challenging and interesting questions in the study of ancient cultures. Both have played important roles in the evolution of civilizations.

CLASS STRUCTURES

Almost all societies have some form of class distinction, according to which people are defined by such things as wealth, ancestry, or occupational function. Differentiation by class is quite limited in preagricultural societies. Typically, among hunters, gatherers, and herders, all members of the group perform similar functions (although, as described in Chapter 2, labor is, in most cases, divided by gender) and have similar skills. Most possessions are shared or owned commonly. Thus, members of these societies remain more or less equal. Exceptions include chieftains and elders (who provide leadership) and priests or shamans (who provide religious guidance and, often, medical care).

True class distinction generally coincides with a society's adoption of agriculture. Agriculture encourages permanent settlement and technological advancement. Because land and the tools and livestock needed to work it are so important, agriculture makes the concept of private property meaningful. Agriculture also leads to the creation of food surpluses, meaning that, unlike in pre-agricultural societies, substantial numbers of people not directly involved in food production can be fed. These people are free to develop other skills for the benefit of their society and themselves. As noted in Chapter 2, this gives rise to the specialization of labor.

Certain social roles—such as political or military leadership—are inherently more powerful than others. Also, some occupations come to be more valued than others. This situation gives rise to the phenomenon of social stratification, in which upper and lower classes emerge. A culture's system of ranking social classes is known as a hierarchy. Each society judges for itself which classes are more important and which are less so. Each society also has its own way of determining how classes interact with each other, how difficult it is for an individual to move from one class to another (the concept of social mobility), and what benefits or disadvantages each class possesses. Religion often plays a role in justifying social hierarchies. In most societies up to 600 C.E. (and even later), the privileged, or elite, classes were quite small. Social stratification tended to be rigid, meaning that upward social mobility was difficult. Certain civilizations, such as India, had extremely strict arrangements, called caste systems, in which movement from one class to another was impossible. In most early civilizations, lines between classes were very sharply drawn. Upper classes typically enjoyed many legal and financial advantages, such as more lenient treatment before the law and immunity from taxation.

At most times and in most parts of the world, political power, religious leadership, and important social functions have been in the hands of males, especially since the rise of settled agricultural and urban cultures. Societies in which male domination prevails are called patriarchies. A small minority of early societies gave more political, religious, and social power to women. These matriarchies, however, were rare. There are a few archaeologists and anthropologists who have tried to prove that most preagricultural societies were originally matriarchal, but their theories are not accepted by most scholars. In either case, from the development of agriculture onward, the gender division of labor has remained an important (and unfortunate) way, along with class, that societies differentiate certain members from others.

> **NOTE**
>
> Up to 600 C.E., the vast majority of people in most societies were peasants and farmers. Still, an increasing percentage of those societies' members performed other functions. Ruling classes, generally in the form of royal families, emerged to run governments that became more complicated as time passed. Other examples of more specialized occupations in early societies include soldiers, priests, craftspeople, artisans, scribes, and accountants.

FORMS OF GOVERNMENT

Few communities, no matter how primitive, fail to provide themselves with a form of leadership. Even the least advanced group will have some kind of chief or war leader. As societies grow into civilizations, they develop more complex forms of government. Although details vary, most political systems fall into one of a few basic categories.

Perhaps most common before the modern era was **monarchy**, or government led by a single ruler—typically a king, queen, emperor, or empress. In premodern eras, the monarch's power was often justified in religious terms: Egyptian pharaohs were said to be the sun god's incarnation, Chinese emperors ruled with the so-called Mandate of Heaven, and many European kings claimed to govern according to the principle of "divine right."

Most monarchs govern with the assistance of a small upper class, known as the **nobility** (or **aristocracy**). This political elite assists the monarch with political administration, economic development, military defense, and other matters that he or she cannot take care of directly or alone. In cases where the monarch's powers are relatively weak, he or she often rules in tandem with a **parliament** (or some sort of lawmaking body) or according to the rules of a constitution or both. Before around 1000 C.E., however, such arrangements were extremely rare. In most instances, monarchical rule is hereditary (as is noble or aristocratic status). Monarchies in which the monarch possesses an unusual amount of power—or all of it—are referred to as autocratic or despotic. In highly decentralized conditions (as in medieval Europe or preunification of Japan), monarchies often degenerated into feudal systems, in which the local authority of individual nobles outweighs the central authority of the monarch.

Also prominent was **oligarchy**, or rule by the few. In oligarchic systems, political power rests in the hands of a small elite group, generally chosen from the wealthy or the aristocracy.

Two forms of government remained fairly uncommon before modern times: the republic and democracy. Often thought to be identical, the two can actually be substantially different. A **republic** (from the Latin term *res publica*, meaning "public thing") is a state in which all or most adult citizens (generally, until recently, only males) play some role in government. However, the republican form of government does not guarantee that all citizens will play an *equal* role in government. For example, the votes of a republic's upper class may count for more than those of lower classes (as in ancient Rome). Or members of the lower classes may be allowed to vote but not to run for office. Unlike a republic, a **democracy** grants more or less equal political rights and opportunities to all adult citizens, that is, until the modern era, all adult male citizens (the word comes from the Greek phrase for "rule by the many"). It is possible for a republic to be fully democratic, but it does not have to be (the modern United States is considered to be a democratic republic). One of the very few democracies to exist before the modern age was the Greek city-state of Athens.

A government dominated by a religious elite is known as a **theocracy**.

Nations (also **nation-states** or countries) are states run by centralized governments and united by uniform legal systems and a sense of common national identity. Generally, a nation-state's population (or the majority of the population) shares a common language, ethnicity, religion, and cultural heritage. Not all societies are nation-states in the modern, technical sense. Especially during the ancient period and even later, states tended to be less centralized, and they were thought of as a monarch's personal property. The concept of nationhood is a relatively modern phenomenon.

SLAVERY

One of human society's most shameful institutions is the ownership of human beings by other human beings, or **slavery**. Until comparatively recently (the 1800s), slavery was widespread. In some parts of the world, it still exists today. Before and around 600 C.E. (and long afterward), most societies around the world practiced slavery or engaged in and benefited from economic activities reliant on it.

Slaves performed a number of functions. These were divided mainly into household tasks and hard labor (especially jobs associated with construction or agriculture). Questions such as the severity of slaves' treatment, the length of their service, and the degree to which they had legal rights or protections depended on the laws and customs of each society.

People fell into slavery in many ways. Some were prisoners of war or captives taken during raids into enemy territory. Some were debtors who were sold—or sold themselves—into slavery. Slaves were sometimes kidnapped or pressed into service by force. In some societies, slave status was hereditary, passed on from parent to child.

Trade in slave labor went on in almost every major society. Regional networks grew up around the globe for the exchange of slaves. Prior to 1000 C.E., particularly important slave markets appeared in the Mediterranean, Africa, China and the Far East, and the Arab world. From the 1400s through the 1800s, Europeans and Americans transported millions of slaves from Africa to North and South America. This infamous **Atlantic slave trade** is discussed in further detail in Units Four and Five, Chapters 18 and 26.

An institution similar to slavery existed in many times and places—**serfdom**. In serf-holding societies, the majority of a country's peasants would be unfree. Serfs were not technically slaves. They had more freedoms and protections than slaves (who were seen in most law codes simply as property). Still, serfs were bound to the land they lived on, unable to move or change profession without permission of the land's owner. Whether or not they had theoretical legal protections, serfs were, in real life, often vulnerable to many of the same abuses that slaves were. In some parts of Europe (especially Russia), serfdom persisted until the 1800s.

WAR

Regrettably, one of the most—if not *the* most—straightforward modes of human interconnection is **war**. Exactly when humans began to engage in organized violence is unknown. Most scholars speculate that combat emerged among hunter-gatherer societies during the Stone Age, growing out of the cooperative efforts needed to track and kill large animals.

From the beginning, wars were fought for a variety of reasons. These included competition over resources such as hunting grounds, water sources, and livestock. Fear and hatred of other groups caused conflicts, as did the desire for captives to use as slaves or for forced labor.

During the Stone Age, few if any societies maintained any type of professional military organization. Instead of forming armies, hunter-gatherer and herding societies assigned the responsibility for fighting to all or most able-bodied males. However, during the Bronze Age, the character of warfare changed. The advent of agriculture, the increased permanency of farming communities, and the rise of cities made it possible and necessary to create a specialized class of soldiers for the protection of a civilization's territory and property. Improved metallurgical techniques gave these new soldiers better weapons and armor.

Therefore, by the 3000s and 2000s B.C.E., sizable and well-organized armies, led by professional generals and officers, had begun to appear in many parts of the world, especially the ancient Middle East and China. Military skills and equipment increased in sophistication and complexity. From the Bronze Age onward, war became a driving force in world history—and one of the most striking, most important ways in which societies, over the course of centuries, have interacted.

> **THE FALL OF EMPIRES**
>
> Empires like Rome, Persia, Han China, and the Abbasid Caliphate collapsed because of a complex mix of reasons—generally a combination of *internal* and *external* factors. Examples of the former include economic crisis, civil war, social tensions, and unwise political leadership (sometimes an environmental problem, such as climatic shift or the appearance of a new disease, plays a role). The most obvious external factor is military threat, whether from raiders, nomads, or an enemy state. Outside aggression is most likely to bring down an empire if it is already weakened by internal problems. Also, the larger an empire becomes, the more likely it is to suffer what many call imperial overreach: The task of holding far-flung territories together stretches the imperial authority too thin, and the empire falls, or at least loses outlying territories.

TRADE

A powerful motivator of interaction between societies is **trade**, or the exchange of goods. From prehistory onward, human communities have found it mutually beneficial to buy, sell, or barter resources with each other. Trade takes place within societies, bringing cities, villages, and rural communities into closer contact. Societies also trade with other societies, creating connections and interdependencies throughout large areas of the world.

As long as the economic terms are relatively fair and equal, trade generally leads to increased prosperity or advantage for all parties. Economic relationships also stimulate the exchange of ideas, information, and cultural practices between civilizations. In many cases, healthy economic relationships between societies and states have helped to preserve peace. Conversely, disputes over trade have frequently led to hostility, even war. In times of conflict or disagreement, it is common for enemies to attempt to deprive each other of the ability to trade, either by means of blockade (physically interfering with a society's ability to move goods across its borders) or sanctions (refusing to trade with a society).

Until the invention of railroads and modern roads, the movement of goods overland was quite difficult. **Water transport** was much easier. Therefore, trade tended to flourish along rivers, lakeshores, and the coastlines of oceans and seas. In the premodern era, key international trade routes sprang up in the **Mediterranean Sea**, the North and Baltic seas, the Arabian Sea and **Indian Ocean**, the river systems of western Europe (especially the Rhine and Danube), the river basins connecting Scandinavia and Russia with the Black Sea, and East Asia's Pacific shore. Land routes included the **caravan routes of the Sahara desert and the Arabian peninsula**. The longest and most important overland trade route was the **Silk Road**. This network stretched more than 5,000 miles, linking China with the Mediterranean coast of the Middle East—and, by extension, Europe.

Principal African-Eurasian Trade Routes, ca. 200 B.C.E.–200 C.E.
During this time, merchants sold goods along a vast trade network that spanned from England in the northwest, to western Africa, Central Asia, and as far east as the Han Empire.

RELIGIOUS INTERACTION

Every society develops or adopts some kind of belief system in order to address questions of ethics, morality, and humanity's place in the universe. The world's major religions are described in Chapter 5. It should be noted here, however, that religious beliefs cross borders very easily, allowing different cultures and civilizations to affect each other profoundly. Sometimes, religions spread peacefully, through cultural contact or deliberate **proselytizing and missionary activity**. In other cases, religious faiths are brought to other societies by means of aggression and war.

As societies interact, they often absorb some of the deities and basic religious concepts of their neighbors, even if names and details change. This borrowing took place among many of the native populations of Africa, South America, and North America. Throughout Eurasia, many religious ideas are shared by the mythologies of the various descendants of the Indo-Europeans, who spread throughout Europe and Asia thousands of years ago. Famous examples of religious borrowing in the ancient Western tradition include the adoption of Sumerian gods and goddesses by the Babylonians, as well as the Romans' use of Greek deities, with slightly modified names.

All the world's key religions had traveled far from their original birthplaces by 1000 C.E. Hinduism was prominent not only in India, but throughout Southeast

Asia. Buddhism spread from India to all of East Asia, including China, Korea, and Japan. Confucianism and Daoism, which originated in China, influenced religious and philosophical thought elsewhere in East Asia. Judaism, Christianity, and Islam burst out of the Middle East to have huge effects on North Africa, Asia, and Europe (later, Christianity and Judaism would be exported to the Americas as well).

THE MIGRATION OF PEOPLES

Human populations rarely develop in isolation, especially in times when communities are less settled. The mass movement, or **migration**, of large numbers of people in the early periods of global history has had a tremendous effect on the ethnic and cultural makeup of most of the world's major societies, even today.

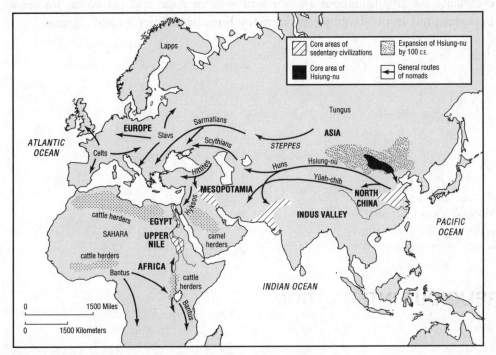

The Movement of Peoples in Eurasia and Africa After 2000 B.C.E.
Migration played a major role in the formation and development of early civilizations. Migrations often led to war and conquest, but they also facilitated cultural interaction and the spread of technology, science, languages, and religions.

As described in Chapter 2, humanity originated in Africa, and then spread to all the other continents (excepting Antarctica). *Homo sapiens sapiens* moved into the Middle East and much of Asia around 100,000 years ago. Perhaps as far back as 50,000 years ago, settlers crossed from Southeast Asia to Australia. By 40,000 years ago, there were numerous human communities throughout Europe. Most scholars think that humans did not reach the Americas until comparatively late. Scientists estimate that *Homo sapiens sapiens* first came to the Americas 15,000 years ago (perhaps earlier). At that time, peoples from Asia crossed an ice shelf or land bridge that spanned what is now the Bering Strait, the narrow waterway separating the tip of Russia from Alaska. By 8000 B.C.E., humans had settled in almost all parts of the globe.

After the settlement of these continents, the regions that experienced the greatest and longest-lasting waves of mass migration were Africa, the Pacific, and Eurasia. From 2,500 to 5,000 years ago, the Bantu peoples began to spread throughout sub-Saharan Africa. Starting sometime around 2500 B.C.E., the epic migration of the Polynesians from Southeast Asia throughout the vast expanse of the Pacific Ocean led to the settlement of literally thousands of islands. In Eurasia, a number of peoples, mainly from Central Asia, migrated outward, deeply affecting the ethnic and linguistic makeup of many European and Asian peoples. In particular, Europe was flooded by a tremendous influx of invaders, from approximately the 200s C.E. to 1000 C.E.—a period known as the **Great Age of Migrations**. During this time, a variety of Germanic and Asiatic peoples moved toward and into Europe. Although they were generally seen as a threat—and often perceived as barbarians—many of these peoples eventually settled throughout Europe and western Asia, and played an immensely important role in the development of many Eurasian ethnicities and cultures.

QUICK REVIEW

1. Why were trade routes particularly extensive in Eurasia?

    (A) There were so many communities that could potentially be linked by them.
    (B) Eurasia was where most goods were produced.
    (C) Europeans did not yet know how to build roads.
    (D) Russian tsars built all these routes using forced labor.
    (E) Trade routes were not well developed at all in Eurasia.

2. Which of the following statements about gender relations in the premodern era is most accurate?

    (A) Across all societies, women were subservient to men to the same degree.
    (B) In some societies, women enjoyed more rights than in others.
    (C) Because of the widespread worship of the mother goddess, in most societies, women were politically dominant.
    (D) Organized religions tended to strengthen gender equality.
    (E) The emergence of agriculture weakened gender division of labor.

3. What is diffusion?

    (A) the assimilation of a minority ethnic group into a larger, more homogeneous population
    (B) the splitting of the atom
    (C) the conquering of one civilization by a much more powerful one
    (D) the spread of foods, trade goods, concepts, norms, practices, and inventions among different peoples
    (E) none of the above

4. What role did the aristocracy usually play in monarchies during the premodern era?

    (A) It usually opposed the monarchy's goals.
    (B) It worked in the interests of its constituents, the peasants.
    (C) It tended to assist monarchs with such tasks as political administration and defense.
    (D) The aristocracy is another word for the monarchy, so it acted as king.
    (E) The aristocracy was an early middle class.

5. Which of the following is an example of a democracy?

    (A) the city-state of Sparta
    (B) republican Rome
    (C) the Mauryan Empire under Ashoka's rule
    (D) Byzantium
    (E) none of the above

6. Which of the following distinguishes slavery from serfdom?

    (A) Serfs tended to have legal protections, whereas slaves were generally seen as property.
    (B) Serfdom was practiced only in Europe, while slavery appeared worldwide.
    (C) Slavery continues to persist, but serfdom was abolished by around 1700.
    (D) all of the above
    (E) none of the above

7. What factors would cause a professional class of soliders to appear in a society?

    I. Because farming meant that land needed to be protected.
    II. Because the society was nomadic and thus more vulnerable to attack.
    III. Because urban areas were built up that needed to be guarded.
    IV. Because agriculture led to labor specialization.

    (A) I and II only
    (B) I, II, and III
    (C) I, III, and IV
    (D) all of the above
    (E) none of the above

8. Leading up to 1000 C.E., what was the world's most vital overland trade route?

   (A) the Silk Road
   (B) the Sahara Desert
   (C) Main Street USA
   (D) the Sahel
   (E) the Trans-Siberian

9. According to scientists, modern humans reached _____ by crossing a land bridge spanning the Bering Strait approximately 15,000 years ago.

   (A) Africa
   (B) Australia
   (C) Greenland
   (D) North America
   (E) Scandinavia

10. During the so-called Great Age of Migrations,

   (A) humans moved back to Africa.
   (B) many Germanic and Asiatic peoples moved into Europe.
   (C) many Europeans moved to Asia to seek a more temperate climate.
   (D) humans moved out of Africa into Indochina.
   (E) Polynesians moved to mainland Asia.

Answers

1. **(A)** In early times, continents such as Australia, North America, and South America were inaccessible to people living in Europe, Asia, and Africa. However, the people of the latter three continents were able to—and had incentive to—interact with each other.

2. **(B)** Different societies treated women differently. While women rarely ever achieved actual equality, they often had certain rights and privileges.

3. **(D)** One of the key ways societies develop is to interact with and learn from other societies.

4. **(C)** While aristocrats sometimes quarreled with, and even opposed, monarchs, they generally helped the monarch to govern. The benefit to the aristocracy was greater power and status.

5. **(E)** Democracy was extremely rare in the premodern era. The best example would have been the Greek city-state of Athens.

6. **(A)** Most law codes granted serfs some sort of legal rights and protections, although they were not always observed in practice. Both systems existed worldwide, and both persisted well past 1700.

7. **(C)** In primitive and nomadic cultures, most adult males shared the burden of defending their societies. Cities and settled regions tended to rely on professional, more specially skilled armies.

8. **(A)** While overland trade routes crossed the Sahara, the Silk Road was longer, joined a greater variety of societies, and transported a larger assortment of goods.

9. **(D)** The Bering Strait joins the northeastern tip of Asia with Alaska. The Americas are thought to have been settled by Asiatic nomads crossing over the land bridge that used to exist there.

10. **(B)** The Great Age of Migrations helped bring an end to the Roman Empire and profoundly shaped the fate of Europe in the medieval era.

Religious Traditions and Belief Systems

CHAPTER 5

- Polytheism versus monotheism
- Judaism (the Torah and Talmud)
- Hinduism
- Buddhism
- Daoism
- Confucianism
- Christianity (the Bible)
- Islam (the Qur'an)

Integral to the growth of any civilization is the development of belief systems that enable social groups to address questions of ethics, morality, spirituality, and the possibility of an afterlife. Religions play positive and negative roles. They give societies a sense of unity, pride, and inspiration. Missionary activity and proselytizing efforts have often led to dynamic and fruitful interactions across cultures. On the other hand, clashes between different faiths (or denominations within faiths) have frequently resulted in bigotry, persecution, and war. In positive and negative ways, religion continues to be an indispensable factor in the functioning of civilizations.

POLYTHEISM

Ancestor Worship And Other Early Forms Of Religion

Almost without exception, the earliest societies' belief systems were polytheistic, meaning that they involved the worship of more than one deity. Among the oldest forms of **polytheism** are ancestor worship and the veneration of spirits. Examples of the latter are totemism (identification of the self with animal symbols), shamanism (a belief in spirit worlds, common in Central Asia, Siberia, and the Americas), "dreamtime" (a spiritual concept peculiar to the Australian aborigines), Shinto (native to Japan), and animism (a worship of life forces prevalent in Africa, the Pacific Islands, and parts of Asia).

Pantheons

Certain civilizations developed elaborate pantheons of gods, each of whom had a distinct personality and function. Among the best-known are the Sumerian-Babylonian deities, shared by many peoples of the ancient Middle East; the Egyptian gods, whose worship was bound up with ritual preparation for the afterlife; the Olympian deities worshipped by the Greeks (and, in modified form, by the Romans); the Vedic gods of ancient India; the Teutonic and Norse gods worshipped in northern Europe; and the "celestial bureaucracy" of deities venerated in China.

Transition to Monotheism: Zoroastrianism

Most of these polytheisms faded away, remaining only as bodies of myth and legend. A few, such as Hinduism and some forms of Buddhism, survive as major religions. One faith that represents a partial commitment to **monotheism** (worship of a single god or goddess) is **Zoroastrianism**, founded in ancient Persia by the priest Zoroaster (also Zarathustra), sometime in the 500s B.C.E. Basing his teachings on a collection of texts called the Avestas, Zoroaster proposed the worship of only one god, Ahura Mazda, the "wise lord." Later, Ahura Mazda's son Mithra was venerated as well. The enemy of Ahura Mazda was Ahriman, the god of darkness. Zoroastrianism flourished in Persia until the 600s C.E., when the expansion of Islam drove it out. It lingers today mainly in India, among the small religious community known as Parsis. However, basic concepts from Zoroastrianism are thought by most religious historians to have played a role in shaping later Jewish thought and, by extension, early Christianity.

JUDAISM

The First Monotheistic Faith

Judaism emerged among the Middle Eastern people known as the **Hebrews** (the terms *Jews* and *Jewish* were not commonly used until the 900s B.C.E.). This religion is generally considered to have been the world's first monotheistic faith—that is, the first to devote itself to the worship of one deity alone. Along with Christianity, which grew out of it, **Judaism** forms a key part of the Western world's ethical, intellectual, and cultural foundation.

Abraham's Covenant

According to Judaic tradition, the patriarch **Abraham**, who lived near the Sumerian city of Ur, entered into a covenant with the god YHWH (often rendered as Yahweh or Jehovah). YHWH swore to make the Hebrews his "chosen people" and to lead them to the "promised land" of Canaan (present-day Israel). Sometime between 2000 and 1850 B.C.E., the Hebrews left Ur and journeyed westward. Abraham's leadership was carried on by his son Isaac and Isaac's younger son Jacob (who took the name **Israel** and whose sons are considered to be the founders of Israel's Twelve Tribes).

Slavery in Egypt, Exodus, and Moses's Leadership

In approximately 1700 B.C.E., during a time of famine, the Hebrews migrated to Egypt, an event narrated in the story of Jacob's son Joseph. Over time, the Hebrews became the Egyptians' slaves, but around 1300 to 1200 B.C.E., under the prophet **Moses**, escaped from Egypt. This exodus is remembered in the celebration of **Passover**, the most important holiday in the Jewish faith. Moses and the war leader Joshua took the Hebrews back to Canaan. During the journey, Moses is said to have handed down from YHWH the principles of Jewish law, including the **Ten Commandments**, revealed to him on Mount Sinai. He is also considered the author of the **Torah** ("Teaching"), the first five books in the Hebrew scriptures (the Tanakh). The Torah was later incorporated by the Christian Bible as the first five books of the Old Testament.

The Hebrew Kingdoms: Freedom and Conquest

Consolidation of the homeland followed. The Hebrews were ruled at first by judges, then by kings, starting with Saul. The Hebrew kingdom reached its zenith under its second monarch, **David** (ca. 1000–961 B.C.E.), and his son **Solomon** (ca. 961–922 B.C.E.). David, a talented military commander, united the kingdom of Israel and created a Hebrew capital at Jerusalem. He was also a skilled musician, and many of the religious songs known collectively as the Psalms are attributed to him. **Solomon** increased Israel's prosperity by taking advantage of its location at the crossroads of Middle Eastern trade routes. In Jerusalem, Solomon dedicated to YHWH the great Temple, the heart of Jewish religious life for centuries.

After Solomon's death, the Hebrew kingdom split into two lands: Israel and Judah. The Hebrews were then conquered by a number of invaders, including the Assyrians (722 B.C.E.), the Babylonian Empire of Nebuchadnezzar (587 B.C.E.), the Persians (539 B.C.E.), Alexander the Great (333–331 B.C.E.), and the Romans (66–64 B.C.E.). Under Nebuchadnezzar, the Hebrews were uprooted from their lands, and Solomon's Temple was torn down (a second temple was built during the 530s and 520s B.C.E.). In the face of their conquerors, all of whom were polytheistic, the Jews, guided by prophets and rabbis ("teachers"), remained true to their monotheistic worship. They also came to believe that a savior, or Messiah ("anointed one") would someday appear to free them from oppression and exalt the name of YHWH.

Roman Rule and the Jewish Diaspora

During the years of Roman rule, the Judaic tradition gave birth to the new faith of Christianity, based on the teachings of Jesus of Nazareth (see the section on Christianity). Shortly thereafter, attempts to rebel against the Romans led to the dissolution of the Hebrew state. During the Jewish Wars of 70–73 C.E., the Romans deprived the Jews of their homeland, destroyed the second Temple, and forced them into a **diaspora** that lasted until the middle of the twentieth century. While some Jews remained in the Middle East, others scattered throughout Europe, Asia, and the rest of the world.

Jewish Principles

In addition to its emphasis on the worship of a single god, Hebrew scripture outlines a strict code of conduct and places a high premium on righteous behavior. The same can be said about the Talmud ("Instruction"), the main collection of Jewish laws and commentaries upon them. Among the ancient Hebrews, legal practices operated on a retributive principle—an eye for an eye, a tooth for a tooth—that was common throughout the ancient Middle East. Dietary restrictions were strict, as were rules governing sexual practice. Although women were respected in the home, Hebrew society as a whole was rigidly patriarchal. As did most people of the eastern Mediterranean, the Hebrews practiced slavery on a limited basis, but Jewish scripture also insisted on charity, social responsibility, and concern for the poor.

> **NOTE**
>
> Until the establishment of the modern state of Israel in 1948, Jews were linked not by geography but by shared cultural heritage, continued dedication to the monotheistic worship of YHWH, and observation of the laws and customs laid out by scripture.

HINDUISM

Born in India, **Hinduism** is an extremely complex, polytheistic faith. Arguably, its roots extend further back in time than those of any other religion still practiced today. Rather than being a single faith in the Western sense—founded by a single individual or group, following a single god or set of gods, recognizing a single body of scripture—Hinduism is a synthesis of many religious traditions. Today, the vast majority of the people of India are Hindu. Sizable Hindu minorities live in Pakistan, Bangladesh, and Sri Lanka. There are Hindu populations in South and Southeast Asia, as well as in emigration throughout the world.

Vedic Roots of Hinduism and Early Hindu Scriptures

No precise date can be assigned to the birth of Hinduism. It evolved over hundreds of years from a combination of the religious practices of the Indus River people, other ethnic groups native to the subcontinent, and Aryan invaders. From this mixture emerged the tradition of **Vedism**, commonly regarded as the foundation of Hinduism. At the core of Vedism are four Aryan scriptures called **Vedas**, meaning "knowledge." The Vedas began to appear in written form after 1500 B.C.E. but are thought to have existed in oral form as far back as 4500 B.C.E. The oldest is the Rig-Veda, which includes over 1,000 hymns and stories about the gods.

Hinduism itself began to take shape after 900 B.C.E., as a result of profound transformations in Vedic thought. New texts appeared, particularly the Upanishads (written between 900 and 500 B.C.E.), essays and poems outlining Hinduism's basic concepts. Also influential was the **Law of Manu** (compiled between 200 B.C.E. and 200 C.E.), best known for its support of the caste system.

Along with new scripture, literary texts that were also religious in nature appeared. One such story was the Ramayana (ca. 350 B.C.E.), a tale describing the adventures of Rama, the seventh incarnation of the god Vishnu. Equally important, if not more so, is the Mahabharata (composed between 200 B.C.E. and 200 C.E.), a grand epic of 90,000 stanzas, making it perhaps the longest poem in the world. The Mahabharata depicts a great war between two royal houses. Its most famous section is the **Bhagavad-Gita** ("Song of the Lord"), a poetic dialogue between the young prince Arjuna and the demigod Krishna, who lectures Arjuna on the concept of moral duty.

Hindu Doctrine

The basic concepts of classical Hinduism were in place no later than the 200s B.C.E., after the Vedic and Upanishadic traditions merged and spread throughout India.

At the center of time and space is the World Soul, or Brahman. All things that exist are reflections of the Brahman's perfection. Every living creature has its own soul, known as atman. However, the material world is an illusion (maya). It causes suffering and prevents the individual soul from perceiving or being connected with the World Soul. The goal of existence is to rejoin one's atman with the Brahman, allowing oneself to be absorbed into perfection.

Union with the Brahman is accomplished by undergoing a cycle of life, death, and rebirth called the wheel of life (samsara); spiritual perfection is attained by this process of **reincarnation**. According to the law of deeds (**karma**), a person's actions in one life will have consequences in a future life. When a person has achieved a sufficient understanding of moral duty (dharma), he or she gains release (moksha) from samsara. Liberated from the cycle of life and death, the atman is free to join with the Brahman.

Union with the Brahman can be attained in a number of ways. Early Vedic scriptures placed great value on ritual obedience to the gods and the priestly class (brahmins). Later scriptures, such as the Upanishads, argued that ordinary men and women could take greater responsibility for their own spiritual development.

Hindu Deities

In addition to the Brahman, Hinduism recognizes hundreds of gods and goddesses, making it a polytheistic religion. However, Hindus consider all deities to be avatars, or incarnations of the Brahman. By the 200s B.C.E., three gods in particular gained the largest followings: Brahma, Vishnu, and Shiva. Technically the most important is Brahma the Creator, the masculine personification of the Brahman, or World Soul.

Vishnu the Preserver is a savior figure, a great friend to humanity. In various avatars, he appears in classical India's greatest literary works. In his seventh incarnation, he is Rama, the hero of the Ramayana. His eighth incarnation is Krishna, the demigod who teaches the prince Arjuna about moral responsibility in the Bhagavad-Gita. Shiva the Destroyer is the god of creation and destruction. He reflects the duality of life and death; he is depicted in paintings and sculptures as a dancer.

Goddesses are important in Hinduism. All female deities are considered incarnations of the great mother goddess, Mahadevi Shakti. Her most famous avatars are Parvati (wife of Shiva), Durga (a warrior goddess), Lakshmi (Vishnu's wife), and Kali (a goddess of death).

The Caste System and the Place of Women

The Indian caste system was given religious justification by Vedic thought and Hindu theology. The caste system's origins date back to the Aryan invasion of India. The Aryans relegated menial tasks and manual labor to the darker-skinned natives. From the 800s to the 600s B.C.E., this scheme grew into a rigid system of social stratification involving four distinct classes. At the highest level were the priests (brahmins). Near the top were the warriors and political rulers (kshatriyas). Commoners (vaishyas), such as farmers and artisans, were next. Servants, serfs, and members of the lower class (shudras) made up the lowest of the four main castes. As time went on, another category, the untouchables—who performed degrading tasks such as the handling of human waste and burial of the dead—was formed. Over the centuries, the caste system grew increasingly complex.

In the Hindu hierarchy, males were thought superior to women (although the Hindu code of behavior required that women be treated with respect, and women played a vital role within the family unit). Men performed the family rituals, had a monopoly on education, and were allowed to own property. Women were considered legal minors even as adults and could not own property. Many women married in childhood, and divorce was rare. The most extreme form of female subservience to men was the sati ritual (also known as suttee), by which wives were required to throw themselves on the funeral pyres of their dead husbands. This practice was discouraged by India's colonial masters, the British, during the nineteenth century. It was outlawed by the Indians themselves in the twentieth century.

The Practice of Sati.
The ritual of sati (or suttee) was a long-standing Hindu tradition. When a man of high caste died, his widow was expected to be burned to death on her husband's funeral pyre. Only in the twentieth century was this practice fully abolished.

Acceptance of one's social situation was considered to be virtuous. Performance of caste duties was an essential part of dharma, or moral duty. Good behavior as a member of a lower caste in one life would result in good karma, increasing the likelihood of being reborn into a higher caste. The Law of Manu is the most famous expression of Hinduism's religious argument in favor of the caste system.

BUDDHISM

Originating in India, the numerous forms of **Buddhism** have spread worldwide. This complex religion is followed in China, Japan, Sri Lanka, Tibet, Korea, and elsewhere in southern and eastern Asia. Although the foundations of Buddhism are associated with the teachings of one person, the variety of beliefs and theologies that fall into the category "Buddhist" is staggering. Broadly speaking, there are two major schools of Buddhist doctrine: Theravada (also known as Hinayana) and Mahayana.

Religious Transition in India

Buddhism was one of several movements born in India during the 500s B.C.E., as the long transition from Vedism to classical Hinduism stirred up religious debate. During this century of great spiritual ferment, many teachers experimented with various ways of achieving union with the World Soul. One religious path that emerged during this time—and might have grown into a larger faith, if not for the simultaneous appearance of Buddhism—was Jainism, established by Mahavira (ca. 540–468 B.C.E.), who preached a doctrine of nonviolence and asceticism, or self-denial.

Siddhartha Gautama and the Birth of Buddhism

The individual who founded Buddhism was Siddhartha Gautama (ca. 563–483 B.C.E.), born into a noble family from northern India. At the age of twenty-nine, Gautama ventured outside his palace, only to be appalled by the pain and poverty experienced by the common people. In shock, he abandoned his aristocratic life to seek an answer to the question of human suffering. Having been born into one spiritual extreme—sensuality and a love of worldly things—Gautama sought his answers in the opposite extreme: fasting and asceticism. After years of self-deprivation, he decided that neither extreme led to salvation. He chose instead a "middle way" of moderation and peace.

While following this middle way, Gautama is said to have achieved enlightenment. He took the name Buddha, "the awakened one," and began to preach. A community of followers spread his teachings; and, after his death, his creed went beyond the borders of India to the rest of Asia.

Buddhist Doctrine

In its earliest form, Buddhism was less a religion than a philosophy. At no time did the Buddha make claim to divinity. Instead, his goal was to correct what he saw as the worst features of Vedism and Hinduism. He also intended to purify concepts such as karma and reincarnation by reducing the role that the priestly brahmins and their complicated rituals played in spiritual life. As a result, the Buddha's teachings either draw on or depart from the fundamental ideas contained in Hindu theology.

Like Hinduism, Buddhism postulates that souls evolve toward spiritual perfection by means of samsara, the wheel of life. However, the Buddha rejected the caste system and argued that any person could achieve liberation, without the aid of priests or rituals. All that was necessary to attain enlightenment was to realize the Four Noble Truths and to follow the Eightfold Path of good conduct (as well as the Five Moral Rules).

By following this moral code, any person can reach enlightenment. In Buddhist terms, liberation from samsara is called **nirvana**, the literal meaning of which is "to extinguish." According to the original teachings of the Buddha, the result of nirvana is not a union of the individual soul with the World Soul. Instead, nirvana leads to a state of superconsciousness, in which one's self is dissolved into the all-encompassing life spirit that transcends place and time.

> **NOTE**
>
> The Four Noble Truths are as follows:
> (1) human existence is inseparable from suffering;
> (2) the cause of suffering is desire.
> (3) suffering is extinguished by extinguishing desire;
> (4) desire may be extinguished by following the Eightfold path (know the truth; resist evil; do nothing to hurt others; respect all forms of life; work for the well-being of others; free your mind of evil; control your thoughts; practice meditation). In addition to the Eightfold Path, the Buddha described Five Moral Rules (do not kill any living being; do not take what is not given to you; do not speak falsely; do not drink intoxicating drinks; do not be unchaste).

Theravada and Mahayana Buddhism

After the Buddha's death in 483 B.C.E., the tradition he founded split into various denominations, roughly divided into two large movements. The older is Theravada Buddhism ("Way of the Elders"), also referred to as Hinayana ("Lesser Vehicle"). Prominent in South and Southeast Asia, Theravada remains closer in spirit to the Buddha's actual teachings. It emphasizes simplicity, meditation, and an interpretation of nirvana as the renunciation of the self. Gods and goddesses have little place in Theravada, and the Buddha himself is not considered to be a deity.

The second and newer movement, Mahayana ("Greater Vehicle") Buddhism, is widespread in northern and northeastern Asia, especially in Japan, Korea, Tibet, and parts of China. Mahayana forms of Buddhism tend to be elaborate and complicated, involving more ritual and symbology than the Buddha himself intended. Part of this change resulted from the fact that Buddhism, upon reaching new lands, often blended with local religions. Moreover, many later Buddhists found the austerity of the original teachings to be of little spiritual comfort, and they began to argue that means of salvation that the Buddha himself had not spoken of were possible.

In some Mahayana denominations, the concept of nirvana came to resemble traditional ideas of heaven. Concepts of hell, or some kind of punishment in the afterlife, appeared. Whereas the Buddha made little mention of gods or goddesses, many Mahayana forms developed complex pantheons of deities, and the Buddha himself became godlike in nature. Adherents of Mahayana also prayed to bodhisattvas (souls who had achieved nirvana but chose to remain in the earthly realm in order to help living humans reach salvation). Worshippers came to rely more heavily on priests, ceremonies, and new scriptures. The obvious irony is that many of these additions were very much like those aspects of Hinduism of which the Buddha himself had disapproved. Nonetheless, Mahayana traditions flourished and developed into a respected, highly popular branch of Buddhist theology.

DAOISM (TAOISM)

Daoism appeared in China during the 500s B.C.E. Like Buddhism (in its original form), Daoism was less a religion and more a philosophical system, whose founding figure made no claim to divinity. However, Daoism had a mystical strain that grew more pronounced as time passed.

The Founders of Daoism

Traditionally, the founder of Daoism is considered to be **Laozi** (Lao-tse), the "Old Master" (ca. 604 B.C.E.). Laozi may or may not be an actual historical figure. He is also said to have written Daoism's central text, the **Tao-te Ching**, although most scholars believe this collection of writings was compiled in the 300s or 200s B.C.E. Another figure associated with the development of Daoism is **Zhuangzi** (Chuang-tse), known to have lived approximately from 369 to 286 B.C.E.

Following the Dao

To follow Daoism is to follow "the way," or "the path," the two most common translations of **dao**. Daoist belief maintains that the universe is governed by an invisible, yet irresistible force that can be sensed intuitively. Daoist thought is deliberately antirational, using parables and paradox to train the worshipper to perceive the world in nonlogical ways. (The most famous Daoist paradox is found in the writings of Zhuangzi, who asks himself if he is a man who has just awoken from a dream that he was a butterfly, or a butterfly still dreaming that he is a man.)

A Daoist seeks wisdom in nature, poetry, and spontaneous behavior. He or she is not concerned with politics, money, or material possessions, because all of these are illusory and meaningless. Daoism places an emphasis on individuality, since each person pursues the dao in his or her own unique way.

Daoist Ritual

After a time, Daoism became associated with mystical and magical practices, such as alchemy and fortune-telling. The I-Ching, or "Book of Changes," is a Daoist text used in reading the future. Daoism's most famous symbol is the yin-yang, a circle whose black and white halves are divided by a double-curved line, serving to illustrate that nothing is absolute, and that opposites flow into each other.

A flexible religion, Daoism has traditionally coexisted with other faiths. It is not uncommon for a worshipper to blend elements of Daoist worship with Buddhism and Confucianism. Since Daoism and Confucianism arose in China at approximately the same time, the relationship between the two has generally been a tight one, even though their philosophical outlooks are, for the most part, diametrically opposed.

Daoism spread throughout its native China. Certain elements were transported to parts of Asia where China had a strong cultural influence, especially Japan and Korea.

CONFUCIANISM

Confucianism: Religion or Philosophy?

Of the world's major belief systems, **Confucianism**, which developed in China during the 500s B.C.E., is the least religious. In fact, lacking any objects of worship or clergy, Confucianism resembles more an ethical code based on secular principles. Confucianism's founders believed in the existence of gods, spirits, and heaven but gave little place to them in their philosophical system. They argued that a morally concerned person should be interested in how he or she acted in the material world. What happened beyond one's physical life was of less importance.

Confucian Texts

Confucianism grew out of the teachings of the sage K'ung Fu-tzu, better known as Confucius (ca. 551–479 B.C.E.), who lived during the politically chaotic Zhou (Chou) dynasty. A minor aristocrat, he served as a government official. Upon retiring from state service, he began to ponder the nature of the relationship between the individual and society at large. He gathered a group of disciples, and these followers captured his thoughts and words on paper. Although K'ung Fu-tzu is traditionally considered to have authored the Confucian classics (books on history, divination, ritual, and poetry), in actuality he left behind no works of his own. His *Analects* ("Selected Sayings") are recordings of conversations with his students.

A second Confucian theorist was Meng-tzu, or Mencius (371–289 B.C.E.). His commentaries helped the Confucian movement reach its highest level of sophistication.

Confucian Principles

Confucianism proposes that a harmonious society can be created by a combination of benevolent rulership from above and good behavior from below. The well-being of the group comes before that of the individual. Order and hierarchy are paramount. Good government is the responsibility of the ruler, and as long as the ruler performs his duties well, his people have an obligation to obey him. Meng-tzu taught that a just ruler possesses the **Mandate of Heaven**, a moral justification for his authority. Unjust rulers who abuse their power lose the Mandate of Heaven, and can therefore be removed by their people.

Ideally, society operates the same way a model family does, with junior members paying respect to their elders. Confucianism regards the family unit as the most important institution in any civilization; if the home is blessed by **filial piety**, society at large is healthy. This vision is reflected in the five relationships K'ung Fu-tzu described as most important to social tranquility: the ruler should be just, those who are ruled should be loyal; the father should be loving, the son respectful; the husband should be righteous, the wife obedient; the older brother should be genteel, the younger brother humble; the older friend should be considerate, the younger friend deferent.

Confucianism also established the female as the subservient sex. Men ruled society, fought wars, and acted as scholars and ministers. They could keep more than one wife and divorce any wife who failed to produce a male heir. Women were exclusively homemakers and mothers. Laws prohibited women from owning property, and they were not provided financial security through a dowry system. However, Confucianism allowed women to have a limited education.

Implicit in all these relationships are the concepts of reciprocity and mutual respect. Those who are superior may expect deference from those below them, but only if they themselves treat those below them well. Likewise, those who are inferior may expect good treatment from those above, but only if they are properly deferent. Central to Confucian thought is a "golden rule" similar to the one found in Christianity: in the *Analects*, K'ung Fu-tzu declares, "Never do to others what you would not like them to do to you."

Confucianism, Neo-Confucianism, and Chinese Political Life

Confucianism coexisted with and at times competed with Daoism and Buddhism. Several times, it gained, lost, and regained its status as an official, imperially sanctioned code of conduct. By the 600s C.E., a newer variation of the creed, called Neo-Confucianism, appeared. Even during those years when it was not in official favor, Confucianism continued to be tremendously influential. China's traditional emphasis on filial piety, social hierarchy, and respect for authority stems in large part from Confucianism and has persisted into the modern era, even under the Communist regime.

CHRISTIANITY

The Judeo-Christian Tradition

Historically and philosophically, **Christianity** is a child of Judaism. The relationship between the two faiths has often been troubled, but it has always been intimate. Both religions, in the form of the **Judeo-Christian tradition**, have formed the bedrock of Western culture for two millennia.

The Life and Ministry of Jesus

The founder of Christianity was **Jesus of Nazareth** (ca. 4 B.C.E.–29 C.E.), later known as the Christ (from the Greek translation of the term *messiah*). Details about Jesus come from the Gospels, the first four books of the Bible's New Testament. Jesus was born into a Jewish family of humble background. As an adult, he became a wandering teacher and gathered an inner circle of disciples.

Jesus spoke of upholding Jewish laws and traditions but also sought to reform them. To him, obeying rabbis and observing customs were not enough to please YHWH (in later Christian usage, God). Jesus taught that the sincerity of one's belief mattered more than giving large offerings of money, wearing proper dress, or following dietary guidelines. He maintained that charity, compassion, and forgiveness were of paramount importance. He reinforced this message in the **Sermon on the Mount** ("Blessed are the poor in spirit . . .") and in what came to be known as the **Golden Rule** ("Do unto others as you would have them do unto you").

During his ministry, Jesus claimed to be the Christ, or the Messiah foretold by Hebrew prophecy. Although many Jews expected the Messiah to be a political ruler who would restore the Hebrew state, Jesus had a heavenly kingdom in mind instead. He spoke of himself as the "Son of God," whose teachings would redeem those who followed his words.

The teachings of Jesus proved immensely popular, especially among the common people and the poor. On the other hand, his claims to be the Messiah and his questioning of tradition angered conservatives within the Jewish religious establishment. Also, rumors that Jesus had assumed the title King of the Jews (a misinterpretation of what he meant by being the Messiah) made Roman authorities suspicious. According to the Gospels, when Jesus preached in Jerusalem during the Passover season, Jewish religious authorities demanded that the Roman procurator, Pontius Pilate, arrest him. Pilate, fearing the political repercussions of Jesus's ministry, agreed. Jesus was tried for blasphemy and treason. Found guilty, he was put to death by the Romans. The method of execution was crucifixion, and the instrument of Jesus's death—the cross—is the Christian faith's most important symbol.

The Early Christian Church

Before his arrest, Jesus had claimed he would return from the dead before returning to God, his Father, in heaven. After his crucifixion, Jesus's closest followers began to preach that he had indeed been resurrected (an event celebrated during Easter, Christianity's central holiday). This veneration of the risen Jesus, which soon came to be known as Christianity, was carried on at first by his closest disciples, such as **Peter** (considered to be the first pope) and the authors of the Four Gospels (Matthew, Mark, Luke, and John). Other adherents of the new faith spread the words of Christ as well. These figures, instrumental in establishing the early Christian church, are known as the apostles. The apostles told the story of Christ's Crucifixion and Resurrection. They also foretold the Second Coming, when the physical world would come to an end, the Kingdom of Heaven would be established, and all souls would be subjected to a Day of Judgment. Good Christians would live with God and Christ in heaven; evildoers and nonbelievers would be damned to hell.

Roman law made early Christianity illegal. Despite those obstacles, Christianity gained a larger following over the next three centuries, not just in Judaea, but throughout the Middle East and the Roman Empire. Playing a crucial role in the early church's organization was the apostle **Paul**. Born Saul of Tarsus, Paul, originally a persecutor of Christianity, changed his name after a sudden conversion to the new faith. With Peter, Paul worked from approximately 45 to 64 C.E. to establish new centers of worship. His greatest contribution was to widen the appeal of Christianity beyond the circle of its original Jewish worshippers. By decreeing that Christians did not have to observe Jewish law (including dietary restrictions and the circumcision of male believers), Paul made it easier to convert Greeks and other non-Jewish peoples. This flexibility allowed the new religion to expand faster.

Christianity caught on among many groups, especially among those who felt powerless in Roman society: noncitizens, slaves, the poor, commoners, and women. The new religion was open to all, and it held out the hope of a happy afterlife to those whose lives in the present were drab or miserable. Although organized Christianity later became male-dominated, the early church gave women a sense of belonging and, within limits, influential roles within apostolic communities. As time passed, however, a strict interpretation of the story of Adam and Eve assigned the blame for humanity's "original sin" to women as a whole. Paul's writings on women put them in a secondary position. Women were to obey men, and they were not allowed to occupy the positions of highest leadership within the church (including priesthood). Cultures that adopted Christianity were affected by this worldview for centuries to come.

Roman Persecution of Christianity

In spite of Christianity's appeal and organizational success, to worship as a Christian remained dangerous for more than three hundred years. Christians devised secret codes and held services in hidden places, often in underground chambers called catacombs. Roman persecution was a constant peril, and many Christians were arrested and executed. Worshippers who died for their faith were known as martyrs. Ironically, the campaigns of persecution, rather than destroying the new religion, only strengthened the followers resolve. Moreover, the bravery and dignity often attracted new converts.

Legalization and the Formal Organization Of Christianity

In 313 C.E., legal status was granted to Christianity by the **Edict of Milan**, handed down by the emperor Constantine. In 380 C.E., Christianity became the official religion of the Roman Empire, and in 392 C.E., it was proclaimed the empire's only legal faith. Free from persecution, the church set up a formal hierarchy of priests and bishops, with the pope (the bishop of Rome) at the top. Only men could serve as clergy. The church also found it necessary to establish a body of dogma, an officially agreed-upon set of beliefs. Important issues included the nature of Christ (considered to be both fully human and fully divine) and the doctrine of the Trinity (the belief that God exists in the three persons of God the Father, Christ the Son, and the Holy Spirit). Beliefs not declared to be part of dogma were condemned as heresy.

Another task was to compile the books of the Bible, which came to consist of two main parts: the Old Testament (the Hebrew Torah, stories from Jewish history, and the writings of Hebrew prophets) and the New Testament (the Four Gospels, episodes from the history of the early Christian Church, and letters written by the Apostles). Decisions about dogma and the Bible were made at a series of councils held during the 300s C.E. and afterward. The priests and scholars who attended the councils or helped to clarify and defend the councils' decisions are referred to as the church fathers. Among the most famous are Jerome (347–420 C.E.), whose Vulgate Bible was the first Latin translation of the holy book, and Augustine (354–430 C.E.), whose *City of God* is considered to have laid the intellectual foundation for further Christian doctrine.

Christianity After the Fall of Rome

With the collapse of the Roman Empire during the 400s C.E. came a new era for the Christian Church. In the Middle East and North Africa, where the Roman legacy was carried on by the Byzantine Empire, metropolitan centers such as Antioch, Alexandria, and Constantinople were the great centers of Christian worship. In the west, where Europe was collapsing into political confusion, the headquarters of the Christian Church was Rome.

Although the Christian Church called itself catholic, or universal, it was, in reality, divided. Doctrinal disagreements, geographic separation, and the passage of time caused the Western and Eastern churches to grow apart after the 500s C.E. In the Great Schism of 1054 C.E., the Western and Eastern churches broke with each other formally. Eastern Orthodoxy remained the faith of the Byzantine Empire, and it was adopted by most Christians in the Middle East, Russia, Ukraine, and much of eastern Europe. Roman Catholicism remained the favored form of Christianity in western Europe. During the Middle Ages, the Roman Catholic Church became one of the most important institutions in Europe, providing Europeans with a sense of religious unity, preserving Latin manuscripts from the Roman era, and exerting a tremendous sway over secular and political affairs. Further splits within the Western Christian church would come later, during the 1500s and 1600s C.E. However, during the medieval era, its influence remained paramount.

ISLAM

The Origins of Islam

The youngest of the world's major religions (and not actually established during this "Foundations" period), Islam transformed itself with amazing speed from a local faith into a cultural, social, and political force of global dimensions. A monotheistic form of worship that originated in the Middle East, Islam is linked with Judaism and Christianity in many ways, and the relationships that have prevailed among the three of them have frequently been stormy, even tragic. Nonetheless, the three faiths contain many similarities and possess an eventful shared history.

Islam arose in the Arabian Peninsula during the 600s C.E., a time when Arabia was sparsley populated and its desert interior largely unexplored. Arabia's few major settlements were built up around oases and coastal towns serving as centers of the caravan trade that linked the region with the rest of the Middle East. From Arabia, the new religion spread rapidly throughout the eastern Mediterranean. By 1000 C.E., its influence stretched from Spain and Africa's Atlantic coast to the borderlands of India in the east.

Mohammed and His Teachings

The founder of Islam was **Mohammed** (also Muhammad), a merchant from the Arabian town of **Mecca**. Born in 570 C.E., Mohammed began to meditate in the mountains near Mecca when he turned forty. In 610 C.E., he experienced a profound vision. According to Mohammed, the archangel Jobril ("Gabriel" to Jews and Christians) appeared to him, delivering the word of **Allah** (Arabic for "God").

With the help of family members such as Ali (his cousin and son-in-law), Aisha (his favorite wife), and Abu Bakr (Aisha's father and his father-in-law), Mohammed preached and gathered a religious community. In 622, he and his followers were forced out of Mecca by local religious authorities, fleeing to the city of Medina. This flight—the **Hegira**—remains a key event in the early history of Islam, and it marks the beginning of the Islamic calendar. Mohammed's community flourished in Medina, and by 630, he and his followers returned to Mecca and converted the city. In 632, Mohammed died, but the religion he had founded survived and grew.

The Principles of Islamic Faith

Mohammed's faith drew directly upon Judeo-Christian images and concepts. He taught that there is one god, Allah. He believed that there is an afterlife and a final judgment in which believers go to heaven and nonbelievers to hell. Islam pays respect to figures from Jewish and Christian faith. Arabs, like the Hebrews, consider Abraham to be their patriarch and Abraham's son Ismail (Ishmael) to be their direct ancestor. Prophets of Allah include Adam, Noah, Moses, David, Solomon, John the Baptist, and Jesus. Islamic teaching instructs Muslims to respect Jews and Christians as "people of the book."

These similarities notwithstanding, Mohammed went on to formulate his own tradition. He claimed to be the last of twenty-eight prophets sent by Allah to reveal His teachings to humankind, and the only one to receive Alla's full and perfect message. The name of the religion itself, *Islam*, comes from the Arabic phrase "to submit to God." Likewise, the term *Muslim*, which describes a follower of Islam, means "servant of God," or "one who has submitted to the will of God."

Submission to Allah involves living by the five **Pillars of Faith** described by Mohammed. These are to declare that "there is no god but Allah, and Mohammed is his prophet"; to pray five times, facing in the direction of Mecca; to fast during the holiday of Ramadan; to give alms to the poor; and to make a pilgrimage (hajj) to Mecca at least once in one's lifetime.

Other Islamic traditions include abstinence from alcohol and pork; avoiding the portrayal of human or animal figures in art; and polygamy (Muslim men are allowed to take up to four wives). There are also restrictions on how women are allowed to dress or appear in public; a strictly observant Muslim woman is to guard her modesty and veil herself when in public. In modern life, these traditions have been loosened or abandoned by many Islamic communities. A number of Muslim nations have become more secular and allow a less stringent observance of these practices. Even in earlier times, male domination of women in Islamic societies was offset by the command that men treat women with respect. Women also enjoyed the right to inherit, have dowries, and own property.

The teachings of Mohammed are contained in the **Qur'an** (Koran), or "Recitation." Muslims consider the Qur'an to be the word of Allah, transmitted directly by Mohammed, so every word is considered sacred. The Arabic that Mohammed spoke is the holy language of Islam. Other important texts in the Islamic tradition are the Hadith, a collection of the proverbs of Mohammed, and the **Sharia**, a codification of traditional Islamic law.

The Expansion of Islam

The expansion of Islam during the 600s, 700s, and 800s C.E. went hand-in-hand with military conquest and political domination. Early Islam made no distinction between political allegiance and religious affiliation; to be a Muslim meant also to belong to a political and social community (*umma*) linked by religious belief. After Mohammed's death in 632, it was decided that the **umma** was to be governed by a **caliph** (*khalifa*), or "successor," who was both a religious and political leader. The first caliph was Mohammed's father-in-law, Abu Bakr.

Before Mohammed's death, most of Arabia had converted to Islam. The first three caliphs—Abu Bakr, Umar (Omar), and Uthman—broke out of Arabia and brought Islam to the rest of the Middle East and beyond. By the end of the 700s C.E., Muslim forces had swept through the Middle East, destroying the Persian Empire, threatening Byzantium, and bringing under Islamic rule Iraq, Syria, Palestine, Egypt, most of north Africa, parts of the Caucasus Mountains, the region that is today Pakistan, Spain, and parts of Italy. From the 600s to the 1200s C.E., this vast territory was ruled over by two Islamic states, or caliphates: the Umayyad Caliphate (661–750 C.E.), centered at Damascus, and the Abbasid Caliphate (750–1258 C.E.), whose capital was Baghdad. The zenith of Islamic civilization, as a single political and religious entity, came during the first 300 years of the Abbasid Caliphate, roughly the years between 750 and 1050 C.E.

> **TIP**
>
> Islamic theology divides the world into two states: dar al-Islam ("house of peace") and dar al-Harb ("house of war"). The former includes those lands where Islam is the dominant faith. In early times, the expansion of dar al-Islam was encouraged. Many moderate Muslims now consider dar al-Islam to be a wider community including all places where their religion can be practiced freely.

Islamic Denominations

Triumph and expansion did not prevent major splits within the Islamic faith. From 656 to 661 C.E., disputes among Mohammed's family led to civil war. The final result was the establishment of the Umayyad Caliphate, under Muawiyah (661–680 C.E.). The majority of Muslims accepted Muawiyah and his successors as legitimate. They refer to themselves as **Sunni**, the "people of tradition and community." To this day, more than 80 percent of all Muslims are Sunni. However, the followers of Mohammed's son-in-law Ali (who was killed in the war) considered the Umayyads to be usurpers. They formed a minority denomination that still exists today, known as the **Shiites**, from *Shi'at Ali*, or "party of Ali."

Another Islamic movement is **Sufism**, a mystical tradition that appeared during the 700s and 800s C.E. Sufism places a premium on fasting, prayer, and meditation as ways to grow closer to Allah. It is especially prominent in Iran.

The Geography of Islam

Several holy places are connected to Islamic worship. One of them, Jerusalem, is also shared by Judaism and Christianity, a fact that has led to considerable friction. According to Islamic tradition, Mohammed ascended to heaven from Jerusalem. The holiest site in the Islamic faith is Mecca: Mohammed's birthplace and home to the shrine known as the Kaaba, or Black Rock. Making a pilgrimage, or hajj, to Mecca is one of Islam's five Pillars of Faith. Observant Muslims pray to Mecca five times a day. Medina, to which Mohammed fled during the Hegira, is also a key center of faith.

Islam is most famously associated with the Middle East, and the vast majority of the people who live there are Muslim. However, as a legacy of Islam's rapid and extensive spread during its first three centuries, there are Muslim communities worldwide. Countries with Islamic majorities include most of the nations of North Africa, Pakistan, Indonesia (the country with the largest Muslim population), and others. Sizable Islamic minorities can be found around the globe.

QUICK REVIEW

1. Which of the following is an example of a pantheon?

    (A) the Twelve Apostles of the New Testament
    (B) the first five American presidents
    (C) a group of miltary heroes
    (D) the Vedic gods and goddesses of ancient India
    (E) nature according to Zen worshippers

2. The Christians incorporated the Jewish books of the Torah as

    (A) the first five books of the New Testament.
    (B) the first five books of the Old Testament.
    (C) the first half of the Qur'an.
    (D) their official prayer book.
    (E) none of the above

3. Which of the following is NOT related to the Jewish faith?

    (A) a belief that a Messiah would appear and free them from oppression
    (B) the Torah
    (C) monotheism
    (D) the Eightfold Path
    (E) the Tanakh

4. Which of the following is an accurate statement about Hinduism?

    (A) It draws from many different religious traditions.
    (B) It was founded in isolation from other religions.
    (C) It originated in China.
    (D) It was founded in 1500 B.C.E.
    (E) It is monotheistic.

5. What is a major similarity between Hinduism and Buddhism?

    (A) Both religions support a caste system.
    (B) Both religions accept that souls reach spiritual perfection through a cycle of life, death, and reincarnation.
    (C) Both embrace the Four Noble Truths.
    (D) Both follow the Five Moral Rules.
    (E) These two religions are diametrically opposed.

6. Daoist thought is

    (A) based on reason.
    (B) proclaimed by the one god, Dao.
    (C) based exclusively on Confucianism.
    (D) largely antirational.
    (E) intrinsically linked to Islam.

7. Scholars largely learn about Jesus from

    (A) Roman archives.
    (B) oral histories.
    (C) books written by the ancient Egyptians.
    (D) the Gospels.
    (E) Greek myths.

8. What contributed most to the spread of early Christianity?

    (A) The Roman Empire exempted the first Christians from paying taxes.
    (B) Christians decreed that new followers did not have to observe Jewish law.
    (C) Christians befriended Emperor Nero, who proclaimed Christianity a state religion.
    (D) Christian armies swept across Europe and forced the conquered peoples to accept the new religion.
    (E) Christians found adherents in the upper classes of Roman society.

9. According to Muslims, how did Mohammed receive the word of Allah?

   (A) He was born speaking God's wisdom.
   (B) He received on his deathbed.
   (C) An archangel delivered him the word through a vision.
   (D) His mother transmitted Allah's wisdom to him.
   (E) He received Allah's words as he wandered through the Sahara.

10. After Mohammed's death, the Muslim community began to be ruled by a caliph, who was

   (A) a religious leader.
   (B) a political leader.
   (C) thought to be the reincarnation of Mohammed.
   (D) both a political and religious leader.
   (E) none of the above

Answers

1. **(D)** A pantheon is a relatively formalized group of polytheistic deities. Other examples include the Olympian gods of Greece and the deities of Norse myth.

2. **(B)** Because Christianity grew out of the Judaic tradition, it was only natural that Jewish scripture be included in the Bible.

3. **(D)** Judaism is the world's first fully monotheistic faith, and prophecies regarding the messiah are an important part of it. The Tanakh is Jewish scripture, the first five books of which are the Torah. The Eightfold Path is a Buddhist concept.

4. **(A)** The origins of Hinduism are uncertain. The Vedic foundations of Hinduism represent a blend of beliefs, customs, and rituals of India's many ethnicities and cultures.

5. **(B)** Buddhism began as a modification of and departure from Hinduism. The two share many of the same concepts and are clearly not diametrically opposed.

6. **(D)** A Chinese philosophy that emphasizes instinct and paradox, Daoism is explicitly antirational. It coexists with Confucianism but is very different, and it has nothing to do with Islam.

7. **(D)** Although they contain many inconsistencies and cannot be accepted as fully verifiable historical documents, the Gospels remain the chief source for details about the life of Jesus.

8. **(B)** An early obstacle to the recruitment of Christians was Jewish law, which required males to be circumcised and imposed strict dietary restrictions. Removing those requirements made it easier to adopt the new faith. Nero was a great enemy of Christianity; early on, Christianity was not spread by force; and it was the lower classes who originally found Christianity appealing.

9. **(C)** According to Islamic teachings, in 610 C.E., Mohammed was visited by the archangel Gabriel, who is said to have revealed the teachings of Allah.

10. **(D)** In theory, political and religious authority were one and the same for early Muslims.

Unit Two: Review Questions

SAMPLE ESSAY QUESTIONS

1. Compare and contrast the organization, characteristics, and collapse of ancient Rome and Han China.

2. Describe and analyze how patterns of social and economic organization changed during the Neolithic era.

3. Compare and contrast the ways civilization took shape, despite political decentralization, in two of the following regions: sub-Saharan Africa, classical India, and Mesoamerica.

4. Analyze the cultural and political changes and continuities that characterized Egypt and Mesopotamia during the ancient era.

MULTIPLE-CHOICE QUESTIONS

1. Which of the following is true of Japan during the Nara period?

   (A) Japan was culturally isolated from China.
   (B) The Japanese embraced Buddhism.
   (C) Korea conquered Japan's southern islands.
   (D) Christian missionaries arrived in the port city of Nagasaki.
   (E) The Japanese established a new capital at Edo, today known as Tokyo.

2. The Indian Ocean

   I. is the world's second-largest ocean.
   II. is the site of a vibrant system of trade and cultural exchange.
   III. can be reached from the Atlantic and Pacific oceans.
   IV. was under Roman control for several centuries.

   Which are correct?

   (A) I, III, and IV
   (B) I, II, and IV
   (C) II, III, and IV
   (D) II and III
   (E) all of the above

3. What do the Code of Hammurabi and Roman law have in common?

   (A) They both derived mainly from religious principles.
   (B) They both represented important steps away from the arbitrary exercise of power.
   (C) They both operate on the retributive principle of an "eye for an eye."
   (D) They both provided all social classes with equal treatment.
   (E) They were both inherently democratic.

4. Which of the following is an incorrect description of agricultural societies?

   (A) Agriculture allowed humans to manipulate their environment as never before.
   (B) Women probably played a key role in promoting the transition from hunting and gathering to agricultural societies.
   (C) Agriculture promoted permanent settlements.
   (D) People began producing their own food nearly 12,000 years ago.
   (E) Agricultural societies were less organized than hunter-gatherer societies.

5. Civilization is marked by

   I. an intellectual tradition, generally including a system of writing.
   II. an economic system that makes available basic goods and services.
   III. a tendency to use violence to resolve conflict.
   IV. a moral code.
   V. a form of political organization.

   (A) I, II, III, and IV
   (B) II, III, IV, and V
   (C) I, II, IV, and V
   (D) I, III, IV, and V
   (E) all of the above

6. What developments are true of classical China (before 1000 C.E.)?

   I. The supreme ruler was an emperor.
   II. Han rulers installed an effective bureaucracy, postal service, and tax-collecting system.
   III. Improved infrastructure and fortifications helped defend China from invasion.
   IV. Trade expanded greatly during the Tang dynasty.

   (A) I, II, and III
   (B) II, III, and IV
   (C) I, III, and IV
   (D) II and III
   (E) all of the above

7. Early Islamic political thought included the belief that

(A) Jews and Christians deserved to be treated with violence.
(B) Women should be equal in status to men.
(C) Church and state should be kept scrupulously separate.
(D) God's sociopolitical and religious community should be one and the same.
(E) Slavery was abhorrent in the sight of Allah.

8. Which sub-Saharan kingdom was a major center of trade around 600 C.E.?

(A) Zulu
(B) Mali
(C) Ghana
(D) Nigeria
(E) Egypt

9. Which of the following is true of Central Asia prior to 600 C.E.?

(A) It was home to many nomadic peoples, many of whom were skilled at horseback warfare.
(B) It gave rise to many urban cultures.
(C) Genghis Khan began his campaigns of conquest there.
(D) The Silk Road bypassed this dangerous region altogether.
(E) It was the birthplace of Judaism.

10. Which of the following is true of slavery?

(A) Monotheistic societies tend to forbid it.
(B) Slaves were used exclusively for agricultural labor.
(C) Technically, slaves had more freedoms than serfs.
(D) Slave trades prevailed in Africa, Eurasia, and the Americas.
(E) Slavery ended worldwide during the 1600s.

11. Which of the following is NOT a reason why the adoption of agriculture tends to lead to class distinction?

(A) Most members of society stay involved in food production.
(B) It promotes technological advancement.
(C) People are free to develop other skills beside food production.
(D) It encourages permanent settlement.
(E) none of the above

12. Why are the Bantu important to African culture?

(A) They ruled Egypt for thousands of years.
(B) They built the major cities of Tunisia.
(C) They come the closest to resembling a common cultural source in sub-Saharan Africa.
(D) They were the first civilization to use numerals.
(E) all of the above

13. In an oligarchy

(A) one ruler controls an entire nation.
(B) a small elite group holds political power.
(C) the people elect representatives to vote on their behalf in a national legislature.
(D) the aristocracy governs along with a monarch.
(E) military rule is the dominant form of government.

14. In what city-state did democratic government emerge before the modern era?

(A) Athens
(B) Sparta
(C) Rome
(D) Venice
(E) Thebes

15. Why is the period between 200 and 1000 C.E. known as the "Great Age of Migrations"?

    (A) Millions of barbarian tribes migrated to China.
    (B) The Bantu migrated to northern Africa.
    (C) Peoples from Asia crossed a land bridge to North America.
    (D) A large number of Germanic and Asiatic peoples moved toward and into Europe.
    (E) all of the above

16. According to the map on page 82, to which of the following areas did the main African-Eurasian trade routes NOT extend?

    (A) Central Asia
    (B) Siberia
    (C) China
    (D) North Africa
    (E) Spain

17. The truths that the Buddha claimed either draw on or depart from the fundamental principles of which belief system?

    (A) Christianity
    (B) Hinduism
    (C) Islam
    (D) Judaism
    (E) Hellenism

18. "The ruler should be just, those who are ruled should be loyal. The father should be loving, the son respectful."

    This principle is likely part of which belief system?

    (A) Christianity
    (B) Hinduism
    (C) Daoism
    (D) Buddhism
    (E) Confucianism

19. Which answer places events from Islamic history in the correct order?

    (A) Gabriel's revelation to Mohammed; the Hegira; the establishment of the Abbasid Caliphate; the split between Sunni and Shiite Muslims
    (B) the Hegira; the establishment of the Abbasid Caliphate; Gabriel's revelation to Mohammed; the split between Sunni and Shiite Muslims
    (C) the Hegira; the split between Sunni and Shiite Muslims; Gabriel's revelation to Mohammed; the establishment of the Abbasid Caliphate
    (D) Gabriel's revelation to Mohammed; the Hegira; the split between Sunni and Shiite Muslims; the establishment of the Abbasid Caliphate
    (E) the establishment of the Abbasid Caliphate; the Hegira; the split between Sunni and Shiite Muslims; Gabriel's revelation to Mohammed

20. Which of the following could NOT be a feature of polytheistic worship?

    (A) a willingness to blend practices and rituals from more than one religion
    (B) a belief that all living beings are animated by divine energy
    (C) a rigid insistence on the worship of one deity
    (D) the veneration of a wide variety of nature spirits
    (E) the identification of each member of a clan with a different totemic animal symbol

Answers

1. **(B)** The Nara period was a time when China (through Korea) had a great impact on the development of Japanese culture, especially with the export of Buddhism to Japan. The arrival of Christian missionaries and the establishment of Edo (Tokyo) took place centuries later.

2. **(D)** The Indian Ocean is accessible from west and east; it has long been home to one of the world's great trade networks.

3. **(B)** Neither code was democratic, and the Hammurabic code treated people differently, depending on their status. Both were more secular than religious in nature, and Roman law did not subscribe explicitly to the "eye-for-an-eye" principle. What both codes have in common is that they set into place legal principles that remained consistent, regardless of the ruler's will.

4. **(E)** A hallmark of agricultural society is that it is more complex and requires greater social organization than herding or hunter-gatherer societies.

5. **(C)** While civilizations often resort to violence, the tendency to do so is not considered a prerequisite for the creation of a civilization. Moreover, primitive societies engage in violence as well.

6. **(E)** All of the answers attest to the development of a complex, long-standing, and advanced civilization in China.

7. **(D)** Islam considers Jews and Christians to be "people of the book," and while Muslims have used force against them, scripture does not particularly justify violence against them. Women were not given equal status, and slavery was permitted (although enslaving fellow Muslims was forbidden). Caliphs wielded both secular and religious authority, making (D) true and (C) false by definition.

8. **(C)** This is a matter of factual knowledge. Egypt and Mali are not sub-Saharan.

9. **(A)** Nomadic peoples such as the Aryans and Huns emerged from Central Asia to affect more settled societies profoundly. Urban civilizations did not appear in Central Asia until relatively late, and Genghis Khan's campaigns did not begin till the 1200s C.E. The Silk Road ran through Central Asia; Judaism, of course, was born farther to the west, in the Middle East.

10. **(D)** Slavery was practiced on all the inhabited continents, and it has never completely disappeared. Major religions often sanctioned it. Slaves were used for many purposes, and their legal status was generally lower than that of a serf.

11. **(A)** If most members of a society remain involved with food production, class distinction is not taking place. By creating food surpluses, agriculture allows greater numbers of people to make their living by some other means.

12. **(C)** The Bantu are the closest thing sub-Saharan Africa has to a common ancestral ethnic group.

13. **(B)** Oligarchy means "rule by the few"; it refers to rule by an aristocratic class without a monarch in place.

14. **(A)** Democratic governments were extremely rare before the 1800s and 1900s C.E. While Rome and Venice were republics, neither was a democracy. The only possible answer from this list is Athens.

15. **(D)** Migration played an important role in the early history of human societies worldwide. The "Great Age of Migrations" refers specifically to the westward movement of Germanic and Asiatic tribes.

16. **(B)** The map shows the extensive network of trade routes in Africa and Eurasia. One of the few areas those routes did not penetrate to was Russia and the Siberian subcontinent. This question tests elementary map-reading skills.

17. **(B)** Both Hinduism and Buddhism arose in India; the Buddha's original intention was to improve upon Hindu practices in his search for truth.

18. **(E)** This is a classic statement of Confucian principle. Political hierarchy, filial piety, and the parallel between a properly governed society and an orderly family are all present.

19. **(D)** This question calls for basic chronological knowledge. Islam was born with Mohammed's visions. He was then forced to flee from Mecca to Medina (the Hegira). After Mohammed's death, the Sunni majority and Shiite minority split. The founding of the Abbasid Caliphate came later.

20. **(C)** By definition, polytheistic faiths involve the veneration of many gods or spirits. Answer (C) is a perfect description of monotheistic practice.

UNIT THREE

WORLD CULTURES MATURING

(600–1450)

Unit Overview

GENERAL REMARKS

Broadly speaking, the period between 600 and 1450 was a time when newer world civilizations matured, largely on the foundations of older cultures that had collapsed or faded away. It was also an age when world civilizations came into ever-increasing contact with each other.

As shown in Unit Two, Chapter 3, many of the world's classical civilizations failed or fell into decline between the 200s and 600s C.E. These include the Roman Empire (with the Greek influence it had kept alive), Han China, and India's Mauryan and Gupta empires. The same process continued up to about 1000 C.E., as other societies considered "classical"—such as Tang China, Heian Japan, and the Abbasid Caliphate—weakened or collapsed.

In other words, between approximately 600 to 1000, the classical period had ended, or was in the process of ending, in almost all areas of the world. New civilizations were created on the foundations of the great classical cultures. In some cases, as in medieval Europe, after the fall of Rome, a lengthy period of backwardness, decentralization, and chaos followed the collapse of a classical civilization. In others, as in China, the transition was less traumatic or at least lasted a shorter time. Whatever the case, mature, sophisticated, advanced cultures—many of them building on the legacy left behind by their classical predecessors—were appearing throughout the world during the period between 600 and 1450.

One important historical question is whether these civilizations are best studied as **nation-states** (countries as formally defined political entities, in the modern sense of the word) or **cultural units** (less formal, defined not so much by political boundaries as by shared traditions, religion, ethnicity, government by a larger imperial or regional authority, and sometimes language). Examples of the latter include the Islamic world, European Christendom, sub-Saharan Africa, and Mesoamerica.

Another general trend was increased connection and communication between world cultures. Although the Americas remained isolated from the rest of the world, vibrant and stimulating systems of interaction and exchange appeared among the civilizations of Africa, Europe, the Middle East, Central Asia, Southeast Asia, and the Far East. Trade, religious influence, technological exchange, cultural and artistic interaction all marked this era. The movement of nomadic and migratory peoples, such as the Vikings and Mongols, greatly affected more settled societies. (A key question of interest on the AP exam will be how **nomadic movement** as a cause of historical change compares to the importance of **cities** during this period.) Even though the world was not yet as joined together as it would later become—with the Europeans' encounter with the Americas and greater improvements in communications and transport technology—extensive systems of global interaction were emerging between 1000 and 1450.

BROAD TRENDS
Global Power and International Relations

- With the exception of the Americas, the major civilizations of the world were coming into increased contact with each other.
- Nomadic and migratory populations (especially the Vikings, Mongols, and Polynesians) continued to have a profound impact on large parts of the world.
- The most advanced and politically influential civilizations during these years were China (especially during the Tang, Song, Yuan, and Ming periods) and the Ottoman Empire.
- Nations of medieval Europe, particularly in the west, gained in power and sophistication.
- Major states and empires—such as Mali, Ghana, Great Zimbabwe, the Delhi Sultanate, the Aztecs, and the Incas—flourished, but for a comparatively short time.
- During the 1200s and 1300s, the Mongols radically altered the balance of power in Eurasia. Their empire, one of the largest in history, brought together vast portions of Europe and Asia. For a time, the Mongols imposed not just political unity but a measure of economic and cultural connectedness not seen since the days of ancient Rome or Han China.
- The invention of gunpowder gradually started to change the equation of world power.

Political Developments

- Most forms of government remained nonrepresentative. Monarchies and oligarchies were most common.
- A few nations managed to place formal restrictions on the power of the monarch—concrete legal systems or lawmaking bodies that shared governmental authority—and still remain centralized. England, with its Magna Carta and Parliament, is an excellent example.
- Most states were not nations in the modern sense of the word. Many were decentralized. Others were multicultural empires joined only by the fact that a single civilization had conquered them all.
- Feudalism became a common form of political (as well as economic) organization in decentralized areas. The best-known examples are medieval Europe and the Japanese shogunates.
- Urban centers played a larger role in the political life of most cultures.

Economic and Environmental Developments

- Most societies remained fundamentally agricultural. The vast majority of people resided in the countryside and made their living by farming.
- However, artisanry and craftsmanship were becoming increasingly important.

- This helped give rise to a slow (but steady) trend: urbanization, or the growth of cities.
- Trade and commerce—even banking—were becoming a basic part of economic life in developed societies.
- The growing importance of trade and commerce made merchant classes larger and more influential in most societies.
- Trade and commerce led to the creation of intercultural and international trade networks. Among the most important were the Mediterranean, the Hanseatic League, the Silk Road, trans-Saharan caravan routes, the gold trade along the Niger River, Indian-Persian economic exchange, the Indian Ocean, and Pacific trade networks.
- Certain cities became important centers for intercultural and international trade. They include Venice, Cairo, Mombasa, Zanzibar, Samarkand, Canton (Guangzhou), Malacca (Melaka), Timbuktu, and Calicut.
- Massive epidemics (pandemics), struck Eurasia. The most famous was the wave of bubonic plague that swept China, the Middle East, and Europe (the "black death") in the 1300s.

Cultural Developments

- Distinct artistic and cultural traditions were developing in each major region of the world.
- The civilizations possessing the greatest degree of scientific knowledge and cultural sophistication were China, the Middle East, Japan, and Muslim Spain.
- Europe underwent great cultural development, especially during the Renaissance.
- China and India exerted a tremendous cultural and religious influence over their neighbors. Buddhism, Hinduism, and art and architectural styles spread from these countries to Southeast Asia, Korea, Japan, Tibet, and elsewhere.
- The Middle East played a large role in spreading knowledge, scholarship, music, art, and architecture to North Africa and Europe. Middle Eastern cultural influence on medieval and Renaissance Europe was considerable.
- Travelers and explorers created links between societies and increased geographical and cultural knowledge. Examples include Zheng He (Cheng Ho), Marco Polo, and Ibn Battuta.
- The invention of block printing in China (perhaps Korea) began to alter cultural life not only in Asia but elsewhere as this new innovation spread.
- Even more dramatically, the invention of the movable-type printing press in Europe, during the 1430s, led to an information explosion, the rapid spread of knowledge and ideas, and a revolution in intellectual life.

Gender Issues

- Women continued to occupy a secondary role in most societies. Women's political rights were minimal or nonexistent.
- Women had sharply defined occupational roles. They were largely assigned to the domestic sphere and seen primarily as childbearers and homemakers. Most work women did outside the home—such as weaving, food gathering, or farm chores—was seen as low status.

- However, in the majority of world civilizations, women possessed at least some freedoms, including legal and economic rights: in many cases, the right to divorce abusive husbands, the right to a dowry, the right to inherit and own property.
- In many societies, women played certain informal, but important, roles. They managed households and family finances, supervised the education of children, and influenced their husbands.
- Being in certain occupations or classes allowed women some respect or escape from male domination. Noblewomen played influential roles in most societies, often as cultural patrons, sometimes as political advisers to their husbands. Priestesses and nuns often enjoyed high status as well as an intellectual life, although their conduct was strictly regulated.
- In some African societies, women enjoyed a great deal of respect, and family trees were matrilinear (traced through the mother), rather than patrilinear.
- In most societies, upper-class women lived easier lives but found themselves more constrained by religious and cultural restrictions on their behavior. Lower-class women, whose lives were much harder, were often less bound by those restrictions because the rules of "proper" behavior applied less to them.
- Societies that feared magic or witchery tended to blame women (especially elderly ones) disproportionately for such things.

QUESTIONS AND COMPARISONS TO CONSIDER

- Differences and likenesses of various world trading systems.
- Intellectual and cultural developments in different societies, and the ways in which societies influence each other (for example, the Middle Eastern influence on medieval European culture or India's influence on Southeast Asian religion, art, and architecture).
- How important is the nation-state (as opposed to larger cultural units) as an object of study during this historical period?
- How did political and social development in western Europe resemble and/or differ from that in eastern Europe?
- Comparisons and contrasts between European and Japanese feudalism.
- Comparisons and contrasts between one of the major European states (or western Europe as a whole) and one of the major African states.
- How did Europe's encounter with sub-Saharan Africa differ from and/or resemble the Islamic world's encounter with it?
- The differences and likenesses between the Mongol Empire and earlier conquest states, such as Rome or Han China.
- The successes and failures of the Roman Catholic Church, the Eastern Orthodox Church, and the Islamic caliphates in their attempts to create a large, multinational civilization united by religion.
- Comparisons and contrasts between Islam and Christianity, not just in terms of doctrine, but also both faiths' impact on social and political organization, gender relations, and views of how nonbelievers should be treated.
- The role of nomadic movement as a cause of historical change during these years compared with the role played by the growth of cities during the same time frame.

Europe During the Middle Ages and the Renaissance

CHAPTER 6

- The medieval period (Middle Ages)
- Feudalism and serfdom
- Roman Catholicism and the ideal of Christendom
- Formation of European states
- The Crusades
- Trade, commerce, and urbanization
- The Black Death (bubonic plague)
- Aristotle and Greco-Latin learning
- Scholasticism
- The movable-type (Gutenberg) printing press
- The Renaissance (classicism and humanism)

The medieval period of European history, also known as the **Middle Ages**, is considered to have lasted from approximately 500 to 1500. Often, the **medieval era** is broken down into three phases: the Early (ca. 500–1000), High (ca. 1000–1300), and Late Middle Ages (ca. 1300–1500). Not all historians, however, use these labels. Also, the question of periodization is complicated by the fact that during the Late Middle Ages, certain parts of Europe—particularly Italy—began to experience the famous cultural rebirth known as the **Renaissance**.

Whatever one calls the various periods of the medieval era, certain trends are clear. The years from 500 to 1000 were a time of political decentralization and overall backwardness. From 1000 to 1300, Europe enjoyed a general revival. Nations became better defined, the economy grew healthier, and the level of technological and cultural knowledge improved. The concept of Europe as a single civilization joined by a common cultural heritage and the Christian religion took greater shape during these years.

The period between 1300 and 1500 was a complex one, marked by crisis and advancement. On one hand, Europe was struck by social unrest, constant warfare, and, in the form of the so-called Black Death, one of the worst epidemics in world history. On the other hand, the Renaissance began, ushering in a period of artistic and intellectual achievement.

FEUDALISM AND THE MANOR SYSTEM

The Origins of Feudalism

In the aftermath of Rome's fall, Europe became politically decentralized. No single ruler was strong enough to provide Europe with central authority, and monarchs typically did not have the power, money, or military strength to govern their lands effectively. The solution was the system of **feudalism**, in which lords and monarchs (lieges) awarded (infeudated) land to loyal followers (vassals). In exchange, the vassals guaranteed that their parcels of land (fiefs) would be governed, that law and justice would be dispensed, that crops would be grown, and that the land itself would be protected. Feudal retainers often subdivided (subinfeudated) their fiefs into smaller units, granting them to people they could rely on. Feudalism remained at the heart of medieval European politics for centuries.

Feudal Nobility, the Manor System, and Serfdom

The retainers to whom monarchs gave large land grants developed into Europe's **noble** (or **aristocratic**) **class**. Structurally, the feudal nobility resembled a pyramid. At the top was the monarch. Below him (or her) were powerful nobles, and below them were lesser nobles. All members of the feudal nobility were theoretically tied to the monarch by bonds of loyalty and landownership, and they were supposed to help provide political leadership.

The feudal nobility also served a military function. One of feudalism's goals was to provide an army of foot soldiers (recruited by nobles) and an elite force of armored cavalry (**knights**) formed by the nobles themselves. Horses and weapons were so costly and the training so specialized that only members of the upper classes could afford to become knights. According to the code of chivalry, the knight was to be a virtuous, Christian warrior who served his lord loyally, treated the lower classes with justice, and acted gentlemanly toward women. Songs and legends, such as those of King Arthur's Round Table, provided examples of how real-life knights were supposed to conduct themselves. Chivalry did restrain the knight's most violent behavior, but in actuality, the code was often broken, and it tended to be more myth than reality.

The feudal system involved more than the ruling class. The vast majority of people in medieval Europe were peasants. The basic unit of feudal landholding was the **manor**, which typically included the lord's residence (an estate or castle) and the peasants' village. Surrounding the residence and village were fields for farming, as well as woodland where food would be gathered and animals hunted (generally a privilege reserved for the lord).

Economically, the feudal system relied on the labor of the peasants. Most peasants in Europe during the Middle Ages were **serfs**. Although serfs were not technically slaves, they were legally unfree. They were not allowed to change residence or profession without permission. Most of their work benefited not themselves but the lord. A portion of their own crops and livestock had to be given to the lord. In addition, serfs had to spend a certain number of days per month fulfilling various labor obligations: building roads, clearing forests, gathering firewood, or most commonly, farming the lord's private fields. Serfs had to pay fees to use any of the manor's facilities that were owned by the lord, including the water mill, the bread oven, the cider press, and the smithy. In times of war, serfs also had to fight: lords would recruit foot soldiers from among them. Overall, living conditions were harsh.

A Medieval Tournament.
The military and political backbone of medieval Europe's feudal system was the knight. High-born and trained from youth in cavalry warfare, the knight was the state-of-the-art warrior of his era. Knights also made up Europe's noble class. Knights honed their military skills—and cultivated the arts of chivalry—at tournaments such as the one portrayed here.

The Time Line of Feudalism

Feudalism persisted throughout the medieval period, and its effects were felt long afterward. Ironically, it outlasted its original purpose. Even after political units began to centralize and resemble modern nations, many feudal practices remained in place. Serfdom took many centuries to disappear, especially in central and eastern Europe. The knightly class transformed into an aristocratic nobility that remained a permanent part of European politics and society until the 1800s and even 1900s. Feudalism set into place class differences that survived as tensions between the poor and powerless on one hand and the rich and powerful on the other.

THE IDEAL OF CHRISTENDOM

The Unifying Influence of Christianity

One of the few things binding European nations and communities together following the fall of Rome was the Christian faith, which acted as a unifying force throughout the continent, both culturally and politically.

Rome itself was one of the two major headquarters of Christian worship. The other was Constantinople, capital of the Byzantine Empire. By 1054, doctrinal differences and geographical distance led to the Great Schism, which separated Christians into two churches: **Roman Catholicism** and **Eastern Orthodoxy**. The former was dominant in central and western Europe; the latter was prominent in the Middle East and the Greek and Slavic parts of eastern Europe.

The Catholic Church shaped medieval society in key ways. Its monasteries preserved many Latin and Greek manuscripts left over from the Roman era. These included scientific and philosophical essays, literary works, and a wealth of learning that otherwise would have been lost. The church also provided the people of Europe with a sense that, despite national and linguistic differences, they were linked by a single faith. This gave a much-needed feeling of cultural cohesion to Europe at a time of extreme decentralization.

The Medieval Papacy and the Political Power of the Catholic Church

The leader of the Catholic Church was the pope, technically the bishop of Rome. At the lowest level of church organization was the priest, who served the needs of an individual community. Only men could become priests. Above the priest was the bishop, who presided over a large territory and supervised many priests. Archbishops and cardinals were powerful church officials who advised the pope. Also part of the church hierarchy were monks and nuns.

After 1000, the Catholic Church became immensely powerful politically. (This is in contrast with the Eastern Orthodox Church, which, in general, viewed itself as subservient to worldly authority.) The pope governed a sizable territory in central Italy, the Papal States. Many popes, especially Innocent III (1198–1216), went to great lengths to assert that the authority of the papacy was superior to that of kings and emperors. The popes had moral authority and the right to determine what was **heresy**, exclude worshippers from the Catholic Church (**excommunication**), and issue calls for holy wars (**crusades**). The ultimate goal of medieval popes was to join the nations of Europe into a single Christian community. Referred to as **Christendom**, this community was to be governed by the pope, with kings and emperors subject to his rule. The Catholic Church never realized this ideal, but for several hundred years, the popes heavily influenced how European monarchs ruled their countries.

The Catholic Church owned vast amounts of land. Combined with its right to collect tithes from the general population, this made the church very wealthy. Another way the church exercised worldly power was control over education, thought, and culture. In 1231, the **Holy Inquisition**, a set of special courts with wide-ranging powers, was established to hunt out and punish heresy and religious nonconformity.

> **NOTE**
>
> Most institutions of learning were connected in one way or another with the Catholic Church. It was dangerous for any scholar or artist to write, say, or produce anything that ran counter to Catholic doctrine.

Monasticism

A prominent feature of medieval Christianity (both Catholic and Orthodox) was **monasticism**, the formation of religious communities whose members (monks and nuns) are not ordained as priests. The first European monasteries stressed contemplation and seclusion. This approach (the Benedictine model) remained dominant from the 500s through the late 1100s. In the early 1200s, new orders, such as the Dominicans and Franciscans, were established to carry on the work of the Catholic Church in the wider world.

THE WESTERN MONARCHIES AND THE EASTERN FRONTIER

Early Kingdoms and the Carolingian Empire

It took several centuries after the fall of Rome for stable nations to form. Short-lived kingdoms, founded by warlords and barbarian chiefs, rose and fell frequently during the 500s and 600s. Internally, decentralization kept states weak, as did external threats such as Viking raids and Muslim invasions.

One of the earliest European nations was the Frankish kingdom, which, by the 700s, grew into the Carolingian Empire. The Franks were a Germanic tribe who, under their king Clovis (465–511), acquired a large empire, including parts of what is now Germany, France, and the Low Countries. Clovis converted his people to Catholicism, and although the kingdom weakened after his death, it did not die away. It grew powerful once again under Charles Martel (688–741), a great military leader who successfully turned back Muslim invaders at the **Battle of Tours** (732), one of the most influential battles of the medieval era. Charles Martel established the Carolingian dynasty, and his son Pepin strengthened the kingdom's ties with the Catholic Church.

Even more successful as a nation-building monarch was Pepin's son **Charlemagne** (768–814), whose name means "Charles the Great." Charlemagne defended Frankish territory against Viking, barbarian, and Muslim attacks. He greatly expanded the kingdom and transformed it into the Carolingian Empire (the pope crowned him Holy Roman Emperor in 800). He was an active supporter of education and culture, much of which he entrusted to the church. By the standards of the day, the Carolingian Empire was strong and well organized. It was still a feudal state, however, and, in 843, Charlemagne's three grandsons divided the empire into smaller parts. The concept of the "holy" and "Roman" empire—a viable state allied with the church and, like Rome before it, able to provide relatively centralized authority—also survived.

> **NOTE**
>
> Charlemagne's legacy was to provide an example of capable leadership for future monarchs.

Other early nations emerged in the late 800s and 900s. Saxon kings united large parts of England. The Capetian dynasty came to rule the area around Paris and gradually gained control over more of France. The eastern, Germanic portion of Charlemagne's realm reformed itself as the Holy Roman Empire, which went on to rule most of central Europe for centuries to come.

The Vikings

An important factor that shaped the development of early medieval European nations was the appearance of the **Vikings**, expert sailors and fierce warriors from Scandinavia. Owing mainly to overcrowding in their homelands, large numbers of Vikings poured out of the north from the 800s through the 1100s. One of the few peoples of this era who could navigate on the open ocean, the Vikings roamed far and wide. They raided and conquered land throughout most of coastal Europe, as far south as the Mediterranean.

> **NOTE**
>
> By forcing nations such as England, France, and the Holy Roman Empire to defend against their attacks, the Vikings (although not on purpose) prompted those nations to centralize more than they had during the early medieval period.

The Vikings colonized Iceland and Greenland. Around 1000 C.E., voyagers led by Leif Eriksson even reached what is today Canada. The Vikings also settled in parts of England, Scotland, and Ireland. They created long-lasting kingdoms in northwestern France and Sicily. A group of Vikings established a trade route from Scandinavia to Byzantium, through Russia. In the process, they created the first Russian state.

England and France

In the west, the most stable states were England and France. For four centuries, the political leadership of both countries was intertwined. In 1066, Normans (descendants of Vikings who had settled in France) led by William the Conqueror, invaded England, defeated the Saxon king, and established their rule there. Because William and his successors were connected to the French throne by blood ties and feudal obligations, there was much confusion and competition between England and France over land and political legitimacy until the middle of the 1400s.

The **Norman Conquest** brought French-style feudalism to England and helped create a rich cultural fusion, not only Celtic and Anglo-Saxon but also Latin-based, in the British Isles. By medieval standards, England became quite centralized, and it did so despite the fact that significant checks were put on the power of the king. (Normally, the less powerful the monarch, the less centralized the state.) During the 1100s, the English adopted a single law code (common law) and the concept of jury trials. In 1215, the **Magna Carta**, imposed on the king by his barons, guaranteed the nobility certain rights and privileges, limiting the monarch's might. Later in the 1200s, the English nobility won the right to form a **Parliament**, which eventually became a representative lawmaking body that governed in conjunction with the king. In the 1200s and 1300s, English monarchs extended their rule to Wales and Scotland. Ireland would follow later.

In France, the Capetian kings centralized their nation by increasing their own power (the typical route to premodern nation building). Originally, the Capetians ruled only a tiny part of France. England controlled large territories, such as Aquitaine and Brittany, while large and economically important regions such as Flanders and Burgundy remained independent. Generations of Capetian monarchs expanded the size of the French kingdom, beat the English in a number of wars (including the Hundred Years' War, mentioned below), and gained control over Burgundy and other stubborn regions. By the mid-to-late 1400s, France was large and centralized, and the French kings were among the most powerful in Europe. Unlike their English counterparts, French monarchs were not limited or obligated to share power in any legally meaningful way.

The political event that most affected England and France during the fourteenth and fifteenth centuries was the **Hundred Years' War** (1337–1453). The war's first years coincided with the onset of other European crises, including social uprisings and the Black Death. Until the early 1400s, the English won a number of victories, gaining control over more than half of France. Only after the 1420s did the French king, helped by the warrior maid Joan of Arc, drive the English out. The war ended most of the awkward connections between the French and English royal families.

> **NOTE**
>
> Victory over the English helped the French kings to centralize their power at home.

The Holy Roman Empire and Italian States: Decentralization

Important states formed in central and southern Europe, but they were less centralized. Dominating the middle of Europe was the Holy Roman Empire, a multicultural monarchy in which the crown passed back and forth among a group of German noble families. The empire was founded in the 900s by the heirs of Charlemagne. Its name was inspired by the theoretical ideal of a state that was large and powerful ("Roman") and brought a variety of peoples into a single Catholic ("holy") community. The emperor was supposed to work in partnership with the pope, but in real life, the two clashed more often than they cooperated.

The Holy Roman Empire was one of medieval Europe's largest states, but the emperor's powers were comparatively weak. His position was not hereditary—he was chosen by the empire's most powerful noble families. The empire's population was ethnically diverse (German, Italian, Hungarian, Slavic, and more), and the empire itself consisted of dozens of duchies, kingdoms, and principalities (almost 200 in the mid-1300s), and each duke, king, and prince guarded his autonomy carefully. Two things helped the empire to centralize somewhat in the 1300s and 1400s. The Golden Bull (1356) asserted the rights and powers of the various rulers under the emperor, but it dramatically reduced the number of states allowed to elect the emperor (from all of them to seven). Also, the **Habsburg** family of Austria emerged as a major player in imperial politics during the late 1200s; by 1438, the Habsburgs gained permanent control over the imperial throne (which remained theirs until 1918).

Even more decentralized than the Holy Roman Empire was Italy (which was not an actual country). Parts of northern Italy were under the Holy Roman Empire's control. Some areas in the south passed in and out of the hands of other foreigners, including the French, Spanish, Muslims, and Byzantines. The parts of Italy that remained free were governed by dozens of city-states; Italy was one of the most urbanized parts of Europe. Its cultural level was high as well (it was the birthplace of the Renaissance). Italy's position in the Mediterranean—which enabled trade with the Middle East and Egypt (and, by extension, the Far East, China, and the Indian Ocean)—allowed its cities to develop strong commercial economies. The chief city-states of medieval and Renaissance Italy were Florence, Milan, and Venice in the north, and Naples in the south. Also important was Rome, the heart of the Papal States. **Venice**, which called itself the "Most Serene Republic," created one of this era's richest and most powerful maritime and commercial empires.

> **NOTE**
>
> From the 1300s onward, the Holy Roman Empire served as Europe's military bulwark against the long wave of Turkish attacks from the east.

Spain and Portugal

The medieval development of Spain and Portugal was shaped above all by the fact that they had been taken over by Muslim invaders, known as the Moors, during the 700s. From 1031 onward, the people of Spain and Portugal fought the Moors in a long struggle known as the **Reconquista**. The legend of El Cid, an eleventh-century general and one of Spain's great heroes, grew out of this reconquest. By the end of the 1200s, the Spanish had pushed the Moors into Granada, the southernmost part of the country. For the next 200 years, the Moors held out in Granada, until they were expelled completely in 1492, by the armies of Ferdinand and Isabella.

The effects of the Moors and the war against them were many. Spanish territory was liberated gradually, region by region, and each newly freed area remained independent, delaying centralization. By the 1400s, there were about half a dozen Spanish kingdoms, not counting Portugal. Only late in the 1400s, when the rulers of the two largest kingdoms, **Ferdinand of Aragón and Isabella of Castile**, married and joined their lands together, did Spain take shape as a single country. Another result of the Reconquista was intense religious intolerance. The war caused Catholic authorities in Spain to be extremely rigid in terms of doctrine and hostile to nonbelievers. Muslims and Jews (whom the Moors had welcomed to Spain) were persecuted, and, by the end of the 1400s, forced to convert to Catholicism or leave the country.

The Moorish presence brought benefits as well. Islamic culture was more advanced than that of medieval Europe, so Spain was able to take advantage of the medical, scientific, and technological knowledge brought there by the Muslim conquerors (as well as the Jewish scholars and professionals who came with them). The Spanish city of **Córdoba** was one of Europe's greatest centers of learning and science, thanks to the long-standing Muslim presence there.

Portugal, an independent principality, began its tradition of world exploration during the 1400s, starting a trend that would sweep the globe. (For more, see Chapter 14.)

> **NOTE**
>
> Spanish art and architecture were also affected by the Moorish style, elements of which still persist today.

Byzantium and Eastern Europe

The farther east, the less centralized European nations became, with the exception of the Byzantine Empire, the crossroads between Christian Europe and the Islamic Middle East. **Constantinople** was a tremendously important trading center, linking Mediterranean Europe with the Middle East and, by extension, the overland routes (such as the Silk Road) and sea lanes that joined the Middle East with China, India, and the East Indies.

Although Byzantium was far superior to the rest of Europe in terms of economic and cultural advancement, it entered a long period of political and military decline. In the eleventh century, a new enemy, the Seljuk Turks, appeared on the eastern frontier. From the Battle of Manzikert (1071) onward, the Seljuks, then their more dangerous successors, the Ottoman Turks, slowly but unceasingly stripped territory away from Byzantium. By the 1400s, Constantinople itself was under threat; in 1453, the Ottomans seized it. The Byzantine Empire was destroyed, its capital became the Turkish city of Istanbul, and the Ottoman Empire went on to conquer large parts of southeastern Europe, clashing for centuries with the Holy Roman (Austrian) Empire.

Territories on Europe's eastern and northern fringe tended to be more poorly defined, politically speaking. Much of this had to do with the stress of invasions from the east. Mongol attacks in the mid-1200s and constant pressure from the Ottomans during and after the 1400s took their toll and, in many ways, held back the political development of nations. Countries such as Hungary, Sweden, and Poland were exceptions: they were stable and sophisticated, at least for the time being. More typical were the Russian lands, farther to the east. During most of the medieval era, Russia was a loose confederation of city-states, governed by constantly feuding princes. The Mongol invasions of the 1240s placed the Russians under the domination of the Golden Horde; not until the mid-1400s did Russia become free. Only after that did a Russian nation begin to take shape, under the leadership of the tsars of Moscow.

THE CRUSADES

The Concept and Origin of Crusading

Among the powers of the medieval popes was the ability to request monarchs to provide troops and money for holy wars known as **crusades**. Crusades were fought for a number of reasons: to convert nonbelievers to Catholicism, to crush Christian movements the papacy considered heretical (infamous crusades of this type were fought in southern France during the early 1200s), and to resist attacks by foreigners who were not Christian (especially Muslims).

Many underlying factors motivated the Crusades:

- Genuine religious fervor on the part of both Muslims and Christians
- Geopolitical conflict between Europe and the Middle East
- The Europeans' desire to become more involved in the international trade network stretching from the Mediterranean to China
- Personal ambitions of Europeans hoping to gain wealth and land in the Middle East
- Racial and religious prejudice

> **NOTE**
>
> The best-known crusades, and the ones generally referred to when the term "the Crusades" is used, are those fought by European Catholics against the Muslims of the Middle East and North Africa from 1095 to 1291.

The Crusading Experience

The spark of the **First Crusade** (1096–1099) came in 1095, when the Byzantine Empire asked Christian Europe for military assistance against the Seljuk Turks, who had recently captured Jerusalem. To increase his chances of receiving aid, the Byzantine emperor exaggerated rumors of Turkish atrocities in the Holy Land. Pope Urban II responded by summoning the **Council of Clermont** and calling upon the knights of Catholic Europe to retake Jerusalem and the Holy Land from the Turks. In 1096, a massive army of Crusaders traveled to Constantinople, then through the Middle East, fighting Muslim forces along the way. In the summer of 1099, the Crusaders reached Jerusalem and placed it under siege. After taking the city, the Crusaders, in one of the bloodiest episodes in military history, butchered almost every Muslim and Jew within its walls (as well as a number of native Christians whom they mistook for Muslims). A key reason for the First Crusade's success was lack of unity among Turks, Arabs, and other Muslim peoples.

After the First Crusade, the Europeans established four Christian states known as the Latin Kingdoms. While they lasted, the Latin Kingdoms served as a military and political foothold in the Middle East. They also enabled Europeans to become involved in the lucrative commercial economy that made the region so wealthy.

The Christians maintained their presence in the Middle East for two centuries. However, the Muslims became eager to expel the Europeans; once they united their efforts, they began to do so. The many crusades that followed were generally responses to successful Muslim campaigns. Jerusalem, for example, fell back to the Muslims in 1187. Especially after 1200, European crusades lost their focus (the Fourth Crusade of 1202–1204 turned into a sack of Christian Constantinople) or failed miserably (like the ill-fated Children's Crusades). In 1291, the Europeans abandoned their last major outpost (Acre) in the Middle East.

Effects of the Crusades

Long-term effects of the Crusades include the worsening of the relationship between the Muslim and Christian worlds. Also important was the greater awareness of the wider world, especially the lands of the east, that the Crusades stimulated among the Europeans. Along with this came an increased knowledge of—and desire for—the economic wealth to be gained by greater interaction with the Middle and Far East. Moreover, the crusading ideal—the notion that Christian warriors were fighting a holy war on behalf of a sacred cause—contributed to the powerful myth of knighthood and chivalry that emerged in Europe during the Middle Ages.

URBANIZATION, TRADE, AND SOCIETY

While the early medieval era was a time of social and economic backwardness, significant gains were made during the High and Late Middle Ages. However, the latter period was a time of social crisis as well.

Population Growth, Trade, and Commerce

From 1000 to 1300, population growth in Europe was considerable. Advanced agricultural techniques—such as the three-field system of crop rotation and the invention of better plows—caused the food supply to increase.

Trade and commerce became a larger part of the European economy. Political stability made **banking**, the movement of goods, and the creation of **markets** safer and more convenient. Because the movement of goods was easier by water than by land, **trade routes** tended to follow rivers and coastlines. One major network, centered on Italy, sprang up throughout the Mediterranean, and did much to connect Europe with the commerce of the Middle and Far East (as noted earlier, the Crusades did much to stimulate this). Other important networks formed along the Rhine River, in the North Sea and English Channel (especially between England and Flanders), and throughout the Baltic Sea. Trade in the Baltic was dominated by the **Hanseatic League**, a group whose influence stretched from England in the west to Russia in the east. The relatively new practice of banking made trade more feasible and dependable. Powerful banking houses were run by the Medicis in Italy and the Fuggers in central Europe.

European Trade Routes During the Late Medieval Period and the Renaissance.
European desire for more direct access to the goods of East and South Asia prompted the great wave of exploration that began during the 1400s and continued during the 1500s and 1600s.

Urbanization

Another social trend was **urbanization**. Although the majority of people in medieval Europe remained in the countryside, working as peasants and serfs, an increasingly large number were moving to cities. Existing cities grew larger, and new cities were founded at a great rate. Some parts of Europe, particularly Italy and Flanders, urbanized more quickly than others.

Cities were excellent sites for trade. They attracted artists, writers, and scholars. Because urban populations included shopkeepers, artisans, tradespeople, and laborers of all sorts, the growth of cities also encouraged specialization of labor. Most skilled trades in medieval cities were organized according to the **guild system**. Guilds were labor groups that maintained a monopoly on their respective trades. They restricted membership, established prices, set standards of quality and fair practice, and provided pensions.

Cities were often overcrowded and polluted, and many people lived in poverty. There were benefits to city life, however, including cultural opportunities and the chance to gain greater wealth. A key advantage was immunity from feudal obligations, especially serfdom: typically, if a person left the countryside and lived in a city for a year and a day, he or she was released from status as a serf (as reflected in the popular saying, "city air makes you free").

Social Stress and Black Death in the Late Medieval Period

Although trade and urbanization continued to expand during the Late Middle Ages, these were also years of great social stress. A wave of uprisings and revolts swept Europe from the early 1300s through the early 1500s (including the peasant Jacquerie of 1358 in France; the Wool Carders' Revolt in Florence, in 1378; and, in 1381, Wat Tyler's Rebellion in England). The causes of such disturbances were many. A general cooling of the climate, referred to by environmental historians as the Little Ice Age, affected harvests and made life in the countryside difficult. More (and longer) wars were being fought, armies were growing larger, and the new gunpowder weaponry of the day was extremely expensive. More peasants were forced into military service (especially during the Hundred Years' War). The taxes of common people also increased. During the last half of the 1400s, religious disagreements and dissatisfaction with the Church sometimes led to rebellion.

> **NOTE**
>
> In the cities, rapid growth often meant greater numbers of poor and unemployed citizens.

Another manifestation of social stress was a sharp rise in the persecution of people thought to be witches. Catholic authorities sought to root out suspected witchcraft, issuing a manual in the late 1400s, *The Hammer of Witchcraft*, to aid in spotting and trying witches. Ordinary people were caught up in the hysteria as well. Most of the victims of witch hunts were women.

Social trauma also came in the form of the **Black Death**, the popular name for the bubonic plague. The arrival of bubonic plague in the mid-fourteenth century ranks as one of the greatest medical disasters in European history. After killing millions of people in China, the disease traveled westward to the Middle East. It reached Europe in 1347 on a ship landing in Sicily.

In 1347 and 1348, the plague ravaged southern Europe. By 1349 and 1350, it spread to central Europe and the British Isles; it was felt in Russia and Scandinavia

NOTE

Many people saw the plague as a sign that the world was coming to an end; others accused Jews of poisoning or bewitching Christians and persecuted them harshly.

NOTE

In this era of poor hygiene and limited medical knowledge, many women—as many as 10 to 15 percent—died in childbirth.

from 1351 to 1353. The disease's deadliness and rapid spread caused tremendous panic throughout Europe. This initial bout of the plague killed 25 to 30 million people, roughly one-third the population of Europe. For centuries afterward, the plague recurred periodically in Europe (although no attack was as bad as the first).

Women in Medieval Europe

As a rule, women were subservient to men in all parts of Europe during these years. How much freedom or how many rights a woman enjoyed depended mainly on her social status.

Women of lower classes cared for the household and assisted with farmwork. They bore children and raised them. Women of low birth also worked as servants for upper-class families. One of the few peasant women to leave an individual mark on medieval Europe was the French war leader **Joan of Arc** (ca. 1410–1431).

In most parts of medieval Europe, women had some property rights. They could own and inherit land and property. They often received dowries (although in some places and times, it was the woman's family that had to provide a dowry to the husband-to-be). Women could separate from their husbands, although obtaining divorces and annulments was difficult, especially for women of the upper classes. Women had protection, although not always equality, before the law.

Women could enter religious life; they could not become priests in either the Catholic or Orthodox Church, but they could become nuns. The majority of nuns were from the landed aristocracy. To marry off daughters, noble families had to provide potential husbands with land, money, or a title; an aristocratic family with many daughters was often unable to pay for all of them to get married. The most common solution was to place younger daughters in convents. Women who preferred intellectual pursuits sometimes found safe haven as nuns. For example, **Hildegard of Bingen** (1098–1179), celebrated for her mystical writings and songs, became abbess of a German convent.

Aristocratic women, while not legally the equal of men, could exert much informal political and cultural influence. If an aristocratic woman was heir to rich property or a kingdom, she was an extremely desirable match. Noblewomen often managed their husbands' estates and financial accounts. Frequently, the mothers of young kings whose fathers died early served as regents and advisers until their sons came of age.

Some women ruled in their own right, as queens. This situation was not common, and countries whose legal systems were based on tribal Germanic (Salic) law, such as France and the Holy Roman Empire, did not allow women to inherit thrones. However, women would come to rule England, parts of Spain, Russia, and elsewhere. The most famous example of a politically important woman during the Middle Ages was **Eleanor of Aquitaine** (ca. 1122–1204). A dynamic, intelligent woman, Eleanor married Louis VII of France and then Henry II of England. She had much influence over politics in both countries. She was also a great patron of art and music.

MEDIEVAL CULTURE

For many years, it was traditional to view the medieval period as the Dark Ages, a time almost completely lacking in culture or sophistication. More recently, it has become standard to recognize the richness of medieval culture, especially during the High and Late Middle Ages. Even so, medieval Europe lagged behind Byzantium and the Islamic world in terms of cultural attainment.

Catholicism and Classicism as Influences on Medieval Culture

The most important factor shaping medieval culture was the Catholic Church, which administered institutions of learning (monasteries, then universities) and was the largest employer of artists, architects, and musicians. Art and ideas that were not in line with church doctrine could be banned—and could lead to severe punishment.

Another influence on medieval culture was the classical learning and literature preserved from ancient Greece and Rome. During the Middle Ages (and long afterward), Latin was Europe's language of learning and culture. (Europeans had much less knowledge of Greek until later, when Arab and Jewish translators made materials in that language more accessible.) Medieval scientific thought was dominated by the theories of the ancient Greeks (mainly through Latin translations). Of special importance was **Aristotle**, whose writings on science, philosophy, ethics, and politics were adapted by Christian scholars and placed at the center of the medieval worldview. Greek science taught the Europeans much, but it also encouraged some mistaken ideas, especially the **geocentric theory**, which argues that the sun revolves around the earth.

Eventually, increased familiarity of European artists and scholars with Greek and Roman texts helped give birth to the Renaissance.

> **NOTE**
>
> Ironically, Aristotle had written about the **scientific method** (in which hypotheses have to be tested by observation and experiment), but medieval Europeans tended to ignore this part of his thinking and accepted most Greek science, errors included, as unquestioned fact.

Art, Architecture, and Literature

Most medieval art was religious in nature. Icons, or religious paintings, were largely inspired by Byzantine styles, even in Catholic Europe. Early church music was mainly plainsong (also known as Gregorian chant): human voices unaccompanied by instruments. Over time, arrangements became more complex, and instruments were used by the end of the Middle Ages. The greatest achievement of medieval architecture was the cathedral, which required skill, money, and decades to build. The prevailing styles were **Romanesque** (thick walls, small windows, square build) and **Gothic** (tall, slender spires; large stained-glass windows; ornate carvings; flying buttresses).

In the secular sphere, the medieval Europeans were great builders of castles (although many were modeled on Byzantine and Middle Eastern designs). Troubadours and minstrels appeared in the eleventh and twelfth centuries and popularized nonreligious music (favorite songs were about love, as well as legends of King Arthur, Charlemagne's knight Roland, and El Cid of Spain).

One trend encouraged by troubadours and minstrels—then later authors like Dante Alighieri of Italy (1265–1321), the English poet Geoffrey Chaucer

(1340–1401), and Christine de Pisan (1364–1410), who wrote in French and Italian—was the increased use of native, or **vernacular**, languages. Although Latin remained the language of the educated elite, it became more acceptable to write serious poetic and literary works in the vernacular. This stimulated a growth in literacy and made literature available to a wider range of people.

Cathedral of Notre Dame, Paris, France.
One of the best-known landmarks of Paris, the Cathedral of Notre Dame provides a quintessential example of the Gothic style of church architecture.

Philosophy and Intellectual Life

The principal school of philosophy in medieval Europe was **Scholasticism**, which attempted to reconcile reason (logic, the senses, and the learning of ancient Greeks and Romans like Aristotle) with faith in God and Christianity. The greatest of the Scholastics was the Italian monk Thomas Aquinas (1225–1274).

The overall level of learning in Europe was boosted by the appearance of **universities**, starting in Italy during the 900s. Although they were at least partly under church influence, universities provided Europe with havens of learning and the exchange of ideas.

NOTE

European intellectual life was also enriched by the Jewish and Muslim thinkers of the Middle East and Moorish Spain, such as Maimonides, Avicenna, and Averroës (see Chapter 7).

The Printing Press

In 1436 or 1437, a new invention revolutionized European culture and the intellectual life of the entire world. This was the printing press developed by German inventor Johannes Gutenberg. The concept of printing by carving images and words into blocks of wood had originated in China (perhaps Korea) centuries before, and was known to the Europeans. However, block printing was costly and unwieldy. Gutenberg created a **movable-type printing press,** in which individual, reusable metal characters could be placed in a frame to form text. The printing press raised literacy rates, spread information, increased the impact of new ideas and scientific theories, and encouraged the expansion of libraries and universities. It played an indispensable role in the Renaissance, the Protestant Reformation, and a general explosion of knowledge that transformed Europe and the West for centuries.

THE RENAISSANCE

The Concept of the Renaissance

During the early 1300s, an important cultural and intellectual revival began in parts of southern Europe, especially the city-states of the Italian peninsula. This revival became known as the **Renaissance,** or "rebirth." By the end of the 1400s, it was spreading from Italy to the rest of Europe. It is considered to have lasted until approximately 1600.

As noted previously, it was common until recently to think of the medieval era as a time of minimal cultural advancement. Consequently, the Renaissance was often viewed as a revolution, a sudden explosion of new ideas and learning. Because historians now have a better appreciation of medieval culture, it has become standard to see the Renaissance more as a gradual cultural and intellectual evolution. Nonetheless, it did represent a significant change.

The Cultural Outlook of the Renaissance

One of the hallmarks of Renaissance culture was **classicism:** a greater understanding of and admiration for Greco-Roman literature and learning. Of course, medieval Europeans were familiar with this heritage. What changed during the Renaissance was that a greater number of people probed more deeply into Latin sources and, thanks largely to translations provided by Jews and Arabs, the learning of the Greeks.

Renaissance thought was more secular than that of the medieval era. The authors and artists of the Renaissance did not ignore religion; even if they had wanted to, doing so would have been dangerous, thanks to the church's influence. Still, Renaissance writings and artworks placed a greater emphasis on worldly matters.

Similarly, another feature of Renaissance culture was **humanism,** a Greco-Roman concept that went hand-in-hand with the classical revival and Renaissance secularism. Humanism, the conviction that to be human is something to celebrate, ran counter to the church-dominated medieval view that to be human was to be tainted with sin and that worldly life was less important than heavenly afterlife.

Causes of the Renaissance

Why did the Renaissance occur first in Italy? One cause was the urban sophistication of the Italian city-states. Another was the commercial strength of the Italian cities, which generated excess wealth sufficient to support a sustained cultural revival. Italy's success in trade and commerce also gave birth to a class of patrons who, though not always of noble blood, were rich, educated, and eager to improve their status by sponsoring artists and writers (the most famous example is the Medici family of Florence). Italy's position as a naval and economic crossroads in the Mediterranean brought it into contact with new ideas and advanced knowledge from the outside world more quickly than the rest of Europe.

Major Figures and Trends of the Renaissance

Important figures in the early Italian Renaissance were the poet Petrarch (1304–1374), the author Giovanni Boccaccio (1313–1375), and the painter Giotto (ca. 1267–1337). As the Renaissance matured, key individuals included the architect Filippo Brunelleschi (1377–1446), the political philosopher Niccolò Machiavelli (1469–1527), the artist and scientist Leonardo da Vinci (1452–1519), the painter and sculptor Michelangelo (1472–1564), and the painters Raphael (1483–1520) and Titian (1477–1576).

Renaissance architects attained a high degree of engineering skill, boosted by a better understanding of mathematics and a deeper knowledge of the techniques of the Greeks and Romans, who had been master builders. Renaissance painters achieved an astonishing level of realism in their work, compared with the art of the medieval era. In painting, as in architecture, increased familiarity with mathematics enabled painters to work out the laws of perspective. The result was a convincing depiction of a three-dimensional subject on a two-dimensional surface. Better paints and equipment, the technique of foreshortening, and the effective use of light and shadowing also increased the quality of Renaissance paintings.

The Spread of Renaissance Culture

By the 1400s, the Italian Renaissance was exerting its influence on the rest of Europe. Travelers, especially northern students attending Italian universities, carried with them techniques drawn from the art and literature of the south. The invention of the movable-type printing press in the 1430s dramatically increased the speed and scope by which information could be produced and transmitted throughout Europe, and the printing press deserves much of the credit for spreading the ideals of the Renaissance far beyond Italy. The Renaissance took hold in southern France, and then all of France, as well as England, Spain, the Holy Roman Empire, Poland, Hungary, and elsewhere. By the late 1400s, it was possible to speak of a northern Renaissance. This northern Renaissance had a profound impact on the rest of Europe, especially with regard to the religious controversies of the 1500s that led to the Protestant Reformation.

QUICK REVIEW

1. Why were knights drawn principally from the nobility?

   (A) Nobles were smarter than commoners.
   (B) Monarchs did not believe that commoners could think strategically.
   (C) The weapons and equipment required for the knighthood were too costly for anyone but members of the nobility.
   (D) Only noblemen could serve as foot soldiers (knights-in-training).
   (E) none of the above

2. Which of the following is an accurate statement about feudalism in Europe?

   (A) It was discontinued by the 700s C.E.
   (B) Serfs were allowed to own land.
   (C) The basic unit of feudal landholding was the village.
   (D) Feudalism led to major class differences in society.
   (E) Serfs embraced the practice of chivalry.

3. In what area did the Vikings NOT settle?

   (A) England
   (B) the Arabian Peninsula
   (C) Sicily
   (D) France
   (E) Greenland

4. In 1215, the Magna Carta

   (A) was the most complex world map of its kind.
   (B) sailed to India seeking out trade.
   (C) granted English nobles certain rights and privileges.
   (D) granted English commoners voting rights.
   (E) none of the above

5. Which of the following is NOT true of the Hundred Years' War?

   (A) Joan of Arc helped drive the English from France.
   (B) One of its causes was the political entanglement of the English and French royal families.
   (C) For a time, England gained control over more than half of France.
   (D) The war had little effect on domestic affairs in England or France.
   (E) Victory over the English helped the French kings to centralize their country.

6. Which of the following is NOT a reason for the Crusades?

   (A) racial and religious prejudice
   (B) geopolitical conflict between Europe and the Middle East
   (C) the Black Death
   (D) religious fervor
   (E) the personal greed of many Europeans to gain wealth and land

7. The Hanseatic League

   (A) was a trade union based in the Mediterranean region.
   (B) fought in the Middle East during the Crusades.
   (C) was a powerful banking house in Italy.
   (D) dominated trade in the Baltic region.
   (E) traded in diamonds.

8. Women in medieval Europe

   (A) all lacked property rights.
   (B) had equality before the law, especially in matters of reproductive rights.
   (C) had some legal protections, but their rights depended on where they lived and which class they belonged to.
   (D) were allowed to become priests in Catholic Europe.
   (E) could enter religious life only in Orthodox Byzantium.

9. Flying buttresses and slender spires are characteristics of _____ architecture.

(A) Gothic
(B) Romanesque
(C) modern
(D) Moorish
(E) Art Nouveau

10. Today, many historians view the Renaissance as

(A) a revolution.
(B) a gradual but significant change in cultural and intellectual ideas and trends.
(C) a sudden explosion of new ideas in the arts, sciences, and scholarly pursuits.
(D) a radical shift in what was once practiced in the arts.
(E) none of the above.

Answers

1. **(C)** Knightly warfare was highly skilled combat that required horses and costly gear. High social status and wealth were needed to afford not only the weapons, armor, and horses but also the time to train.

2. **(D)** Serfdom was first established in the 700s C.E., and serfs neither owned land nor had any part of the chivalric code. The manor was the basic unit of feudal landholding. What feudalism did was to entrench class differences for centuries to come.

3. **(B)** This is a matter of simple factual knowledge, although the question illustrates the wide range of Viking migration.

4. **(C)** An early stepping stone in the creation of England's parliamentary monarchy, theMagna Carta formally limited the powers of the English king. It should not be mistaken, as it often is, as the moment that created democracy in England; it did next to nothing for the common people.

5. **(D)** The early years of the Hundred Years' War coincided with the Black Death. Moreover, the increased burdens of higher taxes and troop recruitment caused major peasant uprisings in both countries.

6. **(C)** The Black Death arrived in Europe from the Middle East, but half a century after the major Crusades had ended. All the other answers help to explain European motives.

7. **(D)** A cooperative venture begun by German city-states, the Hanseatic League grew into one of medieval and Renaissance Europe's great trade networks. It was dominant in the North and Baltic seas.

8. **(C)** Almost never was the treatment of women 100 percent just or unjust. Although women's rights and privileges were more limited than those of men, they did exist. Much depended on social status, as well as place of origin.

9. **(A)** Cathedral building was one of the Europeans' great cultural achievements during the Middle Ages. The technically advanced Gothic style represented the pinnacle of that achievement.

10. **(B)** The Renaissance used to be regarded as a radical departure from the medieval "dark ages." With greater appreciation for the attainments of the medieval era, it has become more common to see the Renaissance as an evolutionary change, not a revolutionary one.

Islam in the Middle East and Africa

CHAPTER 7

- The Sunni-Shiite split
- The Abbasid Caliphate
- Trans-Saharan caravan routes
- The Arab slave trade
- Mali and Timbuktu
- The Seljuk and Ottoman Turks
- The conquest of Constantinople
- Ibn Battuta

Prior to 600 C.E., the dominant civilizations in the Middle East were the Byzantine Empire and Persia. Suddenly, the political and religious landscape of the Middle East—and much of Eurasia—was transformed by the appearance of Islam.

During the 600s and 700s, military conquest carried the new faith out of Arabia, where it was born, to Spain and Morocco in the west, and the borderlands of India in the east. The Islamic caliphate aspired to unite all worshippers into a single political community called dar al-Islam (much as popes strove to do in Christian Europe). The golden age of classical Islam lasted from the middle of the 900s to about 1000, and is associated with the Abbasid Caliphate.

> **TIP**
>
> The key tenets of Islam, as well as the place of women in the Islamic world, are discussed in Chapter 5.

Although the Abbasids retained theoretical control over the Islamic world until the Mongol conquest of 1258, their power started to wane before that. Islamic culture remained advanced, but, politically speaking, the years after 1000 were a period of decline.

Another characteristic of these years was political confusion. From 1000 to the 1400s, many Islamic states rose and fell. Other Middle Eastern peoples, such as the Persians and Turks, began to rival the Arabs as forces in the Islamic community. Outside enemies and invaders added to the chaos. Finally, by the end of the fifteenth century and beginning of the sixteenth, the Islamic world—at least the Middle East and North Africa—would be reconsolidated under Turkish groups, specifically the Ottomans. However, even under the Ottomans, Islam was never again united the way it had been under the Abbasids.

THE EXPANSION OF ISLAM AND THE FIRST CALIPHATES

As described in Chapter 5, Mohammed and his followers spread Islam throughout Arabia in the 620s and 630s. Later in the 600s, Muslim forces conquered Sassanid Persia, weakened the Byzantine Empire, and converted most of the Middle East to Islam. By the early 700s, the Muslims had brought under their sway Iraq, Syria, Lebanon, Palestine, Egypt, most of North Africa, Spain, parts of Italy, Central Asia, and India's western frontier (present-day Pakistan).

Muslim territory was ruled by the caliph ("successor"), the title assumed by the new religion's leaders after Mohammed's death in 632. The caliphate was theocratic; its authority was political as well as religious. Three caliphs (Abu Bakr, Umar, and Uthman) reigned before the Sunni-Shiite split (656–661). After that, power passed to the Umayyad Caliphate (661–750), which governed from Damascus, in Syria, and continued Islam's military expansion. The Umayyad caliphs made Arabic the official language of the Muslim world and imposed a tax on those who did not convert to Islam. A series of rebellions led to the Umayyads' decline.

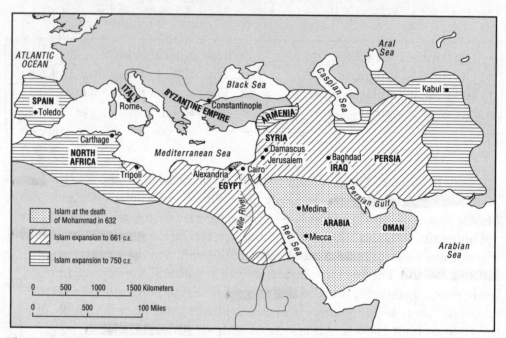

The Birth and Expansion of Islam, 632–750.
Born in Arabia, the dynamic new faith of Islam triumphed throughout the Middle East, where it is still dominant. It then continued to expand, both eastward and westward.

The Abbasid Caliphate

Following the Umayyad dynasty was the Abbasid Caliphate (750–1258), which established a great capital at Baghdad and presided over the golden age of classical Islamic culture.

The caliphs were strong and provided peace and stability throughout the Islamic empire. Economic unity prevailed (as it had throughout the empires of Persia, Rome, and Han China). Muslim manufacturers were among the most skilled in the world (especially at the production of steel). As described at the end of this chapter, the level of cultural advancement was extremely high. The most famous and best loved of the Abbasid caliphs was Haroun al-Rashid (776–809).

The political unity of the Abbasid caliphate began to disintegrate during and after the 900s. Geographic overextension, the difficulty of ruling millions of people of such diverse ethnicities, and the Sunni-Shiite split all contributed to the gradual breakup of the caliphate. Nomadic movements in North Africa, Syria, and

> **NOTE**
>
> The first two and a half centuries of Abbasid rule were the high point of Islamic civilization as a single political entity.

Iraq destabilized the caliphate as well. As early as 875, Persia and Central Asia came under control of a non-Arabic dynasty (the Samanid). In 909, a Shiite caliphate (the Fatimids) rose up in Egypt and ruled there till 1171. Spain achieved independence briefly from 929 to 976.

At the same time, Baghdad itself was under military threat. It fell to several conquerors, including the Seljuk Turks, who kept the Abbasid caliph in place as a figurehead. Military stress continued, tearing the caliphate apart. (The Abbasids' weakness largely accounts for the European crusaders' success in seizing Middle Eastern territory.)

The final blow came from the Mongols, who invaded the Middle East in the mid-1200s (for more on the Mongols, see Chapter 10). In 1258, the Mongols captured Baghdad and killed the last Abbasid caliph. Afterward, the Middle East splintered into many separate states. Eventually, it was united, but only partly, by the Turks.

ISLAM IN SAHARAN AND SUB-SAHARAN AFRICA

The Spread of Islam to Africa

Islam reached the eastern parts of North Africa (especially Egypt) in the 600s and 700s. Over the next few hundred years, it spread through the Sahara, and even to sub-Saharan Africa. Some of northeastern Africa remained Christian: the Nubian kingdoms of Kush and Axum (until the 1300s and 1400s), Ethiopia, and the Coptic Christians of Egypt. However, most converted to Islam.

Islam was brought to Africa by Arab traders—either overland (along the trans-Saharan caravan routes or by sea, along the continent's Indian Ocean coastline. In most cases, conversion was peaceful, although it was sometimes carried out by force. In addition, much of the commercial activity that brought Islam to southern Africa was connected with the extensive Arab slave trade. Trade northward consisted of slaves, salt, ivory, and animal skins. Trade southward included manufactured goods like glass, metalwork, and pottery.

As for the west, Islam took root not just in the Sahara, but also sub-Saharan Africa, during the eleventh century. Here, the most dedicated converts were the Berbers, desert nomads and hardened warriors. From Marrakesh, in present-day Morocco, Berber clans extended Muslim authority far to the south beyond the Sahara.

> **NOTE**
>
> Many of the Swahili city-states of Africa's east coast were home to large Muslim communities. After the 1100s, Middle Eastern culture was one of the many elements that contributed to the incredible diversity of East African civilizations.

Mali

By the 1300s and 1400s, Islamic states in western sub-Saharan Africa included Songhai, Kanem-Bornu, and many Hausa city-states. The biggest and most powerful was Mali (ca. 1250–1460), along the Niger River basin, an important north–south trade route for centuries. Founded in the mid-1200s by the conqueror Sundiata, and blessed with sizable deposits of gold and metal ore, Mali became a key center for trade in western and northern Africa.

Conversion to Islam proved beneficial. Politically, it enabled good trade relations with Arab states to the north. It also created a group of educated scholars who acted as public servants.

Mali's products were highly valued. They included gold, salt, ivory, animal skins, and slaves. The chief commercial outpost (though not the capital) was **Timbuktu**, a stopping point for caravans and traders traveling in all directions. The main commodity here was salt. Timbuktu was also a renowned center of religious studies and Islamic scholarship.

Mali's most powerful ruler was **Mansa Musa** (1312–1337), famous throughout Europe and Africa as one of the world's wealthiest monarchs (a Spanish map of 1375 referred to Mali as home to the "richest and noblest king in all lands"). Mansa Musa more fully systematized the government. By the early 1400s, Mali was under foreign attack, and its territory was steadily shrinking. Its might collapsed by the end of the century.

Culturally speaking, Mali (like most parts of Africa) was home to a strong tradition of oral storytelling and song making. One of Africa's most famous epic poems from this period comes from Mali, the *Son-Jara* (also known as the *Sundiata*). It dates from the 1200s, and it tells of the many exploits of the chieftain Son-Jara (Sundiata), founder of the Mali state.

THE RISE OF THE TURKS

Originating on the open steppes of Central Asia, the nomadic tribes known collectively as the Turks began to exert a signficant influence on the Middle East, starting around 1000 C.E. By the 1400s, the Ottoman Turks would be the dominant political force there.

Mamluks and Seljuks

Most Turkish tribes were adept at horse combat. Many Turks were brought to the Middle East by the Arabs to serve in their armies. These cavalry warriors were called **Mamluks**. They became dedicated converts to Islam and were among the best soldiers in the Middle East. By the eleventh century, there were many Mamluks in Asia Minor (present-day Turkey). In 1250, a large group of them migrated to Egypt and established a kingdom there.

In the eleventh century, the **Seljuk Turks** moved westward. They captured Baghdad in 1055 (but kept the Abbasid caliph in place as a figurehead). In 1071, the Seljuks defeated the Byzantine Empire at the Battle of Manzikert. They then took most of Asia Minor, Syria, Lebanon, and Palestine (including Jerusalem). Seljuk successes crippled the Byzantine Empire and ushered in its long period of decline. However, Turkish victories prompted European Christians to begin the Crusades in 1095.

Crusaders and Mongol Assaults

The early Crusades and the establishment of the Latin Kingdoms (see Chapter 6) threw the Middle East into political confusion. Until the mid-1100s, neither the weakened Abbasids nor their many political rivals proved capable of organizing effective resistance. One of the Middle East's great leaders during this time was the Kurdish general **Saladin**, who recaptured Jerusalem in 1187 and drove back the Third Crusade (1189–1192).

By the 1200s, the Mamluks, Arabs, and Seljuks had gotten better at fighting the crusaders. The Latin Kingdoms shrank steadily, and the Europeans were expelled by the end of the century.

However, an even greater crisis emerged in the form of the **Mongols** (see Chapter 10). As described earlier, the Mongols moved into the Middle East in the mid-1200s and, in 1258, seized Baghdad and destroyed the Abbasid Caliphate. Only in 1260 was the Mongol advance halted: that year, a Mamluk army defeated the Mongols at the Battle of Ain Jalut (Goliath Springs) in Syria. The Mongols took no more territory but established a state (the Il-Khan Empire) that lasted until 1349. For a long time, no single state—Mamluk, Seljuk, or Mongol—was strong enough to centralize the Middle East.

The Ottomans

The group that eventually dominated the Middle East, the **Ottoman Turks**, rose to prominence in the 1300s and 1400s. As early as the 1200s, the Ottomans, who served the Seljuks as vassals, settled northwestern Asia Minor. By the century's end, they had their own independent state, founded by the sultan Osman I (1280–1326).

The Ottomans also conquered southeastern Europe and what remained of the Byzantine Empire. Attacks on the Balkans began in the late 1300s, and the Ottoman fleet of galleys (oared warships, often rowed by prisoners or slaves) captured many ports and islands in the eastern Mediterranean. Finally, in 1453, Ottoman armies under Sultan Mehmet II, using the world's largest and most advanced gunpowder artillery, captured Constantinople. The **fall of Constantinople** ended the 1,100-year history of the Byzantine Empire and set the stage for a long, intense struggle against Christian Europe during the late 1400s and 1500s.

> **NOTE**
>
> During the 1300s and 1400s, the Ottomans took over most of the Middle East, including Mamluk Egypt and the territory held by the Seljuks and Mongols.

ISLAMIC CULTURE

For all its political failures, the Abbasid Caliphate presided over the golden era of Islamic culture. Compared with its neighbors—Europe, sub-Saharan Africa, the steppes of Central Asia—the Islamic world was far more culturally advanced during the 700s through the 1200s. The Islamic world's only cultural and intellectual rivals during these years were India and China.

Mathematics and Science

The mathematical and scientific aptitude of the Muslims was great. Under the Abbasids, the use of so-called Arabic numerals (which actually originated in India) became widespread. Islamic scholars were also adept at medicine. In the 900s, the physician Razi compiled the *Hawi*, the most thorough medical encyclopedia of its time. Even more famous was the Persian scientist Ibn Sina, known to the West as Avicenna (980–1037), whose *Canon of Medicine* remained in wide use until the 1600s, both in Europe and the Middle East. The fact that many stars in the night sky bear Arabic names attests to the skill of Muslim astronomers. One reason for the Ottomans' great military successes was a

> **NOTE**
>
> The term *algebra* comes directly from Arabic, and the Muslims were equally expert at trigonometry.

high degree of expertise with gunpowder weaponry, which required a good working knowledge of metallurgy and chemistry.

Philosophy

The Islamic world produced many philosophers: some Muslim, some Jewish (but accepted as citizens and recognized for their accomplishments). Like the Scholastics of medieval Europe, Islamic philosophers investigated the relationship between human reason and religious faith.

The two most famous thinkers came from Muslim Spain. Ibn Rushd, better known as **Averroës** (1126–1198), played an indispensable role in Islamic and European cultural life. A celebrated doctor, Averroës translated and analyzed the works of the Greek philosopher Aristotle, reintroducing his ideas to Europe. A second philosopher was **Maimonides** (1135–1204), a Spanish rabbi. Maimonides wrote commentaries on Jewish scripture and, like Averroës, encouraged the dissemination of Aristotle's ideas throughout Europe. His most famous work, *Guide to the Perplexed*, attempted to reconcile the rationality of Greco-Roman thought with Jewish theology (as Thomas Aquinas would do with Christian thought).

Islam's Influence Over Culture

As in Christian Europe, religion played a large cultural role. Muslim authorities controlled what was acceptable art or literature. Because the **Qur'an** forbids the worship of graven images, Islamic art during these years tended to feature geometric patterns and shapes rather than human or animal figures (although this was not a hard-and-fast rule). Religious colleges (**madrasas**) were centers of learning and education. Much intellectual activity in the Islamic world involved debates and commentaries on the Qur'an, the sayings of Mohammed, and Islamic law (**Sharia**).

Islamic Literature

Among the classics of Islamic literature from the Abbasid years is *The Thousand Nights and a Night*, known in the West as ***The Arabian Nights***. The work includes the tales of Sindbad the Sailor, Ali Baba, and Aladdin. Also important is the *Rubaiyat* of **Omar Khayyám** (ca. 1038–1131). Famous as a mathematician and astronomer, Khayyám composed this collection of bittersweet, meditative poems in the early 1100s.

Another masterpiece was *Travels*, the journal of **Ibn Battuta** (1304–1368), the Islamic world's greatest explorer. Born in Morocco, Ibn Battuta spent 30 years visiting Mecca, Persia, Mesopotamia, Turkey, Central Asia, Spain, Timbuktu, India, China, and Sumatra, a journey covering more than 75,000 miles.

From Persia came **Sufism**, a mystical strain of Islam that places an emphasis on attaining union with Allah by means of ritual disciplines and spiritual exercises (especially chanting and dancing). The best example of Sufi thought and belief can be found in the poetry of Rumi (1207–1273).

> **NOTE**
>
> Arabic was both the holy language of Islam and the principal language of cultural and intellectual life, just as Latin was for the Christians of medieval Europe. However, starting in the 800s and 900s, Persian joined Arabic as a major language in Islamic thought and literature.

QUICK REVIEW

1. A chief characteristic of Islamic states from 1000 to 1400 was

    (A) political unity.
    (B) the consolidation of democracy.
    (C) political chaos.
    (D) steady strengthening of political power.
    (E) the weakening of Turkish control over Islamic lands.

2. Which of the following is true of the Abbasid Caliphate?

    (A) It presided over the golden age of Islamic culture.
    (B) It heavily persecuted Jews and Christians.
    (C) It provided firm leadership when European crusaders invaded.
    (D) It forbade commercial relations with China.
    (E) It established a separate Muslim state in the western Sahara.

3. Which of the following places in Africa remained Christian despite the spread of Islam on the continent?

    (A) Marrakesh
    (B) Swahili city-states
    (C) Mali
    (D) Ethiopia
    (E) Tunisia

4. After the mid-1200s, Mali

    I. was soon conquered by Arabs, who installed an administration that was controlled from Turkey.
    II. stopped acting as a trade center.
    III. became a key trade center and controlled a major communications network.
    IV. was led by Christians.

    (A) III only
    (B) IV only
    (C) I, II, and III
    (D) III, and IV
    (E) I and II only

5. Timbuktu was renowned for its

    (A) gold and its role in opposing the slave trade.
    (B) salt reserves and Islamic scholarship.
    (C) large harbor.
    (D) glass and ceramic architecture.
    (E) many Gothic churches.

6. The Turkish military campaigns

    (A) crippled the Holy Roman Empire.
    (B) crushed the Mongols.
    (C) introduced Islam to the Middle East.
    (D) weakened the Byzantine Empire.
    (E) none of the above

7. The cavalry warriors who went on to establish their own state in Egypt in the 1200s were

    (A) the Ottomans.
    (B) the Mongols.
    (C) the Mamluks.
    (D) the Seljuks.
    (E) the Berbers.

8. Which of the following contributed to the military success of the Ottomans?

    (A) They practiced guerrilla warfare.
    (B) They had a fleet of oceangoing sailing ships.
    (C) They allied effectively with the Mongols.
    (D) They ceased relying on cavalry troops.
    (E) They had well-made gunpowder weaponry.

9. In what way were philosophers in medieval Europe and the Islamic world similar?

   (A) They both believed in Christianity.
   (B) They both studied the relationship between reason and faith.
   (C) They both introduced astrology into their studies of metaphysics.
   (D) They were both persecuted by their rulers.
   (E) They were required to be members of the clergy.

10. Why did Islamic art during this period usually feature geometric patterns and shapes rather than depictions of living things?

   (A) The Qur'an forbids the worship of graven images.
   (B) Depiction of living beings was not seen as fashionable.
   (C) Artists were not yet properly skilled to draw human figures.
   (D) Geometric shapes were seen to be more godlike.
   (E) none of the above

Answers

1. **(C)** The Islamic world stayed politically united only until the 900s C.E. The Abbasid Caliphate gradually disintegrated until its destruction in 1258. Only in the 1400s did the Ottoman Empire reunify the Middle East.

2. **(A)** The Abbasid Caliphate weakened politically after 900, when various parts of the Islamic Empire broke away and achieved autonomy. Abbasid resistance to the Crusades were ineffective. Political difficulties aside, the Abbasid era was a culturally advanced one, and Muslim authorities tended not to treat nonbelievers with violence (although they did tax those who did not convert).

3. **(D)** This is a matter of factual knowledge. Egyptian Copts also remained Christian.

4. **(A)** From 1250, when Sundiata established his state there, until the 1400s, Mali was one of the greatest and wealthiest kingdoms in Sub-Saharan Africa. Although Islamic, it was not controlled by Turks or Arabs.

5. **(B)** The great commercial center of Mali, Timbuktu shipped salt all along the Niger River trade route. It was also a renowned center of Islamic learning.

6. **(D)** Of the military outcomes described, only the crippling of the Byzantine Empire can be attributed to the Turks. The Seljuks started Byzantium's decline by defeating it at the Battle of Manzikert (1071).

7. **(C)** Brought to the Middle East to serve in Arab armies, the Mamluks gained control of Egypt in the 1200s. In 1260, they halted the Mongol advance into the Middle East.

8. **(E)** Advanced technology and metallurgical skill enabled the Ottomans to equip themselves with state-of-the-art gunpowder weaponry—including the artillery they used to capture Constantinople in 1453.

9. **(B)** The question of how intellect and logic could be reconciled with religious belief preoccupied thinkers in the Islamic world, as it did the European Scholastics.

10. **(A)** Although, in practice, the depiction of living beings was not absolutely prohibited, it was discouraged because the Qur'an (like the Bible's Ten Commandments) frowns on the artistic depiction of animals and humans as objects of worship.

China, Japan, and East Asia

CHAPTER 8

- The Tang dynasty and Song Empire
- The silk industry
- The Silk Road and the Indian Ocean trade network
- The Grand Canal
- Canton and Chinese urbanization
- The invention of gunpowder
- Neo-Confucianism
- Foot binding
- Kublai Khan and the Yuan Empire
- Marco Polo
- The Ming dynasty
- Zheng He
- Nara and Heian Japan
- The shogunates and the samurai class
- Rice-paddy farming
- Block printing

After the fall of the Han dynasty in 220 C.E., China alternated between periods of political unity and fragmentation. Imperial collapse in China tended not to be as traumatic as the fall of Rome was for Europe, but it did cause turmoil. Between 589 and 906, China enjoyed a political revival under the Sui and Tang dynasties. However, after the fall of the Tang, it once again split into various empires and states. This disunity lasted for several centuries. Not until the late 1200s would the country be joined together again.

During the 1200s, China, like the rest of Eurasia, was rocked by the explosive military expansion of the Mongols. It was conquered by the Mongols—indeed, Mongol rule played a significant part in the country's reunification. After the mid-1300s, China underwent even greater centralization under the Ming dynasty. Whatever the political situation, the growth of China's cities—among the largest and wealthiest in the world—continued.

Other countries of East Asia, especially Japan, Korea, and Vietnam, passed in and out of the Chinese political orbit, but were constantly influenced by their larger neighbor. At times they were under China's direct control, at others they were free. China also exerted a strong artistic, literary, and religious pull on them. As time passed, all three became more independent politically and culturally.

THE SUI AND TANG DYNASTIES

The first strong dynasty to emerge after the fall of the Han was the Sui (589–618). Despite its short life, the Sui reunified China and expanded its borders in a burst of military conquest.

Even stronger was the **Tang Dynasty** (618–906). Under the Tang, China became larger than ever before. Emperors like Xuanzong (712–755) extended China's rule to parts of Central Asia, Mongolia, Manchuria, Tibet, and, to the south, the Pacific coast. Like the Han Dynasty, Tang China forced many of its neighbors into a **tributary system**, in which Korea, Vietnam, Japan, and others had to make regular monetary payments to avoid punishment.

The Tang economy was very strong thanks to an advanced infrastructure (good roads, waterways, and canals—especially the **Grand Canal**, which the Sui dynasty created to link the Yellow and Yangzi rivers, and the Tang rulers expanded). Increased trade stimulated the Tang economy. In particular, the **silk industry** made the Chinese (who kept the secret of silk production to themselves for centuries) exceptionally wealthy. Greater control over the southern coast allowed China to take greater part in the **Indian Ocean trade network**. The Chinese also traded with the Middle East and the Mediterranean by means of the 5,000-mile **Silk Road**.

The Tang rulers were cultural patrons. Emperor Xuanzong sponsored the creation of the **Han Lin Academy of Letters**, a key institution of learning. The Tang exerted a strong artistic and religious influence over its neighbors, including Korea and Japan.

During the 800s, a series of peasant rebellions and military disasters weakened the Tang. In 906, the dynasty collapsed completely, and several centuries of disunity followed.

SONG (SUNG) CHINA

The Song Empire and Its Rivals

Following the Tang breakdown, China fragmented into separate states until the late 1200s. The largest and longest lasting was the **Song (Sung) Empire**, which ruled east-central China, from the Yellow River in the north to the Vietnamese border in the south. The Song lasted until 1279 but lost land steadily, because of war with its neighbors.

Until 1121, the primary threat to the Song was the Liao Empire to the north. The Song paid a tribute of silk and cash to the Liao, but then destroyed them with help from the **Jurchen**, who lived even farther to the north. Unfortunately for the Song, the Jurchen proclaimed their own empire (**the Jin**) and turned on the Song. The Song gave up much territory, withdrawing to the south. This smaller Song state survived until the Mongol conquest of the 1270s.

Song Society and Economics

Despite its political troubles, the Song Empire was culturally and economically impressive. It enjoyed steady population growth and **urbanization**, becoming the world's most heavily urbanized society—home to the largest cities on earth, several of them with a million or more inhabitants. Although its economic ties with Central Asia and the Middle East lessened, Song China was still connected with the trade routes (such as the Silk Road) that extended to those regions.

If contact with the Middle East lessened, the Song became more involved with the Pacific coast and Southeast Asia. The port of **Canton** (now **Guangzhou**) became one of the world's busiest and most cosmopolitan trading centers. Song China's large trading vessels, known as junks, cruised the eastern seas and Indian Ocean, carrying silk and manufactured goods.

Song Culture and Religion

Song China was the most scientifically and technologically advanced society of its time, with the possible exception of the Abbasid Caliphate. The Song Chinese were excellent mathematicians and astronomers. Song scientists developed accurate clocks, as well as a working **compass** (first used for navigation at sea in 1090). The most striking example of Song China's scientific and technological expertise was the celestial clock of Su Song (built in 1088), an eighty-foot-tall structure that told the time of day, the day of the month, and the positions of the sun, moon, planets, and major stars. It was the first device in world history to use a chain-driven mechanism (powered by flowing water). Also during the Song period, the Chinese invented **gunpowder**, pioneered the use of paper currency (which they called "flying money"), and made use of **block printing** (a practice they may have adopted from the Koreans).

Concerning religion, a great revival of Confucius's teachings—**Neo-Confucianism**—took place during the Song period. Neo-Confucianism was an important unifying factor in a poiltically divided China. It reinforced Chinese culture's tendency toward hierarchy and obedience, and put a premium on education and cultured behavior. Most governmental officials gained their posts by scoring well on rigorous civil service examinations, a Confucian practice. A new form of Buddhism emerged as well: **Chan** (known as **Son** in Korea and **Zen** in Japan). Chan stressed simplicity and meditation, and became very popular, both in China and abroad.

> **TIP**
>
> The most striking example of Song China's scientific and technological expertise was the celestial clock of Su Song (built in 1088), an eighty-foot-tall structure that told the time of day, the day of the month, and the positions of the sun, moon, planets, and major stars. It was the first device in world history to use a chain-driven mechanism (powered by flowing water).

Women in Chinese Society

Neo-Confucianism, along with Chinese tradition, was used to justify the greater subordination of women, especially upper-class women, whose families were most likely to follow Confucian dictates. Earlier, a husband's family had to produce a dowry for a new bride; now the reverse became the norm. Marriages were arranged, mainly to the groom's benefit.

The best-known aspect of Chinese subjugation of women was **foot binding**. This painful practice, which kept women's feet tiny and dainty but in the process crippled them, was firmly established by 1200, and it continued into the early 1900s.

Women of the lower classes were generally freer than those of the upper classes, but they still occupied a secondary status compared with men. On the other hand, women of all classes had inheritance and property rights, and retained control over their dowry after divorce or a husband's death. Still, the social position of Chinese women was decidedly second-class. (One dramatic exception was Empress Wu Zhao, the only woman ever to rule China in her own right. However, even she was forced off her throne in 705.)

THE MONGOL CONQUEST AND YUAN CHINA

As discussed in Chapter 10, almost all of Eurasia was affected in the 1200s by the sudden and successful military expansion of the Mongols. As **Genghis Khan** and his sons began their conquests, the Chinese states were among their first targets.

The Mongols attacked the Chinese states in 1211. They steadily accumulated territory, even after Genghis Khan's death in 1227. By 1234, the Mongols had captured almost all of western and northern China, and they threatened what remained of the Song Empire. The Song continued to resist for several decades.

In the 1260s, Genghis Khan's grandsons quarreled among themselves and began to divide the Mongol Empire. China and Southeast Asia fell to **Kublai (Khubilai) Khan**, who moved his capital from Mongolia to the Chinese city of Beijing and proclaimed the **Yuan Empire** (1271–1368). Kublai Khan conquered the rest of China, including the Song state, which fell in 1279.

Although Kublai Khan called himself the Great Khan of the Mongols, he and the Mongol leadership adapted themselves to Chinese ways: They adopted Buddhism and, as an official language, Mandarin Chinese. Indeed, Kublai Khan can be considered the reunifier of China as a single state.

Kublai Khan reigned until 1294 and made Yuan China rich and powerful. Most of his military campaigns succeeded, although he was unable to conquer Japan (which he tried to take in 1274 and 1281) or Java (which he fought in 1293). Kublai Khan forced most of China's neighbors to pay tribute, and the Yuan Empire resisted attacks from other Mongol states in Central Asia.

Kublai Khan rebuilt China's bureaucracy and economy. He repaired roads and canals and built new cities (including the resort of Shangdu, famous in the West as Xanadu). Kublai Khan also restored trade with the west. The **Silk Road**, which had fallen into inactivity, emerged again as a vital trade route. The Venetian merchant **Marco Polo** visited Kublai Khan's China in the 1270s.

The Yuan state was not so fortunate after Kublai Khan's death. During the early 1300s, China suffered tremendous population loss (estimated at 30 to 40 percent), owing to the appearance of **bubonic plague** (which traveled west to the Middle East and Europe, where it was known as the Black Death). Economic decline resulted from the population loss. A series of civil wars broke out in the 1340s, and a final rebellion overthrew the Yuan in 1368.

THE EARLY MING DYNASTY

Triumph of the Ming

The rebel who brought down the Yuan Empire, Zhu Yuanzhang, had been a soldier, a bandit, and a priest. After becoming emperor in 1368, he took the name **Hongwu** (1368–1403) and established the **Ming Dynasty** (1368–1644), one of the longest-lasting and most famous in Chinese history. His son **Yongle** (1403–1424) was also a strong ruler.

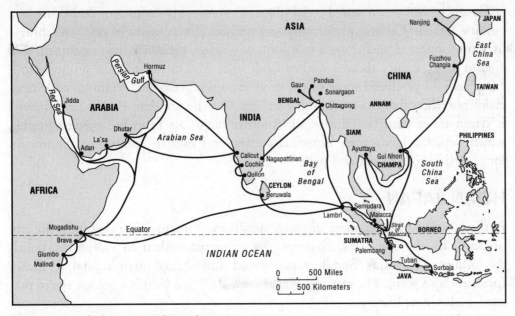

The Voyages of Zheng He, 1405–1433.
China's greatest mariner, Zheng He, sailed several times from China to Arabia and East Africa. He explored, established diplomatic relations, and exacted monetary tribute from weaker states.

At home, Hongwu and Yongle recentralized the country and repaired the damage done by the wars of the 1300s. Once again, the population grew, and the economy recovered. As a way of restoring imperial legitamacy, Yongle transformed Beijing into a magnificent capital by building the **Forbidden City**, which served for centuries as the imperial residence and seat of government—and still stands at the heart of Beijing.

Abroad, the early Ming rulers expanded China's borders. Like earlier dynasties, they maintained a tributary system. They forged alliances with kingdoms in Vietnam (Annam and Champa) and Korea (the Yi). When the Mongol warlord Timur, who defeated the Delhi Sultanate (see Chapter 11), attacked China, the Ming drove him away.

Not only was Ming China's army large and effective, its navy was for a time a potent instrument of diplomacy and intimidation. From 1405 to 1433, the admiral and explorer **Zheng He** (Chang Ho) made seven long voyages to Southeast Asia, India, the Middle East, and East Africa. He expanded Chinese trade, gained much knowledge about the outside world, and forced fifty states and cities to pay tribute. After Yongle's death, however, the Ming rulers—distracted by the land-based threat of Nomads to the north—lost interest in exploration and naval expansion. This can be seen as a global turning point: had the Ming continued to exploit their power at sea, China might have started a wave of worldwide exploration and colonization, as the nations of Europe were on the verge of doing.

Ming Art and Culture

Culturally, the Ming years remain famous as a time of artistic grandeur and intellectual dynamism. Chinese art, religion, and literature continued to exert an influence on countries such as Korea, Vietnam, and Japan (although China's cultural sway over Japan had lessened since the eleventh century).

Confucianism was restored to its place of prominence, rejoining Buddhism as a guiding force in Chinese philosophy and religion. Great works of classical Chinese literature appeared, including a new form of writing, the novel (one example is *The Golden Lotus,* a story about a wicked landowner who mistreats those around him). Ming artisans produced some of the most exquisite glassware, ceramics, and, especially, porcelain that the world has ever seen (it is no accident that the word *china* is synonymous with fine dishware). Another major art form was scroll painting, which depicted landscapes, historical scenes, and human and animal figures on long, vertical rolls of silk and paper.

HEIAN JAPAN

In the 600s C.E., the Japanese imperial family, the Yamato, still ruled from the city of Nara. By the late 700s, however, the emperors wished to escape the political influence of Nara's Buddhist priesthood and shifted their capital to Heian (present-day Kyoto). The classical Heian period (794–1185) is a golden age in premodern Japanese history.

The Heian era gave rise to an unusual and complex form of government: the emperor—considered to be the descendant of Japan's Shinto gods, and therefore sacred—lost political power but remained important as a symbolic figurehead. Real power rested with whatever noble family gained the position of chancellor (*kwampaku*) and, with it, the duty of "protecting" the emperor. The chancellor kept the emperor in seclusion and ruled in his name.

Heian Jingu Shrine, Kyoto, Japan.
Kyoto, the old capital of Japan, still contains many of the architectural masterpieces from the Heian era (794–1185), when the city was known by that name. Heian was a major center of Buddhist worship and scholarship, and hundreds of shrines and temples were built there. This shrine is one of many examples of the religious architecture of the period.

From 858 onward, the ruling family in Heian Japan was the **Fujiwara clan**, which gained permanent custody over the chancellorship and imperial family. During the 1000s and early 1100s, the Fujiwara presided over a peaceful, prosperous, and culturally brilliant nation. Japanese painting reached a high level of skill, and one of the classics of world literature, **Lady Murasaki's *The Tale of Genji***, an epic about love and Japanese court life, dates to this period. Many of Japan's classical prose writers were women. Men considered poetry to be a more elevated art form.

Early in the Heian period, Japanese culture was influenced in many ways by China. Japanese religious life was shaped by the importation of Buddhism and, to a lesser extent, Confucianism and Daoism, all of which coexisted with Japan's native faith, Shinto. China's system of ideograms influenced the Japanese alphabet, and the poetry, painting, and architecture of Tang China had a great impact on Japanese style. After about 1000, the Japanese began to develop a more independent cultural tradition.

Unfortunately for the Fujiwara, their pursuit of cultural refinement and preoccupation with court life led them to neglect military affairs. For decades, the Fujiwara delegated military responsibilities to various warrior clans (from whom the samurai class would emerge). By the 1100s, these warrior clans were quarreling among themselves and, at the same time, with the Fujiwara.

The Heian regime was destroyed by the **Taira-Minamoto war** (1156–1185), fought by two warrior clans who supported rival claimants to the emperor's throne. The Fujiwara were driven from power by 1160. The Taira gained the upper hand at first, but were eventually defeated by the Minamoto, who created a new government known as the shogunate. The conflict marked Japan's transition from classical age to medieval period (as the fall of Rome did for Europe). It also inspired one of Japan's epic works of literature, *Tales of the Heike*.

FEUDAL JAPAN AND THE FIRST SHOGUNATES

Upon defeating the Taira, the Minamoto moved the capital to Kamakura, far from Heian, and established a decentralized military government. As before, the emperor was a symbolically important figurehead, but real power belonged to the **shogun** ("great general").

Two shogunates governed Japan before the country's breakup in the 1500s: the Kamakura (1185–1333) and the Ashikaga (1336–1573), which, after a short civil war, moved the capital back to Kyoto (formerly Heian). The shogunates were feudal systems, in which the shogun shared power with landowning warlords called **daimyo**. Like the knightly aristocracy of medieval Europe, the shogun and daimyo came from a warrior class known as the **samurai** ("one who serves"). To belong to the samurai class was a great privilege. Just as European knights (in theory) lived by the ideals of chivalry, the samurai followed a strict code of loyalty, honor, and bravery called **Bushido** ("way of the warrior"). Bushido was even more stringent and hierarchical than European chivalry; the most extreme penalty for violating it was ritual suicide (seppuku, or hara-kiri).

The change in government affected the status of upper-class women in Japan. The Heian court had placed great emphasis on cultural brilliance and elaborate manners, and women were able to have a certain social and political influence. The rougher warrior ethic of the shogunates allowed women fewer opportunities. Unlike European chivalry, the code of Bushido did little to encourage respectful treatment of women.

During the 1200s and early 1300s, the Kamakura shoguns kept order in Japan. They even repelled Kublai Khan's two attempts to invade from China (1279 and 1281). The Ashikaga shoguns were politically weaker and allowed greater decentralization. Starting in the mid-1400s, a series of civil wars began to tear Japan apart; by the 1500s, the country was almost completely disunified, with most daimyo ruling their lands independently. Only in the very late 1500s and early 1600s would Japan be reunified.

Under the Ashikaga, trade and commerce flourished in Japan, and an important merchant class emerged. As in China, urbanization proceeded rapidly. New forms of Buddhism arrived, especially **Zen** (**Chan**), which proved popular among the samurai class. Pure Land (Jo Do) Buddhism, which promised a heavenly afterlife, gained a large following among the lower classes. The philosophical simplicity of Zen affected several important cultural practices, such as the *cha-no-yu* tea ceremony, landscaping (rock gardens and bonsai trees), and haiku poetry.

KOREA AND VIETNAM

Like Japan, Korea and Vietnam fell under the cultural and religious (and, at times, political) influence of China. As in China, agricultural production in Korea and Vietnam mainly involved rice cultivation. As with Japan, Korea's and Vietnam's art, literature, and architecture were shaped by China. The writing systems of all three countries—*hiragana* and *kanji* in Japan, *hangul* in Korea, and *chu nom* in Vietnam—were based at least somewhat on Chinese ideograms. From China came Confucianism and various forms of Buddhism.

Korean kingdoms, among them the Jogosean (Old Choson), formed as early as the 2000s B.C.E. By the 500s C.E., they had developed a long, tangled relationship with China. Silla, for example, the first kingdom to unite the entire peninsula, was a close ally of Tang China and collapsed when the Tang fell. Koryo, the next state, had ties with the Song, then was invaded by the Mongols. It won its freedom by the mid-1300s but collapsed soon after. The Korean kingdom of Yi (1392–1910), enjoyed close ties with Ming China. Many scholars speculate that **block printing** was invented in the Koryo state and then passed on to the Chinese. It was also through Korea that much of China's influence on Japanese culture was transmitted.

The Vietnamese had contact with the Chinese as early as the 200s B.C.E. Close ties formed between Tang China and the Vietnamese states of Annam and Champa. At various points after 1000, Annam and Champa were under Chinese rule, paid tribute to China, or allied with China.

The widespread practice of **rice-paddy farming**, or growing rice by means of wet cultivation, originated in Southeast Asia—most likely in Vietnam—around 500 B.C.E. Before this, rice had been grown dry. Wet cultivation led to increased crop yields and spread to other parts of Asia, including China and Japan. In this way, the Vietnamese kingdoms had a profound agricultural and environmental impact on a vast portion of Asia.

QUICK REVIEW

1. For many years, the Chinese enjoyed a virtual monopoly on the production of:

   (A) rice.
   (B) porcelain.
   (C) silk.
   (D) cinnamon.
   (E) bamboo.

2. Which of the following is NOT acknowledged to be a Chinese invention?

   (A) gunpowder
   (B) the stirrup
   (C) the compass
   (D) chain-driven machinery
   (E) none of the above

3. Which of the following is true about Chinese women in the period between 1000 and 1400 C.E.?

   I. Women of the lower classes tended to be freer from restrictions than those of the upper classes.
   II. Neo-Confucianism reinforced the secondary status of women in Chinese society.
   III. Although women were generally subordinate to men, several of them ruled China in their own right.
   IV. The binding of women's feet was practiced more widely.

   (A) I only
   (B) III only
   (C) II and III
   (D) I, II, and III
   (E) I, II, and IV

4. Mongol conquest had what effect on China?

   (A) The Mongols eradicated most traces of traditional Chinese culture.
   (B) The Mongols carried out numerous atrocities against the Chinese population.
   (C) The Mongols shut down foreign trade along the Silk Road.
   (D) The Mongols reunited and revitalized the Chinese state.
   (E) The Mongols outlawed Buddhism in favor of Islam.

5. What pandemic killed 30 to 40 million of Yuan China's population and then traveled westward to the Middle East and Europe?

   (A) bubonic plague
   (B) cholera
   (C) leprosy
   (D) tuberculosis
   (E) Spanish flu

6. The early Ming emperors

   (A) were culturally brilliant but politically decadent.
   (B) lost much of China's territory to its neighbors.
   (C) were dynamic conquerors.
   (D) ignored naval power and exploration.
   (E) neglected art and culture in favor of warfare.

7. Which of the following is NOT true of Japan's Heian period?

   (A) Under a figurehead emperor, the Fujiwara clan controlled governmental affairs.
   (B) The warrior ethos of the Heian court gave aristocratic women few opportunities to exert their influence.
   (C) During the later Heian period, Japanese culture became less dependent on Chinese influence.
   (D) Lady Murasaki's famous novel, *The Tale of Genji*, was written during this time.
   (E) It came to an end as the result of the Taira-Minamoto war.

8. When the first shoguns ruled Japan,

   (A) real power rested with the emperor.
   (B) political authority was in the hands of Buddhist monks.
   (C) the emperor's power was symbolic.
   (D) the shoguns served as Shinto priests.
   (E) none of the above

9. Which of the following is true of Zen Buddhism?

   (A) It originated in Japan, then traveled to Korea and China.
   (B) It had comparatively little impact on Japan.
   (C) It displaced the Shinto religion.
   (D) It became popular among the samurai of Japan.
   (E) Its emphasis on heavenly afterlife appealed to lower classes.

10. Rice-paddy cultivation

    (A) is extremely labor-intensive.
    (B) probably originated in Vietnam.
    (C) led to increased crop yields.
    (D) all of the above
    (E) none of the above

Answers

1. **(C)** One of China's most profitable commodities was silk, the production of which is extremely complicated. The Chinese jealously guarded this secret for centuries.

2. **(B)** The stirrup is thought to have originated in Central Asia. The other inventions are associated with Song China, whose scientists and engineers were extremely skilled. The Chinese may have invented block printing, but this is not certain (some credit the Koreans).

3. **(E)** Only one woman (Wu Zhao) governed China in her own right, Neo-Confucianism encouraged the subordination of women, and foot binding (thought to keep women's feet "dainty" and "ladylike") began to catch on during these years. Lower-class families were less likely to obey all the dictates of Neo-Confucianism, and female labor was too valuable for the lower classes to afford the "luxury" of foot binding.

4. **(D)** Under Kublai Khan, the Mongol leadership adapted itself to Chinese culture and established the Yuan state. Kublai Khan presided over expansion, unification, cultural development, and economic growth.

5. **(A)** Best known in the West as the Black Death that struck Europe in the 1340s, the fourteenth-century wave of bubonic plague—one of history's greatest medical disasters—originated in China, caused great devastation there, and did the same in the Middle East.

6. **(C)** While the later Ming emperors became decadent, rulers like Hongwu and Yongle actively and successfully expanded Ming power by means of military might and sponsored wide-ranging naval expeditions, such as the voyages of Zheng He. They were also great cultural patrons, and the Ming Dynasty is renowned for artistic and cultural brilliance.

7. **(B)** The highly refined Heian court was dominated by the Fujiwara clan. Art, culture, and court ritual were very important, and women enjoyed a comparatively high degree of status. China's influence over Japanese culture never ended, but it lessened considerably.

8. **(C)** The shogun was a military leader, one of whose duties was to protect the emperor (who remained symbolically important). As the Fujiwara clan had done during the Heian period, the shoguns dominated the emperors and used them as figureheads to legitimate their own authority.

9. **(D)** Originating as Chan Buddhism in China, Zen spread to Japan. Its austerity and simplicity resonated with the samurai warrior.

10. **(D)** One of Asia's most important agricultural practices, rice-paddy (or wet) cultivation probably arose in Vietnam and spread throughout Southeast and East Asia. Though it requires great effort, it greatly boosts crop production.

South and Southeast Asia

CHAPTER 9

- The Delhi Sultanate
- The importation of Islam to India
- The Indian Ocean trade network (Calicut, Malacca)
- Burma, Thailand, and Annam
- The Khmer Empire and Angkor Wat
- Hinduism, Buddhism, and Islam in Southeast Asia
- Borobudur
- The Polynesian migration

South and Southeast Asia are regions of remarkable ethnic and cultural diversity. India and the lands that surround it are environmentally and geographically diverse as well. India measures 2,000 miles east to west and 2,000 miles north to south. In the north are mountains and forest. The center is cut by the Ganges and Indus river basins. The southern third is more tropical. The entire climate of the Indian Ocean region is affected twice per year by huge seasonal rainstorms called monsoons (which occur in June–July and December–January). Most of Southeast Asia is tropical in climate.

Until the modern era, Southeast and South Asia were often politically fragmented. India in particular was seldom unified as a single state. In other parts of South Asia, kingdoms and states tended to rise and fall rapidly. Culture, tradition, language, and religion served as unifying factors more than politics did.

> **NOTE**
>
> By itself, the Indian subcontinent is home to people of several races, dozens of different languages, and many minor and major religions.

INDIA AND THE DELHI SULTANATE

Between 600 C.E. and 1200 C.E., India was disunified. The Gupta Empire, the last state to provide any sort of unity, collapsed in 550 C.E.

The next group to unite a large part of India were Muslim invaders, who reached the northwest frontier (the Indus valley and Afghanistan) in the 700s and converted it to Islam. By the 900s, Muslims were escalating their attacks on the Indian border.

In 1022, Muslim armies, led by Afghan warlords, began the conquest of northern India, a process that continued for the next two hundred years. In 1206, the Muslims captured the city of Delhi, and most of northern India fell into their hands. Muslim generals established the Delhi Sultanate (1206–1520s).

The major impact of the Muslim invasions and the establishment of the Delhi Sultanate was to introduce Islam into India. Islam did not displace earlier faiths like Hinduism and Buddhism, but joined them as one of the country's major religions. (One interesting development is that, in India, Muslim women tended to enjoy more property rights than Hindu women,

> **NOTE**
>
> Technically, the Delhi Sultanate was part of the Abbasid Caliphate (see Chapter 7), but only until the caliphate's destruction in 1258.

153

especially those of low caste; it was also possible for Muslim women in India to divorce and to remarry after their husbands died.)

There were religious conflicts under the Delhi Sultanate. At first, the sultans imposed their new faith harshly. They became less severe over time, but Hindu and Muslim populations did not tend to mix, and tensions—sometimes outright violence and persecution—characterized the relationship. Islam's influence was greatest in the north and along the west coast.

Politically, the Delhi Sultanate grew from the mid-1200s to the mid-1300s, by which point it controlled most of India. Afterward, the sultanate shrank. Many regions in the south broke away. In 1398, the Central Asian warlord Timur (see Chapter 10) attacked and captured Delhi itself. When he departed, after a year of plundering, the city was in ruins. The Delhi Sultanate survived, but barely. It grew steadily smaller, then, in the 1520s, succumbed to new invaders from the north.

OTHER INDIAN STATES

Although India's ethnic complexity makes it hard to generalize, for many years, the northern parts of the country were populated by Indo-Europeans (largely descended from the Aryas who invaded ca. 1500 B.C.E.). The south was inhabited by darker-skinned peoples of Dravidian origin.

Independent Southern States

Various states and kingdoms emerged in the south of India, independent of the larger governments in the north. Among them were the Tamil kingdoms on the Indian Ocean coast: they formed around the 100s B.C.E. and survived for 2,000 years.

In the 1300s, even more states emerged in the south, most of them breakaways from the Delhi Sultanate. Bengal became an independent Muslim state in 1338. Gujarat, a Muslim city on the western coast, declared independence from the sultanate in 1390 and flourished as a trading center in the Indian Ocean network. The Vijayanagara Empire (1336–1565) and the Malibar city-states formed Hindu enclaves on the Indian coast. The former controlled many southern ports and the island of Sri Lanka. The latter ruled much of the southwestern coast. The most important of the Malibar cities was Calicut.

Indian Ocean Trade

One of the world's most vibrant commercial economies centered on the Indian Ocean trade network, which joined East Africa, Arabia, the Persian Gulf, India, the Malay peninsula, Indonesia, China, and Japan. From west to east, this exchange network covered an expanse greater than 6,000 miles.

In the west, a zone controlled largely by Arab traders, goods came from Africa and the Middle East. Africa provided ivory, animal hides, timber, gold, and slaves. From the Middle East came textiles, carpets, glass, and Arabian horses. The middle zone was dominated by Indian cities and kingdoms. India offered precious gems, elephants, salt, and cotton cloth. From Sri Lanka (Ceylon) came cinnamon. Other spices, as well as exotic woods, came from Indonesia. In the east, China traded silk, porcelain, and paper. Japan was a major source of silver.

Major ports in the Indian Ocean network included Sofala, **Mombasa**, and Mogadishu in East Africa; Jidda, Mecca, and Ormuz in Arabia and Persia; the Gujarati port of Cambay and the great Malibar metropolis of **Calicut**, both in western India; and **Canton (Guangzhou)** and Hangzhou in China. By means of the Red Sea and Suez isthmus, the Indian Ocean trade network connected to the Mediterranean and the trade networks flourishing there.

The Indian Ocean Trade Network Before 1500 C.E.
The arrival of Portuguese traders just before 1500, then the massive influx of other Europeans, changed the economic patterns of this region forever.

SOUTHEAST ASIA

Geographically, Southeast Asia consists of three zones: the mainland; the Malay Peninsula; and the island chains of the Indian Ocean and South China Sea. The climate is tropical, and much of the terrain is mountainous or blanketed by rain forest.

Between 3000 B.C.E. and 2000 B.C.E., Malays and other peoples arrived, from China, India, and elsewhere. Local inhabitants practiced agriculture by around 2000 B.C.E. The early peoples of Southeast Asia were also skilled bronze workers and navigators (the island peoples traveled great distances in sophisticated outrigger canoes).

Southeast Asian States

Major states emerged in Southeast Asia before and around 500 C.E. These included Burma, the Thai kingdom, and the Vietnamese states of Champa and Annam (see Chapter 8). Most of these states were culturally and economically influenced by China, India, or both. They traded spices (cinnamon, nutmeg, cloves, and pepper), especially for silk from China, and took part in the vast Indian Ocean and Pacific trade networks.

> **NOTE**
>
> Thanks to contact with India and China, most Southeast Asian states adopted Hinduism, Buddhism, and sometimes both. Before 1000 C.E., Islam also appeared in Southeast Asia.

The Khmer and Srivijayan Empires

For years, the two most developed states in Southeast Asia were the Khmer Empire (500s–1454 C.E.) in Cambodia and the Srivijayan Empire (500s–1100s C.E.) of Sumatra.

The Khmer civilization emerged in Cambodia and Laos by the 500s C.E. and reached its peak during the Angkor period (889–1454). The Angkor rulers were militarily aggressive, expanding the Khmer state into parts of Burma and the Malay Peninsula. Culturally and religiously, the Khmer were influenced primarily by India. They adopted both Hinduism and Buddhism, building more than 21,000 temples. The Khmer state collapsed in the 1400s, when Cambodia was conquered by neighboring Thailand.

In the Indonesian islands to the south, the **Srivijayan Empire** took shape. From the island of Sumatra, the Srivijayans expanded, gaining control of the maritime trade routes between Indonesia and the Malay Peninsula by the 600s. They then took over

> **NOTE**
>
> The city complex of **Angkor Wat**, with its ornate palaces and pagodas, covers forty square miles.

NOTE

The Srivijayan Empire declined in the 1000s and 1100s, weakened by outside enemies, then displaced by a new empire. In the 1200s, Islam arrived in the Indonesian islands. It remains a dominant faith there to this day.

parts of the Malay Peninsula, as well as the Indonesian island of Java. Like the Khmer Empire in Cambodia, the Srivijayan Empire was influenced by India and accepted both Hinduism and Buddhism (although Buddhism was dominant). The Srivijayans' greatest architectural legacy is the Buddhist temple complex of **Borobudur**, built on the island of Java from 770 to 825. Borobudur is in the shape of a mountain over 100 feet high; every level represents a stage on the path to enlightenment.

Political Changes, 1200s–1400s

Political change came to Southeast Asia from the 1200s through the 1400s. The Chinese and Mongols made repeated attacks from the north. Thailand expanded, conquering the Khmer state in Cambodia. The Vietnamese state of Annam became a military power after the early 1400s.

NOTE

By the 1500s, Burma emerged as a great power, with an army of more than half a million.

After 1400, the economic powerhouse of Southeast Asia was the city of **Malacca (Melaka)**, located on the narrow waterway separating the Malay Peninsula from Sumatra. It connected the Indian Ocean with the South China Sea and was, therefore, a crucial nexus in the Indian Ocean trade network. Founded in 1400, Malacca was controlled by China, then the Thais. It enjoyed a brief period of freedom before being conquered by European colonists—the Portuguese—in 1511.

THE POLYNESIAN MIGRATIONS

One of history's most epic journeys was the **Polynesian migration** across the Pacific from approximately 2500 B.C.E. to 900 C.E. Originally from Southeast Asia, the Polynesians left their homes in the Philippine and Indonesian islands around 4,500 years ago.

NOTE

In a process lasting over 3,000 years, the Polynesians spread eastward across a 20,000-mile expanse, settling thousands of islands. The region known as Oceania is populated mainly by their descendants.

Early Polynesian Culture

The original Polynesians were root farmers, growing taro and sweet potatoes and supplementing their diet with pigs, chickens, and fish. Their social organization was hierarchical. Tribes were led by powerful chiefs. Polynesian religion was animistic and concerned with avoiding improper behavior, or **taboo** (*tabu* or *kapu* in Polynesia).

Because so much of their life was based on the sea, the Polynesians were expert sailors and navigators. Their **outrigger canoes**, which could sail more than 120 miles per day, allowed them to travel vast distances over open water. Not only could the Polynesians navigate by the sun, moon, and stars, they possessed an intimate knowledge of tides, currents, and wave patterns (even creating maps woven from twigs and grasses to represent the ocean's rhythms).

The Migrations

Why the Polynesians began their long migrations is unknown; most scholars speculate that ecological crisis drove them from their homes. Certainly environmental necessity kept them going once they started. When the Polynesians settled an island, the population would grow to such a point that part of the tribe (sometimes all of it) would have to move onward to keep from depleting all the resources.

The first wave of migration took the Polynesians to the island chain of Micronesia, east of the Philippines. Then, around 2000 to 1300 B.C.E., some Polynesians moved to Melanesia, east of New Guinea and Australia and including Fiji.

Another major wave of migration took the Polynesians to the oceanic expanse that now bears the name Polynesia. Polynesia is bounded by an imaginary triangle, with Hawaii at the north, New Zealand to the southwest, and Easter Island to the southeast. By 300 to 400 C.E., Polynesians had settled **Easter Island**, building their famous statues of human heads. By the 1500s, environmental stress and tribal war destroyed the Easter Island civilization. More successful was Polynesian settlement of New Zealand, where the **Maori** culture, established around 800 C.E., survived and prospered. A warrior society, the Maori became the largest single Polynesian subculture by the 1700s.

QUICK REVIEW

1. Until the modern era, India

   (A) enjoyed relative political unity.
   (B) was not often united into a single state.
   (C) experienced cultural homogeneity.
   (D) was dominated by a single religion.
   (E) was highly urbanized.

2. Over two hundred years, between the 1000s and 1200s, the _____ seized parts of northern India.

   (A) Muslims
   (B) British
   (C) Mongolians
   (D) Chinese
   (E) Pakistanis

3. For centuries, the northern sections of India were populated by _____ and the southern parts by _____ .

   (A) peoples of Dravidian ancestry, Indo-Europeans
   (B) Pakistanis, Africans
   (C) Tibetans, Chinese
   (D) the British, the French
   (E) Indo-Europeans, peoples of Dravidian ancestry

4. Indian Ocean trade tied together all of the following areas directly EXCEPT

   (A) East Africa.
   (B) the Arabian Peninsula.
   (C) the Persian Gulf.
   (D) Russia.
   (E) India.

5. Southeast Asian states

   I. included the Khmer and Srivijayan empires.
   II. adopted Hinduism or Buddhism or sometimes both.
   III. traded spices for silk from China.
   IV. took part in Indian Ocean trade.

   (A) I, II, and III
   (B) II and IV only
   (C) III and IV only
   (D) III only
   (E) all of the above

6. Angkor rulers of Cambodia

   (A) were not motivated to expand their borders.
   (B) focused on internal economic development.
   (C) were militarily aggressive.
   (D) encouraged the spread of Christianity.
   (E) ruled well into the nineteenth century.

7. The following religion arrived in Indonesia by the 1200s and soon became dominant there:

(A) Daoism
(B) Zen Buddhism
(C) Islam
(D) Hinduism
(E) none of the above

8. Ancestors of the Polynesians largely came from

(A) China and Japan.
(B) the Philippine and Indonesian islands.
(C) Portugal.
(D) Scandinavia.
(E) Australia and New Zealand.

9. According to most scholars, why did the Polynesians migrate so widely?

(A) They were constantly threatened by Muslims.
(B) They were belligerent by nature and sought out other lands to conquer.
(C) They were cannibals.
(D) They wanted to avoid depleting their resources.
(E) none of the above

10. Which of the following is true about Islam in India?

(A) The Delhi Sultanate introduced Islam to India peacefully.
(B) Islam's influence over India faded away after the collapse of the Islam Sultanate.
(C) Islam displaced Hinduism and Buddhism almost completely after the 1200s.
(D) Muslim women were just as restricted in their behavior as Hindu women.
(E) After being harshly imposed by the Delhi Sultanate, Islam came to coexist with Hinduism as a major faith.

Answers

1. **(B)** Ethnic and linguistic diversity, along with political disunity, prevailed in premodern India. Unifying states such as the Gupta Empire and Delhi Sultanate were the exception rather than the rule.

2. **(A)** Muslim invaders conquered and converted India's northwest frontier from the 700s to the 900s. Starting in 1022, they invaded India itself, establishing the Delhi Sultanate in the 1200s.

3. **(E)** The general rule is that, ethnically, northern India bore greater traces of the Aryan-Indo-European incursions of 1500 B.C.E., while Dravidian cultures remained dominant in the south. The Indian caste system helped to perpetuate ethnic differences.

4. **(D)** The Indian Ocean trade network was one of the widest-ranging and most cosmopolitan in history. All the areas listed were drawn directly into it except for Russia (which was largely disunited and isolated during much of this era).

5. **(E)** All of these are true of Southeast Asia between 600 and 1450 C.E. The Khmer and Srivijayan states were important regional powers. Most of Southeast Asia took part in Pacific and Indian Ocean trade, and most were influenced by Hinduism and/or Buddhism.

6. **(C)** The Khmer actively pursued military expansion, especially into Burma and the Malay Peninsula.

7. **(C)** Islam's impact on Indonesia is still evident today. In fact, Indonesia is now the world's most populous Islamic nation (although many other faiths are still observed there as well).

8. **(B)** The Polynesians originated in the islands of Southeast Asia, then spread outward across the Pacific.

9. **(D)** Environmental factors had much to do with encouraging the Polynesian migrations. Environmental mismanagement also helped destroy the Polynesian culture on Easter Island.

10. **(E)** The Delhi Sultanate brought Islam to India by force. Treatment became less severe over time, and only part of the population (especially in the north) converted. Not bound by the caste system, Muslim women in India had a greater degree of freedom than Hindu women.

The Mongol Empires

- Genghis Khan
- The Mongol Empire and the Pax Mongolica
- The Silk Road (Samarkand)
- The breakup of the Mongol Empire
- Kublai Khan
- Timur

During the 1200s, almost all of Eurasia was swept by a whirlwind from Central Asia: the Mongols. United for the first time in their history by Genghis Khan, the Mongols burst out of their homeland in the 1210s, beginning one of the most successful military campaigns of all time. At its peak, the Mongol Empire was the largest conquest state that has ever existed, stretching across most of Asia, as well as parts of the Middle East and Europe.

By the late 1200s and early 1300s, the Mongol state broke apart into smaller units. The nomadic Mongols were adept at warfare but less so at nation building. This makes for an interesting contrast between their empire and states like Rome and Han China.

Nonetheless, the Mongols had a tremendous impact on Europe and Asia during the 1200s and 1300s. They destroyed and created nations. They shaped the social and political development of many civilizations. Also, for a time, the Mongol states provided a degree of unity—or at least connectedness—to a huge part of the Eurasian landmass. It is increasingly common for historians to speak of the thirteenth century as a period of **Pax Mongolica** (or Pax Tatarica): the "Mongol (or Tatar) Peace." Although the notion of peacefulness may be exaggerated, there is no denying that the Mongols temporarily tamed the vast spaces of Eurasia, affecting many of its great civilizations.

GENGHIS KHAN AND THE RISE OF THE MONGOLS

The Mongols (also Tartars or Tatars) were a group of nomadic tribes from the steppes, or open plains, of Central Asia. They herded livestock. They were excellent horsemen and archers.

The Mongols are frequently perceived as having been barbaric, even bloodthirsty. This is a stereotype. While the Mongols did not have a sophisticated society before their great wave of expansion, they proved adept at **cultural borrowing**. From their neighbors and the people they conquered, the Mongols adoped a law code, a written script, new religious practices, and better technology.

Before 1200, the Mongols, who numbered between 1.5 and 3 million, were divided into more than thirty disunited, often warring tribes. In 1206, the Mongols were united by the warlord Temujin, better known as **Genghis Khan** (also Chingiz, Jenghiz, or Chinggis), which means "ruler of limitless strength." Genghis Khan reorganized the Mongol armies and, shortly after seizing power, led them on their great campaign of conquest.

The Mongol Empires, 1294 C.E.
By 1294, the Mongols, a nomadic people, had conquered most of Asia and key portions of Europe and the Middle East. Mongol control over these territories had a major and lasting effect on many parts of Eurasia.

THE FIRST WAVE OF CONQUEST

Mongol conquests began in 1211. The first target was northern China; by 1215, the Mongols had breached the Great Wall and seized the city of Beijing. The Mongols also moved against Central Asia, capturing the great Silk Road trading center of Samarkand. By Genghis Khan's death in 1227, the Mongols controlled a large state encompassing present-day Mongolia, much of Central Asia, and northern and western China. His heirs would enlarge the empire even further.

What accounted for the Mongols' success? It used to be thought—incorrectly—that the main reason was great numbers. The early Mongol armies were large (about 80,000 to 100,000 troops) but not so large that they could easily have overwhelmed such a large territory. Mongol warriors were talented cavalrymen and archers, and they could fire from horseback, galloping at full speed, forward or backward. The Mongols (and their horses) were possessed of great endurance and hardiness. They organized their armies efficiently into tightly knit military units based on groups of ten. The Mongols were also quick to adopt advanced military technology and techniques from their more advanced neighbors. This was especially the case with siege warfare, which the Mongols learned from the Chinese and Central Asian states.

THE SECOND WAVE OF CONQUEST AND THE PAX MONGOLICA

Genghis Khan's heirs continued the wars of conquest. Genghis's third son, Ögödei, ruled the Mongols as Great Khan till 1241. He greatly expanded the empire and built a new capital, Karakorum, for it.

In the east, Ögödei's armies moved farther into China, threatening the Song Empire (which the Mongols defeated in the 1260s). Ögödei also forced Koryo, or Korea, into tributary status.

Ögödei had even more ambitious goals in the west. In 1236, he sent a large invasion force to seize as much of Europe as possible. From 1237 to 1240, the Mongols conquered most of Russia and Ukraine. From 1240 to 1242, they took over parts of Bulgaria, Romania, and Hungary. When they tried to push into Poland and Germany, however, they overextended themselves. Also, Ögödei died in 1241, and the succession struggle ended the invasion effort. Russian and Ukraine remained under Mongol rule as tributary states for two centuries.

As described in Chapter 7, the Mongols, commanded by Hulegu, invaded the Middle East in the 1250s, toppling the Abbasid Caliphate in 1258 and advancing until 1260, when they were stopped by a Mamluk army at Ain Jalut.

At their zenith, the Mongols ruled an empire that stretched from Poland in the west to Korea in the east, and from Siberia in the north to Vietnam in the south. Over this massive expanse, the Mongols imposed a single political authority, encouraged economic exchange, made travel conditions safer, and imposed legal order. Silk Road trade, which had fallen off, now revived and flourished, and cities like Samarkand became crucial economic centers, with merchants, missionaries, and travelers of all professions and ethnicities passing through. Among these was the Venetian merchant and explorer Marco Polo.

Many historians refer to this brief semi-unification of Eurasia as the Pax Mongolica, or "Mongol Peace." It was maintained not just by force but by a surprisingly high level of administrative skill. Helped by their habit of cultural adaptation, the Mongols borrowed a written language (Uighur, a Turkic dialect); their law code (the *yasa*, from China); paper currency (from China); and new religious beliefs (Buddhism and Islam). The Mongols used their own skill with horses to create one of the premodern world's fastest and most efficient postal systems (the *yam*).

BREAKUP OF THE MONGOL EMPIRE

A Chinese proverb is often quoted to describe the Mongol Empire: "One can conquer an empire on horseback, but one cannot govern it from there." Even recognizing their underappreciated political strengths, it must be said that the Mongols were better at conquest than they were at governing. Soon after its size and power peaked, the Mongol Empire, spread too thin, began to break apart.

In 1260, the last khan to rule over a united Mongol empire (Mongke) died. Civil war broke out, and the empire's four largest units became independent states. The homeland, which went to Kublai Khan, included Mongolia, China, and territories to the east and southeast. The Golden Horde ruled over Russia and parts of eastern

Europe until the mid-1400s. The Il-Khan Mongols converted to Islam and ruled much of the Middle East until the rise of the Ottoman Turks in the late 1300s. A Mongol state, the Jagadai Khanate, governed Central Asia well into the 1400s. Like the Il-Khans (with whom they often struggled), the Jagadai became Muslims.

A later Mongol warlord was the Jagadai khan **Timur** (also known as Tamerlane). From 1370 to 1405, Timur rose up and attempted to repeat the military triumph of his ancestor Genghis Khan. Quickly, he conquered Central Asia, Persia, northern India (including Delhi), southern Russia, and parts of the Middle East. The expansion ended with Timur's death, but his descendants ruled over Central Asia—and the Silk Road cities of Samarkand and Bukhara—until the 1500s.

QUICK REVIEW

1. Genghis Khan's chief role in the Mongols' history was

   (A) to conquer Russia.
   (B) to topple the Abbasid Caliphate.
   (C) to unite the Mongol tribes.
   (D) to convert the Mongols to Islam.
   (E) to take over western Europe.

2. The Mongols were skilled in _____, but not in _____.

   (A) warfare, nation building
   (B) administration, warfare
   (C) archery, horsemanship
   (D) nation building, cultural borrowing
   (E) architecture, painting

3. The most effective Mongol troops were

   (A) cavalry armed with bows and arrows.
   (B) heavily armored lancers.
   (C) light infantry using javelins.
   (D) pikesmen.
   (E) musketeers.

4. Why were the Mongols successful at conquest?

   I. They had the largest army of all time.
   II. They adopted advanced technology quickly.
   III. They organized their armies efficiently.
   IV. They were talented cavalrymen.

   (A) I, II, and III
   (B) II, III, and IV
   (C) I and III only
   (D) I only
   (E) all of the above

5. Which of the following territories did the Mongols NOT conquer?

   (A) Russia
   (B) Ukraine
   (C) Bulgaria
   (D) Romania
   (E) France

6. What fate did Russia experience at the hands of the Mongols?

   (A) It drove off an attempted invasion.
   (B) It was conquered, but only briefly.
   (C) It formed an alliance with the Mongol Empire.
   (D) The Mongols ignored Russia.
   (E) It was ruled by the Mongols for two centuries.

7. Which of the following is an accurate statement about Mongols' cultural adaptation?

   (A) They tended to adopt the religions of the people they had defeated.
   (B) They learned equestrian skills from the Europeans.
   (C) They adopted the Persian language as their written script.
   (D) They borrowed portions of a law code from the French.
   (E) They began dressing like Russians.

8. The Mongols' economic policy included

   (A) banning outside trade.
   (B) emphasizing agriculture over commercial activity.
   (C) imposing heavy tariffs on trading partners.
   (D) maintaining trade along the Silk Road.
   (E) building a large fleet of merchant vessels.

9. Which of the following is true of the Mongol state?

   (A) The Mongols adopted Uighur as their written script.
   (B) The Mongols established one of the most efficient postal systems in premodern history.
   (C) The Mongols made use of paper currency.
   (D) all of the above
   (E) none of the above

10. Why did the Mongol Empire break up?

   (A) The Mongols reverted to pastoralism.
   (B) The Mongols were unable to administer such a large territory effectively.
   (C) After Genghis Khan died, his successors were too incompetent to rule.
   (D) Russia conquered Mongolia.
   (E) none of the above

Answers

1. **(C)** Although Genghis Khan was a skilled war leader in his own right, he did not personally lead armies into Russia or against the Abbasids, and the Mongols never conquered western Europe. It was by uniting the Mongol tribes that Genghis Khan truly changed the course of history.

2. **(A)** During the 1200s, Mongol armies conquered many lands. They succeeded largely thanks to their talents as cavalrymen, their skills in archery, and their ability to adopt advanced military technology and techniques from peoples they had defeated. However, by 1260 Mongol unity collapsed with the death of Khan Mongke, and civil war ensued. During the late 1300s, the Ottoman Turks gained control of many lands the Mongols once ruled.

3. **(A)** As mentioned above, Mongol armies excelled on horseback and in archery. The Mongols as well as their horses both enjoyed great endurance. However, they were not known for using the weapons mentioned in the other answers.

4. **(B)** Although the Mongols did not have the largest army of all time, they did adopt advanced technology from conquered peoples, organized their armies into tightly knit military units, and were excellent horsemen.

5. **(E)** The Mongols conquered parts of eastern Europe but their rule never extended as far west as France. By the 1240s, when they were in reach of western Europe, they were overextended, far from home, and fighting on unfamiliar terrain.

6. **(E)** The Mongols conquered Russia in the 1240s, and their rule ended in the mid-1400s, when the city-state of Moscow gained the upper hand.

7. **(A)** The Mongols often chose to follow Buddhism or Islam, both of which had originated in areas they had conquered. They used the Turkic language of Uighur, not the Persian language, as their written script.

8. **(D)** Encouraging economic exchange, the Mongols revived trade to continue along the Silk Road, which ran through Central Asia. They were not known for encouraging maritime trade, though.

9. **(D)** In the 1200s, the Mongols maintained a high level of administrative skill as rulers of a vast empire. They facilitated communications by use of the language Uighur and an efficient postal system, and printed paper currency for economic transactions.

10. **(B)** By the late 1200s, the Mongols had overextended themselves. As a result, they failed to administer their large empire effectively. Also, the civil war of 1260 ruined the unity the Mongols had enjoyed for several decades.

Sub-Saharan Africa

CHAPTER 11

- The Sahara Desert and Africa's sub-Saharan regions
- The Bantu
- Matrilinear societies
- The Arab slave trade
- Trans-Saharan caravan routes
- Ghana and the gold trade
- Great Zimbabwe
- The Indian Ocean trade network (Mombasa and Zanzibar)
- Swahili as a lingua franca

Not just physically, but culturally and politically, Africa is divided by the Sahara Desert. As described in Chapter 7, most of Saharan Africa and the northern continent fell into the orbit of the Islamic world. The story of sub-Saharan Africa is more complex.

A geographical note: The AP World History course subdivides Africa into the following regions: North Africa (covered in Chapters 7, 15, and 23), West Africa, East Africa, Central Africa, and Southern Africa. The latter four are dealt with in Chapters 11, 18, and 26.

INTRODUCTION TO SUB-SAHARAN AFRICA

Factors Restricting the Growth of Major Sub-Saharan States

In sub-Saharan Africa, the development of strong, sizable political units occurred later and more slowly than in other parts of the world. Much of this had to do with the tremendous variety of ethnicity there, where more than 2,000 languages and dialects are spoken.

One of the few common threads shared by many—but not all—peoples of sub-Saharan Africa is descent from the Bantu tribes. Around 1000 B.C.E., the Bantu began to move out of their homeland in west central Africa. Their descendants settled in almost all parts of the continent south of the Sahara. With the passage of time, however, each smaller group developed its own distinct language and cultural tradition.

Environmental factors also limited the growth of major states. The fluctuating climate of sub-Saharan Africa and human susceptibility to insect- and animal-borne diseases (especially malaria and sleeping sickness) in sub-Saharan regions were obstacles to population growth.

Basic Features of Sub-Saharan Societies

Most sub-Saharan communities were small. Social life revolved around the village. Food was provided by means of a combination of hunting, herding, and limited agriculture. It appears that most African societies gained the skill of **metalworking** on their own, rather than having it taught to them by outsiders, as was commonly thought until recently.

As in most early civilizations, women in sub-Saharan Africa tended to be subservient to men. Women were often valued, though, for their labor as fieldworkers (while men tended cattle) and for producing heirs. Women also were respected for storytelling abilities and their role in educating young people about moral values and religious beliefs. Interestingly, in Africa, lineage was sometimes **matrilinear**, rather than patrilinear. Women often inherited property, and the husband was required to move into his wife's house. Rules of behavior between the sexes tended to be more informal than in the Middle East, China, or India.

Art and Culture

African tribes possessed a high degree of skill in carving and sculpture, especially in wood and ivory. Metal sculpture became more common over time. By the thirteenth and fourteenth centuries, West African artists were creating masterpieces out of bronze and iron. In Ife, in present-day Nigeria, metalworkers formed bronze and iron statues by first designing molds with melted wax. These sculptures may have influenced the work of metalworkers from the West African state of Benin. Such artists are famous for their sophisticated and detailed bronze, brass, and copper sculptures of heads, ornaments, animal figures, and reliefs depicting court life.

Architecture in Africa varied across regions owing to diverse cultural influences. In sub-Saharan Africa, Greater Zimbabwe stood out for its impressive stone buildings and walls. The stones were carefully cut, then set in place without mortar. In Mali, fourteenth-century builders used timber as skeletons in reinforcing mud mosques that still stand today. The architecture of Zanzibar is distinguished by the use of coral to decorate buildings.

African literature of this period was preserved by **oral tradition**. Professional storytellers chronicled history and social custom. They also acted as entertainers and served as advisers to kings. The most famous epic of sub-Saharan Africa from these years is *Son-Jara* (or *Sundiata*), from Mali (see Chapter 7).

Most native African religions were animistic (see Chapter 5), based on the worship of the spirits of animals and ancestors.

Islam and Contacts with North Africa

As time passed, the increased interaction between North Africa and sub-Saharan Africa included trade. Unfortunately, it also included slavery: for hundreds of years, **Arab slavers** penetrated to the south, forcing Africans into bondage. By the eleventh century, some traders in the Sahara owned more than a thousand slaves apiece.

Islam became part of sub-Saharan life, sometimes by force (as in Ghana), sometimes peacefully (as in Mali). Mali's great city of Timbuktu was an important center of Islamic scholarship. Muslims brought religion and trade to the cities of the eastern coast and previously isolated parts of southern Africa. Still, in comparison to North Africa, which became almost completely Muslim, sub-Saharan Africa was less heavily influenced by Islam.

WEST AND CENTRAL AFRICA

Ghana

In West Africa, the state of Ghana, founded in the 500s C.E., continued to be strong and prosperous. When Europe began minting coins during the 1200s, Ghana's gold gained in value, and it became a major supplier of gold to the world economy. Koumbi Saleh, one of Ghana's capitals, hosted a prosperous Muslim community of merchants linked to the trans-Saharan trade route. Ironically, iron and copper were more useful, and thus more valuable, to Africans than gold was. So caravans carried iron and copper across the Sahara as well as the precious metal.

Over time, Ghana's ecological and demographic conditions weakened its society. As its population grew, food production failed to meet demand in what was by then an extremely arid environment. All of this left Ghana vulnerable to Muslim conquest, the immediate cause of its downfall.

Central African States and Great Zimbabwe

In Central Africa, a few large city-states became home to advanced civilizations. Among them were Kongo and Benin.

From the 1250s to the 1450s, the most powerful of these states was the one that emerged around the cities of Mutapa and Great Zimbabwe. Politically linked, the two cities controlled seven hundred miles of the Zambezi river basin.

The larger and more important city was Great Zimbabwe (ca. 1000–1400). Its name means "sacred graves of the chiefs," and it was crucial as a political and religious center. It was a great walled city, encircling 193 acres and home to approximately 20,000 people.

Great Zimbabwe was immensely wealthy, thanks to large deposits of gold and diamonds. Gold was shipped east to Sofala, where it became part of the East African–Indian Ocean coastal trade complex (see Chapter 9). Archaeologists have found in the ruins of the city gold, jewelry, copper ornaments, birds carved out of soapstone, iron tools, Chinese ceramics, and Persian artworks. Such an assortment shows how extensive trade was in the area at the time.

Rumors of Great Zimbabwe's wealth—and of lost treasures and hidden mines—persisted for hundreds of years, long after the city itself collapsed in the mid-to-late 1400s.

THE EASTERN COAST

East Africa and the Indian Ocean Trade Network

As part of the large Indian Ocean trade network, the East African coast was open to a remarkable variety of cultural and economic influences. East Africa gained its wealth from a diverse selection of desirable goods like ivory. Slaves were part of the economy as well. Through trade, African societies had an impact on the outside world. As early as the Roman era, East Africa had commercial ties with India and the Mediterranean. By the tenth and eleventh centuries, African-made goods were reaching China, by way of the Indian Ocean trade network. Chinese maritime trade expanded during the early Ming dynasty (see Chapter 8), and many Chinese vessels made their way to the East African coast.

The Diversity of East African City-States

City-states flourished on the East African shore between 1000 and 1500. Nearly forty urban centers were sprinkled along the 1,500-mile stretch of coast running from Mogadishu (in today's Somalia) to the south. They were all multiethnic. Beginning in the 1100s, Persians and Arabs migrated to Mogadishu and pressed southward, mixing with the local Africans. The East African city-states were politically independent. Many were ruled by Arab sheiks, who led rich mercantile families. Key cities included **Mombasa**, Sofala, and **Zanzibar**.

TRANSNATIONAL LANGUAGES

Throughout history, certain languages have risen up to allow communication between cultures whose native tongues are very different. The term *lingua franca* is often used to describe them. Examples include Latin; Arabic; Swahili; the sign language used by Native American tribes on the Great Plains; and, increasingly in our own time, English. A language achieves the status of lingua franca for various reasons. In some cases, it is the shared religious language of people who are ethnically different; in others, it is the tongue that most effectively facilitates trade in a multilingual region. Sometimes it is imposed from above by a military or imperial power (like Spanish in Latin America or English in India).

East African cities were also diverse in terms of their populations, which included native Africans; Arabs, Turks, and other Middle Easterners; and Indians and others from South and Southeast Asia. A tremendous amount of ethnic, religious, cultural, and linguistic mixing occurred along the East African coast. Muslims moved in large numbers to the area, starting in the mid-to-late 600s. Islam became important but did not displace local religions. The most widespread language in the region was **Swahili**, which became the lingua franca, or common tongue, for much of the entire coast. East Africa was a vibrant area with a booming economy from approximately 1200 to 1500. Even Indonesians, in search of better economic opportunities, crossed the Indian Ocean to settle on Madagascar, an island off the southeast coast of Africa.

By the early 1500s, the arrival of European colonists and explorers would change everything, not just for East Africa but for the entire Indian Ocean basin.

Christianity in East Africa

Christianity existed as a dominant, even official, religion in two parts of northeastern Africa. The Copts, a Christian minority, formed communities in Egypt and Sudan.

Ethiopia (also known then as Abyssinia) was not only the oldest African state but, for many centuries, a Christian kingdom. Rumors about the wealth and Christianity of the Ethiopian monarchs gave rise in Europe to the legends of Prester John: a mythical Christian king in Africa who possessed fabulous wealth. These legends were among the factors that spurred on the age of exploration.

QUICK REVIEW

1. Which of the following helps explain why strong and sizable political units developed later and more slowly in sub-Saharan Africa than in many other regions of the world?

   (A) Language was not yet developed.
   (B) People in Africa had not yet evolved sufficiently to develop political units.
   (C) There were many cannibals in this part of Africa.
   (D) There was a vast array of languages and dialects spoken.
   (E) none of the above

2. How did women in the small communities of sub-Saharan Africa tend to be treated?

   (A) They were seen as political equals.
   (B) They were valued as fieldworkers and for educating children.
   (C) They were treated as goddesses.
   (D) More women served as chiefs than men.
   (E) Women tended the cattle and so had much power.

3. African tales of this period were preserved through

   (A) oral tradition.
   (B) scroll painting.
   (C) writings on large slabs of stone.
   (D) stories written on bronze statues.
   (E) manuscripts kept in pyramid-shaped archives.

4. The immediate cause of Ghana's downfall was

   (A) environmental calamity.
   (B) the Crusades.
   (C) its takeover by the Portuguese.
   (D) Muslim conquest.
   (E) the slave trade.

5. How do researchers know that Great Zimbabwe was so wealthy at one time?

   (A) It left behind written accounts of its history.
   (B) Explorers testified to its great wealth.
   (C) Gold, jewelry, and other valuable items have been found in its ruins.
   (D) It still exists, and has remained wealthy for hundreds of years.
   (E) none of the above

6. As far back as what era did East Africa have commercial ties with India and the Mediterranean region?

   (A) the 1700s
   (B) the 1400s
   (C) the Sumerian era
   (D) the Egyptian Old Kingdom
   (E) the Roman era

7. Which of the following is an accurate statement about East African cities during this period?

   (A) The area was not ethnically diverse.
   (B) The most widely used language was Swahili.
   (C) The area never enjoyed a booming economy.
   (D) Islam had not yet reached the shores of East Africa yet.
   (E) East African city-states were all under the rule of a single Arab sheik.

8. The Copts were and still are a _____ minority in predominantly Islamic Egypt.

   (A) Jewish
   (B) Buddhist
   (C) Christian
   (D) Muslim
   (E) agnostic

9. Which of the following is an accurate statement about slavery at the time in sub-Saharan Africa?

   (A) By the 1200s, some traders owned more than a thousand slaves apiece.
   (B) Slavery was confined to Timbuktu, at least until the 1400s.
   (C) Only Muslims could own and sell slaves.
   (D) The people who were enslaved tended to live in East Africa.
   (E) Slavery had not arrived in this region of the world yet.

10. How did African societies gain the skill of metalworking?

   (A) Muslims taught Africans the skill.
   (B) Western Europeans taught Africans this skill.
   (C) African societies learned this skill only after they were enslaved.
   (D) They gained it on their own without outside help.
   (E) none of the above

Answers

1. **(D)** The remarkable ethnic and linguistic diversity of sub-Saharan Africa made it difficult for united states to take shape.

2. **(B)** This answer describes the traditional roles of women in sub-Saharan societies. Although they were not treated with equality, sub-Saharan African women tended to enjoy more freedom and respect compared with women in China, the Middle East, or India.

3. **(A)** Sub-Saharan Africa's linguistic diversity discouraged the development of written scripts. In their absence, traditions, songs, and stories were passed down orally.

4. **(D)** Long-term environmental changes weakened Ghana and left it vulnerable, but the short-term cause of its downfall was Muslim invasion from the north.

5. **(C)** This is one instance when archaeological research helps historians understand old cultures and how they lived.

6. **(E)** Trade among these three regions is known to have gone on as far back as the days of Rome.

7. **(B)** East African cities were wealthy, cosmopolitan, and very diverse. The common language that emerged, in order to facilitate trade and general contact, was Swahili.

8. **(C)** While most of North Africa is Muslim, small communities, including Egypt's Copts and most Ethiopians, remain Christian.

9. **(A)** This answer gives some sense of the scale of the slave trade in sub-Saharan Africa, which was run mainly, but not wholly, by Arab slavers, and involved both West and East Africa.

10. **(D)** For a long time, the prevailing scholarship had it that sub-Saharan societies were too primitive to have gained knowledge of metalworking without having it brought or taught to them by outsiders. Recent archaeological evidence has disproven this idea.

The Americas

CHAPTER 12

- The pre-Columbian era
- The Anasazi
- Cahokia and the Mississippian civilization
- The Olmecs, the Maya, and the Aztecs

- Pyramids and human sacrifice
- Tenochtitlán and Mesoamerican urbanization
- Terrace farming and llama herding in the Andes
- The Incas and Machu Picchu

nlike the peoples of Eurasia and Africa, who interacted with and influenced each other, the early societies of North and South America developed in isolation. Settled by the descendants of Stone Age travelers who crossed from Asia over a land bridge that joined Alaska with Siberia—then disappeared with a rise in ocean levels—North and South America remained geographically separated from other continents for thousands of years.

By about 9000 B.C.E., the entire length of the Americas, north to south, had been settled. The passage of time, geographical spread, and environmental diversity caused the social groups scattered through the Americas to develop unique cultural, social, and linguistic characteristics.

Major areas of settlement included North America's eastern woodlands, desert Southwest, and open plains; the deserts and jungles of Mexico and Central America; and the Andes Mountains of South America. Before 600 C.E., as discussed in Chapter 3, advanced civilizations emerged in all these areas. Many of these societies are unusual in that they are among the few to reach an advanced state without developing systems of writing (such as the Incas and the Mississippians) or inventing the wheel.

The geographical isolation of the Americas continued until the end of the 1400s. Only with the voyages of Christopher Columbus did the societies of North and South America come into sustained contact with outsiders. (In the historiography of the Americas, the period before 1492 is referred to as the **pre-Columbian era**.) The arrival of the Europeans changed the Americas beyond recognition. In the meantime, between 1000 and 1450, several major civilizations emerged or reached their peak of development.

NORTH AMERICA

In North America, most Native Americans (known popularly by the erroneous term "Indians") were nomadic or seminomadic hunter-gatherers divided into tribes. Around 1000 C.E., the number of tribes—and the differences between them—increased dramatically and grew until about the 1500s.

The role of women in most North American tribes seems to have been defined relatively loosely. Because most of these groups were not yet fully agricultural, the gender division of labor was not as sharply formed as in the more developed empires of Central and South America. Women tended to gather berries and roots, weave, make pottery, and raise children. However, their status was not necessarily secondary to that of men, at least not formally.

Not counting what is today Mexico, two regions of North America became home to advanced societies. One was the Southwest, where settlement seems to have begun in the 300s B.C.E. Unusually for pre-Columbian North America, many Southwestern cultures were agricultural (learning the practice from more sophisticated societies in Mexico). The most famous Southwestern people were the **Anasazi**, who inhabited the region from about 400 (perhaps earlier) to 1300. They lived in complex dwellings known as pueblos—sometimes built on the open flatland, sometimes high up in the caves of canyons. The Anasazi believed that humans emerged from the earth, so they held religious ceremonies in underground chambers called kivas. This practice was passed on to tribes that later settled in the Southwest. Women in Anasazi communities may have had the right to own property.

To the north and east, sophisticated societies emerged in the Ohio and Mississippi river valleys. These groups built large **earth mounds**, presumably for religious and ceremonial purposes. The first was the Adena culture (ca. 500 B.C.E.–100 C.E.), followed by the larger Hopewell culture (ca. 100–400). After 600, the region's most advanced culture was the Mississippian civilization (ca. 700–1500). Like their predecessors, the Mississippians built great mounds. They also built cities, the largest of which was **Cahokia**, located in what is now western Illinois; by 1200, it had a population of over 30,000.

Between 1250 and 1500, the Mississippian culture was in decline (for unknown reasons, Cahokia was abandoned around 1250). At the same time, Native Americans began to organize themselves into smaller hunter-gatherer groups. These evolved into the major Native American tribes that remain familiar today. The arrival of European settlers and explorers in the late 1400s and 1500s forever changed the lives of all Native Americans.

MEXICO AND CENTRAL AMERICA

It was in Mexico and Central America (or Mesoamerica) that major civilizations in the Americas first developed. Agriculture, in the form of maize (corn) and potato cultivation, was practiced there as early as 5000 to 3000 B.C.E. The region's first dominant society was the **Olmecs** (ca. 1200 B.C.E.–400 B.C.E.), who, like the Sumerians in Mesopotamia, left behind a religious and cultural tradition that profoundly influenced later Central American peoples (see Chapter 3). The Teotihuacán culture (ca. 100 B.C.E.–750 B.C.E.), near what is now Mexico City, created one of the largest urban centers in the world at the time.

Thanks to the pattern set by the Olmecs, there was a high degree of cultural continuity among the peoples of Mesoamerica, all the way through the 1500s C.E. Most Central American societies tended to be hierarchical dictatorships ruled by kings and priests. They were not unified nations but city-states that shared a common culture, interacted economically, and also warred with each other frequently.

Women were subject to rigidly defined gender roles. A few upper-class women gained stature as priestesses or used noble status to exert informal influence. Aztec women could own property and sign contracts independently of their husbands. Still, most women were restricted to roles traditionally assigned to females.

Many of the peoples of Central America—most famously the Maya and the Aztecs—erected large **pyramids** for religious purposes. Unlike the ancient Egyptians, who used pyramids as tombs for the dead, the Maya and Aztecs built pyramids as temples and places of **human sacrifice**.

States in Pre-Columbian Central America, ca. 1200 B.C.E.–1200 C.E.
This map demonstrates that, in Central America, many civilizations developed, rose, and fell in succession. The Olmecs set the pattern for cultural development here, followed by the Maya, Toltecs, and Aztecs.

The Maya

Around 250 C.E., a new culture, the Maya, emerged in present-day Guatemala, Honduras, Belize, and southern Mexico. The Mayan lands were governed by independent city-states and rival kingdoms, such as Tikal, Palenque, and Uxmal. At its peak, the Mayan population reached three million.

The polytheistic religion of the Maya, which included human sacrifice and the worship of serpent gods and jaguar deities, derived partly from the Olmec tradition.

The Maya devised an elaborate hieroglyphic script, the most advanced system of writing in the pre-Columbian Americas. Superb astronomers and mathematicians, they invented an ususual but intricate and accurate calendar. They were gifted architects.

The reasons for the Mayan collapse remains a mystery. Theories include land overuse, nearby volcanic activity, disease, and inter-city warfare. Following the Maya were the Toltecs (ca. 968–1156), an aggressive warrior society that conquered central Mexico until civil war and external invasion finished off their civilization.

The Aztecs

The next major group in Central America—and the last before the arrival of the Europeans—were the Mexica, better known as the **Aztecs** (ca. 1300–1520). The chief city of the Aztecs was the metropolis of **Tenochtitlán** (on the site of what is today Mexico City). At the height of Aztec power, Tenochtitlán had a population of half a million; and its marketplace, a thriving center of trade, could hold more than 60,000 people.

The Aztecs were even more warlike than the Toltecs before them. During the 1300s, the Aztecs began conquering an empire of more than 125,000 square miles. They ruled over a population of 10 million.

Aztec religion remains the culture's most famous feature. The Aztecs built pyramids to serve as temples and worshipped many of the same gods as the Mesoamerican peoples before them. Key deities included the jaguar god and the feathered serpent (Quetzalcoátl, who also appeared as a light-skinned, bearded man). Most important was the sun god, Huitzilopochtli, who took the form of a giant hummingbird. The Aztecs believed that the reappearance of the sun every morning depended on their devotion to Huitzilopochtli. They also believed the sun drew its energy from human blood, so they practiced human sacrifice on an extremely large scale. Victims included prisoners of war but also ordinary Aztec citizens. Historians estimate that, by the end of the 1400s, over 20,000 people per year were ritually slain.

The Aztec thrived in Central America until the early 1500s, when the Spanish arrived. The defeat of the Aztecs led to Spanish domination of Mexico and Central America until the 1800s. The Spanish conquest is described in Chapter 19.

SOUTH AMERICA

The ecological diversity of South America is staggering. Climates range from tropical to cool and arid. Terrain types include jungle, desert, mountains, grassland, and the vast Amazon river basin.

Early Andean Civilizations

The environment in which complex South American societies first developed was mountainous. It was on the west coast, in the **Andes Mountains,** that civilizations first took shape. At first glance, the rugged terrain might seem too inhospitable to encourage the growth of advanced societies. However, that very ruggedness demanded a high degree of cooperation and efficient coordination of human labor, giving rise to a number of major cultures, both before and after 600 C.E.

Most of these societies appeared in the northwest Andes, in what is today Ecuador, Bolivia, and Peru. Among the earliest was the **Chavin** (ca. 850–250 B.C.E.). Later civilizations include the Nazca (100–800 C.E.), the Moche (200–700 C.E.), the Huari (ca. 500–1000), the Tiahuanaco (ca. 500–1000), and the Chimu (ca. 800–1465).

Andean Civilizations, ca. 850 B.C.E.–1532 C.E.
The earliest major civilizations of South America emerged in the Andes Mountains, on the continent's western coast. The last and greatest was the Incan Empire.

Features of Andean Civilizations

Most Andean societies had certain features in common. Most were organized into clans called *ayllu*. Smaller groups cooperated by taking on rotational labor obligations for the entire clan. The Andean peoples practiced animal husbandry, breeding llamas, alpacas, and vicuñas for transport, food, and wool.

Women in Andean societies were greatly constrained in their rights and freedoms. Wives were considered little more than domestic servants. Lower-class women worked as weavers, farmers, and child rearers. One alternative was to become involved in religious life. Especially in Incan society, many young girls were chosen to serve in temples.

Andean cultures also grew crops, but cultivating land was difficult in such a mountainous region. To overcome this difficulty, Andean peoples used a method of terrace farming, in which flat surfaces were carved, staircase fashion, out of the mountains' sloped sides. Terrace farming was labor-intensive, but it allowed farmers to work in environments not naturally favorable for agriculture.

Another noteworthy feature of Andean societies is that most of them accomplished a high level of cultural sophistication without developing a system of writing. To keep financial records and accounts, Andean civilizations used an elaborate system, called quipo, of knots tied in cords.

The Incas

All these features were passed on to the most famous Andean civilization, the Incas (ca. 1300s–1536). The Incas rose quickly during the 1300s to build a huge empire in the Andes, subduing many of the peoples already mentioned. In less than a hundred years, Incan territory grew into a massive expanse covering 3,000 miles north to south, from Chile to Ecuador, and stretching from the Pacific coast to the upper Amazon.

Even in such mountainous terrain, the Incas created an elaborate system of transport and communications, including more than 13,000 miles of roads. The Incas also constructed large cities, including the capital, Cuzco, and the fortress and temple complex of Machu Picchu. The ruler was known as the Great Inca. He was considered the sacred descendant of the sun god, and to look at him directly was an offense punishable by death.

The Incas worshipped a number of deities, but chief among them was the sun god. The Temple of the Sun in Cuzco was the largest place of worship. It was laid out in the shape of a puma, and the interior was lined with gold. The temple was staffed by thousands of *acllas*, or "virgins of the sun." These were young women chosen each year from throughout the empire to serve as acolytes.

The Incan civilization enjoyed its heyday during the 1400s and early 1500s. After that point, the Incas—like the Aztecs in Mexico—were brought down by the Spanish. The conquest of the Incas is detailed in Chapter 19.

QUICK REVIEW

1. Why are many societies of the Americas considered unusual?

   (A) Their form of governance was not based on hierarchies but on equality before the law.
   (B) Most reached an advanced state of civilization without developing systems of writing.
   (C) Women acted as the warriors.
   (D) They were more brutal to outsiders.
   (E) They all spoke the same language, Spanish.

2. How were Southwest Native Americans different from those in the eastern woodlands?

   (A) They built large earth mounds instead of cliff dwellings.
   (B) They tended to be physically larger.
   (C) They were more warlike.
   (D) They were agriculturalists, not hunter-gathers.
   (E) They were known to be noticeably lighter-skinned.

3. Which of the following Native American societies built large mounds and are thought to have used them for religious purposes?

   (A) the Sioux
   (B) the Mississippians
   (C) the Pueblos
   (D) the Apache
   (E) the Hopi

4. Most of the Central American societies

   I. tended to be despotic.
   II. were often politically fractured.
   III. had a low level of trade with other peoples of the region.
   IV. had a high level of trade with other peoples of the region.

   (A) I, II, and III
   (B) I, II, and IV
   (C) I and III only
   (D) II and IV only
   (E) I and IV only

5. How did the Maya MOST differ from other pre-Columbian societies in the Americas?

   (A) They devised the most advanced system of writing.
   (B) They practiced human sacrifice more actively than their neighbors.
   (C) They were the first to manufacture iron weapons.
   (D) They were monotheistic.
   (E) They refrained from building pyramids.

6. Which of the following was the Aztecs' principal god?

   (A) the lion god
   (B) the jaguar god
   (C) the sun god
   (D) the feathered serpent god
   (E) the moon god

7. In South America, where did the first complex societies develop?

   (A) along the Amazon River
   (B) on the southern grasslands
   (C) on offshore islands
   (D) along the Brazilian coast
   (E) in the Andes Mountains

8. What major features did Andean civilizations have in common?

    I. They developed written forms of language.
    II. They were organized into clans.
    III. They practiced animal husbandry.
    IV. Women tended to have equal rights with men.

    (A) I, II, and III
    (B) II, III, and IV
    (C) I and IV only
    (D) II and III only
    (E) I only

9. What environmental factor did Incan rulers have to overcome to build their empire?

    (A) desert heat and aridity
    (B) thick jungle
    (C) rough mountainous terrain
    (D) the constant eruption of nearby volcanoes
    (E) none of the above

10. The Incas and Aztecs were conquered by the

    (A) Maya.
    (B) Spanish.
    (C) French.
    (D) Russians.
    (E) Mexicans.

Answers

1. **(B)** Examples of civilizations in the Americas that lacked systems of writing include the Incas and Mississipians. They were also unusual because many did not use wheels for transport purposes.

2. **(D)** Unlike most Native Americans in North America, peoples of the Southwest tended to be agriculturalists. They probably learned farming techniques from their neighbors to the south, in Mexico.

3. **(B)** Unlike the other four societies listed in this question, only the Mississippians are known for their great mounds. The largest mound in North America is located in what was once the Mississippian city of Cahokia in western Illinois.

4. **(B)** Most Central American societies were ruled by priests and kings, and city-states often fought each other. However, peoples of this region often interacted peacefully in terms of trade.

5. **(A)** The Mayan writing system was more sophisticated than that of the Aztecs, for example. Mayan hieroglyphs included phonetic symbols and ideographs. The Mayan calendar indicates a complex understanding of astronomy and mathematics.

6. **(C)** The sun god, named Huitzilopochtli, appeared to the Aztecs in the shape of a large hummingbird. The Aztecs sacrificed humans on a large scale to appease him.

7. **(E)** The first complex societies in South America lived in the northwestern Andes in what is now the countries of Ecuador, Bolivia, and Peru. These societies included the Nazca, Moche, Huari, Tiahuanaco, and Chimu.

8. **(D)** As mentioned above, these societies lacked a written language. They were organized into clans called *ayllu*, which were further broken down into smaller groups, each obligated to fulfill a certain kind of labor for the entire clan. The Andean societies also herded animals, such as llamas. They sometimes grew crops, although the mountainous conditions often made farming difficult.

9. **(C)** The Incas linked together their vast and mountainous territory through a complex system of communications and transport, including thousands of miles of roads.

10. **(B)** The Spanish conquered the Incas and Aztecs between 1519 and 1536. The Maya were no longer a distinct civilization at this time, and the other groups on this list were not involved in colonizing South America.

Unit Three: Review Questions

SAMPLE ESSAY QUESTIONS

1. Women were treated in different ways by different societies during the period between 600 and 1450. Choose two of the regions listed below and compare and contrast how women were treated by them.

   East Asia
   the Middle East
   Central America
   India
   sub-Saharan Africa

2. Discuss how one of the following regions changed between 600 C.E. and 1450 C.E., with an emphasis on how the arrival of Islam affected the region.

   East Africa
   India
   West Africa
   Spain

3. Compare and contrast the organization and characteristics of the Mongol Empire with those of the Abbasid Caliphate.

4. Describe and analyze changes and continuities in the European cultural and intellectual outlook between 1000 and 1500.

MULTIPLE-CHOICE QUESTIONS

1. In what way or ways did the Catholic Church affect the development of medieval Europe?

   I. Its monasteries preserved important manuscripts from the Greek and Roman eras.
   II. It prevented Muslims from taking over any parts of continental Europe.
   III. It gave the peoples of a politically divided Europe something in common culturally.
   IV. It promoted the use of Latin, which became the language of learning in Europe.

   (A) I only
   (B) I and IV
   (C) II, III, and IV
   (D) I, III, and IV
   (E) all of the above

2. Which of the following is true of the Holy Roman Empire during the late medieval period?

   (A) It was the most centralized monarchy in Europe.
   (B) It formed a long-lasting alliance with the Ottoman Turks.
   (C) It consisted of nearly 200 smaller states, many of them quite autonomous.
   (D) It was governed from Rome by the pope.
   (E) none of the above

3. Which of the following was NOT a major consequence of the Moorish occupation of medieval Spain?

   (A) The Moors brought with them advanced knowledge of medicine and science.
   (B) The Moors Christianized Spain.
   (C) The Moors profoundly affected Spanish art and architecture.
   (D) The Moors provided a haven for Jewish scholars and professionals.
   (E) The Moors withdrew from different parts of Spain at different times, delaying the country's centralization.

4. Scholastic philosophers in medieval Europe

   (A) sought to reconcile Christian faith with the worldview of the ancient Greeks and Romans.
   (B) dismissed Greco-Roman learning as pagan superstition.
   (C) considered the teachings of Plato and Aristotle to be more insightful than Christian doctrine.
   (D) rebelled against the intellectual constraints imposed upon them by the Catholic Church.
   (E) embraced Muslim beliefs and argued in favor of religious tolerance.

5. Which of the following is true of cities in medieval Europe?

   I. Urbanization and the revival of trade were interrelated processes.
   II. Cities in western Europe were larger and more prosperous than older cities in the eastern Mediterranean.
   III. In most parts of Europe, serfs who escaped to a city and lived there for more than a year became free.
   IV. Urban governments actively combated poverty by establishing extensive welfare systems.

   (A) I only
   (B) III only
   (C) I and II
   (D) II and IV
   (E) I and III

6. What ethnic group restored some degree of centralization to the Middle East after the fall of the Abbasid Caliphate and the Mongol invasions?

   (A) the Turks
   (B) the Kurds
   (C) the Arabs
   (D) the Circassians
   (E) the Berbers

7. Which do historians consider the major achievements of Islamic culture during the Abbasid Caliphate?

   I. Muslims eradicated heretical offshoots, such as Sufism.
   II. Muslims imported "Arabic" numerals from India and made their use widespread.
   III. Muslims greatly increased understanding of astronomy and mathematics.
   IV. Muslims created masterpieces of world literature, such as the *Rubaiyat*.

   (A) I, II, III
   (B) II, III, IV
   (C) I and III only
   (D) II and IV only
   (E) all of the above

8. The technique of block printing is thought by many to have emerged in _____ rather than China.

   (A) Burma
   (B) Mali
   (C) Korea
   (D) Thailand
   (E) Japan

9. The Song Dynasty

   (A) is best known for its scientific and technological prowess.
   (B) united China's lands under a strong, stable empire that lasted several centuries.
   (C) successfully resisted the Mongols and remained outside their sphere of influence.
   (D) suffered terribly as a result of the bubonic plague.
   (E) isolated China from the rest of the known world.

10. China's most important port city during the Song and Yuan eras was

    (A) Beijing.
    (B) Nanjing.
    (C) Harbin.
    (D) Canton.
    (E) Tientsin.

11. Which of the following is NOT true of the Japanese shogunates?

    (A) Like European chivalry, the code of Bushido placed emphasis on obedience and loyalty.
    (B) The dominant class was the warrior aristocracy known as samurai.
    (C) Land was held by powerful lords called daimyo.
    (D) The status of women became lower than it had been during the Heian period.
    (E) Samurai frowned upon Zen Buddhism for what they considered to be a pacifist attitude.

12. The Delhi Sultanate

    (A) introduced the caste system to India.
    (B) eventually gained control of the entire Indian subcontinent.
    (C) successfully resisted the assault of the Central Asian warlord Timur.
    (D) all of the above
    (E) none of the above

13. With what religion is the Indonesian temple of Borobudur associated?

    (A) Buddhism
    (B) Hinduism
    (C) Islam
    (D) indigenous polytheism
    (E) Jainism

14. What were some examples of the Mongols' cultural borrowing during the Pax Mongolica?

    I. the adoption of advanced law codes
    II. the adoption of a written language
    III. the adoption of new religious practices
    IV. the adoption of nomadism

    (A) I and II only
    (B) II and III only
    (C) I, II, and III
    (D) II, III, and IV
    (E) none of the above

15. The Mongol assault on the Middle East

    (A) was repelled immediately.
    (B) resulted in the creation of a khanate that lasted only a few years.
    (C) succeeded in toppling the Abbasid Caliphate, but was finally stopped by a Mamluk force.
    (D) enveloped the entire Middle East.
    (E) led to a second assault on central and western Europe.

16. What was the principal commodity traded by Ghana?

    (A) gold
    (B) ivory
    (C) timber
    (D) slaves
    (E) coffee

17. Which of the following is true of East Africa's city-states?

    I. Swahili was used as a regional lingua franca.
    II. Substantial numbers of Muslims settled there.
    III. They formed a integral part of the Indian Ocean trade network.
    IV. They were cosmopolitan, multiethnic urban centers.

    (A) I and II
    (B) II only
    (C) III only
    (D) II, III, and IV
    (E) all of the above

18. The first inhabitants of the Americas

    (A) sailed to South America across the Pacific.
    (B) arrived in eastern Canada after voyaging across the Atlantic.
    (C) crossed a land bridge to Alaska across what is now the Bering Strait.
    (D) emerged there on their own.
    (E) reached the Brazilian coast on rafts from Africa.

19. Which of the following did the Maya and Aztec NOT have in common?

    (A) a cultural tradition influenced by the Olmec
    (B) human sacrifice
    (C) pyramid building
    (D) a sophisticated written script
    (E) veneration of similar deities

20. Upon what unusual animal did Andean societies rely for food, wool, and other transport?

    (A) the ibex
    (B) the llama
    (C) the wildebeest
    (D) the water buffalo
    (E) the bison

Answers

1. **(D)** These manuscripts contained significant scientific ideas, philosophical essays, literary works, and other types of secular learning that otherwise would have been lost. In addition, Europe was more culturally unified because of the Catholic Church's strong influence at the time.

2. **(C)** The population of the Holy Roman Empire consisted of many different peoples, and it was quite decentralized. Its people shared a historical memory of ancient Rome and a common religion, Roman Catholicism. However, it was not governed from Rome.

3. **(B)** The Moors were a Muslim people who invaded Spain in the 700s. They were not expelled from Spain until 1492, and they left behind an enduring cultural legacy.

4. **(A)** The school of philosophy known as Scholasticism tried to reconcile reason and scientific learning of the Greeks and Romans with religious faith. The best-known Scholastic was an Italian monk named Thomas Aquinas.

5. **(E)** Cities attracted artisans, tradespeople, laborers, and merchants. As cities grew, so did specialization of labor and the development of new skills. Also, fairs and markets grew in cities as more people arrived to sell their goods.

6. **(A)** The Ottoman Turks began to dominate the Middle East in the 1300s and 1400s. By the 1500s, nearly the entire Middle East was under Ottoman control. The Ottoman Empire collapsed as a result of World War I.

7. **(B)** The Abbasid Caliphate is recognized as the golden era of Islamic culture. The Muslims had a sophisticated understanding of astronomy and mathematics and created masterpieces of world literature written at the time. Sufism was not heresy, but a respected part of Islamic culture.

8. **(C)** Although Korea was under the cultural and religious influence of China at this time, block printing was likely first created by Koreans, then later adopted by the Chinese.

9. **(A)** Song scientists furthered knowledge in the fields of astronomy and mathematics. They also invented accurate clocks, the compass, and gunpowder. The Song state was relatively weak, politically speaking, and the bubonic plague struck China later.

10. **(D)** Canton was one of the world's busiest commercial centers during this time. Goods from throughout Asia flowed through its port and were often carried by large trading vessels called junks.

11. **(E)** Zen, or Chan, Buddhism actually was quite popular among samurai. Followers of Zen Buddhism are not necessarily pacifists.

12. **(E)** The Delhi Sultanate was established by Muslim generals in 1206 in India. Under their rule, Islam was introduced to India, although the regime did not abolish other existing religions, such as Hinduism and Buddhism. However, Hindus and Muslims often did not mix socially, and tensions flared between the two religious groups in some areas of India.

13. **(A)** The temple is shaped like a mountain. Each level marks a stage on the path to spiritual enlightenment according to the Buddhist faith.

14. **(C)** The law code the Mongols used was borrowed from a number of cultures, including the Chinese, and was written in the Turkic language. Also, the Mongols often adopted the religions of the people they ruled, including Buddhism and Islam. They were originally nomads.

15. **(C)** In the 1250s, the Mongols vanquished the Abbasid Caliphate. Then in 1260, the Mongolian commander Hülegü was defeated by Mamluk cavalrymen at the Battle of Ain Jalut.

16. **(A)** Ghana, in West Africa, enjoyed a period of relative prosperity in the 1200s largely thanks to the fact that it was the world's chief supplier of gold. Ghana also gained economically from its sales of iron and copper to markets in Africa.

17. **(E)** East Africa was open to a vast array of diverse cultural and economic influences. While Islam was the most important religion in the region, other religions existed there too. People largely communicated through the Swahili language, and inhabitants of the city-states in East Africa participated in an active Indian Ocean trade network.

18. **(C)** Between 15,000 and 30,000 years ago, Stone Age people traveled from Asia across a land bridge joining Alaska with northeastern Siberia. The land bridge disappeared as ocean levels rose. Once reaching Alaska, social groups scattered south throughout the Americas in search of better living conditions.

19. **(D)** The Maya created a complex written system of hieroglyphics, while the Aztecs never adopted a written language. The other answers are examples of things the two civilizations did have in common.

20. **(B)** Andean societies, such as the Incas, used llama for food, transportation, and clothing and other woven goods. The other animals on the list were not found in this mountainous region.

UNIT FOUR

WORLD CULTURES
INTERACTING
(1450–1750)

Unit Overview

GENERAL REMARKS

Between 1450 and 1750, the world's civilizations became truly connected for the first time in history. The most significant trend of this era was the emergence of a fully global system of exchange and interaction. Regrettably, much of this interaction consisted of warfare, exploitation, and slavery. Nonetheless, trade, discovery, cultural interchange, and the faster and easier movement of peoples brought the various societies of the world into greater proximity. One can accurately speak of world cultures interacting, for good and for bad, during this period.

One of the primary causes of this greater interaction was the massive and sustained effort of the Europeans to explore the rest of the world. Driven by scientific curiosity, the quest for power, the hope of spreading Christianity, and, above all, a desire for wealth, European mariners sought out oceanic trade routes that would link them directly with China, India, Japan, and elsewhere in the Far East. During the 1400s and 1500s, European explorers reached all these places. They also encountered the Americas: a "New World" that had, for thousands of years, lain outside the bounds of knowledge of the peoples of Asia, Africa, and Europe.

Within decades, European traders, missionaries, and conquerors had spread throughout the world. The Europeans became the first in history to sail around the globe, and they established a presence in many parts of coastal Africa, Southeast Asia, and the Far East. Most dramatically, European colonizers conquered and transformed the Americas. The opening of the Americas to the rest of the world was done brutally and out of greed, but it also played a tremendous role in shifting the world's economic, linguistic, religious, and cultural patterns. It changed forever the environments of the Americas, Africa, and Europe, as new animals, new foods, and new diseases were brought back and forth in a development known as the Columbian Exchange.

Another major trend of this era was the rise of Europe. Until the 1400s, Europe had been relatively weak and backward, compared with civilizations such as China and the Ottoman Empire. During the 1500s and 1600s, however, Europe pulled even with China and the "gunpowder empires" of the Islamic east (Ottoman Turkey, Safavid Persia, and Mughal India) in terms of scientific advancement, global power, and wealth. During the 1700s, Europe overtook these other cultures, becoming the strongest, most technologically adept, and richest civilization in the world. By the middle of the 1700s, Europe was well situated to dominate the vast majority of the globe, militarily and economically—which it did in the 1800s.

Technological development and scientific knowledge increased in many parts of the world during this time. Economic and technological practices that can be considered proto-industrial were appearing in such places as Europe and China. The foundations for the rapid and thorough industrialization and mechanization of many societies during the late 1700s and 1800s were laid during the 1600s and early-to-mid 1700s.

In addition, agricultural techniques in most societies improved dramatically. In Europe, it is common to speak of an "agricultural revolution" during this era. Worldwide, improved agriculture helped lead to a significant population increase. The rate of growth was the fastest ever seen to that date, as the world population rose from 350 million in 1400 to 610 million in 1700.

BROAD TRENDS
Global Power and International Relations

- During the first centuries of this era (the 1500s and 1600s), global might was concentrated in China and the Islamic world's "gunpowder empires" (Ottoman Turkey, Safavid Persia, and Mughal India).
- The nations of Europe, especially in the west and north, grew steadily more powerful. By the early 1700s, they were overtaking the civilizations listed previously in terms of military, scientific, and technological aptitude.
- The most dramatic and global development of the era was the European campaign to explore (and, where possible, conquer and colonize) the rest of the world. In particular, the European encounter with the Americas—and the incorporation of the Americas into the world economic system—transformed the world.
- European colonization of the Americas, the African coast, and parts of Southeast Asia set the stage for a massive burst of imperial activity during the 1800s. During the 1700s, European colonization led to the emergence of a truly global economic system. It also created a worldwide system of military competition among European powers for global dominance. Some of the European wars of the 1700s—especially the Seven Years' War (1756–1763), which raged not only in Europe, but also North America and India—can, in a sense, be considered history's first "world wars."
- The increased importance of gunpowder weaponry meant that, from this time forward, technological aptitude and military strength would be intimately connected.

Political Developments

- In many parts of the world, political organization became more centralized and sophisticated. Many of the features of modern government, such as bureaucracies, agencies, admiralties, treasuries, general staffs, state banks, and other institutions, began to appear.
- Nation-states in the contemporary sense of the word began to emerge. Nation-states were solid political units with relatively fixed borders, a sense of national

unity, and populations that were mostly (though never completely) homogenous in terms of language and ethnicity.

- Europe began to experiment with new forms of monarchy: absolutism and parliamentarism.

Economic and Environmental Developments

- Social diversification resulted from the growing importance of nonagricultural ways of making a living. Banking, commerce, trade, shopkeeping, artisanry, and craftsmanship all led to the creation of a middle class (often referred to as the bourgeoisie) in many societies, but especially in Europe. This middle class was small to begin with, but steadily grew in numbers and importance.

- More economic importance began to be placed on trade, commerce, and money, rather than land (which had been the traditional source and measure of wealth).

- In several civilizations, primarily Europe, proto-industrial modes of production began to appear, especially during the 1700s. By the late 1700s, the concept of capitalism was beginning to emerge as well. Both these trends would have a profound impact on the 1800s.

- Europe's exploration and colonization of the Americas created a new major trade network in the Atlantic. This economic system linked Europe, Africa, North America, and South America. Indirectly, it was connected by trade with the Middle East and Asia.

- During the 1500s and 1600s, Spanish and Portuguese extraction of precious metals (especially silver) from the Americas affected economies around the world. Over time, this huge and relatively sudden influx of gold and silver coinage into the economies of so many societies created a glut of precious metals. Many civilizations, from Europe to China, experienced severe inflation as a result of this trend during the 1600s.

- By far the most unfortunate by-product of this era's economic trends was the birth and growth of the Atlantic slave trade, which, from the late 1400s to the late 1800s, resulted in the capture and forced deportation to the Americas of perhaps 12 million Africans.

- The Columbian Exchange brought new foods, plants, and animals from North and South America to Africa and Europe. In particular, the importation of corn and potatoes dramatically altered the diets and agricultural practices of Europe. To North and South America, the Europeans brought new technology, the horse, and Christianity. By bringing African slaves to the New World, the Europeans also imported foods, cultural practices, and religious beliefs from Africa. The Europeans also brought diseases, such as smallpox and measles, to which the peoples of the Americas had no immunity. It is estimated that up to 25 percent of the pre-Columbian population of the Americas perished within decades from the diseases brought to the New World by European conquerors and colonizers.

- World population growth was considerable during these years. From 1400 to 1700, the world's population increased from 350 million to 610 million. The increase was due mainly to improvements in agricultural technique in most world cultures, as well as a general warming of the global climate. The parts of the world that grew the most were Asia and Europe.

Cultural Developments

- Most major societies had by now developed well-defined artistic and literary traditions. Increased technological aptitude enabled the production of arts and crafts of very high quality.
- The level of scientific knowledge and technological achievement was especially high in civilizations such as China, Ottoman Turkey, Mughal India, and Safavid Persia.
- Europe made exceptional strides in terms of scientific knowledge and technological achievement. The Renaissance, the Scientific Revolution, and the Enlightenment all furthered the intellectual growth of Europe, to the point that, during the late 1600s and 1700s, it overtook the civilizations listed above.
- The steadily increasing influence of the printing press led to the rapid spread of information, scientific knowledge, religious debates, and new ideas. By creating more materials to read—and more incentive to read—the printing press helped to boost literacy rates.
- Europe experienced a religious earthquake, the Protestant Reformation, that had a profound impact not just on matters of faith, but also cultural life, military and political affairs, and economics. The split between Protestants and Catholics affected the ways in which Europeans spread Christianity to other parts of the world.
- In addition to the cultural, religious, and artistic interchange that went on among the societies of Africa, Europe, and Asia, the European encounter with the Americas led to even greater cultural interaction. The movement of Europeans and Africans (mainly slaves) altered the patterns of North and South American ethnicity, religion, language, art, and music. The changes were positive and negative, and in all cases significant.
- As a result of their Age of Discovery, the Europeans established a presence in almost all parts of the world during this era. Consequently, European colonies and trading missions spread European culture to Africa, Asia, and the Americas.

Gender Issues

- Throughout most parts of the world, women continued to occupy a secondary status, in terms of social roles, economic opportunities, and political influence.
- In most societies, marriage remained a primarily economic arrangement. Marriage ties were often a way to gain or transfer wealth and property. Marriage also ensured the inheritance of one's goods and assets by legitimate heirs.
- In a limited, gradual sense, parts of Europe began to develop a greater awareness of the injustice of the position of women.
- Also in Europe, individual women or women of small but important segments of society (aristocratic women or women of the emerging middle class, for

example) managed to gain educations, become active in business, make scientific discoveries, or become artists and writers.

- In most societies, women discovered or developed ways to gain influence or advance their desires in informal, often subtle ways (advising husbands and sons, educating children, running or helping to run businesses, managing household finances, and so on).
- A handful of Europe's most important monarchs during this era—Elizabeth I, Maria Theresa, Isabella, and Catherine the Great, for instance—were female.

QUESTIONS AND COMPARISONS TO CONSIDER

- Compare one or more major European monarchies from this period with an Asian empire (such as Ottoman Turkey, Ming China, or Mughal India).
- Contrast Russia's relationship with western Europe with the way one of the following interacted with the West: Mughal India, the Ottoman Empire, Tokugawa Japan, or China.
- Consider various forms of monarchy during this era and how they were legitimated (divine right, constitutionality, Mandate of Heaven, etc.).
- Compare the growing Atlantic slave trade with other systems of unfree labor (for example, serfdom in medieval Europe, serfdom in Russia, or the Arab slave network in Africa).
- Examine the likenesses and differences between the global economy that emerged after European exploration and the international trading networks that existed beforehand (also compare and contrast both with the globalization of the world economy during the late twentieth and early twenty-first centuries).
- Compare the European Age of Discovery with earlier efforts at exploration, such as Zheng He's or Ibn Battuta's.
- What features distinguish the kingdoms and empires of Africa or the Americas from those in Europe and Asia? What features did they have in common?
- Compare the different approaches of various European nations to colonization (both in the Americas and worldwide).
- How were empires built by Europeans? By African states? By Asian nations?

Europe: Reformation, Absolutism, and Enlightenment

CHAPTER 13

- The Protestant Reformation and Catholic Counter-Reformation
- Absolute monarchies versus parliamentary monarchies
- The movable-type (Gutenberg) printing press
- The scientific revolution and the heliocentric theory
- The Enlightenment (Age of Reason)
- The agricultural revolution and the Columbian exchange
- Urbanization and the appearance of a middle class
- Mercantilism, capitalism, and proto-industrialization
- The Atlantic slave trade

The years between the mid-1400s and late 1700s—often referred to as Europe's early modern period—were years of political, religious, intellectual, and socioeconomic transformation. European nations grew stronger and more stable. New Christian churches, the Protestant denominations, were born. Until approximately 1600, the Renaissance spread northward from Italy, affecting all of Europe. Afterward, the scientific awareness and intellectual sophistication of Europe (at least its upper classes) increased by leaps and bounds. The continent's population grew and diversified. Europeans improved their agricultural techniques, and their technological aptitude increased, and they took the first steps in building modern industrial and commercial economies.

In addition, Europe's global power skyrocketed during the early modern period. The Europeans did not invent gunpowder weaponry, nor were they the first to use it successfully. In the long term, though, they used it most efficiently. Also, as described in Chapter 14, it was during these years that Europe, unlike any other major civilization, explored most of the globe, then conquered and colonized a vast portion of it. In the 1400s, Europe was simply one of many major civilizations, and a relatively small, weak one. By the end of the 1700s, it was among the most powerful; and its military, diplomatic, and economic might would only increase in the 1800s.

THE PROTESTANT REFORMATION AND ITS AFTERMATH

The Crisis of European Catholicism

For more than a thousand years, there had been only one major Christian denomination in most of Europe: Roman Catholicism. (Eastern Orthodoxy was important in Byzantium and eastern Europe.) As described in Chapter 6, the Catholic Church enjoyed an immense amount of prestige, power, and wealth during most of the medieval era.

During the 1300s and 1400s, the church entered a period of long-term crisis. For most of the 1300s, the papacy was transferred by force to the French city of Avignon, making the church look weak. For forty years in the late 1300s and early 1400s, there were rival popes, each claiming allegiance from all Catholics, causing great confusion. The church hierarchy grew notoriously corrupt in the 1400s, selling church offices and granting certificates of forgiveness for sins (indulgences) in exchange for money. As years passed, more people came to see the church as hypocritical and too concerned with money and power. This feeling grew both among ordinary people and scholars, monks, and priests. Until the early 1500s, though, the church proved able to crush any opposition.

The Protestant Churches

Real change began in 1517, when a German monk, **Martin Luther**, protested the sale of indulgences in his hometown. In his Ninety-five Theses, Luther launched a general attack against church abuses and certain parts of Catholic doctrine. When the church ordered him to recant, or retract, his criticisms, he refused and was excommunicated. Quickly, what started as a simple dispute grew into a complete rupture of the Catholic Church. In the 1520s, Luther, now a fugitive, founded a new church, Lutheranism, the first of Europe's Protestant denominations.

With the **Protestant Reformation** under way, other movements soon emerged. The French scholar **John Calvin** established a theocratic community in the Swiss city of Geneva and preached an even more extreme form of Protestantism. Calvinism caught on in France (the Huguenots, an oppressed minority), the Dutch Republic (the Reformed Church), parts of England (the Puritans), and Scotland (the Presbyterians). In England, Henry VIII, previously a staunch defender of Catholicism, declared his country to be Protestant (mainly for political and marital reasons, not religious ones), forming the **Church of England**, also known as the **Anglican Church**.

Many beliefs and practices separated Protestants from Catholics. In the beginning, Lutheran and Calvinist churches favored institutional simplicity, in contrast to the bureaucracy and political power of the Catholic Church. Protestants did not venerate the saints or the Virgin Mary the way Catholics did. Rituals and sacraments were less important to them. Priests were allowed to marry. Most important was the concept of **salvation by grace**, the belief that only God's grace—not good works, observance of rituals, or the power of the pope—could bring a worshipper to heaven. (Calvin's doctrine of **predestination** took the idea further, arguing that whether a person would be saved or not was known to God from the beginning of time.) This belief accounted for the lack of emphasis on ritual and sacraments. It also led Lutherans and Calvinists to emphasize a pure, sincere relationship with God. They were encouraged to read the Bible for themselves (unlike Catholics), making education and literacy important to them.

Not all Protestants thought alike. Calvinist churches tended to be more puritanical and severe. In many ways, the Anglican Church was not far removed from the Catholic Church. During the religious wars of the 1500s and 1600s, Lutherans sometimes fought Calvinists. In England, the Anglican majority persecuted the minority Puritans almost as heavily as it did English Catholics.

The Catholic Counter-Reformation and Religious War

In response to the Protestant Reformation, the Catholic Church underwent change in the mid-to-late 1500s, a process known as the Catholic Counter-Reformation (sometimes simply the Catholic Reformation). At the Council of Trent (1545–1563), the church worked to eliminate the worst of its financially and spiritually corrupt practices. To increase its appeal and compete with Protestant churches for worshippers, the church sponsored the creation of impressive religious art and architecture (helping give birth to the Baroque movement). The church also stiffened religious discipline: it reaffirmed the authority of the pope, gave new powers to the Holy Inquisition, and created an Index of Forbidden Books. It also approved the formation of a new religious order, the Jesuits (Society of Jesus), whose priests and monks worked tirelessly as missionaries, teachers, and diplomats to combat Protestantism.

From the 1520s through the 1640s, Europe was plagued by a series of religious wars, as the papacy and Catholic monarchs attempted to halt the Protestant tide and even force Protestants to return to the Catholic fold. The first serious conflicts were in Switzerland (where civil war erupted in the 1520s) and the Holy Roman Empire (where, in the 1540s and 1550s, Catholic forces won but were forced by political factors to compromise and allow some German states to remain Protestant). Religious violence rocked England and Scotland from the 1530s through the first half of the 1600s. The Dutch war of independence from Spain, which began in the 1560s and lasted eighty years, was motivated largely by the desire of the Dutch to remain Calvinist, even in the face of Spanish religious oppression. During the last half of the 1500s, France tore itself apart in a series of bloody civil wars between the Catholic majority and Calvinist (Huguenot) minority. The failed attack of the Spanish Armada in 1588 was part of Spain's attempt to defeat Elizabeth I and destroy English Protestantism. The last and deadliest of the religious wars was the Thirty Years' War (1618–1648), which pitted Spain, the Holy Roman Empire, and Catholic German states against the Dutch, the Danes, the Swedes, and Protestant German states (England lent financial support but did not fight). For political reasons, Catholic France sided with the Protestant powers, who won in the end.

> **TIP**
>
> Europe's religious wars were particularly brutal. All sides felt justified by their beliefs in committing horrible atrocities. These wars tended to last a long time, and they frequently involved women, children, and other civilians. They took place at the same time that Europe's armies were growing larger and starting to use **gunpowder weaponry** full-scale, a fact that made them even deadlier. After the Thirty Years' War came to its close in 1648, religious strife and persecution did not end, but the age when major wars were primarily about religion was over.

Religious Divisions in Europe, ca. 1600.
For centuries, Christianity had been divided into two large denominations, Eastern Orthodoxy and Roman Catholicism. In most of Europe, the latter had been predominant. Starting with the Protestant Reformation in 1517, however, new religious rifts began to appear. By the end of the sixteenth century, western and northern Europe were divided into Catholic and Protestant camps, as shown in this map.

ABSOLUTE AND PARLIAMENTARY MONARCHIES

The Fading of Feudalism and The Emergence of European Nation-States

Although traces of feudalism survived, European countries in the early modern period were becoming more like **nation-states** in the contemporary sense: solid political units with fixed borders, a sense of national unity, and mostly (though never completely) homogenous populations in terms of language and ethnicity.

Much of this had to do with the strengthening of central state institutions. During the Middle Ages, institutions had been weak (if not nonexistent), forcing monarchs to resort to the feudal system. By the 1500s onward, however, this power structure was changing. Especially by the 1600s and 1700s, European states were developing **bureaucracies**, such as tax-collecting bodies, central banks, general staffs (for the army), admiralties (for the navy), and various ministries and cabinets. Although monarchs and aristocrats still controlled most positions of power, governments were becoming more rational and bureaucratic. Combined with advancements in communications and transport, the development of stronger state institutions allowed monarchs to centralize in a way they had not been able to during the Middle Ages.

Centralizing Rulers

During the late 1400s and 1500s, many rulers went to great lengths to centralize political power. Frequently, this meant competing with the noble (aristocratic) class, which was anxious to keep for itself the feudal privileges it had been granted during the medieval era. Monarchs who were especially successful in building strong states during these years include

- England: Henry VIII (founder of the Anglican Church and booster of English naval power) and Elizabeth I (who secured Anglicanism's place as England's official church, encouraged exploration, repelled the Spanish Armada of 1588, and sponsored Renaissance figures, such as Shakespeare)
- France: Louis XI (who conquered Burgundy) and Henry IV (who ended France's religious wars and granted Protestants the right to worship)
- Holy Roman Empire: Charles V (the Habsburg ruler who also governed Spain, encouraged colonization of the Americas, won wars against France and the Turks, and attempted to oppose Martin Luther and Protestantism)
- Spain: Philip II (son of Charles V; although it failed to conquer England in 1588, Spain under Philip II was the most powerful nation in Europe and benefited from its colonial exploitation of the Americas)
- Russia: Ivan III (who threw off Mongol rule and united Russia under Moscow's governance) and Ivan IV (known as "the Terrible" for the extreme violence he used to gain control over his noble class)

Many of these rulers also emerged as strong—if not always successful—military leaders during the Protestant Reformation and the religious wars following it.

By the 1600s and 1700s, two major forms of monarchy emerged. The more centralized form was absolutism, the less centralized was parliamentarism.

Absolute Monarchy

In absolute monarchies, the monarch is, at least in theory, all-powerful. There are no legal limitations to his or her power (although, in real life, even absolute monarchs were restricted in their actions by informal factors, such as a weak personality, uncooperative nobles, or an unreliable army). Absolutism in Europe was typically justified by the doctrine of divine right, according to which the monarch reigns by the will of God. (This is similar to the Mandate of Heaven in China, although divine right theory places no obligation on the monarch to rule justly.)

Europe's archetypal absolute monarch was Louis XIV of France, the Sun King who ruled from 1661 to 1715 (Louis ascended the throne in 1638, but he was only five years old at the time). Louis XIV created a highly centralized bureaucracy and national economy. He broke the power of his aristocracy and made it obey him. He built the largest army and navy that Europe had seen in centuries. He turned Paris and his palace of Versailles into grand, impressive centers of power. In many ways, Louis illustrated the strengths and weaknesses of absolute monarchy. He was an intelligent, forceful man who used his extensive powers to make France better-organized, better-run, and mighty. On the other hand, he involved France in too many wars, damaging the economy he had worked so hard to improve. Near the end of his reign, he persecuted the French Protestants, to whom his grandfather had guaranteed religious freedom.

France remained an absolute monarchy until the French Revolution of 1789. Other countries created absolute monarchies, attempting to imitate what Louis had done in France. In the late 1600s, the Austrian Habsburgs turned the Holy Roman Empire into an absolutist monarchy. Leopold I built great palaces around Vienna, centralized his government and economy, and fought wars against the Turks. (In 1683, the Turks nearly destroyed Austria in the **Siege of Vienna** but were turned back; afterward, the Austrians and their allies pushed the Turks steadily to the east.) The constant Turkish pressure on Austria's eastern frontier provided a good excuse for greater imperial control. In the eighteenth century, Maria Theresa and Joseph II carried on the tradition of absolutism in Austria.

The small but militarily powerful German state of Prussia became an absolute monarchy during the late 1600s and 1700s. **Frederick the Great** (1740–1786)—a great general as well as a skilled ruler—was one of the most effective absolute monarchs of his time. His victory over Austria, France, and Russia during the **Seven Years' War** (1756–1763) is considered to be one of the greatest military triumphs in European history. As with all absolute monarchs, however, the price Prussia paid for Frederick's talents was greater dictatorship and decreased freedoms.

The largest nation in the world, Russia, also emerged as an absolute monarchy. Thanks to Moscow's tsars, Russia already possessed a tradition of strong central authority. It was, however, economically, culturally, and scientifically backward compared with the West. (One effect of Mongol rule had been to cut Russia off from Europe during the Renaissance.) During the late 1600s and early 1700s, **Peter the Great** not only centralized political power but forced rapid, Western-style modernization on Russia. He also changed Russia's geopolitical orientation. Earlier, Russia had been mainly isolated from Europe and concerned with events in Asia. However, by fighting and winning a long, hard war with Sweden, Peter gained a place for Russia in the European diplomatic system. From 1700 onward, Russia would be Europe's great power of the east. It would become more European in nature, although never completely so. The other great absolute ruler of eighteenth-century Russia was Catherine the Great, who gained an international reputation for her intellectual achievements and military conquests.

Parliamentary Monarchy

Other governments, such as those in England and the Dutch Republic, took another direction. Even as these states centralized and modernized, the rulers became less powerful. These monarchies were known as **parliamentary monarchies**, because the ruler governed in conjunction with some kind of lawmaking body appointed by the aristocracy, elected by some or all of the people, or some combination of both.

During and after their war of independence from Spain, the Dutch wavered back and forth between centralized and decentralized rule. Either way, the *stadholder*—an executive leader who was not quite a king—had to share power with a larger council called the States General.

Even more famous was the system that emerged in England (which joined with Wales, Scotland, and Ireland to form Great Britain in the early 1700s). Since the 1200s, England's monarchs had been compelled to share power with the legislative body known as Parliament. Parliament gradually assumed greater powers until, in the 1600s, the balance of power shifted in its favor. The English Civil War (1640–1649) was partly about religion (Anglican vs. Puritan) but more about power (king vs. Parliament). The forces of Parliament won the civil war, killed the king (Charles I), and established the Commonwealth, ruled by Parliament (then by the general Oliver Cromwell).

When the royal family returned to England in the Restoration of 1660, the rivalry between monarch and Parliament remained (the three-way religious struggle between Catholic, Puritan, and Anglican caused problems as well). Another uprising—the Glorious Revolution of 1688—followed, and another king (William I, also the ruler of the Dutch Republic) was invited to take the throne. In this case, however, the invitation was conditional: William I had to agree not only to an act of religious toleration but also to a **Bill of Rights**, which curtailed the powers of the monarch and made Parliament the dominant partner in English politics. From 1688 onward, Parliament grew steadily stronger, while the monarchy grew steadily weaker and more symbolic.

The advantages of parliamentary monarchy are clear from the English and Dutch examples. Both nations developed strong economies, powerful navies, urbanized societies, and intellectual and cultural outlooks that were relatively open and free from religious persecution. Although poverty and inequality existed in both countries, society was more flexible, and social advancement was more feasible than in absolute monarchies.

THE PRINTING PRESS, THE SCIENTIFIC REVOLUTION, AND ENLIGHTENMENT PHILOSOPHY

The Northern Renaissance and the Baroque

The level of intellectual sophistication rose constantly in Europe during these years. The Renaissance, which had begun in Italy during the 1300s, spread to the rest of Europe and continued till approximately 1600. Important figures in this later, **northern Renaissance** included the Dutch philosopher Desiderius Erasmus (known for his debates with Luther, as well as his satirical novel *In Praise of Folly*), the Spanish novelist Miguel de Cervantes (author of the classic *Don Quixote*), the English cleric Thomas More (who invented the term *utopia* in his book of the same name), and, also from England, the poet and playwright **William Shakespeare**.

The cultural style that followed the Renaissance was the **baroque**, which dominated painting and architecture from the early 1600s through the early 1700s. In music, it lasted longer, until the mid-to-late 1700s. Baroque culture emphasized the bold, the dynamic, the colorful, and the impressive. Another major trend of this era was the birth of opera.

The Movable-Type Printing Press and Its Effect on European Culture

A prime cause of early modern Europe's remarkable cultural growth was Johannes Gutenberg's movable-type printing press, invented in Germany in the 1430s (see Chapter 6).

The spread of Renaissance ideas from Italy to the rest of Europe was due largely to the printing press. The press had even more of an impact on the religious debates that preceded, then caused, the Protestant Reformation: Because an increasing number of people could read the Bible itself, not to mention the hundreds of essays and articles written for and against church reform, religious ideas had a much wider effect than they could have had before.

Renaissance Science and the Heliocentric Theory

Europe's scientific and technological aptitude increased during the early modern period. During the late Renaissance, certain thinkers and scholars were moving away from the intellectual orthodoxy of the Middle Ages, in which a fixed set of ideas from the age of ancient Greece and Rome (especially selected theories from the writings of Aristotle) were combined with Catholic doctrine.

During the mid-1500s, despite the continued control of the Catholic Church over European intellectual life, individuals such as the Flemish doctor Andreas Vesalius and the Polish astronomer Nicolaus Copernicus began to cross important scientific boundaries. Vesalius did pioneering work in the field of human anatomy. Copernicus provided mathematical proof for the heliocentric theory, according to which the earth and other planets revolve around the sun. The Catholic Church favored the geocentric theory, in which the earth—home to what the church considered God's greatest creation, human beings—was at the center of the universe. It took more than another century before the heliocentric theory was accepted as fact throughout Europe.

The Scientific Revolution

The pace of scientific discovery accelerated during the 1600s and early 1700s, which are commonly spoken of as a time of Scientific Revolution in Europe. Early in the 1600s, thinkers such as René Descartes of France and Roger Bacon of England laid the groundwork for modern formal logic and revitalized the ancient concept of the scientific method.

Also in the 1600s, the German astronomer Johannes Kepler and the Italian physicist Galileo confirmed and popularized Copernicus's theories. (Kepler also proved that the planets move in elliptical, not circular, orbits.) In doing so, they ran afoul of the Catholic Church; Galileo was tried by the Inquisition and forced to reject his own scientific conclusions in public. (Protestant nations such as England and the Dutch Republic were safer havens for scientific pioneers; only in the 1700s did it become less risky for those in Catholic countries to challenge church doctrine.)

Many of the ideas that make up humankind's basic understanding of science were discovered or proven during the Scientific Revolution. They include the states of matter (liquid, gas, or solid), the question of whether light consists of waves or particles, the fact that living creatures are made of cells, the existence of capillaries, the concept of the vacuum, and the science of statistics. Among the scientific instruments invented or perfected during these years are the telescope, the microscope, the pendulum clock, the thermometer, and the barometer.

The person who represents the Scientific Revolution at its peak is **Isaac Newton** (1642–1727) of England. Newton is famous for a number of ideas and discoveries, including his laws of motion, his thoughts on the concept of gravity, and his role in inventing the mathematical system of calculus. The publication of his mathematical work *Principia* (1687) is considered one of the most important moments in European intellectual history. Just as important, however, is the fact that Newton, more than any other figure of the Scientific Revolution, understood scientific thought as a totality. Newton took the discoveries and theories of his day and tied them together into a single system of thought—Newtonian physics—backed up by mathematical proof. Not until Einstein's development of the theory of relativity in the early twentieth century would Newton's fundamental principles be seriously challenged or altered.

The Age of Reason (The Enlightenment)

During the 1700s, the educated public of Europe (still a small segment of society, though it was growing) felt it was living in a culturally and intellectually advanced era. Europeans—at least the middle and upper classes—considered themselves to have left behind what they thought of as the intellectual crudeness and superstitious darkness of the Middle Ages and even the 1500s and 1600s, with their wars of religion. The Europeans of this era put great faith in the power of human logic and rationality, as well as the recent discoveries of the Scientific Revolution, to solve problems and understand the world around them. Accordingly, it was common to refer to the 1700s as the **Age of Reason** or the **Age of Enlightenment**.

Enlightenment culture valued not just science but also philosophy and ideas about how to make human society and government more just, efficient, and humane. Philosophical societies, salons, and literary circles appeared in all the major cities of the Western world during the 1700s, from Boston and Philadelphia in the United States to St. Petersburg in Russia. Among the most important centers of Enlightenment thought were Edinburgh, London, and, most famously, Paris.

Women played a significant role in the Enlightenment. More women from the upper (and even middle) classes were gaining educations and proving that they were intellectually equal to men. A number of women became renowned for important Enlightenment writings and activities, including **Mary Wollstonecraft** of England (author of *A Vindication of the Rights of Women*) and Catherine the Great, Empress of Russia. Upper-class women, particularly in France, played a key part in organizing and hosting the salons at which much Enlightenment discussion and debate took place.

Among the most prominent Enlightenment philosophers were John Locke of England (an early figure), and **Voltaire**, Denis Diderot, and the Baron Charles de Montesquieu (from France). A later Enlightenment figure was Jean-Jacques Rousseau, also of France. All of these thinkers, as well as others, shared a faith in order and logic.

Beyond that, however, not all of them had the same ideas about politics and society. All believed that government should be rationally organized and fairly regulated. Most believed in freedom of expression, opinion, and religion. Some, however, were monarchists (they simply felt that the monarch should govern according to law, not tyranny). Others, such as Rousseau, believed in granting more political power to ordinary people, although Rousseau viewed women as inferior to men.

Some Enlightenment philosophers remained Christian (although they opposed religious war). Others, especially Voltaire, opposed organized religion as a flawed human institution, and some became atheists altogether. Nonetheless, their common emphasis on reason and progress bound Enlightenment thinkers together. As described in Chapter 20, Enlightenment ideas played a crucial role in motivating several revolutions at the end of the 1700s, including those in America and France.

SOCIETY AND ECONOMICS

Population Growth and Class Diversification

The 1500s and 1600s were a time of demographic and economic crisis in Europe. Ecologically, Europe experienced a cooling period referred to by historians as the Little Ice Age, and famines were common. The wars of religion not only caused many combat deaths but also spread disease and caused mass starvation. Agricultural techniques remained relatively primitive. Populations declined or stayed level, depending on year and region.

Many changes came during the 1700s. Environmental conditions improved. New foods from the Americas, especially corn and the potato, revitalized European agriculture (on this Columbian Exchange, see Chapters 14 and 19). New ideas and methods for effective food production also emerged; this agricultural revolution included soil aeration, the systematic use of manure, the adoption of iron plows instead of wooden ones, and the scientific rotation of crops. The number and severity of famines decreased, and crop yields grew larger.

As a result, Europe's population grew considerably during the 1700s. In addition, it began to diversify. As before, the vast majority of Europeans were peasants. At the top, royal families and noble classes made up a tiny (but powerful) segment of society. However, a steadily increasing percentage of people in Europe made their living as craftsmen and shopkeepers—or even merchants, bankers, and professionals, such as doctors and lawyers. Such people formed a growing (but still relatively small) middle class. A related development was increased urbanization. All these trends would accelerate in the 1800s.

Mercantilism, Capitalism, and Proto-Industrialization

The economic philosophy that prevailed during most of the early modern period was mercantilism, which advocated strict state control over economic activity and the exploitation of colonies (as sources of raw materials and as markets for the home country's manufactured goods).

As part of the Enlightenment, a new economic theory appeared, based on the concept of free trade, competition, and the market forces of supply and demand:

capitalism. The most famous of its early supporters was the Scottish economist **Adam Smith**, who made a case for the new doctrine in *The Wealth of Nations* (1776). Capitalism became the Western world's dominant approach to economics in the modern era.

Although true, full-scale industrialization did not occur in Europe until the end of the 1700s, a growing number of people were becoming involved in manufacturing during the early and mid-1700s (and even the late 1600s). They were also making use of machines and methods like cottage industry in ways that can be considered proto-industrial. This **proto-industrialization** was the immediate precursor to the Industrial Revolution of the late 1700s and early 1800s.

A final note about early modern European economics: because of the Age of Exploration, international trade became a key part of European economic activity. A great deal of Europe's wealth during these years was directly or indirectly connected with the **Atlantic slave trade**.

Women in Early Modern Europe

The status and rights of women changed considerably in early modern Europe. On the whole, women of the upper class gained greater access to education and participated more actively in intellectual life. Many women in the emerging middle class became more educated and assumed a greater economic role as business partners, bookkeepers, and operators of various enterprises. Women of all classes gained more control over when and whom they married, as well as divorce, childbirth, inheritance, and similar issues.

In no sense, however, were women considered equal to men, intellectually or economically. Nor did they have equal status or rights. Rates of death during childbirth were still high. Women made up the majority of victims—approximately 75 percent—in the witch hunts of the 1500s and 1600s. Both Catholicism and the new Protestant faiths maintained that women were inferior to and more sinful than men, and both used arguments based on scripture to reinforce these notions.

Women made significant progress in cultural and intellectual life. Many Catholic nuns maintained a high level of education. Protestantism's emphasis on literacy led upper- and middle-class women to gain at least some degree of learning.

A number of painters were women. Women took part in scientific work, although they were not allowed to become university faculty (except on extremely rare occasions) or join scientific societies. Women also turned to writing and philosophy, especially during the eighteenth century. Like Mary Wollstonecraft and others, they played a crucial part in the Enlightenment.

Some of the most important monarchs of early modern Europe were women. Among them were Isabella of Castile, Elizabeth I of England, Maria Theresa of Austria, and Catherine the Great of Russia.

QUICK REVIEW

1. Which of the following best describes the general European sentiment toward religious affairs just before the 1500s?

    (A) Most people felt a devout, unquestioning allegiance to the Catholic Church.
    (B) Many people were turning toward Calvinist forms of worship.
    (C) Most people had become altogether apathetic about religion.
    (D) Many people doubted the Catholic Church's ability to provide spiritual leadership.
    (E) Most people were turning toward the teachings of Martin Luther.

2. Which of the following is NOT part of Lutheran doctrine?

    (A) Good works are sufficient as a means of achieving salvation.
    (B) Clergy should be allowed to marry.
    (C) Rituals and sacraments are less important than one's relationship with God.
    (D) A good believer should read the Bible diligently.
    (E) Salvation can be attained only by the grace of God.

3. What European country below did NOT develop an absolute form of monarchy during the 1600s and 1700s?

    (A) the Austrian Empire
    (B) the Netherlands
    (C) Spain
    (D) France
    (E) Russia

4. Which of the following is most likely to be a feature of parliamentary systems of monarchy?

    (A) higher levels of political repression
    (B) greater degree of religious intolerance
    (C) rigid class structures
    (D) elimination of poverty
    (E) flexible social systems

5. Europe's so-called Scientific Revolution accomplished which of the following?

    (A) led to the triumph of the geocentric theory
    (B) promoted the scientific theories of Aristotle and Galen
    (C) built on Descartes's and Bacon's revival of the scientific method
    (D) immediately swept away Catholicism's authority over intellectual affairs
    (E) provided universal education for the population of Europe

6. What grand and dynamic artistic and musical movement was largely associated with the Catholic Counter-Reformation?

    (A) the Renaissance
    (B) the baroque
    (C) rococo
    (D) romanticism
    (E) surrealism

7. Which of the following is NOT true about the emergence of capitalism in Europe?

    (A) One of the earliest advocates of capitalism was Adam Smith.
    (B) The rise of capitalism paralleled the rapid growth of Europe's middle class.
    (C) Capitalism operated according to the principle of economic competition.
    (D) Capitalist theory favored the lessening of governmental control over economic activity.
    (E) Capitalism involved greater governmental control over economic activity.

8. Which of the following applies to the early development of industrialization in Europe?

    (A) A period of proto-industrialization during the 1600s and 1700s preceded the Industrial Revolution.

    (B) The steam engine fueled industrial development during the late 1600s.

    (C) There was almost no industrial or proto-industrial activity in Europe before the end of the 1700s.

    (D) European industrialization was hindered by the rise of capitalism.

    (E) Initiative on the part of the aristocracy was chiefly responsible for Europe's early industrialization.

9. Enlightenment thought is best characterized by which of the following?

    (A) a complete rejection of religious faith

    (B) a conviction that logic and reason were capable of solving social and political problems

    (C) active advocacy of the rights of women to vote

    (D) support of the established political order

    (E) a deep faith in religious principles

10. Who among the following was associated with Enlightenment philosophy?

    (A) Shakespeare

    (B) Voltaire

    (C) Erasmus

    (D) all of the above

    (E) none of the above

Answers

1. **(D)** A growing number of Europeans began to believe that popes and priests were more concerned with wealth and power than spiritual leadership. This disillusionment with the Catholic Church paved the way toward the Protestant Reformation.

2. **(A)** The Lutheran doctrine does not recognize that an individual's completing good works would ensure one's place in heaven. Instead, a believer must trust in God that he or she will be saved. The other answers are examples of other aspects of Lutheran doctrine.

3. **(B)** The Netherlands became a parliamentary democracy. Its inhabitants enjoyed a relatively high amount of religious freedom, and a wider variety of intellectual and cultural practices were tolerated than in many other parts of Europe at the time.

4. **(E)** More flexible social systems emerged from parliamentary systems of monarchy because governments had less power to interfere with diverse cultural and social practices, and social mobility was more feasible than in absolute monarchies.

5. **(C)** Although the Scientific Revolution did not bring about universal education for all Europeans, or quickly overturn religious dogma in science, it ushered in a renewed interest in the ancient concept of the scientific method as opposed to blind acceptance of the ancients' often mistaken scientific teachings. Doing away with the geometric theory was one of the Scientific Revolution's signal accomplishments.

6. **(B)** Baroque art and architecture were supported by the Catholic Church to increase its appeal to average worshippers in its competition with Protestant churches for souls. The Baroque style of religious art and architecture was very ornate and moved many people with its splendor and powerful presentation.

7. **(E)** Capitalism, unlike mercantilism, advocates a smaller role for government in economic affairs. All the other answers accurately describe capitalism.

8. **(A)** Proto-industrialization wa a part of European economic life as early as the 1600s. The steam engine did not appear until the 1700s; the middle class, not the aristocracy, did the most to encourage industrialization; and capitalism helped, not hindered, the process of industrialization.

9. **(B)** Enlightenment thinkers chose to rely on human reason and logic to solve problems, rather than superstitions and religious doctrine. On other issues, their opinions often varied.

10. **(B)** Voltaire (1694–1778) was a writer and philosopher who criticized religious fanaticism and championed toleration. His plays, such as *Candide*, were witty and sarcastic. They often attacked religious intolerance.

Age of Discovery, Age of Imperialism: The Western Campaign of Exploration and Colonization

---

CHAPTER 14

- Exploration, colonization, and the rise of the West
- The compass and improved naval technology
- Gunpowder weaponry
- Trade and missionary activity
- Slavery and resource extraction
- Major explorers and conquistadors
- Trading companies

Between the early-to-mid 1400s and the mid-to-late 1700s, the nations of Europe accomplished what no other civilization had done: they explored the wider world around them, discovered how to sail around the globe, and mapped the planet's major oceans and landmasses.

With this knowledge came might and wealth. From the beginning of their campaign of world exploration, the nations of Europe conquered, colonized, and forced open foreign markets. European explorers and generals were aided by superior technology, the vulnerability of many non-Europeans to European diseases, and, in many cases, sheer ruthlessness.

The legacy of Europe's age of exploration is mixed. On one hand, exploration gave the nations of Europe an unprecedented amount of geographical and scientific knowledge. Colonization made Europe rich and powerful. It was during the years of exploration—and largely *because* of exploration—that Europe ceased to be one of the smallest and weakest of the world's important civilizations, and started to become the dominant culture on the planet.

On the other hand, Europe paid a great moral and ethical price for the knowledge and power it gained from exploration and colonization, which went hand-in-hand with war, greed, prejudice, religious intolerance, and slavery. Many parts of the world remained under European rule for hundreds of years. Even now, the long-standing tensions left over between Western nations and their former colonies continue to have an impact on international relations.

> **NOTE**
>
> In general, the environments, populations, economies, and political systems of many peoples of the world were altered enormously by Europe's outward expansion. The effects of the Europeans' sudden incursion into other parts of the globe are detailed in other chapters in this unit.

ECONOMIC MOTIVATIONS AND TECHNOLOGICAL CAPABILITIES

Why and how did the Europeans become the first to explore the world? For many centuries, the peoples of Europe had been much less technologically and scientifically advanced than their neighbors in the Middle East or countries such as China. Any observer during the medieval era would have thought it unlikely that Europe, only a short time later, would emerge as the leader in world exploration.

Until the 1400s, Europeans' geographic knowledge was limited. They knew the Mediterranean, Baltic, and North seas well. Africa, the Middle East, Asia, and even Russia were unknown, inaccessible, or impassable. For the time being, the only outlet was the Atlantic Ocean, which was frighteningly unfamiliar.

Economic Motives for Exploration

The Europeans' primary motivation for exploring was economic. During the Middle Ages, the nations of Europe had become aware of the fabulous wealth of other parts of the world, especially to the east. Europeans also knew how sophisticated and desirable many eastern goods were.

> **NOTE**
>
> Mediterranean trade, greater knowledge about the Middle East gained during the Crusades, and the tales of Marco Polo all whetted European appetites for the wealth of far-off places such as China, the Indies, and Japan.

By the 1400s, Europeans were dreaming of silk, metal goods, spices, fruit, jewels and precious metals, and other items unknown or in short supply in their own lands. If they could reach the Far East directly, rather than trading with middlemen in the Middle East, they would be able to gain access to these goods and make tremendous profits.

New Navigational and Maritime Technology

If Europeans were interested in exploring by the 1400s, they needed the technology and knowledge to do so. Already by the 1300s, Europeans had learned the secret of the compass from the Chinese. Better knowledge of the stars (gained largely from the Arabs) and better navigational instruments, such as the astrolabe and sextant, made it possible for European sailors to venture farther from shore without getting lost.

Naval technology improved as well. During the 1300s and 1400s, the Europeans began to build large, long ships, allowing them to sail faster, carry larger food supplies, and cover greater distances. Larger ships were also able to crest the huge waves of the open ocean without capsizing or breaking apart. Finally, large stern rudders and advanced systems of sails and rigging allowed ships to travel in almost any direction the captain wanted to go, even if the wind was not favorable.

Finally, European nations were beginning to use gunpowder weapons by the 1300s and 1400s. Although it was not until the 1500s and 1600s that Europeans invented the huge gunships that let them to carry massive firepower to every part of the globe, European sailors and soldiers came equipped with muskets, pistols, and small artillery pieces. Not only could they use gunpowder weapons at sea, but they would be able to use them against less technologically advanced native populations when they reached new lands.

THE IBERIAN WAVE OF EXPLORATION: SPAIN AND PORTUGAL

The first European nations to explore the wider Atlantic world were Portugal and Spain. Both were on Europe's Atlantic frontier, close to Africa and the islands off Africa's coast. They also had a great deal of maritime experience in the Mediterranean, thanks to trade and a long series of naval wars against the Ottoman Turks.

Portuguese and Spanish exploration during the 1400s and early 1500s proceeded in two ways. First, the Portuguese attempted to reach the lands of the Far East by inching their way down the coast of Africa, rounding the continent, and then sailing across the Indian Ocean to Asia. Second, and in the meantime, the Spanish—competing with the Portuguese—attempted to find their own route to Asia by sailing west, around the world. Famously, the Spanish found the continents of North and South America instead, as well as an ocean previously unknown to them: the Pacific. Quickly, both countries figured out the relationship between the Atlantic and Pacific oceans.

> **NOTE**
>
> By the 1520s, the Europeans succeeded in sailing around the globe for the first time in human history.

Henry the Navigator and Portugal's Exploration of West Africa

The Portuguese began Europe's age of exploration thanks mainly to their prince, known popularly as Henry the Navigator (1394–1460). He and his successors sent out many voyages to the west and south, attempting to find a sea route to India and the Far East. The Portuguese claimed several Atlantic island groups, including the Madeiras and Azores, and traveled down Africa's western coast, conquering and exploring. They seized the Moroccan port of Ceuta in 1411, and soon afterward, the Cape Verde Islands. The Portuguese continued to expand along Africa's western shore, taking over or domineering areas like Kongo (see Chapter 18). In 1488, Bartholomeu Díaz reached the southern tip of Africa. In honor of the completion of his first leg of the journey to India, the Portuguese named the tip of Africa the Cape of Good Hope.

Spain, Christopher Columbus, and the New World

The Spanish, distracted by the Reconquista (see Chapter 6), were not as quick as the Portuguese to start exploring. Falling behind meant that, if the Spanish wanted their own sea route to Asia, they would have to try something different. The result was the famous voyage of the Italian captain Christopher Columbus in 1492, sponsored by King Ferdinand and Queen Isabella.

What Columbus proposed was to sail west in order to reach China and India. The boldness of his plan lay not in the idea that the world was round, because that was well known to most educated Europeans. What made his proposal striking was his belief that the world was small enough that an expedition would be able to sail from Spain to Asia without getting lost or running out of food and water. He set sail in August 1492, and his ships reached the islands of the Caribbean on October 12, 1492.

> **NOTE**
>
> Europe's encounter with the New World—the continents of North and South America—changed forever the history of the entire globe.

Columbus remained convinced all his life that he had found the Indies (hence the mistaken term Indians for Native Americans), but the Spanish and Portuguese realized quickly that what he had found were lands completely unknown to them.

Spanish and Portuguese Exploration, 1492–1529.
The first European nations to colonize the wider world were Spain and Portugal. Their successes are attested to in this map. The north–south lines of demarcation were established by the papacy, to whose authority both nations, being Catholic, submitted.

The two countries turned to the pope to determine who would be allowed to claim which parts of the New World. In **lines of demarcation** agreed to in 1494 and 1529, the pope gave jurisdiction over most of South America and all of North America to the Spanish. The Portuguese received only Brazil.

Reaching India and Circumnavigating the Globe

By the end of the 1490s, the Spanish and Portuguese had two worlds to explore and conquer.

The Portuguese continued to sail eastward to India from the southern tip of Africa. In 1498, Vasco da Gama became the first European to reach India by sea. The profit from his voyage equaled sixty times the original investment, an indication of how lucrative the business of exploration eventually became.

Shortly thereafter, the Portuguese captain **Ferdinand Magellan** (sailing for Spain) led an expedition that tied together all previous efforts of the Spanish and Portuguese. Magellan was inspired by the 1513 discovery of Panama by the Spanish explorer Vasco de Balboa, the first European to sight the Pacific Ocean from the New World. Hoping to cross both oceans, Magellan's ships left Europe in 1519 and traversed the Atlantic. They rounded South America and made their way through the Pacific, returning to Europe in 1522 (although Magellan himself died along the way).

Spanish and Portuguese Colonization

Having reached Africa, Southeast Asia, and the Far East on one hand and the New World on the other, the Spanish and Portuguese began to establish a colonial presence in all these areas. In the Far East and Southeast Asia, many countries were too strong or too advanced for the Portuguese to conquer, and for the most part they settled for trade. Still, the Portuguese seized some areas, including the Indian port of Goa (1510), the thriving commercial center of Malacca (1511), and the island of Sri Lanka. As they had in West Africa, the Portuguese took over much of the East African coast, setting up strongholds in cities such as Mombasa and Zanzibar.

In the New World, the Portuguese moved into Brazil during the early 1500s. The Spanish built up their power in the Caribbean, using islands such as Cuba, Puerto Rico, and Hispaniola (today Haiti and the Dominican Republic) as bases.

The North and South American mainland fell to the **conquistadores**—generals who brought huge parts of both continents under Spanish control. Florida fell to Juan Ponce de León after 1513. From 1519 to 1521, **Hernán Cortés** waged a remarkably effective and brutal campaign against the Aztecs.

NOTE

Columbus's mistake is the reason that the American continents are not named after him, but after Amerigo Vespucci, who consciously mapped their coasts as new landmasses.

TIP

More details on how the Spanish and Portuguese treated their new colonies are contained in future chapters, especially Chapters 18 and 19.

The Aztec capital, Tenochtitlán, became Mexico City, headquarters of what the Spanish now called New Spain. Later, California, Arizona, New Mexico, Colorado, Texas, Missouri, Louisiana, and Alabama were taken over by other conquistadores, such as Hernando de Soto, Francisco de Coronado, and Álvar Cabeza de Vaca. Farther to the south, in the 1530s, **Francisco Pizarro** destroyed the mighty Incan Empire.

Both in Africa and the New World, Portuguese and Spanish colonies were originally intended to boost their home countries' power and wealth through the exploitation of raw materials. From the start, the Spanish and Portuguese attempted to use Native Americans as slaves. When that effort failed, they brought slaves to the New World from Africa.

THE NORTHERN WAVE: FRANCE, THE DUTCH REPUBLIC, AND ENGLAND

During the 1500s, other European nations began to explore and colonize. The most important were France, the Dutch Republic, and England.

For decades, the Spanish and Portuguese jealously guarded their geographic knowledge and navigational techniques. They were especially anxious to lock the countries of northern Europe out of Atlantic exploration. At stake were military power, immense wealth, and Catholic-Protestant rivalry.

Only after the middle of the 1500s were the French, Dutch, and English able to steal enough information, shadow enough Spanish and Portuguese ships, and gain enough knowledge about sea routes to begin their own exploration and colonization. During the 1500s and 1600s, for the French, English, and Dutch to explore and colonize typically meant also fighting the Spanish and Portuguese—either at sea or on land—as the new arrivals tried to take colonial territories away from the older powers.

> **NOTE**
>
> During the early 1500s, the only area that France, the Dutch Republic, and England were able to explore and settle was the northern coast of North America, which the Spanish saw as less desirable. One reason these countries explored here was their hope of finding an alternative route (a "northwest passage") to Asia through the Arctic.

French Exploration and Colonization

In the 1520s, the Italian captain Giovanni da Verrazano, commissioned by the French, surveyed North America's Atlantic coast. From 1534 to 1541, Jacques Cartier traced the course of the St. Lawrence River, the first step in France's settlement of Canada. France established its first cities in Canada in the early 1600s: Port Royal in Nova Scotia (1605) and Quebec, founded by Samuel Champlain (1608).

Later in the 1600s, the French moved southward, exploring the Great Lakes and major rivers. In 1673, Louis Joliet and Father Jacques Marquette, traveling west from the Great Lakes, discovered the Mississippi River and mapped its northern reaches. In 1682, René Robert de la Salle sailed

French, English, and Dutch Colonization by 1700.
By 1700, France, England, and the Netherlands had gained many imperial footholds in North America, South America, the Caribbean, Africa, and Asia.

NOTE

The principal reason for colonizing Canada was its rich supply of animal furs.

down the entire length of the Mississippi, claiming land for France, even though much of this territory was already under Spanish control. During the late 1600s and 1700s, the French took much of the Mississippi basin and some of the coast of the Gulf of Mexico away from the Spanish. This large expanse was called Louisiana (different from the state of the same name).

Dutch Exploration and Colonization

Dutch exploration was, at first, closely tied to the war of independence against Spain. Dutch strategy in the late 1500s and early 1600s was to fight the Spanish at sea and, if possible, disrupt connections with their colonies. The Dutch did the same to the Portuguese and, by the 1590s, were seizing colonies from them: the Spice Islands in 1595, the Southeast Asian port of Malacca in 1641, the island of Sri Lanka, much of West Africa, and a number of Caribbean islands. To manage their colonies in Asia, the Dutch formed the **Dutch East India Company** (1602). The Dutch also invaded Indonesia, where they maintained a colonial presence for hundreds of years. They ran pepper and spice plantations on the island of Sumatra. On Java, they established the colonial capital of Batavia (1619), now the Indonesian capital, Jakarta.

NOTE

In 1624, Dutch settlers purchased the island of Manhattan from the local Native Americans and built a city there called New Amsterdam. That city eventually became New York, after the English took it from the Dutch in the mid-1600s.

The Dutch colonized North America as well. In 1609, they commissioned the English sailor Henry Hudson to explore the bay and river that now bear his name.

English Exploration and Colonization

Although England did not begin a major campaign of exploration until after the mid-1500s, it established legal claim to parts of North America as early as the 1490s, thanks to the voyages of John Cabot, who attempted to find an Arctic passage to Asia through Canadian waters. During the mid-to-late 1500s, the English fought a series of naval wars with the Spanish, seeking to harass Spanish colonies or capture Spanish treasure ships returning from the New World. The English gained much navigational and geographic knowledge from these wars.

NOTE

Francis Drake, raiding Spanish ports, became the first Englishman to sail around the world (1577–1580).

In the 1600s, the English established their own colonies in North America, from the Carolinas to the Canadian border. Two colonies failed during the 1580s, but the English settlement of Jamestown, led by John Smith, gave the English a foothold in the New World. English Puritans, the so-called Pilgrims, came to America as well, seeking religious freedom. The first such Pilgrims sailed across on the *Mayflower,* which landed at Plymouth Rock in 1620.

The English made incursions into South Asia as well. Their first expedition to the Indies came in 1591. Shortly afterward, the English founded the **British East India Company** (1600) to manage economic—and, later, military—relations with South and Southeast Asia. The English were in northwestern India by 1608 and would gradually take over more of the subcontinent. The English seized the Southeast Asian port of Malacca from the Dutch in 1795.

NOTE

The English were eager to turn their colonies into genuinely permanent settlements (something other colonizing powers were for a long time less interested in doing).

As with the Spanish and Portuguese, the countries of the northern wave were eager to gain military strength and, especially, economic wealth from their colonies. Exploitation of natural resources—and of the native populations—was the norm. Like the Spanish and Portuguese, the French and English brought slaves to the New World from Africa (see Chapters 18 and 19).

QUICK REVIEW

1. Which European nation first began a sustained campaign of exploration?

   (A) France
   (B) Portugal
   (C) the Netherlands
   (D) England
   (E) Austria

2. What made Christopher Columbus's proposed voyage in 1492 unusual was

   (A) his new theory that the world was round.
   (B) that his recent invention, the compass, would shorten sailing times across the Atlantic.
   (C) his idea that the world was small enough for a ship to sail west from Europe to Asia.
   (D) his hope that an undiscovered continent lay to the west of Europe.
   (E) his intention to circumnavigate the globe.

3. Which of the following helped encourage the Europeans to explore the wider world?

   (A) Marco Polo's reports of the riches found in China
   (B) exposure to Middle Eastern trade during the Crusades
   (C) a desire for foodstuffs, especially spices, not available in Europe
   (D) all of the above
   (E) none of the above

4. What was Portugal's principal colony in Latin America?

   (A) Chile
   (B) Ecuador
   (C) Mexico
   (D) Belize
   (E) Brazil

5. Whose authority arbitrated Spain's and Portugal's rival claims in the New World?

   (A) the pope
   (B) the Holy Roman Emperor
   (C) the Prince of Portugal
   (D) the United Nations
   (E) the King of Spain

6. Which parts of the New World did the French colonize during the 1500s and 1600s?

   (A) Mexico and Brazil
   (B) Massachusetts and New York
   (C) Canada and the Mississippi Valley
   (D) the mid-Atlantic coast
   (E) Canada and Cuba

7. Primarily from which country did the Dutch seize colonies in Southeast Asia?

   (A) Spain
   (B) Portugal
   (C) England
   (D) France
   (E) none of the above

8. Which Spanish conquistador conquered the Aztecs and took Mexico for Spain?

   (A) Cortés
   (B) Pizarro
   (C) Coronado
   (D) Ponce de León
   (E) Cabeza da Vaca

9. Which of the following became England's first successful colony in North America?

   (A) Plymouth Rock
   (B) Charleston
   (C) Pennsylvania
   (D) Jamestown
   (E) New York

10. Early on, what factor played the greatest role in determining where France, England, and the Netherlands were able to explore and colonize?

    (A) their climatic preference for cooler environments
    (B) their relative technological backwardness in comparison to Spain and Portugal
    (C) their peace treaties with Spain and Portugal
    (D) the authority of the pope
    (E) Spain's and Portugal's temporary monopolies on navigational knowledge

Answers

1. **(B)** Portugal was geographically well positioned to embark on exploration by sea, as it is located on the Atlantic and is not far from Africa. Portugal also explored the Mediterranean, in pursuit of trade and in naval battles against the Ottoman Turks.

2. **(C)** The Spanish desired their own sea route to the Far East. Columbus assumed that his expedition could sail from Spain to India or China without running out of supplies or getting lost at sea.

3. **(D)** The Europeans wanted to explore new lands for various reasons, and all three of those listed here are correct.

4. **(E)** In the early 1500s, Portugal began colonizing Brazil. Like the Spanish, the Portuguese wanted to increase their country's wealth and power by exploiting the natural resources of South America.

5. **(A)** The pope acted as arbiter because both countries were predominantly Roman Catholic and the church still had political influence over them at the time.

6. **(C)** Owing to Jacques Cartier's early exploration of the St. Lawrence River, the French began to gain a foothold in Canada in the 1500s. By the 1600s, the French had established cities in what is now Nova Scotia and Quebec. In the late 1600s, French explorers discovered the Mississippi River. The French later managed to wrest control of some parts of the Mississippi basin from the Spanish.

7. **(B)** The colonies the Dutch seized from the Portuguese from the late 1500s to the mid-1600s included the Spice Islands, Malacca, Sri Lanka, colonies in west Africa, and some Caribbean islands.

8. **(A)** From 1519 to 1521, Cortés conquered the Aztecs in Mexico by using brutal methods. The Spanish renamed the Aztecs' capital Mexico City and called the area New Spain.

9. **(D)** First settled in 1607, Jamestown in present-day Virginia was England's first permanent colony in North America. Jamestown's economic success was due to the fact that the area's main crop was tobacco, which the English exported and sold to Europeans for high profits.

10. **(E)** For several decades, the Spanish and Portuguese successfully guarded their knowledge of geography and navigational technology. Spain and Portugal wanted to ensure their military power, wealth, and religious rivalry, but by the 1500s the other European powers also began to gain ground in the New World.

Islamic Empires in the Middle East and North Africa

- The gunpowder empires
- The Ottoman Empire and the sultan
- The capture of Constantinople (Istanbul)
- The janissaries
- Suleiman's conquests
- The siege of Vienna
- The millet system
- The harem

The unity of the single Islamic state, the Abbasid Caliphate, stretching from Spain to India, vanished during the 1200s. Decades of chaos and confusion followed, as Mongol warriors invaded and the Seljuk and Ottoman Turks rose up as regional powers.

Afterward, however, strong Islamic empires emerged in place of the fallen caliphate: the Ottoman Empire, the Safavid Empire in Persia, and the Mughal Empire in India (the last is described in Chapter 17). All three were highly centralized, technologically advanced, and militarily powerful. They are commonly referred to as the "gunpowder empires," because of their mastery of new weaponry and their effective use of it in accumulating regional might.

The grandest and most influential of the Islamic states was the Ottoman Empire. It was also the longest lasting, with a geopolitical role to play on three continents: Africa, Asia, and Europe. Its neighbor to the east, Persia's Safavid Empire, was also impressive. However, it was not as strong as the Ottoman state, and it did not survive nearly as long.

THE OTTOMAN EMPIRE

The Ottoman State

The Ottoman Turks, originally nomads migrating from Central Asia, established their own state in 1280. They rose in the late 1300s and 1400s to gain hegemony over most of the Middle East, restoring central authority to the region.

TIP

See Chapter 7 for more information about the Ottoman Turks.

Centralized authority was provided by the sultan. He ruled with the help of an elaborate bureaucracy, run by ministers called vizier (*wazir*), headed by the grand vizier, and provincial governors (beys and pashas). In the early 1500s, Selim I (1512–1520) claimed religious as well as political authority for the sultan, equating the Ottomans' right to rule the Islamic world with that of the Arab caliphates of bygone years.

The Islamic World's Gunpowder Empires, ca. 1629–1707.

The Blue Mosque, Istanbul, Turkey.
Officially the Sultan Ahmed Mosque, this seventeenth-century masterpiece is popularly known as the Blue Mosque. One of the great landmarks of Istanbul, the Blue Mosque is one of the many places of Islamic worship the Ottoman sultans constructed there after Mehmed II took the city, formerly Constantinople, from the Byzantine Empire. The Blue Mosque is unusual in having six minarets, rather than the usual four.

The sultan's position was hereditary, although the eldest son did not always inherit, largely because the sultan typically did not marry but fathered heirs with a number of concubines. A concubine whose son became the sultan's heir was known as the queen mother and generally enjoyed influence as an adviser to the sultan and her son. When a new sultan came to power, he often killed his brothers to eliminate potential competition. The preferred method of execution was strangling.

The Ottoman Military

The Ottoman Empire was a mighty conquest state. Under a series of militarily active sultans, it moved into southeastern Europe, and its navies gained sway over the eastern Mediterranean. One of the Ottomans' great triumphs was the destruction of the Byzantine Empire in 1453. That year, the army of Mehmed II captured the city of Constantinople, after bombarding it with 26-foot-long cannons that fired ammunition weighing 1,200 pounds. Mehmed turned Constantinople into his new capital, Istanbul.

Further conquests followed. Selim I moved into North Africa. Ottoman forces pushed farther into Europe, along the Danube River. They seized the Romanian province of Wallachia in 1476, then paused for the next four and a half decades (this time was spent fighting in the Middle East and Africa, as well as consolidating domestic affairs).

A larger and more successful thrust into Europe came under **Suleiman I the Magnificent** (1520–1566), greatest of the Ottoman sultans. Suleiman resumed the Ottoman assault on the Danube and Romania, Hungary, and the Holy Roman Empire. By 1529, the Ottomans had reached the outskirts of Vienna, where Christian armies finally stopped them. The Turks were pushed back somewhat, but they now controlled a vast part of southeastern Europe. Moreover, the Turkish fleet enjoyed almost complete superiority in the Mediterranean until the end of the 1500s—and remained a deadly enemy even afterward. The Ottoman presence in Europe lingered into the early 1900s.

During the 1500s and first two-thirds of the 1600s, the Ottoman Empire was at its military and organizational peak. As one of the Islamic world's three "gunpowder empires," Ottoman Turkey was for a time innovative in its adoption of military technology and capable in administering its armies and navies.

The sultans supplemented the traditional cavalry (outdated and not entirely trustworthy) with elite soldiers called **janissaries** (from *yeni cheri*, or "new troops"). They were essentially slaves but given many privileges. The infantrymen were equipped with muskets, and they received advanced training. For many years, the janissary system, although harsh, kept Ottoman Turkey at the forefront of world military affairs.

> **NOTE**
> Janissaries were recruited at childhood from conquered Christian communities, converted to Islam, and raised to be loyal to the sultan.

Diversity and Religious Policy

Also during the 1500s and early 1600s, the Ottomans were efficient at governing their large territory as well as the diverse population that lived there. The Ottomans ruled not only Sunni Muslims but also members of the Shiite minority. They governed Jews, in addition to Christians: Orthodox, Catholic, Protestant, and smaller denominations. Many tongues—especially Turkish, Arabic, and Persian—were spoken in the empire.

Both for political and economic reasons, the sultans practiced relative religious tolerance: non-Muslims were allowed to convert to Islam if they wished but were not forced to do so. They did not have equal rights, they were not permitted to serve in the military, and they had to pay a special head tax. There were occasional abuses. Still, non-Muslims were, on the whole, not treated badly. Ottoman policy kept the peace, and the extra tax revenue was economically beneficial. Each religious group (Muslims included) was grouped into an administrative unit called a *millet* ("nation"): There was one for Jews, another for Orthodox Christians, and so on.

Women in the Ottoman Empire

Among the Ottoman elite, women played influential but informal roles. The sultan's mother (the queen mother) ran the household, controlled marriage alliances, and could even be involved in diplomatic relations with foreign officials.

Despite its popular reputation, the harem ("sacred place") was not simply a collection of concubines for the sultan's pleasure. It was a complex elite social network. Male members of the harem (mostly eunuchs) were trained for military or administrative positions, while concubines were educated to read the Qur'an, to sew, and to perform music. Members of the harem were ranked by status, and some could leave the harem to marry officials. Few of the women in the imperial harem were used for sexual purposes. In fact, most of them were members of the sultan's extended family. These women also gained influence over male rulers by raising them as boys and training them to respect their guidance.

> **NOTE**
> Many members of the harem were originally slaves (slaves could not be Muslim) or prisoners.

Outside the imperial family, women on the whole were not seen in public. However, they had the right to own property, retain it after marriage, and could buy, sell, and inherit real estate. They could also testify for themselves in court.

The Long Decline of the Ottoman Empire

The last truly gifted Ottoman sultan was Suleiman the Magnificent. In addition to being a talented commander, he was an excellent domestic ruler. Because of his gift for governance, he is often referred to as Suleiman the Lawgiver. Few of the sultans who followed had Suleiman's qualities, and many were mediocre or worse.

NOTE

By the 1800s, the Ottoman Empire was, in a bit of black humor, routinely referred to as the "sick man of Europe."

In the late 1600s, the Ottomans made one last attempt at a major European offensive. The attack almost succeeded but was turned back in 1683. That year, the Turks, as they had in 1529, reached Vienna, capital of the Holy Roman Empire. The siege of Vienna was seen at the time as a great turning point; had the city fallen, even more of Europe would have been open to Muslim conquest. At the last minute, Vienna was saved by a massive Austrian counteroffensive (greatly assisted by other Catholic allies, especially the Poles, whose cavalry played a key role in the battle). Afterward, the Europeans pushed the Ottomans back to the east. The Turks were not expelled from Europe, but lost much territory from 1683 to 1718.

During the 1700s, the Ottomans fought the Europeans—especially the Austrians and Russians—frequently. However, they never again seriously threatened Europe, and their power declined steadily during the 1700s and 1800s.

Ottoman Culture

NOTE

Thanks in part to Europe's Scientific Revolution (see Chapter 13) and in part to the Turks' own complacency, the Ottoman Empire started to fall behind the nations of Europe in terms of learning and innovation.

The culture of the Ottoman Empire was sophisticated. Its level of intellectual advancement was high. However, after the 1500s and early 1600s, the Ottomans lost the scientific and technological advantages they had enjoyed over their European neighbors.

Nonetheless, the Ottomans were skilled at art, literature, and music. Perhaps the field at which they excelled the most was architecture. The best-known Ottoman architect is Sinan: during the mid-1500s, he designed eighty-one mosques with large domes and tall, thin minarets. The Turks were also renowned for their mosaics.

NORTH AFRICA UNDER THE OTTOMAN EMPIRE

Just as North Africa had converted to Islam from the late 600s onward, much of the region fell to the Ottomans. In the early 1500s, Selim I conquered Egypt and claimed authority over all Muslims in North Africa.

The Turkish presence in North Africa was mainly restricted to the coast. To the south, the Ottomans made sure to control the trade routes crossing the Sahara. They also supervised trading towns along the Niger River and other waterways. Beyond that, the Turks ruled relatively lightly, leaving day-to-day government to local governors called pashas.

NOTE

Moving westward from Egypt, the Ottomans took most of Africa's northern coast. They captured the ports of Tripoli, Tunis, and Algiers, as well as many other cities.

THE SAFAVID EMPIRE IN PERSIA

Since Islam's early days, the land of Persia (now Iran) had been an important part of the Muslim world. It had been absorbed by the Arab caliphates and then, from the 1200s to the 1400s, controlled by various Mongol and Turkic warlords. At the beginning of the 1500s, under a new empire, it regained its independence.

In 1501, a fifteen-year-old boy rose to power in Persia, took the ancient title of shah, and proclaimed the Safavid Empire. Devoted Shiites, the Safavid shahs converted the majority of the Persian population to that denomination. Safavid Persia was commercially vibrant; the beautiful city of Isfahan was a great center of trade for silk, ceramic tile, and especially Persian rugs.

Militarily, the early Safavids were innovative and well organized. Like Ottoman Turkey and Mughal India, Safavid Persia was one of the Islamic world's gunpowder empires. Abbas I the Great (1587–1628) added gunpowder infantry (similar to the Ottoman janissaries) to his army.

Like the Ottoman Empire, Safavid Persia declined in the late 1600s and 1700s. The dynasty fell in 1723.

QUICK REVIEW

1. What group rose to dominate the Middle East during the 1400s and afterward?

   (A) the Safavid Persians
   (B) the Egyptian Mamluks
   (C) the Berbers
   (D) the Ottoman Turks
   (E) the Kurds

2. What was the greatest military triumph of the Ottoman Empire during the 1400s?

   (A) the invasion of Albania
   (B) the capture of Constantinople
   (C) the siege of Vienna
   (D) the battle of Mohács
   (E) the annexation of Moldavia

3. The janissaries were

   (A) elite gunpowder troops recruited from Christian communities.
   (B) aristocratic cavalry units from the Egyptian provinces.
   (C) mercenary crossbowmen from East Asia.
   (D) artillery specialists.
   (E) skilled naval commanders.

4. Which of the following applies to Suleiman I?

   (A) He was known as the Magnificent.
   (B) He led a highly successful campaign of conquest in southeastern Europe.
   (C) He was a wise and skilled domestic ruler.
   (D) all of the above
   (E) none of the above

5. What best describes the religious policy of the Ottoman rulers?

   (A) ruthless suppression of non-Islamic faiths
   (B) relative tolerance of religious minorities
   (C) complete acceptance of non-Islamic faiths
   (D) expulsion of non-Islamic minorities
   (E) gradual conversion from Islam to Christianity

6. The basic unit of religious categorization in the Ottoman Empire was

   (A) the exarchy.
   (B) the parish.
   (C) the *umma*.
   (D) the caste.
   (E) the *millet*.

7. What was one of the ways the sultans legitimated Ottoman rule?

   (A) by asserting the religious authority of the caliphs
   (B) by claiming the Mandate of Heaven
   (C) by means of the theory of divine right
   (D) by instituting democratic reforms
   (E) by stirring up tensions between Muslims and Christians

8. What moment marked the high point—and the end—of the Ottoman advance into Europe?

   (A) the 1476 capture of Wallachia
   (B) the 1521 seizure of Belgrade
   (C) the 1526 siege of Mohács
   (D) the 1683 siege of Vienna
   (E) the 1718 treaty of Passarowitz

9. Which of the following is true of the Ottoman harem?

   (A) It existed solely for the sultan's pleasure.
   (B) Except for the sultan and young boys, no males were involved in harem life.
   (C) Concubines and the queen mother exerted a substantial degree of informal influence.
   (D) all of the above
   (E) none of the above

10. Which of the following characterizes the Ottoman Empire during the 1700s?

   (A) healthy economic growth
   (B) steady political decline
   (C) successful military expansion
   (D) innovative semidemocratic reform
   (E) modernization within the Islamic establishment

Answers

1. **(D)** The Ottoman Empire was the most influential, largest, and longest-lasting Islamic state in world history. In the late 1400s and early 1500s, the Ottomans conquered parts of the Middle East and held control of these territories until the Paris Peace Conference, which ended World War I, stripped them of their Middle Eastern possessions.

2. **(B)** The Muslim Ottomans conquered Constantinople in 1453, destroying the Christian Byzantine Empire in the process. Constantinople soon was renamed Istanbul, which became the new capital of the Ottoman Empire.

3. **(A)** The Ottoman sultans recruited the janissaries to supplement the traditional, outdated cavalry. The janissaries were converted to Islam and raised to be loyal to the sultans. They helped maintain the Ottomans' military domination.

4. **(D)** Suleiman I is the most famous Ottoman sultan largely because of the three reasons listed here. During his reign, the Ottomans conquered lands of Eastern Europe. He was an effective lawgiver at home.

5. **(B)** The sultans practiced religious tolerance less out of humanity but for political and economic reasons. The Ottomans governed large territories filled with populations from diverse religious and social backgrounds and needed their cooperation.

6. **(E)** The word *millet* can be translated as "nation." Each religious group had its own administrative unit, which the Ottomans created largely for tax purposes and to keep track of different populations.

7. **(A)** By giving themselves status equal to the earlier caliphs, sultans claimed both religious and political authority over their territories.

8. **(D)** In 1683, the Ottomans besieged Vienna. However, they were not destined to control the city. The Austrians waged a successful counteroffensive, and the Europeans soon pushed the Ottomans back east.

9. **(C)** The queen mother was the mother of the sultan's heir. Concubines exerted informal influence by raising future male rulers and training them to respect their advice. Males, generally eunuchs, took part in harem life.

10. **(B)** By the 1700s, the Ottoman Empire began its steady decline in political influence and had lost much of its territory in eastern Europe. In the 1800s, the Ottoman Empire was considered by many to be the "sick man of Europe."

China, Japan, and East Asia

- The Ming dynasty
- The Manchu conquest and the Qing dynasty
- The European arrival in East Asia
- Silk and tea production
- Canton and trade protectionism
- Daimyo, samurai, and Japanese feudalism
- The reunification of Japan
- The Tokugawa Shogunate
- Social stratification versus urbanization and the merchant class
- Nagasaki and Japanese isolationism

Between the 1400s and 1700s, China and Japan consolidated their position as the dominant powers of East Asia. Under the Ming dynasty, established in 1368, China reached a peak of cultural grandeur and elegance. After 1644, when a younger dynasty, the Qing (Manchu), arose, the Chinese continued to enjoy a high level of artistic and intellectual sophistication and even greater military and political prominence in Asia.

Japan began this period disunited and divided. For more than two centuries—the mid-1300s through the late 1500s—Japan tore itself apart in feudal wars and civil conflicts. Finally, during the late 1500s and early 1600s, Japan reunified. The regime that completed the reunification, the Tokugawa Shogunate, established strict control over Japanese politics and society, and ruled till the mid-1800s.

In the international context, the Chinese and Japanese remained only dimly aware of a major change: Despite their cultural advancement and political consolidation at home, both countries slipped in terms of global power, losing the scientific and technological advantages they had possessed during the period between 1000 and 1450. This power shift, resulting from a certain stagnation, left both countries, especially China, vulnerable to foreign influence and domination during the 1800s.

MING CHINA

In 1450, the **Ming Dynasty** was almost a century old. From its foundation in 1368 to the early 1400s, Ming China had been a politically dynamic and militarily active state, conquering neighbors and exploring faraway lands. It was economically prosperous. Its population grew steadily during the late 1300s and 1400s, recovering from the wars and diseases of the late Yuan period.

Although Ming China remained powerful during the 1500s and early 1600s, its principal strengths during these years were cultural. As described in Chapter 8, the artistic and intellectual achievements of the Ming were impressive: literary masterpieces, fine porcelain ("china"), architecture, and the revival of Confucianism.

During the Ming period, the first European explorers began to arrive. As Portuguese traders and captains arrived in Asia, they established commercial ties with the Ming. The Spanish and Dutch arrived later. China was too large and powerful for the Europeans to conquer, they established embassies and trading houses there. Catholic (particularly Jesuit) missionaries were important as well.

The 1600s were a time of rapid decline for China. The late Ming rulers were weak and allowed the government to decentralize and then unravel. The Portuguese and Spanish traded with silver from North and South America, and the sudden, massive influx of precious metal triggered inflation, then economic breakdown. At the same time, agriculture yields shrank (perhaps because of a worsening of soil quality or a general cooling of the climate). The population grew more quickly than the land's ability to support it, and famines occurred regularly.

Finally, revolution and war drove the Ming to collapse. Serious military threats came from nomads and other invaders from Central Asia, Mongolia, and Manchuria. The huge cost of defending China's borders drained the economy. A massive peasant revolt, lasting from 1636 to 1644, toppled the dynasty. The last Ming emperor committed suicide, after first trying to kill his family.

The peasants' victory, however, was short-lived. Within weeks, enemies from the north, the Manchus, swept into northern China, took Beijing, and established a new dynasty.

THE QING (MANCHU) CONQUEST OF CHINA

The Manchus and the Establishment of the Qing Empire

The **Manchus** were from Manchuria, the large region northeast of China. Although related to the Chinese, the Manchus were ethnically distinct. For many years, the Manchus (who made up less than 5 percent of the population) created an ethnically based system of social stratification, in which the Chinese, as subjects, had to wear certain clothing and tie their hair in long braids, or queues. Males had to shave their foreheads, as reflected in a proverb of the time: "lose your hair or lose your head."

The empire established by the Manchus was called the **Qing** (or Ch'ing, 1644–1911). It included Manchuria and, then, after 1644, northern China. Skilled warlords, the Manchus continued their conquests. By 1683, they had taken southern China and the island of Formosa (now Taiwan).

The Manchus also controlled or added to their tributary system areas such as Mongolia, Tibet, Nepal, Burma, Vietnam, and much of Central Asia. Qing expansion to the north brought the Chinese into contact with Russia, which was moving deeper into Siberia by the 1600s and 1700s. It took much negotiation for the Chinese and Russians to arrive at a mutually acceptable boundary.

Qing Economics and Foreign Contacts

Full-scale trade with European nations began under the Qing, during the 1690s. Foreign trade was closely regulated by the state, and by the 1750s, most of it was allowed to take place only in one city, the port of **Canton**. Along with silk and porcelain, China's most important commodity was **tea**. While the Qing Empire sent a high volume of exports to other nations, it allowed few imports. This policy of **trade protection** gave China a highly favorable balance of trade.

The Qing regime sharply limited foreign contacts, economic or cultural, with ordinary Chinese. Desiring to maintain a favorable balance of trade, the Qing strove to prevent the Chinese population from developing an appetite for foreign goods. Also suspicious of outside influences (and because of their strong support of Confucian ideals), the Qing banned Christianity in 1724. Another reason for limiting foreign contacts was cultural arrogance: like the Ming before them, the Qing considered China to be the center of the world and superior to all nations. In their eyes, Europeans were barbarians. China would pay heavily for this attitude in the 1800s.

Emperors Kangxi and Qianlong

During the late 1600s and early 1700s, the Qing emperors were capable rulers, good administrators, and strong centralizers. The Emperor **Kangxi** (1662–1722) is widely considered one of the greatest monarchs in Chinese history: a skilled general, a just lawgiver, and a sponsor of culture and learning. Kangxi bolstered the imperial authority of the Qing by patronizing Confucianism, with its emphasis on respect for authority. Unlike many of the rulers who followed, he appreciated the importance of the West's growing technological aptitude. Another eighteenth-century ruler, Qianlong (1735–1796), was the last intelligent, dynamic ruler the Qing had. He strengthened China's borders, fostered economic growth, and promoted scholarship and art.

After Qianlong, the quality of the Qing rulers declined. They grew more complacent and less active. Also, as during the late Ming period, the Chinese population grew much faster than the economy (population surpassed 300 million by 1799). Over time, national wealth was barely sufficient to support the population. For all but the upper classes, poverty worsened. Despite its strength as a regional power, Qing China was slipping backward in terms of technological innovation, scientific advancement, and global power—a danger the emperors succeeding Kangxi and Qian long failed to perceive properly. By the 1800s, China would be increasingly open to European and American influence, then domination.

FEUDAL WAR AND REUNIFICATION IN JAPAN

As discussed in Chapter 8, Japan was governed after 1185 by military rulers called **shoguns**, who held power on behalf of the emperor, whose position was essentially symbolic. Although the shoguns preserved order and kept the country relatively unified in the late 1200s and early 1300s, decentralization became an increasingly serious problem in the late 1300s and 1400s. In theory, the Ashikaga Shogunate (1336–1573) ruled the country. In reality, Japan was becoming steadily more feudal, breaking down into semi- or wholly independent states ruled by the landed aristocracy, or daimyo. As most feudal nobles in Europe had been knights, most Japanese daimyo belonged to the samurai elite.

In the 1460s, Japan descended into an even more chaotic period of anarchy and civil war that lasted till the late 1500s. During this Era of Independent Lords, the shogun was weak, daimyo fought daimyo, and samurai who lost or left their masters (*ronin*) became mercenaries or turned to banditry. The economy suffered, and crime rates rose. Starting in the 1540s, Portuguese, Spanish, and Dutch traders, as well as Catholic missionaries (including the Jesuit Francis Xavier, who did much to promote his faith in Asia), arrived. The shoguns' political weakness allowed foreigners and their Christian beliefs to gain substantial influence. The Europeans also introduced gunpowder weaponry.

The reunification of Japan took more than fifty years (1560 to 1615) and involved the military and diplomatic efforts of three politician-warlords. Oda Nobunaga, one of the first Japanese generals to use gunpowder weapons (especially at Nagashino in 1573), conquered east and central Japan but was assassinated in 1582. Following him was Toyotomi Hideyoshi, who rose from humble origins to reunify almost the entire country. A clever politician, he centralized power from his capital, Osaka, and restored order (at the cost of harsh social stratification). In 1598, when he died, his son was only a child, and civil war broke out once again. The victor was Tokugawa Ieyasu, a brilliant, ruthless commander. He appointed himself shogun in 1603 and completed the full unification of Japan in 1615 (a process that included forcing Hideyoshi's son to kill himself). The Tokugawa shoguns would rule Japan for two and a half centuries.

THE TOKUGAWA SHOGUNATE AND THE CONSOLIDATION OF JAPAN

The Tokugawa Shogunate lasted from 1603 to 1868. After so many years of disunity, order and stability were its main priorities. The Tokugawa era is also known as the Great Peace (or the Pax Tokugawa).

Centralization, Dictatorship, and Social Stratification

As Hideyoshi had done before him, Ieyasu centralized the country. He established a new capital at the city of Edo (modern-day Tokyo). As before, the emperor remained a figurehead. Peace came at the price of dictatorship, as well as increased social stratification. Japan's class system became more rigid than ever before, and until the mid-1700s, it was almost impossible for a person to move from one class or profession to another. One tool the Tokugawa used to enforce this policy was a renewed emphasis on Confucianism. Ordinary citizens were forbidden to own weapons; the samurai retained the privilege of owning swords. The Tokugawa maintained a strict monopoly on gunpowder technology and kept the number of guns in Japan as small as possible.

Under the Tokugawa, women lived under increased restrictions, particularly if they belonged to the samurai class. Wives had to obey their husbands or face death. They had little authority over property and received less education than men, although they were encouraged to follow artistic and cultural pursuits. Among the lower classes, gender relations were more egalitarian. Peasant men and women both worked in the fields, and women gained respect as homemakers and mothers. Even so, as in earlier eras, girl children were less valued and sometimes either put to death or sold into prostitution. Some women gained status as **geishas**, special courtesans who were highly valued for their musical, artistic, and conversational skills.

Japanese Isolationism

Many Portuguese, Spanish, and Dutch traders and missionaries entered Japan in the late 1500s, and Christianity became quite popular. However, many Japanese (like the Chinese) considered Europeans barbaric. More important, Japanese authorities suspected foreign ideas (including religious ones) and feared the possible effects of uncontrolled importation of gunpowder weaponry. Both Nobunaga and Hideyoshi started the process of restricting foreign access to Japan, even persecuting (and crucifying) Christians on several occasions.

The Tokugawa shoguns continued this policy of **isolationism**. Christianity was officially discouraged. A national seclusion policy was instituted in the 1630s, and from 1649 until the 1720s, foreign traders were allowed entry only into one city, the port of **Nagasaki**. A brief period of openness followed and then Japan sealed itself off again until the 1850s.

Economics, Society, and Culture

Despite the Tokugawa regime's oppressive nature, it had many accomplishments to its credit. It restored and kept the peace. The population grew rapidly. Rice and grain production more than doubled between 1600 and 1720. Tokugawa Japan became highly urbanized (Edo was one of the world's largest cities), and the shoguns built an elaborate network of roads and canals. Economic growth was impressive: The Japanese became great producers of lacquerware, pottery, steel, and quality weapons.

During the 1600s, and especially the 1700s, the **merchant class** became increasingly wealthy and powerful (an exception to the general rule of social stratification). As for the samurai class, peace brought with it difficult transitions. At the price of obedience, samurai kept their social prestige; but in a modernizing society not at war, there was little need for a warrior elite with traditional combat skills. Some samurai were released from service by their daimyo lords; others found that the value of their land decreased as the country's economic center of gravity shifted to the cities. Masterless samurai (ronin) sometimes turned to banditry, and there were occasional samurai uprisings. Most samurai, however, remained loyal, even if their traditionalist mindset kept many of them from embracing social and economic change.

In the cultural sphere, the samurai class maintained many of the traditions and styles mentioned in Chapter 8. There was some European influence on architecture (especially castle building, which had to adapt to the introduction of gunpowder) and painting (more emphasis on the laws of perspective). Among the urban classes, a new form of drama, **kabuki theater**—which featured acrobatics, swordplay, and scenes of city life—became popular. It was very different from the older, more refined Noh drama favored by the upper classes.

QUICK REVIEW

1. Who was Francis Xavier?

(A) a Portuguese warlord who conquered Macao

(B) a Jesuit missionary who traveled widely in Asia

(C) a Spanish colonial administrator in Canton

(D) a Dominican priest who advocated equal rights for all Asians

(E) an Italian composer influenced by Asian music

2. Which of the following adversely affected Ming economics during the first half of the 1600s?

(A) inflation caused by the glut of silver coming from Spanish and Portuguese colonies in the New World

(B) the financial strain caused by the need to defend China's long frontiers

(C) the decline of agricultural yields and disturbances in the countryside

(D) all of the above

(E) none of the above

3. Which of the following is true about the Qing Dynasty?

  I. The Qing rulers were ethnically distinct from most of China's inhabitants.

 II. The Qing came to power in China by peaceful means.

III. The Qing forced ordinary male citizens to wear their hair in queues.

IV. The early Qing rulers were militarily active.

(A) I and II only

(B) I and III only

(C) I, III, and IV

(D) II, III, and IV

(E) all of the above

4. Upon what belief system did Qing rulers rely to strengthen their imperial authority in China?

(A) Confucianism

(B) Daoism

(C) Pure Land Buddhism

(D) Hinduism

(E) shamanism

5. How is Kangxi's rule over Qing China best characterized?

(A) He is famous for military resistance to European colonizers.

(B) He used forced labor to rebuild the Great Wall.

(C) He sponsored the arts and solidified central authority.

(D) He launched naval expeditions into the Indian Ocean.

(E) He wrested much Siberian territory from Russia.

6. How would one best characterize Japan's political situation during the 1400s and 1500s?

(A) a condition of peace and prosperity

(B) a state of disunity and civil war

(C) a time of tight political cohesion

(D) a division of the country between two warring factions

(E) a dominance of politics by religious authorities

7. Which of the following is NOT true of Japan's samurai class?

(A) The samurai class evolved into a military aristocracy.

(B) Samurai followed a rigid code of behavior called Bushido.

(C) Samurai were philosophically attracted to the simplicity of Zen Buddhism.

(D) Samurai without masters to serve were known as *ronin*.

(E) Samurai favored an open society and greater mobility for all classes.

8. Which of the following is true of Japan's relations with the outside world in the 1600s?

   (A) Japanese merchants persuaded the shoguns to allow free trade with Europeans.
   (B) When foreign trade was permitted, it was generally restricted to the port of Nagasaki.
   (C) Christianity never gained a following among the Japanese.
   (D) Foreign traders and missionaries showed very little interest in Japan.
   (E) The Tokugawa shoguns encouraged the activities of Christian missionaries.

9. What characterized the politics of the Tokugawa Shogunate?

   (A) rigid social stratification backed by a dictatorial government
   (B) a gradual opening of Japanese economic and intellectual life to the outside world
   (C) ruthless extermination of political enemies and racial minorities
   (D) a high degree of social mobility
   (E) a move toward limited forms of participatory democracy

10. Which social class began to gain a substantial amount of new social and economic influence in seventeenth-century Japan?

   (A) the peasantry
   (B) the industrial working class
   (C) the merchant class
   (D) the urban poor
   (E) artisans and craftspeople

Answers

1. **(B)** One of the first members of the Jesuit order founded by Ignatius Loyola, Francis Xavier traveled to Southeast Asia in the 1540s. He spent the rest of his life in Asia as a missionary and teacher, ensuring that Catholicism gained a permanent foothold in South and East Asia. He visited most of Southeast Asia and Japan, then died while trying to gain permission to enter China.

2. **(D)** All these reasons contributed to the decline of the Ming dynasty, which collapsed in the 1640s. A huge peasant revolt lasting eight years was the immediate reason for its downfall.

3. **(C)** The Qing, an empire founded by the Manchus, came to power shortly after the Manchus invaded northern China in 1644. The Qing forced Chinese men to wear their hair in long braids and to shave their foreheads.

4. **(A)** Confucianism emphasizes respect for authority not only inside the family unit but also within the state. Qing emperors patronized Confucianism to fortify authority in China, and the Tokugawa shoguns used it to justify social stratification.

5. **(C)** Kangxi was successful because he was a strong centralizer, as well as a talented general, a just lawgiver, and a patron of culture and scholarship. He did not fight the Europeans or invade Siberia. Construction of the Great Wall and the launching of naval expeditions took place under other dynasties.

6. **(B)** Beginning in the late 1300s and early 1400s, Japan broke down into a patchwork of independent or semi-independent feudal states. Japan was not reunified until 1615, when a powerful commander, Tokugawa Ieyasu, captured Osaka.

7. **(E)** Japan's samurai class, a traditional warrior elite that guarded its social and military privileges carefully, was not concerned with civil rights and increased social mobility. The other answers on this list are accurate.

8. **(B)** Japan's rulers distrusted foreigners and so were isolationists. Therefore, they kept tight reins over trade, especially restricting Europeans' access to the country. Christianity, despite obstacles raised by the shoguns, made inroads into Japanese society.

9. **(A)** As already mentioned above, the Tokugawa Shogunate maintained its rule and peace in Japan through authoritarian control and social stratification. It did not open to the outside world willingly.

10. **(C)** The merchant class grew wealthier and more influential in Japan in the 1700s, as Japan grew to produce such desirable goods as lacquerware, pottery, steel, and weapons.

South and Southeast Asia

- Gunpowder empires
- The Mughal Empire
- The Indian cotton trade
- The Indian Ocean trade network
- Sati
- The rise of Sikhism
- The European arrival in South and Southeast Asia
- The British East India Company
- The Maori and the Aborigines

Between 1450 and 1750, South and Southeast Asia experienced, on the whole, greater political centralization. These areas were also confronted by the sudden appearance of European explorers and merchants in the late 1400s and early 1500s. Both developments changed the region considerably.

The largest and most powerful states in the region were in India. In 1450, India was ruled by the Delhi Sultanate, which was declining rapidly. In the 1520s, invaders from the north destroyed the Delhi State and established in its place the even stronger state: the Mughal Empire, which survived into the mid-1700s.

As before, India and the rest of South and Southeast Asia were characterized by an incredible diversity of ethnicity, language, and religion (major faiths included Hinduism, several forms of Buddhism, Islam, and more). In many ways, this diversity enriched India and its neighbors. However, it also created deep social and cultural divisions, which often caused conflict and strife.

MUGHAL INDIA

As detailed in Chapter 9, the Delhi Sultanate had been weakening steadily during the 1300s and 1400s. The final blows against it came in the early 1500s.

Babur the Tiger and the Mughal Empire

Starting in 1520, **Babur**—a Mongol warlord in the tradition of Genghis Khan and Timur—launched a full-scale invasion of India from the north. Known as the Tiger, Babur quickly defeated the Delhi Sultanate.

In 1526, after the battle of Panipat, Babur established his own government, the **Mughal Empire**, which he ruled until his death in 1530. His successors conquered most of the rest of India, and the empire continued for the next 200 years. Its name comes from the Persian word for *Mongol* (the word *mughal* is often spelled *mogul*, which, in English, still refers to any rich or powerful individual).

229

Like the Delhi sultans, the Mughals were Muslims, making their state one of the three great Islamic empires of the era, along with the Ottoman Empire and Safavid Persia (see Chapter 15). Like the Ottoman and Safavid states, Mughal India was a **gunpowder empire**, using military force and advanced weaponry to maintain power, both at home and abroad.

In its prime, the Mughals expanded steadily southward, ruling India from their famous Peacock Throne. Their first capital was Agra; later, the capital moved to Delhi, which was restored to its former glory. The Mughal rulers centralized India. The economy thrived thanks to a boom in the Indian cotton trade. The early Mughals were religiously flexible, allowing Hindus and Buddhists to practice their own faiths, even under Muslim rule. Only during the last years of the empire did this approach change.

Mughal India was culturally vibrant. Its architectural brilliance is illustrated by India's most famous landmark, the **Taj Mahal**, the white marble mausoleum built in Agra by Shah Jahan in memory of his wife. In painting and literature, there was a fusion of Persian and Indian styles.

> **TIP**
>
> Mughal India was similar to other Islamic empires of the day in that, while it was more technologically and scientifically advanced than most parts of the world during the 1500s and first half of the 1600s, it lost ground, especially to the nations of Europe, during the late 1600s and afterward.

Women in Mughal India

The effect of Mughal rule on women was mixed. On one hand, the Mughals allowed women certain rights. Female aristocrats were awarded titles, earned salaries, owned land, and ran businesses. Some received an education and expressed their creative talents openly. Women of all castes were permitted to sell their woven products. They could inherit land.

However, the Mughals restricted women's rights through **Sharia**, or Islamic law. These practices tended to coincide with restrictions that Indian society had already placed on women, such as cloistering women inside the home, as in the case of Hindu upper-class women. The Hindu practice of **sati** remained legal (although Akbar the Great attempted to outlaw it), and women were instructed to serve under their husbands.

Akbar the Great

Mughal rule reached its peak under **Akbar the Great** (1556–1605), grandson of Babur. Akbar completed the conquest of India. A great commander, Akbar used gunpowder weapons to gain control over most of the subcontinent.

Akbar created an efficient nationwide bureaucracy. The tax codes and legal system operated fairly. Akbar's reign was one of prosperity.

Akbar was also famed for religious tolerance. He allowed non-Muslims to worship as they wished, abolished the tax paid by non-Muslims, and encouraged friendly relations among Muslims, Buddhists, and Hindus. He even sought advice from the Catholic priests who arrived with European traders. Akbar ensured that a specific percentage of government officials were Hindu, and he married a Hindu princess.

Decline of the Mughal Empire

The Mughals' fortunes took a downward turn during the late 1600s and early 1700s. Akbar's great-grandson, **Aurangzeb** (1658–1707), a militant Muslim, abandoning the policy of religious tolerance, reimposed the tax on non-Muslims and forced thousands to convert to Islam against their will. His policy caused tremendous civil strife. This, in turn, had an adverse effect on the economy. Aurangzeb's intolerance also turned one religious minority, **the Sikhs,** into a rebellious and warlike group. The Sikhs' religion, which stressed the power of prayer and meditation, had been founded in the 1400s by the teacher Nanak. During the 1500s and early 1600s, the Sikhs had been peaceful. When Aurangzeb killed their leader in 1675, they revolted, founded their own state in Punjab, and developed a strong warrior tradition.

The Mughal state declined during the 1700s. The social and economic effects of religious struggle continued. Provinces broke away and became independent. In 1739, an Iranian marauder sacked Delhi and carried away the Peacock Throne, symbol of Mughal glory and power.

Arrival of the Europeans

European interference in Indian affairs steadily increased. The Portuguese trader Vasco da Gama arrived in 1498 (see Chapter 14). More Portuguese, then Spanish, came to South Asia. They were followed by the Dutch and then the French and English, who arrived in the 1600s. During the 1500s and early 1600s, the gunpowder empire of the Mughals was strong and technologically advanced enough to keep the Europeans in their place.

During the 1600s, however, the balance of power shifted. The English built textile factories at Fort William (near Calcutta, in the northeast) and Madras. The western gateway port of Bombay (now Mumbai) was ceded to the **British East India Company** (one of the most politically powerful corporations in world history) in 1661. The Dutch East India Company established bases in Ceylon (now Sri Lanka). The French created a great garrison and trading center at Pondicherry, on the east coast. The Europeans profited by gaining control over the trade of Indian cotton for spices from the East Indies.

European, particularly English, control over India increased during the 1700s. Until after the 1750s, the European presence was concentrated mainly on the coastline. However, starting in the 1740s, large numbers of French and British troops were fighting each other in India, for the "right" to colonize the entire subcontinent. By the 1750s, the English had defeated the French; they then turned to the conquest of India itself. They triumphed over the Mughal state easily, although they kept Mughal rulers in charge of certain parts of India as puppets. In a short time, one of the world's mightiest empires had been transformed into a weak colonial possession.

SOUTHEAST ASIA

Kingdoms of Southeast Asia

Like India, the nations of Southeast Asia solidified politically. They also faced the arrival and constant encroachments of European explorers and colonizers.

Strong states in the region during these years included Thailand (which conquered the neighboring Khmer state in Cambodia), the Vietnamese nation of Annam, and Burma (which maintained the largest army in Southeast Asia). Vietnam and Burma became tributary states of Qing China. The islands of Indonesia were politically and economically important, until they submitted to Dutch colonial control.

Buddhism and Hinduism were dominant religions. Islam was important as well, especially in Indonesia, where it became the majority faith.

The European Presence in Southeast Asia

Europeans arrived in Southeast Asia after 1498, when Vasco da Gama reached India. The Portuguese quickly took over whatever parts of Southeast Asia they could: Malacca, Goa, Sri Lanka, and more. Where they could not conquer, they traded. The same was true for the Europeans who followed: the Spanish, Dutch (who took over Indonesia), French, and English. Because they were smaller and less advanced than India, it was harder for the nations of Southeast Asia to remain free from European colonization—although many managed to do so, at least until the 1800s, when European imperialism became even harder to resist. The Jesuit priest **Francis Xavier** came to Southeast Asia in the 1540s and spent the rest of his life cementing a Catholic foothold throughout Asia.

Australia and Its Neighbors

Farther to the south, the English encountered the continent of Australia. In 1770, the British mariner and explorer **James Cook** charted the east coast of Australia and claimed the continent for his country. The nearby islands of New Zealand (home to the Polynesian **Maori**) and Tasmania came under English control as well.

Full-scale settlement of Australia began in 1788. For years, the population consisted mainly of soldiers, government officials, and criminals "transported" to the colony as punishment. In 1830, Britain claimed the entire continent of Australia. The rate of settlement increased, as free settlers joined the colony seeking their fortunes. Mainly sheep farmers, Australians pushed into the interior and displaced the original inhabitants, the **Aborigines**, who had lived there for tens of thousands of years. The confrontations between colonists and Aborigines were often violent and one-sided, ending with the dispossession and ill treatment of the natives.

QUICK REVIEW

1. In sixteenth-century India, the Delhi Sultanate gave way to which government?

(A) the Gupta Empire
(B) the Srivijayan Kingdom
(C) French rule
(D) the Mughal Empire
(E) British rule

2. The founder of the Mughal Empire was

(A) Aurangzeb.
(B) Babur.
(C) Akbar.
(D) Jahan.
(E) Nanak.

3. What major faiths were most prominent in South Asia's religious landscape during the sixteenth and seventeenth centuries?

(A) Hinduism, Islam, and Buddhism
(B) Christianity and Buddhism
(C) animism, Buddhism, and Zoroastrianism
(D) animism, Hinduism, and Zoroastrianism
(E) Islam, Christianity, and animism

4. A boom in what commodity led to increased prosperity in the Mughal Empire during the 1600s and 1700s?

(A) nutmeg
(B) coffee
(C) cotton
(D) wool
(E) cloves

5. The most famous architectural legacy of the Mughal Empire is

(A) the Red Fortress of Gwalior.
(B) the temple of Borobudur.
(C) the Great Gate of Mumbai.
(D) the Taj Mahal.
(E) Gandhi's Tomb.

6. Which of the following is true of Akbar's reign in India?

I. He completed the Mughal conquest of India.
II. He improved India's tax code and legal system.
III. He pursued a policy of religious tolerance.
IV. He married a Hindu princess.

(A) I, II, and III
(B) II, III, and IV
(C) I and IV only
(D) II and III only
(E) all of the above

7. The most striking aspect of Aurangzeb's reign was

(A) his continuation of Akbar's policy of religious tolerance.
(B) his ruthless suppression of Muslim beliefs.
(C) his ruthless suppression of non-Muslim beliefs.
(D) his democratization of the political system.
(E) his abolition of the caste system.

8. How did the Mughal Empire come to an end?

(A) It was subdued by the British, who retained some Mughal rulers in place for political purposes.
(B) It collapsed owing to a global shift in the cotton trade during the 1700s.
(C) It was completely eradicated by French colonists.
(D) Outside invaders from the Himalayas sacked the capital and destroyed the empire.
(E) none of the above

9. The majority religion in Indonesia is

    (A) Christianity.
    (B) Islam.
    (C) Hinduism.
    (D) Buddhism.
    (E) Sikhism.

10. Australia's colonial population was made up largely of what group during the 1700s and early 1800s?

    (A) religious dissidents
    (B) gold miners
    (C) Scottish refugees
    (D) convicts
    (E) Irish peasants

Answers

1. **(D)** The Mughal Empire ruled India for over two centuries. The Mughals were Muslims who used military force and gunpowder technology to maintain power.

2. **(B)** Babur was a Mongol warlord who invaded India from the north beginning around 1520. He ruled parts of India for ten years, and his heirs moved southward to conquer much of the rest of India.

3. **(A)** Buddhism and Hinduism were the dominant religions among the populations of South Asia. However, Islam grew in popularity in this region.

4. **(C)** The Indian economy thrived under the Mughals owing mainly to a boom in the cotton trade during this period. When the Europeans arrived in India in the 1600s, they gained control over the cotton industry, trading for spices from the East Indies.

5. **(D)** The Taj Mahal was built in 1648 in Agra as a memorial to the wife of Shah Jahan. It is still one of India's foremost landmarks.

6. **(E)** Akbar used heavy artillery to amass control over nearly the entire subcontinent of India by the early 1600s. He also ensured that the government bureaucracy ran efficiently. He was extremely tolerant.

7. **(C)** Aurangzeb abandoned earlier policies of toleration. He forced thousands of his subjects to convert to Islam, causing much strife.

8. **(A)** By the 1750s, the British had expelled their French rivals from most of India. The Mughal rulers who remained in place after the British took over more of India acted as their puppets.

9. **(B)** Indonesia is now the world's largest Muslim country by population.

10. **(D)** The British transported convicts to Australia as punishment. The other British groups who emigrated there included soldiers and government officials.

Sub-Saharan Africa

CHAPTER 18

- The Songhai state
- The kingdom of Kongo
- The Asante (Ashanti) kingdom
- The Zulu
- The gold and ivory trades
- The Indian Ocean trade network
- The Boers (Afrikaners) and the apartheid system
- Abstraction in African art
- The Arab slave trade
- European exploitation of Africa
- The Atlantic slave trade, the Middle Passage, and triangular trade

Starting in the early 1400s, Africa came under the increased influence of the exploring powers of Europe. Along the western and eastern coasts, Portugal, then other European nations, seized cities, built fortresses, and established permanent colonies. For centuries, Europeans exploited Africa economically, taking gold, spices, ivory, and other resources through trade and by force. Most shameful was the Atlantic slave trade, which began in the 1400s, as Portugal started transporting Africans overseas for use as forced labor. Quickly, more nations became involved, and the size and number of slave shipments grew astronomically, with the slave trade persisting well into the 1800s. Its effect on Africa, the Americas, and the economies of Europe was profound.

For the time being, however, the interior of Africa remained largely free from European control. Not till after the mid-1800s would Europeans penetrate much beyond the coasts. Certain African nations grew strong and thrived. On occasion, Africans were able to defeat European forces and stop colonists and slavers from moving deeper into the continent. Nonetheless, the economic impact of European imperialism was felt even in the interior, as were the effects of the slave trade.

WEST AND CENTRAL AFRICA

The Songhai State and Kongo

By the mid-1400s, the previously dominant power in West Africa, Mali, was fading. In its place, the Muslim kingdom of Songhai (previously a part of the Mali Empire), rose up. The first of its powerful kings, Sunni Ali, conquered neighboring territory in the 1460s and asserted control over many trade routes and the key city of Timbuktu. Songhai's most famous ruler, Askia Mohammed (1493–1528), came to the throne by deposing the last Sunni ruler (the name *askia*, which he adopted after coming to power, means "usurper"). A skilled general, Askia Mohammed continued to expand Songhai's boundaries. He centralized power by creating a complex bureaucracy, and he sponsored art, scholarship, and the building of many mosques. He encouraged trade, and the growing merchant class generated wealth by exchanging salt for gold. A fictionalized account of his reign, *The Epic of Askia Mohammed*, is one of the classics of the West African oral tradition. Songhai prospered until the late 1500s. Civil war followed the peaceful reign of Askia Daoud, and Morocco conquered the divided kingdom in 1590.

Taking shape around 1400, the kingdom of **Kongo** grew out of Bantu-descended communities that had existed since 1000 B.C.E. The state extended from the Atlantic coast to the western edge of what is now the modern state of Congo. Prior to European contact, its economy was based on ivory, cloth, pottery, and metal.

In 1483, the Portuguese arrived in force, and although they did not conquer Kongo outright, they compelled it—largely by taking hostages—to enter into a long and complex relationship with Portugal. The king, Nzinga a Nkuwu, converted to Catholicism and took the name João I. Later monarchs followed the same example, adopting European names and the Christian faith. For many years, Kongo existed not as a colony, but as a state forced into economic and political partnership with an outside power. This relationship cost Kongo some of its autonomy, but also helped make it powerful. (Much the same is true of the Asante kingdom, discussed below.) During most of the 1500s, Kongo expanded and centralized, establishing an elaborate system of provinces and duchies to govern its population of approximately 500,000. Its large army acquired modern weaponry—and many mercenaries—from Portugal. Kongo helped to satisfy Portugal's growing appetite for African slaves, mainly by using its army to fight its neighbors and enslave thousands of prisoners of war.

Internal disputes and succession struggles weakened Kongo in the late 1500s and early 1600s, and again in the mid-1600s. Even so, Kongo managed to reduce Portuguese dominance: In 1622, with help from the Dutch, it expelled the official Portuguese presence. Periodic conflicts followed until Kongo's decisive defeat of Portuguese armies in 1670. The country went through various phases of unity and disunity throughout the 1700s and most of the 1800s, until, near the end of the century, it was fully colonized.

The Europeans and West and Central Africa

All of West Africa was affected by the arrival of the Europeans in the 1400s. First the Portuguese and then the Dutch, English, and French landed on the African coast, began trading, and built permanent outposts. The original purpose of the Portuguese had been to find their way south and east to India. As they became interested in Africa for its own sake, the Europeans sought to gain control over the **gold and ivory trades** that extended throughout West and Central Africa and the upper Zambezi River.

Women in West and Central Africa

As mentioned in Chapter 11, several African groups, particularly in West Africa, were **matrilineal** in organization, and women took part in leadership. In some instances, women became rulers. For example, **Queen Nzinga** (1582–1663) ruled the Mbundu peoples in what is now Angola. She was respected for defending her people against the Portuguese.

In West African trading villages, women took part in market activities. Sometimes women's councils administered the markets.

In North African cities, where Islam dominated, upper-class women were more likely to be cloistered and made to wear veils. However, economic necessity compelled lower-class women to work outside the home.

The Emergence of the Slave Trade

From the late 1400s onward, the development of African nations, the patterns of African trade, and the history of entire tribes were shaped by the growing European presence. The strongest states in West Africa—Oyo, Benin, Dahomey, Kongo, and Asante—were those that cooperated with the European slave trade, by warring on and imprisoning other African tribes, and then selling the captives to European slavers.

In particular, the **Asante (Ashanti)** kingdom, founded by Osei Tutu in 1680, became immensely powerful because its leaders sold gold and slaves to Europeans in exchange for muskets and gunpowder. West Africa was nicknamed the Gold Coast in recognition of the lucrative exchange of gold for slaves. Asante was one of the few parts of Africa where both minerals and agricultural resources were found in abundance.

Even states and tribes in Equatorial Africa, beyond the direct impact of Europeans on the coast, were affected. The trade networks that connected Equatorial Africa with the west coast were redirected or destroyed by the Europeans. Some West Africans began to raid Equatorial Africa for goods to trade with Europeans. Worst of all, the Europeans' desire for slaves frequently led West Africans to fight their neighbors in Equatorial Africa in search of prisoners to sell into slavery.

SOUTHERN AFRICA

Before the arrival of the Europeans, the southern tip of Africa had been settled by various tribes, mainly descended from the Bantu (see Chapter 3). The Portuguese rounded the tip of Africa in 1488, establishing an outpost on what they called the Cape of Good Hope.

During the 1600s, control of the region passed from the Portuguese to the Dutch. Dutch settlers known as **Boers** (also Afrikaners) arrived in 1652 and became firmly established as farmers and traders; their language evolved into a dialect called Afrikaans. Even more so than most white Europeans, the Boers possessed a strong sense of racial superiority and looked upon Africans and other peoples of color as inferior. Over the centuries, the Boers' harsh treatment of native Africans developed into the infamous system of **apartheid**.

WOMEN IN POWER

Many women throughout history have held political power on an individual basis. Examples include Cleopatra, Elizabeth I, Catherine the Great, Nzinga, Cixi, Golda Meir, Indira Gandhi, and Margaret Thatcher. Matrilineal societies, like those found in parts of West Africa, have often afforded women more respect and authority than they enjoy elsewhere. An interesting question, however, is whether this means that women are treated *equally*. Many queens and empresses come to power only because male alternatives are not available, and it does not necessarily follow that they can (or even want to) use their position to improve the overall condition of women. Even in modern democracies, women tend to be underrepresented as elected officials. In discussing how women have influenced historical developments, be sure not to overgeneralize from the often atypical experiences of powerful individuals; until very recently, sexism and inequality have been the norms in most times and places.

The Boers enslaved the nearest African tribe, the Xhosa, a peaceful herding people. As the Boers expanded to the north, they encountered a stronger and more warlike people, the Zulu. Many wars broke out between the Boers and the Zulu. By the early 1800s, the entire region came under British control, although the Boers continued to live there. This awkward, three-way situation caused much conflict during the 1800s.

EAST AFRICA

As discussed in Chapter 11, the towns and states of East Africa were part of the vibrant, cosmopolitan Indian Ocean trade network. From the 1400s onward, this system continued to exist, although the arrival of European merchants and conquerors changed conditions considerably.

The Portuguese, the first to arrive, originally viewed East Africa as a platform for reaching the Indies. For example, in 1498, the East African port of Malindi was Vasco da Gama's jumping-off point to Calicut, in India. Soon, however, the Portuguese realized the advantages of having permanent bases in East Africa. Not only would bases allow them to reach India more efficiently, it would give them tighter control over trade in the Indian Ocean basin, especially in spices.

In the early 1500s, the Portuguese conquered a chain of cities along the East African coast, turning them into colonies. These included Malindi, Sofala, Mozambique, and Mombasa. Arabs expelled the Portuguese from Mombasa in 1728, but Portugal's presence in the region remained strong for hundreds of years. Others, including the English, later colonized East Africa as well.

AFRICAN CULTURE

Africa did not have a unified approach to art, although it is possible to make some generalizations. Sculpture was its most dominant medium. African art was also concerned with human adornment, as in masks and elaborate beadwork. Moreover, much of African art has been abstract, or not made to recreate visual reality (long before abstract art became a popular concept in the West).

Between 1450 and 1750, artists continued to produce wood carvings, sculptures, metalwork, and paintings. European traders brought home with them carved ivory pieces and textiles, which were admired by distinguished art patrons. Textile arts were prevalent in places like the West Congo basin. While textiles were considered prestige objects, owned by the elite, they were also sold to people of the lower classes.

Finely woven basketry, often done in intersecting geometric patterns, was treasured by royal families in East Africa. Basketry of high value was produced in Rwanda and Burundi. In the seventeenth and eighteenth centuries in Christian Ethiopia, kings commissioned artists to produce churches with brightly colored wall paintings of holy events. One of the most famous of these churches is the Church of Debre Berhan Selassie in Gondar, Ethiopia.

African architecture was influenced by Arabs and European colonists, who built fortresses and residences in East and West Africa.

THE ATLANTIC SLAVE TRADE

As in most parts of the world, slavery had existed in Africa for many years. African tribes often enslaved members of other tribes. In addition, the large **Arab slave trade** had for a long time extended throughout the Sahara and southward.

The Origins of the Atlantic Slave Trade

The arrival of the Europeans, however, changed the character of slave trading in Africa. The Portuguese began this process, but other European nations followed suit. Over time, the Atlantic slave trade became a central part of the European economy and a primary factor in Europe's ability to generate such great wealth from the 1500s onward.

Starting in 1441, the Portuguese began to enslave Africans, taking them to Portugal and selling them in Europe. The number of slaves brought directly to Europe was relatively small. During the 1500s, however, slaves began to be taken to the Americas, and the numbers grew.

This new slave trade involved important changes. It took Africans farther from home. It became far greater in scale. Also, while unjust, earlier forms of slavery had not always involved hard labor, and owners took some care of slaves, at least as pieces of property. The Atlantic slave trade involved a greater degree of manual labor, and treatment of slaves tended to be harsher.

Reasons for the Expansion of the Atlantic Slave Trade

Several factors increased the demand for African slaves. One was the labor-intensive nature of planting, harvesting, and refining sugar. During the 1500s, Portuguese and Spanish colonies in Brazil and the Caribbean became major centers of **sugar production**, and the desire for slave labor there became more intense.

Also during the early 1500s, it became clear to the Spanish and Portuguese that, in the New World, Native Americans were not well suited as slaves. In addition, by 1542, the Catholic Church had abolished the system that allowed the Spanish to enslave Native Americans (see Chapter 19). If the Spanish and Portuguese wanted a source of slave labor—not just for sugar cultivation but also for **mining**, agricultural work, and menial labor—they had to turn elsewhere. Africa seemed an ideal source.

The Growing Scope of the Atlantic Slave Trade

Roughly 1,000 slaves per year were taken from Africa in the late 1400s, and more than 2,000 per year in the 1500s. It is estimated that at least 325,000 Africans were enslaved by Europeans in the 1400s and 1500s.

The Atlantic slave trade mushroomed in scale during the 1600s and 1700s. More than a million slaves were transported from Africa in the 1600s, and at least 6 million were taken in the 1700s. It is thought that, in total, no fewer than 12 million Africans became slaves in the New World between the mid-1400s and the late 1800s. Thirty-seven percent went to Brazil (the largest slaveholding country), 15 percent to Spanish America, 41 percent to non-Spanish parts of the Caribbean, and 5 percent to the southern colonies of British North America, where they grew crops such as cotton and tobacco.

The Middle Passage

Slaves were captured and shipped to the Americas under notoriously appalling conditions. Many were captives or prisoners of war, herded like animals to the coast and sold to European slavers by other Africans. Most were separated from their families; many were mixed in with members of other tribes, who spoke different languages and followed different customs.

On the West African coast, slaves were loaded onto ships to make the infamous **Middle Passage** across the Atlantic. The more slaves a ship could carry, the greater its profits, so slaves were packed into boats as tightly as possible. Chained, lying on their backs, surrounded by hundreds of other bodies, all in darkness, slaves endured a nightmarish sea journey for weeks. Upon arrival in the New World, they would be taken to slave markets and sold. In the early years, up to 25 percent of slaves perished during the Middle Passage. During the 1700s and 1800s, slavers cut the average death rate to 10 percent or less—not for humane reasons but because each dead slave was a financial loss.

Atlantic Slavery, the Triangular Trade, and the World Economy

By the 1700s, African slavery had become a crucial element in European economic life and global trade. Until the early 1800s, no major nation made slavery or the slave trade illegal. Moreover, slaves were an integral part of the economic system known as **triangular trade**. European manufactured goods (metalware, cotton textiles, processed alcohol such as gin and rum, firearms) would be brought to Africa and exchanged for gold, ivory, timber, and slaves. The gold, ivory, and timber would be brought back to Europe, while slaves were sold in the Americas.

The Middle Passage therefore comprised the second leg of this triangular trade. In the Americas, slaves would be traded for furs and other materials, such as tobacco, raw cotton, sugar, and silver (typically grown or mined by slaves—and thus, slaves were not only commodities in the triangular trade network but unwilling producers in it as well). These materials would be brought back to Europe. This system was paramount in the growth of European wealth.

QUICK REVIEW

1. Which of the following is NOT true of the Songhai state?

   (A) It had a strong merchant class that traded salt for goods like gold.
   (B) Its rulers converted to Catholicism under pressure from arriving Europeans.
   (C) It had previously been a state within the powerful Mali Empire.
   (D) Its rulers centralized the state and created a complex bureaucracy.
   (E) Islam remained the dominant faith there.

2. What goods did European traders primarily seek in West Africa?

   (A) gold and ivory
   (B) bananas and mahogany
   (C) oranges and ivory
   (D) coffee and gemstones
   (E) ivory and gemstones

3. Which of the following best characterizes Africa's relations with Europe between 1450 and 1700?

   (A) European powers controlled the entire continent.
   (B) The European impact on Africa remained minimal during these years.
   (C) The effects of the Atlantic slave trade were felt only in West Africa.
   (D) The Europeans' direct influence was felt mainly on the coasts, while the African interior remained largely free.
   (E) Only North Africa fell under European influence.

4. What effect did the Portuguese presence have on the kingdom of Kongo?

   (A) The Portuguese persuaded Kongo to stop enslaving its neighbors.
   (B) The Portuguese conquered Kongo outright during the 1500s.
   (C) The Portuguese compelled Kongo's rulers to convert to Catholicism.
   (D) The Portuguese protected Kongo from Dutch encroachment.
   (E) The Portuguese enslaved most of the Kongo population by 1700.

5. The Asante kingdom grew strong by which of the following means?

   (A) cooperating with Europeans engaged in the Atlantic slave trade
   (B) purchasing and using gunpowder weapons
   (C) increased involvement in the West African gold trade
   (D) all of the above
   (E) none of the above

6. Which European power first colonized parts of East Africa?

   (A) Portugal
   (B) Spain
   (C) England
   (D) France
   (E) the Netherlands

7. What art forms were most prominent in sub-Saharan Africa?

   (A) painting and composed music
   (B) sculpture and textiles
   (C) written literature and painting
   (D) textiles and written literature
   (E) sculpture and composed music

8. Which of the following is true of the Boers?

   (A) They were English settlers in South Africa.
   (B) They were Arab merchants in East Africa.
   (C) They were Dutch settlers in South Africa.
   (D) They were French settlers in East Africa.
   (E) They were Spanish colonists in North Africa.

9. Besides the Europeans, which other group ran a major slave trade in Africa?

   (A) the Turks
   (B) the Persians
   (C) the Sri Lankans
   (D) the Syrians
   (E) the Arabs

10. The New World country that imported the largest percentage of African slaves was

   (A) Brazil.
   (B) Virginia.
   (C) Canada.
   (D) Cuba.
   (E) Haiti.

Answers

1. **(B)** The Songhai state remained Muslim. It grew out of the Mali Empire and became a great power in West Africa.

2. **(A)** Parts of West Africa were known as the "gold coast" and "ivory coast" because of the economic importance of commodities there.

3. **(D)** Initially, the Europeans did not venture very far inland because they were able to extract valuable resources, including minerals and slaves, nearer to the coast. They built permanent outposts on the coast and traded there as well.

4. **(C)** The Portuguese did not take over Kongo until the late 1800s. Over the course of a long and complex relationship, they "persuaded" Kongo's rulers to convert to Christianity and pressured Kongo to enslave other Africans and sell them to Portugal.

5. **(D)** The Asante kingdom grew strong largely because of their contacts with Europeans. All three of these answers are correct. The Asante benefited as well from living in a region that had an abundance of minerals and agricultural resources.

6. **(A)** The Portuguese first colonized the area because they wanted to use it as a stopping-off point on the way to the Indies. Later, however, they found that they could gain better control over the Indian Ocean basin by setting up permanent bases there.

7. **(B)** In sub-Saharan Africa, sculpture and textiles were of particularly high quality. So were ivory and wood carving. Artistic abstraction was very common here and, in later centuries, influenced Western Art.

8. **(C)** The Boers came to sub-Saharan Africa in the 1650s to farm and trade with ships sailing around Africa. The Boers possessed a very strong sense of racial superiority and enslaved the Xhosa people. Later, the area came under British control, but the Boers remained there.

9. **(E)** Even before the Europeans arrived in sub-Saharan Africa, Arab traders had created a slave trade there and in the Saharan region as well.

10. **(A)** During the 1500s, the Portuguese began importing African slaves to Brazil because they needed the labor in sugar cultivation, one of the country's major industries. Also, European colonizers found that Native Americans were not well suited as slaves, so they sought out slaves in Africa.

The Americas as "New World"

- The conquistadors and New Spain
- Gunpowder weaponry and horse warfare
- The importation of smallpox and measles
- Seville's House of Trade and the viceregal system
- The encomienda system
- Silver mining and sugarcane cultivation

- Plantation monoculture
- The Atlantic slave trade
- The North American fur trade
- The French and Indian Wars
- Indentured servitude and "transportation"
- The Columbian Exchange

As described in Chapter 14, North and South America, which had existed in a state of isolation for thousands of years, came into contact with the rest of the world after the middle of the 1400s. European explorers arrived, considering themselves to have discovered what they thought of as the New World. Of course, the concepts of "discovery" and "New World" were meaningless to the Americas' original inhabitants. Equally meaningless was the name given to them by the Europeans: "Indians" reflected Columbus's mistaken belief that he had reached Asia during his voyages of the 1490s.

During the 1500s and afterward, the Spanish and Portuguese, then other Europeans, turned the Americas into their own spheres of influence. The Europeans also brought the Americas into contact with the rest of the world, economically, culturally, ecologically, and politically.

Most notably, the Europeans made North and South America part of a developing network of trade and exchange that was expanding literally around the world. Traders, settlers, explorers, and slaves came to the Americas, as did new technology, knowledge, and cultural traditions. The environment of the Americas changed forever, thanks to the Europeans' exploitation of the continents' resources—and their introduction of new diseases, plants, and animals. Conversely, the new foods and natural resources (especially precious metals) extracted from the New World had a significant impact on civilization worldwide—not just in Europe but also Asia and Africa. This so-called **Columbian Exchange** proved to be one of the most significant global developments during the period from 1450 to 1750.

NEW SPAIN

After the 1492 voyage of Columbus, the papal **lines of demarcation** granted jurisdiction over the entire New World to Spain, with the exception of Brazil, which went to Portugal.

The Spanish first established themselves on the islands of the Caribbean. Military expeditions led by **conquistadores** led to the creation of New Spain on the mainland of North and South America. The conquistadores took over Florida and most of what is today the southern and southwestern United States, including Texas and California. Their most striking victories were the conquest of Montezuma (Moctezuma) II and the Aztecs by **Hernán Cortés**, from 1519 to 1522, and the destruction of the Incan Empire between 1531 and 1536 by **Francisco Pizarro**. The former allowed the Spanish to turn Mexico City (built on the site of the Aztec capital, Tenochtitlán) into New Spain's principal headquarters. The latter opened up South America for future conquests.

> **NOTE**
>
> Starting in 1535, New Spain was governed as a viceroyalty (*viceroy* means "in place of the king"). By the 1700s, three new viceroyalties—Peru, New Granada (northern South America), and La Plata (southern South America)—had been added.

Reasons for Spanish Success

Even with very small forces, the Spanish defeated large and powerful cultures in the Americas quickly and decisively. With their **horses and gunpowder weapons**, conquistadores such as Cortés and Pizarro enjoyed a military advantage that outweighed their lack of numbers. The Spanish (especially Cortés) were also adept at **divide-and-conquer tactics**, whereby they stirred up rivalries among native tribes and allied with some against others.

What most enabled the Spanish conquest was disease, particularly **smallpox** and **measles** (the same was true of the Portuguese in Brazil). Having no immunity to these new illnesses, native peoples died in massive numbers. Anywhere from one-quarter to one-half of the original population perished, and the survivors were even more vulnerable to Spanish invasion.

Exploitation, Forced Labor, and Slavery

The conquistador Cortés famously explained that he had come to the Americas for "God, gold, and glory." Although converting Native Americans to Catholicism was considered important (especially to offset the loss of worshippers to Protestant churches in Europe), Cortés's second motivation—economic exploitation—was Spain's highest priority in the New World.

At first, the conquistadores governed the territory they conquered, sending one-fifth (*la quinta*) of their profits back to Spain. The viceregal system placed the New World colonies under Madrid's direct control. All colonial economic activity was run by the **House of Trade** in Seville.

Above all, the Spanish extracted **precious metals** from the Americas: **gold** and, even more important, **silver**. The largest silver mines were dug near Mexico City and at **Potosí**, Bolivia's "mountain of silver." Agriculture was important as well. Chief crops included **coffee**, bananas, tomatoes, corn, potatoes, and most crucial, **sugarcane**, which was turned into rum and molasses. The Spanish (and Portuguese) made use of **plantation monoculture**: the intensive cultivation of a single crop on large estates (known as haciendas, estancias, or latifundia).

Mining, labor-intensive sugarcane farming, and plantation monoculture required large numbers of manual laborers. At first, conquistadores resorted to the **encomienda** system (which declared all peoples in the Americas Spanish subjects) as a way of forcing Native Americans to work as slaves. This practice ended by the 1530s and 1540s, not only because Native Americans proved unable and unwilling to work as slaves but also because the Catholic clergy protested the cruelty resulting from the encomienda system. The book *Tears of the Indians*, by the monk Bartolomé de las Casas, did much to sway Spanish opinion about the plight of Native Americans. The encomienda was abolished in 1542. As described in Chapter 18, the result was to persuade the Spanish (like the Portuguese) to turn to Africa as a source of forced labor, leading to the escalation of the **Atlantic slave trade**.

> **NOTE**
>
> Plantation monoculture is environmentally damaging (it wears out soil); it leads to long-term economic backwardness (by discouraging countries from diversifying their resource base) and, worst of all, encourages unfair labor practices (including slavery).

Ethnic Diversity and Social Stratification

The arrival of the Spanish increased the racial diversity of the Americas. Pure-bred Spanish who settled in the New World were known as *peninsulares*. Those of Spanish descent born in the colonies were criollos (better known as creoles). When Spanish and Native Americans intermarried, their families were known as mestizos, or "mixed." Other mixed races were mulattos (Europeans and African blacks) and *zambos* (Native Americans and African blacks). This intermixing of ethnicities and traditions has made Latin American culture very rich.

Unfortunately, during the centuries of Spanish rule, these groups were organized into a rigid social hierarchy, with European Spaniards at the top and those of mixed blood and native ancestry near the bottom. Slaves were on the lowest rung of the social ladder.

PORTUGUESE BRAZIL

Brazil, the one major territory in the New World allotted to Portugal rather than Spain, was discovered by accident in 1500 by Pedro Cabral, whose ship blew off course in a storm. At first, the Portuguese considered Brazil unimportant and established an outpost there only in 1532. By the mid-1500s, the Portuguese came to recognize Brazil's economic potential.

Native populations were decimated by Portuguese conquerors, falling victim to superior technology and new diseases. Portugal's treatment of the natives, a mixture of labor exploitation and mass conversion to Catholicism, was similar to Spain's. Various ethnic mixes of European, Native American, and African emerged. **Plantation monoculture** was dominant.

> **NOTE**
>
> Many of the same trends found in New Spain applied to Brazil.

Mining was important in Portuguese Brazil, as were the forest industries of the Amazon basin. For years, however, the most important resource was **sugarcane**. The labor-intensive nature of sugarcane cultivation prompted the Portuguese to use African slaves, first on their islands off the African coast and then Brazil. The first boatload of slaves to be brought directly from Africa to the New World arrived in 1518 (although African slaves had been brought there indirectly before then). Brazil was the largest importer of African slaves, and it was the last country in the Americas to outlaw slavery—not until 1888.

DUTCH AND ENGLISH NORTH AMERICA

The Dutch in the Americas

NOTE

The Dutch cultural presence—in the form of place names and well-to-do families (knickerbockers)—remain today.

As noted in Chapter 14, in the late 1500s, the Netherlands and England started attempting to break the Portuguese and Spanish monopoly on global trade routes and overseas colonization. They also began to settle in the New World.

The Dutch took over a number of islands in the Caribbean and seized part of northwestern Brazil from the Portuguese. In 1621, the Netherlands established the Dutch West India Company, twin to the older Dutch East India Company.

Farther to the north, the Dutch founded New Netherlands, in the region explored and claimed by Henry Hudson on their behalf. In 1624, Peter Minuit purchased the island of Manhattan from a local Native American tribe. Here, the city of **New Amsterdam**, capital of the new colony, grew into a thriving commercial center. The colony's leader was Peter Stuyvesant. In 1664, the Dutch lost New Netherlands to the English, who gave New Amsterdam another name: New York.

English Colonies and Permanent Settlement in the New World

Like the Dutch, the English moved into the New World as part of their commercial and military rivalry with Spain. They established a presence in the Caribbean, particularly on the islands of Barbados, Trinidad, and Jamaica.

Successful colonization of North America began at Jamestown, Virginia, in 1606. Economic activity was important, although many colonies were established by religious minorities, especially Puritans and Quakers, fleeing persecution at home. The *Mayflower* Pilgrims' Plymouth colony was founded in 1620; the nearby Massachusetts Bay Colony followed in 1628, and Boston was founded in 1630. The English seized New Amsterdam in 1664, renaming it New York. The colony of Pennsylvania, organized in 1682 by William Penn, was home to the English New World's largest city, Philadelphia.

The English took raw materials from the New World: sugarcane from the Caribbean; timber, corn, and potatoes (which caught on in England's oldest and closest colony, Ireland); and in the southern colonies, tobacco, which proved remarkably profitable. In addition, England, more so than other European nations, viewed the New World as a place to encourage large-scale **permanent settlement**. English colonies in the Americas became politically sophisticated, developed strong systems of local government, and, by the 1700s, felt a deep sense of local, even independent, identity.

NOTE

After the American Revolution, England deported its criminals to Australia.

Slaves were used by English colonists in the New World, especially in the Caribbean and the southern mainland. English criminals were often punished by "transportation," or exile, to the Americas. One institution that brought labor to the English New World was **indentured servitude**: would-be colonists who could not afford passage across the Atlantic would agree to work for a period of time for the families that paid their way. This was more common in the northern colonies.

FRENCH CANADA AND LOUISIANA

The French colonial presence in the New World began in **Canada**, in the 1500s and early 1600s, as Jacques Cartier, Samuel Champlain and other explorers charted the St. Lawrence River and established outposts like Quebec and Montreal (see Chapter 14).

In the 1600s, the French laid claim to the vast **Louisiana** territory, which included the Great Lakes and the Mississippi basin. In the south and along the Gulf of Mexico, they challenged the Spanish. The main priority of the French in North America was the **fur trade**: French colonists were great hunters, trappers, and woodsmen (*voyageurs*).

The French maintained island bases in the Caribbean, including Martinique, Guadeloupe, and Saint Domingue (today Haiti). Sugarcane production was the economic mainstay here.

By the mid-1700s, France had lost much of its territory in the New World. Its principal enemy was England, although Spain was a foe as well. Despite allying with a number of Native American tribes, French colonists lost several conflicts with English settlers, including Queen Anne's War (1701–1714), King George's War (1740–1748), and the **French and Indian Wars** (1756–1763), an offshoot of the Seven Years' War in Europe.

As a result of the third conflict, the English took over Canada (the province of Quebec stubbornly retained its French heritage). The Louisiana region was handed over to Spain, although the French got it back briefly in the late 1700s. French culture remains important in eastern Canada, the northern fringe of the United States, and the state of Louisiana. There, the Cajuns are descendants of the Canada's Acadians, who were expelled and forced southward by the English after the French and Indian Wars.

> **NOTE**
> The French were also more adept than other Europeans at cooperating with Native Americans (especially the Hurons and Algonquins), learning their ways, and adapting themselves to local customs and environments.

THE RUSSIAN-AMERICAN COMPANY

Europe's least famous colony in North America was Russia's. After conquering Siberia in the 1500s and reaching the Pacific coast in the 1600s, the Russians set their sights on Alaska and other areas. In the 1730s and 1740s, the **Bering expedition**, organized by the Russian government, surveyed the waters separating Siberia from North America. Afterward, Russian hunters and soldiers moved into the Aleutian Islands and Alaska.

The **fur trade** stimulated Russian settlement of North America. The Russians established a permanent colony in Alaska in 1784. They created the **Russian-American Company** and moved down the Pacific coast, building fortresses as far south as northern California.

> **NOTE**
> At least 80 percent of the Aleutians' native population is said to have perished due to Russian colonization, thanks to violence, the spread of disease, and alcoholism.

> **NOTE**
> Russia's presence in the New World lasted until 1867, when it sold Alaska to the United States.

THE COLUMBIAN EXCHANGE

Europe's encounter with the Americas led to one of the greatest demographic and ecological transformations in world history, known commonly as the **Columbian Exchange**.

The exchange of foods, plants, and animals shaped the environments of Old World and New World alike. From Europe came sheep, goats, cattle, and pigs, which increased the meat and milk supply in the Americas. The Europeans also brought the **horse**, which provided labor and transport and radically changed the lifestyle of Native Americans who lived on plains and grasslands. **Coffee**, which came from Arabia and Turkey and had already been transplanted to Africa, was found to flourish in South America. The southeastern part of North America joined Egypt and India as one of the world's great sources of **cotton**. Wheat, olives, and grapevines were brought to the Americas as well.

NOTE

Among the effects of this exchange was the mass transfer of populations. Millions of slaves and hundreds of thousands of colonists came from Africa and Europe to the New World. Once in the Americas, their interaction with the indigenous peoples led to complex and rich ethnic and cultural mixing.

From the Americas came manioc (which became a staple in Africa), squash, sweet potatoes, peppers, beans, peanuts, and vitamin-rich tomatoes. Caribbean **sugarcane** displaced the Old World's sugar beet as a primary source of sugar and became central to the world economy (and the Atlantic slave trade). **Tobacco** and cacao (for making chocolate) became eagerly sought luxury goods in Europe. Because they were easy to grow and yielded many calories per acre, **corn** (maize) and **potatoes** were the New World crops that most affected Eurasia and Africa.

World Boundaries in 1453 and 1700.
In 1453, major states and empires were concentrated in Eurasia and small territories in Africa and the Americas. By 1700, large civilizations had spread into Russia, more portions of the Americas, and deeper into Africa.

NOTE

The death rate caused by European diseases is thought to have been at least 25 percent of the Americas' pre-Columbian population; some estimates run as high as 50 percent.

Tragically, the transfer of diseases, such as **smallpox** and **measles**, brought to the New World from Europe, was part of the Columbian Exchange. Environmentally isolated from Eurasia and Africa for so many centuries, the inhabitants of the Americas had no immunity to these new illnesses. The one disease Europeans may have brought back from the New World is the sexually transmitted disease syphilis (although there is much scholarly debate about the origins of this disease).

QUICK REVIEW

1. Spain's principal reason for colonization in the New World was

   (A) economic profit.
   (B) conversion of Native Americans to Catholicism.
   (C) scientific curiosity.
   (D) strategic advantage.
   (E) the desire of the Spanish to settle elsewhere.

2. The main accomplishment of Bartolomé de las Casas was

   (A) to develop a new method of silver mining.
   (B) to discover the fabled Fountain of Youth.
   (C) to help end the harsh treatment of Indians by Spanish conquistadores.
   (D) to revolutionize agricultural technique in the New World.
   (E) to conquer the Incas.

3. The precious metal most sought by the Spanish and Portuguese in the Americas was

   (A) gold.
   (B) copper.
   (C) tin.
   (D) silver.
   (E) nickel.

4. Which of the following best describes the Spanish and Portuguese approach to agriculture in the Americas?

   (A) The Spanish and Portuguese encouraged a balanced cultivation of a variety of crops.
   (B) The Spanish and Portuguese relied on large-scale plantation monoculture.
   (C) The Spanish and Portuguese experimented with a variety of agricultural methods.
   (D) The Spanish and Portuguese were mainly unconcerned with agriculture.
   (E) The Spanish and Portuguese made agriculture their highest priority in the Americas.

5. Which is an example of changes brought about by the Columbian Exchange?

   (A) the exportation of the horse from North America to Europe
   (B) the extraction of silver from South America by the Spanish
   (C) the importation of coffee to the Americas from Europe
   (D) the spread of smallpox to Europe from North America
   (E) the arrival of corn and potatoes from the Americas to Europe

6. Native American victims of the Spanish conquest perished primarily by what means?

   (A) gunpowder weapons
   (B) starvation and famine
   (C) diseases such as smallpox and measles
   (D) mass execution by hanging
   (E) mass execution by burning

7. Peter Stuyvesant was the leader of which colony?

   (A) Hudson Bay
   (B) New Amsterdam
   (C) Pennsylvania
   (D) Quebec
   (E) Roanoke

8. Which European nation was most concerned with long-term settlement of large numbers of people in the New World?

   (A) England
   (B) Portugal
   (C) France
   (D) the Netherlands
   (E) Spain

9. What commodity were the French most interested in finding or harvesting in the New World?

   (A) coffee
   (B) tobacco
   (C) sugar
   (D) fur
   (E) rum

10. What European power colonized Alaska and the Aleutian Islands?

    (A) Great Britain
    (B) Russia
    (C) Spain
    (D) Portugal
    (E) Belgium

Answers

1. **(A)** The Spanish explored and colonized North and South America largely for reasons of profit. They were motivated to extract natural resources of this region, although converting Native Americans to Catholicism was also a goal.

2. **(C)** De las Casas wrote a book that protested the inhumane treatment of Native Americans by the Spanish. This book helped sway the opinion of Spanish authorities, who changed labor regulations in 1542.

3. **(D)** Precious metals were the most important natural resource that the Spanish extracted from the Americas. Although the Spanish mined gold, they mined more silver than any other precious metal and exported it to Europe and the rest of the world. A resulting silver glut affected the global economy in the 1600s.

4. **(B)** Such a system allowed the Spanish and Portuguese to grow large quantities of a single crop cheaply. Labor in the plantation system was cheap because the Europeans paid Native Americans little or used slaves. Unfortunately, monoculture eventually harms the environment and fails to diversify a country's resource base.

5. **(E)** Corn and potatoes had a major impact on European diets because they provide a high calorie yield per acre grown. This situation meant more food for less work and therefore more profits.

6. **(C)** Native Americans had never been exposed to these illnesses. Therefore, they did not have the time to work an immunity to them and died in significantly high numbers. The high population loss also weakened the ability of Native Americans to resist the Spanish.

7. **(B)** Under Stuyvesant's leadership, the Dutch colony of New Amsterdam prospered and enlarged. However, after the English defeated the Dutch in 1664, the English took control of the colony and renamed it New York.

8. **(A)** The English saw their colonies as more than areas from which to extract valuable natural resources. Instead, they built permanent settlements, which developed strong systems of local government. By the 1700s, this trend led colonists to feel a growing sense of independence from England.

9. **(D)** Initially, like the Spanish, the French were mainly interested in economic extraction, as opposed to establishing permanent settlements as the English had. Most French colonists in North America were hunters and trappers who harvested skins and pelts for the European market.

10. **(B)** The Russians began to settle Alaska and the Aleutian Islands in the 1700s. A growing number of Russian hunters and soldiers soon inhabited the Aleutian Islands and then settled in Alaska.

Unit Four: Review Questions

SAMPLE ESSAY QUESTIONS

1. Compare and contrast the Ottoman Empire and Ming China. Pay special attention to the question of how such grand and powerful civilizations could, by the 1700s, have fallen so far from the position of global might and technological leadership they had enjoyed in the 1400s and 1500s.

2. How did the rise of the Atlantic slave trade affect Africa, economically, politically, and demographically, between 1450 and 1750?

3. Compare and contrast Kongo and Mughal India, both in terms of their internal policies and their relations with the outside world, focusing on the period between 1450 and 1750.

4. What changes did Japan undergo between 1450 and 1750?

MULTIPLE-CHOICE QUESTIONS

1. Which of the following is NOT a reason Europeans joined Protestant churches during the Reformation?

   (A) Many felt that the Catholic Church was too concerned with wealth and power.
   (B) Roman Catholic priests stopped performing rituals.
   (C) Many people saw the Catholic Church as hypocritical and corrupt.
   (D) Many people saw the Catholic Church as too bureaucratic.
   (E) none of the above

2. What was the purpose of the Counter-Reformation?

   (A) to reorganize and reform the Catholic Church and increase its public appeal
   (B) to avoid reforming the Catholic Church
   (C) to force individuals to adopt Catholicism
   (D) to colonize Africa
   (E) to outlaw abortion

3. One effect of the Protestant Reformation on women in Europe was

   (A) to allow them to become pastors.
   (B) to forbid them from working in businesses or shops.
   (C) to urge them to assert their equality with men.
   (D) to make it more difficult for them to arrange marriages.
   (E) to encourage them to read the Bible and thereby raise their literacy.

4. Why did an increasing number of countries in Europe function more like nation-states beginning in the 1600s?

   (A) Feudalism became more widespread.
   (B) Politics began to decentralize.
   (C) State institutions, especially bureaucracies, central banks, and armed forces, strengthened.
   (D) Populations became more heterogeneous.
   (E) none of the above

5. How did Peter the Great change Russia's geopolitical orientation?

   (A) by focusing its foreign affairs more on Europe than on Asia
   (B) by focusing its foreign affairs more on Asia than on Europe
   (C) by making it a democracy
   (D) by creating a parliament with control over the direction of foreign policy
   (E) by colonizing parts of Africa

6. Which of the following is true of eighteenth-century European society?

   (A) Most Europeans were merchants or involved in global trade in some way.
   (B) The aristocracy grew in numbers.
   (C) The majority of Europeans were peasants.
   (D) The population began to shrink.
   (E) The feminist movement gained momentum in France.

7. How is capitalism different from mercantilism?

   (A) Capitalism focuses on state-controlled wealth accumulation, while mercantilism gives all commercial power to the merchants.
   (B) Capitalism arose earlier than mercantilism.
   (C) Capitalism is a socialist theory, whereas mercantilism is not.
   (D) Capitalism focuses on free trade and the market forces of supply and demand, while mercantilism features state-controlled economic activity.
   (E) Capitalism involves trade on land, whereas mercantilism involves maritime trade.

8. How did Ottoman leaders rule their empire during the 1500s?

   (A) They were religiously intolerant and failed to gain bureaucratic control over their subjects.

   (B) They were fairly religiously tolerant and efficient in governing their territory.

   (C) They allowed local people to vote for their own leaders, as long as they did not oppose Ottoman dominance.

   (D) They carried out a policy to exterminate non-Muslims.

   (E) The Ottoman Empire did not exist in the 1500s.

9. Why did China become more open to foreign influence after the end of the 1700s?

   (A) Its national wealth had declined, and it slipped backward in technological innovation and scientific advancement.

   (B) Its leaders encouraged more imports.

   (C) England promised the Chinese military support.

   (D) The Chinese economy was booming, and China's leaders wanted to increase trade with the West.

   (E) China welcomed Christian missionaries as modernizers.

10. How was Japan reunified by 1615?

   (A) The emperor reasserted his power.

   (B) The threat posed by European invaders compelled it to unify.

   (C) Its politicians settled their disputes for largely economic reasons.

   (D) Three politician-warlords used force and diplomacy to reunite the country.

   (E) none of the above

11. The Mughal rulers

   I. were Muslims.
   II. ruled Thailand.
   III. used military force and advanced weapons technology to maintain power.
   IV. harmed the economy with their corruption.

   (A) I, II, and III

   (B) II, III, and IV

   (C) I and III only

   (D) II and IV only

   (E) all of the above

12. In the early 1400s, what was the main result of Portuguese exploration of West and Equatorial Africa?

   (A) The Portuguese gained control over the gold and ivory trade networks.

   (B) The Portuguese found a route to the West Indies.

   (C) The Portuguese established a position from which to conquer Egypt.

   (D) The Portuguese gained control over the iron trade.

   (E) none of the above

13. Which country did the Boers come from, and in which African region did they settle?

   (A) Tunisia and Central Africa

   (B) the Netherlands and South Africa

   (C) Scotland and Kenya

   (D) France and Algeria

   (E) none of the above

14. Which of the following describes trade in the Indian Ocean during the 1400s?

   (A) Trade and development were in decline.

   (B) The Indian Ocean swarmed with pirates, who prevented trade from taking place.

   (C) There was no trading system in this area at the time.

   (D) The area was a vibrant and cosmopolitan system of economic and cultural exchange.

   (E) East African cities were under the control of Spanish colonists.

15. What increased the European demand for African slaves from the 1500s onward?

   (A) Sugar cultivation in Brazil and the Caribbean became an increasingly important part of the Europeans' colonial economies.
   (B) European settlers in the New World became convinced that Native Americans were not suited for slavery.
   (C) Slaves were central to the triangular trade system in the 1600s and 1700s.
   (D) The *encomienda* system was abolished soon after the Spanish established their rule over most of the New World.
   (E) all of the above

16. Which of the following was NOT a part of the triangular trade system?

   (A) the so-called Middle Passage that brought slaves to the Americas
   (B) colonial raw materials that went to Africa
   (C) European manufactured goods that went to Africa
   (D) slaves traded for raw materials in the Americas
   (E) raw materials sent back to Europe from the Americas

17. Why were the Spanish able to conquer large and powerful Native American societies so quickly and decisively?

   I.   The Spanish had more sophisticated military technology.
   II. Native Americans tended to be pacifists and did not put up a fight.
   III. The Native Americans died in great numbers from European diseases.
   IV. The Spanish used effective divide-and-conquer tactics.

   (A) I, II, and III
   (B) II, III, and IV
   (C) I, III, and IV
   (D) I and III only
   (E) II and IV only

18. According to the two maps on page 248

   (A) the size of Russia had contracted greatly between the 1450s and the early 1700s.
   (B) the Incas still controlled the west coast of South America even in the 1700s.
   (C) Great Zimbabwe still existed by 1700.
   (D) the same dynasty led China in the early 1700s as in the 1450s.
   (E) both the Holy Roman and the Ottoman Empires existed in some form between the years 1453 and 1700.

19. What was a major consequence of plantation monoculture?

   (A) Slaves were underused.
   (B) It yielded low profits.
   (C) Many different crops were harvested on the same plot of land.
   (D) It led to environmental degradation.
   (E) Farmers became more susceptible to disease.

20. Which of the following INCORRECTLY matches a European power with one of its major colonies?

   (A) England—Louisiana
   (B) Russia—Alaska
   (C) Spain—Mexico
   (D) Portugal—Brazil
   (E) the Netherlands—Indonesia

Answers

1. **(B)** Early Protestants believed that less emphasis should be placed on rituals and sacraments than was the case in the Catholic Church. For example, they opposed the Catholic veneration of saints because they thought that such a practice interfered with a pure and sincere relationship with God.

2. **(A)** The Counter-Reformation occurred during the mid-to-late 1500s in response to the growth of Protestantism in Europe. The Catholic Church wanted to regain worshippers by increasing its appeal through such strategies as the creation of impressive art and architecture. Also, the Catholic Church stiffened religious discipline and revived the Holy Inquisition. The Jesuits order was formed and came to play an active role in European life.

3. **(E)** Protestant leaders were not interested in advocating gender equality. However, they did often encourage women to read the Bible. In the process, more women learned how to read and write.

4. **(C)** During the 1600s, centralization continued in European nation-states, and their governments became more bureaucratic. They collected taxes from their subjects; the taxes paid for bigger governments and more powerful armies.

5. **(A)** In attempting to westernize Russia, Peter the Great chose to focus Russia's foreign affairs more on Europe than Asia. By his death in 1725, Russia had become a key member of the European state system and a military power.

6. **(C)** In Europe at this time, the population grew thanks to the Agricultural Revolution, and there was greater social diversification. Still, most people remained peasants.

7. **(D)** Mercantilism is an economic system that benefits the state first and foremost. For example, trade is structured so that the state reaps the greatest amount of profits. Conversely, capitalism is an economic system that financially benefits individual owners of the means of production and capital, and the state is less likely to interfere in economic transactions.

8. **(B)** During the 1500s, the Ottomans continued their military conquests into eastern Europe. They ruled over a diverse number of people and felt that they could best administer these regions if they allowed a semblance of religious tolerance.

9. **(A)** At the end of the 1700s, China's population was growing more steadily than its economy. As a result, poverty increased and the country declined in terms of technological and scientific advancements and its geopolitical influence.

10. **(D)** For years, Japan was in political turmoil. Anarchy reigned. Three Japanese rulers used force and diplomacy to unify the country between 1560 and 1615. The ultimate unifier of Japan was Tokugawa Ieyasu.

11. **(C)** The Mughals ruled India, not Thailand. Particularly under the reign of Akbar the Great, from 1556 to 1605, the Mughals governed the country efficiently. They maintained power as well through military force and advanced weaponry. However, in the 1700s, the Mughal state declined owing to unrest in the provinces and growing European advances.

12. **(A)** The Portuguese aimed to control these networks, which existed throughout West and Equatorial Africa. During the 1500s, they conquered the Shona people's Mwene Metapa dynasty as a way to dominate the gold trade along the upper Zambezi River.

13. **(B)** The Boers are of Dutch ancestry. They also are called Afrikaners. They first settled in South Africa in 1652 in order to farm the land and establish trade along the coast.

14. **(D)** The Indian Ocean trading system thrived at this time. The Portuguese in particular established permanent bases in East Africa,

not only for use as a launching pad to India but also to gain tighter control over trade in the region.

15. **(E)** Several factors increased the European demand for African slaves from the 1500s onward.

16. **(B)** Under the triangular trade system, Africa became a major source of raw materials and slaves. Manufactured goods were produced in Europe and then brought to Africa and exchanged for gold, ivory, timber, and slaves.

17. **(C)** Native Americans, with no immunity to new diseases brought by the Spanish, died in very high numbers. Native Americans could not compete with the Spanish in military technology, and divide-and-conquer tactics weakened possibilities for effective alliances among groups.

18. **(E)** The Holy Roman Empire was later referred to as the Austrian Empire. It collapsed in 1918 as a result of World War I. The Ottoman Empire, already in decline in the 1800s, also collapsed because of World War I.

19. **(D)** Monoculture damaged the environment because of the emphasis it places on cultivating one crop. The other choices are factually wrong, as slaves were used widely, profits were high in the sugar industry, and farmers did not become more susceptible to disease as a result.

20. **(A)** The French first settled Louisiana, after traveling across the Great Lakes and down the Mississippi River. The Louisiana Territory became the property of the French crown in 1663. In 1803, the American government purchased this land from the French for approximately $15 million.

UNIT FIVE

WORLD CULTURES
IN THE MODERN ERA
(1750–1914)

Unit Overview

GENERAL REMARKS

During the 1750–1914 period, the world entered the modern age. In this, it was led by the nations of the West, consisting of Europe and the United States.

Exactly what defines **modernity** is a question of debate among historians. In popular terms, the word *modern* is used simply as a synonym for "contemporary" or as a way to describe one's own times. In historical terms, the word *modern* is used to describe an era characterized by certain features. Different scholars outline modernity's features in different ways, but most agree that they include the following:

- In politics, there is a move away from traditional monarchy and toward greater political representation. The end result in most societies is some form of democracy or at least the appearance of democracy.
- In economics, mechanization and industrialization become driving forces. There is a shift from feudalism and mercantilism to capitalism. Rather than being based primarily on agriculture, economies are based increasingly on industry and commerce.
- In society, there is class transformation, as old aristocracies gradually fade away, in favor of new elites whose status derives from wealth. New classes expand or emerge, especially the middle class and industrial working class. As agriculture gives way to industry, societies become urbanized. Population growth accelerates in the modern era.
- In culture, a scientific, secular worldview becomes dominant. In arts and letters, styles change more rapidly and radically than ever before.

In all these things, Europe, with the United States, moved forward first. Great political upheavals such as the **American Revolution** and the **French Revolution** began the long process of expanding political representation and giving more people a greater voice in politics. It was in Europe that the **Industrial Revolution** began, and it was there that capitalism emerged. Both transformed the economies of the world. Population growth, class diversification, and urbanization were hallmarks of Western social development during the late 1700s and throughout the 1800s. The foundations for modern culture and intellectual life had been laid in Europe during the 1700s, during the Scientific Revolution and the Enlightenment.

To varying degrees, modernization reached the rest of the world in the nineteenth and early twentieth centuries. A few non-Western nations adapted well and quickly, such as Japan. Some, including the Ottoman Empire, China, and the nations of Latin America, modernized slowly or half-heartedly. Other civilizations, most notably those of Africa and Southeast Asia, lagged farther behind. No matter the pace, however, change eventually came to all these regions.

Another overarching development between 1750 and 1914 was the **rise of the West** as the world's dominant civilization. Not only did rapid industrialization and modernization make the West prosperous and technologically advanced, they made it powerful as well. European (and American) imperialism gave control over most of the world's habitable territory to the nations of the West. Many areas that had originally been colonized during the Age of Exploration—such as North and South America—became free during the late 1700s and early 1800s. However, a **new imperialism** swept over East Asia, Southeast Asia, Central Asia, the Middle East, the Pacific, and Africa during the 1800s and early 1900s. Seeking markets and raw materials, armed with industrial-era weaponry, the nations of the West established control over a vast portion of the globe. Never before in history had a single civilization become so powerful. As impressive as imperialism was practically, however, it carried with it a steep moral and ethical price. Imperialism was inextricably bound up with warfare, racial prejudice, economic rapacity, and slavery. Many of the harmful effects of Western imperialism are still felt in regions such as Africa, Latin America, and Asia to this day.

By the end of the nineteenth century, Europe—wealthy, sophisticated, militarily dominant—was at the peak of its power. Unbeknownst to them, Europe's nations were about to fall from that pinnacle. The young United States was overtaking Europe in economic and military strength. New philosophies, scientific theories, and cultural movements were calling into question the traditional certainties and values of the Western world. Most important, Europe was moving toward war. The conflict resulting from the diplomatic tensions of the late 1800s and early 1900s—World War I—was the worst war ever fought to that date. The world war did much to start and then speed up the process of European decline.

BROAD TRENDS

Global Power and International Relations

- The technological, economic, and military rise of the West—Europe and the United States—completely altered the balance of global power. World affairs were increasingly determined by foreign-policy and military developments in Europe, especially during the 1800s.
- The United States broke away from English rule during the late 1700s. During the 1800s, it dominated the North American continent and became a world power.
- The Spanish and Portuguese colonies of Central and South America freed themselves from European rule during the early 1800s.
- In North Africa, the eastern Mediterranean, and the Middle East, the gradual collapse of the Ottoman Empire presented the nations of Europe with a troubling and destabilizing diplomatic issue known as the Eastern Question.

- European (and U.S.) imperialism—the "new imperialism" of the mid-to-late 1800s—gave the nations of the West unprecedented global dominance. In 1815, the nations of the West controlled 35 percent of the world's habitable territory. In 1914, they controlled 85 percent.
- The one non-Western nation that developed an effective, modern, colonial empire was Japan, in the late nineteenth and early twentieth centuries.
- In Europe, the new nations of Germany and Italy appeared.
- By the end of the 1800s, diplomatic tensions, nationalism, and competition over colonies made it increasingly likely that the nations of Europe would go to war. An alliance system formed. The level of aggression rose steadily. World War I resulted in 1914.

Political Developments

- The hallmark of modern political life is greater popular representation.
- This trend first got underway in the West. It began in the late 1700s, primarily with the American and French Revolutions.
- During the 1800s, especially after the 1848 revolution, politics in Europe and the West became increasingly representative. By the end of the century, Great Britain, France, and the United States, along with a few smaller countries, had become democracies (although women could not yet vote). Even in nondemocratic states, bureaucracies and parliamentary bodies were becoming an increasingly important part of government, even more so than the will of individual rulers and monarchs.
- Other parts of the world tended to be slower in moving away from traditional autocracies or monarchies. A few, such as Japan and the Ottoman Empire, did so, developing parliamentary forms of monarchy by the start of the twentieth century. The nations of Latin America developed parliamentary governments in theory, but many of those slipped into dictatorship or military rule.
- Much of the non-Western world spent most of the nineteenth century under European (in some cases, U.S.) colonial domination.

Economic and Environmental Developments

- Economic life was transformed by the phenomenon of industrialization, which displaced agriculture as the largest and most important sector of the economy. Industrialization swept Europe in the late 1700s and early 1800s, then spread to the rest of the world. The Industrial Revolution began in England.
- The dominant mode of economic organization in the West became free-market capitalism. Along with industry, commerce and banking—the foundations of a money-based economy (as opposed to a land-based one)—grew in importance.
- Industrialization transformed class structures. The traditional aristocracy, with its status based on land and family prestige, faded. Among the lower classes, the proportion of peasants and farmers shrank. The middle class grew tremendously, gained great wealth, and diversified. A new lower class, the industrial working class, was born.

- Industrialization led to urbanization. Cities grew in size, and more cities were established.
- For any society, the first decades of industrialization were typically painful for the lower classes. Working conditions were poor, and wages were low. Over time, however, industrialization greatly raised the average prosperity of a society's population, and even the lower classes began to benefit after some time.
- The non-Western world adopted industrialization at varying speeds and in different ways. Sometimes, European imperial powers introduced it to their colonies. In other cases, rulers of free non-Western nations tried to impose industrialization from above.
- One of the bedrocks of the world economy during the late 1700s and most of the 1800s was slavery. Africa was the primary victim of slave trading. The East African and Atlantic slave trades continued into the 1870s and 1880s, respectively.
- Industrialization vastly increased humanity's impact on the environment. Pollution levels rose.

Cultural Developments

- Starting in the West, a scientific, secular worldview became paramount. The technological and scientific advancements of the Industrial Revolution, as well as the theories of scholars such as Charles Darwin, accelerated this process.
- Greater access to public education became a normal part of life in western Europe, northern Europe, Canada, and the United States throughout the 1800s. Literacy rates rose as a result. The same is true for many other parts of the world during the late 1800s.
- There was a tremendous movement of peoples during this period. In particular, there were massive waves of emigration from Europe and China to North and South America during the mid-to-late 1800s and early 1900s. The United States was the preferred destination, but Canada, Argentina, and Chile took in many immigrants as well.
- Nationalism became a powerful cultural attitude in Europe and then elsewhere. By the end of the 1800s, nationalist movements were becoming prevalent in non-Western parts of the world dominated by foreign colonial rule.
- The non-Western world began to adopt many of the artistic and literary forms of the West, especially print culture and writing styles, as well as architecture. Conversely, styles from Asia, Africa, and the Middle East had an influence on Western culture, particularly in painting, sculpture, and décor.
- In Europe and the Americas, the pace of cultural change sped up considerably. By the end of the 1800s and the beginning of the 1900s, new artistic and literary trends were emerging at a rapid rate. Increasingly, new artistic and literary trends were about breaking rules and defying conventions.

Gender Issues

- Although in most societies, the status of women remained secondary, the 1750–1914 period saw great changes in gender relations.

- In the West, a greater awareness of the unequal treatment of women began to spread, starting around the late 1700s. This was stimulated partly by the theories of Enlightenment philosophy, as well as the active role played by women in the American and French revolutions.
- During the late 1700s and early 1800s, the Industrial Revolution profoundly altered the conditions under which women worked. The Industrial Revolution shifted the workplace away from the farm, where men and women both lived and worked, to mines, factories, and other spaces away from the home. This shift created a domestic sphere and a separate working sphere away from the home.
- In Europe and the United States, women of the lower classes were generally compelled to enter the workplace (most frequently textile factories). These women also bore the double burden of serving as the primary homemakers and caregivers for their families.
- After the mid-1800s, the number of working women in Europe and North America declined. Women of the middle and upper classes had rarely worked to begin with. As wages for industrial workers rose (making those jobs more desirable to men) and as laws restricting the number of hours women and children could work were passed, the number of lower-class working women fell. A cult of domesticity, stressing that a woman's place was in the home, while a man's was in the workplace, dominated Western culture—especially among the middle and upper classes—during the mid-to-late nineteenth century.
- Certain occupations were open to women, such as child care (governesses), teaching, domestic household work (servants and maids), nursing, and artisanry.
- Strong and vigorous women's movements appeared in Europe, Canada, and the United States. They agitated for suffrage (the right to vote), equal opportunity to work, equal pay, temperance, and other causes.
- A handful of European nations—but no major ones—gave women the right to vote before World War I.
- The move toward women's equality tended to be slower in non-Western societies. In some, however, the educational level of women rose, as did the extent of property rights. As in the West, women worked, especially in certain occupations, such as agricultural laborers, servants, teachers, nurses, and so on. As non-Western parts of the world industrialized, lower-class women tended to enter the workplace, as they did in the industrial West.

QUESTIONS AND COMPARISONS TO CONSIDER

- Compare revolutions in two or more of the following countries: America, Haiti, France, Mexico, and China.
- Discuss the response of non-Western parts of the world such as China, India, Japan, and the Ottoman Empire to imperial encroachments and foreign pressures (especially from Europe and the United States) during this period.
- Compare the status of women in the West and that of women in other parts of the world. Also, in western Europe, compare the roles and conditions of upper- and middle-class women with those of the peasant and working classes.

- Describe the various approaches taken by various Western powers to colonization. Also, how does the late-nineteenth-century wave of imperialism (the "new" imperialism) compare to earlier waves of colonization?
- Discuss the various ways in which non-Western states attempted to modernize and adopt industrial practices. How important is the question of whether industrialization was imposed on a society from above, by the ruler, or emerged from below?
- Take a close look at Japanese industrialization and European industrialization. How were they alike, and how did they differ?
- How did Western intervention in Latin America differ from Western intervention in Africa during the 1750–1914 period?
- Examine the nationalist and anticolonial movements in non-Western parts of the world. Compare and contrast their methods and their successes and/or failures.

The Europeans at Home: Revolution, Reaction, and Reform

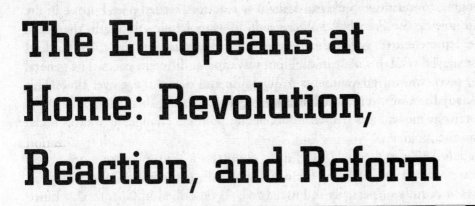

CHAPTER 20

- The Atlantic revolutions and the French Revolution
- The Napoleonic wars, the Congress of Vienna, and reaction
- The Industrial Revolution
- Increased representation (reform versus revolution)
- Women's movements and female suffrage
- Nationalism and the unifications of Italy and Germany
- Anti-Semitism (pogroms; the Dreyfus Affair)
- Romanticism, realism, and artistic modernism
- Charles Darwin and the theory of natural selection
- Albert Einstein and the theory of relativity
- Sigmund Freud and psychology

From 1750 to 1914, the European political order changed dramatically. In the mid-1700s, all of Europe's major nations were monarchies. Although a handful were parliamentary, allowing for some level of popular representation, most were absolute—meaning that, in theory, the monarch had few if any restrictions on his or her power. In general, monarchs shared power only with aristocratic noble classes. In any given country, the nobility made up an extremely small proportion of the overall population but controlled most of the country's wealth, owned most of the nation's land, and enjoyed virtually all influence over politics.

From the 1770s through the 1810s, this state of affairs was shaken apart by a wave of **Atlantic revolutions.** The most famous took place in Britain's North American colonies (see Chapter 27) and France, but there were others as well. Although not all their goals were met, the revolutions dealt a death blow to absolute monarchy in most of Europe. Another effect was that an ever-increasing number of people began to dream of—and fight for—social and political systems that treated them fairly and gave them more voice in government. Another factor that changed ordinary Europeans' social and economic aspirations was the **Industrial Revolution,** which happened at the same time as the political revolutions in America and France and is described in Chapter 21.

Although a conservative backlash, known as **reaction**, settled over Europe in the decades following the French Revolution and its Napoleonic aftermath, the desire for more representative government never died. Each nation, its rulers and its people, struggled with this issue in different ways and at different paces. The general trend, however, was for governments to liberalize and democratize over time. This was especially the case after the **revolutions of 1848**. During the second half of the century, reform movements helped to accelerate political change, as well as social and economic progress.

By the late 1800s and early 1900s, most countries in Europe were more or less representative, and a few were, by the day's standards, democratic. Most European economies were fully or partially industrialized. As described in Chapter 22, European powers, thanks to their imperial successes, dominated a vast amount of the rest of the world. These years marked the peak of Europe's global might. Underlying diplomatic and strategic tensions, however, gave rise to World War I (1914–1918): the huge cataclysm that started the process of toppling Europe from its position of world power.

THE FRENCH REVOLUTION AND THE NAPOLEONIC ERA

Long-term Causes of the French Revolution

The causes of the **French Revolution** (1789–1799) are many and complex. Deep, long-term factors included

- The wide social and economic gap between ordinary citizens (known as the Third Estate) and the country's elite, the Catholic clergy (**First Estate**) and the aristocracy (Second Estate)
- The unfair tax system, from which the wealthy First and Second Estates were exempt
- The frustrated ambitions of the middle class, who had wealth and education but, because they belonged to the Third Estate, were barred from social advancement
- The influence of the Enlightenment (see Chapter 13), whose philosophers, many of whom were French, made powerful arguments in favor of fair government, equal treatment of citizens, the separation of governmental powers, and civil rights

Added to these causes were the political ineptitude of the last two absolute monarchs of France, Louis XV and Louis XVI, and a long-standing financial crisis in France. Another ingredient was the American Revolution (1775–1783), which France supported (adding to its financial troubles) and which the French people admired. Little did the French government realize that by helping the American revolutionaries, it would encourage revolution in its own country shortly afterward.

The Estates General and the Early French Revolution

The immediate cause of the French Revolution was the impending bankruptcy of the government. Saddled with debts piled up by the previous king, having spent even more money on America's revolution, unable to tax the rich First and Second Estates, and burdened with a wife, Marie Antoinette, who spent lavishly, **Louis XVI** (1774–1792) could not solve France's financial crisis. By 1787 and 1788, inflation, unemployment, food shortages, and rising prices were tormenting the entire country.

In May 1789, desperate for a solution, Louis XVI summoned the **Estates General**: a national assembly of delegates from each estate. The delegates of the Third Estate— mainly middle-class lawyers—came to Versailles expecting to negotiate seriously about changing the tax system and granting equal rights to all classes. By June, however, it was clear that neither Louis XVI nor the First and Second Estates were prepared to compromise. This clash of wills sparked ten years of revolution.

In late June, the delegates of the Third Estate, with liberal members of the First and Second Estates, declared themselves to be a new government, the **National Assembly**, and vowed not to leave Versailles until the king granted them a constitution. In July, the people of Paris and other major cities rose up in support of the assembly, as did peasants in the countryside. The Paris revolt, **Bastille Day**, is celebrated as the moment France liberated itself from absolute monarchy. Over the summer, the assembly assumed power in Paris.

The first two years of the revolution were a relatively moderate time. Louis XVI was allowed to remain king, but with the reduced powers of a parliamentary monarch. Guided by Enlightenment ideals and the American Declaration of Independence, the assembly guaranteed basic civil liberties in the **Declaration of the Rights of Man and the Citizen**. Future assemblies were to be elected by popular vote. Aristocratic status and privileges (especially exemption from taxes) were done away with, lands owned by the Catholic Church were nationalized, and church and state were separated. Policy was guided by the motto Liberty, Equality, and Fraternity.

There were, however, problems. At first, the rights proclaimed by the revolution, including the vote, applied only to white, Catholic, adult males. Only with time did Jews, Protestants, and blacks gain those rights. In addition, despite the many key roles women played in toppling the absolutist regime, the revolution never granted them those rights (or the vote). More practically, the assembly failed to solve worsening economic problems. Louis XVI, encouraged by Marie Antoinette, secretly plotted **counterrevolution**, as did many former aristocrats. Other countries, fearing that their people would follow the French example if the revolution succeeded, threatened war.

Moreover, the victorious revolutionaries could not agree on how to change France. Liberal nobles and clergy, with much of the middle class, were satisfied with parliamentary monarchy and moderate change. The rural population, happy to have equal rights and to limit the power of the king, wanted economic relief but not deeper social change. The urban lower classes (known as sans-culottes) and certain middle-class idealists were more radical. They wanted to end the monarchy altogether, drive out or persecute former aristocrats (even liberal nobles), change society more thoroughly (some favored abolishing Catholicism), and export the revolution to other countries by force. Resolving all these desires would prove impossible.

Radicalism, the Reign of Terror, and the Directory

From the spring of 1792 through the summer of 1794, the French Revolution took a sharply radical turn. In April 1792, France went to war with Austria and Prussia; other countries, including Britain, joined in, and France would remain at war for almost the entirety of the next quarter century. The economy worsened, and early military failures caused mass hysteria. Remaining aristocrats and political moderates fell under suspicion, as did the royal family. Radical parties became more influential.

In the fall of 1792, a new constitution created a new legislature (the National Convention), stripped the king of all powers, and proclaimed the French Republic. Elections brought the radical parties to power. Most important were the Jacobins, led by Maximilien Robespierre, a fanatically idealistic lawyer. In January 1793, Louis XVI was executed for treason (Marie Antoinette was killed in October). The Jacobins created an executive body, the Committee of Public Safety, which assumed dictatorial powers, persecuted enemies, and attempted the radical transformation of French society. It expanded the war effort, mobilized the economy for combat, and carried out the modern world's first national draft. Civil war erupted in the countryside (especially the Vendee), as peasants rebelled against conscription and the radicals' efforts to eradicate Catholicism.

Between the summer of 1793 and the summer of 1794, Robespierre and the Committee, supported by the urban sans-culottes, carried out a Reign of Terror, searching for counterrevolutionaries and traitors. In this panicked, witch-hunt atmosphere, civil liberties were largely ignored. More than 300,000 people were arrested without warrant and tried without jury or appeal. Between 30,000 and 50,000 were killed, many beheaded by the guillotine. In July 1794, a coup within the committee overthrew Robespierre (who was guillotined) and ended the Terror.

For the next five years, a more moderate government called the Directory ruled revolutionary France. The military situation stabilized, and the Directory attempted to restore order after the chaos caused by the Terror. However, the middle-of-the-road Directory was unpopular, and it was overthrown in 1799, bringing an end to the revolution.

Napoleon Bonaparte

Among those who ousted the Directory was a talented and popular general, Napoleon Bonaparte, who quickly seized power for himself. Napoleon claimed to follow the ideals of the French Revolution, but in reality, created a dictatorship stronger and more efficient than the absolute monarchy had been. Indeed, in 1804, Napoleon had himself crowned emperor of France.

Evaluating Napoleon's reign is difficult. He was arrogant and autocratic, with little respect for democracy or constitutional rule. His wars lasted for years, cost untold amounts of money, and killed millions of people. On the other hand, he modernized France in many ways, creating institutions that still exist today, such as the Bank of France and the Civil Law Code (known then as the Napoleonic Code, still the foundation of modern French law). Until his wars went badly in 1812, his military skills made France immensely rich and powerful.

Napoleon is best known for his military career. After coming to power, he continued the wars France had begun during the revolution. His chief enemies were

Britain, Austria, Prussia, and Russia. From 1805 through 1811, his victories made France the most powerful nation in Europe: the only major nations not under his control were Britain and Russia.

Several factors brought about Napoleon's downfall: his inability to counter British naval power, a guerrilla war in Spain and Portugal, and, finally, an overambitious invasion of Russia in 1812. He was defeated, captured, and exiled in 1814. In 1815, he escaped and had to be beaten again at the Battle of Waterloo. After years of captivity, he died in 1821.

Successes, Failures, and Long-term Effects of the French Revolution

What made the French Revolution and its Napoleonic aftermath so important? After all, in many ways, the revolution failed. The dream of a popularly elected government faded, only to be replaced by the harsh Committee of Public Safety, the semidictatorial Directory, and the unmistakably dictatorial Napoleon. After Napoleon's defeat, the old royal family was restored to power. Moreover, it is hard to argue that liberty, equality, and fraternity were achieved by means of Jacobin terror and the guillotine.

On the other hand, the French Revolution did away with absolute monarchy. Kings, queens, and emperors continued to sit on European thrones, but in no major country, with the exception of Russia, were they all-powerful. As time passed, monarchs yielded more of their power to ministries, parliaments, and legislatures.

Also, the French Revolution (like the American Revolution before it) inspired other **Atlantic revolutions**. Uprisings in Ireland, Belgium, the Netherlands, and Poland attempted to follow the American and French examples. They failed, but revolutions in Haiti and Latin America succeeded (see Chapter 27). Even Napoleon spread revolutionary ideals throughout Europe by writing constitutions for the countries he conquered.

In the end, the greatest legacy of the American and French revolutions was to cause people to demand greater popular participation in government and to force nineteenth-century governments to be more attentive to those demands. The rulers of the 1800s might not give into all of their subjects' desires, but they could no longer ignore them as they had before. As time passed, ordinary people became more successful in getting their voices heard and their demands met. The story of European politics during the 1800s and early 1900s is primarily *this* story.

REACTION AND REFORM: POLITICS IN EUROPE, 1815–1914

The Congress of Vienna and the Principle of Reaction, 1815–1848

Real change would have to wait for several decades. After the defeat of Napoleon, the leaders of Europe gathered at the **Congress of Vienna** (1814–1815) to settle the peace. Not only did they redraw the map of Europe, but Britain, Austria, Prussia, and Russia restored prerevolutionary governments wherever possible (including in France) and agreed to cooperate in preserving the **military diplomatic balance of power**. The experience of the French Revolution and the Napoleonic wars convinced most politicians that any kind of liberalism led automatically to political chaos and war; to them, the best way to maintain order was to oppose any kind of democratic change. This arch-conservative stance was called **reaction**, and its principal spokesman was the Austrian statesman **Klemens von Metternich**, who hosted the congress.

The resulting Congress System helped to keep the peace in Europe until the early 1850s. However, stability came at the price of stifling political change and civil liberties. Although monarchies were no longer absolute, freedom of expression and freedom of the press were restricted, secret police forces became common, and censorship was heavy. Trade unions and workers' associations were illegal (just as the industrial working class was expanding), and political parties were outlawed in many countries.

Even in western nations such as Britain and France, political controls tightened. Less than 5 percent of the British population could vote or run for Parliament, and the Congress of Vienna brought the kings back to France. Change in both countries was slow. In Britain, it took place by means of gradual reform. (In 1832, the First Reform Act slightly expanded the vote and improved the electoral system's districting and operation. In the 1820s and 1830s, the home minister, Robert Peel, ushered in a series of limited social and political changes.) France lurched forward by means of periodic revolution (in 1830, 1848, and 1871).

In central and eastern Europe, the level of repression was much greater. On behalf of his emperor, Metternich ruled Austria with an iron hand. Prussia, now a leading German state, was militaristic and authoritarian. Russia remained an absolute monarchy; there were no meaningful checks on the tsar's power. In addition, Russia continued the practice of **serfdom**, the system of unfree agricultural labor that had died away elsewhere in Europe decades, if not centuries, before. In addition to being inherently unjust, serfdom was inefficient and kept Russia socially and economically backward.

The Revolution of 1848

The **Revolution of 1848**, which shook almost every country on the continent to its political roots, is a great dividing point in nineteenth-century European history. Underlying causes include

- popular impatience with over three decades of reactionary rule
- social and economic pressures caused by the **Industrial Revolution** (see Chapter 21)
- the growing strength of **nationalism**
- a long series of economic downturns and bad harvests that caused the decade to be known as the "hungry forties" (the Irish Potato Famine is the best-known of these crises)

The 1848 revolution began in France, where the king was deposed, and Napoleon's nephew (Louis Napoleon, later Napoleon III) became president. It spread to the rest of Europe (prompting Metternich's famous quote about revolution: "Every time France sneezes, Europe catches cold"). Only Britain (which was flexible enough to avoid revolution) and Russia (which punished liberals and radicals harshly enough to make revolution too dangerous) remained immune. Uprisings broke out in Prussia, Austria, most of the German states, and many parts of Italy. Nationalism caused a number of areas ruled by the Austrian Empire (Italian cities, Czech Bohemia, Croatia, and Hungary) to rise up.

By the end of 1848 and early 1849, all the revolts were crushed or faded away. Historians often speak of 1848 as "the turning point that did not quite turn." Still the revolutions of 1848 had their effects. They compelled Prussia and Austria to grant constitutions. They demonstrated the growing political importance of nationalism and laid the foundation for the later unifications of Italy and Germany. They inspired **Karl Marx** to write *The Communist Manifesto*. Most of all, the revolutions hammered home for good the earlier lesson of the French Revolution: that the political, social, and economic demands of ordinary people had to be taken seriously, if not met.

Representative Government and Unifications, 1848–1914

During the second half of the century, most European countries moved closer to representative forms of government. Britain and France became democracies (defined by **universal male suffrage**, or a politically meaningful vote for all adult males). Even in less representative regimes, political power began to spread outward to larger numbers of governmental advisers, ministries, and agencies.

Britain under Queen Victoria gradually extended the vote to the middle and lower classes by means of the **Second** (1867) and **Third** (1885) **Reform Acts**. Under prime ministers Benjamin Disraeli and William Gladstone, the Conservative and Liberal parties took turns granting economic concessions and fairer labor laws to the lower classes. By the early 1900s, the working class had enough political influence that a new party, Labour, was founded to serve its interests. Britain in the late 1800s had the world's greatest empire and was extremely prosperous. It wrestled, however, with the questions of women's suffrage and Irish nationalism.

France's progress toward democracy was less consistent and less gentle than Britain's. In the republic that existed for a short time after 1848, all adult males could vote. In 1851, however, the president, Louis Napoleon, staged a coup and crowned himself Napoleon III. He was not an absolute dictator (although he increased censorship), and he helped to modernize Paris and industrialize the country. He abdicated after losing the bitter **Franco-Prussian War** (1870–1871). From that time, France has remained a democratic republic. However, democracy did not solve all of France's problems. France was rocked by corruption and financial scandals. Worst of all was the **Dreyfus Affair** (1894–1906), in which the army and government made a Jewish officer into a scapegoat after military secrets were discovered to have been leaked to Germany. The controversy divided the left (which maintained Dreyfus's innocence) from the right (which was convinced of his guilt) and exposed the ugly streak of anti-Semitism in modern European society.

Nationalism profoundly affected politics in Italy, Germany, and Austria. The **unification of Italy** took place in the 1860s thanks to a combination of clever diplomacy by the statesman Camillo Cavour, the military leadership of Giuseppe Garibaldi, and popular patriotism. Under Victor Emmanuel II, Italy became a constitutional monarchy.

The **unification of Germany** was spearheaded by Prussia under the leadership of **Otto von Bismarck**, one of the century's most skilled diplomats. Nationalist sentiment spurred unification, as did a series of short, decisive wars against Denmark (1864), Austria (1866), and especially France (1870–1871). War with Austria made Prussia paramount in the German-speaking world; victory in the **Franco-Prussian War** removed all obstacles to unification. The new German state had a parliament (the Reichstag), and all adult males technically had the vote, although the electoral system was heavily stacked in favor of the upper classes. Germany rapidly became a strong, modern, industrialized state, but under Bismarck, it was very conservative politically. Craftily, Bismarck offered the lower classes generous economic concessions (pensions, insurance, shorter workdays) to keep them from being attracted to trade unions or socialism.

After 1848, the Austrian emperor was forced to liberalize somewhat, and a parliament was established in 1861. A multinational empire, Austria had to confront many ethnic tensions throughout the late 1800s and early 1900s, as the nationalist aspirations of minority populations such as Czechs, Poles, Slovaks, Croats, Serbs, Hungarians, and others mounted. In the **Augsleich** ("Compromise") of 1867, the Hungarian minority, Austria's largest, won equal status, and the country was renamed the Austro-Hungarian Empire. As in other parts of Europe, **anti-Semitism** became an ugly part of political life; at the turn of the century, the mayor of Vienna ran several successful campaigns on an openly anti-Jewish platform.

Even autocratic Russia was forced to change somewhat. Defeat in the Crimean War prompted Alexander II, a moderate liberal, to modernize the country with a series of "great reforms." The most important of these was the **emancipation of the serfs** (1861), which ended a morally reprehensible practice and allowed some economic progress. Sadly, Alexander II was assassinated by terrorists, and the extremely conservative rulers who succeeded him, including the last tsar, Nicholas II, undid many of his reforms. A serious uprising in 1905 almost toppled Nicholas II; he survived but was forced to create and share power with an elected, semiparliamentary body called the Duma. However, he kept the Duma weak and took every opportunity to avoid cooperating with it. Anti-Semitic persecution escalated in turn-of-the-century Russia, and **pogroms** (violent raids on Jewish settlements) became increasingly common.

Women's Movements

The English author **Mary Wollstonecraft** is considered the founder of modern European feminism. Her 1792 treatise, *A Vindication of the Rights of Women*, insisted that women, like men, possessed reason and were therefore entitled to equal rights. During the French Revolution, the playwright Olympe de Gouges argued in her "Declaration of the Rights of Woman and the Citizeness" that women should have the same rights as men. The government dismissed her proposal, and she died during the Reign of Terror.

Larger women's rights movements emerged in the 1830s in Europe and the United States. Early on, they focused on reforming family and divorce laws to allow women to own property and file for divorce. This initial effort did not reap quick results, as women did not gain full property rights in Britain until 1870, Germany until 1900, and France until 1907.

Soon, feminists were seeking better access to higher education and jobs. The first professions open to women (beyond domestic servitude, already dominated by women) were teaching and nursing. Women also led the way in campaigning for temperance, the abolition of slavery, and aid for orphans and the poor.

By the middle of the nineteenth century, women began to seek political rights, most notably suffrage, the right to vote. As a rule, European and American **suffragette movements** were led by women of the upper classes. The most vocal women's movement was Britain's, led by Emmeline Pankhurst. Major figures in the U.S. movement were Susan B. Anthony and Elizabeth Cady Stanton. American and Canadian women not only called for the right to vote, they agitated for better working conditions for women, child welfare, and temperance (in the early 1900s, Margaret Sanger began her controversial campaign for public support of birth control). Almost no countries gave women the vote until late in World War I or afterward. Exceptions include Norway, Finland, and a handful of U.S. states.

INTELLECTUAL AND CULTURAL CURRENTS

In contrast to long-lasting cultural and intellectual movements such as the Renaissance and the Enlightenment, trends and styles in the 1800s and 1900s changed constantly. Such rapid evolution has been a hallmark of modern Western culture.

The principal cultural movement of the late 1700s and early 1800s was **romanticism.** A backlash against the rational Enlightenment, romanticism emphasized emotion, passion, heroism, and the imagination.

In the mid-1800s came numerous scientific discoveries that changed the outlook of the Western world. The most important was the work of English naturalist **Charles Darwin.** On the basis of research conducted around the world on a British naval expedition, Darwin explained the biological process of evolution with his **theory of natural selection.** In *On the Origin of Species* (1859), Darwin caused a scientific and cultural storm by arguing that evolution is a random process in which physical changes that increase an animal's chance for survival are passed on to that animal's offspring. Darwin stirred up even greater controversy in 1871, when, in *The Descent of Man*, he applied the principles of natural selection to human beings and postulated that humans and apes share a common evolutionary ancestry. Darwin's ideas, along with discoveries in other sciences, including geology and archaeology, did much to erode faith in traditional religion and encourage a more secular worldview in the West.

The culture of the late 1800s and early 1900s was characterized by diversity and innovation. Turning away from realism in the 1870s, **modernist** artists and writers (including Vincent van Gogh, Paul Gauguin, Vasily Kandinsky, and a young Pablo Picasso) broke the rules of traditional culture and experimented with a dazzling array of new styles: symbolism, impressionism, post-impressionism, and on the eve of World War I, expressionism, cubism, and even abstraction. Asian and African art exerted a powerful influence on this generation of artists.

TIP

Famous romantics include Lord Byron, Ludwig van Beethoven, Victor Hugo, Richard Wagner, and Pyotr Tchaikovsky. Around the 1840s, romanticism, while it did not die away, yielded its place of prominence to **realism.** Realists were concerned with everyday life, social problems (such as poverty), and the psychology of their characters. Realist authors include Charles Dickens, Gustave Flaubert, Leo Tolstoy, and Fyodor Dostoevsky.

During most of the 1800s, Western culture was characterized by faith in progress and excitement about new technology and science. For the most part, especially among the general public, this sense of optimism continued until the eve of World War I. However, in some ways, the turn of the century was a time of intellectual crisis and uncertainty. German philosopher Friedrich Nietzsche proclaimed famously that "God is dead," and argued that all systems of morality were valueless in the materialistic modern age. Quantum theory and **Albert Einstein's theory of relativity**, elaborated in 1905, opened up new (and disturbing) questions in the field of physics for the first time since the days of Isaac Newton. The early theories of the Austrian physician **Sigmund Freud** about dreams and the subconscious advanced the new science of psychology, but his insights made many people uneasy, both before and after World War I.

Aristide Bruant at Les Ambassadeurs (1892), by Henri de Toulouse-Lautrec.
French painter and poster artist Henri de Toulouse-Lautrec (1864–1901) was one of many artists who, during the late 1800s, departed from the strictly realist styles of the early and middle nineteenth century. Like many of France's impressionist and post-impressionist painters, Toulouse-Lautrec was influenced by foreign art, most particularly Japanese prints.

QUICK REVIEW

1. Which social class(es) in France did NOT pay taxes before the revolution of 1789?

   (A) the First Estate
   (B) the Second Estate
   (C) the First and Second Estates
   (D) the First and Third Estates
   (E) the Third Estate

2. During the French Revolution, the sans-culottes were

   (A) radical revolutionaries who came from the urban mob.
   (B) liberal aristocrats who sided with the Third Estate.
   (C) peasant counterrevolutionaries who led the first stage of the revolution.
   (D) middle-class lawyers and merchants who led the first stage of the revolution.
   (E) an elite force of bodyguards attempting to protect the royal family.

3. Which of the following remain(s) a part of Napoleon's legacy as ruler of France?

   I. the Bank of France
   II. the Academie Française
   III. the university system
   IV. the Civil Law Code

   (A) I and III only
   (B) II and III only
   (C) I, II, and IV
   (D) I, III, and IV
   (E) II, III, and IV

4. The principal architect of the Congress System that prevailed in Europe during the first half of the 1800s was

   (A) Metternich.
   (B) Cavour.
   (C) Bismarck.
   (D) Gladstone.
   (E) Castlereagh.

5. Great Britain's First Reform Act did which of the following?

   (A) It gave all adult males the vote.
   (B) It improved districting and the operation of the voting system.
   (C) It granted women the right to vote.
   (D) It abolished the House of Lords.
   (E) It provided for voting by secret ballot.

6. The Dreyfus Affair

   (A) was a scandal that rocked the British financial world.
   (B) was a diplomatic crisis that nearly spoiled Germany's relationship with Austria.
   (C) was a miscarriage of justice that split French society and demonstrated a spirit of anti-Semitism there.
   (D) was a court case in Russia involving a serial murderer.
   (E) was a love triangle that embarrassed the Hungarian aristocracy.

7. According to the terms of the 1867 Augsleich, the Austrians agreed to rule their empire jointly with

   (A) the Hungarians.
   (B) the Croats.
   (C) the Czechs.
   (D) the Serbs.
   (E) the Slovenes.

8. The hallmark of Alexander II's reign in Russia was

   (A) his victory in the Crimean War.
   (B) his suppression of peasant revolts in Siberia.
   (C) his creation of Russia's first constitution.
   (D) his establishment of Russia's first university.
   (E) his emancipation of Russia's serfs.

9. Which of the following best describes the struggle of nineteenth-century feminists in Europe and the United States?

   (A) Feminists were concerned only with gaining the right to vote.
   (B) Feminists struggled for the vote but also for social reform in areas such as education and temperance.
   (C) Feminists chose to focus mainly on social reform, ignoring the struggle for the vote.
   (D) Feminists gained the vote in several major nations just before World War I.
   (E) Feminists failed to gain the vote anywhere until after World War I.

10. Charles Darwin's accomplishments can best be summed up as follows:

   (A) He was the first to propose the theory of evolution.
   (B) He single-handedly caused Western civilization to experience widespread doubt regarding the Christian faith.
   (C) He successfully argued against the theory of evolution.
   (D) He was the first to explain satisfactorily the concept of evolution, by means of the theory of natural selection.
   (E) He was the first to explain satisfactorily the concept of evolution, by means of genetic theory.

Answers

1. **(C)** In France, the First Estate was the Catholic clergy, and the Second Estate was the aristocracy. The fact that these two privileged social classes were exempt from paying taxes was a cause of the French Revolution.

2. **(A)** The lower-class radicals were tired of rising prices and food shortages. They stormed the streets of Paris and rioted in 1789, and later supported the Reign of Terror.

3. **(D)** Napoleon's rule ushered in many state institutions that still exist today, such as the Bank of France, the University System, and the Civil Law Code. However, the Academie Française was founded in 1635, before Napoleon's time.

4. **(A)** Klemens von Metternich was an Austrian politician. He conceived of the Congress System, or Concert of Europe, as a way of achieving a balance of power in Europe that would stave off future wars.

5. **(B)** Although the First Reform Act improved districting and the operation of the voting system for Parliament, it did not achieve the ambitious goals listed in the other answers. Later Reform Acts expanded voting rights. The House of Lords still exists today as the upper house of Parliament.

6. **(C)** The Dreyfus Affair was a major political controversy in France at the turn of the nineteenth and twentieth centuries. A Jewish officer named Dreyfus was falsely accused of spying for Germany. The affair not only exposed anti-Semitism in France, it also showed how deeply divided the country was at the time.

7. **(A)** The Hungarians were the largest and most powerful minority group in the Austrian Empire in the mid-1860s. In 1867, they forced the Austrian government to grant them equal status within the empire. *Augsleich* means "compromise."

8. **(E)** Alexander II emancipated the Russian serfs in 1861. He also lessened state censorship, reformed the legal system, and increased the powers of local government. Unfortunately, the two tsars who followed worked to undo many of his reforms.

9. **(B)** Feminist movements in the United States, Canada, and Europe all focused on attaining suffrage. However, women were also interested in improving educational opportunities for their children and outlawing the sale and distribution of alcohol.

10. **(D)** Although Darwin was not the first scientist to propose the theory of evolution, he did explain more thoroughly the biological process of evolution by introducing his theory of natural selection. Genetic theory was developed later. Darwin's work was one of many factors that promoted a more secular worldview in the West.

Industrialization and Worldwide Economic Trends

CHAPTER 21

- Industrialization and the Industrial Revolution
- Proto-industrialization versus traditional artisanry
- The steam engine and the mining and textile industries
- Steamships, railroads, and the telegraph
- The gradual application of electric and petroleum power
- The factory system and interchangeable parts
- Rise of the middle (bourgeois) and working (proletariat) classes
- The stimulation of population growth and urbanization
- Effects on women
- Capitalism (Adam Smith)
- Trade unionism
- Socialism and communism (Karl Marx)
- Global ramifications of Western industrialization
- The cotton gin's impact on the Atlantic slave trade

Until the end of the 1700s, the economies of the world's major civilizations were principally agricultural, and their societies were rural. Over the centuries, trade and commerce, as well as arts and crafts, had become increasingly important—but compared with agriculture, they remained relatively minor.

In Europe and the United States, this state of affairs changed dramatically during the end of the 1700s and the first half of the 1800s. The mass production of goods by means of machine power—industrialization—became a key part of Western economies. The importance of trade and commerce skyrocketed, and a growing number of people moved from rural areas to the city. Capitalism became the dominant economic system. Taken together, these changes form what is commonly known as the **Industrial Revolution**. Its first stage coincided roughly with the political revolutions taking place in America, France, and the Atlantic world (see Chapters 20 and 27). Although industrialization was a "revolution" only in a metaphorical sense—it was a decades-long process with no clear-cut beginning and no real end—it changed life in Europe and the rest of the world as thoroughly as the political revolutions did. It placed new machines and inventions at the disposal of ordinary people. It affected old social classes and created new ones. It changed the way millions of people worked, where they lived, how they understood political problems, and how they viewed themselves.

> **NOTE**
>
> By the late 1800s and early 1900s, the United States and most European nations—especially in the north and west—were industrialized, modernized, and urbanized. By that time, industrialization had also become important in other parts of the world.

THE INDUSTRIAL REVOLUTION

Background to Industrialization

The Industrial Revolution is considered to have begun in England in the 1780s with the successful application of the **steam engine** to two sectors of the economy: **mining** and **textiles**.

Many things combined to spark industrialization in England. Already from the late 1600s, proto-industrial practices (methods more productive than traditional artisanry and craftsmanship) had been in place. Machines such as the flying shuttle and the spinning jenny, which sped up the manufacture of cotton, were invented as early as 1733 and 1764. England was already relatively urbanized, and a set of harsh agricultural laws, the **Enclosure Acts** (which, in favor of wealthy landowners, fenced off large amounts of farmland that had once been common property) impoverished many farmers and forced them to relocate to the cities—creating a large pool of available labor. Environmental change played a role as well: the depletion of forests in England and Ireland (timber was used both for fuel and to build ships for the Royal Navy) increased dependency on coal, and efficient coal mining required machine power, especially to pump water out of mine shafts. Other factors working in England's favor were an excellent system of roads and canals and a strong tradition of trade and commerce.

Steam Power and Beyond: The Industrial Era Begins and Matures

What was needed by the end of the 1700s was a power source greater and more reliable than wind, water, or muscle to drive new machines in factories and mines. In 1782, the Scottish inventor **James Watt** patented a steam engine that was both powerful and cost-effective. The first stage of the Industrial Revolution involved the integration of Watt's steam engine into the textile and coal-mining industries.

The next stage of the Industrial Revolution, which lasted roughly until the middle of the 1800s, involved the universal application of steam power—and, more slowly, electricity—to all areas of economic activity. Industrialization also spread to other parts of Europe, as well as to North America. Key trends of this second phase include

- The modernization of transport, thanks to **steamships** (1807) and **railroads** (the 1820s)
- The modernization of communications, beginning with the **telegraph** (1837)
- The **factory system**, which systematized, mechanized, and increased the scale of production
- The concept of **interchangeable parts**, pioneered by two Americans, the inventor Eli Whitney and a gunsmith, Samuel Colt

Although the Industrial Revolution is considered to have ended around the mid-1800s, the **industrial era** continued throughout the rest of the century and gave birth to a huge wave of invention. Crucial innovations of this phase include the vulcanization of rubber (the 1840s); the **Bessemer process** (the 1850s), which made steel production cheaper and easier; the wider use of **electricity** (Thomas Edison's lightbulb came in 1879); the commercial use of **petroleum** (starting in 1859); the birth of chemical industries; the **internal combustion engine** (the 1860s–1870s), which led to the automobile; the **telephone** (1876–1879); the **radio** (1895–1901); and the **air-**

plane (1903). Warfare industrialized as well, with modern rifles, better artillery, and the machine gun. In the countryside, the **tractor** helped cause an agricultural boom.

Industrialization occurred first and most thoroughly in western Europe (especially Britain, the Low Countries, France, and Germany), as well as the United States. Southern and eastern Europe lagged behind. Britain led the world in industrial production for most of the 1800s. By the end of the century, Germany and the United States were catching up, then surpassing, Britain.

The Social and Environmental Effects of Industrialization

The Industrial Revolution and its aftermath vastly transformed Western society. Especially between the 1780s and 1840s, the effects were as traumatic as they were important. For the lower classes, the birth pangs of the modern industrial era were extremely painful.

The economic clout of the traditional aristocracy, whose wealth had been based primarily on land, was diminished by industrialization. The class that benefited most was the **middle class** (or bourgeoisie), especially bankers, merchants, and factory owners who drew direct profits from industrial growth.

The Industrial Revolution gave birth to a new class, the **working class** (or proletariat). During the first decades of industrialization, this working class bore the heaviest economic burden. The labor of the proletariat allowed the Industrial Revolution to move forward, but until the second half of the 1800s, the working class was badly treated and barely compensated. Workers received low wages, lived in squalid and crowded housing, worked long shifts (fourteen hours a day, six days a week, was not unusual), coped with unsafe working conditions (risk of fire, dangerous machines, exposure to poisonous or harmful substances), and had no pensions, safety laws, or insurance. Child labor was common.

In the countryside, industrialization caused social divisions as well. More land came to be owned by well-off farmers and homesteaders who were essentially middle class. Under them were poor agricultural laborers who formed a rural working class of sorts. (In Russia until 1861, the system of **serfdom** still prevailed, and **slavery** persisted until 1865 in the southern United States.)

Only after the 1840s (about the time the Industrial Revolution ended) is industrialization considered to have brought about meaningful improvements for large numbers of people in Europe and America. Various laws and measures began to give relief to the working class—although completely fair treatment and full social and political equality were still distant goals, achieved only after hard effort and not until the late 1800s or even 1900s. The general level of prosperity rose during the second half of the 1800s and, with it, the overall standard of living, even for the lower classes. The fruits of industrial-era science and technology also became more available after mid-century. At least in major cities, many features of modern life became available, including bus service, streetlights (gas, then electric), citywide sewage systems, icebox refrigeration, indoor plumbing, steam heating, canned food, and medical advances (vaccination, germ theory, antiseptic surgery, anesthesia).

Related social trends are massive **population growth** and **urbanization**. Europe's population grew from 175 million (187 million, by some estimates) in 1800 to 266 million in 1850 and 423 million by 1900. Similar growth took place in the United States. European cities that existed grew larger; in 1800, London reached the 1 million mark, as did

Paris in the 1830s. Many new cities sprang up, such as Liverpool and Manchester, precisely because of the Industrial Revolution. By the mid-1800s, England and Wales were urban societies, meaning that 50 percent or more of the population lived in cities. At that time, the level of urbanization had reached 25 percent in France and the German states, and it continued to grow, as it did in the Low Countries and the United States. While urbanization is generally associated with social advancement, it had its seamier side during the industrial era: cities were typically very polluted and very crowded, and the lower classes lived in slums or shantytowns where sewage was primitive or nonexistent. Diseases such as **cholera**, **tuberculosis**, and typhoid ran rampant in such conditions.

> **NOTE**
>
> The **environmental impact** of industrialization was (and remains) complex and huge.

Population growth and urban concentration affected the environment as did the industrialized nations' voracious appetite for resources and raw materials (wood, coal, metals, petroleum, and more). Pollution reached unprecedented levels; and unlike today, there were few laws and regulations to combat it. As non-Western parts of the world industrialized, they repeated this pattern. The early stages of human-caused climate change (global warming) are thought to date to the nineteenth-century industrial takeoff.

Women and Industrialization

Before the Industrial Revolution, European women of the lower (and sometimes middle) class worked with men on the farm or in the family business, so motherhood and homemaking were not full-time pursuits. The Industrial Revolution altered that reality, turning husbands into wage earners and wives into homemakers. By the late 1800s, it had created a sharply defined **domestic sphere** for women and, for men, a **separate workplace**.

This evolution took time. In the early 1800s, husbands and wives (and often children) in working-class families had to labor in factories or mines to make ends meet. Before 1870, women made up 50 percent of the textile workforce. Ironically, this meant that lower-class women had more opportunity to work than those of the middle and upper classes. However, "opportunity" was not a matter of privilege or right; it was economic necessity, and working women earned much lower pay than men.

Throughout the 1800s, most working women remained in traditional types of female labor, such as domestic service or agricultural work. Most were single, not married. Some single women, desperate for jobs, left Europe for Australia, the United States, or Canada. By the late 1800s, large numbers of poor women worked outside the home.

Increasingly, though, as salaries improved in industry (making these jobs more desirable to men) and laws restricted the number of hours women could work, more working-class women stayed at home. Fewer middle-class (and almost no upper-class) women worked.

Around the turn of the century, with the rising standard of living, a mass consumer society began to emerge. Products such as sewing machines and cast-iron stoves freed up time for women of all classes to pursue activities outside the home.

ECONOMIC THEORIES AND MOVEMENTS

Industrialization coincided with the rise of **capitalism** in the West. **Adam Smith's** *The Wealth of Nations* appeared in 1776, just before the Industrial Revolution began. Capitalism encouraged free trade and political liberalism (at least for the middle classes), and it led to the creation of great wealth in the Western world. On the other hand, capitalism was based on competition, and left unregulated, it could be cruel to those who lost (like the early working class).

Smith and the other classical economists who favored capitalism argued that the laws of supply and demand—the "**invisible hand**," to use Smith's metaphor—should be left to operate freely, with minimal government intervention. (Note that Germany, where state control of the economy was pronounced, broke this rule and still became an industrial powerhouse.) Smith himself insisted that governments should take measures to fight extreme poverty, a point often forgotten today. Other economic thinkers of the day maintained that little could be done about poverty. Thomas Malthus of England wrote in his influential *Essay on Population* (1799) that poverty was one of the inevitable consequences of population growth. David Ricardo's "**iron law of wages**" was even more pessimistic: any employer, he said, will naturally pay workers no more than what is needed to allow them to survive. To force employers to pay higher wages would make things worse: they would fire workers, who Ricardo then predicted would starve. Such theories caused economics to be nicknamed the "dismal science" and were used for a long time by middle- and upper-class industrialists to justify oppressive labor practices.

> **NOTE**
>
> Economic thought and social movements asked how economic progress could be made to benefit the largest possible number of people without endangering the generation of wealth.

By the middle of the century, especially after the **Revolution of 1848**, it was clear that pure, dog-eat-dog capitalism could not remain as it was without causing severe social and economic stress. But how should it be changed? Liberals and reformers sought to soften capitalism's hard edge by agreeing to fairer labor laws and social welfare measures. For workers, a more radical option (by the standards of the day) was the **trade union** movement. In the early 1800s, unions were illegal in Europe and the United States, and workers risked injury and arrest if they joined unions or went on strike. Compared with socialism, though, the union movement was a less extreme way to struggle for political rights and better treatment in the workplace (higher wages, five-day work week, shorter hours, safety regulations, pensions, and employee insurance). In the late 1800s and early 1900s, unions earned legal status in most countries and gained greater economic and political strength. Political parties dedicated to the needs of workers, such as Labour in Britain, formed.

Even more extreme was **socialism**, which rejected capitalism and denied the validity of private property. (Most radical of all was anarchism, which rejected all forms of government.) Many varieties of socialism appeared in the 1800s, all sharing the belief that economic competition is inherently unfair and leads to injustice and inequality. The most influential form of socialism is **communism**, originated by the German philosophers **Karl Marx** and Friedrich Engels and most famously outlined in *The Communist Manifesto* (1848) and *Das Kapital* (1867–1894). Marx and Engels argued that all historical development was driven by a **class struggle** between the upper class (which controls capital, or the means of economic production) and the lower class (which is forced to labor for the upper class). They predicted that the age of industrial capitalism, with its struggle between bourgeoisie and proletariat, was the final stage of human history before the realization of socialism. Society would then move on to communism, an economic state of perfect justice, equality, and prosperity. To achieve socialism, however, Marx and Engels believed that revolution would be needed, so they advocated the overthrow of capitalism, by force if need be.

> **NOTE**
>
> Marxism captured the imaginations of thousands of workers and intellectuals, and it became one of the modern era's most influential doctrines.

THE GLOBAL IMPACT OF INDUSTRIALIZATION

Industrialization and Imperialism

Western industrialization and imperialism (see Chapter 22) were intimately connected in several ways. First, industrialization gave Western nations the wealth, technological aptitude, and scientific knowledge to conquer and colonize other parts of the world. Particularly, it placed new weapons in the hands of Westerners: gunboats, artillery, quick-firing and accurate rifles, and machine guns, all of which made Western imperialism difficult for poorly armed native forces to resist.

Second, if industrialization gave the West greater ability to conquer and colonize, it also provided more motivation. Industrialization required ever-greater amounts of raw materials: iron ore, coal, rubber, metals, timber, and chemicals, all of which could be stripped from other parts of the world. The growing importance of steamships made it necessary for Western nations to maintain naval bases and refueling stations around the globe. Moreover, as Europe and America produced more manufactured goods, they needed overseas markets to sell them to. All these needs spurred the Western nations' intense burst of imperial activity during the 1800s, especially the second half.

The Influence of Industrial Nations Over Nonindustrial Nations

Even in parts of the world that Europe and America did not conquer or colonize, industrialization often had a profound effect. In many parts of Africa, Asia, and Latin America, Western businessmen and industrialists struck deals with aristocrats or the political elite to exploit local resources. These bargains typically involved the large-scale growth or extraction of a small set of crops or natural resources. This kind of **monoculture** generally damages the environment and retards the development of a healthy, diverse economy. It also exploits these countries' native workers: Western payments or investments end up in the pockets of a small number of local elites, rather than adding to the national well-being.

NOTE
In the tropics, the derogatory slang for countries with monoculture economies is "banana republic."

In the long term, most non-Western parts of the world came to imitate industrial methods of production. Western colonizing powers exported industrial practices to their imperial possessions. Political leaders in free nations came to see industrialization as a way to gain wealth and power. In such cases, industrialization was typically imposed from above by the ruler. The worldwide adoption of industrialization worldwide continued through the twentieth century and continues today.

Industrialization and the Atlantic Slave Trade

Another global effect of early industrialization concerns the **Atlantic slave trade**. The 1793 invention of the **cotton gin** by the American engineer Eli Whitney transformed the international textile trade. One of the factors limiting growth in the textile trade was the fact that raw cotton still had to be cleaned by hand. The cotton gin changed this situation, enabling the full mechanization of the textile industry, which phenomenally boosted England's demand for raw cotton. Although Egypt was a major source of cotton, an equally important supplier was the American South, where cotton was grown and harvested mainly by slaves. Most economic historians argue that, before the 1790s, slavery was becoming less profitable in the American South and might have died away relatively quickly and easily. The advent of the cotton gin, combined with increased English demand, revived the profitability of slave-based production. Therefore, slavery in America was prolonged for decades—necessitating civil war to end it—largely because of the textile trade's industrialization.

QUICK REVIEW

1. The Industrial Revolution is generally considered to have begun in

   (A) France.   (D) Belgium.
   (B) Germany.   (E) the United States.
   (C) England.

2. The widespread application of what device played the largest part in beginning the Industrial Revolution?

   (A) the electric turbine
   (B) the water wheel
   (C) the internal combustion engine
   (D) the windmill
   (E) the steam engine

3. The Enclosure Acts affected the Industrial Revolution by

   (A) driving peasants off their land and thereby creating the workforce needed for factories and mines.
   (B) bankrupting wealthy landowners, convincing them to turn to manufacturing.
   (C) increasing the land under cultivation, destroying trees, and increasing reliance on coal for fuel.
   (D) educating peasants and turning them into skilled workers.
   (E) setting more land aside for new factories and mines.

4. What was the first major trade to be fully power-driven and industrialized?

   (A) the canning of food
   (B) the textile industry
   (C) the production of rubber
   (D) the manufacture of glass
   (E) the leatherworking trade

5. The Bessemer process allowed the cost-effective and reliable production of

   (A) steel.   (D) aluminum.
   (B) fine cotton.   (E) concrete.
   (C) rubber.

6. What effect did nineteenth-century industrialization have on Europe's aristocratic class?

   (A) Industrialization made the aristocratic class more powerful.
   (B) Industrialization had little effect on the aristocratic class.
   (C) Industrialization gradually weakened the power and prestige of the aristocratic class.
   (D) Industrialization suddenly weakened the power and prestige of the aristocratic class.
   (E) Industrialization had no effect at all on the aristocratic class.

7. Which of the following was NOT among the Western world's industrial leaders during most of the nineteenth century?

   (A) Austria
   (B) England
   (C) Belgium
   (D) the United States
   (E) the western German states

8. Who was the originator of the "iron law of wages"?

   (A) Adam Smith
   (B) Thomas Malthus
   (C) Robert Owen
   (D) David Ricardo
   (E) Karl Marx

9. Which of the following best characterizes standard Marxist doctrine?

(A) Economic competition leads to the highest possible level of prosperity for all.

(B) The struggle between propertied classes and laboring classes is the determining force in all human affairs.

(C) Any interference with the natural operation of supply and demand is harmful.

(D) It is possible to achieve social justice and economic equality within the capitalist framework.

(E) There is no avoiding the fact that there will always be impoverished classes in every society.

10. How did industrialization affect the Atlantic slave trade?

(A) Reliance on machines caused the slave trade to end somewhat earlier than it would have otherwise.

(B) Industrialization had little or no effect on the slave trade.

(C) Industrialization of the textile trade increased the demand for U.S. cotton and revived slavery for several decades.

(D) Industrialization quickly ended the slave trade.

(E) Steam power allowed the British and U.S. navies to stop the slave trade altogether before the 1850s.

Answers

1. **(C)** Proto-industrialization was especially prevalent in England. England had a well-developed transportation system at the time and was already heavily urbanized. It also had a large pool of industrial labor compared with that in other European countries.

2. **(E)** More powerful steam engines were developed near the end of the 1700s. They provided energy to machines that were key to producing manufactured goods in factories.

3. **(A)** The Enclosure Acts were passed by wealthy landowners in the British Parliament. These laws were enacted to privatize and fence off a great amount of farmland that had been common property before. Farmers were forced to pay rent or forfeit their farms.

4. **(B)** In England in the 1780s, the steam engine, patented by a Scottish mechanic, James Watt, in 1782, was used to power machines in the textile industry. Coal mining also relied on Watt's steam engine beginning in the late 1700s.

5. **(A)** The Bessemer process was perfected in the 1850s. It was a cheap and easy way to produce steel. The mid- to late 1800s was a period when new energy sources, new raw materials, and new inventions for industrial use emerged.

6. **(C)** Industrialization gradually weakened the power and prestige of the aristocratic class as trade, commerce, and manufacturing superseded landownership as the key means of generating wealth. The middle classes benefited most from industrialization; they were the merchants, bankers, factory owners, and industrialists.

7. **(A)** European areas that industrialized more slowly tended to be in the south and east, such as Spain, Portugal, southern Italy, and the Austrian Empire. They remained largely agricultural.

8. **(D)** Ricardo wrote that employers, if they are rational and want to make profits, will not pay their workers any more than subsistence-level wages. He warned that interfering with the "iron law" would lead to economic ruin.

9. **(B)** Marx criticized capitalism and economic competition. He argued that the class struggle of the nineteenth century was the final stage of history before the emergence of socialism and, later, communism.

10. **(C)** Unfortunately, industrialization did not lead to the emancipation of African slaves. In the American South, slaves grew and harvested cotton. The invention of the cotton gin and England's increased demand for cotton made slave-based cotton production very profitable.

The Europeans Abroad: Imperialism, Nationalism, and Foreign Policy

CHAPTER **22**

- The new imperialism
- Social Darwinism and the "white man's burden" concept
- The Monroe Doctrine and manifest destiny
- The British East India Company and the Indian Mutiny
- Foreign concessions in China and the Boxer Rebellion

- Japanese imperialism and the Russo-Japanese War
- The Great Game
- The Eastern Question
- The Scramble for Africa and the Berlin Conference
- Nationalism, competition for empire, and the European alliance system

---

One of the most astounding political facts of the nineteenth century is that, while, in 1815, the nations of the West—Europe and America—controlled 35 percent of the world's habitable territory, they controlled 85 percent by 1914. The nineteenth century was truly an age of empire, in which the West came to achieve dominance over a larger portion of the globe than any civilization had before.

Western imperialism was nothing new. European powers had been conquering other parts of the world since the 1400s. From the 1700s onward, the United States had grown "from sea to shining sea" by means of warfare and subjugation of the native population. From the mid-1800s to the early 1900s, however, imperialism took on a more aggressive and systematic character; and many historians refer to this as the **new imperialism**.

Imperialism remains one of the Western world's longest-lasting and most controversial legacies. As a practical undertaking and a military enterprise, the West's domination of the world was impressive, and it made Europe and America powerful and rich. On the other hand, imperialism was inseparable from bloodshed, racial prejudice, and slavery. As the English-Polish author Joseph Conrad wrote in the novel *Heart of Darkness*—one of the classic literary depictions of European imperialism—"The conquest of the earth, which mostly means the taking it away from those who have a different complexion or slightly flatter noses than ourselves, is not a pretty thing when you look into it too much." Moreover, Europe's and America's campaigns of colonization left deep political scars around the globe, many of which have not yet healed even in the twenty-first century.

Whether abroad or at home, European foreign policy became increasingly aggressive. During the first half of the 1800s, the balance of power achieved by the Congress of Vienna largely kept the peace. After 1850, however, several wars broke out among the European powers: the Crimean War (1853–1856), in which Russia fought France and Britain; the wars of Italian unification, which entangled France, Austria, and several Italian states; and the three wars Prussia fought to unify the German states, especially the Franco-Prussian War (1870–1871).

Much of this aggression was caused by the growing intensity of **nationalism**, a relatively new cultural phenomenon that placed a premium on patriotic sentiment. Another cause was competition over imperial possessions, especially as the century drew to a close and the amount of desirable territory left to be conquered shrank. On the surface, relative stability was maintained from 1871 to 1914, a period in European history known as the Long Peace. Underneath, however, the potential for conflict grew with every passing year. The **European alliance system** emerged during the 1890s and early 1900s as a result of this growing sense of foreign policy crisis. It was also a principal factor in the complex background of World War I.

CAUSES OF IMPERIALISM

A variety of interrelated factors enabled and motivated the new imperialism of the 1800s. They apply to the nations of Europe, and to a degree, the United States.

One set of factors was economic. As discussed in Chapter 21, industrialization gave the West the ability to conquer and more reasons to do so. Industrialization made Western economies hungry for **raw materials**, many of which could be seized from less powerful nations by force. Also, Western nations needed **markets** for the goods they produced and thought colonies would serve well (in retrospect, economic historians have determined that this was a mistaken belief and that colonies were less suitable as markets than other industrialized countries).

A second factor was **military superiority**. Industrialization gave Western armies and navies ocean-going fleets powered by steam (and, later, petroleum), modern rifles, machine guns, rapid-fire and long-range artillery, and more. Only rarely could native populations resist Western military forces. Also, because modern ships required elaborate repair bases and fueling facilities, Western navies needed control over islands and ports around the world to maintain **sea power**.

A social factor prompting imperialism was Europe's rapid **population growth** during the 1800s. One outlet for excess population growth was emigration to the Americas, and, as discussed in Chapter 28, millions of Europeans made that choice. Another outlet, however, was to leave the homeland and go to the colonies.

Scientific and technological aptitude were also instrumental. In this case, knowledge was power. A new wave of exploration during the 1700s and early 1800s added to Western nations' understanding of Africa, Asia, the polar regions, and the Amazon basin. Better maps and geographical familiarity made it easier for Westerners to conquer these areas. In addition, medical advances made it possible to penetrate tropical regions more deeply. Previously, diseases such as sleeping sickness, yellow fever, and **malaria** had prevented Westerners from controlling the interior of Africa and Southeast Asia. The development of effective treatments for these illnesses (especially **quinine**, which relieved the symptoms of malaria) changed this situation.

Finally, a complex set of cultural factors motivated the West to build empires. A sense of racial superiority was widespread among white Europeans and Americans, who believed they were entitled to conquer and colonize "backward" or "primitive" peoples. Cecil Rhodes, who did much to colonize Africa, said famously of his British homeland, "I contend that we are the finest race in the world, and the more of it we inhabit, the better it is." In some cases, this belief was "justified" by crude prejudice. A more sophisticated but still misguided doctrine of **social Darwinism** was also used to argue in favor of imperialism. Social Darwinists implied that it was natural for technologically advanced peoples to conquer those who were less so. (Darwin himself denounced this idea as a perversion of his theories.)

Yet another cultural impulse behind imperialism was a genuine conviction that white Westerners had a duty to teach and modernize the darker-skinned, supposedly primitive peoples of Africa and Asia. The English poet Rudyard Kipling gave this sentiment its most famous label: the **White Man's Burden**. The French spoke of their civilizing mission (*la mission civilisatrice*). This attitude was well-meaning and heartfelt, but also condescending. European and American missionaries, doctors, scientists, and colonial officials sometimes did much good in the places they visited. However, they did so out of at least a subconscious sense of racial superiority, and they often trampled on or eradicated native cultural practices and beliefs.

EUROPE'S OVERSEAS EMPIRES

Western Approaches to Imperialism

Almost the entire non-Western world was either colonized during the nineteenth century or fell under the influence of Western nations. By far the largest and most widespread empire was Britain's. (A famous motto of the time: "The sun never sets on the British Empire.") France had a sizable empire, as did Belgium and the Netherlands. Although Austria is not commonly thought of as a colonizing power, its empire was in eastern and southeastern Europe. Russia conquered Siberia, much of the territory to its south, and for a time, parts of North America. After 1870, new countries such as Germany and Italy began to build overseas empires, in an attempt to catch up with older imperial powers like Britain and France.

Different powers treated their empires differently. The British are considered to have had the most enlightened approach, relatively speaking. Although they took their colonies by force and exploited them economically—and were prone to the same sense of racial superiority as other Westerners—they interfered less with local customs than other colonizers. In keeping with their sense of the White Man's Burden, they introduced positive social reforms and useful scientific and technological knowledge. Likewise, the French subscribed to the notion of *la mission civilisatrice*, but were less consistent about it. The Portuguese and Belgians were known to be especially harsh, even cruel, masters, particularly in Africa. Germany and Italy were also brutal. The latter used poison gas in conquering parts of North Africa.

The Americas

North America fell mainly under the sway of the United States, which conquered the entire Western frontier during the nineteenth century. Motivated by the doctrine of **manifest destiny**—the belief that it was entitled to the entire center of the continent between Atlantic and Pacific—the United States fought Mexico, negotiated borders with British Canada, and warred on Native Americans, driving them to defeat and onto reservations. In its way, this was no less an imperial campaign than what European nations did in Africa or Asia. The Spanish lost their empire in North America when Mexico launched a revolution in the 1810s and 1820s. The Russians gave up their North American possession, Alaska, to the United States in 1867.

The **Latin American wars of independence** freed Mexico, Mesoamerica, and South America from Spain and Portugal in the early 1800s (see Chapter 27). However, much of Latin America came under the sway of the United States, which did not conquer the region but considered it part of the U.S. sphere of influence. The **Monroe Doctrine**, issued in 1823, formally stated that the United States would not permit European interference in the Western Hemisphere. U.S. economic and political influence over Central and South America increased throughout the 1800s. At the end of the century, in 1898, the **Spanish-American War** gave the United States control over Cuba, Puerto Rico, and the Virgin Islands, making it an imperial power in Latin America.

Southeast Asia

The vast expanse of Asia was colonized and influenced by a variety of powers. The region that had been longest under European control was Southeast Asia. The Dutch tightened their grasp over Indonesia. France took over Indochina, the area that is today Laos, Cambodia, and Vietnam. By the mid-1880s, the British controlled Burma, the Malay Peninsula (with the great trading center of Singapore), and northern Borneo. Farther to the south, Britain reigned over the continent of Australia. The Philippines had belonged to Spain since Magellan's voyage of 1521, but the United States took them in 1898, following the Spanish-American War. Later in the century, Germany seized a number of small Pacific islands for use as naval posts.

India

The heart of the British Empire was India. Britain and France quarreled with each other over hegemony in India during the 1700s. At the battle of **Plassey**, in 1757, the British won a major victory over the Mughal Empire, enabling them to consolidate their military presence in India and leading to a decline of French influence. Over the next decades, the British went on to conquer most of the subcontinent. Until the late 1850s, India was not administered directly by the British government but by the semiprivate **British East India Company**, one of the richest and most powerful business ventures in world history. In 1857, however, the **Indian Mutiny** (also known as the **Sepoy Rebellion**)—which failed but shocked the British badly—persuaded the government to assume full control over the colony. India was exceptionally important to Britain, in terms of national pride, strategic position, and economic benefit. During the late 1800s, one-quarter of the wealth generated by the British Empire came from India.

China

China, despite its vast size and immense population, fell victim to almost every European nation, as well as to the United States. China was not technically colonized. However, thanks to military defeat at the hands of the British and other foreigners during the middle of the 1800s, it was compelled to open its borders and trade with other countries at highly disadvantageous terms (see Chapter 24). It gave up pieces of territory such as **Hong Kong** (a British colony from 1842 until 1997, when it returned to Chinese rule), as well as Manchuria and Korea. The British, French, Americans, Germans, Russians, and others were allowed to establish **foreign concessions:** large districts in coastal cities where Western, not Chinese law, prevailed. Foreign ships were allowed to sail as far up Chinese rivers as they pleased. The balance of trade was lopsidedly in favor of the foreigners. The Chinese rose up to resist foreign domination in the failed **Boxer Rebellion** of 1900. In 1911, the Manchu Dynasty collapsed, its weakness due in large part to foreign meddling.

Japan Resists Western Imperialism

Unlike most Asian nations, Japan resisted Western imperialism, becoming an imperial power itself. Isolated until 1853, when the U.S. Navy forced it to resume diplomatic and economic relations with the wider world, Japan chose to adopt the science, technology, and military know-how of the West, especially under **Emperor Meiji**. Not only did Japan avoid foreign takeover, it began to build its own Asian empire. It defeated China in 1895, taking the island of Taiwan and occupying Korea. More shockingly, Japan dealt Russia a humiliating defeat in the **Russo-Japanese War** (1904–1905), gaining control over more of the Asian mainland, as well as a number of islands (see Chapter 24).

Central Asia and the Great Game

Much of Central Asia—the wide expanse of desert and mountains through which the Silk Road had run—fell to Russia, which felt the need to protect its southern frontier. Because Russia lacked warm-water ports, it hoped to drive to the Indian Ocean and gain an outlet to the sea. The Islamic khanates and cities of Turkestan, Bukhara, Samarkand, and the Afghan border were taken by the Russians between the 1820s and 1880s. Russian imperialism in this region greatly disturbed Britain because it placed the Russians within striking distance of the Middle East, much of which was in the British sphere of influence. More important, Russian encroachments on Central Asia threatened the lines of communication between Europe and India, which the British were determined to protect at all costs.

For most of the 1800s, Britain and Russia were locked in an intense campaign of espionage and diplomatic intrigue known as the **Great Game**, a term coined by the poet Rudyard Kipling (Russians called it the Tournament of Shadows). The Great Game never resulted in outright war, but it created a deep rivalry between Britain and Russia until shortly before World War I.

The Middle East and the Eastern Question

For centuries, the Middle East and most of North Africa had been in the hands of the Ottoman Empire. However, the Ottoman Empire was collapsing, and the **Eastern Question**—how to fill the power vacuum caused by the Ottomans' decline—became a central issue in global politics (see Chapter 23). During the last half of the 1800s, large portions of this region were seized by Europeans, especially the French and British. Algeria, Tunisia, and most of Morocco became French. Part of Morocco fell to Spain, while Italy captured Libya.

The most important territory was Egypt, which became a British protectorate in the 1880s. During the 1870s, Egypt, an autonomous part of the Ottoman Empire, had fallen under French and British influence. Both countries financed the construction of the **Suez Canal**, which opened in 1869. Control over the canal—a vital link between Europe and the Mediterranean on one hand and the Red Sea and the Indian Ocean on the other—was crucial, and the British used economic pressure to gain political control over Egypt. They also established control over the Sudan, and both countries became part of the Anglo-Egyptian Administration. To the east, Persia, which had remained independent of Ottoman rule, was divided into two spheres of influence by Russia and Britain. The global importance of the Middle East—based largely on its geographic position between Europe and Asia—increased dramatically with the **discovery of petroleum** there in 1908. Middle Eastern oil still plays a key role in modern geopolitics.

> **TIP**
>
> The global importance of the Middle East—based largely on its geographic position between Europe and Asia—increased dramatically with the **discovery of petroleum** there in 1908. Middle Eastern oil still plays a key role in modern geopolitics.

The Scramble for Africa

Africa experienced the most intense burst of European imperialism near the end of the century (see Chapter 26). Until the 1880s, only Africa's coastlines had been directly colonized or exploited. Gold, ivory, foodstuffs, and especially slaves had been wrested from Africa, either by military force or economic pressure. Although slavery and the slave trade had been made illegal by most Western nations following the French Revolution and Napoleonic Wars, both institutions continued throughout the 1800s. Slavery was practiced in the United States until the Civil War of the 1860s, and even afterward, it continued in parts of the Caribbean and South America. Not until Brazil outlawed slavery in 1888 did the **Atlantic slave trade** end completely. More than 2 million slaves were transported from Africa during the 1800s, bringing the likely total of African slaves captured from the late 1400s to the late 1800s to at least 12 million.

The character of African colonization changed remarkably after 1880. From then until the 1910s, European nations raced to take over territory in Africa. Thanks to better maps, industrial-era weapons, and effective tropical medicines, European colonizers penetrated every part of what the West thought of as the "dark continent." This so-called **Scramble for Africa** became so intense that it almost sparked war in Europe several times. The Berlin Conference (1884–1885), presided over by Otto von Bismarck, laid down guidelines for African expansion and, for a time, preserved peace. Still, competition over African territory caused diplomatic crises among the European powers during the early 1900s, especially the **Boer War** (1899–1902). For the Africans, the sudden and overwhelming influx of Europeans spelled disaster. Tribe after tribe, country after country, fell to the Germans, Italians, British, French, Belgians, and others. By 1914, only two nations in Africa remained free: Liberia, whose independence was guaranteed by the United States because it had been founded by freed American slaves, and Abyssinia (Ethiopia), which armed itself with modern weapons and drove off Italian efforts to conquer it. Within three decades, the rest of the continent had been brought under Europe's imperial sway.

The Balkans

Even parts of Europe were vulnerable to imperial predation. Southeastern Europe—the **Balkans**—lay at the crossroads of several empires. Although this area was the most economically and culturally backward of Europe, the imperial ambitions of Russia, Austria, Italy, and the deteriorating Ottoman Empire all centered on it. The level of competition among these powers steadily escalated. Complicating the situation was the intense wave of **nationalism** that swept most of southeastern Europe during the nineteenth century. Starting with the **Greek war of independence** in the 1820s, the various minorities ruled by the Ottomans, Austrians, and Russians constantly agitated for greater independence—and, if they had independence, they craved more territory. To realize their goals, many of these peoples were willing to risk war. By the early 1900s, the nationalist ambitions of many Balkan peoples—especially the Serbs—had become a destabilizing force in European politics. Not only were two Balkan wars fought in 1912 and 1913, but the events that triggered World War I took place there.

AGGRESSION AT HOME: NATIONALISM, WARFARE, AND ALLIANCE SYSTEMS

The Balance of Power in Nineteenth-Century Europe

As noted above, the European **balance of power** had been maintained during the first half of the 1800s. Even the wars of the mid-1800s were short and limited in intensity. Ironically, it was during the Long Peace of 1871 to 1914 that tensions worsened. Although this era gave birth to the modern Olympic Games (starting in 1896) and the Nobel Peace Prize (first awarded in 1901), the turn of the century was marked by saber rattling, **jingoism** (a British nickname for belligerent patriotism), and **brinksmanship** (a diplomatic term referring to a country's willingness to risk war in order to get its way).

Factors Destabilizing the European Balance of Power

Several factors upset Europe's diplomatic stability in the late 1800s and early 1900s. One was the force of **nationalism**, which in most countries transformed patriotic sentiment into aggressive tendencies. Another was **competition over empire:** as the 1800s came to an end, there were fewer places for European nations to expand. Especially in Africa, the jostling for new conquests came close to starting war several times in the early 1900s. A third destabilizing force was the ambitious nature of German foreign policy. An economic and military powerhouse, despite having been united only in 1871, Germany came to believe that it deserved what it called "a place in the sun": equal military and imperial status with older nations such as Britain and France. This was the case especially under **Wilhelm II**, who came to the throne in 1888 and dismissed the skilled and cautious diplomat **Otto von Bismarck** in 1890. Under Wilhelm II, Germany became openly aggressive and forceful, making the rest of Europe extremely nervous.

The Creation of Europe's Turn-of-the-Century Alliance System

From the 1880s to the 1910s, the **European alliance system** took shape, dividing Europe into two armed camps. Germany and Austria formed an alliance in 1879; joined by Italy in 1881, they formed the Triple Alliance. (Italy dropped out of this coalition in World War I, but the Austro-German partnership held firm.) In response, France, bitter about defeat in the **Franco-Prussian War** (and the resulting loss to Germany of the border provinces Alsace and Lorraine), allied in 1894 with Russia, which viewed Austria as a threat in the Balkans. Geographically, France and Russia had their rivals surrounded.

Until 1907, Britain remained unaligned. Thanks to the **Great Game**, it viewed Russia as an enemy, and it had little affection for France. After 1890, though, it felt increasingly alarmed by Germany. Wilhelm II's aggressive imperialism and, even worse, his expansion of the navy (which menaced the root of Britain's global power, control of the seas) soured Anglo-German relations and shifted British strategy. In 1907, the British informally joined the Franco-Russian alliance, forming the Triple Entente ("understanding").

At this point, any crisis between two countries could potentially involve all of Europe's major powers, the likelihood of war increased. Worsening the problem was Germany's strategy in case of war, the **Schlieffen Plan**. Facing the dilemma of a two-front war, German generals planned a rapid, massive attack against France. Once France was defeated, the Germans and Austrians could deal with Russia at their leisure. To work, the Schlieffen Plan would have to be executed with lightning speed. In the event of a crisis, Germany would have little time to make decisions or resort to diplomacy, and thus, the outbreak of war became even more probable.

QUICK REVIEW

1. Which of the following best describes the broad trends in European foreign policy during the 1815–1914 period?

   (A) European nations were highly warlike in the aftermath of the Napoleonic conflicts but became more peaceful after mid-century.
   (B) The post-Napoleonic treaties kept the peace until the 1850s, then a series of short but important wars broke out until 1871, followed by a four-decade period of peace.
   (C) There was constant war in Europe from the 1850s until the end of the century.
   (D) There were no major wars on the European continent between the defeat of Napoleon and the beginning of World War I.
   (E) none of the above

2. Which of the following did NOT encourage or enable the "new" imperialism of the late 1800s?

   (A) a sense of racial and cultural superiority
   (B) industrial-era military technology
   (C) the need to maintain far-off naval bases and refueling stations
   (D) the essays of Sigmund Freud
   (E) new medical treatments for tropical diseases, such as malaria

3. Which of the following nations is considered to have treated its colonies most poorly?

   (A) Belgium
   (B) Great Britain
   (C) France
   (D) the Netherlands
   (E) Austria

4. The role that the United States played in Latin America during the 1800s and early 1900s can best be described as

   (A) colonial overlord over most of the region.
   (B) strictly hands-off.
   (C) encouraging and nurturing.
   (D) warlike and aggressive.
   (E) economically and politically interventionist.

5. Which European power colonized Indochina?

   (A) Great Britain
   (B) Germany
   (C) Italy
   (D) the Netherlands
   (E) France

6. During the first half of the 1800s, which institution administered Great Britain's colony in India?

   (A) the British East India Company
   (B) the British crown
   (C) the British army
   (D) Lloyd's of London
   (E) the Bank of England

7. Which Asian nation proved most successful at resisting foreign domination?

   (A) China
   (B) Laos
   (C) Japan
   (D) Burma
   (E) Malaysia

8. Which European powers were enmeshed in the so-called Great Game?

   (A) Great Britain and Russia
   (B) Russia and France
   (C) Italy and Germany
   (D) Austria and Italy
   (E) Austria and Russia

9. Which country's collapse was at the heart of the Eastern Question?

(A) Persia's
(B) the Ottoman Empire's
(C) India's
(D) Afghanistan's
(E) China's

10. The number of slaves taken from Africa to the Americas between the late 1400s and late 1800s is most likely somewhere around:

(A) 1 million
(B) 35 million
(C) 12 million
(D) 22 million
(E) 6 million

Answers

1. **(B)** European foreign policy was marked by aggression in the mid-nineteenth century. The Crimean War pitted Russia against Britain and France. The wars of Italian unification involved several Italian states, France, and Austria. The Franco-Prussian War was one of three wars at the time fought over German unification.

2. **(D)** Freud wrote about human psychology. The ideas of Charles Darwin, another key thinker, were misused to justify ideas of racial superiority ("social Darwinism"). Darwin himself denounced the concept of social Darwinism.

3. **(A)** Belgian king Leopold II cared far more about making profits in the Belgian Congo than about treating its inhabitants humanely. He spent his own fortune to ensure that Belgium gained monopoly control over the region's rubber and ivory trade. In the process, Belgian authorities brutally murdered thousands of Congolese people.

4. **(E)** At this time, the United States brought Latin America under its own sphere of influence. Under the Monroe Doctrine of 1823, the United States declared that it would prohibit European countries from interfering in matters concerning the Western Hemisphere. Later in the century, the United States became a colonizing power in Latin America when it took control over Cuba, Puerto Rico, the Virgin Islands, and other islands in the region.

5. **(E)** Under Napoleon III, the French seized Indochina, the area that today is Laos, Cambodia, and Vietnam. In 1954, after suffering defeat at the hands of the Vietnamese nationalists led by Ho Chi Minh, France pulled out of the region.

6. **(A)** The British East India Company administered India for Britain until 1858. As a semiprivate company, it was one of the world's wealthiest and most powerful business ventures. The Indian Mutiny in 1857 compelled the British to take full control over India.

7. **(C)** Japan successfully resisted European attempts at domination. Instead, it adopted scientific, technological, and military advances from the West to pursue its own imperial ambitions. In the late 1800s and early 1900s, it defeated China, increased its dominance over Korea, and defeated Russia.

8. **(A)** The so-called Great Game was an intense competition between Russia and Britain for influence over Central Asia. It involved espionage and diplomatic intrigue. These tensions never resulted in outright war, although the rivalry lasted until shortly before World War I.

9. **(B)** The Eastern Question concerned how Europe's major powers would fill in the power vacuum left behind by the decline of the Ottoman Empire. Egypt was arguably the most important part of the empire, particularly because of the fact that whoever gained control of Egypt would also have control over the Suez Canal, completed in 1869.

10. **(C)** The exact number of Africans forcefully transported to the Americas during this time is not known. However, historians have estimated that at least 12 million were and that more than 2 million slaves were taken from Africa in the 1800s alone.

The Middle East

- Decline of the Ottoman Empire
- The janissaries
- The Tanzimat Reforms
- Nationalism and the Eastern Question
- The Suez Canal
- The Young Turks
- The Madhi
- The Great Game

The Middle East, with Islamic North Africa and Central Asia, underwent a fundamental transformation between the early 1700s and early 1900s. Before 1700, the Ottoman Empire, feared and respected throughout Eurasia as a great power, reigned supreme over most of this region. Where it did not, states such as Persia and the khanates of Central Asia stood strong and free.

After 1700, military setbacks at the hands of European enemies weakened the Ottoman Empire. Its European possessions gradually slipped away. Internal decay allowed outlying territories in North Africa to gain autonomy. Those territories were then taken into British, French, and Italian empires, further eroding Ottoman power. By the nineteenth century, the failing Ottoman Empire had earned an unflattering nickname: the "sick man of Europe." Periodic reform efforts kept the state alive during the 1800s but did not stave off decline. More reform came at the beginning of the 1900s, but World War I would destroy the Ottoman Empire, which was then transformed into the modern Turkish state.

In the meantime, how to deal with the steady collapse of the Ottoman state—and still maintain the European balance of power—became one of the crucial foreign policy issues of the 1800s. This Eastern Question puzzled and perplexed diplomats for decades.

European imperialism also dealt blows to other states in the Middle East and neighboring regions. Egypt, the Caucasus, Persia, and Central Asia came under European—mainly British and Russian—control during the 1800s.

THE DECLINE OF THE OTTOMAN EMPIRE

The Ottoman Empire sustained a heavy set of blows in the late 1600s and early 1700s. In 1683, the Turks nearly succeeded in capturing Vienna, capital of the Austrian Habsburgs. They failed, and in the next three and a half decades of fighting, lost battle after battle and much territory, including Hungary and Transylvania. The treaties of Karlowitz (1699) and Passarowitz (1718) left the Turks greatly diminished in Europe.

Occasional conflicts with Austria continued to sap Ottoman strength. Even worse were the periodic wars the Turks fought with Russia, especially against Peter the Great in the 1710s and Catherine the Great in the late 1700s. With each new struggle, the Turks lost more territory.

Internal Decay and Attempted Reform

Internal troubles also damaged the Ottoman state. Mediocre rulers and governmental corruption had weakened the political system during the 1600s and continued to do so in the 1700s. The dilemma was that sultans who wished to improve or modernize the system met with opposition from influential groups and officials with vested interests in the traditional way of doing things.

This was especially the case with the armed forces. The **janissaries**, who had been so innovative and effective in the 1500s and 1600s, became backward and complacent in the 1700s and early 1800s, refusing to adapt to new technology and tactics. Unfortunately for the empire, the janissaries were, until the 1820s, powerful enough to prevent any change for the better. For example, when Selim III tried to reform the bureaucracy and modernize the army and navy, the janissaries, fearing the loss of their privileged position, assassinated him in 1807.

Later sultans were more effective at changing the system. From the 1820s onward, the Ottoman leadership made some progress in modernizing the political system, the economy, and the military. The sultans boosted Western educational principles, scientific knowledge, and technological expertise. To a degree, they also secularized, against the protests of the traditional Islamic clergy. In the late 1820s, Mehmed III created a professional, European-style army and navy and then subdued the janissaries.

From 1839 through 1876, the Ottoman government introduced a wide-ranging set of changes known as the **Tanzimat reforms.** These reforms emphasized greater religious tolerance for the non-Muslims *millets* (social groups categorized by religion) living in the empire, reform of the legal system, the creation of schools that would teach Western science and technology, the establishment of national telegraph and postal systems, and more. The Tanzimat reforms even included discussing the possibility of a constitution. Another effect of the Tanzimat reforms was to give women greater access to education. Public schools were founded for women. In addition, more women (although still a small number) began to enter public life in the late 1800s.

Still, such limited change was not enough to solve the empire's deep-seated internal and external problems. The Tanzimat reforms and other such measures alienated conservatives and traditionalists, who found them too extreme. Yet they did not do enough to satisfy the growing numbers of forward-looking politicians and military officers who wanted more change than the sultan was willing to make. By the early 1900s, this generation of modernizers, known as the **Young Turks**, would, from within the regime, play a decisive role in ending the sultan's rule.

Revolts, Rebellions, and the Gradual Disintegration of the Ottoman Empire

Long before this, external problems such as rebellion and war were disintegrating the Ottoman Empire. In the early 1800s, an upsurge of nationalism, combined with political turmoil caused by the Napoleonic Wars, led to many uprisings in Turkish-controlled Europe. Serbia revolted in 1807, and even though the revolt failed, the Serbs remained restless.

More seriously, the **Greek war of independence** began in 1821. By 1827, France and Britain, responding to Christian Europe's outpouring of sympathy for the Greeks, aided the rebels (earlier, the poet Lord Byron had helped turn the war into an international cause by leaving England to fight and die on the side of the Greeks). Russia, sharing Greece's Eastern Orthodox faith, also joined the war. Defeated by this coalition, the Ottomans were forced to recognize Greek independence in 1832. At the same time, the Ottoman government had to cope with the rebellion of Muhammad Ali in Egypt and the growing autonomy of possessions in western North Africa.

The Eastern Question

From the 1820s onward, the steady collapse of the Ottoman state presented the nations of Europe with a geopolitical challenge became known as the **Eastern Question**. Although the Turks had been Europe's enemies since the 1300s, the Ottoman Empire was now seen as a satisfactory regime to have in place in the Middle East. It was no longer a real threat, it was predictable, and for the time being, it held together many volatile parts of Asia and Europe. To destroy it or allow it to fall apart quickly might cause chaos or give birth to a new state that was strong and hostile.

Another aspect of the Eastern Question was that the nations of Europe did not wholly trust each other. The Ottoman Empire sat at a geographically crucial juncture: the crossroads of Europe and Asia, the joining of the Black and Mediterranean seas, and the Suez isthmus, which linked the Mediterranean with the Indian Ocean and Asia. If one European country took too much advantage of the Ottomans and seized too much territory from them at one time, it would upset Europe's fragile **balance of power**. Informally, the nations of Europe agreed to solve this part of the Eastern Question by not acting too suddenly or decisively in the region. The Ottomans' decline was to be managed carefully and slowly. If necessary, the European powers would prop up the empire if it seemed in danger of immediate collapse.

The complexity of the Eastern Question was illustrated many times. The Europeans took so long to help Greece in the 1820s because they feared causing too much damage to the Ottoman Empire at once. Soon after joining the Greeks *against* the Turks, Britain and France gave aid *to* the Turks by helping contain Muhammad Ali's revolt in Egypt; they worried that Muhammad Ali would be too formidable an enemy if he toppled the Ottoman sultan. Sometimes the Eastern Question pitted the Europeans against each other; when Russia annexed Ottoman territory in the early 1850s, Britain and France fought alongside the Turks in the Crimean War (1853–1856), the first time since Napoleon's defeat that European powers had clashed with each other.

Tensions worsened after 1870. The construction of the **Suez Canal** in 1869 increased the strategic and economic importance of Egypt, as well as Britain's and France's interest in the region. Italy's unification in the 1860s meant yet another European power with ambitions in the eastern Mediterranean. Moreover, Balkan **nationalism** intensified in the late 1800s. The Balkan Crisis (1876–1878) nearly destroyed the Ottoman Empire: when Romania, Bulgaria, Serbia, and Montenegro revolted against the Ottomans, Russia went to war on their behalf, beat the Turks, and imposed a harsh treaty. The rest of Europe, not wanting Russia to defeat the Turks too decisively, intervened. At the Congress of Berlin (1878), the four rebel nations gained their freedom, but the European powers compelled Russia to offer a more generous treaty to the Turks. Once again, the Eastern Question was dealt with through a combination of opportunistic land grabbing and balanced management.

The Ottoman Empire's Final Years

Domestically, the Ottoman Empire, steadily losing territory and constantly interfered with by the powers of Europe, suffered great difficulties as the 1800s came to an end. As the twentieth century began, the sultan's days were numbered. A group of pro-Western army officers, with a modern, secular outlook, began to form. They called themselves the **Young Turks**, and they were deeply dissatisfied with the sultan's failures to reform and strengthen the Empire. Led by Enver Pasha, the Young Turks seized control in 1908, neutralizing the last sultan and establishing a parliamentary government. The Young Turks modernized the military, aligned themselves with Germany, and began a series of social, economic, and political reforms.

However, the Young Turks could not save the Ottoman Empire. Between 1911 and 1913, the Italians seized the Ottomans' last provinces in North Africa, and a coalition of Serbia, Greece, and Bulgaria defeated the Ottomans in two Balkan Wars. Finally, during World War I, the Young Turk government sided with the Germans. Defeated by the Allies in 1918, the Ottoman Empire collapsed altogether, and its Middle Eastern possessions rebelled or were stripped away by the French and British. The empire was replaced by the modern Turkish state during the 1920s.

EGYPT AND NORTH AFRICA

At its peak, the Ottoman Empire ruled most of Islamic North Africa. Even before the late 1700s, the empire's grip here was weakening owing to distance and the desire of cities such as Tripoli, Algiers, and Tunis for greater autonomy.

Things worsened with the Napoleonic Wars. In 1798, France sent Napoleon to capture Egypt and the Suez isthmus. He easily defeated Egyptian and Turkish armies, temporarily deposing the Mamluks who ruled Egypt on the Ottomans' behalf. Although the English restored the regime, Ottoman authority in Egypt was badly damaged.

The Revolt of Muhammad Ali

In 1805, the rebellion of **Muhammad Ali** freed Egypt from Ottoman rule. An officer in the Turkish forces, Muhammad Ali seized power and began to modernize Egypt until his death in 1839. He created a Western-style military, modernized agriculture (especially cotton), boosted industrialization, and recruited large numbers of European professionals to work for him and teach his people new skills. Muhammad Ali transformed Egypt into one of the world's greatest suppliers of cotton, although he worked his peasants oppressively to do so.

Muhammad Ali threatened the Ottomans even more seriously when he tried to expand his borders. He took the Sudan, then went east, capturing the Sinai, Syria, parts of Arabia, and northern Iraq. He threatened the Ottoman capital, Istanbul. Afraid that he would topple the Ottomans completely, France and Britain stepped in. Recognizing Muhammad Ali as the hereditary prince (khedive) of an autonomous Egypt, the Europeans convinced him not to expand further—and in so doing, saved the Ottoman Empire. Even so, the empire had been badly injured.

European Imperialism in North Africa

As the 1800s passed, the western parts of North Africa, now cut off from the Ottoman Empire by Egypt, fell out of the Ottomans' hands and into those of European imperialists. The French seized Algeria in 1830; more than 150,000 French settled there by the mid-1850s (France considered Algeria to be as important to it as India was to Britain). Later, the French established a protectorate over neighboring Tunisia. Morocco fell to the French and Spanish late in the century. Finally, Libya was conquered by Italy during the Italo-Turkish War (1911–1912). Incidentally, this was the first war in which airplanes were used in combat.

The Suez Canal and English Dominance Over Egypt and Sudan

Egypt fell out of the Ottoman orbit only to be sucked into the European sphere of influence. Muhammad Ali's grandson Ismail, also a reformer, decided to build a canal across the Suez land bridge that linked the Mediterranean with the Red Sea. Ismail's other modernizing efforts, which included building schools and hospitals, were helpful to Egypt. In the short term, building the Suez Canal led to European domination. A French engineer, Ferdinand de Lesseps, designed the canal, and British and French companies supervised the construction, which lasted from 1854 to 1869. The **Suez Canal** was a marvel of modern construction, and it revolutionized international shipping. However, thousands of Egyptians died during the construction, and the French and British held most of the shares in the company that owned the canal. The British bought up many French shares and, in 1875, all of Egypt's. Control over these shares gave Britain an excuse to interfere in local politics. In 1881, the Egyptian military revolted against the khedive. Under the pretext of protecting their investment in the canal, the British assumed control over the region, establishing a protectorate called the Anglo-Egyptian Administration. Although the khedive technically ruled Egypt, the British controlled the government. (For other examples of Western economic dominance over regions that were not technically colonies, see Latin America and China during the late 1800s and early 1900s.)

The British extended the Anglo-Egyptian Administration southward, bringing the Sudan under its control. In the 1880s and 1890s, British authority was opposed by a religious leader and Islamic rebel known as the **Mahdi** (Arabic for "one who is rightly guided"). In 1895, the Mahdi's army massacred a British force at Khartoum, one of Britain's most stunning imperial defeats. In 1898, the British beat the Mahdi at Omdurman in a classic imperial battle in which a small European army, armed with modern rifles and machine guns, mowed down a much larger but poorly armed indigenous force.

From the late 1800s until after the end of World War II, Egypt and North Africa remained in European hands.

PERSIA, THE CAUCASUS, AND CENTRAL ASIA

Much the same pattern that applied to the Ottoman Empire and North Africa applied to the rest of the Middle East.

The Decline and Partition of Persia

Like the Ottomans, the Persians had created a mighty gunpowder empire, the Safavid state (see Chapter 15). It remained strong through the early 1700s, but then found itself at the mercy of outside powers. To the north was Russia, which, as it modernized and Westernized, seized Persian territory in a number of wars. In the late 1700s and 1800s, Russia took portions of the Caucasus Mountains, which lay between the two countries, absorbing Armenia, Georgia, and Azerbaijan. The first two, Christian states living under the Islamic Persians, had asked Russia for help (but had not wanted to become part of the Russian Empire as they did).

The Qajar Dynasty, which ruled Persia from 1794 to 1925, was unable to resist foreign control, even though it technically ruled the country. (In this, its situation resembled China during these years.) In the 1800s, Britain and Russia cynically divided Persia into spheres of influence, allowing them to balance their rivalry in the region and flank the Ottomans. The northern zone went to Russia, the southern zone to Britain. This arrangement lasted until after World War II. British investment in Persia was heavy, especially after the discovery of oil reserves 1908.

The Russian Conquest of Central Asia

From the 1820s through the 1880s, the Russians waged a long, intense campaign of conquest and colonization in Central Asia, home to the Silk Road khanates and city-states. The Russians conquered these regions for several reasons: nationalistic pride, natural resources (Central Asia is a great cotton-producing region), strategy (the Russians feared having a long, open southern frontier), and the hope, never realized, of driving to the Indian Ocean to establish warm-water ports. In long, bloody wars of pacification, the Russians took Tashkent (1865), Samarkand (1868), and Bukhara (1868), driving all the way to the Afghan border.

As discussed in Chapter 22, Russian ambitions here distressed the British: Russia threatened Britain's lines of communication to India and drew near to India itself. The resulting **Great Game** of espionage and diplomatic maneuver caused much Anglo-Russian rivalry until the early 1900s.

QUICK REVIEW

1. The successful rebellion of which Ottoman territory in the early 1800s demonstrated the empire's weakness and also gained much sympathy from the European public?

   (A) Serbia
   (B) Romania
   (C) Greece
   (D) Bulgaria
   (E) Albania

2. Until the 1820s, what institution or group stood in the way of the Ottoman sultans' efforts to reform?

   (A) the janissary corps
   (B) the admiralty
   (C) the Young Turks
   (D) the grand vizier's chancellery
   (E) the grenadiers

3. The actions of Muhammad Ali had what effect on the Ottoman Empire?

   (A) He conquered North Africa for the sultan.
   (B) He kept North Africa from breaking away from the empire.
   (C) He assassinated the sultan and assumed control over the empire.
   (D) He revolted against the empire, gaining freedom for Egypt.
   (E) He gained freedom for Tunisia and Algeria.

4. What part of North Africa became France's most prized colony?

   (A) Morocco
   (B) Algeria
   (C) Tunisia
   (D) Libya
   (E) Egypt

5. Which of the following is NOT true of Ottoman reform between the 1820s and 1870s?

   (A) The sultans considered the possibility of granting a constitution.
   (B) Many of the changes were known collectively as the Tanzimat Reforms.
   (C) Schools began to teach Western science and technology.
   (D) Greater religious tolerance was encouraged.
   (E) It included no improvements for women.

6. The 1869 completion of _____ vastly increased the geopolitical importance of Egypt?

   (A) the Suez Canal
   (B) the Aswan Dam
   (C) the Giza Canal
   (D) the Luxor Bridge
   (E) the Alexandria Dockyards

7. Which group deposed the Ottoman sultan in 1908?

   (A) British commandos
   (B) Sufi assassins
   (C) the Young Turks
   (D) the janissary corps
   (E) Russian spies

8. Who led a large, religiously motivated army against the British in the Sudan during the late 1800s?

   (A) Muhammad Ali
   (B) the Mahdi
   (C) Enver Pasha
   (D) Ismail
   (E) Rumi

9. Which European power conquered Central Asian city-states such as Bukhara and Samarkand?

    (A) France
    (B) Italy
    (C) Great Britain
    (D) Germany
    (E) Russia

10. What Middle Eastern state did the British and Russians divide into two spheres of influence during the 1800s?

    (A) the Ottoman Empire
    (B) Persia
    (C) Egypt
    (D) Syria
    (E) Lebanon

Answers

1. **(C)** Lord Byron's public championing of the Greeks' battle for freedom helped achieve Greece's independence from the Ottomans in the late 1820s. France, Britain, and Russia all came to Greece's aid against the Ottomans.

2. **(A)** The conservative janissaries refused to adapt to the new technology and tactics of the emerging industrialized age. In 1807, they assassinated Sultan Selim III when he tried to reform the bureaucracy and modernize the armed forces.

3. **(D)** Egyptians under Muhammad Ali vanquished Ottoman rule during the 1805 rebellion. He created a Western-style military and improved the economy, including turning Egypt into one of the world's top cotton-producing states.

4. **(B)** Algeria became France's key conquest. The French seized Algeria in 1830, and over 150,000 of its citizens settled there by the mid-1850s. The French did not relinquish their hold on Algeria until 1962.

5. **(E)** The Tanzimat Reforms somewhat improved the lives of women. They gave women better access to education, and more women were allowed to enter public life as a result.

6. **(A)** The Suez Canal links the Mediterranean with the Red Sea—and, by extension, it links the Mediterranean with the Indian Ocean and Asia. Thus, the canal is very important geopolitically to whoever controls the waterway.

7. **(C)** The Young Turks were a group of pro-Western army officers with a modern, secular worldview. They were dissatisfied with the sultan's failures to reform and strengthen the Ottoman Empire. Under Enver Pasha, the Young Turks seized control of the empire in 1908.

8. **(B)** The Mahdi was a Muslim leader in the Sudan who rebelled against the British in the mid-1880s. The British, under General Horatio Kitchener, defeated the Mahdi at the battle of Omdurman in 1898.

9. **(E)** From the 1820s to the 1880s, Russia colonized Central Asia by force. The Russians seized city-states then for nationalistic pride, natural resources, and strategic reasons.

10. **(B)** The British and Russians agreed to partition Persia (modern-day Iran) during the 1800s. In this way, they achieved a balance of power in the region while also outflanking the Ottoman Turks. The Russians controlled the northern zone, which bordered its own territory, and the British controlled the southern zone.

China and Japan

- The decline of Qing China
- The tea and opium trades
- The Opium Wars, the concessions system, and the Open Door Policy
- The Taiping Rebellion
- The Dowager Empress Cixi and the Boxer Rebellion
- Sun Yat-sen and the Nationalist Party

- The Tokugawa Shogunate
- Matthew Perry and the opening of Japan
- The Meiji Restoration and Japan's industrial modernization
- The Russo-Japanese War

As with the rest of the globe, the European presence in East Asia increased dramatically from the late 1700s through the early 1900s. The major states there, China and Japan, reacted to this development in very different ways.

Famously, Napoleon Bonaparte referred to China as a sleeping dragon. By that, he meant that with its huge population, vast size, and rich resources, China had the potential to become one of the world's mightiest nations. However, under the rule of the late Qing (Manchu) emperors, China continued to slumber, and its power decreased rather than increased. Deluded by a sense of its own grandeur, based on past accomplishments and old traditions, the Qing leadership did little to modernize and industrialize. This backwardness left it vulnerable, and, during the 1800s, China suffered repeated defeats at the hands of Western powers. Although China was not actually conquered and colonized, it was forced to grant so many privileges and economic concessions to outside powers that its integrity as an independent nation was compromised. The Qing state weakened internally during the 1800s and collapsed in 1911.

By contrast, Japan responded effectively to the challenge posed by the West. When the United States and the nations of Europe forced its markets open to the world in the 1850s, Japan chose to learn from them. From 1868 onward, under new leadership, the Japanese modernized, industrialized, and militarized. They preserved their independence. By the 1890s and early 1900s, Japan was an imperial power, expanding its sphere of influence in East Asia. As several wars during these years proved, Japan became the first non-Western nation in the modern era capable of rivaling Europe and America in military ability and strength.

QING (MANCHU) CHINA IN DECLINE

The Peak of the Qing Dynasty

The Qing, or Manchu, rulers who had conquered China from the north in 1644 had been mighty, ruthless leaders. The dynasty's peak, however, had been the long reign of Kangxi (1662–1722). Emperor Qianlong (1736–1795) was the Qing's last strong, competent ruler.

During the last half of the 1700s, Qianlong defended China's long borders, kept the empire's far-flung regions under control, improved economic growth, and sponsored art and learning. During his reign, one of the greatest novels in Chinese literary history appeared: Cao Xuequin's *Dream of the Red Chamber* (1791). This novel, which depicts upper-class family life in eighteenth-century China, narrates the tragedy of two young lovers caught up in the decline of a wealthy and powerful clan.

Internal Decline of the Qing

Unfortunately for the Qing, several negative trends weakened China simultaneously almost immediately after Qianlong's death. The quality of leadership declined steeply, as weak, incompetent emperors took the throne.

More widely, the government became riddled with corruption. The cost of maintaining border defenses along the northern and western frontiers became increasingly burdensome. The economy worsened, and population growth was too rapid (China had 300 million people at the beginning of the century, and 400 million by the end). Popular discontent with the Qing and bad economic conditions broke out into open revolt several times. One such occasion was the White Lotus Rebellion (1796–1804), which took years for the authorities to suppress.

Chinese Foreign Trade Before the 1830s

At the same time, an external problem made itself felt: increased economic and diplomatic pressure from the West, particularly from Britain. As late as the 1810s, the Chinese had the upper hand in their relationship with the West. China was too strong to conquer, and it enjoyed an enormous advantage in its balance of trade.

Europeans could trade with China only in a small number of designated ports and cities (including Kiakhta in the north and Canton on the southern coast). The Chinese accepted only a tiny selection of Western goods in trade. In return, they sold the nations of the West silk and porcelain. The most profitable commodity was tea, which the Chinese sold in immense quantities to the outside world, especially Russia and Britain. In exchange, the West paid China vast amounts of silver bullion.

For years, Westerners complained about these conditions and requested the Chinese to allow them to sell more goods in China. In 1793, a British delegation led by Lord Macartney made such a request, but it was denied. Famously, Macartney, in order to meet the Emperor Qianlong, was compelled to lower himself onto one knee, and he was referred to by the Chinese not as an ambassador, but as a tribute-bearer. When Macartney asked that the British be allowed to sell more of their goods to China, Qianlong replied, "Your country has nothing we need." In 1816, a similar mission under Lord Amherst received much the same response.

Tea Harvesting in China.
For hundreds of years, silk, then porcelain, had been China's chief commodities in trade. During the 1600s and 1700s, however, tea began to overtake both in importance. The tea trade played a great role in global economics during the 1700s and 1800s. During those centuries, "all the tea in China" became the most popular slang phrase to describe unimaginable wealth. Shown here is the traditional method of harvesting and processing tea in China.

The Qing's refusal to bargain was partly tough business sense. However, it also had to do with feelings of superiority: the Qing leadership believed that the emperor was the Son of Heaven, that China was the **Middle Kingdom** and the center of the universe, and that all outsiders were barbarians. What the Qing failed to realize, however, was that the Western "barbarians" were, by this point, much more scientifically and technologically advanced than the Chinese—and had stronger navies, better weapons, and more effective armies. The days when the Chinese could intimidate foreigners into accepting such an embarrassing and unprofitable imbalance of trade were about to end.

The Opium Wars and Foreign Domination of Qing China

Meanwhile, the British, followed by other Europeans, found a clever, if unethical, way to break into Chinese markets: the **opium trade.** Opium had been known in China since the early 1700s, but it was not yet widely available. The British changed this situation in the 1820s and 1830s by flooding China with opium grown in northeastern India. With lightning speed, opium became the drug of choice among Chinese of all classes. The British made fantastic profits, and the balance of trade swung suddenly in Britain's favor. Over time, other countries—including France, Portugal, and the United States—sold opium to China, but Britain controlled 80 percent of the trade.

The Chinese government was outraged. The trade was illegal. It reversed the balance of trade, and silver bullion, instead of flowing into China, flowed out at an alarming rate. Moreover, opium addiction was so widespread that it affected economic productivity: on any given day, millions of farmers and workers would be so incapacitated by the drug that they could not work. The Chinese protested to the West. One official lamented, "The foreigners have brought us a disease which will dry up our bones, a worm that gnaws at our hearts, a ruin to our families and persons. It means the destruction of the soul of our nation."

The Qing government tried to strike back by arresting dealers, seizing opium supplies, and intercepting boats carrying the drug. The problem for the Chinese was that any aggressive action might give the foreigners an excuse for war. This is what happened in 1839, when the Chinese navy blockaded Canton, one of the few ports where foreigners were allowed to trade. This action sparked the first **Opium War** (1839–1842), between Britain and China. The British won easily, then forced the humiliating Treaty of Nanking on the Chinese. The Qing government was required to open five more ports to foreign trade, lower tariffs on British goods, and grant extraterritorial rights to areas in China where the British lived and worked (British, not Chinese, law prevailed in these areas). In addition, China had to surrender **Hong Kong** to Britain.

The conflicts over opium and trade did not end in 1842. More fighting, including a second Opium War (the so-called Arrow War), and a Franco-British expedition to Beijing took place between 1856 and 1860. Treaties arrived at between 1858 and 1860 legalized the opium trade, opened more ports to foreign trade, and granted greater powers to the Portuguese, French, British, Americans, and Russians, who set up **economic concessions** on Chinese territory. During the late 1800s, China grew weaker and had to give more privileges to foreign traders. Late in the century, Japan, Germany, and Italy gained concessions as well. Much territory along the Chinese coast was extraterritorial, meaning that it was legally under foreign, not Chinese, control. By 1898, foreign vessels were allowed unrestricted travel up the rivers of China.

The Taiping Rebellion

Serious internal problems dogged the Qing at the same time foreign pressure increased. The worst was the **Taiping Rebellion** (1850–1864), the costliest and most devastating civil war in world history. The Taiping Rebellion lasted almost a decade and a half. It claimed somewhere between 20 to 30 million lives, making it the second deadliest war in history, next to World War II.

The uprising was started by Hong Xiuquan, a Cantonese clerk educated partly by Protestant missionaries. An aspiring government official, Hong failed his civil service examination. The shock seems to have caused him to have visions, in which he became convinced that he was Jesus Christ's younger brother, destined to establish a "heavenly kingdom of supreme peace"—the meaning of the word *taiping*—in China.

Hong's rebellion began in 1850. An extraordinarily magnetic leader, Hong attracted several followers who organized an effective modern army. Hong's vision of a new China also proved appealing to millions of ordinary Chinese who resented the Qing's high taxes, its arbitrary and oppressive rule, and the fact that the Manchu emperors were essentially foreign rulers. At their peak, Hong and the Taiping leaders controlled one-third of China.

The Taiping Rebellion waned after 1860. Competent generals took over the Qing war effort, and the government was assisted by a foreign force—the Ever-Victorious Army—commanded by an American soldier of fortune, Frederick Townsend Ward, and then the English general Charles "Chinese" Gordon. Quarrels among the Taiping leadership hurt the movement as well. By the early 1860s, the Taiping forces were in retreat. Hong committed suicide by taking poison in 1864, and the remaining Taiping leaders were captured and executed.

The Leadership of Dowager Empress Cixi

The Taiping Rebellion left China in ruins, and the Qing government was thrown into chaos. Not until 1878 did a strong leader emerge—unfortunately, one who adamantly opposed modernization. The dowager empress **Cixi** "ruled" China from 1878 to her death in 1908. A concubine to the emperor in the 1850s, Cixi became a major figure at the Qing court. In 1878, she placed her nephew Guangxu on the imperial throne and gained the position of regent. She did not rule China in her own right, but controlled her nephew—and the government—long after Guangxu became an adult.

Under Cixi's influence, Qing rule became more oppressive. China's outlying possessions—Tibet, the Gobi Desert and Mongolia, Chinese Turkestan—began to slip away, gain greater autonomy, or fall into foreign hands. At home, Cixi opposed all reform, which she regarded as pro-Western treason. In 1898, when her nephew, the emperor, began to listen to reform-minded advisers, she acted harshly. As soon as Guangxu's short-lived Hundred Days' Reform began, Cixi struck back by placing her nephew under house arrest and executing the reformers.

Western Spheres of Influence in China, 1910.
Starting in the early-to-mid-1800s, Great Britain, then other Western nations, pressured China into opening its markets and yielding up economic and political control over much of its coast. These concessions grew in size and number during the 1800s and early 1900s, reaching their peak just before the collapse of the Qing dynasty in 1911.

The Sino-Japanese War and the Open Door Policy

All this time, foreign domination of China increased, especially as the new nations of Germany and Italy pushed for a greater share of Chinese trade. Germany took the major port of Tsingtao. Japan defeated China in the Sino-Japanese War (1894–1895). In 1898, the United States, with its **Open Door Policy**, arranged for all Western nations to have equal access to Chinese markets. Such a policy reduced much of the pressure that European nations were placing on China to open up further, but it also meant that foreign control continued.

Missionaries in China

Another result of increased foreign influence in China was a rise in the level of missionary activity there. From the late 1800s through the mid-1900s, it became more common for Protestant and Catholic clergy and volunteers to travel from Europe and the United States to China in order to spread Christianity and teach Western languages. In this way, they interfered with and even eroded traditional Chinese culture.

However, missionaries also brought scientific and technological knowledge, treated diseases and ailments with modern medicine, and helped eliminate oppressive cultural practices, such as female **foot binding**. Missionary activity proved to be an illustration of imperialism's mixed legacy of positive and negative impact.

The Boxer Rebellion and Last-Ditch Attempts at Reform

Finally, in 1900, Chinese anger at foreign influence burst out of control. Making things worse were a severe drought, which damaged agriculture and hurt farmers, and widespread unemployment in the cities. What followed during the summer was the **Boxer Rebellion**, so called because many of the rebels were Chinese "boxers," or martial-arts experts.

Most of the rebels' rage was directed at foreigners, especially in the capital, Beijing, where rebels attacked foreign residents and besieged foreign legations. In the end, the rebellion was put down, mainly by foreign troops. In revenge, the foreign communities in China burned a number of temples. They also forced the Qing government to pay a heavy financial penalty.

Too little, too late, even Cixi recognized the need for at least some reform. In 1905, she formed a committee to investigate the possibility of writing a constitution. She and Guangxi both died in 1908, but the reform effort continued under China's last emperor, Henry Puyi. Local assemblies were formed, and elections for a national assembly were planned for 1910.

Sun Yat-Sen, the Collapse of the Qing, and the Chinese Republic

However, reform came too late to save the Qing dynasty. Efforts to change were too weak and feeble. Opposition groups of many types had formed in China, especially among younger Chinese who opposed Manchu domination of their race and favored Western-style modernization. The most important of these revolutionaries was **Sun Yat-sen** (1866–1925), the father of modern China. During the early 1900s, Sun Yat-sen united a number of opposition groups into a movement called the Revolutionary Alliance. Sun hoped to carry out a government takeover that would progress from military revolt to the formation of a constitutional democracy. His movement was founded on three ideas, which he called People's Principles: Nationalism (meaning opposition to Manchu rule), Democracy, and People's Livelihood.

The Qing regime collapsed in 1911. In the fall, a major uprising began in the central Chinese industrial region of Wuhan. Although Sun Yat-sen was actually in the United States at the time, his movement was at the forefront of the rebellion. The uprising spread, and Sun returned from America. A Chinese Republic was founded in early 1912, with Sun as its president. His party was now called the **Nationalist Party (Kuomintang)**. For the first time in recorded Chinese history, the country was ruled not by an imperial dynasty or foreign conqueror, but by a politician brought to office by popular action.

The Chinese Republic, however, had a short and stormy history. Sun was forced to step aside as president shortly after coming to power. Confusion, decentralization, political breakdown, and civil war characterized the 1910s through the 1940s. In 1949, the republic would be destroyed, and a communist government would take its place.

ISOLATION AND PARTIAL MODERNIZATION IN TOKUGAWA JAPAN

The Tokugawa Shogunate in the Eighteenth Century

In the 1750s, Japan was ruled by the **Tokugawa Shogunate**, which had taken power in the early 1600s. As before, supreme authority technically rested with the emperor, but real power belonged to the shogun, who ran the country in the emperor's name. Under the Shogun were the remnants of the **samurai** class, the warrior aristocracy from Japan's feudal era.

In the 1600s and early 1700s, the Tokugawa shoguns had been strong, dynamic rulers. They had centralized Japan and transformed it from a constantly warring collection of disunified states into a single country at peace. The Tokugawa shoguns were highly dictatorial, creating a rigidly stratified society that restricted social mobility, kept ordinary citizens out of politics, and allowed few personal freedoms. Tokugawa Japan also isolated itself from the rest of the world. By the 1720s, the only country Japan had formal relations with was Korea. Informal ties were maintained with China, and the government allowed some foreign trade at the port of **Nagasaki**.

> **TIP**
>
> The Tokugawa shoguns were highly dictatorial, creating a rigidly stratified society that restricted social mobility, kept ordinary citizens out of politics, and allowed few personal freedoms.

Partial Modernization in Tokugawa Japan

In the late 1700s and early 1800s, Tokugawa Japan partially modernized, both economically and socially. Population growth was steady. Japan, already a society of cities, experienced even more urban growth. Kyoto and Osaka were major centers, and the capital, Edo (present-day Tokyo), had a population of well over a million. Agriculture practice was rationalized, allowing fewer people to grow more food. This reform led to further urbanization and freed up a labor force just as proto-industrialization began in Japan.

Trade, commerce, and manufacturing became increasingly important. A national infrastructure—more roads, canals, and ports—began to emerge. The **merchant class**, soon to be a modernizing middle class, grew in number, wealth, and influence. Despite the country's international isolation, some Japanese gained an awareness of Western scientific and technological knowledge.

Partial modernization placed the shogun and the samurai in a dilemma. It made Japan more prosperous and more advanced. On the other hand, the spread of new foreign learning, the movement of people from countryside to city, and the increased social and economic clout of the merchant class undermined the power and land-based wealth of the traditional aristocracy.

Therefore, the regime allowed some modernization, but not as much as Japan was capable of. In particular, members of the samurai class—whose military prowess was based on skill with traditional weapons, such as swords—were anxious to preserve the state's monopoly on gunpowder weaponry. How long the Tokugawa leadership would have kept up this approach is impossible to say. In the early 1850s, however, external forces compelled Japan to change.

The Opening of Japan and the Overthrow of the Shogunate

In 1853, American gunships appeared off the Japanese coast. Their commander, **Commodore Matthew Perry**, requested Japan to open its economy to foreign trade. Although the Americans' words were friendly, the threat of naval bombardment lay behind them. After some debate, the shogun agreed to end his country's decades-long isolation. Over the next five years, European nations persuaded the Japanese to open up to them as well. For a time, it appeared that Japan might fall victim to the same kind of Western economic pressure that was crippling China.

Painfully aware of what was happening to China, certain samurai leaders, particularly from the southern provinces of Satsuma and Choshu, urged the shogun to stand up to foreign intimidation. This Sat-Cho Alliance gained a following at the Edo court and pressed for the severance of all ties with the West. It also took matters into its own hands. In 1867, a Choshu coastal fortress fired on Western ships, and the ships fired back. The resulting scandal gave the Sat-Cho Alliance the pretext it needed to move against the last shogun, who had just come to power. In January 1868, the Sat-Cho staged a military uprising and overthrew the shogunate. Meiji, who had just become emperor in 1867, was the first emperor in nearly a thousand years to enjoy full imperial powers.

THE MEIJI RESTORATION AND JAPANESE ASCENDANCY

The **Meiji Restoration** of 1868 began Japan's modern age. Although the rebellion that brought Meiji to power was initially anti-Western, even the most xenophobic members of the new government realized that, in order to avoid Western domination, Japan would have to adopt Western learning, economics, and military methods. In addition, the emperor himself was personally inclined toward Westernization. What followed was a revolution from above, in which Meiji's government radically altered Japanese politics, economics, and social organization.

From Feudalism to Constitutional Monarchy

In 1871, Meiji abolished feudalism. Although individual samurai continued to serve in positions of power, hereditary privileges were done away with. Government stipends to the samurai, a privilege of the past, were eliminated. Former samurai were forbidden to wear swords, their traditional symbols of authority, in public.

The rigid social hierarchy of the Tokugawa regime ended. Modern laws (the Civil Code of 1898) were drawn up. The Constitution of 1890 created an elected parliament, the Diet. Owing to property qualifications and other restrictions, suffrage was quite low, around 5 percent, and the emperor had a great deal of power over the Diet. The civil code and constitution also made little room for the rights of women, who were largely confined to a secondary status (industrialization gave many lower-class women jobs, but these were low-paying, low-status positions). In effect, Meiji and his successors created an oligarchy (rule by the few) that was less repressive and restrictive than the Tokugawa regime but hardly representative.

Industrialization and Economic Modernization

Meiji and the emperors who followed him also altered the economy beyond recognition. Agricultural productivity increased. The major change, however, involved industrialization. Meiji sent young members of the upper class to visit or study in Europe and America, to learn engineering, economics, and military science. He created a Ministry of Industry in 1870 as well as state banks to finance his industrialization campaign. New railroads, steamships, ports, and canals were constructed every year. Huge corporations called **zaibatsu**, sponsored largely by the state, came to dominate the economic landscape. The government encouraged not just large-scale industry but also private enterprise, spurring the growth of a larger middle class.

Economic growth came at a price. For farmers, taxes increased. Working conditions for the industrial lower classes were oppressive, just as they had been during the first decades of Europe's Industrial Revolution. Sweatshop environments, low wages, and unsafe labor practices prevailed, especially in textile mills and coal mines. In one mine near Nagasaki, workers toiled in temperatures of up to 130 degrees Fahrenheit, and were shot if they tried to escape. Unions of any type were forbidden.

Social and Class Transformation in Japan

Social transformation was a major part of the Meiji Restoration. The traditional privileges of the samurai class were taken away. Access to political positions was increasingly dependent on merit, competence, and civil service examinations. Meiji's reforms and Japanese industrialization increased the size and power of the merchant and middle classes, much as industrialization did in the West. The feudal prejudice against trade and artisanship faded away.

Things changed for the lower classes as well. The farming population decreased, but their taxes increased considerably. The industrial working class grew steadily. On one hand, their working conditions could be dreadful. They were barred from full political participation by the Constitution of 1890. However, the lower classes also benefited in some ways from the Meiji reforms. The new tax system of 1872 funded a national educational system. Commoners, who previously had not been allowed to handle or learn how to use weapons, were now allowed to serve in the military. Overall, Japanese society adopted Western dress, fashions and manners, the Western calendar, and the metric system. The population boomed, growing from 35 million in 1873 to 55 million in 1918.

Japanese Militarism and the Russo-Japanese War

Meiji Japan also became increasingly militaristic. Nationalist sentiment ran high during the late 1800s and 1900s, helping spur the desire for empire building. The government-sponsored religion of **State Shintoism**, a modern revival of Japan's ancient faith, emphasized Japanese superiority and veneration of the emperor as a descendant of the gods. Japan wanted markets for its manufactured goods. A resource-poor island, Japan also needed raw materials to continue industrial growth.

Japan's expansion began in the 1870s. It forced Korean ports open to trade, much as the West had done with China and Japan itself. From China, it took the Ryukyu Islands, which include Okinawa, the most cherished of Japan's overseas possessions. In the 1880s and early 1890s, Japan modernized its navy and drafted a well-drilled and well-equipped army.

More military successes followed. The Sino-Japanese War (1894–1895) resulted in Japan's occupation of Taiwan and Korea (annexed in 1908). An even more impressive triumph was the **Russo-Japanese War** (1904–1905). Competition over influence in Manchuria caused great tension between the two countries. Russia's rapid expansion in this area and its construction of the Trans-Siberian Railroad, the longest in the world, interfered with Japanese ambitions in the region. The Japanese opened the war with a surprise attack on Russia's Pacific naval base at Port Arthur. Tiny compared to Russia, Japan was nonetheless better prepared for war and had the advantage of fighting close to home. When the war ended, Japan was victorious. It annexed land near Korea, the southern half of Sakhalin Island, and the Kurile Islands.

The Russo-Japanese War marked the first time in the modern era that a non-Western nation had defeated a European power in a full-scale military conflict. In a way, it was an early warning signal that, later in the twentieth century, Europe's peak as the world's dominant civilization would eventually pass—and that its empires would gradually slip away. As for Japan, it entered the new century as a modern, industrial nation and a regional power with a growing empire. Japan would continue to modernize. Unfortunately, its militaristic, nationalistic streak would widen as well, and its imperial ambitions would spin out of control.

QUICK REVIEW

1. The last effective ruler of Qing China is considered to be

   (A) Kangxi.
   (B) Qianlong.
   (C) Cixi.
   (D) Guangxu.
   (E) Puyi.

2. Western nations were most upset with Qing China about what aspect of their trading relations?

   (A) the high price of Chinese rice
   (B) China's refusal to allow large amounts of foreign goods to be sold there
   (C) China's sponsorship of the illegal heroin trade
   (D) China's use of slave labor to manufacture its products
   (E) China's reluctance to sell silk and porcelain

3. What was the commodity that Western powers most sought from China during the late 1700s and 1800s?

   (A) rice
   (B) soy sauce
   (C) wine
   (D) tea
   (E) coffee

4. Which of the following resulted from the Opium Wars?

   I. China granted outside powers greater access to its port cities.
   II. China agreed to outlaw opium consumption.
   III. China ceded Hong Kong to Great Britain.
   IV. China allowed Germany to annex Taiwan.

   (A) I only
   (B) I and II only
   (C) I and III only
   (D) I, II, and IV
   (E) I, III, and IV

5. The Taiping Rebellion

   (A) was led by a former clerk who believed he was Jesus Christ's younger brother.
   (B) overthrew the Qing dynasty.
   (C) lasted only a short time and did little damage to China.
   (D) was supported by Great Britain and the United States.
   (E) started because of the secret work of Russian spies in China.

6. Which of the following describes the Tokugawa Shogunate during the late 1700s and early 1800s?

   (A) moving steadily toward economic modernization and greater democratization
   (B) isolated from the wider world and clinging to old samurai traditions
   (C) anarchic and plagued by civil war
   (D) benefiting intellectually and culturally from friendly ties with several Western powers
   (E) extremely warlike, perpetually in conflict with its neighbors

7. The emperor Meiji was

   (A) largely a figurehead, controlled by the shogun.
   (B) a ruthless dictator.
   (C) an extreme traditionalist who opposed most forms of change.
   (D) the founder of the Tokugawa Shogunate.
   (E) the great modernizer who replaced the Tokugawa shoguns.

8. How did Japanese industrialization differ from European industrialization?

   (A) The middle class was unimportant to Japan's industrial growth.
   (B) Female wage earners in Japan were treated with greater equality than their European counterparts.
   (C) Japanese industrialization was directed largely by the imperial regime, whereas in Europe it arose with less government involvement.
   (D) Japanese industrial growth was not accompanied by a trend in urban growth.
   (E) Living and working conditions were much better for Japan's working class.

9. What were the *zaibatsu*?

   (A) huge industrial conglomerates
   (B) the most advanced battleships of their day
   (C) elite military units
   (D) large plantations that dominated Japanese agriculture
   (E) the oldest Buddhist temples in Japan

10. The Russo-Japanese War

   (A) marked the first time in the modern era that a non-Western nation had defeated a Western power.
   (B) resulted from the clash of Russian and Japanese imperial ambitions in Manchuria.
   (C) began with a Japanese surprise attack on a Russian naval base.
   (D) all of the above
   (E) none of the above

Answers

1. **(B)** Qianlong effectively defended China's borders, maintained control over its regions, increased economic growth, and promoted art and learning. However, once he died, the quality of leadership in China declined.

2. **(B)** The Chinese had a large advantage over the West in terms of balance of trade. China was too strong for Western powers to conquer, and it accepted only a small amount of Western goods in trade at this time.

3. **(D)** Tea was China's most profitable commodity. China's top buyers were Britain and Russia. In return for its tea, the Chinese received large amounts of silver bullion.

4. **(C)** As China grew weaker militarily and politically, Germany gained concessions, but Taiwan was not one of them. However, Britain did gain control of Hong Kong. Treaties adopted in the mid-1800s actually made the opium trade legal.

5. **(A)** Hong Xiuquan was a Cantonese clerk educated partly by Protestant missionaries. In the 1850s, he led the Taiping rebels in their quest to overthrow the Qing rulers. The rebellion began to wane after 1860, and Hong eventually committed suicide.

6. **(B)** By the 1720s, Korea was the sole country with which Japan maintained formal relations. Then, in the late 1700s and early 1800s, Tokugawa Japan partially modernized. This modernization included the growth of foreign trade and commerce.

7. **(E)** Emperor Meiji ascended to the throne in 1867, shortly before the last shogun, Tokugawa Yoshinobu, was overthrown. Meiji was the first Japanese emperor in centuries to wield full imperial powers.

8. **(C)** The Japanese government coordinated the process of industrialization. In doing so, it created a Ministry of Industry and state banks, and built a transportation infrastructure to move goods more efficiently.

9. **(A)** These large corporations were sponsored mainly by the state. They came to dominate the Japanese economy. However, the Japanese government also encouraged private enterprise on a smaller scale, spurring the growth of the middle class.

10. **(D)** The Russo-Japanese War of 1904–1905 was a great victory for Japan. Japan was better prepared for war and benefited from fighting close to home. As a result of the war, it annexed new territories and compelled Russia to agree to recognize its sphere of influence in southern Manchuria.

India and Southeast Asia

CHAPTER 25

- The decline of Mughal India
- The British East India Company and the battle of Plassey
- The Indian cotton industry
- The zamindar system
- Sepoys and the Indian Mutiny
- National liberation movements and the Indian National Congress
- The Dutch East India Company and Indonesia
- Singapore and Hong Kong
- French Indochina and *la mission civilisatrice*
- Thailand's continued independence
- The Spanish-American War and U.S. annexation of the Philippines

The proverbial jewel in the crown of the British Empire was India. The conquest and ownership of this country, one of the largest and most populous regions on earth, by a small island nation 5,000 miles away was one of the central facts of nineteenth- and early-twentieth-century life. Throughout the 1800s, British control over India affected global economics, the movement of navies, international relations, and the balance of world power. It gave Britain immense wealth and prestige, and it affected the course of Indian history, changing politics, economic development, social practices, language, and virtually every aspect of Indian culture.

Likewise, the great arc of Southeast Asian nations and islands that stretched between British India and China came under increased Western control in the 1800s. By the end of the century, only a tiny portion of Southeast Asia remained free of foreign domination.

On the other hand, **national liberation movements** were beginning to form by the late 1800s, both in India and the rest of Southeast Asia. For the time being, they were unable to dislodge their foreign masters, but they lay the foundation for the movements that successfully expelled European colonists after World War II.

FROM FOOTHOLD TO MASTERY: THE BRITISH IN LATE-EIGHTEENTH-CENTURY INDIA

During the last half of the eighteenth century, most of India was technically ruled by the once-mighty **Mughal Empire**. However, the Mughals' political fortunes had declined badly since the glory days of the 1500s and 1600s. Many parts of the subcontinent had slipped out from under Mughal rule, becoming independent kingdoms or city-states. Also by the 1700s, increased pressure from European outsiders destabilized what was left of Mughal power.

Anglo-French Competition Over India

In the early 1700s, the Portuguese and Dutch still maintained small settlements along India's coasts. The Europeans most intent on gaining control over India, however, were Britain and France. For the time being, Britain's interests were represented by the **British East India Company**, which, on its own, financed the military takeover and economic development of India.

From the southeastern ports of Pondicherry and Madras (which they captured temporarily from the British), the French tried until the late 1750s to grapple with the British East India Company for hegemony over India. However, French colonial administrators did not get adequate support from the home government in Paris.

Also, at the end of the decade, the British East India Company, under Sir Robert Clive, enlarged its power by scoring key military successes against the Mughals. When Indians attacked the British population of Bengal and jailed many of them, soldiers and civilians alike, in a horrible underground prison known as the **Black Hole of Calcutta**, the British used the event as a pretext for military action. In 1757, at the crucial battle of **Plassey**, Clive defeated a Mughal force more than ten times the size of his own. The Mughals were compelled to grant such extensive military and economic concessions that British superiority on the subcontinent was permanently ensured. The French had no more hope of rivaling the British in India, and their zone of control shrank to the coastal territory surrounding the port of Pondicherry.

Britain's Gradual Conquest of India

Even in 1800, the British held only a comparatively small part of India. Major centers of control were Bombay, the great gateway port of the west coast; Madras, a cloth-making center on the southeast shore; and Fort William, near Calcutta, in the Bengal region of the northeast.

The British East India Company used military and economic power to expand its control and pressure the Mughals to grant it ever-widening tax-collecting rights and administrative powers. Whereas the British at first had footholds only on the coasts, they gradually extended their reach into the interior, especially up the Ganges River in the north. In some regions, the company governed directly. In others, it ruled through the authority of local Mughal officials or friendly natives.

Between the 1760s and 1810s, the company fought a number of campaigns. Major foes included Haidar Ali, who led guerrilla armies in the south; Tipu Sultan, who fought on central India's Deccan Plateau; and the Maharatta princes. Many British generals who became famous in other conflicts—such as Cornwallis, who lost to the Americans at Yorktown, and Wellington, who defeated Napoleon at Waterloo—saw service in these wars.

By 1810, the company controlled almost one-fourth of India, as well as most of Ceylon (now Sri Lanka).

British Administration of India Before 1800

Before 1800, the British East India Company's administration of British India was heavy-handed, even clumsy. Initially, the main goal was to create a local **cotton industry**. The British would process the cotton into cloth and sell it to the East Indies for spices, which were sent back to Britain.

In the beginning, British rule harmed the local population in several ways. Profits generated by Indian raw materials went to Britain, rather than benefiting the local economy. The size and efficiency of British-built textile mills drove out of business local textile enterprises, which were often run by women. Also, British tax law applied to the British zone of control and allowed the authorities to confiscate land from peasants who could not pay their taxes. The British thought they had created a fair taxation system by leaving collection to local native officials called **zamindars**. However, the zamindars lost no time in overtaxing their countrymen and then making themselves rich by using British law to seize land from peasants. Such confiscations became so common in the 1770s that famines struck the countryside, killing approximately one-third of the Indians—mainly peasants—living under British control.

> **NOTE**
>
> As time passed, British economic goals in India became more diverse. British rulership became more adept and in many ways more enlightened. On the other hand, British rule was still imposed by military force and motivated mainly by economic exploitation and strategic concerns. All during the 1800s, the British masters tightened their grip on India.

INDIA UNDER BRITISH RULE: THE 1800s

During the first half of the 1800s, the British extended their control over India. They moved from the coastline and the Ganges River valley into the interior, gaining authority—whether direct or indirect—over the entire country. The British also took outlying northwestern areas, such as Punjab and parts of Afghanistan, after a series of conflicts with skilled warriors like the **Sikhs** and mountain peoples like the Pathans.

Methods of British Control

British colonial authority—referred to popularly as the **Raj**—was complex. Although the British crown was becoming more involved, the British East India Company still assumed primary responsibility for administering and exploiting the expanding colony. Cities such as Bombay and Calcutta were directly governed by the Raj, as were the coasts and large swathes of the interior. In some parts of the interior, the British ruled indirectly, allowing obedient rajas and maharajas to stay on their thrones. In this way, the British ruled some areas at less cost and effort.

Positive and Negative Effects of British Colonial Rule

The British became much better at colonial administration than they had been during the 1700s. They were guided by a combination of selfishness, a desire for efficiency, and the well-meaning but condescending sense of superiority that poet Rudyard Kipling later called the **White Man's Burden**. British economic interests in India, formerly restricted to cotton, now became multifaceted. A wide variety of resources was now sought and exploited. To make their own lives in multifaceted India more comfortable and because they felt it would be better for the native Indians, British colonizers modernized the country in many ways. They created roads, railroads, a telegraph system, and a postal service.

The British also affected India's cultural life. They put into place a quality educational system, partly to raise the level of scientific and technological knowledge, partly to create a group of Western-educated natives who would be loyal to Britain and assist in governing a pro-British India. In the words of the historian Thomas Macauley, who helped create this system, the goal was to educate a native elite that

NOTE

To a degree, the English, simply to keep order, reduced the level of sectarian strife between Muslims and Hindus.

was "Indian in blood and color, but English in taste, in opinion, in morals, and in intellect." For the same reasons, the British created a civil service examination system for Indians who wished to work in the government. The Raj officially discouraged the conversion of Indians to Christianity (although a few British officials violated this policy on an individual basis). Still, the British eliminated cultural and religious (particularly Hindu) practices they felt were inhumane, including **sati** (or suttee,) the practice of burning a widow alive at her husband's funeral; *thuggee* (the ritual assassination of travelers in the name of the goddess Kali); and the **caste system's** harsh treatment of so-called untouchables.

Native Officials and Sepoy Troops

The British went to great lengths to instill loyalty within their native subjects. Their comparatively light touch in religious and cultural practices helped greatly. Whenever possible, the British delegated local political authority to Indians. The British East India Company also trained large numbers of native troops called **sepoys**. Using native troops made it easier for Indians to accept foreign rule; as well, it saved the British a great deal of money and kept them from having to draft large numbers of their own citizens to serve far from home. The number of actual British soldiers and officers in India was quite low.

The British Approach to Colonial Rule

NOTE

Even the benefits of British rule were bestowed because of the Britons' conviction that they were "civilizing" a lesser race.

The British method of imperialism in India—which they tended to follow in other colonies throughout Asia and Africa—is difficult to evaluate. British rule brought many benefits and new learning to the non-Western world, and compared with other imperial nations, the British were relatively humane in their colonial practices. Certainly the British themselves believed that they were doing their colonial subjects good. However, British rule was established by conquest, supported by military might, preserved by divide-and-conquer politics, and done for the purpose of economic exploitation.

The Indian Mutiny (The Sepoy Rebellion)

Whatever the case, tensions between the British and the Indians were present throughout the 1800s. On one occasion, those tensions exploded suddenly and violently: the **Indian Mutiny** (1857–1858), also known as the **Sepoy Rebellion**, ranks as one of the most traumatic events in modern Indian and British history.

Within many sepoy regiments, underlying resentment of British rule broke out into open revolt, owing to rumors that British officers were deliberately trying to undermine Hindu and Muslim religious practices. Legally, the Raj was allowed to require sepoys to serve overseas. In the case of Hindus, crossing large bodies of water would break their caste. Hindu sepoys were not, in fact, sent overseas, but fear that they might be stirred up trouble. It was the perceived violation of Muslim and Hindu dietary restrictions, however, that actually triggered the rebellion. New rifles with greased cartridges were issued to sepoys in 1857. The false rumor that the grease was made from pig and cow fat—unclean to devout Muslims and Hindus, respectively—caused great outrage.

With lightning speed, the initial disturbances became a massive wave of nationwide revolt. Hundreds of thousands of people were killed: British soldiers, British civilians, loyal Indian troops, rebels, and Indian civilians. Massacres and atrocities were committed by both sides.

By 1858, after great effort and a tremendous amount of anxiety that India would be lost altogether, British troops, along with natives who continued to serve the Raj, put down the rebellion.

> **NOTE**
>
> The British were fortunate that the rebels had no clear plan or single leader. Moreover, Hindu and Muslim rebels often failed to cooperate with each other—and sometimes fought each other.

The British Crown Assumes Control

For the rest of the century, British rule over India remained strong and solid. One important change was that the British crown took from the British East India Company all authority over the subcontinent. The British government now oversaw politics, ran the army, and supervised the colonial economy. Victoria, queen of England, took the title empress of India.

Nationalist Movements in Turn-of-the-Century India

Even though British control over India grew more secure, problems simmered under the surface. The British strategy of educating a native elite in the Western style was generally successful, but in some cases backfired. Larger numbers of these educated young people used their knowledge to agitate for freedom. Education exposed many of them to liberal or radical ideas and convinced them that it was hypocritical of the British—with their long tradition of civil liberties and representative government—not to apply those liberties to nonwhite races.

> **NOTE**
>
> The most important of the new nationalist groups was the **Indian National Congress**, formed in 1885. Most members were English-speaking, educated members of the native upper classes.

Eventually, the most famous and influential member of Congress was **Mohandas K. Gandhi**. Trained as a lawyer in London, he lived in South Africa from 1893 to 1915, defending the rights of Indian workers living under the system of apartheid. After returning to India in 1915, he started to preach nonviolent resistance to British rule.

> **NOTE**
>
> Over the next three decades, Gandhi was a central figure in India's quest for freedom.

SOUTHEAST ASIA

Like India, Southeast Asia found itself increasingly in foreign hands during the late 1700s and 1800s. Before 1800, the only large areas firmly under European control were **Indonesia**, or the Dutch East Indies, and the Philippines, which belonged to Spain. By 1786, the British also had a presence in the Malay Peninsula. The Portuguese retained parts of the island of Timor, a tiny remnant of the Indonesian colony the Dutch had taken from them. Dutch rule over Indonesia was the responsibility of the **Dutch East India Company**, which handed much responsibility over to upper-class natives, trained and educated in the Western style.

Malaya and Singapore

As the British tightened their grip on India during the early 1800s, they made parallel advances into nearby Southeast Asia. In exchange for giving up their claims on Indonesian territory, the British were allowed by the Dutch to absorb the Malay Peninsula, which was rich in rubber, tin, oil, copper, iron, and aluminum ore

NOTE

Along with India and, after 1842, Hong Kong, Singapore was one of Britain's most prized possessions in Asia.

(bauxite). In 1819, a British colonial official, Stamford Raffles, established a British outpost on **Singapore**, an island at the peninsula's tip. Quickly, Singapore became an important trading center and fortress; with the advent of steamships, it became a key naval base.

The French Conquest of Indochina

The European incursion into Southeast Asia never ceased. Britain took over Burma, formerly a major power, in 1826. To prevent the British from having an unbroken chain of territorial possessions stretching from India to the South China coast, France responded by moving into **Indochina**, the territory that now encompasses Vietnam, Cambodia, and Laos.

From 1857 to 1859, France pressured Vietnam into accepting foreign rule. Cambodia followed in 1863, and Laos fell in 1893. Indochina was the source of many raw materials, but most profitable to the French were chrome, oil, bauxite, tin, and rubber.

NOTE

The French placed more emphasis on religious conversion than the British.

The French model of imperialism was similar but not identical to that of Britain's. The French exploited the economy, but in accordance with their ideal of *la mission civilisatrice*, they also brought modern science and technology to their colonies in Southeast Asia. They educated—and often converted to Catholicism—a local elite of upper-class, Westernized natives. In contrast, the French resorted more readily to repression and violence to maintain order and carry out policy.

Modernization and Freedom in Thailand

The only state on the Southeast Asian mainland that remained independent throughout the 1800s was Thailand, owing to good leadership and good luck. Like Emperor Meiji in Japan, King Mongkut and his successor, King Chulalongkorn (both made famous in Anna Leonowens's memoir, *Anna and the King of Siam*, a book grossly distorted by Broadway and Hollywood), were modernizing monarchs, introducing industrialization and Western-style reform into their country. Thailand's geographic setting was also fortunate. The country lay between British-controlled Burma and French-dominated Indochina, and both European powers agreed informally to let it serve as a buffer zone between their colonies.

U.S. Annexation of the Philippines

NOTE

The English poet Rudyard Kipling wrote the poem *White Man's Burden* to commemorate the U.S. victory over the Spanish.

The last major colonial takeover in Southeast Asia was the **annexation of the Philippines** by the United States, in 1898, as a result of victory in the **Spanish-American War**. Although the conflict centered on Cuba, the United States sent a fleet under George Dewey to neutralize the Spanish naval forces based at Manila Bay. Dewey decimated the Spanish at sea. Then, with the assistance of native Filipinos (who, at first, saw the Americans as liberators), U.S. troops landed, defeated Spanish ground forces, and occupied the islands.

American victory resulted in Spain's being stripped of all its colonies. This action raised the question of what to do with the Philippines. After great debate, the U.S. government chose to turn the islands into a colony. The United States wished to keep the Philippines from falling into the hands of the Japanese. The islands also provided the United States with a superb naval base in the Pacific, and a way station for trade with China. Moreover, the Americans felt a "moral" obligation, similar to the **White Man's Burden**, to civilize the Filipinos.

Thus, as with European colonizers, imperialism in this case was a mixture of practical selfishness and condescending idealism. The great tragedy was that American colonization was imposed by means of a savage jungle war. A Filipino guerrilla force led by **Emilio Aguinaldo** resisted the American takeover until 1901, and the conflict was exceptionally bloody.

QUICK REVIEW

1. What authority governed British India in the 1700s and early 1800s?

   (A) the Home Office
   (B) the Foreign Ministry
   (C) the British East India Company
   (D) the Colonial Office
   (E) the British General Staff

2. Who were the zamindars?

   (A) native officials who administered parts of India for the British
   (B) freedom fighters who resisted British colonization of India
   (C) Hindu priests who called for a holy war against the British
   (D) Muslim troops who allied with the British against Hindu communities in India
   (E) the pro-British merchant class of eastern India

3. During the late 1700s and first decade of the 1800s, British control over India was restricted to

   (A) Sri Lanka (Ceylon).
   (B) the Ganges Valley.
   (C) the eastern coast.
   (D) the coastlines and the Ganges Valley.
   (E) the Brahmaputra Valley.

4. Among the benefits of British rule in India was/were

   I. An educated native elite.
   II. The abolition of sati.
   III. The construction of telegraphs and railroads.
   IV. Universal male suffrage.

   (A) I and II only
   (B) I and III only
   (C) II and III only
   (D) I, II, and III
   (E) all of the above

5. What were native troops who served under the British authorities in India called?

   (A) brahmins
   (B) sepoys
   (C) thugs
   (D) coolies
   (E) gurkhas

6. The most effective nationalist group to oppose British rule in India, starting in the late 1800s, was

   (A) the Tamil Tigers.
   (B) the Muslim League.
   (C) the Indian National Congress.
   (D) the Independence Party.
   (E) the Indian Liberation Army.

7. What was the Netherlands' chief colony in Southeast Asia?

   (A) Singapore
   (B) Burma
   (C) Macao
   (D) Goa
   (E) Indonesia

8. What key city and naval base was founded by Stamford Raffles for the British at the tip of the Malay Peninsula?

    (A) Hong Kong   (D) Goa
    (B) Singapore   (E) Malacca
    (C) Macao

9. Which Southeast Asian nation managed, through Westernized leadership and good luck, to stay free of foreign domination?

    (A) Laos   (D) Thailand
    (B) Cambodia   (E) Burma
    (C) Vietnam

10. Which Filipino guerrilla leader fought the Spanish, then the United States, late in the 1800s?

    (A) Emiliano Aguinaldo
    (B) Ferdinand Marcos
    (C) Thomas Aquino
    (D) Mateo Buenviaje
    (E) Edward Ramos

Answers

1. **(C)** The British East India Company administered India for Britain until 1858. As a semi-private company, it was one of the world's wealthiest and most powerful business ventures. The Indian Mutiny in 1857 compelled the British to take full control over India.

2. **(A)** Zamindars personally benefited from the British taxation system in India. They overtaxed peasants and then seized land from them when they failed to pay in full. As a result, mass famines occurred that killed approximately one-third of the Indian population in the late 1770s.

3. **(D)** At first, the British only had a foothold on the coasts. Then they worked their way into the interior, particularly up the Ganges River in the north.

4. **(D)** Universal suffrage was not established during the British Raj. However, the three other answers are correct. The British eliminated certain cultural practices they felt were inhumane. Overall, the British arrogantly presumed they were "civilizing" a "lesser race."

5. **(B)** Sepoys were originally trained by the British East India Company to serve the military goals of the British. However, their loyalty had its limits: sepoy regiments rebelled against British rule from 1857 to 1858, when they heard rumors that British officers were trying to undermine Hindu and Muslim religious practices. Tens of thousands of people were killed in this uprising.

6. **(C)** The Indian National Congress was founded in 1885. Most members were educated and English-speaking members of the upper classes. The most famous of its members was a lawyer named Mohandas K. Gandhi, who advocated nonviolent resistance to British rule.

7. **(E)** For several centuries, the Dutch East India Company was responsible for ruling Indonesia. It trained and educated upper-class natives in the Western style, in order to help administer Indonesia for the Netherlands.

8. **(B)** In 1819, the British established an outpost on Singapore, an island off the tip of the Malay Peninsula in Southeast Asia. Singapore soon became an important trading center, fortress, and naval base for the British.

9. **(D)** Thailand was the only major state on the Southeast Asian mainland that remained independent throughout the nineteenth century. Its rulers were modernizing monarchs who introduced industrialization and Western-style reform. Thailand served as an independent buffer zone between Burma and Indochina.

10. **(A)** Aguinaldo fought the U.S. takeover of the Philippines until 1901. American forces suppressed Aguinaldo's soldiers in their successful campaign to colonize the Philippines and establish a key naval base in the Pacific.

Sub-Saharan Africa

CHAPTER 26

- Kongo
- The Asante (Ashanti) kingdom
- The Boers (Afrikaners) and the Great Trek
- The Zulu
- The diamond industry in South Africa
- Zanzibar and the Arab-East African slave trade
- The Atlantic slave trade
- The Scramble for Africa and the Berlin Conference
- The Belgian Congo and the rubber industry
- The Herero Wars
- The Boer War

Like most of the non-Western world, sub-Saharan Africa fell under the increased sway of European imperialism from 1750 to 1914. For several centuries, Africa had already been victimized by the **Atlantic slave trade**. Millions of Africans had been forcibly transported to the Americas. African political systems and economic patterns, even in parts of the continent not directly under foreign control, had been shaped by the slave trade. From the 1400s onward, Europeans had plundered gold, ivory, and other reserves from Africa. They had also established outposts, naval bases, and small colonies on the east and west coasts of the continent.

Nonetheless, Europe's direct influence over Africa, especially south of the Sahara, was comparatively limited until late in the 1800s. After the Napoleonic Wars, the slave trade was made illegal in most Western countries. Although it continued for decades unlawfully, the Atlantic traffic in slaves tapered off and faded away. Moreover, strong African states resisted foreign domination for much of this period (in a sad irony, much of this strength was due to profits made by cooperating with the Atlantic slave trade). Although the Europeans found it relatively easy to take control of North Africa (see Chapter 23) and parts of the coastline, the central and southern interior remained for a long time difficult to penetrate.

Great changes came after 1880. Before then, outside powers controlled approximately 10 percent of Africa. Less than three and a half decades later, in 1914, foreigners controlled the entire continent, with the exception of two small countries. By the middle of the 1800s, explorers and missionaries had gained precise geographical knowledge of the African interior. Better medicines enabled larger numbers of soldiers and settlers to travel to and live in Africa's tropical zones. Industrial-era weaponry increased the Europeans' military superiority over the Africans.

During the 1880s and 1890s, the ever greater intensity of the Western world's competition over empire drove European nations to carve up African territory while there was still room to expand. This **Scramble for Africa** subjugated virtually the entire continent.

NOTE

The long-term political and economic effects of Europe's exploitation of Africa still reverberate in the twenty-first century, long after the continent's decolonization.

The Scramble for Africa also stirred up the combative passions of the Europeans and contributed to the diplomatic tensions that caused World War I.

FREEDOM'S TWILIGHT: AFRICAN STATES FROM THE LATE 1700s TO THE MID-1800s

African States During the Late 1700s and Early 1800s

European hegemony over Africa was a long time in coming. During the late 1700s and early 1800s, a number of states were strong enough to resist foreign domination. Others were useful and cooperative enough that it was worthwhile for the Europeans to work with them rather than fight them. Some of these states, such as Benin, Oyo, Dahomey, **Kongo** (see chapter 18), and Asante (Ashanti), played large roles in the Atlantic slave trade. They helped European traders and slavers capture and transport their fellow Africans.

In the west, a number of states remained independent well into the 1800s. These included the various Hausa, Fulani, and Yoruba states. They formed, broke apart, and reformed, constantly fighting each other in costly civil wars. Among them were the Fulani Empire, Macina, and the Tukolor Empire. All three were Muslim theocracies.

The Asante (Ashanti) Kingdom

The strongest and most unified of the West African states was the **Asante (Ashanti)** kingdom, one of the last to survive as an independent state. Founded in the late 1600s, Asante took part in the flourishing trade in gold and slaves on Africa's west coast. Using profits to buy guns, Asante became a strong military power.

Asante's might increased dramatically during the late 1700s and early 1800s, especially as its African neighbors fought each other or came under foreign control. A large military buildup began under Osei Kojo (1764–1777). During the early 1800s, the Asante threatened European outposts and trade routes along the Gold Coast. They also resisted British, French, and American attempts to destroy the slave trade in the 1820s. By 1823, Britain found itself locked in a series of Asante wars that lasted until the end of the century, when it finally subdued the kingdom.

> **NOTE**
>
> Next to the Zulu, the Asante were the most challenging of the Europeans' native foes in Africa.

South Africa, the Boers, and the Zulu

South Africa had been colonized by the Dutch in the mid-1600s. For a century and a half, these Afrikaner **Boers**, as they called themselves, displaced or conquered native Africans. When the British assumed control over South Africa during the Napoleonic Wars, the Boers were themselves displaced. In the 1830s, the Boers made their **Great Trek** to the north and east and, in the 1850s, founded the Orange Free State and the South African Republic (Transvaal), both of which bordered British South Africa. In the meantime, the Boers and the recently arrived British came into contact with a new native power: the Zulu tribe.

The **Zulu**, a Bantu-speaking people, were relatively quiet and peaceful before 1800. Around 1816, however, a new chieftain, **Shaka**, seized power and united Zulu clans into a single tribe. A gifted military leader, Shaka has been called the

Black Napoleon. Under him, the Zulu became a warlike, conquering tribe. Even after his death in 1828, they remained fearsome.

During the first half of the 1800s, the Zulu defeated neighbor after neighbor, scattering African tribes throughout the southern part of the continent. A significant wave of migration was caused partly by Zulu aggression. The Zulu also fought the Boers and British, and it took several wars for the Europeans to pacify them. The last major conflict, in 1879, was provoked by British officials who hoped to move into the Zulu lands because diamonds had recently been found there.

A particular factor that heightened tensions in South Africa was the discovery of **diamond fields**. Gold deposits were also found. The sudden emergence of such great potential wealth destabilized things by making parties more willing to fight over territory. The British began annexing diamond fields in 1871. Diamond mines cruelly exploited African labor. Workers were rigidly segregated by race, and rights, privileges, and restrictions were race-based.

> **NOTE**
>
> The Zulu armies, led by Cetewayo, eventually lost the **Zulu War of 1879**. It took eight months for the British to win, and one of the early battles, Isandhlwana, in which a British force was massacred to the last soldier, was one of the worst military defeats suffered by a European force in Africa.

East Africa

The East African coast, which had come under Portuguese domination between the late 1400s and late 1600s, enjoyed a period of strength and independence—at least from European control—during the late 1700s and early-to-mid 1800s. For the time being, the large island of Madagascar remained free, as did the Batutsi state in what is today Rwanda.

The Coptic Christian kingdom of Ethiopia, which earlier had allied with Portugal against Muslim conquerors, expelled the Portuguese, largely over questions of religious doctrine, in 1632. For the next two and a half centuries, Ethiopia went into isolation, then modernized under Theodore II, who came to the throne in 1855. As for the rest of the coast, the new power was not European but Arab. In 1728, Arabs drove the Portuguese from the port of Mombasa. Portugal's strength in the region then waned, although it retained footholds along the coast.

By the early 1800s, Omani Arabs had gained tremendous political influence in East Africa. They also controlled the flourishing trade between the East African coast and India. By far the most important East African port was **Zanzibar**, on a small island off the coast of Tanganyika. Its role as an economic powerhouse was demonstrated by the fact that the Omani sultan made it his capital in 1840. Zanzibar's primary trading partner was Bombay. This fusion of Arab, African, and Indian stimulated not just economic interaction but a vibrant cultural interchange as well. Zanzibar's Arab masters also extended their economic influence into Africa's interior, to the west and north.

Among the principal resources that flowed through Zanzibar were cloves, spices, sugar, and ivory. An even more important part of Zanzibar's economy was slavery. Ironically, just as the demand for slaves in the Atlantic was finally withering away (see below), there was a major resurgence in the **Arab–East African slave market**. This resurgence had much to do with the growth of plantation agriculture in the area, fueled by the increased demand for sugar and spices. Between 1875

> **NOTE**
>
> It took decades for the Western powers to eliminate the East African slave trade. Abolition came about as a result of popular outrage, missionary activity (a key figure here was the Scottish explorer and humanitarian **David Livingstone**), and military action. The great slave market in the center of Zanzibar was shut down in 1873. The British took control of the city later in the century.

and 1884, the peak of the East African plantation economy, 44 percent of the total population was made up of slaves.

THE END OF THE ATLANTIC SLAVE TRADE

The Atlantic Slave Trade Becomes Illegal

One of the great changes that came to Africa during the 1800s was the gradual ending of the **Atlantic slave trade**. Its demise resulted partly from economic and practical considerations. It was becoming more difficult and therefore more expensive to obtain slaves.

Equally important was the growing revulsion that slavery caused in many Western countries. For moral, ethical, and religious reasons, an ever-greater number of citizens and politicians were unwilling to continue basing their nations' economies so squarely on slavery. Countries like the Netherlands (1795) and Denmark (1803) began to make slavery illegal.

> **NOTE**
>
> The British did not just ban slavery, but took it upon themselves to act as the Western world's champions of the anti-slavery cause.

The major turning point came when Great Britain, in 1808, resolved to make slavery illegal (slavery was banned in all parts of the British Empire in 1834). During the peace settlements that followed the Napoleonic Wars, the British convinced almost all of Europe and the Americas to outlaw slavery and the slave trade. With the exception of Spain and Portugal, Europe agreed (Russia continued to rely on **serfdom**, but this was a different question). For the most part, the Americas went along as well. Canada (still part of the British Empire) and most of Latin America outlawed slavery. The holdouts were Cuba and Brazil, which did not end slavery until 1883 and 1888. The United States, split between the slaveholding South and the nonslave North, agreed to make the slave trade illegal. The government also worked to restrict the spread of slavery within the United States as the country expanded. Not until after the U.S. Civil War (1861–1865) was slavery made completely illegal throughout the country.

The Atlantic Slave Trade Continues Illegally

The continued survival of slavery in the Americas meant that the Atlantic slave trade, illegal or not, went on during a good part of the 1800s. It has been calculated that 2 million Africans were transported to Brazil, Cuba, and the Caribbean during the 1800s. A small percentage of these were smuggled into the United States as well. The best estimate of the number of Africans enslaved by the Atlantic slave trade between the late 1400s and the 1800s is approximately 12 million.

> **NOTE**
>
> Slavery continued to be a painful problem for Africa throughout most of the 1800s.

As noted above, a market in African slaves flourished in Zanzibar during the 1800s, not ending until 1873. According to some sources, at the end of the nineteenth century, the number of slaves in the Islamic states of West Africa stood at nearly 5 million.

Foreign powers did more than legislate against the slave trade. **Abolition movements**, especially in Britain and the northern United States, pressured their governments to fight slavery actively. Canada served as a haven for slaves escaping from the southern United States. **Missionaries** in Africa, especially those from Britain, campaigned against slave raids and slave markets—both on the Atlantic coast and in East Africa and Zanzibar. A great crusader here was David Livingstone of Scotland.

The British founded special colonies in Sierra Leone and the Gold Coast for freed blacks. Similarly, a group of American blacks and freed slaves settled the nation of Liberia, on the West African coast, with sponsorship from the U.S. government.

In the early 1800s, the British government dispatched the Royal Navy to blockade the West African shoreline, hunt down slave ships, and bombard the coastal fortresses of African states that continued to support the slave trade. Less enthusiastically, France and the United States joined in these antislave trade naval expeditions.

Effects of the Slave Trade on Africa

The slave trade took an immense toll on Africa. Obvious effects included human suffering, population loss, dependence on foreign goods (as opposed to indigenous production), the stirring up of tribal warfare, and the disruption of traditional trade networks and economic practices.

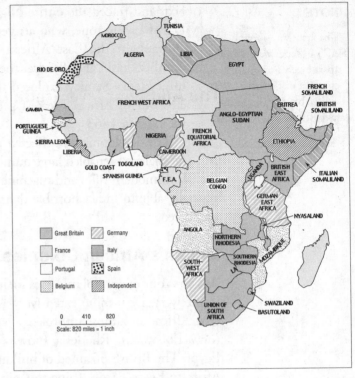

European Imperialism in Africa, 1914.

It is equally obvious how the ending of the slave trade benefited Africa. However, there were also unforeseen, less positive consequences. One was a sharp economic slump—because, as heinous as it had been, the slave trade had been extremely lucrative. Economic weakness left African states more vulnerable to foreign takeover in the late 1800s. Moreover, the antislavery intervention of Great Britain and other nations, however well-intentioned, gave Europeans a pretext for involving themselves in Africa's affairs and thinking of military action as legitimate. This helped pave the way for the rush to conquer all of Africa at the end of the century.

EUROPEAN IMPERIALISM AND THE "SCRAMBLE FOR AFRICA"

Approximately 10 percent of Africa was under foreign control before 1880. Most of this territory lay north of the Sahara or along the coastlines. Suddenly, between 1880 and 1914, the states of Europe were caught up in a breathlessly rapid "**Scramble for Africa**." On the eve of World War I, only two countries—Ethiopia and Liberia—remained free.

Reasons for Europe's Late-Nineteenth-Century Domination of Africa

Many factors motivated and enabled the Scramble for Africa. First, a series of geographic expeditions from the 1770s through the 1860s gave the Western world an unprecedented amount of information about the African interior. Mungo Park of

NOTE

The fact that so many African states were torn apart by civil or intertribal conflicts made them vulnerable to European takeover. So did economic backwardness.

Scotland traced the entire Niger River from 1795 to 1805. The missionary David Livingstone, who arrived from Scotland in 1841, spread Christianity, and fought the East African slave trade, also found time to explore the Zambezi basin and discover the Victoria Falls (1855). Anglo-American adventurer Henry Stanley explored the Congo, while England's John Speke unraveled one of Africa's greatest geographical mysteries by locating the source of the Nile in 1863.

The development of effective treatments for tropical diseases—such as **quinine** for malaria—enabled large numbers of Westerners to move into the African interior. With modern rifles and machine guns, small numbers of European soldiers were generally able to inflict horrible damage on native warriors, even when greatly outnumbered.

Britain's African Colonies

Britain's zone of control in Africa included the Gold Coast, Sierra Leone, and Nigeria in the west. Even more extensive was its collection of colonies in northeastern and East Africa, an almost unbroken chain that included South Africa, Bechuanaland (now Botswana), Rhodesia (now Zimbabwe), Kenya, Uganda, the Sudan, and Egypt. The British dreamed of building a continental railway stretching from South Africa to Egypt ("from **Cape to Cairo**," as the imperialist Cecil Rhodes put it), but they were blocked by the German acquisition of territory on the eastern coast.

Late in the century, Britain gained influence over the rich port of Zanzibar, partly in connection with its efforts to end slavery there. Zanzibar had been claimed by Germany, but Britain received control over it as part of a swap of colonial territories.

Britain's method of African colonial administration was similar to the one it followed in India: a comparatively enlightened **White Man's Burden** approach that made use of an educated native elite, deployed native troops trained in the Western style, and brought new science and industrial technology to the colonies.

The French in Africa

France's African empire was restricted mainly to the Saharan north: Morocco, Algeria, Tunisia, West Africa, and Equatorial Africa. However, it had territories elsewhere, such as Djibouti, part of the Somali coast, and the island of Madagascar. As in Southeast Asia, France acted in accordance with its "civilizing mission" and, for the most part, treated its colonial subjects reasonably responsibly.

The Portuguese

Portugal retained control over its longtime possession in West Africa, Angola. On the eastern coast, where it had once reigned supreme, it took Mozambique. Unlike the French and British, the Portuguese were quite harsh with their African colonies.

Belgium and the Congo

Tiny Belgium gained control over one of the largest African colonies: the vast **Congo** basin. In 1876, **Leopold II** of Belgium, with the Anglo-American explorer

Henry Stanley as his manager, established a private company for the economic development of the Congo. By 1884, the Congo was fully under the company's control. In his will, Leopold left the colony to Belgium.

Leopold's exploitation of the Congo was brutal, and Belgium's record as a colonizing power was among the worst in Africa. Belgian-owned **rubber plantations** overexploited rubber trees and, worse, brutally forced Congolese villagers to meet production quotas. One vile practice was the policy of some overseers to chop off the right hands of Congolese workers who did not harvest enough rubber. Some workers were simply massacred. Belgian occupation led to massive depopulation.

> **NOTE**
>
> Before the Belgians arrived, the area's population was around 20 million. By 1911, only about 8.5 million people remained.

Italian Colonization of Africa

The new nation of Italy had poor luck in Africa. In 1911 and 1912, it seized Libya from the Ottoman Empire in a short war that involved the use of aircraft and poison gas. Before that, in 1896, the Italians had attempted to conquer Ethiopia. King Menelik II, however, had prepared well by purchasing modern rifles for his army and hiring Western mercenaries to train his troops. The Italians were prevented from taking Ethiopia by their humiliating defeat at the Battle of **Adowa**, which ranks as one of the most embarrassing setbacks in the history of European imperialism.

German Colonization of Africa

Also new to the world stage was Germany. In keeping with the military prowess they had shown in Europe, the Germans quickly assembled a sizable empire in Africa. Their possessions included Togoland, the Cameroons, Southwest Africa, and German East Africa (consisting mainly of Tanganyika, off of which the island of Zanzibar lay).

Unfortunately, the colonies left for the Germans were those no one else had wanted. Rather than turning a profit, they actually lost money. The Germans also had to deal with several major uprisings, including the Maji Maji revolt in Tanganyika (1905–1907) and the infamous **Herero Wars** in Southwest Africa (1904–1908). The latter were especially savage, to the point of genocide.

> **NOTE**
>
> Historians estimate that the Germans killed almost 80 percent of the Herero—64,000 of 80,000—by the time they quelled the rebellion.

African Women and European Imperialism

One of the major consequences of colonial rule was that many African families were broken up. Husbands often went to work in mines or on plantations, while wives and children stayed behind in villages and on reserves. Women were left to grow food for their families for mere survival and to care for the sick and aged. Long separations between spouses often led to a rise in the level of prostitution and the spread of sexually transmitted diseases.

In general, African men benefited more than women from the economic changes brought by colonial rule. In regions where colonial officials introduced private property rights, property was given to male heads of households, not women. Most jobs, even those in teaching, were reserved for men, and women were discouraged from running family businesses or selling goods in markets.

Imperialism in Africa and Its Effects on European Diplomacy

The Scramble for Africa quickly stirred up aggression among the Europeans, bringing them numerous times to the brink of conflict.

The German diplomat Otto von Bismarck attemped to cool tensions at the **Berlin Conference** (1884–1885), whose purpose was to agree on boundary lines and set down rules for further expansion into Africa. Needless to say, the lines on the resulting map reflected European desires and had little relation to the traditional territorial boundaries of native African tribes or ethnic groups, none of whom were invited to take part.

The Berlin Conference temporarily helped to prevent war over Africa, but tensions rose in the 1890s and 1900s. In 1896, France and Britain almost came to blows as a result of the Fashoda Incident, in which French troops moving eastward into the Nile Valley encountered British soldiers who regarded the region as belonging to them. The French eventually withdrew, but not before a short war scare. In the early 1900s, Germany's naked ambitions in Africa caused more trouble. Its interference with French and Spanish plans for northwestern Africa led to a Morocco Crisis in 1906 and another one in 1911.

Even worse was Germany's public support of the Dutch Afrikaners in the **Boer War** (1899–1902). Here, fighting had broken out between the British and Boers in South Africa. Although the British had a larger, better-equipped army, the Boers were skilled guerrilla soldiers and excellent sharpshooters, fighting on their home territory. The war was a painful one, with the British forced to pacify the Boer civilian population. More than 120,000 women, children, and male noncombatants (many of them black Africans) were placed in **concentration camps** (the twentieth century's first) by the British. Between 26,000 and 28,000 died, causing an international outcry. The Germans made no secret of their sympathy for the Boers. This public favoritism had the result of worsening Anglo-German relations, already strained because of the two countries' naval race and Britain's anxieties about German imperialism elsewhere in Africa (especially German East Africa, which kept Britain from building a continental railroad from Egypt to South Africa). As noted in Chapter 22, these tensions had profound effects on the alliance system that emerged in the years before World War I.

In this way, the Scramble for Africa backfired on the Europeans. Imperial successes there led to diplomatic problems, which, taken together, helped bring about World War I—the conflict that began the process of breaking down European world power.

QUICK REVIEW

1. Which group in South Africa embarked on the "Great Trek" during the early 1800s?

   (A) the Zulu   (D) the Boers
   (B) the Swazi   (E) the Ngoni
   (C) the Xhosa

2. What transformation did the Zulu undergo during the early 1800s?

   (A) They migrated to northwest Africa.
   (B) They united and militarized under a warlike chieftain.
   (C) They began to industrialize.
   (D) They were conquered and enslaved by the Boers.
   (E) They converted to Islam.

3. The discovery of what resource in South Africa during the last half of the 1800s greatly altered political and economical life there?

   (A) diamonds   (D) silver
   (B) bauxite   (E) copper
   (C) oil

4. What was the fate of Ethiopia at the end of the 1800s?

   (A) It was absorbed into the Anglo-Egyptian Administration.
   (B) It was subdued by Arab slavers.
   (C) It was colonized by the French.
   (D) It tore itself apart in a series of civil wars.
   (E) It successfully resisted European colonizing efforts by modernizing its army.

5. Which city was the center of the East African slave trade?

   (A) Mombasa (D) Sofala
   (B) Zanzibar   (E) Nairobi
   (C) Malindi

6. Which of the following best describes the results of the outlawing of the Atlantic slave trade?

   (A) The slave trade was hindered by the ban, but approximately 2 million Africans were still taken illegally to the Americas.
   (B) No European nations made any real effort to enforce the ban on the slave trade.
   (C) Spain and Portugal took the lead in combatting the slave trade once it was illegal.
   (D) The slave trade dried up almost completely within a decade of being outlawed.
   (E) The United States and France almost went to war over the continuation of slavery in North America.

7. Which is the most accurate statement about European colonization in Africa during the 1800s?

   (A) European powers began the century largely in control of Africa but were pushed out of all but 10 percent by the 1890s.
   (B) Industrial-era weaponry allowed the European powers to conquer all but two countries in Africa by 1880.
   (C) European control over Africa was at roughly the same level in 1900 as it had been in 1820.
   (D) Despite controlling only 10 percent of Africa as late as 1880, European powers had conquered almost the entire continent shortly after the new century began.
   (E) European powers failed to penetrate the interior of Africa, and they took over only 25 percent of the continent by 1900.

8. Which European nation, by exploiting the Congo horribly, gained a reputation as one of the cruelest colonial powers of the imperial era?

   (A) Belgium   (D) Great Britain
   (B) Italy   (E) The Netherlands
   (C) Germany

9. The Germans came close to exterminating which African tribe?

   (A) the Fulani   (D) the Hutus
   (B) the Herero   (E) the Hausa
   (C) the Batutsi

10. The twentieth century's first concentration camps were used by whom in what conflict?

   (A) the French during the Fashoda Incident
   (B) the Germans during the First Moroccan Crisis
   (C) the Italians during their takeover of Libya
   (D) the Spanish during the Second Moroccan Crisis
   (E) the British during the Boer War

Answers

1. **(D)** In the 1830s the Boers completed their Great Trek, which took them to the north and east in South Africa. In the 1850s, they founded the Orange Free State and the South African Republic, which bordered British South Africa.

2. **(B)** In 1816, Shaka seized power and united several Zulu clans into a single tribe. He taught the Zulu how to fight efficiently and, in doing so, turned the Zulu into a warlike, conquering tribe in the region.

3. **(A)** One of the world's largest deposits of diamonds is located at Kimberly, South Africa. This discovery proved to be destabilizing to the South African population, as African labor was exploited and control over the diamond industry stoked racial bigotry among the white colonizers.

4. **(E)** In 1896, Ethiopian troops defeated the Italians at the Battle of Adowa. The Ethiopian king had hired Western mercenaries to train his troops and bought modern rifles for his army as well.

5. **(B)** The resurgence in the Arab–East African slave market was fueled by the growth of plantation agriculture in the region. Zanzibar was the center of the slave trade at the time. The great slave market finally was shut down in 1873.

6. **(A)** Unfortunately, the slave trade did not end overnight, even when it became illegal and the British undertook the work of enforcement. Slaves were still shipped to Cuba and Brazil, and smuggled into the United States, where the slave trade became illegal. Slavery was not outlawed in the United States until after the end of the Civil War.

7. **(D)** The European powers' Scramble for Africa subjugated almost the entire continent of Africa in only a few years' time. White settlers expropriated African grazing lands, and white traders stole cattle and other possessions from indigenous peoples there.

8. **(A)** Belgian authorities overexploited rubber trees and vines throughout the Congo basin. Sometimes, they chopped off the hands of Congolese workers they thought had failed to meet their quotas for harvesting rubber.

9. **(B)** The Germans killed an estimated 80 percent of this tribe during the Herero Wars in Southwest Africa between 1904 and 1908. However successful they were in the end, the Germans' methods were particularly savage and could be considered genocidal today.

10. **(E)** In the Boer War, fighting broke out between the British and the Boers for control over South Africa. The British pacified the Boer civilian population by placing 120,000 women, children, and male noncombatants in concentration camps. Between 26,000 and 28,000 people died in these camps.

Revolution and Consolidation in North and South America

- The Atlantic revolutions
- The American Revolution
- The Monroe Doctrine, the Louisiana Purchase, and manifest destiny
- Slavery in America and the Atlantic slave trade
- Immigration to the United States and the Americas
- The Haitian Rebellion
- The Latin American wars of independence
- The Mexican Revolution
- The Mexican-American War
- Caudillos, monoculture, and dollar diplomacy
- The Spanish-American War
- The Panama Canal

During the late 1700s and early 1800s, the colonies of the New World—the possessions of European powers for three centuries—threw off the ties that bound them politically and economically to their home countries. The **American Revolution**, the **Haitian Rebellion**, and the **Latin American wars of independence** were all part of the great wave of revolutions—including the French Revolution—that struck the Atlantic world during this era. All of them shook the political and economic foundations of the Western world. All were interrelated in terms of intellectual influence and political effect.

However, their results differed greatly. In the north, the American Revolution created an economic and political powerhouse: The United States, the modern world's first major nation to become a democracy, steadily expanded across the continent. Despite internal troubles, even wars, concerning slavery and the suppression of Native Americans, the United States grew in size and might. Like the nations of Europe, it industrialized. Already by the early 1800s, the United States was the dominant power in the Western Hemisphere. By the end of the century, it had acquired overseas territories of its own and was on the threshold of a world power.

As for Latin America, revolution brought freedom, but it did not create nations as well equipped to deal with freedom as the United States was. Despite high ideals and good intentions, most of the new Latin American nations were plagued by dictatorial politics, economic backwardness, poverty, racial prejudice, and frequent revolutions and civil conflicts. In addition, the great power to the north, the United States, became increasingly involved in Latin American economics and politics, and not always for the better.

THE AMERICAN REVOLUTION AND THE BIRTH OF THE UNITED STATES

Causes of the American Revolution

The **American Revolution** (1775–1783) resulted from the combination of several trends in the thirteen British colonies in New England and the mid-Atlantic coast:

- A growing sense of patriotism and national identity. In this sense, the "revolution" was less a revolution and more a war of independence.
- Increased resentment of Great Britain's economic mastery. In particular, the taxes Britain levied to pay for the army it maintained in North America angered many colonists, especially in light of the fact that they lacked representation in the British Parliament.
- The desire of the colonial merchant (that is, middle) class to better itself. Economic freedom from Britain would allow American merchants to become wealthier, thanks to free trade and the new spirit of capitalism.
- The influence of Enlightenment philosophy (see Chapter 13). Most of the leaders who carried out the American Revolution and shaped the government afterward had read the works of Enlightenment thinkers such as Locke, Montesquieu, and Voltaire. The **Declaration of Independence** (1776), by Thomas Jefferson, is considered a classic Enlightenment text.

The American Revolution

Whatever the causes, the American Revolution broke out in 1775, with the twin battles of Lexington and Concord. At first, the poorly trained and poorly armed American forces, led by George Washington, struggled against the professional armies of Britain. By 1777, however, the tide was turning. Although some colonists, nicknamed Tories, remained loyal to the British, popular support for the revolution was high; most members of all classes—lower, middle, and upper—united behind it. The Americans were fighting on their home territory. Not only did European freedom fighters with military experience arrive to train American troops, the Americans used unconventional tactics and guerrilla warfare to counter the British soldiers' training and experience. The British were fighting far from home, at the end of extremely long supply lines.

After America's victory at Saratoga in late 1777, France, Britain's mortal enemy, began to lend military and naval assistance to the American colonists. The assistance of the French fleet against the Royal Navy, Britain's chief weapon, was particularly useful to the Americans.

By 1781, the British war effort was failing. When the main British force was surrounded at Yorktown, the war was effectively over, although peace talks dragged on until 1783. The Americans were victorious—and had won themselves a new country.

The U.S. Constitution and the Formation of the American Government

The next step was to determine a form of government. There was much disagreement over how closely bound together the thirteen colonies would be. Also, who should have power? Should the government be elected? If so, who should be allowed to vote? What should be done about slavery? These questions and others were decided at the Constitutional Convention of 1787. By 1789, the **United States Constitution** had been written and accepted by all thirteen states.

The system that resulted was a democratic republic, in which a federal government shared powers with governments in each state. To prevent a dictatorship, power at the federal level was shared among three branches (a concept borrowed from the Enlightenment philosopher Montesquieu): executive (president), legislative (Congress), and judicial (Supreme Court). State governments, as well as the president and members of Congress, were to be elected. However, democracy in this case—as in all cases before the twentieth century—was not all-inclusive. Elections were indirect. Women and Native Americans could not vote; nor could men who failed to fulfill certain property requirements. Moreover, the U.S. Constitution did not outlaw slavery.

Despite its initial flaws, the U.S. Constitution has remained one of the most successful political documents in world history. It is also the product and cause of a great deal of intellectual and philosophical exchange. Most of the Constitution's general ideals and many of the specific political principles came from England and France, thanks to the influence of Locke, Voltaire, Montesquieu, Rousseau, and others. In turn, the Constitution (and the Declaration of Independence) had an enormous impact on the **Atlantic revolutions** that followed in the 1780s, 1790s, and early 1800s. France's **Declaration of the Rights of Man and the Citizen** drew heavily upon both documents, as did the failed Dutch rebellion of the 1780s. In the early nineteenth century, the revolutionaries of Latin America tried to adapt the Americans' political methods and ideals. Therefore, the American Revolution had a tremendous impact on the rest of the world.

The Growing Global Importance of the United States

The domestic history of the United States is beyond the scope of the AP World History examination. A few points, however, should be made about the new country's effect on global affairs during the 1800s and early 1900s:

- *Inspiring freedom*: America's example of representative government and respect for civil liberties (in spite of flaws, such as slavery) stood out as an example to people in other countries who wished to bring about similar changes.
- *Sphere of influence*: The **Monroe Doctrine** (1823), in which the U.S. government warned the nations of Europe against intervening in the Western Hemisphere's political affairs, was the first step in the United States' creation of a sphere of influence there. The United States quickly became the dominant power in the Americas. By the end of the 1800s, especially after the **Spanish-American War** (1898), the United States' economic and political influence over Latin America was considerable—and, in some cases, imperial.
- *Expansion*: The rapid growth of the United States, from a collection of small colonies on North America's east coast to a vast land sprawling from Atlantic to Pacific, greatly altered the balance of world power. This growth began with the **Louisiana Purchase** (1803) and continued with the **Mexican-American War** (1846–1848). The United States became a huge nation, incredibly rich in natural resources. It was motivated by the ideology of **manifest destiny**, the belief that continental expansion was a natural right.

- *Slavery*: The persistence of **slavery in the American South** was a key factor in allowing the Atlantic slave trade to continue for so long, even after it had been made illegal in the 1810s. It was the underlying cause of the U.S. Civil War (1861–1865).
- *Industrial growth*: During the last two thirds of the 1800s, the United States not only followed Europe in industrializing but surpassed it. Many of the industrial era's key innovations and inventions came from the United States. Also, by the end of the 1800s, America was poised to become the greatest economic power in the world. It was already overtaking Europe's strongest industrial powers, Britain and Germany, in many economic sectors.
- *Immigration*: America's reputation as a land of freedom and economic opportunity drew millions of **immigrants** from Europe and Asia during the 1800s. Between the 1830s and 1890s, an estimated 17 million people (perhaps more) came to settle in the United States. Immigrants continued to arrive during the early 1900s. Combined with the large numbers of Europeans and Asians who emigrated to Latin America during these years, this development had a tremendous demographic effect on the geographic balance of world population.

Developments in Canada

Canada, the other British colony in North America, underwent changes during the 1800s. Although Canada remained loyal during the American Revolution, a desire for greater autonomy made itself felt not long afterward. Armed uprisings took place in 1837 and 1838. Although they failed, they convinced the British that flexibility was called for. In 1840, Upper Canada (now Ontario) and Lower Canada (now Quebec), along with other territories in the east, were joined together as the United Provinces of Canada. However, the United Provinces were not self-governing.

More independence came in the 1860s. Canadian politician John Macdonald became the leader of the country's freedom movement. Thanks largely to his efforts, not to mention British fears that a disgruntled Canada might grow closer to the United States, the home government in London, in 1867, conferred upon Canada **dominion status**, entitling Canada to its own constitution and parliament. The constitution created a confederation of Upper Canada, Lower Canada, Nova Scotia, and New Brunswick.

The British monarch was still the head of state; and, for the time being, foreign affairs were still controlled by Britain. Still, in most respects, Canada was self-governing. John Macdonald became the first prime minister. Over time, confederation was extended to the western provinces, first Manitoba and British Columbia, then Alberta and Saskatchewan. Later, Great Britain used this scheme of dominion status to give similar autonomy to Australia and New Zealand.

THE HAITIAN REBELLION

One of the key moments in the spread of the Atlantic revolutions to Latin America and the Caribbean was the **Haitian Rebellion** (1791–1804), the only large-scale slave revolt to succeed in the New World. The Haitian Rebellion was inspired in large part by the American Revolution and caused directly by events related to the French Revolution.

The island of Haiti, known then as Santo Domingo, had been colonized by the Spanish and the French. Each ruled half of the island, whose economy was based mainly on sugar production. The French half was populated by a mix of French colonists, Creoles (those of French descent but born in the colonies), free blacks (known as *gens de coleur*), and over half a million black slaves. When the French Revolution began in 1789, it threw French Haiti into chaos, mainly because the white colonists and freed blacks, all of whom competed over Haiti's sugar economy, quarreled. In 1791, the slaves of Haiti seized this opportunity to rebel.

By 1793, the leader of the Haitian Rebellion was **François Toussaint L'Ouverture**, often referred to as the Black Washington. Although a slave, L'Ouverture was literate and well-read. He was also a talented military commander. By 1798, he had freed the slaves in French Haiti; he then crossed into Spanish-controlled Santo Domingo and liberated the blacks there as well. At this point, L'Ouverture hoped to make of Haiti a country for free blacks. It would be friendly to France but also independent.

Unfortunately for L'Ouverture, the French government had no intention of allowing Haiti to go free. Over the next four years, the French debated the Haitian question. Then, in 1802, Napoleon Bonaparte decided to send troops to Haiti to retake it for France. Ironically, while a young officer in France's revolutionary army, Napoleon had been an admirer of L'Ouverture, but now the two men were enemies.

The French managed to capture L'Ouverture, who was put in chains and sent back to France, where he died in prison. However, the French failed to conquer Haiti. Unused to fighting in tropical conditions, the French could not quell the Haitian rebels. Yellow fever killed over 40,000 French troops. Finally, in 1804, Napoleon gave up the effort to reconquer Haiti. The French went home in disgrace, and the independent nation of Haiti was born.

The Haitian Rebellion had the effect of helping to inspire rebellion elsewhere in Latin America. It also had one other far-reaching geopolitical impact. Because of his frustration with the fighting in Haiti, Napoleon decided not to maintain major colonies in the New World. Up to this point, France had been the master of central North America: the large Louisiana territory, stretching from the Great Lakes to the Mississippi Delta. In 1803, Napoleon sold it at a bargain price to the United States. President Thomas Jefferson accepted the offer eagerly. Unlike Napoleon, he recognized that the **Louisiana Purchase** would allow the United States to control the North American continent. By helping to convince Napoleon to sell Louisiana, the Haitian Rebellion played a part in bringing about a major shift in global power.

THE LATIN AMERICAN WARS OF INDEPENDENCE

Not long after the Haitian Rebellion, revolution spread to virtually all of Latin America. From 1810 to 1825, Mexico, Central America, and South America gained their independence from Spain and Portugal. As with the American Revolution, reasons for the **Latin American wars of independence** included a growing sense of national identity and local resentment of Spanish and Portuguese economic policies. Also important was the frustration that the European-descended, or *criollo* ("creole"), upper and middle classes felt toward the rigid social hierarchy of Latin American societies, which prevented them from realizing their goal of upward social and economic mobility. Even before the revolutions began, tensions were brewing.

THE CAUSES OF REVOLUTION

Understanding how and why revolutions take place is a daunting task for any historian. Social stress and class differences, economic inequality and poverty, incompetent or oppressive political leadership, and intellectual and cultural forces (religion, nationalism, doctrines, ideologies) are almost always all to be found at the root of any major revolution. Studying and comparing revolutions involves trying to figure out which of these is more or less important in any given case. Another important distinction has to do with whether forces causing revolution come *from above* (top-down), *from below* (bottom-up), or, as is often the case, both. Who are the actual revolutionaries? Do they continue to cooperate after the initial seizure of power, or do they disagree and quarrel among themselves, leading to further struggle?

The spark that set off the Latin American revolutions was lit by Napoleon back in Europe. Between 1807 and 1809, Napoleon invaded Spain and Portugal, toppling the royal governments there. The Spanish king was placed under house arrest, while the Portuguese royal family fled to Brazil. These sudden blows to the Spanish and Portuguese monarchies had a swift and profound impact on Latin American politics. Brazil's transition to independence was relatively smooth. Spain's Latin American possessions, however, rose up in rebellion.

Simón Bolívar and the Liberation of Spanish South America

The most influential revolutionary was **Simón Bolívar** (1783–1830), known throughout Latin America as the Liberator. A member of the creole upper class in Venezuela, Bolívar was inspired by the ideals of the Enlightenment, frustrated by the inefficiency and injustice of Spanish rule, and personally ambitious.

In 1810, Bolívar took control of the independence movement sweeping across northern South America: Venezuela, Colombia, Bolivia, and Ecuador. Unlike many members of the creole elite, who rebelled against Spain for the sake of their narrow class interests, Bolívar realized that no revolt could succeed unless it attracted all classes. In a bold stroke, he promised to fight for the rights of mixed-race Latin Americans, as well as for the emancipation of slaves. This pledge turned a small and largely unsuccessful upper- and middle-class rebellion into a mass war of independence. The military turning point of Bolívar's wars came from 1819 to 1821, when he managed to gain control over Venezuela and Colombia.

At this juncture, Bolívar joined forces with another freedom fighter, José de San Martín, a general turned revolutionary. Between 1816 and 1820, San Martín had freed Argentina, Chile, Uruguay, and Paraguay. Despite political differences—San Martín was more conservative—the two men decided to cooperate, with Bolívar as overall leader. By 1825, royalists had been cleared out of Bolivia, Ecuador, and Peru, and Spanish South America was now free.

Brazilian Independence

In the meantime, Brazil had also become independent. Here, the move toward freedom came from above, rather than below. In 1820, the king of Portugal went back to Europe to reclaim his throne. He left his son, Prince Pedro, as regent. However, he also gave Pedro this advice: "My son, if Brazil starts to demand independence, make sure you are the one to proclaim it. Then put the crown on your own head." Indeed, in 1822, when Brazilians began to agitate for freedom, Pedro declared independence, created a constitutional monarchy, and proclaimed himself Pedro I.

The Mexican Revolution

Mexico and Central America waged wars of independence as well. The **Mexican Revolution** (1810–1823) was complicated by the inability of various social classes to cooperate. It began in September 1810, when the priest **Miguel Hidalgo**, unfurling the flag of the Virgin of Guadalupe, called for independence from Spain. Hidalgo was killed in 1811, but his fight was carried on by another priest, **José Maria Morelos**. Hidalgo and Morelos fought not just for freedom from Spain but also social justice. They wanted equal rights for Indians, mestizos, and slaves (whom they planned to set free). They wanted constitutional rule. Hidalgo and Morelos's platform gained mass support from the lower classes. Unfortunately, their goals were opposed not just by the Spanish but also many upper-class Mexicans, even those who wanted independence. Like Hidalgo, Morelos was killed, in 1815, by conservative Mexicans, not the Spanish.

This meant that Mexico's revolt was completed by the elite, not the lower classes. A conservative colonel, Agustín Iturbide, overthrew Spanish rule in 1820–1821. He then tried to establish a dictatorship, with himself as emperor. He was quickly overthrown, and a Mexican republic was proclaimed in 1823. That same year, the nations of Central America, south of Mexico, established the United Provinces of Central America.

The Caribbean

Only in the Caribbean did Spain retain American colonies. Until its defeat by the United States in the Spanish-American War of 1898, Spain kept islands such as Cuba and Puerto Rico.

POLITICAL CONSOLIDATION IN LATIN AMERICA
Political Difficulties in Nineteenth-Century Latin America

Shortly before his death in 1830, Simón Bolívar commented pessimistically about the revolutions he had helped to make: "We have achieved our independence…at the expense of everything else." In and of itself, freedom did not bring about good government, social justice, or healthy economies. Throughout the nineteenth and early twentieth centuries, Latin America suffered from a number of long-standing and fundamental problems.

First and most immediate was political breakdown. Bolívar had hoped that Latin America would be divided into a small number of sizable states, each governed by constitutional rule. Almost right away, though, Bolívar's large confederations—such as Gran Colombia and the United Provinces of the Río de la Plata—split apart into smaller states.

Second was the failure of constitutional rule in many of the new states. Bolívar drafted constitutions, based on fair political and social principles, for more than a dozen nations. These were influenced by the Napoleonic law code and the ideals of the American and French revolutions, but imposed on Latin American nations artificially. There was no tradition of constitutional rule in Latin America, so civil liberties and political rights had little meaning.

This failing led to a third problem: the prevalence of dictatorial rule. It was typical for military or political strongmen, often known as **caudillos**, to gain control of Latin American governments. They ruled by means of personal charisma, military force, or oppression. Despite the efforts of reformers and liberals, such as Mexico's Benito Juárez, who led the country from 1867 to 1872, conservative dictatorship, rather than representative, democratic government, was the rule in nineteenth-century Latin America.

Economic Backwardness

Another difficulty was economic backwardness. Hundreds of years of Spanish and Portuguese rule had geared Latin American economies to extract raw materials. They generally emphasized **monoculture** or, at best, the development of only a small set of resources. They required large reserves of slaves or cheap labor. These practices continued, as did plantation agriculture. Latin American leaders failed to diversify their economies. Profits tended to benefit only the elite (or foreign investors), while the labor was carried out by large numbers of extremely poor peasants and workers. Moreover, Latin American economies were slow to modernize and industrialize.

Social and Racial Divisions

Social inequality persisted. Although constitutions theoretically did away with the rigid social hierarchies that the Spanish and Portuguese had put in place, people of mixed race, Indians, and blacks were the victims of much prejudice. In many areas, such as Mexico's Yucatán Peninsula and Brazil's Amazon basin, racial tensions led to uprisings and guerrilla wars. Another social problem was economic inequality: the gap between rich and poor had always been wide, and it remained wide or grew even wider in most Latin American societies during the 1800s. In Brazil and Cuba, slavery continued to be legal until the 1880s.

Foreign Influence Over Latin America

Yet another problem was the increased influence of foreign countries over Latin American economics and even politics. This was especially the case with the United States. During the Texas rebellion of the 1830s and the **Mexican-American War** (1846–1848), the United States took vast amounts of territory from Mexico, including Texas, New Mexico, Arizona, and California.

During the 1860s, Napoleon III of France attempted to install a Habsburg emperor, Maximilian, as the ruler of Mexico.

Slavery in Brazil.
From the mid-1500s to the end of the 1800s, Brazil was the largest single importer of slaves from Africa. In particular, the sugar industry was dependent on slave labor. Not until the 1800s did Brazil's government make slavery illegal. Shown here are scenes of the sale and punishment of slaves in Brazil.

Less dramatically, foreign investors, especially from Britain and the United States, worked hand-in-hand with Latin American elites to control Latin American economies, then pocket the profits. This **"dollar diplomacy"** gave Britain and, later, the United States a tremendous amount of influence in the region.

Until late in the 1800s, Spain maintained a presence in the Caribbean, retaining control over islands such as Puerto Rico and Cuba. Spanish treatment of these colonies was harsh. Slavery persisted in Cuba until the 1880s. Cuban freedom movements began to appear. The most famous voice for Cuban independence was the poet José Martí. Spain responded by placing political agitators in **concentration camps**, the modern world's first such prisons (borrowed by the British in the early 1900s, during the Boer War). Spain's influence here would end in 1898, with the Spanish-American War.

The United States also exercised political power in the region, viewing the Americas as its sphere of influence. The **Spanish-American War** (1898) gave the United States an empire of sorts in Latin America, by placing Cuba and Puerto Rico under its protection. It was the United States that built the **Panama Canal** in the early 1900s, another sign of its regional dominance.

> **TIP**
>
> When the Pan-American Union formed in 1889 to promote cooperation among Latin American nations, cynics referred to it as the "Colonial Division of the U.S. State Department."

Limited Modernization and Industrialization

Despite all these problems, Latin America modernized somewhat in the late 1800s and early 1900s. Industrialization came late, but it did come, especially in countries like Mexico and Argentina. Countries such as Argentina, Uruguay, and Chile made it possible for women to gain educations (even, in Chile, law and medical degrees), and extended greater rights to them.

Immigration from Europe and Asia also swelled the populations of Latin American nations. Although countries like Argentina, Brazil, and Chile did not receive the same numbers as the United States, millions settled there during the last half of the 1800s, adding to what was already a diverse social and ethnic mix.

QUICK REVIEW

1. Which of the following is true of the relationship between the American and French revolutions?

   I. French philosophers, such as Montesquieu, influenced the shape of the new American government.
   II. The financial burden of aiding the American Revolution became a factor in causing the French Revolution.
   III. French revolutionaries were inspired by the successful example of revolution in America.
   IV. Thomas Jefferson helped to write France's Declaration of the Rights of Man and the Citizen.

   (A) II only
   (B) II and IV
   (C) I, II, and III
   (D) II, III, and IV
   (E) all of the above

2. Why did Britain grant dominion status to Canada?

   (A) because of armed uprisings and the fear that angry Canadians might join the United States
   (B) out of fairness, because it had already granted dominion status to Australia
   (C) to help prepare for an invasion of the United States
   (D) to prevent the Russians from expanding east out of Alaska
   (E) none of the above

3. One global effect of the Haitian Rebellion was

   (A) to reestablish French control over the Caribbean.
   (B) to bring the British into the conflict on the side of the rebels.
   (C) to place Haiti in authority over Cuba and Puerto Rico.
   (D) to convince France to sell its Louisiana territory to the United States.
   (E) to lead the United States to establish a protectorate over Puerto Rico and the Virgin Islands.

4. What political strategy transformed the South American wars of independence from a limited uprising to a successful mass movement?

   (A) The movement's leaders attracted upper-class support by promising to keep slavery legal.
   (B) The movement's leaders promised equal rights for all and freedom for the slaves.
   (C) The movement's leaders appealed to the middle classes by agreeing to give the vote only to those with property.
   (D) The movement's leaders arrested and sometimes executed those who remained loyal to Spain.
   (E) The movement's leaders attracted the lower classes by calling for a socialist revolution.

5. Which Latin American nation made a smooth transition from colony to independent monarchy?

   (A) Brazil
   (B) Venezuela
   (C) Ecuador
   (D) Colombia
   (E) Uruguay

6. Which of the following best describes Mexico's road to independence?

   (A) A mass movement of the lower classes led to the formation of a participatory democracy.
   (B) A failed mass movement of the lower classes was followed by a successful anti-Spanish rising by Mexican conservatives.
   (C) The Spanish quickly and voluntarily granted Mexico its independence.
   (D) The Mexican army, aided by the young United States, rapidly expelled the Spanish rulers.
   (E) none of the above

7. Who were the caudillos?

   (A) Latin American cattle ranchers
   (B) liberal politicians who safeguarded constitutional rule in Latin America
   (C) wealthy plantation owners who dominated Latin American agriculture
   (D) conservative strongmen who established dictatorships in many Latin American nations
   (E) Indian warriors who rebelled against Latin American governments

8. Where did slavery persist the longest in the Americas?

   (A) the United States and Mexico
   (B) the United States and Cuba
   (C) Cuba and Brazil
   (D) Cuba and Paraguay
   (E) Paraguay and Chile

9. What was the chief result of the Mexican-American War?

   (A) The United States gained huge amounts of territory, including California.
   (B) Mexico took Texas back from the United States for the next fifty years.
   (C) The United States installed the Habsburg emperor Maximilian as ruler of Mexico.
   (D) The United States set Mexican slaves free.
   (E) The United States took the Yucatán Peninsula from Mexico.

10. Which of the following is NOT true of Latin American social and economic life in the last half of the 1800s?

   (A) Plantation monoculture continued to keep Latin American economies relatively backward.
   (B) Economic investment in Latin America helped give the United States much political influence there.
   (C) Even after slavery was abolished, other forms of labor exploitation were common.
   (D) Treatment of blacks, Indians, and those of mixed race was generally free of prejudice.
   (E) Immigration from Asia and Europe swelled the population of Latin American nations.

Answers

1. **(E)** All of these answers are accurate. In these ways, the two revolutions were closely connected in spirit and even financially. Most of the U.S. Constitution's general ideas came from England and France, influenced by such thinkers as Locke, Voltaire, Montesquieu, and Rousseau.

2. **(A)** The British did not want another revolution on its hands in Canada after losing to the American colonists in the previous century. As a result, the British Parliament passed the British North America Act in 1867, which conferred upon Canada dominion status. Dominion status gave Canadians a written constitution and their own parliament.

3. **(D)** As result of the Haitian Rebellion, which proved a major failure for France, Napoleon decided to abandon his colonies in the New World. Thus, Haitian independence had long-term and far-reaching geopolitical implications.

4. **(B)** Simón Bolívar pledged to fight for the rights of mixed-race Latin Americans and the emancipation of slaves. His pledge turned what was originally a limited rebellion into a mass war of independence in Venezuela and Colombia.

5. **(A)** The decision to turn Brazil into a constitutional monarchy came from above rather than through means of a mass rebellion. In 1822, Prince Pedro declared independence and created a constitutional monarchy, with himself as its king.

6. **(B)** In Mexico, Hidalgo and Morelos fought not just for independence from Spain but also for social justice. Their platform gained mass support because they advocated equal rights for Indians, mestizos, and slaves, whom they promised to emancipate. However, in the end, conservative, upper-class Mexicans killed these two popular leaders and overthrew Spanish rule in 1821. A Mexican republic was founded in 1823.

7. **(D)** In Latin America in the 1800s, independence did not guarantee a path to democracy. In fact, dictatorial rule prevailed. Caudillos gained control of several Latin American governments and ruled by means of personal charisma, military force, and oppression.

8. **(C)** The holdouts were Cuba and Brazil. They did not end slavery until 1883 and 1888, respectively. Both depended on slavery in their agricultural industries.

9. **(A)** The Mexican-American War was waged between 1846 and 1848, with the United States as the victor. During this time, the United States took control of what are now the states of Texas, New Mexico, Arizona, and California.

10. **(D)** Social divisions along racial lines continued into the nineteenth century and beyond in many parts of Latin America. People of mixed race, Indians, and blacks were the main victims of much informal racial prejudice. In some areas, racial tensions led to violent uprisings.

Unit Five: Review Questions

SAMPLE ESSAY QUESTIONS

1. Analyze in detail how one of the following areas changed between 1750 and 1914, with particular emphasis on its response and reaction to Western influence and/or takeover.

   sub-Saharan Africa
   India
   Latin America
   the Middle East

2. Compare and contrast the origins, ideals, and outcomes of the French Revolution with those of ONE of the following: the Haitian Rebellion, the Latin American wars of independence, or the overthrow of Qing China.

3. How did economic views and philosophies change in the Western world between 1750 and 1914?

4. Compare and contrast the efforts of non-Western regions to modernize during the 1800s. Choose TWO of the following: China, Japan, Latin America, and the Ottoman Empire.

MULTIPLE-CHOICE QUESTIONS

1. What factors allowed England to become the first industrialized country?

   (A) It already had a developed trade system.
   (B) The depletion of timber caused it to rely more heavily on coal.
   (C) It had a well-developed transportation network.
   (D) It was already heavily urbanized.
   (E) all of the above

2. Which of the following statements would Marxists oppose?

   (A) An iron law of wages dictates that employers should not be compelled to pay workers more.
   (B) Economic competition is inherently unfair.
   (C) Throughout history, the upper classes exploit the labor of the lower classes.
   (D) Free-market capitalism leads to inequality.
   (E) Violent revolution may be necessary to achieve socialism.

3. Which of the following did NOT play a part in causing the French Revolution?

   (A) a wide gap between ordinary citizens and the country's elite
   (B) the unfairness of the tax system
   (C) middle class dissatisfaction with the present state of affairs
   (D) a peasant revolt against the middle class
   (E) the influence of Enlightenment ideas

4. The Congress of Vienna had what larger political and social effect?

   (A) It slowed down the industrialization of Europe.
   (B) It resulted in an informal agreement among European leaders to combat liberalism and political change.
   (C) It forced Europe's remaining monarchs to grant constitutions.
   (D) It outlawed slavery and serfdom throughout Europe.
   (E) It encouraged nationalism and sped up the unifications of Italy and Germany.

5. In what major way did democratization in nineteenth-century France and Britain differ?

   (A) Britain's process was more consistent and less violent.
   (B) France's process was more consistent and less violent.
   (C) Women were granted suffrage in Britain, whereas French women were not.
   (D) Women were granted suffrage in France, whereas British women were not.
   (E) none of the above

6. How did Japan avoid being colonized by Western powers in the late 1800s?

   (A) The samurai class sealed Japan off from the West and successfully resisted external pressures.
   (B) Japan formed a powerful regional alliance with China and Korea.
   (C) Japan's emperors began a campaign of Westernization and industrialization.
   (D) Japan paid tribute to Western powers to avoid invasion.
   (E) Japan convinced Western powers that it had no natural resources worth taking.

7. What MOST attracted Britain's attention to Egypt and the surrounding region in the mid-to-late 1800s?

   (A) the rich gold mines of the Upper Nile
   (B) the strategic importance of the Aswan High Dam
   (C) desire to gain control over the Suez Canal
   (D) the discovery of oil in neighboring Sudan
   (E) none of the above

8. In what ways did African colonization change after 1880?

   I. Competition among Western powers to colonize the continent intensified.
   II. Competition among Western powers to colonize the continent cooled.
   III. The Western powers that attended the Berlin Conference agreed to observe certain basic rules.
   IV. Diplomatic crises caused by competing colonial claims persisted into the twentieth century.

   (A) I, II, and III
   (B) II, III, and IV
   (C) I, III, and IV
   (D) I and III only
   (E) none of the above

9. The European alliance system of the 1890s and early 1900s

   (A) stabilized European diplomacy by ensuring that no one country felt isolated.
   (B) did not include Britain, which pursued a strict policy of isolation.
   (C) paired a coalition of democratic governments against a coalition of autocratic regimes.
   (D) increased the likelihood of war by potentially drawing all of Europe's powers into any single crisis.
   (E) left Germany and Austria in a geographically advantageous position.

10. The map on page 327 illustrates that

    (A) France controlled Cameroon.
    (B) Britain controlled Madagascar.
    (C) Belgium was the only European country to have colonized Central Africa.
    (D) Germany controlled the most amount of territory in Africa, followed by France.
    (E) the only African states that were not colonized by European powers in 1914 were Liberia and Ethiopia.

11. What did the Ottoman Empire have in common with China during the 1800s?

    (A) They were both forced to allow foreign powers to establish commercial enclaves on their territory.
    (B) They both lost the position of technological and scientific superiority they had enjoyed in previous centuries.
    (C) Neither made any attempt at social or political reform.
    (D) Both refused to adopt gunpowder weaponry.
    (E) Opium addiction caused a national crisis in both countries.

12. By the early 1800s, Manchu leaders in China

    (A) were known for economic efficiency.
    (B) were actively pursuing constitutional reform.
    (C) accepted a vast amount of Western goods in trade.
    (D) met with popular discontent and widespread reaction against corruption and economic malaise.
    (E) encouraged opium addiction among the peasants to keep them under control.

13. The political party most involved with the overthrow of the Qing and the foundation of the Chinese Republic was

    (A) the Nationalist Party.
    (B) the Communist Party.
    (C) the Taiping Party.
    (D) the White Lotus Party.
    (E) the Reform Party.

14. Which of the following did NOT happen during the Meiji Restoration?

    (A) The middle class expanded and gained influence.
    (B) The regime allowed labor unions to form.
    (C) The samurai class lost its traditional privileges.
    (D) An industrial working class grew rapidly.
    (E) Commoners could serve in the military.

15. Which of the following is true of missionary activity in the 1800s?

    I. Missionaries were responsible for eliminating sati (the ritual burning of widows) in India.
    II. Missionaries combated the East African slave trade.
    III. Missionaries discouraged the practice of foot binding in China.
    IV. Missionaries converted much of the population of Indochina to Protestantism.

    (A) I only
    (B) I, II, and III
    (C) II, III, and IV
    (D) II and III only
    (E) all of the above

16. Nineteenth-century nationalism did NOT

    (A) spark Balkan uprisings against Ottoman power.
    (B) foster a sense of jingoist patriotism among ordinary Europeans.
    (C) inspire a wave of successful national liberation struggles in Africa.
    (D) help to motivate the imperial campaigns of the Western powers.
    (E) spur the unifications of Germany and Italy.

17. Which of the following accurately describes patterns of immigration during the nineteenth century?

    (A) Large numbers of Europeans and Asians emigrated to the Americas, especially Chile, Argentina, and the United States.
    (B) Many Europeans immigrated to the Americas, but few Asians did so.
    (C) Only the United States allowed immigrants; Latin American nations officially discouraged immigration.
    (D) Immigration had little effect on the demographic profile of the United States.
    (E) Thousands of Americans emigrated to Europe.

18. How did the history of Liberia differ from that of other African countries?

    (A) It was colonized by Europeans long before any other parts of Africa were.
    (B) It was the last African country to be colonized by Europeans.
    (C) Missionaries ran the country's government in the early 1900s.
    (D) It was founded by former slaves with the sponsorship of the United States.
    (E) none of the above

19. Which African peoples put up the strongest resistance to European armed forces?

    (A) the Asante and the Zulu
    (B) the Bantu and the Swazi
    (C) the Ngoni and the Gaza
    (D) the Dahomeians and the Fulani
    (E) the Ndebele and the Tutsi

20. How did abolishing the slave trade in Africa help pave the way toward European conquest there in the late 1800s?

    (A) The pattern of African trade changed, causing many states to lose revenue, suffer economic downturns, and become more vulnerable to foreign takeover.
    (B) Fighting for the abolitionist cause, Europeans set a precedent for future interventions in African affairs.
    (C) Europeans began thinking that military invasions of African territory were justified.
    (D) all of the above
    (E) none of the above

Answers

1. **(E)** England became the first industrialized country for all these reasons. Protoindustrialization was most pervasive there than anywhere else in the late 1700s.

2. **(A)** Marxists advocate workers' rights, so they would disagree with the dictates of the iron law, which benefit the interests of capitalists. Instead, they would argue in favor of the other four points.

3. **(D)** The French middle class shared some of the same grievances with the peasantry. For example, before the French Revolution, both groups belonged to the Third Estate, which meant that they were barred from social advancement and had to pay taxes, unlike members of the aristocracy.

4. **(B)** The Congress of Vienna, which met from 1814 to 1815, was dominated by representatives of Austria, Russia, Prussia, and Great Britain. They acted out of conservative principle. For instance, they agreed that revolution caused war and opposed liberalism as a force that led to revolution.

5. **(A)** During the nineteenth century, the British government gradually gave into popular demands to expand civil liberties and suffrage. Meanwhile, France experienced continuing political instability and periodic revolution in the nineteenth century.

6. **(C)** Japan's rulers acted pragmatically, by choosing to become less isolated from the West. Japan resumed trade ties and diplomatic relations with Western powers while building its own empire in the East.

7. **(C)** The Suez Canal has had great geopolitical significance, as the British understood well in the 1800s. The canal linked the Mediterranean with the Red Sea and, by extension, the Indian Ocean and Asia. Once the British gained a majority of shares in the canal, it used this fact as an excuse to gain control over Egyptian affairs.

8. **(C)** From the 1880s to the beginning of World War I, the European powers engaged in a rapid Scramble for Africa. The late nineteenth century was an era of nationalism, aggression, and imperial competition in Europe. Moreover, Africa was particularly vulnerable to European domination for geographical, political, and economic reasons.

9. **(D)** The result of the European alliance system at this time was to divide the European powers into two armed camps, rather than preserving the peace. Germany, Austria, and Italy formed the Triple Alliance, while Britain, France, and Russia formed the Triple Entente.

10. **(E)** The map shows how widespread European domination was over Africa at this time. Only Ethiopia and Liberia were not colonized by the European imperial powers.

11. **(B)** During the 1800s, the Ottoman Empire was in decline owing to internal problems, including its rulers' failure to modernize thoroughly (although they attempted some reform). During the last decades of the 1800s, China grew increasingly weaker and was steadily forced to hand over more privileges to foreign traders.

12. **(D)** By this time, the Qing dynasty was facing internal decline. The cost of maintaining border defenses along the northern and western frontiers became increasingly burdensome, especially as economic conditions worsened in China.

13. **(A)** The Nationalist Party (Kuomintang) was first led by Sun Yat-sen, who opposed Manchu rule and aimed to create a constitutional democracy in China. In 1912, he became president of the new Chinese Republic, but it never enjoyed political stability.

14. **(B)** The Meiji regime allowed the middle class to expand because it supported private enterprise. However, its rulers did not favor the interests of the working class. Sweatshop environments, low wages, and unsafe labor practices prevailed.

15. **(D)** Christian missionaries championed several moral causes, including opposing the slave trade in Africa and foot binding in China. They did not have the authority to end Sati. Missionaries in Africa, especially from Britain, campaigned against slave raids and slave markets.

16. **(C)** National liberation movements in Africa did not occur until the twentieth century, particularly after World War II. However, national liberation movements did occur elsewhere in the 1800s. For example, peoples in the Balkans rose up against Ottoman rule.

17. **(A)** Immigration had a large effect on the demographic profile of the United States, as well as on that of Chile and Argentina. Many people from Europe and Asia believed that there were greater economic opportunities for themselves and their families in the Americas.

18. **(D)** Liberia was never colonized by an imperial power. Instead, in the 1800s, the American Colonization Society, a group of American blacks and freed slaves, settled Liberia with sponsorship from the U.S. government.

19. **(A)** The Asante became strong militarily because they used profits from their participation in the slave trade to buy guns. During the 1800s, the British were locked in a number of Asante wars. The British did not subdue them until 1900. The Zulu fought both the Boers and the British. In the early 1800s, one Zulu military leader, Shaka, united the clans and taught them how to fight in an organized, efficient manner.

20. **(D)** The antislavery military and political intervention of European powers, such as Great Britain, gave Europeans a further pretext for becoming involved in Africa. It accustomed Europeans to thinking that military action there was legitimate, and thus paved the way for the rush to conquer Africa by the end of the nineteenth century.

UNIT SIX

THE TWENTIETH CENTURY AND CONTEMPORARY WORLD CULTURES (1914–PRESENT)

Unit Overview

GENERAL REMARKS

The twentieth century ranks as one of the most tumultuous eras in world history. It was a time of paradox and contradiction, leading one major historian to refer to it as the "age of extremes." During the twentieth century, a larger part of the world than ever before adopted democratic forms of government (and allowed women to vote), but the most oppressive dictatorships in world history also appeared. The 1900s were an era of unprecedented prosperity but also a time of striking socioeconomic polarity, as the gap between rich and poor widened. The twentieth century witnessed tremendous cultural and scientific advancement but also the worst wars and the greatest arms buildup in human history.

The first half of the twentieth century was dominated by two great military conflicts: the world wars. Both **World War I** and **World War II** caused immense devastation. The latter was the bloodiest and costliest conflict humanity has ever experienced. Both wars led to profound changes in the world balance of power, politically and economically. World War I destroyed several of the great empires of the nineteenth century and sapped Europe's strength. World War II completed the process of weakening Europe, dislodging it from its position of global mastery.

The interwar years were marked by economic crisis, resulting from the **Great Depression**, which emanated outward from the United States. This period also saw the emergence of powerful, extremely repressive dictatorial regimes, such as Soviet Russia, Fascist Italy, and Nazi Germany. For a time, it appeared that **totalitarianism**, not democracy, might be the wave of the future. Starting with the establishment of the Soviet state, **communism** became an important and influential—although, in the end, seemingly unworkable—alternative to **capitalism** as a form of economic organization.

During the second half of the twentieth century, sweeping trends affected the entire world. One, following the collapse of Europe's global dominance, was **decolonization** (or **national liberation**). From the 1940s through the 1970s, those parts of Africa, Asia, and the Pacific that had been under European (and U.S.) imperial control in the 1800s and early 1900s became free. This wave of national liberation created dozens of new nations. In some cases, decolonization proceeded smoothly and peacefully. In others, it was attained by force or disintegrated into violence and political chaos.

Another effect of World War II and Europe's decline as a global power was a new diplomatic alignment, the **Cold War**. In the previous century and a half, world affairs had been determined by the workings of the European balance of power.

After World War II, political and economic power was concentrated in the hands of two large, evenly matched superpowers: the United States and the Soviet Union. This situation of bipolar equilibrium persisted for four and a half decades, dividing most of the globe into two hostile camps.

The twentieth century was an era of modernization. Those societies that were already industrialized when the 1900s began—such as the United States, Canada, western Europe, and Japan—became even more adept at scientific and technological innovation, until, after the 1940s and 1950s, they began to move into postindustrial modes of economic organization and production. Such societies are generally referred to as the **developed world**. A number of other countries, especially in Asia, made great progress in industrializing and modernizing, especially after World War II. The majority of the world's nations, known as the **developing** or **nondeveloped world** (or, in Cold War terms, the **Third World**), remain in a less advanced stage of economic and technological progress. Developed or nondeveloped, modern societies have had an immensely greater impact on the environment. The most noticeable effect today is **climate change** (popularly known as global warming).

During the late twentieth century, there has been an overall rise in the level of wealth and modernization. The economies of the world have also globalized, or grown closer together, to a steadily increasing extent. Despite this, the twentieth and twenty-first centuries have also seen the widest gap between prosperity and poverty to appear in many years, if not in world history. Even within developed nations, social and economic polarity is extreme, and the gulf between the developed and developing worlds is especially wide.

The 1980s and 1990s saw the collapse of communism in Europe and the USSR, and with that, the end of the Cold War. The same decades also witnessed a wave of democratization in many parts of the world, as well as the increased **globalization** of the world economy and the meeting and mixing of ethnicities and traditions, or **multiculturalism**. Mass communications have made the world, metaphorically speaking, a much smaller and more connected place. This is especially due to the relatively sudden proliferation of computer technology, which has caused an **information (or digital) revolution**.

The world's general direction in the early twenty-first century remains unclear. On one hand, many trends, such as the end of the nuclear arms race, economic globalization, the worldwide prevalence of American popular culture, and the spread of mass communications and computer technology, seem to be drawing the world closer together. On the other hand, ethnic violence and **genocide**, extreme forms of nationalism, religious fundamentalism, proliferation of **weapons of mass destruction**, potential tensions between China and the West, and a cooling of relations between Russia and the United States are all factors threatening to pull the world farther apart. The same is true of the terrorist attacks of **September 11, 2001**, on the World Trade Center and Pentagon—the event most likely to be seen in the future as the symbolic beginning of the new century—and the resulting worldwide **war on terror**.

BROAD TRENDS

Global Power and International Relations

- During the first half of the 1900s, two world wars profoundly shaped global affairs.
- After 1914, Europe's position of world dominance was badly weakened by World War I. Nonetheless, Europe retained a position of global importance, as well as its overseas empires, for three more decades.
- The United States, after World War I, became the world's richest and most powerful nation.
- World War II completed the process of dismantling Europe's global dominance. The war left world power divided between two superpowers, the United States and the USSR.
- For four and a half decades after World War II, most of the world was divided into hostile camps, led by the United States and the Soviet Union. This geopolitical struggle was known as the Cold War. Although the superpowers never warred against each other directly, they used other nations as proxies in their struggle. They also engaged in a nuclear arms race, the largest and most expensive weapons buildup in world history.
- From the 1940s through the 1970s, a mass wave of decolonization deprived the European powers of their empires. Former colonies in Asia, Africa, the Pacific, and elsewhere became free. Dozens of new nations were formed.
- During the late 1980s and early 1990s, communism in Eastern Europe and the Soviet Union collapsed. This dramatic development helped bring an end to the Cold War.
- The only remaining superpower in the post-Cold War era is the United States. A rising economic and political power is China, the world's most populous nation.
- The terrorist attacks of September 11, 2001, have begun a new global struggle, the U.S.-led war on terror. It has also sharpened tensions between much of the developed West and the Islamic world, especially the Middle East.
- The gap between high tech and low-level warfare has grown wider than ever before in history. The most advanced armed forces possess weapons of mass destruction, precision-guided ("smart") weapons, and—thanks to what generals call the "revolution in military affairs"—digitally integrated systems. Much of the rest of the world fights low-intensity or guerrilla wars, using only small arms and hand-to-hand weapons.

Political Developments

- The level of popular representation in national governments grew in many countries, especially in the Western democracies.
- Women gained the vote in most Western nations, then in most other countries.
- Between the world wars, democracies tended to be politically weak and economically depressed.

- The most dynamic governments of the interwar period were the new totalitarian dictatorships, which aimed to control as many aspects of their subjects' lives as possible.
- After World War II and during the Cold War, the primary form of political and economic organization in the West (Canada, the United States, and Western Europe) was the democratic state with a capitalist system, although capitalism was modified to varying degrees by social welfare systems.
- A number of regimes, led by the Soviet Union and China, adopted communist economic systems. Their political systems tended to be dictatorial.
- The nations of the so-called Third World, which joined neither the U.S. alliance nor the Soviet bloc during the Cold War, experimented with a variety of political and economic systems.
- During the late 1980s and early 1990s, communism collapsed in Eastern Europe and the Soviet Union. This development ended the Cold War. It also left China as the world's major communist state.
- The globalization of culture and economics has led some scholars to speculate that the nation-state may either fade away altogether or cease to be the primary form of political organization. Whether or not this prediction will prove true, regional diplomatic alliances and regional economic blocs, such as the Association of Southeast Asian Nations and the European Union, have become increasingly important in the late twentieth century and early twenty-first.

Economic and Environmental Developments

- During the first half of the century, the West (Europe, Canada, and the United States) fully industrialized. Certain other parts of the world achieved significant degrees of modernization and industrialization (such as Japan, parts of Latin America, and China).
- A number of countries experimented with communist economies (the Soviet Union, then, after World War II, Eastern Europe, China, North Korea, Cuba, Vietnam, and others).
- During the 1930s, the Great Depression, emanating from the United States, had a tremendously negative impact on the economies of most of Europe and Latin America, as well as Asia and Africa to a lesser degree.
- World War II consumed a huge amount of the world's economic resources during the first half of the 1940s. It is estimated that, at the war's peak, between one-quarter and one-third of the world's entire productive capacity was devoted directly or indirectly to World War II.
- After World War II, a great split between the capitalist West and the communist Soviet bloc (and China) emerged. This split prevailed until the end of the Cold War.
- Also after World War II, a different split emerged between the developed world, whose prosperity steadily grew (with a few minor regressions, such as the economic crisis of the 1970s), and the nondeveloped and developing (or Third) world, which lagged behind. Because so many nondeveloped and developing nations are located near or south of the equator, this disparity is sometimes referred to as the north–south split.

- After the 1950s and 1960s, Western economies began to move from industrial economies to postindustrial economies, based less on manufacturing and more on service, information, and advanced technology (especially computers). This trend continues.
- During the 1970s, a general economic crisis, characterized by energy (particularly oil) shortages, recession, and unemployment struck most of the capitalist West.
- A general rise in prosperity took place in Western economies during the 1980s and 1990s. The same was true in China. The Soviet bloc experienced a severe economic downturn during this time.
- The 1980s and 1990s were also an era of greater economic globalization, as international trade, economic regionalization, and the clout of multinational corporations all became increasingly important. This trend continues and is steadily accelerating.
- The collapse of communism in Eastern Europe and the USSR has forced a number of countries to make a painful, difficult transition from communism to free-market economies. Most of these countries continue to wrestle with this transition in the twenty-first century.
- Escalating industrialization, increased energy and resource consumption, massive engineering projects, and the production of toxic, chemical, and nuclear waste have all helped exponentially to increase humanity's impact on the environment.
- Environmental awareness in the West grew slowly during the early 1900s, then expanded after World War II. Green movements have grown in size and influence.
- The emission of greenhouse gases (especially carbon dioxide) is thought by most scientists to be causing climate change (global warming). The best-known international effort to cooperate in understanding and reversing the trend is the Kyoto Protocol (1997).

Cultural Developments

- Mass media and mass communications technology have transformed the cultural sphere. Cinema, radio, television, and other electronic media have been used to create high art.
- Mass media and communications have also been used to create popular (or mass) culture: music, literature, and so forth aimed at a popular audience for purposes of entertainment.
- The art of the twentieth century was characterized by bold experimentation and the distortion, even abandonment, of traditional norms and conventions.
- During the first two-thirds of the 1900s, largely because of the demoralizing effects of Europe's decline and the world wars, Western high art tended to be marked by uncertainty and pessimism (in contrast to the exuberance and energy of popular, or mass, culture).
- Scientific advancement proceeded at a breathtaking pace and scale. Fields that were especially innovative were physics, biotechnology, rocketry, electronics, and computers.

- After World War II, Western culture began to move beyond the "modern" period into a newer "postmodern" era.
- Worldwide, different cultures have begun to mix, interact, and blend to an unprecedented degree. This celebration and acknowledgement of different traditions and styles is generally referred to as multiculturalism.
- Since the 1990s, the proliferation of personal computer technology, particularly access to the Internet and World Wide Web, has led to an information revolution.

Gender Issues

- Women's movements began to campaign for greater equality and the right to vote during the late 1800s and early 1900s.
- By causing large numbers of women to move into the workplace, World War I greatly accelerated the cause of women's equality.
- Most Western nations gave women the vote shortly after World War I.
- Even more so than World War I, World War II gave millions of women the opportunity to work. Many women also served in the armed forces (mostly in noncombat roles). Their role during World War II significantly boosted women's hopes and chances for more rights and greater equality.
- The development of reliable contraception (especially birth-control pills) gave women with access to it unprecedented control over pregnancy.
- During the 1960s and 1970s, a great feminist movement, agitating for women's liberation and equal rights, swept Canada, the United States, and Western Europe. Since then, women's movements have sought to achieve more than simple legal equality and the right to vote. Their goals have been to reach full cultural and economic equality, changing social norms and behaviors to create a more positive climate for equal gender relations.
- Progress toward equal treatment of women has been uneven in other parts of the world.

QUESTIONS AND COMPARISONS TO CONSIDER

- Discuss the various ways different nations and regions modernized during the twentieth century. Were they industrialized before the 1900s? Did modernization efforts come from the population at large, or were they instituted by the government? Did they have to be put into place by force? Has modernization by force proven effective?
- What kind of impact did the world wars have on the non-Western world? Compare different regions, such as Africa and Asia. How did the wars affect women?
- Compare two or more of the twentieth century's major revolutions, such as the Russian, Chinese, Cuban, or Iranian. Alternatively, compare one or more of these with revolutions in previous centuries. Consider comparing how each affected women.
- Investigate the process of decolonization as it played out in various parts of the world (compare, for example, India and Africa).

- Focus on various national liberation movements and independence struggles during the period of decolonization. What obstacles did various movements face? How did their approaches to liberation and decolonization differ, and how were they alike? Did they use force? If so, how and why?
- How has the legacy of colonialism affected cultural identity and/or patterns of economic development in Africa, Asia, and Latin America?
- How has nationalism in Europe differed from nationalism in decolonizing or formerly colonized parts of the world, both in character and in its political effects?
- Compare the effects of the Cold War on the West, the East, and the so-called Third World. How useful are these labels?
- How has the rise of Western consumer society and economic globalization affected different civilizations outside Europe? Compare, for example, China with sub-Saharan Africa, or Japan with Latin America.
- How does ethnic violence in the late twentieth century compare with the Holocaust?
- Compare the nation-state with regional groupings (diplomatic, economic, military) that have emerged during the late twentieth and early twenty-first centuries.
- What models for economic development in the developing (or Third) world have been proposed and/or attempted? What social and political consequences have they led to?
- Examine Western and non-Western forms of cultural expression. How have mass media and popular culture affected world culture? Which has become more important: multiculturalism or the Americanization of contemporary world culture?
- Consider how high-tech warfare (nuclear arms and other weapons of mass destruction, "smart" weapons, the so-called Revolution in Military Affairs) contrasts but also coexists with guerrilla warfare and other forms of low-intensity conflict.

World War I

CHAPTER 28

- World War I (Allies versus Central Powers)
- Nationalism and competition over empire
- The European alliance system
- Trench warfare and the Western Front
- naval blockade and submarine (U-boat) warfare
- The Armenian genocide
- Total war
- The home front (rationing, conscription, restriction of civil liberties)
- Women's roles and female suffrage
- The Paris Peace Conference, Treaty of Versailles, and the Fourteen Points
- The League of Nations
- The Balfour Declaration
- The Spanish flu

In the late summer of 1914, the nations of Europe went to war. All parties involved expected that the conflict would be short and decisive. As the British press was fond of claiming, "the boys" would be "home by Christmas."

Instead, **World War I** (July 1914–November 1918), known to the people who experienced it as the Great War, lasted more than four years. More than thirty nations joined in the fighting. The war killed up to 10 million soldiers. Between 3 to 5 million civilians perished as well, mainly of disease and starvation caused by the war but also as a result of direct military action. Approximately 28 to 30 million people were wounded or disabled by the war. At war's end, Europe's economies lay in ruins, even those of the countries that had won. The treaties that ended the war redrew the map of Europe and that of the world completely.

It is no exaggeration to say that World War I shattered Europe politically and culturally. Four great empires—the German Reich, Russia's tsarist regime, Austria-Hungary's Habsburg dynasty, and Ottoman Turkey—were destroyed. Russia's wartime suffering led directly to communist revolution; Germany's defeat inspired Adolf Hitler to follow the path of fascism. Even victorious nations such as Britain, France, and Italy were exhausted and demoralized. Barbarity and bloodshed caused by the war hugely shifted European cultural attitudes. The spirit of optimism and faith in progress so prevalent in the nineteenth century vanished, to be replaced by fear, anxiety, and gloom. The Europeans' view of themselves as models of civilized behavior and cultural superiority was exposed as a foolish illusion. The only major nation in the West to escape this malaise was the United States, which remained comparatively undamaged by the war—and even managed to profit from it economically.

Far-reaching social changes resulted from or were sped up by the war. These included the final decline of the aristocracy, the rise of the middle and lower classes, the greater democratization of European politics, the complete industrialization and modernization of European economies, and the granting of suffrage to women.

In global terms, World War I caused a fundamental shift in power. Europe had gained tremendous global might during the last half of the 1700s. In the nineteenth century, it had become the dominant civilization on the planet, and it reached the zenith of its power from 1870 to 1914. After World War I, however, it was clear that Europe would not be able to continue in its position of economic, political, and imperial preeminence for much longer. The United States was on its way to becoming the world's military and economic powerhouse. Europe's imperial possessions were becoming increasingly restless, and although countries such as Britain and France held on to their empires for a while longer, the process of decolonization was unavoidable—the question was when, not whether, it would happen.

Clearly, the war was much more than a straightforward armed conflict. For all these reasons and more, World War I, rather than the calendar year 1900, is generally considered to be, metaphorically speaking, the true beginning of the twentieth century.

BACKGROUND AND BEGINNING

As discussed in Chapter 22, long-term causes of World War I include a potent cocktail of **nationalism**, **competition over empire**, and an unstable **European alliance system** (France and Russia, informally aligned with Britain, against Germany, Austria, and Italy) with the potential to draw all the continent's powers into conflict in the event of crisis.

That crisis came in the Balkans, in Sarajevo, capital of Bosnia: a Slavic province under Austrian authority but with a large Serb population and, therefore, coveted by the young and intensely nationalistic nation of Serbia. On June 28, 1914, a Bosnian Serb student assassinated the heir to Austria's throne, Franz Ferdinand, and his wife.

The assassination caused outrage worldwide but especially in Austria, which blamed Serbia (although it was not officially responsible) and decided to use the murders as a pretext to humble its troublesome neighbor. In July, Austria issued Serbia an ultimatum, a list of humiliating demands, and threatened war if Serbia did not agree to them. Because of the alliance system and a general sense of nationalist belligerence, this regional quarrel rapidly escalated into a continental conflict. Russia, protective of its fellow Slavs (and unfriendly to Austria) supported Serbia. Germany assured Austria of its support (the infamous "blank check"), even if Russia intervened. France was pledged to aid Russia in the event of hostilities.

On July 28, Austria declared war on Serbia. Russia responded by mobilizing its troops. Like clockwork, the alliance system went into operation (Germany's plan for avoiding a long two-front war required immediate action, a factor that sped up the process). Between July 28 and August 4, Serbia, Austria, Russia, Germany, France, and Britain entered the war. Although guilt for the the war was later assigned principally to Germany, many factors contributed to its beginning, and a number of countries share at least some guilt.

COMBAT

The Combatants: The Allies and the Central Powers

The war expanded beyond the original alliance system. The **Allies**, as the Triple Entente now called itself, consisted of Great Britain, France, and Russia. Many of Britain's imperial dominions, including Canada, Australia, New Zealand, and South Africa, took part. Italy abandoned its former partners and joined the Allies in 1915, because

Britain and France promised it Austrian territory. In 1917, the United States would join the Allied war effort; later that year, Russia would drop out of the war. On the other side were the **Central Powers.** These were Germany and Austria, the nations of the Triple Alliance, minus Italy. They were joined by Bulgaria and the Ottoman Empire. Other nations took part in the war, but these were the major combatants.

The Schlieffen Plan, the Invasion of Belgium, and the Battle of the Marne

Germany's **Schlieffen Plan** and its failure shaped the first phase of World War I. Faced with a two-front ground war against France and Russia, as well as the long-term threat of the British navy, Germany made a daring gamble: the Schlieffen Plan sent 75 percent of the German army against France, with the goal of taking Paris in six

World War I in Europe, 1914–1918.
In Western Europe, the basic dynamic of the conflict was determined quite early. Then, thanks to the stalemate of trench warfare, it changed very little until the last months of war. In the east, fighting conditions were much more fluid.

weeks. The rest of the army, with the Austrians, would defend against Russia, which was expected to take months to mobilize fully. To catch the French off guard, the main attack force would move through Belgium, which was neutral.

The illegal invasion of Belgium, which killed many civilians, stained Germany's reputation badly. It enabled Allied propaganda to argue convincingly that the Germans were aggressors, "barbarians," and "Huns."

By early September, the Schlieffen Plan had failed. Belgium resisted more stoutly than Germany had anticipated. The Russians mobilized more quickly than expected. Although German troops came within sight of Paris, the French army made a heroic stand at the Marne River. The battle there saved Paris, foiled the Schlieffen Plan, and dashed any hope of a quick end to the war.

Trench Warfare, the Western Front, and the Eastern Front

In late 1914, two European fronts, the Western Front and Eastern Front, took shape. They were very different. In the west, stalemate prevailed. Both sides were evenly matched and armed with the latest in industrial-era weaponry. Artillery, machine guns, and modern rifles had made the battlefield so deadly that traditional tactics, which involved charging the enemy, were no longer feasible. Military technology disproportionately favored the defensive. The result was **trench warfare,** one of the most horrific styles of combat in human history. For the next three years, fighting on the **Western Front,** while exceptionally bloody, resulted in almost no movement at all. Actions such as the Verdun Offensive and the Battle of the Somme, both in 1916, rank among the most futile operations of all time, resulting in hundreds of thousands of casualties but no useful outcome.

NOTE

By the end of 1914, 500 miles of trenches, bunkers, and barbed wire, separating the Germans from the Allied forces, stretched from the English Channel to the Swiss border.

NOTE

Not until 1917 and 1918 did tactical changes and new weaponry (such as tanks and airplanes) start to end the painful stalemate of trench warfare.

Ordinary life in the trenches could be almost as miserable as combat. Mud, lice, rats, disease, and the smell of dead bodies combined to make the trench experience maddeningly terrible. Eloquent descriptions of trench warfare can be found in literary works such as Erich Maria Remarque's novel *All Quiet on the Western Front*, Robert Graves's autobiographical *Goodbye to All That*, and the work of Britain's so-called "war poets" (Robert Owen, Siegfried Sassoon, Stephen Spender, and others).

Fighting on the Eastern Front was very different. This front was much longer, extending well over a thousand miles, and was less entrenched. Serbia fell to the Austrians. After initial setbacks, the Germans and Austrians moved quickly and efficiently against the Russians, killing, wounding, and capturing millions. They also took hundreds of thousands of square miles of Russian territory. From the beginning, the Russians found themselves in terrible trouble. Bulgaria and the Ottoman Empire joined the war on the side of the Central Powers, cutting Russia off from its allies. By 1917, Russia was nearing the end of its capacity to fight.

Naval Warfare and the Use of Submarines

Considering that the naval race between Britain and Germany had been an underlying cause of the war, it was ironic that there were few traditional ship-to-ship naval battles in World War I. Britain's Royal Navy imposed a blockade on Germany and Austria, causing the starvation of thousands. In response, Germany deployed its most effective naval weapon: the **submarine** (or **U-boat**), which enabled the German navy to do tremendous economic damage to Britain. However, submarine warfare carried with it the danger of destroying neutral ships or killing civilians from neutral countries, so it was diplomatically risky. Over time, Germany's success with submarine warfare would backfire, bringing the United States into the war in 1917.

The Global Dimensions of World War I

The war also took on a global dimension. The war had begun largely because of empire, and its effects spread to Europe's colonies. Many of Britain's imperial dominions, including Canada, Australia, New Zealand, and South Africa, declared war on the Central Powers and took an active part in European and Middle Eastern combat.

France and Britain mobilized native troops in Africa. Although most of them played a support role, performing construction and garrison duties, some saw combat in Africa against German colonial troops. The French also brought African troops to the Western Front (in a classic instance of stereotyped prejudice, the Germans feared these soldiers as cannibals). More than 2.5 million Africans (almost 2 percent of the total population) were involved in the war effort in some way. Britain also mobilized Indian sepoys, Sikhs, and Nepalese Gurkhas for combat in the Middle East.

The fighting spread beyond Europe. There were clashes in Africa. Japan joined the Allied war effort, then took over Germany's island colonies in the Pacific. Australia seized German New Guinea. The most important non-European theater of war was the Middle East. In 1915, the British, using Australian and New Zealander troops, tried to knock Ottoman Turkey out of the war by landing at Gallipoli, southwest of Istanbul. This campaign proved an utter disaster, resulting in 50 percent casualties.

More successful was the effort of the officer T. E. Lawrence, better-known as Lawrence of Arabia, who persuaded Arab princes to rise up against their Ottoman masters. By 1917 and 1918, the British, with their Arab allies, dismantled what was left of the Ottomans' Middle Eastern empire. Before that, however, in 1915, the Ottomans carried out the **Armenian genocide**, using the excuse of potential pro-Russian disloyalty to massacre somewhere between 500,000 to 2 million victims.

The War's Last Stages: 1917 and 1918

The year 1917 was a crucial turning point in several ways. All the original European combatants were exhausted by the fighting. Frustrated by the stalemate and its ability to win surface battles at sea, the German navy turned to unrestricted submarine warfare, hoping to starve Britain out of the war. Economically, the U-boat campaign worked: by the spring of 1917, Britain was reduced to a six-week food supply. Diplomatically, however, submarine warfare was a disaster, as it provoked the United States to declare war in April 1917.

On the other hand, Russia was collapsing. The tsarist regime fell in March, and although the new government attempted to continue the war effort, the Russian army was in full retreat and suffering mass desertions. When Vladimir Lenin and the Bolsheviks staged their Communist revolution in October–November 1917, they immediately took steps to pull Russia out of the war. Germany was now free to send large numbers of troops to the Western Front, where the balance of force was already razor-thin.

The last year of World War I—late 1917 to late 1918—was, therefore, a great military race. The Allies' goal was to get American soldiers across the Atlantic (with German U-boats sinking troop ships) and ready for combat. The German goal was to transfer soldiers from the Eastern Front to the west and use them to knock the weary French and British out of the war before the Americans arrived in large numbers. Whichever side accomplished its goal first would win, and it was not clear until the summer of 1918 who would prevail.

Realizing that time was against them, the Germans launched a massive offensive against Paris in the spring of 1918. As in 1914, this attack was halted by a determined stand at the Marne River. During the summer, American, Canadian, British, and French troops pushed the Germans back. In the fall, the Germans were in full retreat. In early November, strikes and mutinies convinced the Austrian and German governments to surrender. World War I ended on November 11, 1918.

THE HOME FRONT

World War I was a **total war**, meaning that it required nations to involve their populations and mobilize their resources completely in order to carry on the fight. The last such war in the Western world had been the U.S. Civil War (1861–1865). Europe itself had not experienced such a conflict since the days of Napoleon. Against all their expectations, the nations of Europe—and, to a lesser extent, the United States—found that World War I affected their civilian populations deeply and directly. The **home front** became a crucial part of every combatant's war effort.

Conscription

Very quickly, the war required mass **conscription**. Already before the war, most European powers had armies of 1 to 2 million men, larger than ever before in history, but those numbers did not suffice. Even in Britain, which had a long tradition of maintaining an all-volunteer army, substantial conscription was called for. Eventually, the belligerent nations of World War I drafted more than 70 million men. Small numbers of women volunteered to serve in Anglo-American forces but did not take active part in combat. Many women served on the front as nurses.

Economic Mobilization and Rationing

Entire economies had to be geared for war as well. Industrial wartime production required enormous amounts of raw material: iron, steel, petroleum, rubber, cloth, and more. The need for uniforms, weapons, tanks, aircraft, ships, and other wartime necessities was immense. Agricultural production had to be stepped up in order to feed armies and civilians. With so many able-bodied men gone to fight, the strain put on civilians—especially women—to keep national economies functioning was incredible. All major combatants centralized their economies somewhat, placing even private enterprise at least somewhat under state control. Food, strategic materials, and consumer goods were rationed, and the **rationing** grew stricter as time passed.

By late 1916 and early 1917, all European nations were suffering terrible shortages. Britain's food supply was almost depleted by Germany's campaign of unrestricted submarine warfare. Germany and Austria experienced the so-called turnip winter in 1916–1917. Russia, cut off from outside help and supplies by Germany and the Ottoman Empire, was so lacking in food and equipment that, by the end of 1916, its soldiers were sent to the front barefoot and unarmed. They were told to scavenge boots and rifles from soldiers who had died in battle.

Restrictions on Civil Liberties

Another domestic effect of World War I was the **restriction of civil liberties**, even in democracies such as Britain, France, and America. All countries imposed censorship on the press, the mass media, and the mail. Those suspected of espionage or treason could be arrested, tried, and sentenced without due process. In most countries, all political parties agreed to unite behind the war effort and refrain from criticism of the government. Socialist parties and trade unions were supervised and their activities curtailed. Even pessimism or an insufficient display of patriotism could bring a person under suspicion; men who attempted to gain conscientious objector status were often denied, and even if they succeeded, they were often harassed or ridiculed. German-speaking immigrants in Allied nations sometimes suffered persecution.

Women and the War Effort

Perhaps the most striking effect on the home front involved the **role of women**. With so many men serving in the armed forces, farms, factories, and workplaces of all types were left understaffed, just as wartime economic pressures required greater, not lesser, production. In all major countries, women stepped up to take the place of men in the workplace. They served as truck drivers, farmhands, factory workers, munitions workers, and in occupations of all types.

The economic contribution of women to their countries' war efforts was considerable. In Britain, over 1.35 million women who had never worked before took jobs. In the factories of Germany's most important arms producer, Krupp, women made up 38 percent of the workforce. Even France, highly resistant to the notion of giving women equal rights, granted a minimum wage to female textile workers producing uniforms.

NOTE

Once the war was over, however, many of the jobs that had gone to women were given back to the men who returned.

THE PARIS PEACE CONFERENCE

After the war, peace terms were decided at the **Paris Peace Conference**, which lasted from 1919 to 1920. All decisions were made by the leaders of the victorious Allied nations. Delegates from the defeated Central Powers were excluded. The major players were Woodrow Wilson of the United States, David Lloyd George of Britain, Georges Clemenceau of France, and Vittorio Orlando of Italy. The Allies drew up five treaties, one for each defeated power: Germany, Austria, Hungary, Bulgaria, and the Ottoman Empire. The most important was the **Treaty of Versailles**, the agreement reached with Germany and signed on June 28, 1919.

Diplomatic Disagreements Among the Allied Leaders

The Paris Peace Conference was characterized by a clash between American idealism and the European Allies' thirst for revenge. In his words, Wilson's desire was "to make the world safe for democracy" and prevent war in the future. These goals were reflected in his **Fourteen Points**, which called for freedom of the seas, an end to secret treaties, free trade, arms reduction, **decolonization**, the rearrangement of European borders according to the "self-determination" of national groups, and the establishment of an international dispute-resolution body called the **League of Nations**.

By contrast, Lloyd George and, more so, Clemenceau, focused on making Germany pay for the war and keeping it weak in the future. Italy wanted the Austrian land and German colonies it had been promised by Britain and France.

NOTE

All the European victors were opposed to Wilson's goal of decolonization.

The Terms of the Treaties

The treaties that resulted were the product of bitter negotiation and compromise. As Wilson wished, the League of Nations was formed. Ironically, since the U.S. Congress did not ratify the Treaty of Versailles, America never joined the League, a fact that weakened it from the start. Many of the other Fourteen Points were discarded or watered down. Taken together, the main points laid out in the five treaties included

- *Dismantling of Austria-Hungary*: The Habsburg Empire was destroyed. Austria and Hungary became two separate states, and each lost a great deal of territory.
- *New nations*: Mainly out of Habsburg territory, but also out of lands lost by Germany and Russia, new countries were created. These included Yugoslavia ("Land of the South Slavs"), Czechoslovakia, Poland, Finland, Latvia, Lithuania, and Estonia. This was done in accordance with Wilson's principle of **self-determination**.
- *Italy and Austria*: Italy received some of the Austrian territory it was promised, but not all.
- *Population transfer in the Balkans*: Thousands of Turks living in southeastern Europe were expelled and sent to the Ottoman Empire. Likewise, large numbers of Greeks living in the Ottoman Empire were forced to move to Greece.
- *The Middle East*: The Ottoman Empire was stripped of its Middle Eastern possessions, especially the Arab lands. They were placed under temporary French and British control, according to a **mandate system** (the League of Nations

would help supervise these areas, which were to be prepared for eventual independence). This stipulation greatly disappointed the Arabs, who had expected freedom in exchange for their military assistance against the Ottomans during the war. Britain also assumed control over Palestine. In the **Balfour Declaration** of 1917, Britain agreed in principle to the creation of a Jewish homeland in Palestine. However, it delayed indefinitely on this question, in order to avoid antagonizing Arabs throughout the Middle East.

Germany and the Treaty of Versailles

The most important provisions pertained to Germany. The Treaty of Versailles imposed the following terms:

- *War guilt*: Article 231, the **war-guilt clause**, laid chief blame for World War I on Germany (a review of the war's causes should remind the reader that, although Germany deserved a good part of the blame, other nations, such as Austria, did much to start it as well).

NOTE

Article 231 was used to justify the heavy punishments that the Treaty of Versailles imposed on Germany.

- *Loss of territory*: Germany lost approximately 13 percent of its territory, amounting to 25,000 square miles, which had been home to 6 million people. The provinces of Alsace and Lorraine went to France, and other lands went to Denmark, Belgium, and Poland. France and Belgium were allowed to occupy the resource-rich Saar until 1935. The Rhineland, the borderland between France and Germany, was also to be occupied till 1935 and maintained as a demilitarized zone in perpetuity.

- *Loss of colonies*: Germany's colonies were stripped and placed under Allied trusteeship. Only Wilson's efforts prevented France and Britain from colonizing them outright.

- *Disarmament*: France and Britain feared a resurgent Germany and therefore disarmed it. The army was allowed a token force of 100,000 soldiers. It was not permitted any military aircraft, submarines, battleships, or heavy artillery.

- *War payments*: Against Wilson's wishes, France and Britain insisted that Germany pay the full cost of the war, calculated to be $32 billion. According to the initial repayment schedule (which was changed several times), Germany was to make war payments until 1961.

The Paris Peace Conference is considered to have produced a flawed peace. Greed and revenge determined many of the terms of settlement. Ignorance, especially regarding Eastern Europe and the Balkans, where the new regimes tended to be unstable and weak, played a large role in redrawing the world map. Justified or not, the harsh treatment of Germany, especially the imposition of such heavy economic terms, made the peace unacceptable to most Germans and would be a significant factor in the rise of Hitler and the beginning of World War II. (On the other hand, it cannot be said that the Treaty of Versailles *directly* caused either of these events.)

LONG-TERM CONSEQUENCES

The grim immediate consequences of World War I were obvious: 10 million soldiers killed, somewhere between 3 to 5 million civilians killed, and 28 to 30 million people wounded. Financially, the cost of the war was assessed at $32 billion. Countless people, particularly in eastern Europe, where borders shifted constantly, were made homeless or stateless. As a final injury, a global epidemic of **Spanish flu** struck during the closing months of World War I. Then and shortly afterward, the Spanish flu killed almost 20 million people worldwide.

Long-term consequences were as follows:

- *Destruction of Eastern and Central European empires*: The German, Austro-Hungarian, Russian, and Ottoman empires all fell.
- *Communism in Russia*: The tsarist regime was replaced by the communist Soviet Union.
- *Instability in Eastern Europe*: The new nations of Eastern Europe were inexperienced and weak. Nationalist tensions within them ran high. During the 1920s and 1930s, only Czechoslovakia would prosper and remain democratic. The others experienced economic difficulties, became politically authoritarian, and suffered from ethnic strife.
- *Social and political transformation*: Although World War I did not cause this trend, it helped to accelerate it. Even before the war, the political power, social influence, and economic clout of the traditional aristocracy had been vanishing, while that of the middle and lower classes had been rising. In almost all countries of Europe—and even elsewhere—World War I did much to complete this transformation.
- *Further industrialization and modernization of European economies*: War mobilization spurred further industrialization in Europe and North America.
- *Women's suffrage*: Thanks largely to the economic role they played during the war, women gained greater respect not just in the workplace but in the public sphere overall. The most important result was **women's suffrage** in most Western nations, during or just after World War I. Scandinavia, the Low Countries, Russia, Britain, Canada, the United States, and others gave women the vote. France and Italy were alone among the major Western powers in resisting this trend; not until the 1940s did women there get the vote.
- *German resentment*: Almost all Germans regarded the Treaty of Versailles as unfair. Many saw it as illegitimate. Anger about the war payments was universal. Years later, this attitude played an important role in the rise of Hitler and the outbreak of World War II.
- *General decline in European economic and global power*: Although the nations of Europe were still able to maintain the appearance of great powers, they had been badly drained by World War I. Even the victors' economies were in sad shape, and those of the losers were in shambles. France, Britain, Belgium, Portugal, and the Netherlands still possessed their overseas empires but maintaining control over them would become increasingly difficult during the 1920s and 1930s and even more so after World War II.

DISEASE AND WORLD HISTORY

From humanity's earliest days, the presence or spread of disease has played an enormous role in how societies encounter and interact with each other. Pandemics in the form of bubonic plague (which swept from China to Europe in the 1300s and plagued Eurasia for centuries) devastated numerous societies. The demographic impact of the spread of smallpox and measles to the Americas by European explorers and conquerors in the 1400s and 1500s was nightmarishly heavy. Rampant urbanization and overcrowding in the 1700s and 1800s often caused massive outbreaks in cholera and tuberculosis. Until the late 1800s, illnesses like malaria and sleeping sickness prevented European imperial powers from penetrating too deeply into the interiors of Southeast Asia and especially Africa. The modern age has brought with it a better understanding of disease; but it has also given rise to much greater global mobility, a factor that makes the widespread outbreak of epidemics and pandemics faster and more likely than before: The Spanish influenza after World War I, the emergence of AIDS (acquired immune deficiency syndrome), and the recent appearance of SARS (severe acute respiratory syndrome) and avian flu are good examples.

• *Sense of uncertainty and anxiety in European culture*: Even before World War I, the prevailing faith in progress that had characterized Europe's cultural and intellectual life during most of the 1800s had been waning (see Chapter 20). Destruction and despair caused by the war, plus the gloom surrounding Europe's political and economic comedown, made this sense of uncertainty and anxiety worse, bringing it to the forefront of European culture.

QUICK REVIEW

1. Which of the following could BEST be used as evidence to support the argument that Germany was to blame for World War I?

   (A) the assassination of Franz Ferdinand
   (B) the harshness of the Austrian ultimatum to Serbia
   (C) the Germans' "blank check" offer to Austria
   (D) the Anglo-German naval race
   (E) the Zimmerman Telegram

2. Which of the following BEST describes the Schlieffen Plan?

   (A) a massive attack on and rapid defeat of France, then a single-front war with Russia
   (B) a massive attack on and rapid defeat of Russia, then a single-front war with France
   (C) the devotion of equal force and attention to France and Russia at the same time
   (D) a total focus on the strategic threat posed by Britain's Royal Navy
   (E) a flanking move directed against Serbia, which might otherwise knock Austria out of the war

3. Which of the following can be said of the World War I home front?

   I. Trade union activity was curtailed.
   II. Rationing and food shortages were common.
   III. Conscientious objectors and others who opposed the war tended to be badly treated.
   IV. Most combatant nations were forced to resort to mass conscription.

   (A) I only
   (B) II only
   (C) II and III
   (D) I, II, and IV
   (E) all of the above

4. Which of the following is most true about combat on the Western and Eastern fronts?

   (A) Fighting on the Eastern Front degenerated into stalemate, while conditions on the Western Front were much more fluid.
   (B) Fighting on the Western Front degenerated into stalemate, while conditions on the Eastern Front were much more fluid.
   (C) Conditions on both fronts were roughly the same.
   (D) The level of technology on the Eastern Front was significantly higher than on the Western Front.
   (E) There were no aircraft used on the Eastern Front.

5. What can accurately be said of the role of women during World War I?

   I. Substantial numbers of women served in combat.

  II. Providing an effective home front labor force during the war advanced the cause of female suffrage.

 III. Many of the jobs women were assigned during the war went back to men after the war ended.

 IV. Countries with a greater gender bias, such as Germany, barred women from the workplace.

(A) II only
(B) IV only
(C) II and III
(D) II and IV
(E) all of the above

6. Which of the following is NOT true of World War I as a global phenomenon?

(A) Native troops from African colonies were not allowed to fight in Europe.
(B) The Japanese seized German colonies in the Pacific.
(C) British agents effectively stirred up Arab rebellion against Ottoman rule.
(D) Canada, Australia, South Africa, and New Zealand took part in the Allied war effort.
(E) The British made extensive use of Sikh and Gurkha troops.

7. Which group fell victim to genocidal massacre during World War I?

(A) the Palestinians
(B) the Roma (Gypsies)
(C) the Jews
(D) the Armenians
(E) Bosnian Muslims

8. The Treaty of Versailles

(A) disarmed the German army and navy almost completely.
(B) created the new nation of Yugoslavia out of German territory.
(C) allowed Germany to retain its colonies in Africa.
(D) was ratified by all the Allied governments.
(E) divided Berlin into zones of Allied occupation.

9. What best describes the relationship between Woodrow Wilson and his fellow Allied leaders, Georges Clemenceau and David Lloyd George, at the Paris Peace Conference?

(A) Out of gratitude, Clemenceau and Lloyd George agreed to almost all of Wilson's proposals.
(B) Wilson opposed most of the so-called Fourteen Points supported by Clemenceau and Lloyd George.
(C) Wilson's thirst for revenge clashed with the lofty idealism of Clemenceau and Lloyd George.
(D) Clemenceau's and Lloyd George's thirst for revenge clashed with the lofty idealism of Wilson.
(E) Clemenceau and Lloyd George vetoed Wilson's League of Nations but readily agreed to decolonize the French and British empires.

10. After the Paris Peace Conference, Arab leaders

(A) were content with their new-found independence.
(B) were frustrated by the limited autonomy granted them as mandate states.
(C) were overjoyed by the Balfour Declaration.
(D) were grateful to the Turkish government for standing up on behalf of the Middle East at the conference.
(E) were angry that Middle Eastern affairs had not been discussed at all during the conference.

Answers

1. **(C)** Germany and Austria were allies and members of the Triple Alliance (initially with Italy). Kaiser Wilhelm II of Germany supported Austria with an assurance that Germany would support any action Austria might take against Serbia, no matter how rash.

2. **(A)** The Schlieffen Plan called for Germany's sending 75 percent of its army against France, in order to capture Paris and force France from the war in only six weeks. The plan was put into effect in August 1914, but it had failed by early September.

3. **(E)** World War I was a total war, and so even the home front became a crucial part of every combatant's war effort. All of the answers accurately describe what happened in most participating countries. Protecting civil liberties at home, especially the rights of war resisters, was not a government priority.

4. **(B)** On the Western Front, both sides were evenly matched and armed with the latest industrial-era weaponry. Conversely, the Eastern Front was much longer, as it extended over a thousand miles. It was far more fluid, and battles were decisive.

5. **(C)** Because so many men were serving in the armed forces at the time, women filled positions in factories and on farms back home. They contributed to economic production during the war. In return, the cause of women's suffrage was greatly served. However, once the war ended and soldiers returned home, many jobs were turned back to male workers.

6. **(A)** In fact, France and Britain mobilized native troops in Africa during World War I. Most of them played only a supporting role, by performing construction and garrison duties. However, some saw combat in the skirmishes that occurred in Africa against German colonial troops. The French also brought African troops to the western front.

7. **(D)** In 1915, the Ottoman Turks massacred an estimated 500,000 to 2 million Armenians. It is widely considered the first campaign of genocide in the twentieth century.

8. **(A)** The Treaty of Versailles assigned full blame for the war to Germany and stripped it of all colonies and all but a token military. German territory was given away to other nations, but not to Yugoslavia; and Berlin was not occupied or divided after World War I. The treaty was not ratified by the United States.

9. **(D)** Wilson wanted to "make the world safe for democracy," by preventing future wars. On the other hand, Lloyd George and Clemenceau desired to make Germany pay for the war. France wanted to make sure that Germany would never be able to pose a threat to European peace again.

10. **(B)** Arab lands formerly under the control of the Ottoman Empire were placed under temporary French and British control, according to a mandate system. Arabs were disappointed by this arrangement, because they had expected freedom. They also opposed the Balfour Declaration.

The Twenty Years' Crisis: The World During the Interwar Period

- The League of Nations
- Democratic weakness in Europe and U.S. isolationism
- The Great Depression and its global impact
- Totalitarianism
- Soviet communism (Vladimir Lenin and Joseph Stalin)
- Italian fascism (Benito Mussolini)
- Nazi Germany (Adolf Hitler) and anti-Semitic policy
- State capitalism (syndicalism)

- Modernization from above in Turkey and Persia
- Oil in the Middle East
- Nationalists vs. Communists in China (Chiang Kai-shek versus Mao Zedong)
- Japanese militarism, war in China, and the Rape of Nanjing
- The Indian National Congress and *satyagraha*
- Latin America, U.S. influence, and dictatorship

Many historians have argued that World War I and World War II were simply two halves of the same conflict, separated by twenty years of temporary peace. Whatever the truth of that observation, it is undeniable that the peace of the 1920s and 1930s rested on an extremely shaky foundation.

This was certainly the case in Europe, where many of the problems that had been stirred up by World War I were not solved by the treaty settlements that followed. Also, the social, economic, and political forces unleashed by twentieth-century modernization were too strong for many governments—especially those that had been damaged badly by the war or those that had been newly created by the Paris Peace Conference—to handle. Another factor that affected the fortunes of interwar Europe was the **Great Depression**. Starting in the United States in October 1929, the Depression began to affect the economies of Europe (and elsewhere) by 1930 and 1931. The Depression damaged beyond repair many economies and regimes that had already been struggling during the 1920s. As a result, dictatorship, often in its most extreme form, **totalitarianism**, became the rule, not the exception, in European politics during the 1930s.

Elsewhere in the world, powerful political developments were underway. Revolution, modernization, and industrialization caught up with many countries that had not experienced those trends during the 1800s. European possessions in Africa, Asia, and the Middle East began to agitate more actively than ever before for **decolonization** and **national liberation**. Nationalism, dictatorship, and militarism became part of political life in much of the non-Western world.

Finally, by the mid-to-late 1930s, the storm clouds of war gathered. Japanese aggression in Asia, along with German and Italian belligerence in Europe and elsewhere (See Chapter 30), made it more likely with every passing year that a major conflict would break out. The failure of the Western democracies to prevent such a conflict only demonstrates the weakness of the interwar peace.

POLITICAL EXTREMISM AND ECONOMIC DEPRESSION IN EUROPE

Fragile Peace and the Crisis Of Democracy

During the 1920s, peace prevailed in Europe, but it was fragile. Also, at the beginning of the decade, it was incomplete. From 1919 through 1922, there were revolutions, civil wars, and military clashes in Germany, Russia, Poland, Hungary, and the Balkans. Even afterward, peace was preserved mainly by the fact that European nations were too exhausted to fight. The new **League of Nations** provided what little political leadership there was. It was well-meaning and accomplished a great deal of humanitarian work, but it was largely ineffective. It had few powers of enforcement. Also, the United States, now the world's strongest and richest country, refused to join.

Despite treaties during the 1920s intended to outlaw war (such as the Treaty of Locarno and the Kellogg–Briand Pact), there was little political will on the part of liberal democracies to ensure long-term peace. During the 1920s, the absence of any real threat created an illusion that permanent peace had been achieved. That illusion would be shattered during the 1930s.

European democracy did not flourish during the 1920s or 1930s. In 1920, there were twenty-three governments in Europe that could be considered democratic. By 1939, there were only twelve. Most of the new states of Central and Eastern Europe fell victim to political extremism, especially during the 1930s, when inflation and, especially, mass unemployment caused by the Great Depression made it difficult to maintain a healthy form of government. Right-wing dictatorship, as well as ethnic discrimination and class tensions, plagued this part of Europe during these years. As described below, the most famous of these dictatorships emerged in Italy and Germany.

Even in stronger and better-established democracies such as France and Great Britain, times were troubled. During the comparatively easier 1920s, both economies, especially Britain's, were sluggish as a result of World War I's draining effect. Both had borrowed a great deal of money from the United States, and each relied on German war reparations to keep up its own payments. Unemployment, strikes, and deficits became the norm in France during the early 1920s and in Britain during the entire decade.

The 1930s were even worse because of the Depression. By 1932, one British worker in four was out of work. France was not as badly hurt as Britain, but it went through hard times. Particularly during the 1930s, both democracies suffered from a lack of firm political leadership. In Britain, a shaky coalition, the National Government ran Parliament with caution and compromise. Some relief came with the creation of a **modern welfare state**, as social security, pensions, unemployment insurance, and so on, were put into place. In France, elections were frequent, and leadership passed from left to right and back again on a regular basis. During the 1930s, economic weakness and political mediocrity made it difficult for France and Britain to cope with the growing threat of Hitler's Germany.

Communism in the Soviet Union

The general crisis of democracy in interwar Europe meant that the most dynamic regimes tended to be the dictatorships, which grew in number and power during the 1920s and especially the 1930s. The first of the new dictatorships was the Union of Soviet Socialist Republics (USSR), or the Soviet Union, the communist regime that rose to power during World War I, in October–November 1917.

When the tsarist regime of Nicholas II fell in February–March 1917, its place was taken briefly by a moderate Provisional Government that attempted to continue the war against Germany, solve Russia's dismal economic problems, and establish a democratic government. In that its first stage was relatively liberal, the Russian Revolution resembled the French Revolution of 1789.

However, the Provisional Government did not satisfy the desire of the vast majority of the Russian population (80–85 percent of whom were peasants) for economic stability, land reform, and peace. The party that benefited most from popular discontent were the Communists, or Bolsheviks, led by **Vladimir Lenin** and his second-in-command, Leon Trotsky.

In the fall of 1917, Lenin and Trotsky overthrew the Provisional Government. From then until 1921, they pulled out of World War I, formed the Soviet government, and fought and won the terrible Russian Civil War (which pitted the Bolshevik Red Army against their anticommunist enemies, called Whites). From 1921 till his death in 1924, Lenin tightened his grip on power and attempted to modernize the Soviet Union along Marxist lines. One of his major challenges was that, while Marx had predicted that communist revolution would first take place in a mature capitalist society with a large industrial working class, Russia was a backward, barely capitalist nation with a huge peasantry and an extremely small working class. A compromise in 1921, Lenin's New Economic Plan (NEP) took a more gradual approach to socialist development, allowing for limited private trade. It lasted until 1927–1928.

Lenin died in 1924. A half-decade succession struggle followed, during which **Joseph Stalin** defeated Trotsky for control over the Soviet government. Stalin became one of the most oppressive dictators of all time. Overturning the NEP, Stalin rapidly modernized the USSR, starting in 1928. His **Five-Year Plans** were intended to transform the Soviet Union from an agricultural society into a modern industrial state. The **collectivization of agriculture**—the placement of all peasants on state-run farms—was meant to rationalize farming, increase governmental control over the countryside, and harness the labor of the peasants (profits generated by agriculture were used to pay for the Five-Year Plans).

Although the USSR modernized under Stalin, the price was steep. The Five-Year Plans amounted to a state-sponsored industrial revolution, with the same social and economic trauma, but applied with ruthlessness and police brutality. Collectivization resulted in a **Great Famine** in southern Russia, Ukraine, and Kazakhstan that killed approximately 4 million to 6 million people. Later in the 1930s, Stalin carried out a huge campaign of terror, the **Purges**, which resulted in the execution of approximately a million people and the arrest and exile to labor camps (**gulags**) of at least 5 to 7 million. Like most modern dictators, Stalin used propaganda to indoctrinate his subjects and instituted an extravagant cult of personality to glorify himself. The Stalinist experience is an extreme example of rapid modernization, directed from above by dictatorial leadership. In Stalin's case, this approach brought the country far more torment then benefit.

Fascism in Italy

In Italy, dictatorship came from the right. After World War I, Italy was rocked by economic depression and political turmoil. Strikes, communist agitation, and constant governmental turnover brought the country to the edge of chaos. The middle and upper classes, frightened of social breakdown and left-wing revolution, looked for a strong leader to restore stability. They turned to **Benito Mussolini**, the right-wing, anticommunist leader of the Fascist Party.

Fascism, Mussolini's invention, is a difficult political concept to define. It can best be described as right-wing radicalism or revolution from the right, unlike ordinary right-wing conservatism, which seeks to prevent change. Fascism seeks to bring about change. It is anticommunist but also anticapitalist and antidemocratic. Fascism is also often characterized by hypernationalism and a state-sponsored campaign of racial and ethnic bigotry.

In October 1922, Mussolini was placed in charge of the government by the king, who feared the communists. For the next twenty-one years, governing Italy, he became increasingly dictatorial. He coined a new term to describe his style of rule: **totalitarianism**, a twentieth-century form of dictatorship in which the regime, using modern technology and bureaucracy, attempts to control every aspect of its subjects' lives. Compared with other totalitarian rulers, such as Stalin and Hitler, Mussolini was actually mild. Still, he imposed censorship over culture, imprisoned (and sometimes killed) political enemies and dissidents, and used propaganda to create a cult of personality.

On the other hand, Mussolini modernized Italy. He built new highways, sponsored literacy campaigns, fought the Mafia, and brought medicine and technology to backward parts of his country. His chief claim to fame was to have made Italy's notoriously inefficient trains run on time. His economic policy was based on the principle of syndicalism (a form of **corporatism** or **state capitalism**, common in right-wing dictatorships). In fascist economies, corporate leaders, rather than practicing free trade, are required to cooperate directly with the government, and labor unions are suppressed. During the 1920s, Mussolini was considered by many to be an effective, even admirable, leader despite his dictatorial tendencies. During the 1930s, however, the Depression undercut his modernizing efforts. He became more dictatorial and, in foreign policy, more aggressive (see Chapter 30). Also during the 1930s, Mussolini drew closer to the newer fascist regime of Nazi Germany.

Nazism in Germany

Germany's road to dictatorship was longer than Italy's, and the results were infinitely worse. From 1919 to 1933, Germany was governed by a democratic regime, the **Weimar Republic,** which was dogged by economic trouble (hyperinflation during the early 1920s wiped out the value of the German mark), the burden of war payments, widespread resentment of the Treaty of Versailles (which the Weimar regime had been forced to sign), and the rise of extremist political parties.

From the left, the German Communist Party became a powerful threat. From the right appeared **Adolf Hitler** and the **Nazi Party:** an anticommunist, antidemocratic group that, after Mussolini's rise to power in Italy, consciously imitated fascism in many ways. The Nazi Party, also obsessed with the notion of racial purity, hated all minorities, but especially Jews, whom the Nazis viewed as "subhuman" and the source of all of Germany's troubles. In 1923, Hitler and the Nazis made a failed attempt to take over the German government. During the short time he spent in prison, Hitler wrote his infamous memoir, *Mein Kampf* (*My Struggle*).

By the late 1920s, the Weimar Republic appeared to have established a reasonably solid democracy. The Depression, however, ended the calm. Its effects reached Germany in 1930. By 1932, 6 million Germans—almost 40 percent of the workforce—were unemployed. The economic pain, destroying the Weimar Republic's ability to govern democratically, boosted Germany's extremist parties, the Communists and the Nazis. A series of elections in 1932 made the Nazi Party the largest in Germany. In January 1933, Hitler was appointed chancellor of Germany.

> **TIP**
>
> By 1932, 6 million Germans—almost 40 percent of the workforce—were unemployed.

Having risen to power by legal means, Hitler established himself as an absolute dictator within months. In February 1933, the Reichstag building, seat of the German government, was burned down. Hitler took advantage of the resulting panic to declare a state of emergency and pass the Enabling Act (March 1933), which suspended the Weimar constitution and gave Hitler the power to rule by decree for four years (a limit Hitler had no intention of obeying).

With blinding speed, Hitler outlawed all other political parties (especially his archenemies, the Communists), took control of the press and mass media, banned labor unions, imposed a system of state capitalism similar to Mussolini's, built **concentration camps,** such as Dachau, for political opponents and dissidents, and established a secret police, the Gestapo. He managed to end German unemployment by means of a giant program of public works and highway building, as well as a massive increase in arms production.

The Nazi regime also instituted **anti-Semitic policies** (it targeted other racial "undesirables" as well). Jews were forced out of various professions (such as law, civil service, and university teaching), their businesses were boycotted, and they were physically harassed. Before World War II, the most drastic official measures taken against the Jews were the **Nuremberg Laws** of 1935. These laws stripped German Jews of their citizenship and forbade Jews and German non-Jews to marry or have sexual relations of any kind.

In terms of foreign policy, Hitler pursued a highly aggressive diplomatic line. As described in Chapter 30, Hitler's belligerence was the principal reason that the fragile peace of the 1920s began to shatter in the 1930s.

NATIONALISM AND MODERNIZATION IN THE MIDDLE EAST

Even before World War I, the Middle East had been on the threshold of great change. Modernization was coming gradually to the Ottoman Empire. In those parts of the Middle East controlled by outside powers, the force of nationalism was rising. By toppling the Ottoman Empire, World War I brought even greater changes to the region.

The Birth of Modern Turkey

The transformation of the Ottoman Empire into the modern Turkish state had its roots in the efforts of the **Young Turks**, who had seized power in 1908 (see Chapter 23). These pro-Western, modernizing officers and politicians had already started to carry out reform before World War I. During the war, the Turks joined the Central Powers and shared defeat with them. The Ottoman Empire suffered more than 300,000 casualties and saw their Middle Eastern possessions rise up in revolt. It surrendered in October 1918.

After the war, the Turks lost most of their Middle Eastern territories to France and Britain. Greece, with Allied permission, was threatening to seize Turkey's western provinces. In the midst of this crisis, a new leader emerged: **Mustafa Kemal**, a colonel who had fought bravely against the British landing at Gallipoli in 1915. Kemal formed a new government in the city of Ankara, drove the Greeks from the Turkish mainland, and negotiated a new treaty with the Allies. In 1923, the last sultan fled the country, and the Ottoman Empire was no more. In its place, Kemal established the Turkish Republic, becoming its first president. He took the title **Ataturk**, meaning "father of the Turks."

From 1923 till his death in 1938, Ataturk labored to create a modern, secular state in Turkey. He wrote a constitution and, despite the fact that he was quite authoritarian, made the pretense of acting like a democratic ruler. Industrialization, Western dress, and Western education were encouraged. Turkish was written in the Roman alphabet. Church and state were separated, and Islamic law (Sharia) was replaced by a European law code. Women were no longer required to wear the veil. They received the right to vote in 1934, and they were encouraged to become educated and join the workforce. To this day, Turkey's status as the most Westernized and most secular state in the Middle East, next to Israel, is a direct legacy of Ataturk's policies.

> **TIP**
>
> To this day, Turkey's status as the most Westernized and most secular state in the Middle East, next to Israel, is a direct legacy of Ataturk's policies.

Persian Independence and Modernization

Persia went through a change similar to that of Turkey, becoming the modern state of Iran. From 1794 to 1925, Persia was ruled by the Qajar dynasty. In reality, however, the country had been divided into two spheres of influence: Russian in the north, British in the south. After World War I, the British presence in Persia increased, largely because of the oil reserves there. Resentment of foreign domination grew steadily, and a nationalist backlash was inevitable. In 1921, an officer named Reza Khan mutinied against the Qajar rulers and expelled the British. By 1925, he had gained control of the country. He called himself **Reza Shah Pahlavi** and established a new royal dynasty. Like Ataturk in Turkey, Reza reformed his country, which he renamed Iran. Although he was not as much a foe of the Islamic clergy as Ataturk was, he Westernized Iran, boosted education, did away with the veil for women, and, in general, secularized the nation. Like Ataturk, he tended toward authoritarianism

Egypt, North Africa, and Arabia

The political fate of the rest of the Middle East was mixed. Egypt and North Africa remained in British, French, and Italian hands, although nationalist sentiment there was growing. For the time being, the Arabian Peninsula remained under Turkish control. The other Arab states formerly under Ottoman rulership were now placed under French and British control and divided into **mandates**, to be supervised partially by the League of Nations. Syria and Lebanon were assigned to France, while Iraq, Jordan, and Palestine fell to Britain.

This arrangement angered most Arabs, who had thought that, by helping the British fight the Turks, they would gain full independence. Another thing enraging the Arabs was the **Balfour Declaration** of 1917, which publicly stated the British government's intention to create a Jewish homeland in Palestine—whose population, in the late 1910s, was 90 percent Arab.

Change came to all these areas during the 1920s and 1930s. Despite the fact that the British allowed only limited Jewish emigration to Palestine to keep from provoking the Arabs, thousands of Jews flooded into the region, many of them illegally. By 1939, the Jewish proportion of the population had risen from 10 to 30 percent.

In the early 1920s, an Arab prince named **Ibn Saud** drove the Ottomans out of the Arabian Peninsula and then united Arabia's many tribes. In 1932, he founded the kingdom of Saudi Arabia. As the only major Arab state to enjoy full independence, Saudi Arabia was important in and of itself. After 1938, it became even more important, with the discovery of huge oil reserves. Overnight, Saudi Arabia became wealthy and strategically vital.

MILITARISM AND REVOLUTION IN ASIA
The Chinese Republic

In 1911, revolution in China had overthrown the Qing imperial dynasty. Taking its place was the Chinese Republic, governed by the **Nationalist Party (Kuomintang)**. **Sun Yat-sen**, often regarded as the father of modern China, was president.

Quickly, however, the republic disintegrated. In 1912, Sun was forced to give up the presidency to General Yuan Shikai, in order to gain the support of the armed forces. In the face of Yuan's growing traditionalism and dictatorialism, Sun and the Kuomintang found themselves in opposition to the government. In 1913, Yuan disbanded the parliament. In response, the Kuomintang began a revolution. It failed, and Sun fled to Japan. Yuan ruled until his death in 1916. Military officers continued to govern in Beijing until the early 1920s.

The rest of China slipped into anarchy. Warlords and bandits took control of vast stretches of the country. In 1920, Sun and the Nationalists returned to the mainland, establishing a base at Canton and throughout southern China. The **Chinese Communist Party** (CCP), founded by radicals at Beijing University in 1921, became a major force. A deadly external threat came from Japan, whose imperial ambitions grew during and after World War I. Japan already controlled Korea and had a sphere of influence in southern Manchuria. Because it had aided the Allies in World War I, Japan also had their blessing to expand that sphere after the war.

Political control was not the only issue over which Chinese parties struggled. During these years, there was a great clash between traditional values and the desire for modernization. The military government in Beijing attempted to revive Confucian principles, while younger students and intellectuals embraced progressive concepts such as democracy, technology, and science. The clearest example of popular activism came on May 4, 1919, when thousands of students came to **Tiananmen Square** in Beijing to protest against the military government. The immediate cause of the May Fourth Movement was the government's willingness to allow Japan to annex Shantung Province. Underlying that specific issue, however, was the desire for political and social reform. As for China's other major political actors, the CCP was progressive in its outlook, while the Kuomintang was torn between the past and the future.

The Chinese Civil War: Nationalists Versus Communists

By the mid-1920s, the main political forces in China were the Nationalists and Communists. From 1923 to early 1927, both parties cooperated to drive warlords and foreign powers out of China. Sun Yat-sen died of cancer, leaving the leadership of the Kuomintang to **Chiang Kai-shek**, a Western-educated officer who leaned farther to the right than Sun had. By early 1927, the Nationalist-Communist alliance had gained control of all China south of the Yangtze River, including the major cities of Shanghai and Nanjing.

In April, Chiang turned against the Communists, murdering thousands of them in Shanghai. Most of the rest of the party was driven far to the north, under the revolutionary **Mao Tse-tung (Mao Zedong)**. Chiang took Beijing in 1928 and founded a Kuomintang regime that combined Westernization with mild authoritarianism. Chiang proclaimed his allegiance to Sun's principles and made some attempts to create a constitutional government and an industrial economy. However, corruption, backwardness, the threat of Japanese imperialism, and warlord anarchy hampered his efforts.

Full-scale civil war against the Communists would soon resume. Against incredible odds, Mao Tse-tung kept the CCP alive, leading it on the Long March (1934–1935), far to the north. At Yenan, the Communists established a base from which to launch military operations against the Nationalists. Mao's central strategy was to make communism appealing to China's vast peasant masses, rather than concentrate on the small industrial working class in the cities.

Starting in 1931, Japan seized all of Manchuria from China. In 1937, Japanese forces attacked China itself, starting a three-way conflict among the Nationalists, Mao's Communists, and the invading Japanese.

TIP

Mao's central strategy was to make communism appealing to China's vast peasant masses, rather than concentrate on the small industrial working class in the cities.

Japan During the 1920s

In the early 1900s, it seemed possible for Japan to evolve into a democratic parliamentary monarchy. The powers of the Diet increased, and universal male suffrage and a bill of rights were granted in 1925. Freedom of the press expanded. The emperor, Taisho, actively supported democratic reform. The economy continued to industrialize and modernize.

On the other hand, traditional forces remained in place. The upper-class elite retained its oligarchical outlook. Nationalism ran high, and Japan's imperial tendencies grew more intense. Even though the economy was strong and modern, most of Japan's industrial might was concentrated in the hands of a small number of corporate conglomerates called *zaibatsu*. By the 1930s, the four largest *zaibatsu* (including Mitsubishi) controlled 21 percent of banking, 35 percent of shipbuilding, 38 percent of the merchant marine, and 21 percent of the mining industry. The effect of this system was to keep wealth in the hands of a tiny number of rich and powerful industrialists and capitalists. Also, because the *zaibatsu* enjoyed substantial governmental support, economic policy was largely under state influence, in a way not unlike the system of state capitalism practiced in Fascist Italy and Nazi Germany.

Japanese Militarism and the Invasion of Mainland Asia

Increased imperial aggression and the effects of the Great Depression derailed Japanese democratization during the 1930s. Japan's exports plummeted more than 50 percent. Farmers and workers were badly hurt. Nationalism, bolstered by state Shintoism (a bigoted and politicized perversion of Japan's indigenous faith), skyrocketed, and anti-Western feelings sharpened. The slogan "Asia for the Asians" called for the expulsion of colonizing powers such as Britain and France.

In September 1931, Japan took all of Manchuria from China, turning it into a puppet kingdom, Manchukuo. Shortly afterward, Japan withdrew from the League of Nations. In 1932, Japan's prime minister was assassinated by right-wing extremists. Moderates and leftists were persecuted. By 1941, the Japanese military, under Hideki Tojo, had gained control of the parliamentary government. It was able to dominate the young emperor, Hirohito, who had taken the throne in 1926.

The Japanese began a full-scale war in Asia in 1937. In July, the Japanese invaded China, committing dreadful atrocities against the civilian population. The so-called **Rape of Nanjing** in December 1937 climaxed with the massacre of 200,000 to 300,000 noncombatants, including women and children. The Japanese war against China continued throughout the 1930s and World War II. In 1938 and 1939, the Japanese clashed with the Soviets on the Siberian borderland but were turned back. The war then spread to Southeast Asia, as Japan attempted to drive out the French and British, establishing its own empire, which it referred to as the **Greater East Asian Co-Prosperity Sphere**.

Nationalist Movements in South and Southeast Asia

In South and Southeast Asia, most of which remained under British and French colonial rule, nationalism became widespread. In Vietnam, Burma, Indonesia, and elsewhere, anticolonial agitation escalated. Typically, such efforts involved an uneasy alliance of Western-educated, middle-class modernizers with intellectuals and students inspired by the communist ideals of Marx and Lenin. It was similar to the temporary joining of the Nationalists and Communists in China—and, as in China, these alliances typically broke apart.

Gandhi, Nehru, and the Indian National Congress

The most successful freedom movement appeared in British-controlled India. The moving force here was the **Indian National Congress** (later the Congress Party), founded in 1885. After World War I, the movement's dominant figure was **Mohandas K. Gandhi**. Because it had loyally supported Britain in World War I, India hoped it would gain greater autonomy after the war, perhaps even dominion status, as Canada, Australia, and New Zealand had. However, demonstrations and protests, organized largely by Gandhi, led to clashes with the British. In 1919, at Amritsar, British troops fired on unarmed protestors, killing 379 and wounding 1,137. This massacre led to chaos. The British imposed a strict crackdown, and Gandhi went to prison.

For the rest of the 1920s, India balanced on a political knife-edge. The British began to make concessions, such as the Government of India Act (1921), which allowed 5 million Indians to vote and created a new parliament, two-thirds of whose members would be Indian. However, the earlier repression of the British prompted the Congress Party to demand more. India could easily have erupted into bloody revolution. That it did not was due mainly to Gandhi's political and spiritual guidance.

Whether free or in prison, Gandhi—now known increasingly as Mahatma, which means "great soul"—preached the policy of nonviolent resistance. Based partly on Hindu religious principles, this policy was called *satyagraha* ("hold to the truth"). An example of *satyagraha* in action came when the British imposed a high tax on salt. Rather than protest violently, Gandhi led 50,000 people on a 200-mile march to the seashore, where they began to make salt illegally by drying out seawater. When the British arrived, Gandhi allowed himself to be arrested peacefully.

Gandhi was freed in 1931. He continued to work with the Congress Party but as a guiding force rather than as a politician. The political leader, also Gandhi's working partner, was a younger lawyer and intellectual, **Jawaharlal Nehru**. The spiritual, traditional Gandhi and the modern, secular Nehru pressed the British for greater reform. In 1935, the British granted a constitution that was a long step forward on the path to eventual self-rule. In 1937, Gandhi and Nehru began their Quit India campaign, trying to convince the British to leave altogether. The advent of World War II delayed British withdrawal, but India gained its freedom in 1947, soon after the war.

Muhammad Ali Jinnah and the Muslim League

The Congress Party was not the only force pressing for Indian independence. India's Muslims had their own freedom movement. During World War I, Muslims and Hindus had pledged to work together for greater autonomy from the British, but they went their separate ways during the 1920s. In 1930, the **Muslim League**, led by **Muhammad Ali Jinnah**, formed. It paralleled the Congress Party's independence efforts, but its aims were different. The Muslim League called for the creation of a separate Muslim state called Pakistan ("land of the pure"). The failure of the Muslim League and the Congress Party to resolve their differences peacefully led to great bloodshed when independence was finally achieved in 1947. It also lay the foundation for the bitter Indo-Pakistani rivalry that still persists.

DICTATORSHIP IN LATIN AMERICA

Outside Influences on Latin America

Before World War I, modern nations in Latin America, while politically independent, had been economically dominated by outside influences. British and U.S. investors exercised great control over enterprises in Latin America. Most Latin American nations relied on the export of one or two raw materials or agricultural products. Chile was a source of fertilizer and copper; Peru mined copper as well. Chile and Brazil sold steel. Oil was taken out of Mexico, Bolivia, Argentina, and Peru. Argentina produced wheat and beef. Central America grew bananas and other fruit. As it had for centuries, sugar came from the Caribbean and Brazil. Brazil was the source of 75 percent of the world's coffee supply.

In exchange for foreign capital and industrial know-how, political elites in Latin American countries allowed foreigners much influence over local politics. The great mass of the population did the work and saw very few of the resulting profits.

The U.S. Sphere of Influence in Latin America

World War I increased the U.S. role in Latin America's political and economic life. With their economies weakened by the war, countries such as France and Britain no longer had the funds to invest in Latin America. The United Fruit Company and other U.S. corporations became major forces in Latin America.

Strategically, the United States viewed Latin America as its sphere of influence and had done so since the late 1800s. The United States had gained possessions such as Puerto Rico and the Virgin Islands, as well as a protectorate over Cuba, after the Spanish-American War of 1898. U.S. Marines had occupied Haiti. Just as the British had taken control of the Suez Canal, America established a military presence after constructing the **Panama Canal**. Instability in Mexico convinced the United States to militarize the border. The United States sponsored dictators, such as Vicente Gómez of Venezuela and Fulgencio Batista of Cuba, in order to preserve stability. A sense grew among Latin Americans that the people of the United States—the *yanquis*, or "yankees"—were imperialists.

In the mid-1930s, Franklin Roosevelt attempted to reduce U.S. influence over Latin America. His **Good Neighbor Policy** (1935) was intended to accomplish this goal and thereby improve relations with the region. As a token of goodwill, Roosevelt withdrew U.S. Marines from Haiti. For the first time in three decades, the United States had no troops in Latin America.

The Great Depression's Effects on Latin America

Unfortunately, the United States affected Latin America in yet another way during the 1930s. The effects of the Great Depression on the region were devastating. Since Latin American economies were so dependent on exports to the United States, the inability of the United States to purchase Latin American goods caused tremendous damage. Exports were cut almost in half. As in many parts of Europe, the economic pain caused by the Depression had a negative effect on politics, inclining Latin American governments toward extremism and dictatorship.

As discussed in Chapter 27, there was a long-standing tradition of authoritarian rule in Latin America. This trend continued into the 1920s and 1930s, when there were few if any genuine democracies in Latin America. The three largest and wealthiest nations—Mexico, Brazil, and Argentina—all became dictatorial, to one degree or another, during these years.

Dictatorship in Mexico, Brazil, and Argentina

Mexico had been beset by political troubles since the death of the liberal reformist Benito Juárez in 1872. Mexico was embroiled in revolution at the turn of the century, as rebels such as Emiliano Zapata and Pancho Villa fought the dictatorial leader Porfirio Díaz and his successors. Villa's raids across the border prompted U.S. military intervention just before World War I. Not until 1920 was order restored, by the **Institutional Revolutionary Party** (PRI). Its very name a contradiction in terms, the PRI went to great lengths to appear democratic. Its constitution granted universal suffrage and the right to strike. However, the PRI leadership was an oligarchy that chose a president every six years and then arranged an election that guaranteed victory to its candidate.

Under this mild form of authoritarian rule, the upper classes prospered and the country modernized. However, the middle class was small and narrow, while the large lower classes—workers and peasants—lagged far behind the elite. Things improved somewhat under **Lázaro Cárdenas**, who became president in 1934. His land reform, in which more than 40 million acres were taken from the upper class and distributed among the peasantry, made him popular with the lower classes. Cárdenas also stood up to the United States by nationalizing the oil industry. Roosevelt lived up to his Good Neighbor promises and refrained from intervention. In exchange, Cárdenas compensated U.S. companies for their losses, then formed PEMEX, Mexico's state-run oil enterprise.

Authoritarianism became genuinely dictatorial in Brazil. Before 1930, the Brazilian government was dominated by wealthy landowners, most of whom owed their power and riches to the **coffee trade**. The Depression, however, plunged the country into crisis. In 1930, Getúlio Vargas, a cattle rancher, became president and ruled as dictator until 1945. Vargas governed from the far right, imitating Fascist Italy and Nazi Germany. He censored the press and authorized his secret police to torture political opponents. On the other hand, Vargas modernized the Brazilian economy, diversifying it and freeing it from its dependence on coffee. Under him, Brazil became Latin America's most industrialized nation. He was forced out of office by his army in 1945.

Argentina became a military dictatorship during the 1930s. In 1916, Hipólito Irigoyen of the Radical Party was elected president. His reform measures were intended to improve the lot of the lower and middle classes. Labor unions became more active. However, landowners and the upper class sabotaged Irigoyen's efforts and, in 1930, supported the army as it ousted Irigoyen. The military government lasted throughout World War II, but its efforts to return to the old export-based economy failed. Labor unrest increased, and the radical lower classes, the *descamisados* ("shirtless ones"), grew louder and more belligerent. Shortly after World War II, in 1946, General **Juan Perón**, along with his charismatic wife, Eva, would appeal to the lower classes in order to come to power—and then establish his own dictatorship.

QUICK REVIEW

1. Which of the following best applies to the League of Nations between the world wars?

   (A) The league provided strong leadership and effectively kept the world at peace.
   (B) The league was effective at functions such as providing famine relief and dealing with refugee issues but was otherwise weak.
   (C) U.S. leadership of the league enabled it to stop aggression in Ethiopia, Spain, and China.
   (D) No major European powers remained in the league by the middle of the 1930s.
   (E) From within, Adolf Hitler manipulated the league into granting Germany a number of territorial concessions.

2. Which of the following best describes the Communist takeover of Russia in 1917?

   (A) The Communists came to power after assassinating the royal family.
   (B) Defeat in World War I demoralized the country so badly that the population overthrew the tsar and voted the Communists into power.
   (C) Recognizing its limitations, the Provisional Government voluntarily stepped down from power, handing government over to the Communists.
   (D) Taking advantage of widespread radicalism and popular discontent with the Provisional Government, the Communists staged a successful armed insurrection.
   (E) The Communists won the majority of seats in parliamentary elections.

3. Who is generally considered to be the father of modern Turkey?

   (A) Mustafa Kemal Ataturk
   (B) Selim III
   (C) Enver Pasha
   (D) Suleiman the Magnificent
   (E) Reza Khan

4. Which Middle Eastern state became independent AND discovered vast oil reserves, both during the 1930s?

   (A) Egypt
   (B) Jordan
   (C) Syria
   (D) Palestine
   (E) Saudi Arabia

5. Who succeeded Sun Yat-sen as leader of the Nationalist Party?

   (A) Mao Tse-tung
   (B) Yuan Shikai
   (C) Chiang Kai-shek
   (D) Zhou Enlai
   (E) Lu Hsun

6. What was the Long March?

   (A) the epic retreat of the Chinese Communists, thousands of miles to the north
   (B) the Chinese Communists' massive offensive against Beijing
   (C) the years-long propaganda campaign the Chinese Communists waged in the countryside to capture the hearts of the peasantry
   (D) the years-long propaganda campaign the Chinese Communists waged in the cities to capture the hearts of the working class
   (E) the Chinese Communists' last-ditch defense of the city of Guangzhou

7. Before World War II, the most notorious atrocity committed by the Japanese military was

   (A) the strategic bombing of Bangkok.
   (B) the execution of British prisoners taken at Singapore.
   (C) the torture of Nepalese noncombatants in Kathmandu.
   (D) the massacre of Chinese civilians after the capture of Nanjing.
   (E) the refusal of Red Cross packages to U.S. officers captured at Guadalcanal.

8. What is the best description of *satyagraha*?

   (A) a fusion of Marxist ideology and Hindu theology directed against British rule
   (B) the policy of nonviolent resistance, mixed with Hindu principle, preached by Gandhi
   (C) the policy of nonviolent resistance, mixed with Muslim principle, preached by Gandhi
   (D) a fusion of Marxist ideology and Muslim radicalism advocated by Muhammad Ali Jinnah
   (E) Gandhi's ethical justification for the use of violence in resisting British rule

9. The violent suppression of demonstrators by British troops at which city almost plunged India into full-scale civil war?

   (A) Lucknow
   (B) Amritsar
   (C) Meerut
   (D) Calcutta
   (E) Mysore

10. In which Latin American state did the PRI control politics for most of the twentieth century?

   (A) Brazil
   (B) El Salvador
   (C) Mexico
   (D) Guatemala
   (E) Bolivia

Answers

1. **(B)** The League of Nations completed a significant amount of humanitarian work, but it failed to keep the peace in the long run. It was largely ineffective because it had few powers of enforcement. Furthermore, the United States, which became the most powerful and wealthiest state after World War I, never joined.

2. **(D)** Lenin and Trotsky overthrew the Provisional Government by armed force in the fall of 1917. The Provisional Government, despite its democratic goals, had failed to bring economic stability, land reform, and peace. As a result, few Russians supported it. This power vacuum provided the Bolsheviks with an opportunity to seize control of Russia.

3. **(A)** The Turkish colonel Mustafa Kemal, later named Ataturk, helped to defeat the British at Gallipoli in 1915. He later formed a new government in Ankara, drove the Greeks from Turkey, and negotiated a new treaty with the Allies. In 1923, once the Ottoman Empire had fallen, Kemal established the Turkish Republic and became its first president.

4. **(E)** In the 1920s an Arab prince named Ibn Saud united the many tribes living in the Arabian Peninsula. In 1932, he founded the kingdom of Saudi Arabia. At the time, it was the only Arab state that enjoyed full independence. In the late 1930s, with the discovery of vast amounts of petroleum on its soil, Saudi Arabia also became extremely wealthy and strategically important.

5. **(C)** When Sun Yat-sen died of cancer, leadership of the Nationalist Party fell to Chiang Kai-shek. Chiang was a Western-educated officer who later became a staunch anti-Communist. He tried to create a constitutional government in the late 1920s, but owing to China's general backwardness, the threat of Japanese invasion, and warlord anarchy, Chiang never ruled over a politically stable China.

6. **(A)** The Communist leader Mao Tse-tung led his forces on the Long March to northern China in 1934 and 1935. In doing so, he kept the Chinese Communist Party alive and established a base from which the Communists would launch military operations against the Nationalists later in the decade.

7. **(D)** In 1937, the Japanese invaded China in full force. They committed horrendous atrocities against the civilian population. The most notorious example was the so-called Rape of Nanjing in December, which included the massacre of 200,000 to 300,000 noncombatants.

8. **(B)** Mohandas K. Gandhi, who was the dominant figure of the Indian nationalist movement, preached the policy of nonviolent resistance to British authority. In one nonviolent action, Gandhi led 50,000 people in a 200-mile march to the seashore, where they protested the British imposition of a high tax on salt by making salt illegally. Gandhi agreed to be arrested without a fight once British troops arrived on the scene.

9. **(B)** Demonstrations and protests often led to clashes with the British. In 1919, at Amritsar, British troops fired on unarmed protesters, and 379 people were killed. This massacre led to chaos in India. As a result, the British arrested Gandhi and imposed a strict crackdown.

10. **(C)** Although the PRI tried to create the appearance of a democratic government in Mexico, in reality, its leadership was an oligarchy that chose a president every six years, then arranged an election that guaranteed victory to its own candidates.

World War II and the Holocaust

CHAPTER 30

- World War II (Allies versus the Axis)
- Aggression versus appeasement before the war
- Blitzkrieg warfare and the effects of tanks and aircraft
- The Lend-Lease program
- The Greater East Asian Co-Prosperity Sphere
- Pivotal battles (Midway, El Alamein, Stalingrad, the D-Day landings)
- Submarines and the war at sea
- Strategic bombing and the atomic bomb
- War crimes, crimes against humanity, and genocide
- The Holocaust (Final Solution)
- The Cold War

World War II (September 1939–September 1945) was and remains the biggest, costliest, and deadliest armed conflict in human history. Beyond that, its long-term global impact continued to be felt in world politics, economics, and diplomacy for five decades.

Before the war ended, sixty-one nations joined the fighting. They were divided into two coalitions, the **Axis Powers** and the **Allied Powers**. The major combatants were

- The Axis Powers: Nazi Germany, Fascist Italy (joined the war in June 1940; left the war in July 1943), and Japan
- The Allied Powers: Great Britain, France (left the war in June 1940), Canada, Australia, New Zealand, the Soviet Union (joined the war in June 1941), and the United States (joined the war in December 1941).

The war was waged over two-thirds of the entire planet. Economically, it has been calculated to have cost $1.6 trillion in 1940s dollars ($4 trillion to $5 trillion in contemporary terms). By the war's midpoint, somewhere between one-quarter and one-third of the world's productive capacity was directly dedicated to war production.

Concerning the grimmest statistic of all, somewhere between 55 to 60 million people were killed during the war. Almost half of those who died were civilians. World War II involved **genocide** as well. Millions of victims—6 million of them Jewish—perished in the German campaign of racial extermination known as the **Holocaust**.

World War II also shifted the balance of global strength completely. World War I had begun the process of toppling the powers of Europe from their position of dominance; World War II finished it. When World War II was over, only two nations, the United States and the Soviet Union, had the military and economic might to affect the course of world events. The great geopolitical struggle between these two new superpowers, the **Cold War**, was the dominant factor shaping global diplomacy, military affairs, and international trade for four and a half decades. World War II also destroyed the imperial might of the European powers. From the 1940s through the 1970s, a massive wave of **decolonization** swept through the non-Western world, and dozens of nations in Africa and Asia became free.

In addition, World War II changed the patterns of international trade, shifted global wealth to the superpowers (especially the United States), spurred a boom in technological and scientific innovation that would be put to civilian use long after the war was over, brought women into the workplace, and had countless other social, economic, and cultural effects. For these and many other reasons, World War II can be considered not only the largest military enterprise in world history but also the most influential.

THE ROAD TO WAR

Unlike World War I, whose origins were quite complex, World War II resulted from a straightforward pattern of aggression on the part of Nazi Germany, Fascist Italy, and Japan. Especially in Europe, major democracies responded weakly and passively. Hamstrung by the Great Depression, anxious to avoid another global conflict, and simply hoping that each aggressive move would be the last, countries such as France, Britain, and the United States did little to stand up to the dictatorships. This policy of letting aggressors have what they want in the hope they will demand no more is known as **appeasement**. The **League of Nations** proved almost useless in dealing with foreign-policy crises. Here is a timetable of what is often referred to as the road to war:

- 1933:
  —Hitler withdrew from the League of Nations.

- 1935:
  —Hitler openly began to rebuild the German army and navy, violating the disarmament clauses of the Treaty of Versailles.
  —Mussolini invaded Ethiopia, causing international outrage. The League of Nations imposed weak sanctions. They did not prevent Italy from taking Ethiopia; their effect was to anger Mussolini and draw him closer to Hitler.
  —The Soviet Union, fearful of Germany, concluded an alliance with France. Both countries agreed to protect Czechoslovakia. France also signed a treaty to protect Poland. This policy of antifascist cooperation was known as **collective security**.

- 1936:
  —Again violating the Treaty of Versailles, Hitler sent troops into the Rhineland, a demilitarized zone. France and Britain protested but took no action. This lack of response set a precedent, in which Hitler would act and the democracies would appease him.

—Mussolini completed his conquest of Ethiopia.

—The Spanish Civil War (1936–1939) began with Francisco Franco's military uprising against the leftist government. Because Franco was allied with Spanish fascists, Mussolini and Hitler assisted him (the Germans took the opportunity to test tanks, airplanes, and new tactics, including terror bombing). Stalin attempted to aid the Spanish government and expected France and Britain to help him do so. He was disappointed when they did not, and his trust in the Western democracies eroded. Aside from the USSR, only a contingent of volunteers, the International Brigades, joined against the rebels. Franco won, became dictator of Spain, and ruled till his death in 1975.

- 1937:
  —In Japan, the military gained control of the government.
  —Germany, Italy, and Japan formed their alliance.
  —Japan invaded mainland China, where the Japanese committed terrible atrocities, including the **Rape of Nanjing**.

- 1938:
  —Germany annexed Austria in the **Anschluss** ("union").
  —Hitler announced plans to seize the Sudetenland, formerly German territory, given to Czechoslovakia after World War I. Mussolini and Hitler met with Neville Chamberlain, Britain's prime minister, and the French premier at the German city of Munich. The Czechoslovaks were not invited; neither were the Soviets, who, with France, had promised to protect Czechoslovakia from aggression. Britain and France let Germany have the Sudetenland in exchange for Hitler's promise to expand no further. Chamberlain claimed to have guaranteed "peace in our time," but the **Munich Agreement** was **appeasement** at its worst. It also destroyed collective security: Stalin, angry and betrayed, chose not to trust Britain and France any further.
  —Japanese and Soviet troops clashed on the Siberian border.

- 1939:
  —Germany took the rest of Czechoslovakia. By doing so Hitler showed the world how foolish France and Britain had been to believe his promises.
  —Germany took western Lithuania.
  —Italy invaded Albania.
  —The Japanese and Soviets fought again in Siberia.
  —Hitler began to make claims on Polish territory that had formerly belonged to Germany. Realizing that this was where Hitler would act next, France and Britain promised to guarantee Poland's safety.
  —Wishing to avoid a two-front war, Hitler sought to reach an agreement with Stalin before invading Poland. In August, Stalin, no longer trusting Britain and France, agreed to sign a nonaggression pact with Hitler. This **Nazi-Soviet Pact** kept the USSR neutral and opened the way for Hitler to invade Poland.
  —On September 1, 1939, Germany invaded Poland and thus World War II began.

THE AXIS ASCENDANT, 1939–1941

During the first half of the war, the Axis powers were triumphant. In Europe, the only major powers opposing Germany were France and Britain. The USSR had agreed to remain neutral, and the United States, sunk into isolationism, stayed out of the fighting as well. In Asia, Japan expanded its war against China to include a greater war of conquest against British, Dutch, and French colonies in Southeast Asia.

New Technology and World War II

In terms of combat and technology, World War II was very different from World War I. In the latter, military technology had favored the defensive, resulting in the hellish stalemate of trench warfare. By the time World War II began, military technology had developed in such a way as to make warfare more rapid and more dynamic.

At sea, naval aircraft, aircraft carriers, new landing craft that allowed marine troops to invade faraway islands and beachheads, and long-range submarines gave the combatants a truly global reach. On the ground, new artillery and, especially, tanks gave armies tremendous offensive punch, as well as the ability to move quickly. In the air, giant strategic bombers were able to fly thousands of miles and drop unheard-of quantities of explosives, further increasing offensive capacity.

This new technology helped make World War II a fast-paced, decisive conflict. It also had the unfortunate effect of making warfare deadlier and involving civilians to a degree never before imagined.

The need to develop better and more effective military technology had a tremendous effect on civilian technology long after the war was over. Among the many wartime innovations that played a large role in postwar life were radar, sonar; jet aircraft, synthetic materials (such as nylon), rocketry, atomic energy, and computer science.

> **TIP**
>
> Among the many wartime innovations that played a large role in postwar life were radar, sonar; jet aircraft, synthetic materials (such as nylon), rocketry, atomic energy, and computer science.

Blitzkrieg, the Invasion of Poland, and Sitzkrieg

The war began with Germany's invasion of Poland, in September 1939 (although it must be remembered that Japan had been fighting China since 1937). The new offensive character of war could be seen right away in Germany's innovative method of **Blitzkrieg** ("lightning war"), which used tanks and airplanes to penetrate deeply and quickly into enemy territory. Within weeks, the fighting in Poland was over—especially because the USSR invaded the eastern half of the country, in accordance with the Nazi-Soviet Pact.

In contrast to Germany's fast action, Britain and France, although they declared war, did very little. With an outdated World War I mentality, the Allies waited for Germany to attack them, believing that, as in 1914, the defense would prevail. While Britain and France marked time, Germany prepared its attack. The winter of 1939–1940 was nicknamed Sitzkrieg ("phony war").

Germany's Invasion of Western Europe and the Fall of France

In April 1940, Hitler launched his assault on Western Europe. The next several months were stunningly successful. Denmark, Norway, Luxembourg, Belgium, and the Netherlands were defeated in weeks, if not days.

Most amazing of all was the fall of France. The Germans attacked France on May 10. By June 22, the largest and most powerful democracy on the European continent had surrendered. The French had been confident that their great chain of border fortifications, the Maginot Line, would protect them. The German Blitzkrieg sidestepped the Maginot Line and sent tanks streaming into northern France. The defeat of France shocked the world. It also left Great Britain in the seemingly hopeless position of fighting Germany and Italy (which joined the war in June) by itself.

The Battle of Britain

From the summer of 1940 to the spring of 1941, Germany concentrated its attention on Britain. Meanwhile, Italy launched attacks in the Mediterranean, trying to take Greece, Yugoslavia, and Egypt (still under British protection). Hitler's attempt to knock Britain out of the war failed. The Royal Navy protected the British Isles from invasion. When Hitler tried to win the war from the air, the Royal Air Force defended England's skies in the **Battle of Britain**.

Britain held out thanks to the skill of its air force, its use of radar, and economic aid from Canada and the United States (although the United States was neutral, the government of Franklin Roosevelt was sympathetic, and its **Lend-Lease program** of economic assistance kept Britain and, later, the USSR well-supplied throughout the war).

Invasions in the East and Operation Barbarossa

In the spring and summer of 1941, Hitler shifted his focus from Britain to Eastern Europe. Mussolini's wars in Greece, Yugoslavia, and North Africa had gone wrong, and Germany had to assist him. One of Hitler's most skilled tank commanders, Erwin Rommel, was sent to Africa to fight the British in Egypt.

Hitler also had a larger plan in mind: the invasion of the Soviet Union, code-named **Operation Barbarossa**. Although the USSR and Germany had carefully observed their pact of neutrality since August 1939, Hitler, having eliminated France from the war, felt confident enough to fight the USSR, even though Britain had not yet been defeated.

On June 22, 1941, Germany invaded the Soviet Union, starting the largest ground war in history. From this point onward, 60 to 75 percent of the German armed forces would fight on this eastern front. At first, it looked as though the USSR would fall as quickly as France had. German forces surrounded Leningrad, the USSR's second largest city, placing it under the worst siege in modern times. They drove deep into Ukraine and southern Russia. They also reached the outskirts of Moscow, the capital. A last-ditch defensive effort in December halted the German advance, but only barely.

Japanese Aggression in Southeast Asia

In the Pacific, fighting between China and Japan continued. Japan's war effort widened in 1940 and 1941, as French, Dutch, and British misfortunes in Europe made their Asian empires vulnerable. When France fell in 1940, Japan began to threaten its colony in Indochina. Japan's eventual goal was to establish its **Greater East Asian Co-Prosperity Sphere** over the entire Chinese coast, all of Southeast Asia, India, Indonesia, and perhaps Australia and New Zealand.

By the summer of 1941, Japan's takeover of Indochina and increased aggression toward Southeast Asia compelled the United States, already upset at Japanese atrocities in China, to impose economic sanctions. Without steel, oil, and other raw materials from the United States, the Japanese war effort on the Asian mainland would be badly damaged. Japan viewed the embargo as an act of war and in late 1941 began to plan a military assault against the United States.

Pearl Harbor and Japan's Assault on the South Pacific

On December 7, 1941, just as the Soviets were halting the Germans outside Moscow, Japan launched its surprise attack on the U.S. naval installation at **Pearl Harbor**, Hawaii. At the same time, the Japanese bombed and invaded U.S. bases throughout the Pacific and on the Philippines.

By the spring of 1942, the Japanese were masters of the South Pacific and Southeast Asia, having captured Hong Kong, Indochina, Thailand, part of Burma, the Malaysian Peninsula (including the great British base of Singapore), the Philippines, Indonesia (the Dutch East Indies), and hundreds of small Pacific islands. However, the effect of the Japanese attack was to bring the United States into World War II, both in the Pacific and in Europe (several days after Pearl Harbor, Germany joined Japan in declaring war on the United States).

Because Pearl Harbor, however devastating, was not a knockout blow, what the Japanese had managed to do was to rouse one of the world's largest countries—with great humanpower resources and the most productive economy on earth—and involve it in the war. In the long term, neither Japan nor Germany would be able to match America's capacity for military industrialization or mass conscription of troops.

THE ALLIED QUEST FOR VICTORY, 1942–1945
The Shifting Balance of World War II

The second half of the war, 1942 through 1945, was very different in character from the first. Most obviously, a different set of countries was involved. France had dropped out, but the USSR and the United States had joined in. Just as important, a different set of factors came into play. The Axis Powers' advantage lay in the skill and quality of Germany's and Japan's armed forces. Allied advantages, especially once the Soviets and Americans became involved, were geographic size, huge reserves of humanpower, large economies, and abundant natural resources.

This distribution of advantages meant that the longer the war lasted, the more likely it was that the Allies would win. Realizing that time was against them, Germany and Japan had been trying to gain decisive victories between 1939 and the end of 1941. Germany's failure to take Moscow and Japan's failure to cripple America permanently with its initial sweep through the Pacific ended the Axis's chances of ending the war quickly. Although Germany and Japan still held the advantage when 1942 began, all the long-term trends were against them.

The Turning Point: 1942

A handful of battles during the summer and fall of 1942 completely changed the tide of the war. If the Axis had won these encounters, they might have been able to force a favorable end to the war. By losing all three, Japan and Germany wasted vast amounts of irreplaceable troops, weapons, and equipment—and lost the strategic initiative they had enjoyed since 1939. These battles were

- **Midway** (June 1942), a naval battle in which the United States destroyed much of the Japanese aircraft-carrier fleet;
- **El Alamein** (July–November 1942), where the British turned back the drive of German tanks toward Egypt and the Suez Canal;
- **Stalingrad** (August 1942–February 1943), a savage clash on the Volga, where the Soviets prevented Germany from capturing south Russia and oil reserves in the east.

With these victories, the Allies had held on long enough for their advantages—larger populations and larger economies—to become decisive.

The European and Mediterranean Theaters of Combat, World War II, 1942.
From September 1939 until the autumn of 1942, the Axis Powers—Germany, Italy, and Japan—succeeded in seizing the military initiative and keeping it. By the middle of 1942, Nazi Germany had reached the height of its power. The areas shaded in gray mark territory that was controlled directly by Germany before the war, belonged to its allies, or had been conquered by it during the war. Not long after this point, primarily because of defeats at El Alamein and Stalingrad, the tide of war turned against the Germans and their partners.

The Shifting Tide: 1943 and 1944

In 1943 and 1944, the Allies determined the direction and pace of the war effort. In the Pacific, the Americans pushed the Japanese steadily westward. Australia, India, Burma, and large parts of China remained free and joined in the fighting. Guerrilla uprisings in Thailand, Vietnam, Indonesia, and the Philippines hurt the Japanese badly.

On the European and Mediterranean fronts, Britain and America took control of North Africa and then used it as a platform from which to invade Italy, depose Mussolini's Fascist government, and knock Italy out of the war. From the east, the Soviets pushed the Germans out of their country, into Eastern Europe, and toward Berlin.

In June 1944, in the **D-Day invasion** (technically known as Operation Overlord, or the Normandy Invasion), British, Canadian, and American troops, ships, and aircraft crossed the English Channel and landed on the coast of France. On land, Hitler now faced Allied threats from three directions: the eastern front, the Italian peninsula, and Western Europe.

War at Sea and in the Air

At sea, the Allies neutralized the last weapon with which Germany had any real chance of threatening them: the **submarine fleet**, which became ineffective by mid-1943.

In the air, the Allies had complete control of the skies by late 1943. From that point forward, British and American aircraft were able to bomb German-held Europe with impunity. After the summer of 1944, American forces had gone far enough across the Pacific that U.S. bombers were able to pound Japan from the air constantly. This practice of **strategic bombing** caused immense damage and killed tens of thousands of civilians. It remains one of the most controversial aspects of the Allied war effort.

The End of World War II

In 1945, the Axis surrendered. Germany gave up the fight first. Caught between the Anglo-American Allies in the west and the Soviet advance from the east, Hitler chose to commit suicide on April 30. Germany stopped fighting in early May.

Despite the fact that it had no hope of winning, Japan continued its struggle against the Allies. The U.S. Navy and Marines closed in on the Japanese home islands, while U.S. bombers continued their assault from the skies.

America's new president, Harry Truman (who came to the Oval Office in April 1945, when Franklin Roosevelt died), greatly feared that an invasion of the Japanese islands would cost tens of thousands of American and Japanese lives. He hoped to win from the air, but conventional bombardment did not seem to be forcing the Japanese to surrender. In July, an international team of scientists working for the Allies tested the first operational atomic bomb in New Mexico. Truman chose to use the A-bomb against the Japanese.

After warning Japan's government that the United States had a new weapon of terrible power, Truman acted. On August 6, 1945, a B-29 bomber named *Enola Gay* dropped an atomic bomb on **Hiroshima**. The initial blast killed at least 78,000 people and destroyed the entire city center; tens of thousands more died later, of burns or radioactive fallout. When the Japanese government ignored Truman's next request for surrender, the Americans dropped a second bomb on August 9, on the port of Nagasaki. The following week, the Japanese agreed to a cease-fire. They surrendered officially on September 2.

THE HOLOCAUST AND OTHER WAR CRIMES

War Crimes and Crimes Against Humanity

The most grisly aspect of World War II involved the many war crimes committed during the seventy-three months of fighting. Of the 55 to 60 million people who died during the war, approximately half were civilians. A good number were killed by means that fell outside the bounds established by international law or acceptable military behavior. Many of these atrocities were horrendous enough that the phrase "war crime" seemed inadequate to describe them. It was after World War II, therefore, that the phrase "**crime against humanity**" entered the world's legal vocabularies.

The Axis Powers were not the only nations to kill civilians. The Red Army committed many crimes—rape, plunder, wanton destruction of civilian property—as the Soviets advanced through Eastern Europe and Germany. The American and British policy of strategic bombing, both over Japan and German-held Europe, caused tremendous civilian suffering. Some commentators, including many Germans and Japanese, have argued that strategic bombing can be considered a war crime (it should be noted that this is a minority opinion). America remains the only nation that has ever used an atomic or nuclear weapon in wartime, and the question of whether it was necessary to use it against Japan continues to be a matter of controversy.

Japanese War Crimes

Nonetheless, it was the Axis that committed war crimes and crimes against humanity systematically and on a large scale. In Asia, Japan was guilty of a wide variety of atrocities. Even before World War II, Japanese forces had raped, pillaged, and butchered civilian populations in many Chinese cities, most notably Nanjing in December 1937.

As the Greater East Asian Co-Prosperity Sphere widened during World War II, Japanese soldiers continued to terrorize civilian populations, not just in China but in all of Southeast Asia. On many occasions, Japanese armies killed American, British, and Asian prisoners of war, against all legal conventions pertaining to military conduct. Prisoners of war were also used as subjects for Japanese scientific experiments, especially for testing biological and chemical weapons. Finally, the Japanese military rounded up women from Korea and Southeast Asia and forced them to serve as prostitutes, or "comfort women," for Japanese soldiers. After the war, the U.S. military authorities held a series of Tokyo Trials, during which Japanese civilian and military officials were tried for these crimes.

Nazi Atrocities

More infamous were the crimes against humanity committed by the Germans. Prior to the war, the Nazis operated an extensive apparatus of terror, which included a secret police (the Gestapo) and concentration camps (such as Dachau). Dissidents (including Protestant and, especially, Catholic religious leaders who protested Nazi policy) had been imprisoned, even executed, since the early 1930s.

As the war began and then progressed, the Nazis began to "euthanize" medical patients with incurable diseases, venereal diseases, or tuberculosis. They killed homosexuals, people with mental disabilities, and political dissidents. They performed medical and scientific experiments on human subjects, typically to the point of mutilation and death (Jews and Soviet prisoners of war were used most often).

Nazi Racial Policy and Genocide

Most heinous were the Nazi campaigns of **genocide** (a term devised in the 1940s, by a Jewish lawyer, to reflect the special, premeditated nature of the crime). The Nazis targeted a number of ethnic and cultural groups. Roma (Gypsies) and Slavs were among those they considered to be "subhuman" or "undesirable."

Most of all, the Nazis hated the Jews. After Hitler's rise to power in 1933, the Nazis passed a number of anti-Semitic policies that grew worse over time. The worst had been the **Nuremberg Laws** (1935), which deprived German Jews of their civil rights. Before the war, however, violence against Jews was not yet official policy, even though, in reality, thousands of Jews were harassed and beaten and their homes and businesses vandalized during the late 1930s. In November 1938, on Kristallnacht ("Night of Broken Glass"), thousands of Jewish shops, synagogues, and homes throughout Germany and Austria were attacked or burned in a single night.

It was during the war that Nazi anti-Semitic policy escalated to the point of genocide. There were 11 million Jews in Europe before the beginning of the war. In 1939 and 1940, as the Germans brought more of Europe under their control, Nazi authorities began to round up Jews and detain them, either in **ghettos** or in existing concentration camps, such as Dachau. It was sometime in 1941 that the order for genocide came down from above. Although no written orders survive, it is certain that, ultimately, the command was issued by Hitler himself.

The Holocaust

Nazi genocidal policy is popularly referred to by the name given it by the Jews: the **Holocaust**. The Nazis referred to it as the **Final Solution**. Whatever its name, it evolved as follows:

- 1939–1940:
  —Jews were forced to wear the yellow star to identify themselves.
  —Polish Jews were rounded up and placed in ghettos.
  —Other European Jews were imprisoned in concentration and transit camps.
  —Some Jews were sporadically executed or died by random violence.

- 1941:
  —In July, an order "to make preparations for the general final solution of the Jewish problem within the German sphere of influence in Europe" was handed down to the SS (the Nazi security forces).

—The Nazis organized **special action squads** (*Einsatzgruppen*) to follow the German army into the Soviet Union, round up Jews, and execute them by shooting.

—Dissatisfaction with the special action squads grew. This method of execution was considered to be too slow, too wasteful of ammunition, and too hard on the morale of the executioners. Because the squads only buried the bodies instead of destroying them, the danger remained that the victims could later be found.

—Experiments with carbon monoxide and other gases were carried out at various concentration camps in an attempt to find an "efficient" way to kill large numbers of victims. Experimental cremation methods were tested.

—Late in the year, construction of special camps for execution and cremation began.

—A cyanide-based insecticide, Zyklon-B, was chosen as the means of extermination.

- 1942:

  —In January, fifteen Nazi officials met in the suburbs of Berlin. Here, at the **Wannsee Conference**, it was decided to use special **extermination camps**, already under construction in German-held Poland, to eliminate Jews and other undesirables. Among these were Majdanek, Chelmno, Belzec, Sobibor, and Treblinka. The largest and most infamous was **Auschwitz-Birkenau**.

  —The special extermination camps went into operation.

- 1943–1945:

  —Jews from all over Europe were shipped to the extermination camps. Other victims were also taken there. Victims were gassed, their bodies processed, their remains cremated.

  —Soviet liberation of camps in Poland began in 1944. Auschwitz-Birkenau was liberated in early 1945.

  —Camps in the west were liberated by the British and Americans.

In the end, the Final Solution resulted in millions of deaths. Of Europe's 11 million Jews, approximately 6 million were killed. In addition, many non-Jewish victims (especially Roma) perished.

It was mainly to punish these crimes that the Americans, British, and Soviets organized the Nuremberg Trials (1946), which prosecuted Nazi leaders. During these trials, the term *crime against humanity* was codified as law. In 1948, in a collective effort to avoid such atrocities in the future, the United Nations adopted the Universal Declaration of Human Rights.

QUICK REVIEW

1. The term *appeasement* best applies to which of the following episodes?

   (A) Soviet support of the Spanish Republic against Franco's revolt in 1936
   (B) Ethiopia's resistance to Italy's 1935 invasion
   (C) France's and Britain's 1938 agreement with Germany at Munich, regarding the Sudetenland
   (D) France's and Britain's willingness to defend Poland in the fall of 1939
   (E) the Soviet takeover of Estonia, Latvia, and Lithuania in 1939 and 1940

2. The League of Nations' response to Italy's invasion of Ethiopia

   (A) strengthened ties between Italy and Germany.
   (B) boosted the League's prestige.
   (C) showed how France and Britain could stand up against Fascist aggression.
   (D) convinced the USSR to join Japan in an anti-European alliance.
   (E) drew Italy into a closer partnership with Austria.

3. The overall course of World War II is best described as follows:

   (A) The Allies fought well in the beginning, faltered during the middle years of the war, then came back to achieve victory.
   (B) From the beginning, the Axis Powers, facing an Allied coalition that possessed larger armies and economies, had no realistic hope of winning the war.
   (C) Only Italy's military prowess gave the Axis Powers any hope of victory; after the Italian surrender, the war turned in favor of the Allies.
   (D) Axis performance during the early stages of the war was mediocre; it sharply improved in the middle years of the war, and only the invention of the atomic bomb saved the Allies.
   (E) The skill and quality of German and Japanese forces nearly brought about an early Axis victory, but halfway through the war, the Allies, with their long-term economic and demographic advantages, turned the tide in their favor.

4. The failure of collective security convinced Stalin to

   (A) resign all his political posts.
   (B) sign a treaty of neutrality with Nazi Germany.
   (C) declare war on Nazi Germany.
   (D) conclude an alliance with Poland.
   (E) take over Czechoslovakia in an effort to protect the Soviet border.

5. Besides the Jews, what ethnic group suffered the worst losses, proportionally, as a result of Germany's Final Solution?

   (A) Kosovar Albanians
   (B) Estonians
   (C) Hungarians
   (D) Roma (Gypsies)
   (E) Ukrainians

6. What did France erroneously trust to keep it safe from German invasion?

   (A) the French air force
   (B) the Maginot Line
   (C) the Vosges Mountains
   (D) the Belgian army
   (E) the threat of Soviet invasion from the east

7. What city experienced the worst siege not just of World War II but of the entire modern era?

   (A) Leningrad
   (B) Krakow
   (C) Stalingrad
   (D) Dresden
   (E) Nagasaki

8. What was the Greater East Asian Co-Prosperity Sphere?

   (A) an association of British colonies in Southeast Asia
   (B) a military alliance that resisted the Japanese attack on Southeast Asia
   (C) a free-trade zone whose economic activity was disrupted by Japanese invasion
   (D) the name given by the Japanese to the Asian empire they conquered before and during World War II
   (E) the formal name of the Dutch colony in Indonesia

9. If the Axis Powers had won World War II, which of the following Allied operations would they most likely have punished as a war crime?

   (A) British and U.S. strategic bombing of German and Japanese cities
   (B) the D-Day landings in northwestern France
   (C) Soviet conduct during the battle of Kiev
   (D) the U.S. and British takeover of Sicily
   (E) the sinking of Japanese aircraft carriers by U.S. pilots at Midway

10. Japanese war crimes included which of the following?

    I. abuse of Chinese and Southeast Asian civilians
    II. execution of U.S., British, and Australian prisoners of war
    III. forced prostitution of women from Korea and Southeast Asia
    IV. the use of prisoners as subjects in chemical- and biological-weapons experiments

    (A) I only
    (B) I, II, and III
    (C) II and III only
    (D) II, III, and IV
    (E) all of the above

Answers

1. **(C)** In diplomacy, appeasement is the policy of allowing a potential aggressor what it wants in the hope that the aggression will cease. It is sometimes a wise option. In 1938, when the British prime minister, Neville Chamberlain, and his French counterpart accepted Hitler's word that his expansion would stop with the Sudetenland, it was not.

2. **(A)** League of Nations sanctions were too weak to stop Italy from taking Ethopia but punitive enough to make Mussolini angry at Britain and France, the countries that had sponsored the sanctions. He withdrew from the League of Nations and pursued closer ties with Hitler.

3. **(E)** The Axis Powers were incredibly successful during the early years of the war, conquering vast amounts of territory and nearly achieving victory. Only between mid-1942 and early 1943 did a string of key battles improve the situation of the Allies, who were then able to take advantage of their large populations and economies.

4. **(B)** Convinced by the weak response of Britain and France during the Spanish Civil War and the Sudetenland Crisis that neither

country could be relied on as an ally, Stalin concluded that his safest course of action was to agree to neutrality with Hitler, thereby turning him against the West for what he hoped (incorrectly) would be a long time.

5. **(D)** Considered by the Nazis to be "undesirables," like the Slavs and Jews, the Roma, known colloquially as Gypsies, were terribly persecuted by them. It is thought that more than half of Europe's Roma perished in the Holocaust. Roma still suffer severe racial discrimination in central and eastern Europe.

6. **(B)** Guessing wrongly that future wars would, like World War I, be defensive in nature, the French built a massive chain of fortifications along most of their border with Germany. The more innovative and flexible Germans found ways to sidestep this Maginot Line when they invaded in 1940.

7. **(A)** Leningrad, the Soviet Union's second-largest city, was surrounded by German troops in September 1941. It never surrendered but remained under siege until January 1944. At least 1 million people died, many of starvation and winter cold; some estimates put the death toll at 1.5 to 2 million.

8. **(D)** This euphemistic term was coined by the Japanese to describe their expanding zone of conquest. Claiming on one hand to liberate Asia from Western colonizers, the Japanese, who considered Chinese and Southeast Asians to be racial inferiors, imposed their own, much crueler form of imperialism.

9. **(A)** Strategic bombing killed hundreds of thousands of civilians in Japan and occupied Europe. Its military effectiveness and morality remain subjects of controversy even today.

10. **(E)** Overshadowed by the Nazi Holocaust, Japanese war crimes, which were motivated by aggressive, nationalist militarism, and a pronounced sense of racial superiority, included all the atrocities listed here. Just as Nazi crimes were punished at the Nuremberg Trials, Japanese crimes were prosecuted at the Tokyo Trials.

The Cold War

CHAPTER 31

- The Cold War
- The Yalta Conference
- The United Nations
- The containment strategy (the Truman Doctrine and the Marshall Plan)
- NATO versus the Warsaw Pact
- Chinese communism and the Sino-Soviet split
- The domino principle
- The Korean and Vietnam wars
- The Soviet invasions of Hungary and Czechoslovakia
- National liberation and decolonization
- Nonalignment, the third world, and proxy wars
- The Berlin Wall and the Cuban Missile Crisis
- The nuclear arms race, deterrence, and MAD
- Détente
- Solidarity and unrest in Eastern Europe
- Perestroika and glasnost
- The fall of the Berlin Wall
- The collapse of the USSR

The end of World War II fundamentally shifted global power. For over 200 years, the constantly shifting balance of power among six or seven European nations had determined the course of world events. With Europe devastated by the war, only two nations possessed true global strength: the United States and the Soviet Union. Because these two nations were orders of magnitude stronger and wealthier than any great power had been before them, they were referred to as **superpowers**.

The popular name given to the state of rivalry that existed between the United States and the USSR from 1945 to 1991 is the **Cold War**. It divided the world into hostile camps—although its bipolar nature was complicated by the eventual breakup of the alliance between Communist China and the Soviet Union. The Cold War gave birth to a nuclear arms race that brought into the world the deadliest weapons ever seen. The great wave of **decolonization** that took place after World War II (see Chapter 32) was deeply affected by the Cold War, because newly free nations often had to choose between allying with one superpower or another. Although the United States and USSR never went to war with each other, dozens of small and medium-size conflicts were fought worldwide between 1945 and the end of the Cold War, killing an estimated total of 50 million people, more than half of them civilian.

The Cold War finally ended in the late 1980s and early 1990s, with the collapse of communism in Eastern Europe and the breakup of the Soviet Union.

WARTIME DIPLOMACY

The wartime alliance between the United States, Great Britain, and the Soviet Union had been a marriage of convenience. Although the United States and Britain were mutually sympathetic, they cooperated with the USSR and its dictator, Joseph Stalin, only because they needed Soviet help to defeat Hitler. Even during the war effort, many tensions arose between Franklin Roosevelt and Winston Churchill on one hand and Stalin on the other. It was clear to all that things would only get worse after the war ended.

The issues concerning the wartime allies were discussed at three summit meetings: the Teheran Conference (November 1943), the Yalta Conference (February 1945), and the Potsdam Conference (July 1945). The questions dealt with included the following:

- *Second front*: The USSR, which fought the vast bulk of the German army, desperately wanted its allies to open up a second front in western Europe as soon as possible. At Teheran, it was decided to invade France in June 1944.
- *Japan*: In exchange for Asian territory, the Soviets agreed to help fight Japan after Germany was defeated. The Americans struck this deal before the atomic bomb was tested.
- *Division and denazification of Germany and Austria*: Germany was to be occupied and divided into four sectors: British, French, U.S., and Soviet. Berlin, which fell into the Soviet zone, was likewise divided, and the western parts of the city were guaranteed highway, air, and rail access to the other zones. Austria was similarly partitioned. Both countries were to undergo a process of denazification, in which former Nazis would be removed from public offices and positions of authority. Germany was to repay $20 billion in reparations. The division of Germany lasted until the end of the Cold War. Austria was allowed to reunify in 1955.
- *United Nations*: Just as Woodrow Wilson had created the League of Nations after World War I, Franklin Roosevelt hoped to establish a new international body, stronger and more effective than the League had been. This body was to be called the **United Nations.**
- *Fate of Eastern Europe*: By far, this was the most sensitive issue. As they defeated Germany, Soviet troops occupied Eastern Europe. It was clear that Stalin hoped to turn this territory into a Soviet sphere of influence. Roosevelt and Churchill were deeply concerned, but Stalin had millions of troops in the region and to press him too hard on this question was to risk having him drop out of the war before Germany was defeated. At Yalta, Roosevelt and Churchill came up with an awkward compromise. They agreed that the USSR would have informal influence in certain East European nations. In exchange, they asked the Soviets to promise to allow free elections throughout Eastern Europe. Stalin agreed and then broke his promises. Some historians see Roosevelt and Churchill as having betrayed Eastern Europe; others argue that there was little they could have done, considering the situation's military realities.

THE COLD WAR BEGINS, 1945–1949

The first stage of the Cold War can be considered to have lasted from 1945 to 1949. Although there were concerns about other parts of the world, such as Japan, Korea, and China, the focus of the Cold War during these early years was primarily European and Mediterranean. For Europe itself, of course, this was a bitter comedown. From being the shaper of world events, Europe—reduced to the superpowers' battleground—was now shaped by them.

The Cold War Division of Europe, 1957.
From 1945 until 1989, the Cold War divided the nations of Europe—with only a few exceptions—into two camps, one dominated by the Soviet Union, the other led by the United States and its European allies. By the mid-1950s, the so-called Iron Curtain had descended over Europe. The nations of the West were joined by the North Atlantic Treaty Organization, a military alliance, and many also joined in the European Economic Community. The Eastern bloc was held together by the Soviet-imposed military alliance known as the Warsaw Pact, as well as COMECON, an economic union led by the USSR.

The Soviet Absorption of Eastern Europe

From 1945 through 1948, the USSR took over Eastern Europe, installing pro-Soviet, communist governments in the eastern half of Germany and in Poland, Czechoslovakia, Hungary, Romania, and Bulgaria. Yugoslavia became communist as well, but under its stubbornly independent leader, Josip Tito, Yugoslavia broke with the USSR in 1948. Albania, also communist, allied with the Soviets until Stalin's death; the mid-1950s, it isolated itself from both superpowers. In March 1946, Winston Churchill warned of the permanent division of the continent in his famous "**iron curtain**" speech.

All of this was a violation of the Soviets' promises at Yalta. In addition, the USSR was threatening Iran and Turkey in 1945 and 1946. The Yugoslavs were sponsoring a communist rebellion in Greece. This brought the Soviet bloc perilously close to the oil fields of the Middle East, as well as the important waterways of the eastern Mediterranean.

Stalin's policy during these years was simple: to gain as much territory as possible without a fight. Although they kept it as secret as possible, the Soviets had been hurt badly by World War II. They had lost 25 million to 28 million dead. One-third of their entire economy had been destroyed. The USSR could not afford to fight the West. On the other hand, Stalin wanted a buffer zone in Eastern Europe, in order to protect his country from suffering again as it had in World War II. Also, because the United States had atomic weaponry and the USSR did not, Stalin felt even more vulnerable. His goal was to push the Americans as hard as he could, up to the point where they pushed back. The clearest example of this came in 1948, during the **Berlin Blockade**. In March, the Soviets suddenly cut off highway and railroad traffic between West Berlin and the western zones of Germany. It was easy to do this without provoking an actual war. When the United States began to fly airplanes to West Berlin, however, Stalin was faced with a choice: allow the flights to continue or shoot the aircraft out of the skies, an act that would certainly start a war. Stalin backed down, having reached the limit of what the United States would allow.

The U.S. Response: Containment

Until 1947, the United States had no coherent strategy for the emerging Cold War. That year, however, as communist takeover threatened Greece and Turkey, President Harry Truman acted. In March, the United States assisted Greece and Turkey, proclaiming the **Truman Doctrine**, which promised "moral and material aid to any and all countries whose political stability is threatened by communism."

Later in 1947, the United States unveiled the European Recovery Plan (or **Marshall Plan**), brainchild of the secretary of state, General George Marshall. Remembering how, during the Depression, economic suffering had driven many European nations to political extremism, Marshall argued that poverty and homelessness in post-World War II Europe might drive governments to communism. The Marshall Plan pumped over $13 billion into Europe for purposes of economic reconstruction. Even the nations of Eastern Europe were invited to take part in the Marshall Plan, but the USSR forbade them to do so.

Finally, in 1949, the Truman Administration made a military commitment to the Cold War with the formation of the **North Atlantic Treaty Organization** (NATO), which bound the United States, Canada, Britain, and nine other Western European states into a formal strategic alliance (the number of NATO members has grown steadily over time).

All these initiatives were elements in the United States's overarching strategy for dealing with the USSR: **containment**. This term was coined by the diplomat

George Kennan, who argued that the USSR would expand as far as it could, as long as it did not have to fight. Soviet expansion, therefore, could be halted by "long-term, patient, but firm and vigilant containment."

Containment did not necessarily mean war but could also consist of economic and diplomatic support for countries targeted by the USSR. The advantage was that Soviet expansion could be kept in check without risking combat. There were, however, drawbacks. Containment gave the initiative to the Soviet Union: it acted, then the United States reacted. There was no end in sight, meaning that containment would have to be pursued for years, if not decades. It would cost immense amounts of money, especially as the arms race between the two countries escalated. Moreover, as described below and in Chapter 32, the containment strategy affected—and not for the better—how America chose its allies in the developing (or "third") world of Africa, Asia, and Latin America.

The Soviets resisted containment. In response to the Marshall Plan, the USSR formed its own economic union, the Council for Mutual Economic Assistance (COMECON). It also developed its own military bloc, the **Warsaw Pact**, to oppose NATO.

By the end of the 1940s, Europe was sharply divided between noncommunist and communist camps, with only a few nations remaining neutral. By 1949, however, Europe ceased to be the only battleground—or even the primary battleground—of the Cold War.

THE COLD WAR GLOBALIZES, 1949–1968

Nineteen forty-nine was a key year in the history of the Cold War. NATO was established. That summer witnessed the **first Soviet atomic test**, which eliminated America's edge in military technology and started a four-decade nuclear arms race.

The Cold War in Asia and the Third World

Also in 1949, after years of civil war, **Mao Tse-tung** defeated Chiang Kai-shek's Nationalists, completing the **communist revolution in China**. The Nationalists fled to Taiwan. On the mainland, Mao established the People's Republic of China (PRC) and allied with the USSR (on Mao's domestic policies, see Chapter 32). In a matter of months, the Cold War had expanded dramatically: The two largest nations on the Eurasian landmass were now together under the banner of communism, and one of them possessed atomic weapons.

With the situation in Europe largely stalemated, the Cold War's focus shifted increasingly to Asia, as well as Africa and Latin America. The first sign of this shift was the **Korean War** (1950–1953), which began with an invasion of the noncommunist South by the communist North (with support from Stalin and, especially, Mao). The United States led a United Nations army to defend South Korea. After three years of combat and more than a million deaths, the war ended with the country still divided, exactly where it had been before.

As the Cold War took on a more global dimension, the U.S. policy of containment became more difficult. In Asia, Africa, and Latin America, there was already a so-called **Third World** of nonaligned nations, most of them less economically developed than the West or the USSR, and if the Soviets attempted to win influence there, the Americans had to compete. The post-World War II wave of **decolonization** and **national liberation** added new regimes to the Third World, and because they had just freed themselves from Western imperialism or overthrown dictators supported by Western powers, many were inclined to stay unaligned (like India and Egypt) or seek ties with the USSR (for example, Cuba after 1959). American anxieties about the possible global expansion of communism were based on what was popularly known as the **domino principle** (if one country in a region "falls" to communism, the rest will too). As the Soviets, Chinese, and Cuba tried to spread communism throughout the Third World, the United States responded with its own interventions. Unfortunately, America came to choose its Third World allies based mainly on how anticommunist they were, not how democratic—and thus, it supported many dictatorial and authoritarian regimes.

> **TIP**
>
> American anxieties about the possible global expansion of communism were based on what was popularly known as the **domino principle** (if one country in a region "falls" to communism, the rest will too).

After Korea, key Cold War events in the Third World include the **Cuban Revolution** (1959), which heightened tensions by placing a communist regime and Soviet ally only miles off the U.S. coast. The **Vietnam War** (1954–1975) began with the liberation of Vietnam from French colonization and continued with America's attempt to prop up an unpopular government in South Vietnam against revolution and invasion from the communist north. This was classic domino-principle strategy on the part of the United States, which feared the spread of communism throughout all of Southeast Asia. However, the war took a turn for the worse in 1968, and America withdrew in defeat in 1973. For more on Cuba and Vietnam, see Chapter 32.

Superpower Rivalry and the Sino-Soviet Split

In the United States, presidents of both political parties pursued firm and active foreign policies and followed the policy of containment. In the USSR, Stalin died in 1953, and new leadership caused more noticeable changes. Nikita Khrushchev (1953–1964) was less brutal than Stalin. He denounced the crimes of Stalin and (within strict limits) allowed some liberalization at home and in the Eastern bloc. He declared his willingness to be friendlier to the West and even visited the United States. Leonid Brezhnev (1964–1982), who forced Khrushchev into retirement, was more of a hard-liner but still not as harsh as Stalin.

Even so, Cold War tensions and the arms race continued. During the 1950s and early 1960s, Khrushchev showed that liberalization had its limits. In 1956, when Hungary reformed more than the USSR wished, then tried to leave the Soviet bloc, Khrushchev suppressed the **Hungarian uprising** by force. His foreign policy became unpredictable. Encouraged by the Cuban Revolution and angered by the flight of American U-2 spy planes over the USSR (in May 1960, the Soviets shot down a U-2 and captured the pilot, causing an international crisis), Khrushchev pursued a boldly aggressive course in East Germany and in Cuba. In August 1961, the Soviets built the **Berlin Wall**. To demonstrate U.S. determination, the U.S. president John F. Kennedy visited the city and declared in a rousing speech, "I am a Berliner." A bigger and more dangerous showdown came in 1962, when Khrushchev attempted to install nuclear missiles in Cuba. In October, U.S. spy planes uncovered what the Soviets were doing, and Kennedy answered with a naval blockade of Cuba. The resulting **Cuban Missile Crisis** is generally considered to be the moment that brought the world closest to nuclear war. The Soviets backed down and withdrew the missiles; the failed gamble and the resulting loss of prestige played a major role in the ouster of Khrushchev in 1964. (Another factor was the USSR's worsening relationship with China, discussed below.)

Tensions cooled somewhat during the rest of the 1960s, although relations were not friendly. When Brezhnev came to power, he proved more authoritarian than Khrushchev, but also more predictable. In 1968, when Czechoslovakia began a major reform program, the "Prague Spring," Brezhnev cracked down hard, sending in a Warsaw Pact army to restore Soviet control. He justified the intervention by stating that the USSR had the right to "protect communism" in Eastern Europe (in other words, to control the Soviet bloc as it pleased), a stance that became known as the **Brezhnev Doctrine**. However, Brezhnev seemed less likely to threaten Europe outside the USSR's declared sphere of influence. Of course, proxy struggles in the Third World continued, and the U.S. involvement in Vietnam escalated.

Cold War geopolitics grew more complex with the **Sino-Soviet split**, which began in the 1960s and continued till the collapse of the USSR. Even though both nations were communist, the Chinese resented the Soviets' patronizing "older brother" attitude (they also felt that many Russians, being white, treated them as racial inferiors). The Soviets did not give the Chinese the secret of nuclear weapons. (China finally developed its own atomic bomb in 1964.) Mao was upset with what he saw as the softer line of Stalin's successors. By the early 1960s, tensions between China and the USSR were serious (but not yet understood in the West). As the decade ended, the Sino-Soviet border became a militarized zone, and occasional episodes of violence broke out. The United States would exploit this split in the 1970s.

The Arms Race and Space Race

When the USSR ended the American monopoly on atomic weapons in 1949, a long **nuclear arms race** began. During the 1950s and early 1960s, the United States had more weapons, but its advantage narrowed as time passed. By the mid-to-late 1960s, the superpowers reached a state of nuclear parity: they each had roughly the same quantity of weapons, and they each had the ability to drop nuclear bombs from airplanes, fire nuclear missiles from submarines, and launch nuclear warheads on intercontinental ballistic missiles (ICBMs) directly at each other's countries. Britain, France, and China also possessed small nuclear arsenals.

Nuclear weapons made traditional military thinking obsolete and greatly heightened international tensions. Any quarrel that got out of control (as, for example, the assassination of Franz Ferdinand did in 1914) could result not just in a world war but global devastation. Over time, nuclear weapons became most important for how they were *not* used: their **deterrence** value was seen as a way of preventing war between the superpowers. In theory, as long as each side remained convinced that rash or aggressive action would destroy it as well as its enemy, both sides would avoid doing anything that might trigger a serious crisis. This logic was referred to as **Mutually Assured Destruction**, with the appropriate abbreviation MAD.

Because rocket technology was so intimately connected with the development of nuclear missiles, the arms race had much to do with another form of superpower competition: the **space race**. Ostensibly a peaceful scientific venture, the exploration of space became associated with hyperpatriotic pride and military rivalry. At the start, the Soviets had the advantage: they launched the first human-made object into space, the satellite *Sputnik*, in 1957, and they sent the first human into space, Yuri Gagarin, in 1961. However, the United States pulled ahead, becoming, in 1969, the first (and, so far, only) nation to land a crewed spacecraft on the moon.

THE LATE STAGES OF THE COLD WAR, 1968–1991

Détente During the 1970s

Between 1969 and 1979, the Cold War entered a more peaceful phase known as *détente* (a French diplomatic term referring to the relaxation of tensions). The United States, wearied by the Vietnam conflict and plagued by economic recession at home, was relieved to scale back hostilities. The USSR was motivated by the need for U.S. and Canadian grain shipments, as well as fears that America was growing closer to China—President Richard Nixon skillfully exploited the Sino-Soviet split by visiting China in 1972.

Détente did not mean tensions disappeared completely. Conflicts in Africa, Asia, and Latin America raged, with the United States and USSR sponsoring opposing sides. The arms race continued, and nuclear arsenals grew larger. Still, for almost a decade, the Soviets and Americans established a working relationship and, at times, genuinely cooperated. The United States sold grain to the USSR. Both powers cooperated in the enforcement of the **Nuclear Non-Proliferation Treaty** (1968–1969), whose purpose has been to prevent the spread of nuclear weaponry. The United States and USSR signed the first arms-control treaties, such as SALT (1972) and the Anti-Ballistic Missile Treaty (1972). In the Helsinki Accords of 1975, the Soviet government agreed to guarantee its people basic human rights. The superpowers even cooperated in space, during the Apollo-Soyuz mission (1975).

The Early-to-Mid 1980s: The Cold War Resumes

The spirit of détente ended in 1979. That year, the **Soviet invasion of Afghanistan**, which threatened the oil supplies of the Middle East as well as the Indian Ocean coastline, damaged relations between the superpowers. The Afghan War lasted ten years and became a Vietnam-like nightmare for the Soviets. It also destroyed détente. Another point of tension was the **Sandinista revolution in Nicaragua** (1979), which the Soviets supported. The latest arms-control treaty, SALT II (1979), went unratified. In 1980 U.S. President Ronald Reagan swung American foreign policy far to the right.

In terms of the arms race and the risk of nuclear war, the period between 1979 and 1985 was the Cold War's most dangerous time, with the exception of the Cuban Missile Crisis of 1962. The arms race escalated. Third World brushfire wars, terrorist campaigns sponsored by the USSR and its allies, and covert operations carried out by the CIA or the KGB increased in number. Both superpowers publicly

TIP

The Afghan War lasted ten years and became a Vietnam-like nightmare for the Soviets. It also destroyed détente.

expressed hostility. Each boycotted Olympic Games hosted by the other (Moscow in 1980, Los Angeles in 1984). Reagan referred to the Soviet Union explicitly as the Evil Empire. Because the nuclear weaponry of the 1980s was faster, more accurate, and more destructive than ever before, the chances that a diplomatic crisis could result in a full-scale, civilization-destroying exchange mounted.

Unrest and Reform in the Soviet Bloc

In the meantime, the USSR experienced political stagnation and economic slowdown at home (especially because of the arms race and the cost of the war in Afghanistan). In Eastern Europe, there was growing unrest, especially in Poland, where the 1980 creation of the trade union **Solidarity**, led by Lech Walesa, sparked a decade-long protest movement that united workers, intellectuals, and Catholic clergy (Pope John Paul II, originally from Poland, did much to support anti-Soviet agitation in Eastern Europe). Other important dissidents included the playwright Vaclav Havel of Czechoslovakia and, in the USSR, the physicist Andrei Sakharov, as well as his wife, Elena Bonner.

Real change was impossible under the aging Brezhnev and his immediate successors. In 1985, however, a younger, reform-minded leader rose to power in the Soviet Union: **Mikhail Gorbachev**. Gorbachev understood that inefficiency, corruption, and economic weakness were undermining his country. He also knew that the USSR could no longer afford to continue fighting in Afghanistan, keep up with America in the arms race, or even maintain control over Eastern Europe.

During the late 1980s, Gorbachev launched two interrelated reform efforts: *perestroika* ("restructuring") and *glasnost* ("openness"). **Perestroika** involved economic changes similar to the reforms of **Deng Xiaoping** in China (see Chapter 32). Within limits, it reduced central state control over the economy, allowing for some free enterprise and expansion of private property. Such changes worked better in China than in the USSR, partly because of long-ingrained inefficiency in the Soviet system, partly because Deng fought conservative opposition in his government more effectively than Gorbachev did. Another difference was Gorbachev's policy of **glasnost**, which allowed greater freedom of the press, public criticism of political corruption and workplace abuses, and frankness about the USSR's clouded past (especially the Stalin era). He allowed competitive voting, created an elective parliament, and legalized non-Communist political parties. Gorbachev hoped that such freedoms would motivate the Soviet people to work harder to make perestroika succeed. Instead, glasnost made people feel freer to ask for even more change—and to criticize Gorbachev himself when things began to go wrong. (Deng did not permit such social and cultural freedoms in China.)

The Walls Come Down: The Cooling of the Arms Race and the Liberation of Eastern Europe

Gorbachev, hoping to reduce superpower tensions, turned a friendlier face to the West. Although tough discussions lay ahead, the terrible nuclear fears of the previous half decade began to fade. By 1987, Gorbachev and Reagan were negotiating arms-reduction agreements and cooling tensions even further.

Gorbachev also started to loosen the USSR's grip on Eastern Europe. He began economic reform and called for greater observance of human rights. Gorbachev's press secretary joked about the "Sinatra Doctrine," hinting that, instead of upholding the Brezhnev Doctrine, the Soviets would allow East European governments to do things "their way."

In the end, Eastern Europe went free. The key year was 1989. Poland, where Lech Walesa and the Solidarity movement won free nationwide elections, led the way. Hungary followed suit by opening its borders to the West. In Czechoslovakia, Vaclav Havel's dissident movement came to power in the so-called Velvet Revolution. Bulgaria's communist regime resigned. In November, the East German Communist Party collapsed, bringing about the freedom movement's most celebrated, most euphoric event, the **fall of the Berlin Wall**. In December, the deeply repressive regime in Romania was overthrown (in one of the freedom movement's rare moments of violence, the dictator, Nicolae Ceausescu, and his wife were executed). Soon, in October 1990, the map of Europe would be dramatically redrawn by the **reunification of Germany**.

Parallel Freedom Movements

The freedom movement in Eastern Europe inspired or paralleled other freedom movements worldwide in 1989 and 1990. Not all succeeded. In May 1989, the seventieth anniversary of the May Fourth Movement that had demanded progressive reform from the Chinese Republic, Chinese students gathered at **Tiananmen Square** in Beijing. They, too, wanted greater freedoms. The Deng regime refused to grant any concessions and, when the students disobeyed orders to disperse, crushed the demonstrations by sending in tanks. Economic change was allowed but not political change.

The nations of Latin America were luckier. Starting in the late 1980s, they began a wave of democratization that continued into the 1990s. In South Africa, in 1990, **Nelson Mandela**, leader of the African National Congress, was released from prison, where he had been held since 1964. Free elections and the **end of apartheid** soon followed.

The Fall of the Soviet Union, 1989–1991

While Eastern Europe rejoiced, trouble brewed in the USSR. Gorbachev faced two major problems after 1989. At home, perestroika was failing, and discontent with his leadership was rising. Liberals and moderates who had originally supported Gorbachev wanted more change than he was willing to give. On the other hand, he had made enough changes to alienate hard-liners and conservative communists. Abroad, the East European freedom movement encouraged an upsurge of **anti-Soviet nationalism** in the USSR itself. In 1990 and 1991, non-Russian parts of the country (especially the Baltic republics, Georgia, and Ukraine) pushed for greater autonomy or declared independence outright. In one instance, Gorbachev resorted to violence (he sent tanks into Lithuania in 1990), but overall, he did not have the heart to crush independence movements by force. As 1991 progressed, the continued existence of the Soviet nation was in doubt.

A sudden blow came in August 1991, when hard-line members of the regime staged a three-day coup against Gorbachev. Thanks to popular resistance and bold leadership by politicians, including Boris Yeltsin, who rallied people against the coup, the takeover failed. Gorbachev returned to power, but he had been fatally weakened. The breakup of the USSR continued; various republics, including Russia itself, went their own way in the fall and early winter, and Gorbachev was powerless to stop them. In December 1991, Yeltsin (now president of the Russian Republic) and the leaders of Ukraine and Belarus declared the formation of a new, post-Soviet confederation, the Commonwealth of Independent States, which made the USSR irrelevant. Bowing to the inevitable, on December 25, Gorbachev resigned as Soviet leader and declared an end to the USSR itself. Soviet Communism, whose birth in 1917 had been one of the major events of the early twentieth century, did not live to see the twenty-first.

The Fall of the Soviet Union and Formation of the Commonwealth of Independent States, January 1992.

In late 1991, Mikhail Gorbachev was forced to dissolve the USSR. At that time, leaders of the former republics of the Soviet Union, with the exception of Estonia, Latvia, Lithuania, and Georgia, chose to form the Commonwealth of Independent States as a way to maintain ties and attempt a smooth transition from Soviet rule.

QUICK REVIEW

1. What diplomatic alignment did the Cold War replace?

   (A) Europe's traditional balance of power
   (B) the unipolar domination of global power by Germany
   (C) Asiatic hegemony
   (D) global anarchy
   (E) a similar condition of bipolar equilibrium

2. Which of the following is true about armed conflict during the Cold War?

   (A) The United States and Soviet Union declared war on each other several times.
   (B) There were almost no armed conflicts at all during the Cold War.
   (C) There were no armed conflicts during the Cold War.
   (D) Approximately 50 million people died in various small-to-medium conflicts.
   (E) Several tactical nuclear exchanges took place during the Cold War.

3. What was the overall strategy pursued by Stalin and the Soviet leadership during the half decade following World War II?

   (A) to cooperate with the United States peacefully in building an equitable global order
   (B) out of weakness, to allow the United States a free hand in shaping postwar Europe
   (C) to concede control of Asia to the United States but gain full control of Europe
   (D) to achieve dominance over as much of Europe as possible, even if it meant risking war with the United States
   (E) to push for as many concessions as possible from the United States, both in Asia and Europe, but not at the risk of war

4. What was the Truman Doctrine?

   (A) Truman's promise that the United States would go to war to protect any nation from communist takeover
   (B) Truman's commitment to lend aid to countries threatened by communist takeover
   (C) Truman's oath to protect Poland from absorption into the Soviet bloc
   (D) Truman's declaration of war on North Korea
   (E) Truman's public refusal ever to use atomic weapons after Hiroshima and Nagasaki

5. Which of the following helped to make 1949 such an important turning point in the Cold War?

   (A) The USSR tested its first atomic weapon.
   (B) Fidel Castro led the Communists to victory in Cuba.
   (C) The Korean War began.
   (D) Tito withdrew Yugoslavia from the Soviet bloc.
   (E) John F. Kennedy was assassinated.

6. What made the launching of *Sputnik* and the flight of Yuri Gagarin MOST troubling to the United States?

   (A) These events represented blows to national prestige.
   (B) Gagarin's landing on the moon gave rise to fears that the USSR would make territorial claims there.
   (C) Triumphs in the "space race" were technologically linked to progress in the nuclear arms race.
   (D) Both *Sputnik* and Gagarin's spaceship were armed with advanced laser weaponry.
   (E) Both *Sputnik* and Gagarin's spaceship were used to take reconnaissance photographs of U.S. missile silos.

7. The Brezhnev Doctrine was

   (A) the USSR's official protest against U.S. conduct in Vietnam.
   (B) the USSR's ideological justification of its military intervention in Czechoslovakia.
   (C) the USSR's restatement of support for Maoist China.
   (D) the USSR's condemnation of NATO's nuclear-arms buildup.
   (E) the USSR's formal outlawing of all dissident activity within its borders.

8. Which of the following best describes the Soviet relationship with China during the late 1960s and early 1970s?

   (A) Despite Soviet liberalization, China remained friendly with the USSR.
   (B) The Sino-Soviet alliance came to an end, but the two countries remained friendly neutrals.
   (C) The USSR and China persuaded India to join them in a Eurasian alliance.
   (D) The Sino-Soviet alliance broke apart, and the relationship became quite unfriendly.
   (E) The Sino-Soviet alliance remained firmly in place.

9. Détente means

   (A) a heightening of tensions.
   (B) exposing the enemy.
   (C) containment.
   (D) counterespionage.
   (E) a relaxation of tensions.

10. Which of the following would be considered a feature of perestroika?

    (A) the Soviet Union's continuation of the war in Afghanistan
    (B) increased levels of free-market economic activity allowed by the regime
    (C) greater centralization of the USSR's central-command economy
    (D) delegation of greater authority to the KGB
    (E) a crackdown on liberal elements in the media

Answers

1. **(A)** For over 200 years, the constantly shifting balance of power among six or seven European states had determined the course of geopolitics. With Europe devastated by World War II, only two nations possessed genuine military, political, and economic strength, the United States and the Soviet Union.

2. **(D)** Although the United States and its European allies did not formally go to war against the Soviet Union or the People's Republic of China, proxy wars were fought in the Third World. In these wars, including in Vietnam, tens of millions of people died.

3. **(E)** Stalin wanted the Soviet Union to gain control over as much territory as possible without a military confrontation with the United States, which the Soviets could not afford. One of his main objectives was to create a strong buffer zone in Eastern Europe as a way to prevent war.

4. **(B)** In 1947, in response to concerns that communist takeovers in Greece and Turkey were imminent, the Truman administration pledged "moral and material aid to any and all countries whose political stability is threatened by communism." This statement became known as the Truman Doctrine.

5. **(A)** From 1945 to 1949, the United States was the sole nation with nuclear weapons. However, in 1949, the Soviet Union detonated its first atomic bomb. Also in 1949, Mao came to power in China, and Nato was formed.

6. **(C)** In 1957, the USSR launched the first human-made object into space, called *Sputnik*. Rocket technology was closely tied to the nuclear arms race, so the USSR's temporary superiority in this area greatly concerned the U.S. and its allies.

7. **(B)** The Brezhnev Doctrine was issued in 1968, the year the Soviets invaded Czechoslovakia, in order to prevent it from gaining further autonomy. The doctrine stated that the USSR had the right to intervene in the affairs of its East European satellite states.

8. **(D)** Although the USSR and China were both communist regimes, they were locked in a dangerous rivalry during this time. The two countries clashed over border disputes and took different sides in the India-Pakistan dispute.

9. **(E)** The détente era saw a relaxation of tensions between the United States and the Soviet Union, although tensions did not disappear entirely. They signed arms-control treaties and cooperated in a space mission and in organizing educational and cultural exchanges in the 1970s.

10. **(B)** Perestroika was a policy initiated by the Soviet leader Mikhail Gorbachev in the mid-1980s that was meant to restructure the economy to make it run more efficiently and in line with some free-market principles. Later in the 1980s, it also came to involve the restructuring of the political system, to allow for limited democratization.

Divergent Forms of Development in the Postwar World, 1945–1991

- The developed world and postindustrial (service) economies
- Sovietization versus Westernization in postwar Europe
- European economic union (the European Union)
- The 1968 protests
- The economic slump of the 1970s
- National liberation and decolonization
- The developing (third) world and the north-south split
- The Organization of Petroleum Exporting Countries (OPEC)
- The Arab-Israeli conflict
- The Iranian Revolution
- Apartheid
- Indian and Indonesian independence and nonalignment
- Japan, the "little tigers," and economic growth in Asia
- Communism in Vietnam, Cambodia, and North Korea
- Maoist radicalism versus Deng Xiaoping's reformism in China
- The Cuban and Nicaraguan revolutions
- Dictatorship and democratization in Latin America

While the postwar decades were dominated diplomatically by the Cold War (see Chapter 31), individual parts of the world underwent a variety of political and social changes.

One preeminent trend was economic and technological modernization. However, this trend applied unevenly to different parts of the world. The societies of the West, the United States, Canada, and Western Europe, were already the most developed and industrialized in the world and therefore had the capacity to keep modernizing quickly and thoroughly. They became immensely prosperous and advanced, moving into a **postindustrial stage** by the end of the twentieth century. As for regions such as the Middle East, Africa, Asia, and Latin America, modernization, in most cases, was slower. The labels typically given to these regions—the **developing world**, less developed countries, or nondeveloped world—indicate how they lagged behind the nations of the West.

The postwar world was also an era of **decolonization**. World War II completed the process of weakening the grasp that several European nations still had on their empires. From the 1940s through the 1970s, countries such as Britain, France, Belgium, and the Netherlands were convinced or forced to free their colonies in the Middle East, Africa, and Asia. Moreover, many regions that had not been colonized per se but had been economically and/or politically dominated by outside powers began to assert themselves in the postwar era. This made the so-called **Third World**—the developing or newly liberated nations of Asia, Africa, the Mideast, and Latin America—increasingly important in global politics and economics. Unfortunately for many of these states, decolonization has sometimes caused as many problems as it has solved. Not all newly liberated countries were able to develop healthy forms of government and economic organization. Also, many of them were caught up on one side or the other in the politics of the Cold War, as the United States and Soviet Union dueled for global influence.

To this day, many imbalances and inequities between the West and the developing world still persist from the Cold War era. In particular, the great disparity in technological development and the vast gap between the West's affluence and the ghastly poverty of many parts of the developing world remain in place and continue to cause political and economic tension. The geographical placement of most of the developed or developing world has made it common to refer to their divide as the **north–south split**.

RECOVERY IN POSTWAR EUROPE

Europe found itself in a paradoxical situation during the postwar era. On one hand, World War II had ended its global dominance. It had been divided by the superpowers into a Cold War battleground. It lost its remaining colonies. On the other hand, after repairing the damage caused by World War II, most of Europe came to enjoy an unprecedented level of prosperity. This was certainly the case in Western Europe, which became one of the wealthiest and most technologically advanced societies on earth. Even communist-controlled Eastern Europe, which remained more backward, overcame the devastation caused by the war. Albeit more crudely and more slowly than in Western Europe, Eastern Europe's standard of living and level of modernization rose from the 1950s onward.

World War II's Effects on Europe

Wartime damage had been extensive. Millions were dead. A third of the Soviet economy had been destroyed. German cities lay in ruins. At least 50 million people were homeless, and more than 16 million were refugees displaced persons (DPs) without a country. The migration and dislocation caused by World War II was tremendous. Horrendous poverty, marked by shortages of food, clothing, consumer goods, and housing, threatened to plunge Europe into chaos.

In another blow to European prestige, colonies worldwide began to agitate for and win their freedom during the late 1940s and afterward. These national liberation movements and wars of decolonization caused European governments great stress and strain.

Sovietization in Eastern Europe

Despite these effects of war, economic recovery began surprisingly quickly. In the east, owing to the sheer political will of Stalin and the plundering of its new East European satellites (especially the Soviet-controlled zone of Germany), the USSR recovered to prewar economic levels within a decade. The USSR went on to create Soviet-style economies throughout the Eastern bloc. Economies were nationalized and centrally planned. Massive industrialization campaigns began. Collectivization, while not as brutally implemented as in the USSR during the 1930s, brought agriculture under state control.

In both the USSR and Eastern Europe, there was substantial economic growth after the 1940s and early 1950s. **Social welfare systems**, which provided education, medical care, pensions, and other basic services to all citizens, were put in place. However, East European economic production was characterized by poor quality. Consumer goods were constantly in short supply because so much emphasis was placed on weapons production during the arms race against the United States. Because Soviet and East European production was carried out without any regard for the environment, the ecological damage caused by a half century of East European industrialization was nothing short of catastrophic—and remains a problematic legacy. Moreover, the entire system was maintained by means of political repression. Especially under Stalin, Soviet control over Eastern Europe was harsh. There were periods of liberalization, but they were sporadic and temporary. The price of going beyond what the Soviets were willing to allow was demonstrated by the Soviet invasions of Hungary (1956) and Czechoslovakia (1968). Not until the end of the 1980s would the Eastern bloc experience real freedom.

Recovery in Western Europe

Economic recovery was more dramatic in Western Europe. As a first step, the European Recovery Plan (better known as the **Marshall Plan**) infused more than $13 billion into the economies of Western Europe. This infusion helped to rebuild the war-torn nations of Europe. It helped prevent the spread of communism. It also rewarded the United States, because this first dose of economic aid created healthy markets eager to buy U.S. goods.

Growth continued throughout the next two decades. A particular star was West Germany, which rose from the ruins of war to become Europe's economic powerhouse. Ironically, Great Britain, one of the victors of World War II, took a longer time than most European nations to recover (mainly because it had spent so much money fighting World War II). Industrial growth was high. Technological innovation allowed West European economies to move beyond industrial production to service, or postindustrial, modes of economic activity (the same was true in the United States).

As in Eastern Europe, most West European nations put into place social welfare systems or improved on the ones created during the 1920s and 1930s. Although they were not socialist or communist, many West European nations began to experiment with economic systems that were not purely capitalist either. This blend of capitalist and social-welfare (even mildly socialist) practice began to be called the "**third way.**"

Not all developments in Western Europe were positive. Europe was caught in the crossfire of the superpowers' nuclear arms race. For a long time, Germany refused to come to grips with the Holocaust or its Nazi past. Democracies such as France and Italy, mired for decades in widespread official corruption, experienced frequent government turnover. France was rocked by the worldwide wave of **1968 protests** that struck not only Paris but also Mexico City, Prague, and universities throughout the United States. Mild authoritarianism and antiunionism persisted in countries such as Spain, Portugal, and Greece until after the mid-1970s. Great Britain wrestled with nationalist aspirations and, after the late 1960s, terrorism in Northern Ireland.

Economic Union in Western Europe

One way the West Europeans made up for their loss of global might was to devise various forms of union. Over time, the principle of union has enabled Europe to boost its economic strength, increase its diplomatic clout, and (less successfully) work together to prevent the outbreak of war or political extremism.

At first, efforts to unite were economic. In 1952, six nations (Belgium, Luxembourg, the Netherlands, Italy, France, and West Germany) formed the European Coal and Steel Community. In 1957, the same countries agreed to even stronger ties by establishing the European Economic Community, also known as the Common Market. The goal of the EEC was to eliminate internal tariffs and encourage the free movement of money, goods, services, and labor. Eventually renamed the **European Union**, the group expanded (Britain, Ireland, and Denmark joined in 1973, while others were admitted later) and strengthened its ties. By the mid-1990s, it included fifteen members and was moving toward monetary union (see Chapter 34).

Other regional organizations binding Western Europe together include the **North Atlantic Treaty Organization** (NATO, formed in 1949) and the Council of Europe (also 1949).

Economic Crisis During the 1970s

Economic crisis struck the Western world—the United States as well as Europe—in the early 1970s. In 1971, the United States was forced to detach the dollar from the gold standard. This move led to monetary instability across Western Europe, whose trade was so dependent on the U.S. currency. The **oil embargo** of 1973, imposed by the nations of the Middle East (from which Western Europe bought 70 percent of its oil), badly damaged the economies of Europe and the United States.

Both Western Europe and the United States suffered from inflation, recession, and unemployment.

Western Europe During the 1980s and 1990s

During the 1980s, many West European nations moved to the right, in an effort to escape the malaise of the 1970s. The elections of leaders such as Margaret Thatcher in Great Britain and Helmut Kohl in West Germany were part of this general trend. The same is true of the election of Ronald Reagan in the United States. Even France's first socialist president, François Mitterand, was forced to make concessions to the right.

In many West European countries, there was a partial retreat from the social-welfare systems of the past, as Thatcher and other leaders carried out **privatization** of state-run sectors of the economy. Overall, West Europe economies recovered during the 1980s and 1990s. To be sure, unemployment, poverty, socioeconomic inequality, and racial prejudice (stirred up by the large influx of non-European and East European immigration into Western Europe) were problems. Still, by the end of the Cold War, Western Europe was a region in which economic prosperity, healthy democratic government, and technological advancement could be taken largely—although not universally—for granted.

Major leaders of postwar Europe include Charles de Gaulle, president of France during the late 1950s and 1960s. France's most decorated World War II hero, de Gaulle was fiercely independent and resisted American domination of European affairs. Konrad Adenauer, chancellor of West Germany (1949–1963), restored Germany's place in the international community. Willy Brandt (1969–1974), also of West Germany, became famous for his policy of *Ostpolitik* (détente with Eastern Europe). Margaret Thatcher, the first female prime minister of Great Britain (1979–1990), moved British politics and economics to the right, dismantled and privatized much of Britain's nationalized social-welfare apparatus, and worked with Ronald Reagan (and later President George Bush) of the United States in opposing Soviet communism. In France, president François Mitterand (1981–1995) made the socialists, rather than the communists, the respectable voices of the French left wing. Helmut Kohl (1982–1998) of West Germany led his country to economic dominance during the 1980s. His enduring mark on German history is his reunification of East and West Germany in October 1990 after the collapse of communism in Eastern Europe.

DECOLONIZATION AND THE EMERGENCE OF THE DEVELOPING WORLD

One of the most powerful trends of the postwar era was the surge in importance of the **developing world** (also referred to in Cold War terms as the **Third World**). It consisted of nations in Latin America, Asia, Africa, and the Middle East that had lagged behind the countries of the West in economic and political development, had been kept under the political and economic thumb of foreign powers, or had been directly colonized.

Decolonization and National Liberation

Even before World War II, some steps had been taken to decolonize. Britain gave home rule to Ireland in 1922 thanks largely to an armed uprising there in 1916. In 1931, the Statute of Westminster transformed the British Empire into the British Commonwealth, whose members were entitled to varying degrees of autonomy. France and Britain began to allow some of their Middle Eastern mandates and protectorates greater freedom, if not actual independence, during the 1930s.

After World War II, **decolonization** and **national liberation** became major agents of change in Asia, the Middle East, and Africa. World War II pried loose the grip that countries such as Britain and France had kept on their empires even after World War I. From the 1940s through the 1970s, dozens of new nations came into being, having attained freedom from their imperial masters.

Another change in the developing world during the Cold War era was the overthrow (or attempted overthrow) of dictators and oligarchies, many of whom had been installed or supported by foreign governments or economic interests. This was especially the case in Latin America, the countries of which were nominally free but often influenced heavily by the United States. These political conflicts were often referred to as struggles for national liberation, just as actual decolonization campaigns were.

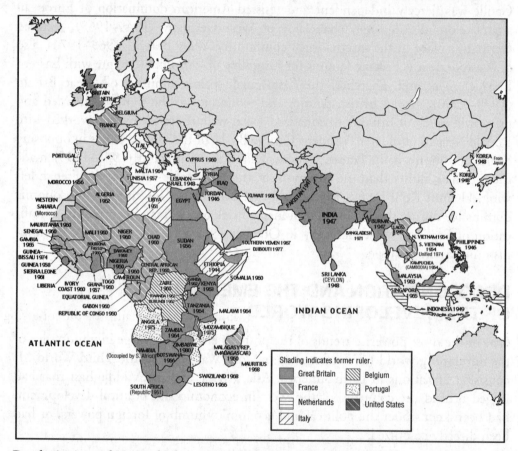

Decolonization and National Liberation in Africa and Asia After 1945.
World War II dealt the final blow to Europe's ability to maintain control over colonial empires. From the 1940s through the 1970s, a great wave of decolonization and national liberation swept Africa and Asia. Freedom was attained in a variety of ways—sometimes peacefully, sometimes by force.

Patterns of Decolonization

The means and results of decolonization varied from country to country. Specific cases are discussed in the geographical sections that follow. There was no set pattern to decolonization. Whether or not a newly liberated nation succeeded in building a healthy political and economic system depended on, among other things, the following questions:

- Did a newly decolonized nation have to fight a war to become free?
- How enlightened had the colonizing power been? Had it educated a native elite, leaving behind politicians, economists, and trained personnel with practical skills? Did the colonizing power assist actively with the transition to freedom? As a rule, Britain had a good record in this respect. To a lesser degree, France did as well.
- Were there serious ethnic, cultural, or religious divisions? In some countries, the colonizing power kept such tensions under control. Decolonization sometimes released them, leading to violence.
- Did a country have natural resources to exploit? Did the government exploit them efficiently? Former colonies that could not compete on the international market often suffered economic difficulties. Also, a newly liberated nation that did not diversify its economy but continued to rely on monoculture or the extraction of a small set of resources tended to recreate the same problems—a gap between rich and poor, economic backwardness, and environmental damage—that colonialism had caused.
- Did a newly liberated country take sides in the Cold War? Often, former colonies turned to one of the superpowers for economic and political support. Because their former masters were typically aligned with the United States and because the Marxist rhetoric of the Soviet Union (and as time passed, China) sounded appealing, many newly liberated countries turned at least for a while to the USSR (or less frequently, China). Superpowers often intervened in the affairs of decolonized nations.

THE MIDDLE EAST

General Patterns in the Postwar Middle East

Developments in the postwar Middle East were dominated mainly by the following factors:

- *The region's strategic and economic importance as the world's key source of petroleum.* Two-thirds of the world's crude oil is produced in the Middle East. The **Organization of Petroleum Exporting Countries** (OPEC), founded in 1960, is dominated by states from this area. Unfortunately, the wealth derived from oil has not led to the elimination of poverty or socio-economic inequality.
- *Contradictions between the urge to modernize and a desire to preserve Islamic tradition.* Long before the September 11, 2001, bombings, **Islamic fundamentalism** had been a force in the Middle East. One of the difficult questions facing the Middle East is how to balance Islamic heritage and Sharia law with progressive social and political practices such as democracy, civil liberties, secular law codes, and gender equality. In particular, how women are treated depends on how this issue is resolved.
- *The destabilizing effect of the Arab-Israeli conflict since 1948.* This remains an intractable, painful, and divisive issue, even into the twenty-first century.
- *Competition between the United States and the USSR for influence in the region during the Cold War.* The Middle Eastern states firmly in the U.S. camp were

Turkey and Israel. All others switched sides, back and forth, depending on where they thought their advantage lay.

- *Authoritarianism.* Dictatorship and human rights abuses have persisted, even in countries that are technically democratic.

Autonomy and Modernization

Even before World War II, the protectorates and mandates of the Middle East had gained freedom or greater autonomy. Saudi Arabia, Iraq, Jordan, Syria, and Lebanon were all free. Egypt and North Africa became independent during the 1950s and 1960s. Egyptian officers staged a coup against the pro-British king in 1952. Libya, taken from Italy by France and Britain during World War II, was also freed in 1952. Morocco and Tunisia gained freedom from France in 1956. Algeria, the African colony France was most unwilling to set free, fought a bitter war of independence from 1954 to 1962.

Turkey and Iran, already independent, continued on their paths toward modernization. More than any other Islamic state, Turkey has remained dedicated to secularism and Westernization. It has integrated itself into European markets, as well as the NATO alliance. Thus, Turkey has served as a gateway between the Western world and the Middle East. Iran did much the same but to a lesser extent and only until 1979, when its pro-Western government was overthrown.

Egypt Under Gamal Abdel Nasser

Independence, oil-based wealth, and geostrategic importance made the states of the Middle East more assertive in the 1950s and 1960s. The most famous example of this new **Arab nationalism** appeared in Egypt, which became an independent republic in 1952. By 1954, Colonel **Gamal Abdel Nasser** had taken control of the government.

A great booster of modernization, Nasser was a proponent of pan-Arabism and tried create a United Arab Republic joining all Arab nations together. This effort failed, but Nasser succeeded in modernizing his country. He also stood up to the West, nationalizing foreign-owned or foreign-controlled industries and businesses.

In 1956, Nasser took the bold step of declaring **Egyptian ownership of the Suez Canal.** This prompted the Suez Crisis, in which French, British, and Israeli troops tried to seize the canal. The United States and USSR, wishing to avoid serious armed conflict in the region, forced the three armies to withdraw, leaving the canal in Egyptian hands. The end result was a blow to British and French prestige, showing how the Cold War diminished European power.

Because Nasser was anti-British, he chose to strengthen ties with the USSR, at least temporarily. Soviet advisers and engineers brought technology and weaponry to Egypt; they also constructed the **Aswan Dam**, the world's largest. However, when the Soviets tried to control Egyptian politics, Nasser expelled them.

Nasser died in 1970. He was succeeded by Anwar Sadat, who drew Egypt closer to the United States and, in 1978, became the first Arab leader to recognize Israel. Sadat was assassinated by Islamic militants in 1981. Since then, Hosni Mubarak has served as president.

The Establishment of Israel and the Arab-Israeli Conflict

One of the most dramatic developments in the postwar Middle East was the **establishment of the State of Israel** (1948) as a homeland for the world's Jews. In 1917, Britain, which gained control over Palestine at the end of World War I, agreed in principle to create a Jewish state there but delayed this decision during the 1920s and 1930s in order to avoid Arab unrest.

After World War II and the horrors of the Holocaust, international sympathy for the Jews, along with strong U.S. support, led to the creation of Israel. Immediately, this stirred up Arab outrage and plunged the Middle East into war. The Israelis had to fight a war in 1948 simply to keep the state that had been given them. This had the effect of displacing Palestinian Arabs, who scattered to Jordan, Lebanon, and throughout the Middle East.

In 1964, the Palestinians gained a semblance of leadership with the foundation of the Palestinian Liberation Organization (PLO), a terrorist group and political movement led by **Yasser Arafat.**

The Arab states fought several wars against Israel, most notably the Six-Day War in 1967 and the Yom Kippur War in 1973. Each time, Israel, with a supremely trained, highly motivated army and strong backing from the United States, defeated the Arab coalitions, taking territory away from Arab states in the process. PLO terrorism was frequent; most infamously, a PLO squad assassinated members of the Israeli Olympic team in 1972.

Not until 1978, when **Anwar Sadat** of Egypt, encouraged by U.S. President Jimmy Carter, agreed with Israeli Prime Minister **Menachem Begin** to recognize Israel in exchange for the return of the Sinai Peninsula, was there an end to outright war in the region. Following Egypt's lead, a number of moderate Arab states began to recognize Israel during the 1980s.

However, problems remained. Throughout the 1980s, the Palestinian population of Israel staged a continuous uprising called the **intifada.** These demonstrations and protests often led to bloodshed. At the same time, terrorist groups acted against Israel as well. Terrorist attacks placed Israel in a difficult position: To avoid a total breakdown of security, it—despite being a democracy, committed to human rights—felt compelled to use violence against civilian agitators, who, while hostile and sometimes dangerous, were poorly armed and often minors.

In 1993 and 1994, the Israelis and Palestinians signed historic peace agreements, one of which called for Palestinian self-rule in parts of Israel. The United States attempted throughout the 1990s to mediate between the two sides and to keep the peace process alive. Nonetheless, tensions remained high, and the peace effort collapsed in 2001, amid violence from both sides.

Iran and Iraq

The most powerful dictatorships in the Middle East were those of Iran and Iraq. Since the 1920s, Iran had been ruled by the secular, modernizing Pahlavi shahs. The last shah, **Mohammad Reza Pahlavi,** ruled from 1941 to 1979. He used Iran's oil wealth to industrialize and modernize. Like the Turkish government, the shah's regime opposed Islamic traditionalism, encouraging Western dress, Western education, the unveiling of women, and the eradication of Sharia law. The shah became an ally of the United States.

Unfortunately, the shah relied on repression to carry out modernization: dissidents were ruthlessly suppressed by the secret police (SAVAK), and the regime was decidedly antidemocratic. By 1979, the shah was in poor health, and his popularity had plummeted; he was seen by many as an American puppet and a disrespecter of Islam. He left the country to seek medical treatment and died of cancer in 1980.

In the meantime, in 1979, the Shiite cleric **Ayatollah Ruhollah Khomeini**, an Islamic fundamentalist the shah had exiled years before, returned to Iran and took control of the country. This **Iranian Revolution** transformed the country into an anti-Western (particularly anti-U.S.), theocratic dictatorship. Famously, the new regime held American hostages captive from 1979 to 1981. At the same time, Iran went to war with neighboring Iraq. The Iran-Iraq War lasted from 1980 to 1988, and devastated both countries. Khomeini died in 1989. The theocracy he created remains in place. Compared with other major revolutions of the modern era, the Iranian Revolution is unusual, if not unique, in being antimodern and religiously based.

Iraq came under the control of **Saddam Hussein** and his Baath Party in 1979. Although his title was president, Hussein became one of the Middle East's most powerful dictators. Originally sponsored by the United States because of his opposition to Iran, Hussein turned his brutality against his own people, his neighbors, and the United States. During his war with Iran, he used poison gas, drafted teenaged children to fight, and killed many civilians. He viciously persecuted Iraq's Kurdish minority.

In 1990, Hussein invaded the oil-rich state of Kuwait and appeared ready to move against Saudi Arabia. In the first major conflict of the post–Cold War era, the first **Gulf War** (1991), the United States led a military coalition to push Hussein out of Kuwait. Between 1991 and 2003, the United Nations imposed trade sanctions, backed by U.S. and allied military action, to prevent Iraq's development of weapons of mass destruction (and to compel Hussein to allow weapons inspections). Hussein's regime was overthrown in a U.S.-led war in 2003.

AFRICA

Decolonization began in Africa mainly during the 1950s and 1960s, somewhat later than in the Middle East or Asia. By the late 1990s, Africa would contain forty-six countries. Security and economic stability in most of them are still affected by the legacy of colonialism.

National Liberation in North Africa

The Islamic states of North Africa became free during the 1950s. Egypt declared independence in 1952, as did Libya. Morocco and Tunisia gained freedom from France in 1956. The long and painful **Algerian War of Independence** (1954–1962) against France completed the process of lifting the colonial yoke from North Africa.

North African states had several advantages over sub-Saharan Africa when it came to decolonization. They were largely, although not completely, homogeneous in terms of religion, ethnicity, and language. They had existed as meaningful political units for a long time, making the transition to nation-state easier. Their colonizing powers also left behind technology and industrial infrastructures (railroads, telegraphs, canals, roads) that proved economically useful, especially in Algeria and Egypt.

Independence in Sub-Saharan Africa

The nations of sub-Saharan Africa had more of a struggle to create successful independent states. Major freedom movements began during the 1940s, in South Africa (the African National Congress); the Gold Coast, or Ghana (Kwame Nkrumah); and Kenya (Jomo Kenyatta).

For the most part, these were nonviolent movements led by intellectuals and labor activists. There were, however, exceptions. The Mau Mau movement in Kenya departed from Kenyatta's approach and killed almost 2,000 people in the 1950s. Violence played a substantial part in the decolonization of Zimbabwe (Rhodesia), South Africa, Rwanda, Zaire (the Belgian Congo), Angola, and Mozambique.

Varying Transitions to Freedom

For the most part, decolonization in the parts of Africa that had been British and French went smoothly. Both Britain and France prepared their colonies for freedom by educating native elites, allowing greater native representation in transitional governments, and minimizing the possibility of interethnic conflict.

Not all went well, however. In Rhodesia, a white-controlled government declared independence from Britain in 1965. It harshly repressed black natives, who responded with violence. Only after a savage conflict was Rhodesia placed under native rule, in 1980, when the country renamed itself Zimbabwe. South African independence from Britain involved serious problems as well.

The worst transitions to independence were made by Belgian and Portuguese colonies. Here, the imperial masters had been particularly exploitative, and neither country took steps to prepare its colonies for independence. Guinea-Bissau gained freedom from Portugal in 1974 but only after a vicious guerrilla war. Angola fought a war of liberation against Portugal from 1961 to 1975. After achieving independence, Angola suffered years of civil war. Likewise, Mozambique fought Portugal from 1965 to 1975, only to descend into a long civil conflict.

Belgium pulled out of Rwanda in 1962, having artificially exacerbated differences between two tribes, the Hutu and Tutsi, who came to hate each other deeply. When the Belgians freed the Congo, postindependence violence was so pervasive from 1960 to 1964 that the United Nations had to intervene. The prime mover in the Congolese independence movement, the Marxist Patrice Lumumba, was assassinated by political rivals (almost certainly with U.S. knowledge, if not complicity) in late 1965.

South Africa and the Experience of Apartheid

As in Rhodesia/Zimbabwe, but for much longer, decolonization in South Africa was tainted by the clash between white and black citizens of the newly free country. The government that declared freedom from Britain was controlled by the white minority, largely descended from Dutch Boers. These Afrikaners practiced the policy of **apartheid** (extreme racial segregation). South Africa is one of the world's richest sources of gold and diamonds. Between the 1960s and the 1990s, the white government of South Africa turned the country into the wealthiest, most modern, and most industrialized on the continent.

However, South Africa became one of Africa's most repressive nations as well. By the 1980s, internal unrest, economic problems, and international revulsion were placing pressure on the South African government to abandon apartheid. The Zulu Confederation, the African National Congress (ANC), and other such groups opposed the white government. The ANC's leader, **Nelson Mandela**, gained the status of sympathetic dissident during his long imprisonment (1964–1990) by the white authorities. His wife, Winnie Mandela, continued the struggle on his behalf. Another moral figure in the antiapartheid movement was Bishop **Desmond Tutu**, a black clergyman in the Anglican Church and a Nobel Peace Prize recipient. In 1990, the government released Nelson Mandela. In 1994, free elections resulted in the ANC's victory. Mandela became the country's president.

Problems Facing Independent Africa

Unfortunately, many of Africa's original aspirations proved difficult if not impossible to attain. Few nations managed to achieve democratic governments, open societies, and economies that led to prosperity for all (or even many) citizens. Some of the problems that have interfered with African modernization include the following:

- *Dictatorship*: Despite beginning as democratic systems, many of Africa's governments degenerated into strongman regimes. Among the most notorious were Idi Amin of Uganda (1971–1979) and Mobutu Sese Seko of Zaire (1965–1997).
- *Corruption*: Dictatorial or not, many African regimes tended to function according to unlawful systems of patronage, nepotism, and graft.
- *Failure to modernize and diversify economies*: Rather than industrialize and diversify, many African regimes generated wealth by continuing to export the natural resources their former colonial masters took from them. This enabled foreign investors great control over African politics. It also kept profits in the hands of political rulers, rather than spreading wealth among the population at large.
- *The Cold War*: As with the rest of the developing world, many African nations became pawns in the global chess game between the United States and USSR.
- *Rapid population growth and food shortages*: The rate of African population growth has outstripped the rate of economic growth. Systems of food distribution are often inadequate, leading to food shortages and famine. The worst famines have been in Somalia and Ethiopia.
- *The HIV/AIDS pandemic*: From the 1980s onward, the HIV virus, which seems to have originated in Africa, has caused millions of deaths. Containing the virus has proven impossible, and African nations are too poor to afford large quantities of the medicines needed to treat it.

- *Lack of cultural or linguistic unity*: In Africa, the lines determining a nation's political borders often do not match where people of certain ethnicities or languages live. Most borders were drawn by European colonizers for their own benefit and convenience, leaving behind confusing varieties of ethnicities, languages, cultural practices, and religions in each country. This makes it difficult for a single state to govern all its people fairly.
- *Intertribal and interethnic conflict*: Frequently, the above problem becomes serious enough that it breaks out into violence. Since the colonial period, most of the wars in Africa have been fought within national borders, not between different countries.
- *Uncontrolled flow of small arms and light weapons*: Although this is a problem throughout the developing world, it is particularly dire in Africa. Small arms feature prominently in armed conflicts, postconflict situations, and everyday life. Thousands of children have been forcibly drafted into militias and paramilitaries.
- *Treatment of women:* In Africa's more developed countries and especially in the cities, women have attained a certain degree of economic and social equality: the right to an education, the right to work, the right to legal divorce and birth control, and so on. However, progress has been slow, and women are still dominated by men, especially in rural areas. In some regions, polygamy is still permitted. One infamous custom, clitoridectomy (female circumcision), is still practiced in some parts of Africa.

ASIA

Among the nations of the developing world, those of Asia have been the most successful in building stable governments and attaining economic prosperity. Regional organizations, notably the Association of Southeast Asian Nations (ASEAN, formed in 1967), have boosted economic, social, and cultural developments and cooperation among their members. Nonetheless, political repression, interethnic and interreligious strife, socioeconomic inequality, and periodic economic crises have caused problems as well. The Cold War also played a role in creating tensions.

The Philippines

In South and Southeast Asia, decolonization campaigns began immediately after World War II. Some were ended quickly, others dragged on. Almost all involved some degree of violence. The first colony in the region to be freed was the Philippines, which, during World War II, had been promised independence from the United States. Freedom was granted voluntarily in 1946. The United States hoped that this would provide an example to colonial powers such as France and Britain.

Indian and Pakistani Independence

India and Pakistan gained their independence next. In this case, Britain handed over power freely. In 1945, the British viceroy, Lord Louis Mountbatten, was ordered to prepare to transfer government to "responsible Indian hands" by 1948. Riots and disturbances, mainly consisting of clashes between Muslims and Hindus, sped up the British timetable.

Indian and Pakistani independence was granted on August 15, 1947. Although the British did not have to be expelled by force, independence still led to violence. Hindu-Muslim conflict cost at least a million lives. In January 1948, **Mohandas (Mahatma) Gandhi**, spiritual leader of the Indian freedom movement, was assassinated by a Hindu extremist who opposed his rhetoric of tolerance between the two faiths.

Despite their difficult beginnings, both nations survived. Pakistan became a modern Islamic republic and a major regional power. However, the original goal of its founder, **Muhammad Ali Jinnah**, has not been attained. Jinnah dreamed of a democratic, modernizing republic that could also remain true to Muslim traditions. Instead, Pakistan has been plagued by corruption, political repression, and military rule. It has also been caught up in a costly and dangerous diplomatic rivalry with its neighbor India. Both India and Pakistan developed nuclear-weapons capability during the 1990s, making their conflict even tenser.

Modern India

India has turned itself into the world's largest democracy. On the other hand, it has also suffered from sprawling inefficiency, an inability to balance population growth with economic growth, and interethnic and interfaith strife. The dominant political force in free India was the Congress Party, led by **Jawaharlal Nehru**, who served as India's prime minister from 1947 until his death in 1964. Unlike Gandhi, who had favored traditional Hindu values (although not religious bigotry) and economic simplicity, Nehru wanted to secularize India and turn it into a modern, educated industrial power.

Diplomatically, Nehru negotiated a difficult position: neighbor to a hostile China and an even more hostile Pakistan and not wishing to be a client of the Soviets, the British, or the United States, Nehru maintained a friendly, cooperative relationship with the USSR, without actually falling into the Soviet camp. As Sukarno had done in Indonesia (see below), Nehru preserved his country's status as a nonaligned nation.

From 1966 to 1975 and again from 1977 to 1984, Nehru's daughter, Indira Gandhi, was prime minister. She continued her father's policies of modernization and political **nonalignment**. Religious strife was her downfall. Her government's actions against the Sikh minority of Punjab provoked Sikh soldiers to assassinate her. From 1984 to 1991, her son, Rajiv Gandhi, served as prime minister, before being killed by Sri Lankan separatists. Since 1991, India's democratic government has continued to struggle with the same problems that Nehru and his descendants did—althogh the country has enjoyed a boom in high-tech industries like computers and film making.

After freeing India, Britain let go of its Southeast Asian colonies. Burma became independent in 1948, Malaysia in 1957, Singapore (which had been attached to Malaysia) in 1965. Hong Kong remained in British hands until 1997, when it was returned to mainland China.

Indonesia

Less willingly than the British, the Dutch and French were forced out of Southeast Asia. After World War II, the Netherlands retained control over the Dutch East Indies, or Indonesia. The charismatic leader of the Indonesian Nationalist Party, **Sukarno**, began to agitate for freedom, and a war of national liberation began in 1945. Afraid that continued combat would lead to a communist takeover of the region, the United States persuaded the Dutch to hand over freedom.

The new nation of Indonesia was born in 1949, with Sukarno as its leader. A huge archipelago, Indonesia is one of the world's largest and most populous nations. It is linguistically and ethnically diverse, although 80 percent of the population is Muslim. At first Sukarno governed democratically, but he became authoritarian over time. Like Nehru, he pursued a nonaligned foreign policy but was far more radical in calling for the Third World to defy the West. Eventually, he drew closer to the Indonesian Communist Party. In 1965, the army, allied with conservative Muslims, staged a coup against Sukarno. It turned into a popular uprising, in which as many as half a million people—mainly Communists—were killed. Sukarno was weakened by the coup, then forced out of office in 1967.

From 1967 to 1998, Indonesia was governed by a military strongman, Suharto. A dictatorial ruler with a record of frequent human-rights abuses, Suharto promoted economic growth, anticommunism, and alliance with the United States.

Vietnam, Laos, and Cambodia

The French attempted for almost a decade to hold on to their colony of Indochina (Vietnam, Laos, and Cambodia). In September 1945, the Vietnamese nationalist and communist **Ho Chi Minh** declared independence. Encouraged by the U.S. promise of freedom to the Philippines and proud of his movement's record of anti-Japanese resistance during World War II, Ho Chi Minh hoped that freedom would be granted without a struggle.

Instead, the French, with U.S. support, tried until 1954 to keep Indochina. Defeated by Vietnamese expertise in guerrilla warfare, the French withdrew. Laos, Cambodia, and Vietnam were given their independence. Vietnam was temporarily divided into a northern communist-dominated zone and a southern noncommunist zone.

Elections were to be held as soon as possible, but the French-educated, Catholic, U.S.-backed leader of South Vietnam, Ngo Dinh Diem, refused to allow elections, knowing that the Buddhist, anti-French peasant masses would vote against him. The North Vietnamese began to fight the south in 1959.

By the early 1960s, the United States was providing substantial military support for South Vietnam; it continued its military intervention for years. In 1968, the United States suffered a serious public-relations setback when the communists staged the Tet Offensive, catching the Americans and South Vietnamese off guard. America scaled back its war effort, withdrawing its troops in 1973. In April 1975, the communists captured the South Vietnamese capital and, with much violence, unified the country under their rule.

Militarism and Authoritarianism in Southeast Asia

Military or authoritarian government became the rule throughout much of Southeast Asia. The Communist **Khmer Rouge** movement in Cambodia took power and carried out a hideous reign of terror that claimed as many as 2 million victims. The U.S.-backed regime of Ferdinand Marcos, which governed the Philippines until the early 1980s, violated civil rights and was extravagantly corrupt. Myanmar (Burma) and Thailand came under military rule. As noted above, Indonesia was heavily authoritarian. Even prosperous and ultramodern Singapore, under prime minister Lee Kuan-yew, emphasized conformity and tradition over freedom and civil liberties.

Japan After World War II

Modernization came to the major nations of East Asia. Japan became the region's surprise powerhouse, just as West Germany, one of the defeated powers of World War II, became the economic dynamo of postwar Europe. At its peak during the 1980s, the Japanese economy was the world's third most productive, after the United States's and West Germany's. Per capita income was among the world's highest, and social services such as education and health care were excellent.

After World War II, Japan was occupied by the U.S. armed forces, which presided over democratic constitutional reform (1947) and the demilitarization of the country. The United States viewed Japan as a strategic anchor of its Cold War policy in Asia and invested in it heavily, both militarily and economically. Politically, Japan became a parliamentary democracy; although the emperor retained his symbolic role, the Diet (parliament) ran the government.

The Liberal Democratic Party came to dominate party politics, and while Japan's democratic system never ceased to function, the Liberal Democrats' influence over the Diet led some commentators to view Japan as slightly oligarchic. Much of Japan's postwar success depended on its population's dedicated work ethic and, through the 1980s, its willingness to place the needs of Japanese society above the desires of the individual.

The 1990s, however, brought not only an economic recession and revelations of deep-seated government corruption but also changes in social attitudes. Younger generations are less willing to conform, to work as selflessly as their parents and grandparents, or to accept traditional social roles. A desire for greater gender equality, in a society where women have generally been expected to play secondary and supporting roles, has also taken hold.

Taiwan, South Korea, and the "Little Tigers"

Like Japan, but to a lesser extent, Taiwan (the Republic of China) and South Korea developed prosperous and free societies. From the 1950s through the 1970s, neither Taiwan nor South Korea was truly democratic. Instead, they were anticommunist regimes that, while parliamentary, concentrated power in the hands of one dominant party. In the case of Taiwan, this was the Nationalist Party (Kuomintang) that had been defeated by Mao's Chinese Communist Party in 1949. Chiang Kai-shek remained in control of the Kuomintang—and thus Taiwan—until his death in 1975. By the end of the 1970s, Taiwan began to democratize.

South Korea remained authoritarian until 1989, when free elections began to be held. Despite their less than democratic nature, both Taiwan and South Korea became allies of the United States because of their staunch anticommunism. They also became economic success stories; along with Hong Kong, Singapore, and Thailand, they became known as the **"little tigers"** for their economic strength (as distinct from the great "tiger" of the Japanese economy).

Both Taiwan and South Korea were extremely important to the United States's Cold War strategic posture. In 1950–1953, the United States spearheaded the United Nations coalition that kept South Korea safe from North Korean invasion. In the 1970s, even though the United States was forced to disclaim its formal recognition of Taiwan in order to establish formal ties with the People's Republic of China on the mainland, the U.S.-Taiwanese relationship has remained strong, both politically and economically.

North Korea

Communism in East Asia came to North Korea after World War II, when the country was divided by the Americans and Soviets. From the 1940s onward, North Korea has remained one of the most isolated and rigidly dictatorial societies on earth. Its long-time leader, **Kim Il Sung** (1948–1994), was an uncompromising Stalinist and ruthlessly oppressive. To the present day, North Korea retains its communist system, although economic collapse and its insistence on maintaining a huge military (which now includes a nuclear-missile capacity) have placed the population in imminent danger of mass starvation.

The People's Republic of China

The People's Republic of China, established in 1949 by **Mao Tse-tung** and the Chinese Communist Party (CCP), has been the most populous communist nation on earth for more than five decades. Like the rest of East Asia, China has modernized—although not as consistently.

China was ruled by Mao from 1949 until his death in 1976. At first, Mao seemed to want to carry out pragmatic social and economic reform. His New Democracy of the early 1950s was greeted with some enthusiasm, as were his initial land reforms. His first Five-Year Plan (1953–1958), which imitated the USSR's five-year plans, led to industrial growth. Collectivization of agriculture began in 1955 but was (at first!) carried out more gradually and humanely than Stalin's collectivization of the late 1920s and early 1930s.

On the other hand, Mao's radical transformation of society, which included persecution of dissenters and so-called class enemies (members of the bourgeoisie or aristocracy), was harsh. Also, his aspirations became overly ambitious by the end of the 1950s, and he began to press too quickly and radically for further modernization. In 1958, Mao began the **Great Leap Forward**, which included a rapid industrial buildup, even more grandiose than the Five-Year Plan's. In the agricultural sphere, it intensified collectivization and called for an utterly unrealistic increase in food production. The trauma, stress, and confusion caused by the Great Leap Forward led to chaos and breakdown in industry. Even worse, agriculture collapsed altogether. The famines that resulted in 1959 and 1960 killed millions (the best estimate is 15 million). The Great Leap Forward was halted in 1960 but not before the damage was done. The program caused splits within the CCP leadership, and opposition to Mao grew. (An interesting exercise is to compare Mao's method of rapid modernization to Stalin's.)

In 1966, Mao embarked on another program of radical modernization, this time in the sphere of society and culture: the **Great Proletarian Cultural Revolution**, which lasted until 1976. The Cultural Revolution has been interpreted by historians as a policy used by Mao and his wife, Jiang Qing (the movement's primary architect), to strike at their political enemies. It also represented their desire to instill absolute revolutionary purity within Chinese society and culture. Censorship was absolute, and indoctrination was crushingly heavy. The one acceptable source of all wisdom was *The Little Red Book*, a collection of Mao's sayings. Young communist activists, known as Red Guards, rampaged throughout the country denouncing and putting on trial any person—university professors, factory foremen, heads of collective farms, writers and journalists, and even politicians—whom they considered to be untrue to revolutionary communist ideals. Victims were demoted, harassed, often arrested and sent to labor camps for "reeducation," and sometimes executed. Even members of the CCP elite were not immune; among those arrested was Deng Xiaoping.

The Cultural Revolution ended only with Mao's death in 1976. A power struggle followed. In 1978, **Deng Xiaoping**, having defeated Mao's widow and her allies (known afterward as the Gang of Four), came to power. Like Mao, Deng was a modernizer. However, while Mao had been idealistic, inflexible, and revolutionary, Deng was pragmatic, willing to compromise, and gradual. Although a communist, Deng was more concerned with China's well-being and growing strength than he was with absolute commitment to abstract Marxist ideals. Famously, he commented that whether a cat is black or white makes no difference, as long as it catches mice.

In contrast to Mao's militant anticapitalism, Deng allowed limited free-market reform in China. Economically, the result was clear: China experienced huge economic growth throughout the 1980s. Wages and standards of living improved. There was, however, a social and cultural effect as well. With greater wealth came the desire for greater freedom, a luxury Deng was not prepared to allow. By the end of the 1980s, China would have to deal with this growing problem. One of this era's most interesting comparisons is the success of Deng's reforms with the failure of Gorbachev's perestroika campaign.

LATIN AMERICA
Dictatorship and Economic Exploitation in Latin America

Latin America had freed itself from colonial domination in the 1800s, so national liberation and modernization here involved the struggle against dictatorship at home and the political and economic influence of the United States.

The Great Depression, despite its generally negative impact, compelled Latin American nations to diversify their economies somewhat. World War II also forced a number of the interwar period's dictators out of power. However, despite some temporary progress toward economic modernization and democratization during the late 1940s and early 1950s, many Latin American countries reverted to exploitative economies and dictatorial government from the late 1950s through the early 1980s. Moreover, in Latin America, "modernization" often led to a concentration of wealth in the hands of a narrow social stratum and weak social justice for the working classes and indigenous peoples.

Military governments and right-wing dictatorships appeared during these decades. By the mid-1970s, only Colombia, Venezuela, and Costa Rica could be considered democratic.

In 1943, military rule was established in Argentina. By 1946, the charismatic **Juan Perón** had come to dominate the military government by appealing to the poor. His wife, **Eva**, whose appeal among the lower-class *descamisados* ("shirtless ones") was great, helped him in this. During the 1950s, Perón became increasingly right-wing, even fascistic. He was overthrown by the army in 1955 and fled to Spain. Perón's popularity remained so high, however, that he was able to return in 1973 and become president until his death in 1974. A brutal military regime ruled from 1976 to 1983. This regime ruthlessly purged leftists, intellectuals, and dissidents, causing at least 30,000 to "disappear" over a decade and a half.

Brazil and Chile also had military regimes from the mid-1960s through the mid-1980s. In Chile, General **Augusto Pinochet** (backed by the U.S. Central Intelligence Agency) led a 1973 coup against the left-wing government of Salvador Allende—who, in 1970, had become one of the few Marxist politicians to come to power by means of democratic election. Pinochet remained in charge until the late 1980s. Like the military dictators of Argentina, Pinochet held the reins of power tightly, using force and violence to eliminate enemies and dissidents.

Mexico, although nominally democratic, was really an authoritarian oligarchy run by the **Institutional Revolutionary Party** (PRI). Its ability to keep the oil-based Mexican economy healthy during the 1950s and 1960s made the PRI's less than democratic nature acceptable to most Mexicans. By the end of the 1960s, however, economic stress, as well as the rising resentment of Indians, Mayans, and other minorities, who felt they were being treated as second-class citizens, stirred up discontent with the government.

The **1968 protests** shook Mexico City (as they did Paris, Prague, and many U.S. universities), showing how the PRI's democratic facade was wearing thin. By the 1980s, the Mexican government was starting to reform gradually but not completely.

Fidel Castro and the Cuban Revolution

Dictatorship from the left appeared in Cuba. In January 1959, the revolutionary movement led by **Fidel Castro** overthrew the right-wing dictator Fulgencio Batista. Within months, Castro had begun to nationalize industry and carry out land reform. His goals were to modernize, industrialize, increase literacy rates, and eliminate socioeconomic inequality. With his second-in-command, the Argentine radical Ernesto "Che" Guevara, he also wanted to combat what he saw as U.S. imperialism in Latin America. Accordingly, the Cuban revolutionaires declared themselves Marxists and turned to the Soviet Union for assistance.

Because of its proximity to the United States, Cuba became a Cold War hot spot from 1961 onward, as demonstrated by the Bay of Pigs incident (1961) and the **Cuban Missile Crisis** (1962). Domestically, the Castro regime's record is mixed. It is undeniable that Cuba has modernized under Castro, and the gap between rich and poor that had prevailed under Batista narrowed considerably. Educational levels have improved, and women (at least officially) are treated with greater equality than before. However, Castro's regime has been rigidly dictatorial and has violated human rights for more than four decades.

Latin America as Cold War Battlefield

Many problems plagued Latin America during the 1970s and early 1980s. Almost all of the military dictatorships found themselves heavily in debt, especially to the United States. Latin America had also become a great Cold War battlefield. Cuba, both on its own and on behalf of the USSR, consistently attempted to export Marxist revolution throughout Latin America. The Soviet Union did the same. For its part, the United States, fearing the spread of leftism directly to its south, made a practice of supporting any Latin American regime that opposed communism. Unfortunately, pro-U.S. regimes in Latin America tended to be right-wing and dictatorial.

One of the clearest examples of how Cold War politics were played out in Latin America during these years was the **Nicaraguan Revolution**. In 1979, the Marxist, Soviet-supported Sandinista movement overthrew the right-wing Somoza dictatorship that had ruled (with U.S. support) since 1937. In response, the U.S. government began to support a right-wing, counterrevolutionary guerrilla movement known as the Contras. In essence, the struggle between the Sandinista government and the Contra movement, both of whom were responsible for political abuses, was a proxy war between the Soviets and the Americans.

Democratization in Latin America

During the late 1980s and early 1990s, a wave of democratization swept Latin America. Much of it was tied to economic improvements, but just as much was due to the cooling down of the Cold War, which reduced the superpowers' anxiety about influence in the region. In addition, the Organization of American States (OAS), a regional organization of approximately forty countries, has promoted democratization, peace, and security in the region.

Argentina's dictatorship fell in 1983, and a free election peacefully handed power over in 1989. Brazil's dictatorship collapsed in 1985. Mexican elections in 1988 prompted the PRI to loosen its monopoly on power. The controversial Pinochet lost power in Chile in 1989.

One of the few exceptions to this trend was Cuba, where Castro's communist regime remained in power, despite the fall of communism in Eastern Europe and the USSR. Latin America's transition to democracy is still not complete. Corruption, backsliding toward authoritarian practice, the widespread economic dependence on illicit drug trafficking (especially in Colombia), and economic instability have troubled many of the region's new democracies. Nonetheless, the struggle to move toward democracy—or continue in that direction—continues.

QUICK REVIEW

1. Which of the following was NOT associated with the Western world's economic malaise of the 1970s?

   (A) oil shortages

   (B) the uncoupling of the U.S. dollar from the gold standard

   (C) levels of unemployment higher than at any time during the twentieth century

   (D) inflation

   (E) recession and general slowdown

2. The loss of which colony during the 1960s caused the French government to collapse?

   (A) Algeria

   (B) Tunisia

   (C) Laos

   (D) Quebec

   (E) Vietnam

3. In which Middle Eastern nation did a Shiite theocracy take over from a secular, modernizing monarchy?

   (A) Iraq

   (B) Jordan

   (C) Syria

   (D) Saudi Arabia

   (E) Iran

4. What Marxist regime devastated Cambodia, killing 1 million to 2 million people?

   (A) the Khmer Blanc

   (B) the Sihanouk Serpents

   (C) the Angkor Brigade

   (D) the Khmer Rouge

   (E) the Viet Cong

5. Where has the HIV/AIDS epidemic proven to be the worst social problem?

   (A) North America

   (B) South America

   (C) Southeast Asia

   (D) the former Soviet Union

   (E) sub-Saharan Africa

6. What was Jawaharlal Nehru's overall policy direction for India?

   (A) to put Gandhi's dream of a spiritually pure, nontechnological India into action

   (B) to cement a firm military alliance between India and the United States

   (C) to modernize, secularize, and democratize India

   (D) to gain more territory for India at the expense of China

   (E) to create a theocratic regime governed by Hindu principles

7. The approach of the United States to Third World countries such as Indonesia, Nicaragua, and the Congo during the Cold War is best summed up as follows:

   (A) The United States ignored communist movements in the Third World as long as they did not pursue a pro-Soviet agenda.

   (B) The United States allied with anticommunist governments and movements, even if they were undemocratic.

   (C) The United States provided sizable aid packages to the poor of Third World countries in order to forestall the emergence of communist movements.

   (D) The United States actively supported socialist parties if they were also democratic.

   (E) The United States maintained a strict policy of nonintervention in the Third World.

8. Which of the following is NOT among the economic powerhouses known during the 1980s and early 1990s as the "little tigers"?

   (A) Singapore

   (B) Vietnam

   (C) Hong Kong

   (D) Taiwan

   (E) South Korea

9. What role did Jiang Qing play in Chinese politics?

(A) She served as a moderating influence on Mao Tse-tung.

(B) She was the prime mover behind the Great Proletarian Cultural Revolution.

(C) She overthrew Mao Tse-tung.

(D) She supported Deng Xiaoping's rise to power.

(E) She became the most eloquent voice among China's anticommunist dissidents.

10. What Central American nation, during most of the 1980s, became a battleground between the U.S.-backed Contra rebels and the Soviet-supported Sandinista government?

(A) Nicaragua

(B) Guatemala

(C) Costa Rica

(D) El Salvador

(E) Honduras

Answers

1. **(C)** Unemployment levels were higher during the Great Depression of the 1930s. The rare combination of inflation and stagnation caused by recession was given the nickname stagflation in the 1970s.

2. **(A)** Algerians waged a war of independence against France from 1954 to 1962. The Evian accords, signed in March 1962 between the warring parties, ended the hostilities and recognized Algeria's independence.

3. **(E)** In 1979, a Shiite cleric, Ayatollah Khomeini, took control of the country. The shah, who had relied on repression to carry out his modernization campaign, fled the country. The Iranian Revolution transformed the country into an anti-Western theocratic dictatorship.

4. **(D)** In 1975, the Khmer Rouge, led by Pol Pot, took control of Cambodia and killed as many as 2 million people in the process. In carrying out plans to eliminate all capitalist elements, the dictatorial regime evacuated cities and forced Cambodians into collective farms. Intellectuals, professional workers, and other city dwellers were murdered.

5. **(E)** From the 1980s onward, the HIV virus, which seems to have originated in Africa, has caused millions of deaths. Containing the spread of the virus has proven to be extremely difficult in many countries of sub-Saharan Africa, where infection rates are among the highest in the world.

6. **(C)** Nehru served as India's prime minister from 1947 to 1964. His goal was to turn India into a modern and educated industrial power. In terms of foreign policy, he preserved India's status as a nonaligned nation, although he also maintained a friendly, cooperative relationship with the Soviets.

7. **(B)** During the Cold War, the U.S. government feared that communism would spread in the Third World. It was especially concerned at times about leftist regimes in Latin America, including Nicaragua and Cuba, because of the region's proximity to U.S. borders. The United States made a practice of supporting any regime that opposed communism, even if it was authoritarian.

8. **(B)** In the 1980s, Vietnam was a communist country. It traded largely with Soviet-bloc countries and so did not open its markets to Western goods or sell its own products on world markets.

9. **(B)** Jiang Qing, Mao's wife, was the chief architect of the Cultural Revolution, a ten-year campaign that was meant to eliminate their enemies and instill revolutionary purity within Chinese society and culture.

10. **(A)** In 1979, the left-wing Sandinista movement overthrew Somoza's right-wing dictatorship. In response, the U.S. government began to support a right-wing, counterrevolutionary guerrilla force known as the Contras.

Social Developments, Cultural Changes, and Intellectual Trends

CHAPTER **33**

- The modern versus the postmodernist (contemporary) period
- Postindustrial (service and high-tech) economies
- Economic globalization (multinational corporations and international trade agreements)
- Socio-economic features of the developed world
- The developing (third) world and the north-south split
- Population growth and modern migration
- Social activism and nongovernmental organizations (NGOs)
- Women's liberation and feminism
- Multiculturalism versus Americanization
- Mass-media technology, the computer, and the information (digital) revolution
- Scientific advancements (quantum physics, genetics, rocketry, computers, robotics)

The twentieth and twenty-first centuries have witnessed an explosion of social, cultural, and intellectual changes. The pace of scientific and technological advancement is faster than ever before. The world's population has grown with breathtaking speed. The world's economies have become increasingly interconnected.

Different parts of the world experienced these transformations differently. As a general rule, the changes of the twentieth and twenty-first centuries can be said to have proceeded along four basic tracks:

- In Western Europe, the United States, and Canada—the West—and Australia and New Zealand, movement has been toward stable democratization, greater economic prosperity, thorough urbanization, commitment to social equality and individual liberties, and the creation of social welfare systems. Scientific and technological achievement has been tremendous. These nations have developed postindustrial economies that emphasize services, consumerism, and cutting-edge technology (especially biotech and computers).

- Prosperous nations in Asia—the so-called tigers, such as Japan and, to a lesser extent, Taiwan, South Korea, Indonesia, and Singapore—have made great strides toward economic and technological modernization. They have urbanized greatly and developed a variety of social services. Their economies are postindustrial and high-tech. In many respects, Japan has equaled or surpassed the West (even though its phenomenal economic growth slowed during the 1990s). However, these societies, although nominally democratic, have been relatively slow to embrace or even tolerate the diversity and individualism that have been the hallmarks of Western societies during the late 1800s and 1900s.
- The Soviet Union and Eastern Europe modernized economically, especially during the postwar era. They urbanized and developed social welfare services. Technological and scientific advancement was considerable. However, Soviet and East European economies remained industrial rather than postindustrial and, in terms of technological finesse (especially with regard to computers), were cruder than Western economies. Moreover, until the collapse of communism in this region from 1989 to 1991, political systems were dictatorial and repressive. Even after the collapse of communism, it has been difficult for this region to move toward democracy and economic prosperity.
- The developing nations of Asia, Africa, the Middle East, and Latin America are all, to one degree or another, striving to attain advanced economic systems, modern societies, and representative forms of government. Some have made progress, attaining a relatively high level of prosperity or functioning democracies, or both. Others are mired in backwardness, poverty, civil war, and dictatorship. Most are somewhere in between. Perhaps the most distinctive case is the People's Republic of China. Communist China has the geography, population, and military capacity of a major power, and its economic growth has been considerable from the 1980s onward. The government is still authoritarian, however, and social and economic progress remains uneven.

With regard to historical labels, it is common to speak of the **modern period** (ca. 1800–1945) as having come to an end, at least in the more developed West. The postwar era and the early twenty-first century are generally referred to by historians as the **contemporary** or **postmodern era**. The modern era was characterized by industrialization, the formation of the nation-state as the primary form of political organization, and the struggle for representative government and economic equality. The postmodern era is characterized by postindustrial and global forms of economic organization, multiculturalism and the blurring of national lines, and an extreme individualism that takes for granted the political and social equality won during the modern era.

One can argue convincingly that this description suits the Western world well. It is more difficult to fit the label "postmodern" to the less developed nations of Africa, Asia, Latin America, and the Middle East, many of which are still in the process of modernizing. This unevenness of social, political, and economic development is in and of itself a major characteristic of twentieth- and twenty-first-century world history.

ECONOMIC GLOBALIZATION

International Trade Before World War II

Systems of international trade had existed long before the twentieth century, and the scope and volume of that trade grew steadily between World War I and the **Great Depression** of the 1930s. The Depression sparked a wave of **protectionism**, as countries sought to shield their own industries and farms by imposing high tariffs on other nations' goods. The most notorious example of protectionism was the United States' **Smoot-Hawley Tariff Act** (1930). This act is widely considered to have spread the Depression to Europe, Latin America, and Asia by destroying the ability of these regions to export goods to the United States. World War II altered the patterns of international commerce in obvious ways.

Foundations of the Post-World War II Economic System

True globalization of the world economy began after World War II. Franklin Roosevelt, guided by the economic principles of John Maynard Keynes (and the convictions of Woodrow Wilson before him), believed that free trade was the key not only to economic prosperity but also to world peace. Nations whose economies interacted equitably, he felt, would be less likely to go to war.

In July 1944, Roosevelt met with Allied delegates at Bretton Woods, New Hampshire. It was here that the International Bank for Reconstruction and Development (the **World Bank**) and the **International Monetary Fund** (IMF), whose purpose was to rebuild Europe and lend assistance to countries in Asia, Africa, and Latin America, were created. In 1958, the first round of the **General Agreement on Tariffs and Trade** (GATT) was held, to establish the working rules governing imports, exports, and economic interaction among participating nations. The Soviet Union and the Eastern bloc refused to join this **Bretton Woods System**, and so their economies were cut off from much of the rest of the world's. Until the international economic crises of the 1970s, currency exchanges were fixed to the value of the U.S. dollar, the world's strongest. In turn, the U.S. dollar was based on the gold standard.

Varieties of Economic Development, 1940s–1970s

Over time, great prosperity came to the United States, Canada, Japan, and the nations of Western Europe. One way Western Europe staged its economic recovery was through **economic union** (the European Coal and Steel Community, the European Economic Community, the European Union), as described in Chapter 32. The reconstruction of war-torn Western Europe—particularly West Germany— was nothing short of incredible. The same was true of Japan.

The rest of the world developed unevenly. In Latin America and Africa, many governments relied on the export of small sets of natural resources or crops, just as they had done as colonies or economic dependents during the 1800s. The Middle East benefited from its dominance on oil production. The **Organization of Petroleum Exporting Countries** (OPEC), formed in 1960, consists mainly of Mideastern nations. OPEC has been one of the most successful and influential international economic coalitions in history.

The economies of the Soviet Union, its East European allies, and Communist China tended to remain largely but not completely isolated from the Western world.

Many nations in Asia, such as Japan, Taiwan, South Korea, Indonesia, and Singapore, were quick to adapt to global capitalism. As Western Europe had done, many Asian nations joined together in regional economic associations. Although the **Association of Southeast Asian Nations** (ASEAN), formed in 1967, was mainly a diplomatic group, it also tightened economic ties. The Asia-Pacific Economic Cooperation Group (1989) did the same.

A general economic crisis struck most of the world during the 1970s. OPEC's **oil embargo** severely affected the energy-dependent economies of the West. Recession and inflation plagued the United States and Western Europe. Although the USSR had its own oil reserves and was safe from OPEC's embargo, inefficiency, food shortages, the cost of the arms race, and governmental corruption sapped the economies of the Eastern bloc. In 1971, President Richard Nixon rocked the international community by taking the U.S. dollar off the gold standard.

Multinational Corporations

Nevertheless, Western economies recovered during the mid-to-late 1980s. Part of this recovery involved the growing strength of **multinational corporations**: huge conglomerates that, while technically "from" a single country, maintained factories, subsidiaries, and distribution networks all over the world, employing foreign workers and selling directly to foreign markets.

For years, the activities of these multinational corporations had been laying the groundwork for further globalization of the economy during the 1980s and 1990s. Critics say that multinational corporations have hurt indigenous populations by exploiting their labor, harming their environments, and preventing their own economies from producing homegrown industries and manufactured goods.

Economic Globalization During the 1990s

The 1990s brought about a high tide of **economic globalization**, at the same time as (and somewhat related to) the collapse of Soviet and East European communism and the democratization of much of the developing world, especially Latin America. The strength of multinational corporations increased. The explosion of computer technology facilitated the electronic transfer of money. Meetings of the **Group of Seven**, or **G-7** (the **Group of Eight**, or **G-8**, after 1998, when Russia joined), an informal association of the countries with the world's largest economies—the United States, Canada, Great Britain, Japan, Germany, France, and Italy—became more frequent and increasingly influential.

In 1995, the GATT regulations were upgraded and strengthened by the formation of the **World Trade Organization** (WTO), whose purpose is to regulate the economic interaction of the more than 100 nations that belong to it.

Regional economic unions became increasingly important. In 1994, the United States, Mexico, and Canada created a zone of free movement of money, goods, services, and labor by means of the **North American Free Trade Agreement** (NAFTA). Moves are afoot to enlarge this zone to include all of the Americas, through the auspices of the Organization of American States (OAS).

Asian nations have tightened their ties as well. By far the boldest experiment in economic integration, however, is Western Europe's. In 1991, the nations of the **European Union** (EU) agreed to the Maastricht Treaty, which provides for the creation of a single currency (the **euro**), the establishment of a European Central Bank, and common policymaking in the fields of immigration, environmental protection, and even foreign affairs and security issues. It took until the mid-1990s for EU nations to ratify the Maastricht Treaty, and friction between member states regarding the details of integration continues. Still, in 2002, many of the EU states abandoned their own currencies for the euro.

Costs and Benefits of Globalization

The costs and benefits of economic globalization are mixed. On one hand, it has generated great wealth, at least in a broad sense and in certain parts of the world. Proponents of globalization argue, with some justification, that free trade helps to preserve peace.

On the other hand, the fact that the economies of all (or most) nations influence each other so strongly means that negative trends in one region—financial crisis in Mexico in 1994 or Asia in 1997, for example, or Russia and Brazil in 1998—can adversely affect the entire world. In addition, it is questionable whether all nations will be willing to subject their individual economic policies to the dictates of the WTO or other international bodies. There have already been bitter disputes over this issue, especially between developing and developed countries.

Finally, globalization threatens to lead to a constant state of economic change and instability. Seeking profits, multinational corporations tend to move to wherever they can produce more cheaply. This means relocating to whatever city or country will provide them with the least expensive labor force, the most advantageous tax benefits or exemptions, and the most lenient environmental regulations. This can also mean the lowering of wages, the sudden unemployment or layoff of local labor forces, and great social stress. Agriculture has been greatly affected by globalization, as farmers in one country find themselves competing with cheap food being imported from other parts of the world. Some critics of globalization also point to its homogenizing effects on culture and fear that their own indigenous cultures are being crushed under the force of foreign (in particular, American) popular culture and values.

Whether or not economic globalization will continue remains to be seen. It most likely will. What also remains to be seen is whether the benefits will eventually outweigh the costs. This is much harder to predict and will remain a major issue into the twenty-first century.

SOCIAL TRENDS AND MOVEMENTS
Basic Features of Western Societies

Social change during the twentieth century was so rapid and thorough that it is difficult to generalize about it. By and large, Western nations and other developed states can be said to have evolved the following social features (albeit imperfectly and/or gradually in many cases):

- Elimination of legal distinctions between social classes.
- The replacement of aristocratic social elites by a professional, white-collar class that attains its elite status through earned wealth and/or educational status (often referred to as meritocracy or technocracy).
- Creation of a large, stable **middle class**.
- Access to at least a minimum standard of living and adequate level of material well-being, even among lower classes.
- **Urbanization**, as well as **suburbanization**.
- Establishment of a **social welfare system** that includes unemployment insurance, pensions, and health care (at least for the elderly, if not the population as a whole).
- Universal educational system.
- Equal political rights for all adult citizens, including females.
- Equal treatment of all citizens before the law.
- Equal rights for minorities (still an ongoing process, even in areas as advanced as the United States, Canada, Australia, New Zealand, Japan, and Europe).
- The participation of **nongovernmental organizations** (NGOs) in the political process. NGOs, representing the interests of various groups in society, pressure governments to implement policies and provide social services.

Standard-of-Living Disparity Between the West and Developing World

With varying degrees of success, countries in the developing regions of Africa, Asia, Latin America, and the Middle East attempted to bring about many of these same changes. Some managed to do so by the end of the century, others did not.

One of the most pressing issues affecting the globe is the vast standard-of-living disparity between the developed world and the **developing world**. Many political scientists and sociologists refer to this as the **north–south split**, because most of the world's advanced, postindustrial societies are located well above the equator.

The gap between the developed and developing worlds causes diplomatic friction, interferes with the smooth and equitable globalization of the world economy, and perpetuates tremendous socioeconomic inequality. An extremely small number of people in the developed nations possesses the majority of global wealth, uses up the bulk of the world's resources, eats a massive share of the world's food, and is responsible for most of the world's energy consumption and pollution. For example, in 1998, the United States alone consumed 25 percent of the world's energy, while its population makes up only 5 percent of the total world population. This trend has been in place during the entire twentieth century and showed no signs of reversing as the century ended.

> **TIP**
>
> In 1998, the United States alone consumed 25 percent of the world's energy, while its population makes up only 5 percent of the total world population.

Major Trends

Other important trends of the 1900s and/or early 2000s:

- *Population growth*: In 1900, the world population was 1.6 billion. At the century's end, that number had risen to 6 billion. Even in the developed world, where birthrates have tended to decline, population has increased. In the developing and less developed worlds, **population growth** has literally exploded. China and India each have populations of over 1 billion. The rate of growth in Africa has averaged over 3 percent per year. Latin America went from 165 million in 1950 to 400 million in the mid-1980s. Cities such as Mexico City, Shanghai, and Buenos Aires are among the most densely populated in the world. Ironically, the true problems resulting from population growth—overconsumption of food and energy and overproduction of waste and pollution—have more to do with the developed world, where population growth is slower.

- *Migration*: Patterns of **modern migration** date to the last half of the 1800s, when millions of immigrants from Europe (and a smaller number from China) flooded to the United States, Canada, Argentina, and Chile. This trend continued through the early 1900s, until the United States instituted stricter immigration policies. The movement of peoples continued after World War II, however, and even intensified. During the late 1940s and 1950s, European refugees and displaced persons (largely from Eastern Europe, where Nazi genocide and then Soviet occupation led to massive population transfers) moved throughout the continent, mainly to Western Europe. All throughout the postwar period, economic opportunity, violence in the developing world (caused largely by brushfire conflicts related to the Cold War), and political repression have led millions of people to leave Asia, the Middle East, Latin America, and Africa for Western Europe and North America. Even as France and Britain dismantled their empires, many of their former colonial subjects migrated from Algeria, India, sub-Saharan Africa, the Caribbean, and elsewhere. Refugees have fled from Asia and Latin America to the United States and Canada, from Africa and the Middle East to Europe. Guest workers from the Middle East (especially Turkey) and elsewhere began to be admitted to Western Europe; by the 1980s, there were more than 15 million. Most recently, the collapse of communism in the former Soviet bloc, as well as ethnic conflict in the former Yugoslavia, has led to a rush of migration from Eastern to Western Europe. Migration has often provided a much-needed labor force and enriched the cultural diversity of the host nation. However, especially when economic times are tight, it has stirred up xenophobia, typically among right-wing extremists.

- *Rise of the consumer society*: In developed societies, inexpensive, mass-produced goods tend to be available to almost all people, even the lower classes. At the same time, fewer people in these societies earn their living by means of agricultural or even industrial production. Consumer societies therefore tend to be based on service, or postindustrial, economies.

- *Social activism*: Demonstrations, protests, and strikes have brought about social, political, and economic change ever since the French Revolution. During the twentieth century, however, **social activism** and the work of NGOs have become increasingly important. The most famous wave of activism came in the 1960s and early 1970s (especially the various **1968 protests** that broke out in Paris, Prague, Mexico City, and U.S. cities and universities). Social activism has toppled colonial regimes (for example, in India), helped to end wars (as in Vietnam), and achieved civil rights (including in South Africa and the American South). It has also been crucial to women's liberation and the environmental movement.

- *Environmentalism*: Ever since the Industrial Revolution, there has been a spirit of environmentalism, striving to prevent the natural world from overdevelopment or destruction. Conservation efforts date back to figures such as Henry Thoreau, Ralph Waldo Emerson, and John Muir. The modern **environmental (or green) movement**, however, is a product of the post-World War II era, when it became clear that pollution, species extinction, and uncontrolled industrialism posed a dire threat to the earth's ecological well-being. Such movements began during the 1960s, both in North America and Western Europe. A major boost came with the publication of Rachel Carson's *Silent Spring* (1962), which warned of the dangers connected with the insecticide DDT. The celebration of Earth Day in 1970 also popularized the environmental movement. NGOs working on behalf of the environment, such as Greenpeace and the World Wildlife Fund, have become globally influential. In some West European countries (particularly Germany), green parties play an important role in national politics. Contemporary environmental efforts, including the Kyoto Protocol are largely focused on the problem of **climate change** (see Chapter 34).
- *Terrorism*: The first major conflict of the twentieth century, World War I, was sparked by a terrorist. Ever since, it has become more common for political movements to achieve their goals by means of violence and assassination. Especially in the post-World War II era, **terrorist activity** has escalated. Major terrorist groups have included the Palestinian Liberation Organization (PLO), the Irish Republican Army (IRA), the Red Brigades (a communist organization in Italy), a variety of anti-Israeli groups (including Hamas and Hizbollah), Chechen extremists, and Al-Qaeda. The first major terrorist act of the twenty-first century and the one that has had the greatest single impact on global affairs is the September 11, 2001 attack on the United States. Al-Qaeda terrorists linked to **Osama bin Laden** hijacked several aircraft and flew them into the World Trade Center and Pentagon, killing over 3,000 people.

> **TIP**
>
> Major terrorist groups have included the Palestinian Liberation Organization (PLO), the Irish Republican Army (IRA), the Red Brigades (a communist organization in Italy), a variety of anti-Israeli groups (including Hamas and Hizbollah), Chechen extremists, and Al-Qaeda.

- *Rise in extreme nationalism, ethnic hostility, and religious fundamentalism*: The most advanced age in human history has also been the most prone to hyper-patriotic **nationalism**, ethnic and religious violence, and **genocide**. The **Armenian genocide** and the **Holocaust** are instances from the first half of the century. The Arab-Israeli conflict, intertribal violence in Africa, and Hindu-Muslim tensions in South Asia have troubled the postwar era. Similar trends have been even more on the rise in the 1990s and early 2000s, as the end of the Cold War has removed many of the restraints keeping ethnic and religious tensions in check (see Chapter 34).

WOMEN AND THE SHIFT IN GENDER RELATIONS

One of the most important trends of the twentieth century—affecting slightly more than half of the world's entire population—is **women's liberation**. Progress here came mainly in the Western world, although other regions have also moved forward, if slowly and partially.

The Early Twentieth Century

Chapters 20 and 28 have already discussed the progress that women's movements in the West made during the late 1800s and World War I in agitating for **women's suffrage**, entering the workplace, and pushing for social, educational, and political equality.

Between 1917 and 1920, women got the vote in almost all Western nations, France and Italy being the most noteworthy exceptions. Except in the USSR (where rapid industrialization required as large a workforce as possible), the rate of female unemployment decreased in the 1920s, as men returned from World War I, and especially in the 1930s, when, during the mass unemployment of the Great Depression, it was considered "wrong" for women to have jobs if men were out of work.

The interwar dictatorships differed sharply in their treatment of women. In the USSR, Marxist ideology called for gender equality. The Soviets observed this ideal to a degree (but far from perfectly), and women made up a large part of the workforce. By contrast, Italian Fascism, German Nazism, and Japanese traditionalism were explicitly hostile to the notion of gender equality. In all three countries, women were expected to be principally mothers and homemakers.

Women and World War II

Famously, World War II brought women into the workplace in even greater numbers than World War I had. The image of "Rosie the Riveter" became a potent symbol of the role of women in U.S. wartime production. In the Soviet Union, women made up nearly 40 percent of the national workforce. Large numbers of American, Canadian, ANZAC, and British women served as war nurses and military personnel (although not combat troops). In the USSR, women served in the military and, in some limited but important cases, saw active duty in combat (mainly as pilots and snipers).

Although there was a temporary dip in female employment afterward, the war had served the purpose of permanently cementing women's place in the working world. Moreover, France and Italy gave women the vote in 1945.

Western Women and Feminism in the Postwar Era

During the postwar era, as Japan, Western Europe, the United States, and Canada moved on to ever-higher levels of economic advancement, women took an increasingly larger role in the workplace and public life. The same was true—and to an even larger degree—in Eastern Europe and the Soviet Union. However, during the late 1940s and 1950s, it was still generally considered that a woman's main roles were that of homemaker, childbearer, and caregiver to children. Even those women who worked suffered widespread gender discrimination: sexual harassment, unequal wages, lack of access to positions of leadership, and so on. The French philosopher Simone de Beauvoir analyzed women's place in modern society in *The Second Sex* (1949), which investigated the deep-seated cultural and biological reasons for male domination of women.

A great step toward equality was taken by women in the Western world during the 1960s and 1970s. This was the era of **feminism**, or women's liberation. Major figures here were Gloria Steinem and Betty Friedan, whose book *The Feminine Mystique* (1963) joined de Beauvoir's *The Second Sex* in providing the movement with an intellectual foundation.

The goal of the women's movement was not just to achieve legal equality but also to eliminate the cultural stereotype of women as the "weaker sex" and to remove social barriers blocking the way toward true equality. Achievements of the women's movement include better and more varied career opportunities, better pay, equal access to higher education, greater respect for women's athletics, a greater role in political life, and the right to birth control, legal abortion, and divorce.

Contemporary Gender Issues

Problems still remain, however. Informal discrimination and sexual harassment have not been eliminated. Access to the highest levels of business and political life is still not complete (a phenomenon commonly referred to as the "glass ceiling").

Moreover, women are still relegated to traditional and secondary roles in many non-Western societies. Although it is a stereotype to say that women are not treated equally in Asia, Africa, the Middle East, and Latin America, the fact remains that Islamic fundamentalism, conservative Catholicism, machismo, old-fashioned views of women as inferior (or wives as servants, even property) constrain women more commonly in these regions than in the West.

THOUGHT, CULTURE, AND SCIENCE

The hallmarks of twentieth-century thought and culture are rapid change and incredible diversity. Other major trends have included **multiculturalism**—the interaction and fusion of the world's various ethnic, artistic, and intellectual traditions—and the effect of **mass media technology** on culture and the arts. Scientific and technological advancement has proceeded at a breathtaking pace. The **information** (or **digital**) **revolution** caused by the computer has vastly altered life in the 1990s and beyond.

Pessimism and Uncertainty in Western Culture

After World War I, art and literature in the Western world tended to be dominated by the themes of uncertainty and anxiety that had already emerged in the late 1800s and early 1900s (see Chapter 20). The psychological theories of **Sigmund Freud**, as well as the philosophical implications of the theory of relativity and the new field of quantum physics, had dampened the overall optimism of the mid-to-late 1800s.

The demoralization caused by World War I increased the spirit of pessimism and relativism (the belief or attitude that there are no objective standards or truths). The best-selling nonfiction book in interwar Europe was the philosopher Oswald Spengler's *The Decline of the West*. The prose and poetry of T. S. Eliot and Franz Kafka dealt with dehumanization in an industrialized, bureaucratized era. By experimenting with stream-of-consciousness prose, authors such as Virginia Woolf, Marcel Proust, and James Joyce attempted to capture the workings of the human mind on the written page. Abstract painters, such as Pablo Picasso, distorted reality to demonstrate that things could be seen from a variety of perspectives. Surrealists, Salvador Dalí and others, placed realistic objects in unrealistic situations to confuse the viewer's sense of reality.

After World War II, the philosophical and literary school of **existentialism**, championed by the playwright Samuel Beckett and the philosophers Albert Camus and Jean-Paul Sartre, proposed that humanity was not guided by any deity, special destiny, or objective morality. Alone in the universe, the individual must learn to create a worthwhile, ethical existence for himself or herself without the benefit of religion or the hope of any life beyond the earthly one.

Mass Media

Mass media came to play an increasingly important role in cultural life. Radio, film, television, the inexpensive production of mass quantities of books, and computers have brought music, drama, literature, and information into the lives of a greater variety of people than ever before. In addition, in the hands of creative directors and filmmakers, cinema has been used to create genuinely great art.

On the other hand, critics of such **mass** (or **popular**) **culture** have argued that it tends to cheapen or dumb down culture by catering to the taste of the lowest common denominator. In addition, mass media have been used for political purposes, such as **propaganda** and indoctrination ("brainwashing"), especially in dictatorships. Even in free societies, critics say, mass media have become powerful tools in the hands of corporate entities, brainwashing people not for political purposes but to advertise goods and make a profit.

Another effect of mass media has been the westernization, even **Americanization**, of global popular culture. Before World War II, the lure of American jazz and Hollywood movies was immensely seductive. Afterward, when America dominated world markets and mass-media technology, Disney, McDonald's, and Coca-Cola, among others, became economic and cultural symbols recognizable not just in the United States but almost literally in every part of the globe. Some intellectuals, especially non-Western ones, have expressed concern about the corporatizing and Americanizing effects of mass culture; the Japanese novelist Yukio Mishima angrily condemned it as "coca-colonization." Others, however, have talked about the potential of mass media to draw people closer together. In the 1960s, Canadian sociologist Marshall McLuhan became famous for writing that modern communications would create a **"global village"**—a prediction that seems to have been at least partly realized, thanks to the Internet and World Wide Web.

Arts and Literature in the Non-Western World

The twentieth and twenty-first centuries have seen the literary and artistic traditions of the non-Western world achieve a status equal to—and in some cases surpassing—those of the West. In addition to maintaining their own indigenous traditions, non-Western authors and artists have adopted Western forms of writing, painting, and composing, often adapting, modifying, and adding native elements to them.

The Mexican painter Diego Rivera created powerful murals that vividly expressed the plight of the working poor, as well as that of Mayans and other indigenous peoples in his country. Chinese author Lu Xun (Lu Hsun) wrote hard-hitting stories about his nation's economic domination by outside powers, as well as the government's inability and unwillingness to care for the lower classes. The Indian poet Rabindranath Tagore, the first non-Westerner to win the Nobel Prize for literature, dazzled readers throughout the world with lyrical, mystical verses based on Hindu concepts.

Non-Western voices in the artistic world grew bolder and more eloquent after World War II. Common themes include the growing pains associated with decolonization, the difficulty of resisting Western (especially U.S.) cultural hegemony, the clash of Western and non-Western culture, and political opposition to one's own politically repressive regime. In *The Interpreters*, the Nobel laureate Wole Soyinka writes about corruption and dictatorship in his native Nigeria. A fellow Nigerian, Chinua Achebe, also takes on themes of decolonization and dictatorship, especially in *Things Fall Apart*. Ama Ata Aidoo describes the place of women in contemporary Ghana in *Changes: A Love Story*.

Cry, the Peacock is Anita Desai's famous treatment of women's lives in India. In Japan, Yukio Mishima, a traditional (but also gay) nationalist, bitterly opposed what he saw as the destruction of Japan's cultural values. His ritual, samurai-style suicide in 1970 elevated him to cult status.

In Latin America, authors such as Gabriel García Márquez and Isabel Allende pioneered magical realism: a richly textured style featuring detailed storytelling.

In the Islamic world, the novelist Naguib Mahfouz won the Nobel Prize for his *Cairo Trilogy*, a vibrant portrait of postwar Egypt. The Indian-born, English-speaking Muslim Salman Rushdie came to world attention in 1988 with *The Satanic Verses*, an irreverent treatment of Islamic orthodoxy. Both Mahfouz and Rushdie fell afoul of Muslim traditionalists. Mahfouz was stabbed by an Islamic extremist in 1984. Rushdie was declared a heretic by Iran's Ayatollah Khomeini, who openly called for Rushdie's assassination and forced him to go into hiding for years.

Science and Technology

Scientific and technological advancement during the twentieth and twenty-first centuries has been constant and spectacular. During the first half of the 1900s, the Western world fully industrialized, moving into a world where petroleum and electricity were the primary sources of energy.

Also in the Western world, great innovation has been made in all fields of science. Progress in certain areas has been most noteworthy. Physics was revolutionized at the beginning of the 1900s. First, **Albert Einstein** developed the **theory of relativity**, making the first major changes to the system of science and mathematics that had been synthesized by Isaac Newton in the late 1600s and early 1700s. Also in the early 1900s came the birth of **quantum physics**. Major figures here included Max Planck, Niels Bohr, Werner Heisenberg, and Enrico Fermi. The work of quantum physicists has completely altered our understanding of astronomy and subatomic particles. It also made atomic weaponry and nuclear energy possible.

Rocketry and space science emerged in the 1900s. Pioneers of rocket science included the American Robert Goddard and Russia's Konstantin Tsiolkovsky. The new science matured during World War II thanks largely to the efforts of German scientists. As discussed in Chapter 31, the nuclear arms race between the United States and the Soviet Union spurred a parallel space race. The move toward a permanent presence in space was encouraged by the USSR's work in developing orbital laboratories and the United States' invention of the space shuttle. Rocket science has also made satellite communications possible.

Another field of special significance is **genetics**, which came into being in the late 1800s thanks to the work of an Austrian monk, Gregor Mendel. The field's great breakthrough came with the **discovery of DNA** by James Watson and Francis Crick in 1953. Since then, scientists have gained an unprecedented wealth of knowledge about how living organisms work. Combined with amazing innovations in computer technology, genetic science has allowed incredible medical advances. In the late 1990s, it also gave humans the power to clone living beings—a practice that is and will continue to be highly controversial.

Yet another significant advancement was the invention of the **computer**, during and shortly after World War II. Computers caused an information revolution that has altered the way people communicate, transact business, entertain themselves, and carry on with their professions. A key innovation was the development of the **Internet**, originally created in the 1960s for U.S. defense research purposes. By the end of the 1990s, a World Wide Web (WWW) had connected millions of users, and it continues to grow. Although a "digital divide" exists between those people who have better access to computer technology in the northern hemisphere and those who have poorer access south of the equator, the worldwide trend is toward greater access for all.

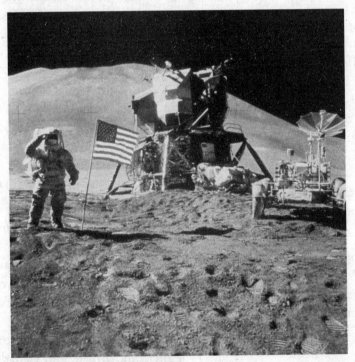

Apollo 15 Mission to the Moon, August 1971.
To this date, the United States is the only nation that has landed crewed spacecraft on the moon. The first moon landing came on July 20, 1969. The Apollo 15 mission, pictured here, was one of the several landings that followed. In recent years, trends in space exploration have included the deployment of crewless probes deep into the solar system (and beyond), long-term space station missions, space shuttle flights, and the use of remote-controlled technology to explore hostile environments, such as the surfaces of other planets.

QUICK REVIEW

1. What international organization has played the most influential role in determining the production level and price of oil in the post-World War II era?

   (A) the Association of Southeast Asian Nations
   (B) the Common Market
   (C) the Organization of Petroleum Exporting Countries
   (D) the European Economic Community
   (E) the World Trade Organization

2. What function does NAFTA serve?

   (A) It creates a free-trade zone that links Canada, the United States, and Mexico.
   (B) It serves as an agreement between Mexico and the United States, preventing illegal immigration from south to north.
   (C) It attempts to regulate the flow of illegal drugs throughout North America.
   (D) It establishes a set of tariffs and trade barriers between Canada and the United States.
   (E) It establishes a free-trade zone that links all the nations of North and South America.

3. In which of the following cities did major demonstrations and social protests break out in 1968?

   (A) Madrid, Glasgow, and Bogotá
   (B) Paris, Mexico City, and Prague
   (C) Quito, Paris, and Bucharest
   (D) Mexico City, Rangoon, and Ottawa
   (E) Bangkok, New York, and Lisbon

4. What step have many northern and western European nations adopted to make up for their diminished diplomatic and economic clout in the post-World War II environment?

   (A) They have constructed their own strategic nuclear forces, jointly controlled by all nations in the region.
   (B) They have created a military alliance that excludes the United States and Russia.
   (C) They have engaged in a new campaign of imperial conquest.
   (D) They have agreed to join together in an economic union, which uses a common currency called the euro.
   (E) They have tightened control over mass-media and entertainment industries.

5. Modern environmental movements

   (A) began only with the publication of Rachel Carson's *Silent Spring.*
   (B) have rarely cooperated with nongovernmental organizations (NGOs).
   (C) have not had an impact on national-level party politics in any major country.
   (D) persuaded the U.S. government to ratify the Kyoto Protocol.
   (E) have stimulated greater public awareness of species extinction and climate change.

6. The image of Rosie the Riveter symbolizes

   (A) the increased involvement of women in the industrial workplace during World War II.
   (B) the postwar trend of home ownership and maintenance by single women.
   (C) the emergence of the women's liberation movement in the 1960s.
   (D) the active combat duty that many American, British, and Canadian women saw in World War II.
   (E) the mobilization of a female workforce to take the place of men during World War I.

7. The effect of the theory of relativity on Western cultural and intellectual life was

   (A) to stimulate popular interest in science.
   (B) to restore a spirit of optimism to arts and letters.
   (C) to increase the sense of uncertainty reflected in arts and letters.
   (D) to convince artists and writers that there was a single objective truth.
   (E) to drive artists and writers to the political left.

8. Mass media have been used for purposes of

   (A) advertising.
   (B) propaganda.
   (C) high art.
   (D) entertainment.
   (E) all of the above

9. Which of the following is NOT true of non-Western art and culture in the twentieth century?

   (A) The fusion of indigenous and Western forms and styles was common.
   (B) Most non-Western intellectuals eagerly embraced the Americanization of global culture.
   (C) Non-Western authors were awarded the Nobel Prize for literature.
   (D) Multicultural influences became increasingly important.
   (E) Many non-Western authors and artists dealt with themes related to national liberation and the legacy of colonialism.

10. The discovery of what substance in 1953 dramatically furthered the progress of genetic research?

    (A) DNA
    (B) amino acids
    (C) RNA
    (D) hemoglobin
    (E) chlorophyll

Answers

1. **(C)** OPEC was formed in 1960, and its members consist mainly of Middle Eastern states. During the 1970s, OPEC's oil embargo adversely affected energy-dependent economies of the West.

2. **(A)** The North American Free Trade Agreement entered into force in 1994. NAFTA has a lower level of economic integration than the European Union does. In other words, unlike the EU, NAFTA countries did not agree to harmonize external tariffs, economic policies, or social policies.

3. **(B)** The most famous wave of social activism began in the late 1960s. It helped bring about civil rights protections for African-Americans in the United States, an end to the Vietnam War, a temporary wave of reform in communist Czechoslovakia, and a strengthening of labor reforms in countries of Western Europe.

4. **(D)** In 1957, six West European countries formed the European Economic Community. As of 2005, twenty-five countries—from both Western and Eastern Europe—are members, and the EEC is now referred to as the European Union. Since 1999, many EU member states have agreed to relinquish their domestic currencies and adopt the euro.

5. **(E)** Since environmental movements first raised awareness of global environmental problems decades ago, hundreds of treaties on the environment have been adopted at the regional and international levels. They include the Kyoto Protocol on climate change and the Convention on International Trade in Endangered Species (CITES).

6. **(A)** World War II brought women into the workplace in even greater numbers than the First World War had. Rosie the Riveter became a potent symbol of women's role in U.S. wartime economic production.

7. **(C)** Einstein's theory of relativity and other scientific findings of the early twentieth century dampened the overall optimism of the mid-to-late 1800s. For example, Pablo Picasso distorted reality to demonstrate that objects and concepts could be seen from a number of different perspectives.

8. **(E)** Mass media have transformed modern communications. They have been put to use in the creation of art, but they have also been used for commercial purposes (advertising), political purposes (indoctrination and propaganda), and entertainment. Those products of mass media not considered high art are referred to as mass culture (or popular culture).

9. **(B)** Typically concerned with preserving and advancing their own cultural traditions, most non-Western authors and artists have also proven adept at adopting Western forms and styles—and those of other cultures—to suit their needs and tastes. Many have been awarded the Nobel Prize for literature (the first was Rabindranath Tagore of India). Many have found the legacy of colonialism to be a rich and important subject. Most are concerned about or opposed to the degree to which American popular culture has proliferated around worldwide.

10. **(A)** In 1953, James Watson and Francis Crick discovered DNA (deoxyribonucleic acid), the substance that determines individual hereditary characteristics and carries the genetic code of all living beings. Understanding DNA has allowed half a century of advances in genetic science, medicine, and biotechnology.

Integration or Fragmentation? Globalism in the Late Twentieth and Early Twenty-First Centuries

- Global integration vs. global fragmentation
- The end of the Cold War
- The September 11, 2001, attacks and the war on terror
- Asymmetrical warfare (terrorism, guerrilla conflict, and small arms versus WMDs and the revolution in military affairs)
- Nuclear proliferation and weapons of mass destruction (WMDs)
- Nationalist aggression and genocide
- Religious fundamentalism
- Environmentalism, climate change, and the Kyoto Protocol
- The United Nations
- Nongovernmental organizations (NGOs)
- Multiculturalism

Are the nations of the world growing closer together or further apart? Enduring symbols of the late 1900s and early 2000s would include the sight of McDonald's golden arches in cities such as Nairobi and Shanghai, as well as the all-pervasive presence of mass media and the Internet in every corner of the planet. One might argue that these are signs of **global integration**.

However, other images of the recent turn of the century would seem to indicate of **global fragmentation**. Ethnic cleansing in the former Yugoslavia. Genocidal butchery in Rwanda. The breakdown of peace talks between Israelis and Palestinians. The terrorist attacks of September 11, 2001, as well as the tensions caused by the resulting war on terror. All of these would appear to signal that world communities are growing apart, not together.

The fact of the matter is that, globally speaking, centripetal and centrifugal forces are both acting on the nations of the world, simultaneously pushing them together and pulling them apart. Which will prevail as the twenty-first century progresses remains to be seen.

DIPLOMACY AFTER THE COLD WAR

In 1992, U.S. President George Bush stated that the **end of the Cold War** had brought about a "new world order." The U.S.-Soviet arms race halted, as did the bipolar division of most of the world into two hostile camps. In this way, the nations of the world were free to emerge from underneath the nuclear umbrellas of the superpowers and associate with each other as they pleased. The risk of nuclear annihilation decreased dramatically, and as described in Chapter 31, the end of the Cold War coincided with a general rise in the level of democratization worldwide.

On the other hand, the end of the Cold War has left the world without a defining diplomatic framework. Instead of two superpowers, only one, the United States, remains. The fact that other countries are now free to join or clash as they wish has made international relations more unpredictable. New diplomatic alignments appear and disappear. Many old alliances have broken or weakened. Others have had to be redesigned. For instance, what purpose does NATO have in Europe now that the threat of Soviet invasion has been removed?

Furthermore, during the Cold War, any conflict anywhere carried with it the risk of superpower involvement and with it the possibility of nuclear war. In its way, then, the Cold War had something of a restraining effect, which contained certain ethnic and cultural pressures, especially within the superpowers' spheres of influence. With the restraining effect of the Cold War removed, many of those hostilities have emerged, breaking out of control in Yugoslavia, Rwanda, Indonesia, and elsewhere. In addition, the post-Cold War years have witnessed the gradual spread of nuclear-weapons capability.

Another point of tension in the post-Cold War era is the strained relationship between the United States and China, the largest remaining communist power on earth. China is not yet a superpower, but its economic growth has been rapid throughout the 1980s and 1990s, and the wealthy commercial center of Hong Kong returned to Chinese rule in 1997. China possesses the humanpower and geographical size eventually to achieve superpower status. Although the United States pursued a policy of engagement with China during the 1990s, trade disputes and diplomatic disagreements have been frequent. U.S. support for Taiwan, which China regards as a breakaway province, is another potential source of conflict. Although the United States does not officially recognize Taiwanese independence, it would probably help to defend Taiwan if China attempted a reunification by force.

As for Russia, America's briefly friendly relationship with it has cooled. During most of the 1990s, Russia was led by Boris Yeltsin, who was then succeeded by a former KGB operative, Vladimir Putin. Russia is still struggling to build democracy and regain its economic footing. Nationalist forces are building, and Russia wishes to retain its sphere of influence in parts of the former USSR (this desire has embroiled Russia in a war with Chechnya since 1995 and caused it to meddle, often unsuccessfully, in the political affairs of countries such as Ukraine and Georgia). On the other hand, its leaders do not want to seem overly aggressive or remain isolated from other parts of Europe. While Russia is, for the moment, too weak to renew its superpower hostility—or nuclear arms race—with the West, it is still an important force in Europe and Asia.

At the time, the end of the Cold War was thought to have brought about lasting global peace. It has not. It would be too much to say that the result has been global anarchy, the post-Cold War years have called for new and creative ways of thinking about diplomacy. As one U.S. government official said during the mid-1990s, "We have slain the dragon; but we now live in a jungle filled with a bewildering variety of poisonous snakes."

SECURITY CONCERNS

War After the Cold War

The end of the Cold War has by no means brought about an era of peace. One major war—the Iraqi invasion of Kuwait and the resulting Gulf War (1990–1991)—took place soon after. War raged in Yugoslavia during the 1990s. In 1999, NATO bombed Yugoslavia in an effort to stop Serb aggression against the Albanian population of the Serbian province of Kosovo. Russia has fought Chechnya.

Just as important, a large variety of brushfire wars, small armed conflicts, and civil disturbances have raged throughout the decade following the collapse of the Cold War, resulting in the deaths of hundreds of thousands. Many of these have been motivated by ethnic hostilities that the Cold War had helped to keep in check. Finally, the **Al-Qaeda attacks on September 11, 2001**, have resulted in a U.S.-led war on terror that spans the globe and looks likely to continue for some time.

Weapons of Mass Destruction

Other troublesome security issues involve **weapons of mass destruction**. From 1987 onward, the United States and Russia have made progress in restricting, even scaling back, the production and testing of nuclear weapons. (Recent tension between the two countries has slowed this process down.) Beyond that, there have been worries that, given the conditions of extreme economic and political breakdown in Russia, nuclear weapons or weapons-grade atomic material might be stolen or smuggled out of the former Soviet Union and end up in the hands of terrorists or rogue governments.

Even more worrisome is the issue of **nuclear proliferation**. Only five countries belong to the "nuclear club," the group of nations officially acknowledged to possess nuclear-weapons capability: the United States, Russia, China, France, and Great Britain. Most nations of the world have signed the Nuclear Non-Proliferation Treaty. Generally, the treaty's effectiveness and longevity have been remarkable.

Nonetheless, several countries, most notably Israel, developed nuclear arsenals during the 1970s and 1980s. In 1998, India and Pakistan, deadly enemies, each tested nuclear weapons, adding new peril to an already dangerous diplomatic situation. North Korea gained nuclear-weapons capability sometime after 2000, and Iran is actively seeking it. How long nuclear proliferation can be contained is one of the most pressing questions of the new century.

The same can be said for other weapons of mass destruction, such as biological weapons (various germs, viruses, and bacteria packaged in a delivery system) and chemical weapons (such as nerve gas and water-based toxins). These are relatively easy weapons to manufacture and deliver and extremely difficult to defend against. During the Cold War, both superpowers abided by international agreements banning the use of biological and chemical weapons. Whether or not all states will choose to honor such agreements, now that the Cold War is over, is an open question.

TIP

There have been worries that nuclear weapons or weapons-grade atomic material might be stolen or smuggled out of the former Soviet Union and end up in the hands of terrorists or rogue governments.

The Proliferation of Small Arms

At the other end of the weapons spectrum are small arms: pistols, rifles, submachine guns, and automatic rifles. During the Cold War, some 50 million people were killed, mainly in the developing world, because of small-scale conflicts of various types. This trend has continued since 1991. Certain parts of the world, such as Africa, Southeast Asia, and Latin America, are awash with small arms. A huge illegal trade in these weapons thrives. Societies in which large numbers of civilians, non-combatants, and members of paramilitary groups—as opposed to regular military forces—have access to heavy weaponry are inherently unstable.

The Revolution in Military Affairs and High-Tech Warfare

One of the most striking features of contemporary military life is the unprecedented disparity between the technological capabilities of the world's most advanced armed forces and those of the least advanced.

The gap between high-tech forces and the lowest level of military capability has always been important, as the West's imperial successes of the 1800s proved. After World War II, however, that gap widened considerably. Nuclear weapons, jet aircraft, third-generation tanks, helicopter gunships, nuclear submarines and aircraft carriers, and global airlift capacity—owned and used by the superpowers and the small group of other nations able to afford them—were a far cry from the assault rifles, grenade launchers, hand-to-hand weapons and other small arms available to most armies or paramilitary groups. On the other hand (as in the nineteenth-century era of imperialism), technological superiority in **asymmetrical wars**—conflicts that pit high-tech adversaries against low-tech enemies—was not always a guarantee of military success. That fact was made painfully clear to the superpowers in Vietnam and Afghanistan, where guerrilla warfare and other irregular forms of combat prevailed.

Computer technology has widened the military gap even further. During the 1990s and early 2000s, the United States and a tiny handful of other nations experienced what generals and strategists refer to as the "**revolution in military affairs**" (RMA). This involved the full integration of computer technology, satellite communications, and precision-guided ("smart") weapons into military operations. Whether such changes will guarantee future victories remains to be seen.

NATIONALIST EXTREMISM, ETHNIC TENSIONS, AND RELIGIOUS FUNDAMENTALISM

One of the forces that the Cold War tended to keep under control was nationalist and ethnic extremism. The collapse of the superpower rivalry has, in many cases, released national, ethnic, and religious pressures, allowing them to boil out of control.

Nationalist Extremism in the West

Even in Western Europe, with its democratic governments and tradition of respecting civil rights, there is a certain level of ethnic tension. Since 1975, the island of Cyprus has been divided between Turks and Greeks, with a United Nations force needed to keep the peace. In countries such as Britain, Germany, France, Switzerland, and Italy, the millions of Turks, Middle Easterners, Africans, Pakistanis, Indians, and Caribbean islanders who live and work there (many of them as **guest workers**) suffer varying degrees of prejudice and discrimination. Right-wing and neo-Nazi groups harass minorities and call for their deportation, especially in times of economic distress. Likewise, much the same applies to the United States, where **anti-immigration sentiment** sometimes rises up in opposition to America's "melting-pot" tradition.

East European Nationalism and the Breakup of Yugoslavia

In Eastern Europe, ethnic tensions are even higher than in the West. Each Eastern European state is home to substantial minority populations, many of which have long histories of conflict. Even the Eastern European states that have made the most progress toward democratization have found it difficult to ensure that the rights of national minorities—Romanians living in Hungary, for example, or Slovaks in the Czech Republic or Russians in the Baltic States—are protected. One group that is heavily discriminated against throughout Eastern Europe is the Roma, better known as Gypsies.

The most striking examples of ethnic hostilities in Eastern Europe are the various wars in the former Yugoslavia. With the collapse of communism in 1989 and 1990, Yugoslavia, an artificial nation created after World War I to unite the southern Slavs—Serbs, Croats, Bosnians, Slovenes, Montenegrins, and Macedonians—began to break apart. Complicating the matter was the fact that these groups practice three religions, Roman Catholicism (Croatians and Slovenes), Eastern Orthodoxy (Serbs, Montenegrins, Macedonians, the Serbian minority in Bosnia), and Islam (the majority of Bosnians). There is also a sizable Albanian minority in Serbia and Macedonia, most of whom are Muslims. All these peoples have a long history of conflict. However, from 1945 until 1980, the communist government of Josip Tito held these conflicts in check and encouraged multicultural coexistence. Even during the 1980s, the various people of Yugoslavia lived together reasonably amicably.

After 1989, **ethnic tensions** began to reemerge. Such tensions were due partly to the stress and strain of communist breakdown but also to the efforts of nationalist politicians (such as the Serbian leader Slobodan Milosevic), who deliberately whipped ethnic hostility out of control for their own purposes. Slovenia, Macedonia, and Croatia declared independence in 1991.

The first Yugoslav war resulted from Serbia's attempt to take territory from Croatia. When Bosnia declared independence in 1992, the Serbian minority there rose up in arms, with assistance from Milosevic and the Serbian government. Their goal was to create a "Greater Serbia."

From 1992 to 1995, while the Serbian-Croatian war came to an end, a second war raged in Bosnia. Serb forces took three-quarters of Bosnia. Even worse, Bosnian Serbs, with full support of Milosevic's Serbian government, carried out the policy of ethnic cleansing. This form of genocide involved the forced deportation of Bosnian Muslims from territories the Bosnian Serbs wanted for themselves. It also included mass executions and the systematic rape of large numbers of women. The Serbian campaign of ethnic cleansing was the worst military atrocity committed in Europe since the Nazi Holocaust. The failure of the United Nations and European community to deal effectively with the crisis was not only embarrassing but called into doubt the ability of international organizations to cope with international conflict in the post–Cold War era. The war in Bosnia was finally ended by the U.S.-sponsored Dayton Accords, in the fall of 1995, when the Serbs backed down under the pressure of U.S. airstrikes and a renewed Croatian offensive.

Another round of fighting came in 1998 and 1999, when Milosevic and the Serbs began another campaign of ethnic cleansing, this time against the Albanian minority living in the Serbian province of Kosovo. For three months in 1999, NATO, in its first-ever military action, bombed Serbia until Milosevic relented. Although, technically, a state of peace exists in the former Yugoslavia, ethnic resentment and bitterness boils just beneath the surface.

Ethnic Violence in Africa, Asia, and the Middle East

Other notorious examples of ethnic violence include the Hutu-Tutsi conflict in Rwanda. In 1994, these two tribes fought each other. In the process, the Hutu killed approximately 800,000 Tutsi men, women, and children. The long-standing effort of the people of East Timor, a Pacific island illegally annexed by Indonesia in 1975, to free themselves has led to great bloodshed. Indonesian suppression of the East Timorese has verged on the genocidal since the 1970s. In 1999, the reign of terror Indonesia visited upon the tiny island was so bloody that it prompted United Nations intervention. Along with a severe currency crisis, the disturbances and scandals connected with East Timorese independence also played a role in toppling Suharto, the dictator who had ruled Indonesia since 1967.

Perhaps the longest-lasting, and still problematic, ethnic clash is that of the Israelis and the Palestinians. The Oslo Accord of 1993, in which the PLO leader Yasser Arafat and the Israeli prime minister Yitzhak Rabin agreed to pursue peace, led to more than half a decade of relative calm in the Middle East. Negotiations came to a deadlock, however, and tensions began to mount once again. In 2001, those tensions broke out into open conflict, as the Palestinians began a second uprising, or intifada.

Religious Fundamentalism

Religious fundamentalism has experienced a revival during the late 1900s and early 2000s. In India, religious conflict among Hindus, Muslims, and Sikhs continues. Policy in Iran is still shaped largely by Islamic fundamentalism. In Afghanistan, Islamic fundamentalism led to the creation of a strictly theocratic government under the Taliban, which ruled from 1989 to 2002. Religious differences are at the heart of the Israeli-Arab conflict in the Middle East and largely at the heart of the ethnic tensions plaguing the former Yugoslavia. They played an overwhelming role in the September 11, 2001 bombings, and they have been heightened by the subsequent war on terror.

Ethnic and religious tensions and violence have to be counted among the fragmenting factors threatening to tear the world apart, rather than bring it together.

ENVIRONMENTAL ISSUES

Despite the existence of vibrant and active environmental movements since the 1960s, environmental problems still remain. In several ways, they have become more pressing during the 1990s and early 2000s.

Environmentalism in the Developed World

In the developed world—the United States, Canada, Western Europe, Japan, and others like them—strict environmental regulations have been put into place from the 1970s onward in an attempt to ensure clean air and clean water for all. Recycling has become common practice. Endangered species have received greater protections. Growing concern about the depletion of the ozone layer led to the elimination of chlorofluorocarbons (CFCs). The ongoing debate about the effect of carbon dioxide and other green-house gasses on planetary climate patterns—**global warming**—has raised awareness about this issue.

Consumption and Pollution in the Developed World

However, the developed world's economies continue to modernize. With that, the rate of consumption among the populations of these countries continues to escalate. This group—a small segment of the world population—eats more, generates more trash, burns more gasoline, uses more electricity, consumes more wood and paper products, and releases more additives and emissions into the air and water than the rest of the people in the world combined.

Modernization and Environmental Problems in the Developing World

Added to this issue is the modernization of the developing world. As large parts of Asia, Africa, Latin America, and the Middle East industrialize and attempt to catch up with the developing world, their rates of energy use and resource consumption have been increasing. These countries also do not have the same clean-air, clean-water, and other regulations in place that nations in the developed world do.

> **THE ENVIRONMENT**
>
> It is common to think of pollution and environmental crisis as modern problems. In fact, societies have affected—and been affected by—the environment from the Stone Age onward. Resource extraction and consumption, as well as pollution, have always been part of the human community. The downfall of civilizations like those of the Indus Valley and Easter Island has been linked directly to environmental disaster or, in the latter case, mismanagement. In countless ways, the industrial era has made humanity's footprint on the environment heavier than ever before: Societies consume more, rely more on machine production and fuel-driven transport, and possess engineering skills that involve the capacity to change the earth in ways unimaginable to preindustrial societies. Currently, climate change (global warming) serves as the clearest demonstration of how profoundly human action has affected the environment.

The Failure of International Environmental Regulations

On the whole, international agreements to take greater care of the environment have met with limited success. A prime example of this is the Kyoto Summit (1997), where over 150 nations gathered to discuss environmental issues, especially the potential dangers of global warming. Although a **Kyoto Protocol** was hammered out, it is still contentious, and many countries, including the United States, have not ratified it. A particular point of conflict is the question of whether or not industrializing countries of the less developed world should be compelled to abide by the same clean-air regulations that nations of the developed world do.

Energy Sources

Another failure has been the inability or unwillingness to develop clean, sustainable sources of energy. Continued reliance on fossil fuels such as coal and especially petroleum has led not only to periodic shortages and economic difficulties but also to continued air pollution. Hydroelectric generation of electric power has its limits. Experiments with wind and solar power—potentially the cleanest sources of power possible—have not been supported by governments or corporations (at times, the latter, whose profits are dependent on oil-based technologies, have actively opposed such experiments).

The only alternative source of energy that has met with any success is nuclear power. This, however, carries with it serious risks, as nuclear accidents at Three Mile Island (1979) in Pennsylvania and Chernobyl (1986) in Ukraine—where 8,000 people were killed immediately and hundreds of thousands were made sick or born deformed afterward—have demonstrated.

Although a variety of environmental issues will confront the nations of the world in the twenty-first century, perhaps the most dangerous and the one that threatens all countries equally is global warming.

REGIONALISM, GLOBALIZATION, AND MULTICULTURALISM

Trends that would seem to encourage the integration rather than fragmentation of world communities include regionalism, economic globalization, and multicultural interaction. All are prominent features of contemporary life. However, they also have their limits.

The United Nations

Regional and international organizations and agencies serve to unite the efforts of countries around the world or in specific parts of the world. The **United Nations**, despite certain failures and flaws, has provided a forum for dispute resolution among the countries of the world since 1945. It oversees peacekeeping missions, monitors the observance of human rights and international treaties, and organizes humanitarian efforts, cultural preservation, and many other activities.

In terms of punitive measures, such as economic embargos, peacekeeping, and peacemaking, the United Nations' record is mixed. It has many successes to its credit, but events in Bosnia, Rwanda, Central Africa, and Sierra Leone have embarrassed it greatly. Its failure to dissuade the United States from invading Iraq in 2003 has called the United Nations' political effectiveness into some question.

Nongovernmental Organizations

A relatively recent trend has been the proliferation of **nongovernmental organizations** (NGOs). These nonprofit groups harness the effort of volunteers and activists locally, nationally, and around the world to work on various causes. Among the best-known NGOs are Greenpeace, the World Wildlife Fund, Amnesty International, Human Rights Watch, the National Organization for Women, Planned Parenthood, the National Rifle Association, and Medecins sans Frontieres (Doctors Without Borders).

Regional Organizations and Alliances

Regional organizations that have fostered international cooperation include the Organization for Security and Cooperation in Europe, the Association of Southeast Asian Nations, the Organization for African Unity, and the Organization of American States. Western Europe has made the greatest efforts to regionalize its economic, military, and political activities. In addition to the European Union and the OSCE mentioned above, many European nations belong to the NATO alliance and the Council of Europe.

Technology as an Integrating Force

Various cultural and technological factors seem to be bringing nations and regions closer together. Mass media technology has greatly increased people's awareness of other parts of the world. Enhanced means of communication—improved telephone networks, satellite transmissions, and above all the Internet and World Wide Web—have made it more possible than ever before for greater numbers of people to be continually in touch with other people in all parts of the globe. Cheaper and quicker modes of transport have enabled people to travel, work, study, or live abroad in vaster numbers than ever before. The celebration of art, literature, music, and traditions from all parts of the world—**multiculturalism**—has become extremely prominent during the 1990s and early 2000s. Cultural fusion and interaction have given multiculturalism even more of a boost.

Economic Globalization

The **globalization** of the world economy continues. The **European Union**, which, as of 2005, includes twenty-five members, has already removed barriers to the movement of people, goods, money, and services. In 2002, many of its members began to use a single currency, the euro. The North American Free Trade Agreement, in operation since 1994, is likely to serve as a model for similar agreements elsewhere. The **World Trade Organization**, formed in 1995, aims to bring the operations of the global economy under a single set of laws, rules, and practices.

However, economic globalization is not complete, nor is it self-evident that the trend is completely positive. Some of the flaws and potential dangers connected with globalization are discussed in Chapter 33. Not all nations belong to the WTO, and even member states quarrel with each other—and with the WTO's rulings. The great gap between the developed and developing worlds still remains—and, at least in some respects, it is widening.

QUICK REVIEW

1. Which of the following nations are suspected or known to possess nuclear weapons?

    (A) Canada, Brazil, Israel
    (B) Brazil, Italy, Russia
    (C) Israel, India, Pakistan
    (D) Pakistan, Zimbabwe, Great Britain
    (E) China, Mexico, France

2. What was the first major armed conflict of the post-Cold War era?

    (A) the Gulf War
    (B) the U.S. assault on Granada
    (C) the NATO bombing of Belgrade
    (D) U.S. intervention in Somalia
    (E) the Soviet invasion of Afghanistan

3. Over what island(s) independence are China and the United States most likely to quarrel in the future?

    (A) Hong Kong
    (B) Taiwan
    (C) Quemoy and Matsu
    (D) Sri Lanka
    (E) the Philippines

4. What ethnic group has met with widespread discrimination and regular violence throughout Eastern Europe since the collapse of communism?

    (A) Germans
    (B) Jews
    (C) Kosovar Albanians
    (D) Serbs
    (E) Roma (Gypsies)

5. Nationalist violence in the former Yugoslavia

    (A) had already caused many deaths under Tito's communist regime.
    (B) had never occurred before the end of the Cold War.
    (C) was purposely stirred up by opportunistic politicians after the collapse of communism.
    (D) was unavoidable because of the deep-seated and irrepressible hatred between ethnic groups.
    (E) resulted from the covert intervention of radical Islamic fundamentalists.

6. The concept of military asymmetry is best illustrated by

    (A) the unprecedented disparity between the technological capabilities of today's most advanced militaries and those of the least advanced.
    (B) the relative smallness of China's nuclear arsenal, compared with America's or Russia's.
    (C) the imbalance caused when a country armed with chemical weapons faces one that possesses nuclear weapons.
    (D) the dilemma faced by a nation when, by itself, it goes to war against a coalition of several countries.
    (E) the clash between a large armed force with a much smaller one.

7. The Kyoto Protocol of 1997 was intended to deal with the problems associated with

    (A) the illegal trade in small arms.
    (B) the HIV/AIDS epidemic.
    (C) the growing number of biological-weapons programs.
    (D) the climatic trend known as global warming.
    (E) the spread of nuclear weapons.

8. Which of the following is NOT true of nuclear energy programs?

   (A) Excluding the problem of nuclear waste disposal, nuclear energy programs provide a cleaner form of energy production than coal-burning plants.
   (B) Incidents at Three Mile Island and Chernobyl have been stark warnings of the risks involved with nuclear energy programs.
   (C) Some countries have been suspected of attempting to convert nuclear energy programs into programs of nuclear-weapons production.
   (D) The disposal of nuclear waste poses an important and difficult environmental problem.
   (E) By the 1990s, nuclear energy programs had been banned in Europe and North America.

9. Which of the following would be considered an integrating trend in global development today?

   (A) the worldwide proliferation of Internet technology
   (B) religious fundamentalism in Afghanistan
   (C) discrimination against Turkish guest workers in Germany
   (D) all of the above
   (E) none of the above

10. In which country did the worst genocide committed in post-Cold War Africa take place?

    (A) Sierra Leone
    (B) Rwanda
    (C) Angola
    (D) Mali
    (E) Nigeria

Answers

1. **(C)** According to the Center for Defense Information, in 2004, Israel possessed approximately 200 nuclear warheads, India possessed approximately 60, and Pakistan between 24 and 48. However, none of these countries signed the Nuclear Non-Proliferation Treaty.

2. **(A)** The United Nations Security Council authorized a coalition of states led by the United States to restore Kuwait's sovereignty after Iraq invaded Kuwait in 1990. U.S. President George H. W. Bush proclaimed that this widespread cooperation among states indicated the dawn of a "new world order."

3. **(B)** In 1978, the United States broke formal diplomatic ties with Taiwan in order to pursue diplomatic relations with China for reasons tied to the Cold War. However, the United States and Taiwan have maintained informal contact through quasi-official agencies and billions of dollars in trade annually.

4. **(E)** Even the Eastern European states that have made the most progress toward democratization have found it difficult to ensure the rights of minority groups, including the Roma. The Roma have faced discrimination in the areas of education, housing, employment, and healthcare in the Czech Republic and Hungary, for example.

5. **(C)** Serbian leader Slobodan Milosevic provoked ethnic hostility for his own political gain in the late 1980s and 1990s. For instance, Bosnian Serbs, with full support of Milosevic's government, carried out the policy of ethnic cleansing of Bosnian Muslims. Such a genocidal policy included mass executions and systematic rape of Muslim women.

6. **(A)** An example of military asymmetry is the conflict between the Israelis and Palestinians. The Israelis have employed sophisticated technology such as fighter jets, tanks, and smart bombs. On the other hand, the Palestinians

use less sophisticated small arms, light weapons, and suicide bombers in the conflict.

7. **(D)** Negotiators in Kyoto agreed to seek reductions in the average national greenhouse emissions of industrialized countries of approximately 5 percent below 1990 levels between 2008 and 2012. Each country has its own specified reduction rate.

8. **(E)** Nuclear power is the only alternative energy source to oil that has met with any success. France is the world's largest (per capita) nuclear power generator.

9. **(A)** The Internet and World Wide Web have made it more possible than ever before for greater numbers of people to be continually in touch with people in other parts of the world. However, many of the world's poorest people, such as those living in sub-Saharan Africa, still lack access to this important technology.

10. **(B)** In 1994 in Rwanda, Hutu militia murdered approximately 800,000 Tutsis and Hutus who objected to the genocide. The UN Security Council failed to authorize a peace enforcement measure in time to prevent the massive bloodshed.

Unit Six: Review Questions

SAMPLE ESSAY QUESTIONS

1. Compare and contrast the impact that World War I had on European imperial power with the effect that World War II had.

2. How have the status of and roles played by women changed between the early twentieth century and the early twenty-first? Focus on one of the following sets of regions:

   the Middle East
   Europe and North America
   South and East Asia

3. Compare and contrast the reform efforts and economic policies of the Chinese leadership after the death of Mao with the campaigns of perestroika and glasnost in the Soviet Union.

4. How have systems of international trade and global economic exchange changed between 1914 and the present?

MULTIPLE-CHOICE QUESTIONS

1. Which of the following was NOT a social change that stemmed from World War I?

   (A) The aristocracy declined in power across Europe.
   (B) The middle and lower classes grew in stature.
   (C) Europeans came to view themselves as models of civilized behavior.
   (D) Europeans' spirit of optimism faded.
   (E) Women were granted the right to vote in most countries.

2. Which of the following was among the communist regimes that survived the Cold War?

   (A) Czechoslovakia
   (B) Bulgaria
   (C) Albania
   (D) North Korea
   (E) Yugoslavia

3. Which of the following was NOT a provision decided at the Paris Peace Conference (1919–1920)?

   (A) breaking up Austria-Hungary
   (B) independence for Palestine
   (C) creation of Yugoslavia
   (D) assigning Germany full blame for World War I
   (E) stripping Germany of its colonies

4. The interwar period in Europe was marked by

   (A) economic depression and weakness within most democratic governments.
   (B) strong support for the policy of collective security.
   (C) growth in the number of democracies, particularly in Eastern Europe.
   (D) an economic boom and the strengthening of capitalism.
   (E) almost complete decolonization of Africa.

5. What effect did the liberation of Eastern Europe in 1989–1990 have on the Soviet Union itself?

   (A) It stifled freedom movements within the USSR.
   (B) It drained badly needed finances from the Soviet economy.
   (C) It greatly boosted Gorbachev's prestige at home.
   (D) It provoked a war between Poland and Soviet Ukraine.
   (E) It provided an example for non-Russian peoples within the USSR who wanted to set themselves free.

6. Fascism can best be described as

   (A) left-wing radicalism.
   (B) socialistic.
   (C) laissez-faire.
   (D) right-wing radicalism.
   (E) moderate.

7. Reza Shah Pahlavi of Iran was similar to Mustafa Kemal of Turkey in that he

   (A) was a democratic ruler.
   (B) proclaimed himself sultan.
   (C) secularized his country.
   (D) turned his country into a theocracy.
   (E) introduced a bill of rights.

8. Which of the following statements accurately describes civilian participation in World War II?

   (A) Nearly half of the war's casualties were civilians.
   (B) Only Jewish civilians were killed in great numbers.
   (C) Most civilians remained far from the battle scenes.
   (D) The warring parties tended to respect international conventions concerning the treatment of noncombatants.
   (E) In the United States, a smaller percentage of women worked outside the home than during World War I.

9. In the 1940s, what was Japan's long-term goal in the Pacific?

   (A) It planned to take over the United States.
   (B) It wanted to control the Chinese coast, all of Southeast Asia, India, Indonesia, Australia, and New Zealand.
   (C) It wanted to regain the Kurile Islands from the USSR.
   (D) It had no other goal but to strengthen trade with its immediate neighbors.
   (E) It wanted to work jointly with Germany in creating a Pacific Rim empire.

10. How did World War II change the patterns of international trade?

   (A) No countries traded with Germany after the war.
   (B) The World Trade Organization was created soon after the war ended.
   (C) The war diminished the European powers' control over world markets.
   (D) The USSR began trading more with Western Europe.
   (E) The United States stopped trading with Asian countries.

11. What kind of geopolitical alignment has the end of the Cold War brought into being?

   (A) the traditional form of balance of power
   (B) a concentration of world might in the hands of three evenly matched powers
   (C) a repetition of the Cold War's bipolar equilibrium
   (D) a state of affairs in which only one nation can be considered a true superpower
   (E) complete anarchy

12. How did Deng Xiaoping's reforms in China differ from those of Mikhail Gorbachev's in the Soviet Union?

   (A) Deng allowed political and cultural liberalization, whereas Gorbachev did not.
   (B) Gorbachev allowed political and cultural liberalization, whereas Deng did not.
   (C) Gorbachev finessed conservative opposition to his reforms better than Deng did.
   (D) Deng's reform plans laid the groundwork for a free-market economy, whereas Gorbachev avoided economic reform.
   (E) Deng gave China's outlying provinces greater autonomy, whereas Gorbachev suppressed all attempts by non-Russian republics to gain more autonomy.

13. What kind of role did many of the so-called Third World nations, including Angola and Vietnam, play in the Cold War?

   (A) They maintained a position of absolute neutrality, remaining on the sidelines.
   (B) They naturally and automatically gravitated toward the Soviet-led communist system.
   (C) They were naturally and automatically attracted toward the American-led democratic nations.
   (D) They became diplomatic and military battlegrounds, over which the two superpowers competed for influence.
   (E) They exerted a great deal of influence over the superpowers' military and diplomatic policies.

14. Lech Walesa's role in ending the Cold War was

(A) to declare martial law in Poland.
(B) to form an armed resistance group that sabotaged the communist regime.
(C) to lead the trade union and social movement known as Solidarity.
(D) to negotiate the withdrawal of Soviet tank forces.
(E) to invite the Soviet army into Poland to put down civic disturbances.

15. According to the map on page 413, which of the following countries did NOT become a member of the Commonwealth of Independent States?

(A) Belarus
(B) Moldova
(C) Russia
(D) Ukraine
(E) Estonia

16. Which of the following statements best describes Europe's political turn to the right during the 1980s?

(A) Leaders, such as Prime Minister Margaret Thatcher in Great Britain, privatized state-run sectors of the economy.
(B) Leaders, such as Chancellor Helmut Schmidt of West Germany, promoted the strengthening of the social welfare net.
(C) Officials became more xenophobic.
(D) Labor unions were given more economic rights.
(E) Taxes were increased.

17. What advantages did North African states have over countries of sub-Saharan Africa in terms of decolonization?

I. They were ethnically and religiously more homogeneous.
II. Their colonizing powers had left behind technology and industrial assets that still proved to be useful.
III. They had been states for a longer time than those in sub-Saharan Africa.
IV. More of their people shared a common language.

(A) I, II, and III
(B) II, III, and IV
(C) II and IV only
(D) all of the above
(E) none of the above

18. Why did apartheid in South Africa end during the 1990s?

(A) White leaders began to realize how unjust the policy really was.
(B) The African National Congress called for its dismantling.
(C) It never succeeded in segregating Africans from whites.
(D) It had succeeded in its goals by then.
(E) White leaders decided that the policy was hurting the country's economy and international reputation.

19. Which of the following factors has NOT interfered with African modernization?

(A) the AIDS/HIV epidemic
(B) lack of cultural or linguistic unity within African states
(C) negative population growth
(D) corruption
(E) interethnic conflict

20. In Latin America, modernization before the 1990s often led to

(A) greater social equality.

(B) better control over illegal drug trafficking.

(C) diversified economies.

(D) a concentration of wealth in the hands of political and economic elites.

(E) the establishment of communist regimes.

Answers

1. **(C)** The Europeans' view of themselves as models of civilized behavior and cultural superiority was exposed as an illusion. The United States was the only Western nation to escape this malaise, owing to the fact that it had remained comparatively undamaged by the war.

2. **(D)** North Korea remains a communist state. The regime's long-range missile development, research into nuclear weapons production, and huge conventional armed forces are of major concern to South Korea and the international community.

3. **(B)** After World War I, Arab lands formerly under the control of the Ottoman Empire were placed under temporary French and British control, according to a mandate system. Arabs felt betrayed by this arrangement because they had expected freedom, including in Palestine, in exchange for their military assistance against the Ottomans during the war.

4. **(A)** In 1920, twenty-three European governments could be considered democratic. However, by 1939, only twelve could be so defined. Most of the new states of Central and Eastern Europe fell victim to political extremism, especially as a result of economic problems during the Great Depression.

5. **(E)** By 1990 and 1991, non-Russian parts of the Soviet Union—particularly Georgia, Ukraine, the republics of Central Asia, and the three Baltic republics—had begun to agitate openly for independence. However, unlike in Eastern Europe, where "revolution from below" spurred the collapse of communist regimes, in the USSR it was political leaders who acted as the architects of the country's collapse.

6. **(D)** Fascism can best be described as right-wing radicalism or revolution from the right. It is anticommunist but also anticapitalist and antidemocratic. It is often characterized by hypernationalism and a state-sponsored campaign of racial and ethnic bigotry.

7. **(C)** As their countries' leaders, Pahlavi and Kemal were similar in that they both were modernizers in Muslim nations. One way of achieving this goal was to secularize their countries.

8. **(A)** One characteristic of twentieth-century warfare was that civilians made up a large percentage of casualties. In World War II, almost half of casualties were non-combatants.

9. **(B)** During this time, Japan had long-term and far-flung imperial pretensions in Asia. The population was experiencing strong nationalist sentiment, and by 1941, the Japanese military had gained control of the parliamentary government.

10. **(C)** Europe was heavily damaged by World War II, both economically and politically. Poverty levels increased, and there was food rationing for years in some countries. The United States emerged as the world's economic powerhouse and assisted its European allies through the Marshall Plan.

11. **(D)** Although Russia inherited the USSR's nuclear arsenal, the United States emerged from the Cold War as the world's sole superpower. The United States holds this distinction because it possesses the strongest military, has the largest economy, and exerts the most political influence.

12. **(B)** Deng encouraged the Chinese people to make money and allowed limited free-market reforms. However, unlike Gorbachev, he did not support democratization, as shown by his regime's crackdown of student demonstrators on Tiananmen Square, Beijing, in May 1989.

13. **(D)** Although the United States and its European allies did not formally go to war against the Soviet Union or the People's Republic of China, proxy wars were fought in the Third World. In these wars, including in Vietnam, tens of millions of people died.

14. **(C)** Before becoming politically active, Lech Walesa was a dock worker in Gdansk, Poland. In the 1980s, Walesa led the trade union movement called Solidarity. It became a focal point for protest and outrage against the Soviet-backed communist regime.

15. **(E)** All three of the Baltic States—Estonia, Latvia, and Lithuania—refused to join the Commonwealth of Independent States after the demise of the USSR. Instead, they sought to gain membership as quickly as possible in European organizations, such as the Council of Europe, NATO, and the European Union.

16. **(A)** Thatcher is an example of a leader in the 1980s who championed right-wing principles, supporting balanced budgets, free trade, privatization of state-run corporations, and deregulation of industry.

17. **(D)** In general, after decolonization, North African states became more economically and politically stable than states in sub-Saharan Africa. The former colonizing powers of North African states tended to leave behind technology and industrial infrastructure such as railroads and canals, whereas this was less often the case in sub-Saharan Africa.

18. **(E)** By the 1980s, internal unrest, economic problems, and international opposition to apartheid forced the South African government to abandon it. In addition, in 1990, the government agreed to free Nelson Mandela, a leader of the African National Congress who had been imprisoned since 1964.

19. **(C)** Africa has one of the world's fastest-growing populations. In many African countries, the rate of population growth has outstripped the rate of economic growth. Many of their citizens are living in poverty and without job opportunities.

20. **(D)** Before this time, many Latin American governments were ruled by military governments or juntas and right-wing dictatorships. These regimes were not accountable to their citizens and so did not care that wealth was concentrated in the hands of political and economic elites.

UNIT SEVEN

MODEL
ADVANCED PLACEMENT
WORLD HISTORY
EXAMINATIONS

Answer Sheet
MODEL TEST 1

Section I

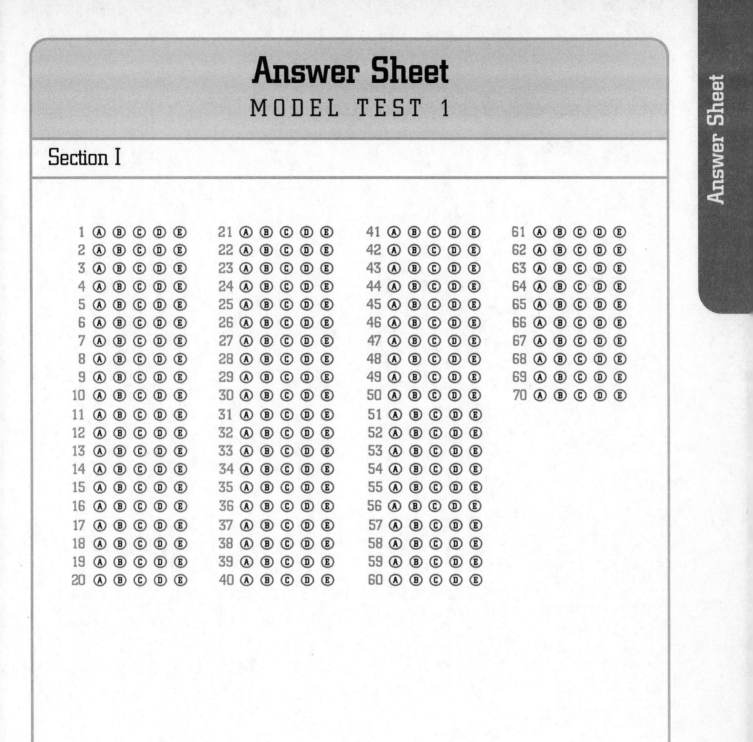

1 Ⓐ Ⓑ Ⓒ Ⓓ Ⓔ	21 Ⓐ Ⓑ Ⓒ Ⓓ Ⓔ	41 Ⓐ Ⓑ Ⓒ Ⓓ Ⓔ	61 Ⓐ Ⓑ Ⓒ Ⓓ Ⓔ
2 Ⓐ Ⓑ Ⓒ Ⓓ Ⓔ	22 Ⓐ Ⓑ Ⓒ Ⓓ Ⓔ	42 Ⓐ Ⓑ Ⓒ Ⓓ Ⓔ	62 Ⓐ Ⓑ Ⓒ Ⓓ Ⓔ
3 Ⓐ Ⓑ Ⓒ Ⓓ Ⓔ	23 Ⓐ Ⓑ Ⓒ Ⓓ Ⓔ	43 Ⓐ Ⓑ Ⓒ Ⓓ Ⓔ	63 Ⓐ Ⓑ Ⓒ Ⓓ Ⓔ
4 Ⓐ Ⓑ Ⓒ Ⓓ Ⓔ	24 Ⓐ Ⓑ Ⓒ Ⓓ Ⓔ	44 Ⓐ Ⓑ Ⓒ Ⓓ Ⓔ	64 Ⓐ Ⓑ Ⓒ Ⓓ Ⓔ
5 Ⓐ Ⓑ Ⓒ Ⓓ Ⓔ	25 Ⓐ Ⓑ Ⓒ Ⓓ Ⓔ	45 Ⓐ Ⓑ Ⓒ Ⓓ Ⓔ	65 Ⓐ Ⓑ Ⓒ Ⓓ Ⓔ
6 Ⓐ Ⓑ Ⓒ Ⓓ Ⓔ	26 Ⓐ Ⓑ Ⓒ Ⓓ Ⓔ	46 Ⓐ Ⓑ Ⓒ Ⓓ Ⓔ	66 Ⓐ Ⓑ Ⓒ Ⓓ Ⓔ
7 Ⓐ Ⓑ Ⓒ Ⓓ Ⓔ	27 Ⓐ Ⓑ Ⓒ Ⓓ Ⓔ	47 Ⓐ Ⓑ Ⓒ Ⓓ Ⓔ	67 Ⓐ Ⓑ Ⓒ Ⓓ Ⓔ
8 Ⓐ Ⓑ Ⓒ Ⓓ Ⓔ	28 Ⓐ Ⓑ Ⓒ Ⓓ Ⓔ	48 Ⓐ Ⓑ Ⓒ Ⓓ Ⓔ	68 Ⓐ Ⓑ Ⓒ Ⓓ Ⓔ
9 Ⓐ Ⓑ Ⓒ Ⓓ Ⓔ	29 Ⓐ Ⓑ Ⓒ Ⓓ Ⓔ	49 Ⓐ Ⓑ Ⓒ Ⓓ Ⓔ	69 Ⓐ Ⓑ Ⓒ Ⓓ Ⓔ
10 Ⓐ Ⓑ Ⓒ Ⓓ Ⓔ	30 Ⓐ Ⓑ Ⓒ Ⓓ Ⓔ	50 Ⓐ Ⓑ Ⓒ Ⓓ Ⓔ	70 Ⓐ Ⓑ Ⓒ Ⓓ Ⓔ
11 Ⓐ Ⓑ Ⓒ Ⓓ Ⓔ	31 Ⓐ Ⓑ Ⓒ Ⓓ Ⓔ	51 Ⓐ Ⓑ Ⓒ Ⓓ Ⓔ	
12 Ⓐ Ⓑ Ⓒ Ⓓ Ⓔ	32 Ⓐ Ⓑ Ⓒ Ⓓ Ⓔ	52 Ⓐ Ⓑ Ⓒ Ⓓ Ⓔ	
13 Ⓐ Ⓑ Ⓒ Ⓓ Ⓔ	33 Ⓐ Ⓑ Ⓒ Ⓓ Ⓔ	53 Ⓐ Ⓑ Ⓒ Ⓓ Ⓔ	
14 Ⓐ Ⓑ Ⓒ Ⓓ Ⓔ	34 Ⓐ Ⓑ Ⓒ Ⓓ Ⓔ	54 Ⓐ Ⓑ Ⓒ Ⓓ Ⓔ	
15 Ⓐ Ⓑ Ⓒ Ⓓ Ⓔ	35 Ⓐ Ⓑ Ⓒ Ⓓ Ⓔ	55 Ⓐ Ⓑ Ⓒ Ⓓ Ⓔ	
16 Ⓐ Ⓑ Ⓒ Ⓓ Ⓔ	36 Ⓐ Ⓑ Ⓒ Ⓓ Ⓔ	56 Ⓐ Ⓑ Ⓒ Ⓓ Ⓔ	
17 Ⓐ Ⓑ Ⓒ Ⓓ Ⓔ	37 Ⓐ Ⓑ Ⓒ Ⓓ Ⓔ	57 Ⓐ Ⓑ Ⓒ Ⓓ Ⓔ	
18 Ⓐ Ⓑ Ⓒ Ⓓ Ⓔ	38 Ⓐ Ⓑ Ⓒ Ⓓ Ⓔ	58 Ⓐ Ⓑ Ⓒ Ⓓ Ⓔ	
19 Ⓐ Ⓑ Ⓒ Ⓓ Ⓔ	39 Ⓐ Ⓑ Ⓒ Ⓓ Ⓔ	59 Ⓐ Ⓑ Ⓒ Ⓓ Ⓔ	
20 Ⓐ Ⓑ Ⓒ Ⓓ Ⓔ	40 Ⓐ Ⓑ Ⓒ Ⓓ Ⓔ	60 Ⓐ Ⓑ Ⓒ Ⓓ Ⓔ	

Model Test 1

SECTION I: MULTIPLE-CHOICE QUESTIONS

TIME: 55 MINUTES FOR 70 QUESTIONS

> *Directions:* Each of the following questions has five suggested answers. Choose the one that is best in each case.

1. Which of the following is an accurate statement about both the Americas and West Africa before 1500?

   (A) Polytheism was the dominant belief system.
   (B) Sorghum and rye were the main food staples.
   (C) Large domesticated animals allowed for extensive agricultural production.
   (D) Trade in bananas and salt was most prevalent.
   (E) A written language was in wide use at the time.

2. Postindustrial modes of economic activity focus MAINLY on providing

   (A) manufactured goods.
   (B) services.
   (C) raw materials.
   (D) plastics.
   (E) biotechnical products.

3. What characterized European social and economic life between the mid-1400s and the mid-1700s?

   I. Mercantilism was the dominant economic philosophy.
   II. Population growth was slow or level during the 1600s but accelerated in the 1700s.
   III. Economic dependence on the Atlantic slave trade decreased.
   IV. Europe's population remained overwhelmingly rural.

   (A) I, II, and III
   (B) II, III, and IV
   (C) I and III
   (D) I, II, and IV
   (E) all of the above

4. Which of the following factors did NOT contribute to major worldwide population growth from 1700 to 1800?

   (A) a decline in infant mortality rates
   (B) the widespread introduction of state-supported systems of health care
   (C) a decline in the number of deadly epidemics
   (D) the introduction of American food crops to Europe and Africa
   (E) the growth in the amount of land under cultivation

5. During and after the 1980s, major Latin American nations such as Chile, Argentina, and Brazil made transitions to what kind of regime?

   (A) democratic
   (B) anarchist
   (C) communist
   (D) fascist
   (E) theocratic

6. The Holy Inquisition was created to

   (A) track down and punish heretics and religious nonconformists.
   (B) canonize followers of Christ.
   (C) build great cathedrals in capital cities of Europe.
   (D) fight the Muslims in the Middle East.
   (E) find the Holy Grail.

7. How did decolonization in British and French colonies differ from that in colonies once ruled by Belgium and Portugal?

   (A) British and French officials better prepared their colonies for freedom and kept violence to a minimum.
   (B) Belgian and Portuguese officials better prepared their colonies for freedom and kept violence to a minimum.
   (C) British and French officials threatened violence, whereas Belgian and Portuguese officials did not.
   (D) Belgian and Portuguese officials allowed native representation in transitional governments.
   (E) Decolonization proceeded in about the same manner for all of these colonies.

8. The Eastern Question from the 1820s onward

   I. forced Great Britain and France to support the Eastern European powers against the Turks.
   II. took into account how destroying the Ottoman Empire might result in the rise of a hostile power in the area.
   III. led European powers to act cautiously toward the Ottomans.
   IV. recognized that the Ottoman Empire was no longer a real threat to Europe.

   (A) I, II, and III
   (B) II, III, and IV
   (C) I and III only
   (D) II and IV only
   (E) all of the above

9. Which invention, above all, allowed the Industrial Revolution to take place?

    (A) the cotton gin
    (B) electricity
    (C) the internal combustion engine
    (D) the steam engine
    (E) the paddle wheel

10. How were trends in New Spain and Brazil similar during colonization?

    (A) Neither used slaves.
    (B) Both European conquerors decimated Native American populations.
    (C) The societies both became ethnically homogeneous.
    (D) Copper mining was a critical part of the economy in both colonies.
    (E) all of the above

11. What global pandemic struck the world just after World War I?

    (A) hepatitis C
    (B) cholera
    (C) the Spanish flu
    (D) the Ebola virus
    (E) the bubonic plague

12. Which of the following statements accurately describes the role of oceans in the development of human societies?

    I. Oceans have, at times, kept societies apart.
    II. Oceans have served as an effective means of transport.
    III. Oceans have stimulated the emergence of networks of trade, technology transfer, and cultural exchange.
    IV. Using oceans, humans could travel completely around the world by the sixteenth century C.E.

    (A) I and II
    (B) I, II, and III
    (C) II and III
    (D) III and IV
    (E) all of the above

13. What made Mali such a powerful state in the 1300s?

    (A) It was known for its huge military forces.
    (B) It profited by cooperating with European slave traders.
    (C) Mali was a great center of Christian worship.
    (D) It was a major center of Islamic instruction and possessed large deposits of gold and metal ore.
    (E) It controlled the spice trade and was a significant center of Buddhist worship.

14. Which of the following did the MOST to encourage European exploration in the 1400s?

    (A) fear that Ming China might gain global supremacy by exploring first
    (B) scientific curiosity
    (C) the desire to seek out direct trade routes to China and the East Indies
    (D) the opportunity to gain new converts to Catholicism in the wake of the Protestant Reformation
    (E) the chance to search for gold, ivory, and slaves in Africa

15. The world's leading producer of cotton around 1700 was

    (A) the American South.
    (B) Flanders.
    (C) India.
    (D) China.
    (E) the Arabian Peninsula.

16. At present, the world's largest democracy, by population, is

    (A) the United States.
    (B) China.
    (C) Russia.
    (D) India.
    (E) Indonesia.

17. Which of the following is a suitable comparison of the political systems in China and Western Europe from 1000 to 1300?

    (A) China was unraveling politically, while in Western Europe the trend was toward unification.
    (B) Leaders in both regions were beginning to colonize parts of Africa at the time.
    (C) While Chinese leaders ruled a unified empire, Western Europe was governed by many monarchies.
    (D) Both regions were undergoing a process of democratization.
    (E) Chinese law instituted civil rights, while Western law focused on protecting the feudal system.

18. Hindu-Muslim tension in the 1940s

    (A) discouraged Nehru and convinced him to abandon the independence movement.
    (B) persuaded the Hindus to plan collaboration with Japan if it occupied India during World War II.
    (C) led to the partition of India and Pakistan.
    (D) delayed Indian independence for the next twenty years.
    (E) was, in the end, resolved without violence.

19. How did the Boers treat Africans?

    (A) The Boers allowed Africans to stay in their ancestral lands.

    (B) The Boers educated Africans in newly built schools.

    (C) The Boers allied with African tribes against the British.

    (D) The Boers worked alongside Africans in designing a democratic system of government.

    (E) The Boers treated Africans harshly and forcefully created a segregated environment.

20. As a result of the first Opium War

    I. the Qing government was forced to open more ports to foreign trade.

    II. the Chinese government had to lower tariffs on British goods.

    III. Hong Kong fell under British control.

    IV. British law took precedence in designated parts of Chinese territory.

    (A) I, II, and III

    (B) II, III, and IV

    (C) I and III only

    (D) all of the above

    (E) none of the above

21. How is the overall effect of World War I on European culture best described?

    (A) Art and poetry in the victorious nations reflected a spirit of triumph and pride.

    (B) Artists and authors quickly put the wartime experience behind them and ignored it.

    (C) A sense of despair and uncertainty came to the forefront of cultural and intellectual life.

    (D) The brutality of the war convinced most artists to reject abstraction and surrealism in favor of more straightforward, realist styles.

    (E) Jazz and other escapist cultural imports from the United States easily allowed the Europeans to forget the trauma of World War I.

22. Before the onset of the Neolithic era, Stone Age societies are NOT believed to have

    (A) domesticated the dog.

    (B) practiced monotheism.

    (C) expressed themselves by means of painting and music.

    (D) constructed dwellings out of wood and stone.

    (E) buried their dead.

23. How were industrialization and imperialism related?

 I. Industrialization gave Europeans better weapons to use in conquering other peoples.
 II. Industrialization forced Europeans to search elsewhere for more raw materials.
 III. Industrialization created more goods, and Europeans felt they needed to open more markets abroad.
 IV. Imperialism led to industrialization.

 (A) I, II, and III
 (B) II, III, and IV
 (C) I and III only
 (D) II and IV only
 (E) all of the above

24. Which of the following are causes or illustrations of social trauma in late medieval Europe?

 I. uprisings and revolts spurred by dissatisfaction with the Catholic Church
 II. the Black Death
 III. peasant rebellions
 IV. rising fear of witches and witchcraft

 (A) I, II, III
 (B) II, III, IV
 (C) I, III, IV
 (D) all of the above
 (E) none of the above

25. Britain's three Reform Acts

 (A) restructured the agriculture sector.
 (B) gave workers more benefits.
 (C) brought Northern Ireland under British control.
 (D) brought Scotland under British control.
 (E) gradually made the country's electoral laws more representative.

26. By the end of the 1920s, why had Japan stopped evolving into a democratic parliamentary monarchy?

 (A) The emperor abolished the Diet.
 (B) The Great Depression and heightened militarism stifled democratic impulses.
 (C) The monarchy was abolished, and the Japanese military took control.
 (D) Japan experienced a left-wing revolution.
 (E) The Japanese people were uninterested in liberal democracy.

27. Dutch colonization in the 1500s and 1600s

 (A) was carried out in partnership with Spanish allies.
 (B) failed to gain a foothold anywhere in Southeast Asia.
 (C) briefly gave the Netherlands control over present-day New York.
 (D) was prompted by harsh religious intolerance in the Netherlands.
 (E) resulted in Dutch rule over Australia until the late 1800s.

28. How did the Russian Revolutions of 1917 resemble the French Revolution?

    (A) Both involved a communist takeover.
    (B) During both, the main organizers were peasants.
    (C) In both, the first stage was more liberal than later stages.
    (D) For both, the goal was the founding of a democratic republic.
    (E) Leaders in both revolutions were bankrolled by ambitious capitalists.

29. The Bretton Woods System was created to

    (A) promote international environmental protection efforts.
    (B) promote international free trade.
    (C) protect Western militaries.
    (D) prevent a nuclear war.
    (E) engage the Soviet bloc in arms control talks.

30. During Japan's feudal period

    (A) the emperor was the symbolic head of the country.
    (B) the shogun held effective power.
    (C) the samurai class was transformed into a new aristocracy.
    (D) all of the above
    (E) none of the above

31. What major factor changed the economic life of East Africa during the early 1500s?

    (A) the depletion of metal deposits
    (B) the arrival of European colonists
    (C) the abolition of the Arab slave trade
    (D) civil war
    (E) invasion by Berber warriors

32. Which of the following ranks as the most remarkable aspect of the reign of Akbar the Great?

    (A) his construction of the Taj Mahal
    (B) his mighty victories in battle
    (C) his many wives
    (D) his dedication to the ideal of religious tolerance
    (E) his establishment of the Mughal Empire

33. What political characteristic did Mexico, Brazil, and Argentina share during the 1920s and 1930s?

    (A) All became democracies.
    (B) All were governed by authoritarian regimes.
    (C) All were monarchies.
    (D) All were ruled by Getúlio Vargas.
    (E) All had experienced communist revolutions.

34. Which eighteenth-century war in Europe spun off so many conflicts elsewhere and had so many global effects that it is sometimes considered a "world war"?

    (A) the Thirty Years' War
    (B) the War of the Spanish Succession
    (C) the Seven Years' War
    (D) the War of the Polish Succession
    (E) the War of the League of Augsburg

35. During most of the nineteenth century, what two countries competed for influence over Central Asia?

    (A) Japan and China
    (B) Germany and Russia
    (C) Britain and Russia
    (D) Japan and Britain
    (E) France and Russia

36. How did the harshness and ruggedness of the terrain in the Andes Mountains affect the way that societies there evolved?

    (A) People were forced to cooperate with each other and work out an effective division of labor.
    (B) Very few buildings or roads were constructed.
    (C) Culture was very primitive.
    (D) There was much fighting over scarce resources.
    (E) Individual families tended to remain isolated, retarding the development of sophisticated societies.

37. What benefits did the discovery of agriculture bestow upon early societies?

    (A) a greater ability to affect the environments in which they lived
    (B) a more reliable way of obtaining a more diverse supply of food
    (C) the ability to establish permanent communities and the reasons to do so
    (D) an increased tendency to cooperate and form more cohesive societies
    (E) all of the above

38. What impact did the Europeans have on West and Central Africa from the late 1400s and after?

    I. Those tribes that cooperated with the Europeans in the slave trade gained in strength.
    II. Some tribes, such as the Asante, received firearms from the Europeans in exchange for slaves.
    III. Trade networks were redirected.
    IV. Some West African tribes raided Central Africa for goods and slaves to sell to the Europeans.

    (A) I, II, and III
    (B) I and III only
    (C) II and IV only
    (D) all of the above
    (E) none of the above

39. Why was the 1904–1905 Russo-Japanese War significant?

(A) Russia was able to secure its foothold in Manchuria for the first time.
(B) It marked the first time that European powers fought in Asia.
(C) It marked the first time in the imperial era that non-Westerners had defeated a European power in a full-scale military conflict.
(D) It was the bloodiest war to date.
(E) Japan's defeat in the war transformed it from a militaristic nation to a more pacifistic one.

World Human Population Growth: 1 C.E.–1999	
Year	*Population*
1 C.E.	200 million
1650	500 million
1850	1 billion
1930	2 billion
1975	4 billion
1999	6 billion

40. According to the chart above, during which of the following intervals did world population grow at the most rapid rate?

(A) 1 C.E.–1650
(B) 1650–1850
(C) 1850–1930
(D) 1930–1975
(E) 1975–1999

41. In what way did Sukarno of Indonesia and Nehru of India share a similar diplomatic approach?

(A) They both fell strictly under the Soviet sphere of influence.
(B) They both fell strictly under the American sphere of influence.
(C) They both remained largely nonaligned in terms of Cold War diplomacy.
(D) They sided with Western Europe against the Americans.
(E) They both considered China their main patron.

42. How did slavery and indentured servitude in the New World differ?

I. Slaves were used only for agricultural labor, whereas indentured servants worked at household tasks.
II. Indentured servants placed themselves in bondage voluntarily, whereas slaves were forced into bondage.
III. Indentured servants were set free once their debts were paid, whereas slaves could be freed only if their masters wished.
IV. There was no practical difference between the two categories.

(A) I and II only
(B) I, II, and III
(C) II and III only
(D) IV only
(E) III only

43. Which of the following is depicted by the map above?

    (A) the spread of French revolutionary ideology across Europe
    (B) the Napoleonic Empire at its peak
    (C) the resurgence of the Habsburg Empire under Franz Josef I
    (D) the map of Europe as determined by the Congress of Vienna
    (E) Europe as it was after the Crimean War

44. Many technological innovations stemmed from World War II, including

    (A) nylon.
    (B) atomic energy.
    (C) computer science.
    (D) radar.
    (E) all of the above

45. Which crop dominated Southeast Asian agriculture in the 1400s?

    (A) rice
    (B) ginseng
    (C) soybeans
    (D) sugarcane
    (E) wheat

46. In what ways did Mustafa Kemal change Turkey?

    (A) He instituted the Islamic law code.
    (B) He abolished suffrage for women and forced them to wear the veil.
    (C) He westernized its culture and legal system.
    (D) He set the country on the road to peace with Greece.
    (E) He agreed to rule alongside the sultan.

47. Which of the following is an example of a technological innovation that occurred roughly simultaneously in two different regions of the world?

    (A) In both the Middle East and China, toolmakers began to mix copper and tin to create bronze sometime between 4000 and 3000 B.C.E.
    (B) Peoples in Europe and the Middle East invented the wheel at the same time.
    (C) The Sumerians and the Celts each invented writing, sometime between 3500 and 3000 B.C.E.
    (D) The Egyptians and the Celts simultaneously discovered the secret of fermenting alcohol.
    (E) Both the Franks and the Flemish invented paper at the same time.

48. The Tanzimat reforms in the Ottoman Empire

    (A) created the janissaries.
    (B) attempted to modernize the empire to a limited degree.
    (C) called for a religious jihad.
    (D) strengthened the military.
    (E) gave officials in North Africa more autonomy.

49. How did the collapse of Han China resemble the Roman Empire's loss of its European lands?

    (A) Both were later absorbed by the Byzantine Empire.
    (B) Their leaders began to rely on astrology to guide their decision making.
    (C) Both fell owing to depletion of natural resources.
    (D) Outside invaders contributed to the collapse of both empires.
    (E) Both collapsed owing to lack of technological innovation.

50. Which statement below does NOT accurately reflect the condition of women between 1000 and 1450?

    (A) Upper-class women in Europe tended to receive educations and manage household affairs in estates and castles.
    (B) At Japan's Heian court, aristocratic women could earn status by means of cultural and artistic accomplishment.
    (C) Certain societies in West Africa were matrilineal, rather than patrilineal.
    (D) In Islamic societies, women of the lower classes were, in practice, less restricted by religious law than those of the upper class.
    (E) The revival of Confucianism allowed Chinese women to gain greater rights and higher status.

51. The Tokugawa Shogunate

    I. promoted democracy.
    II. encouraged interaction with the outside world.
    III. failed to spur economic growth.
    IV. encouraged more social mobility.

    (A) I, II, and III
    (B) II, III, and IV
    (C) II and IV only
    (D) all of the above
    (E) none of the above

52. Which of the following broad changes made the sixteenth century different from the fifteenth century in Europe and the Atlantic world?

    (A) The slave trade began.
    (B) The Renaissance spread to Russia and other regions to the east.
    (C) Absolutism reached its peak in Europe.
    (D) Systematic sugar production was introduced in the New World.
    (E) Triangular trade came abruptly to a halt.

53. How did European and Japanese feudal systems differ?

    (A) Japanese feudalism relied on serfdom, whereas the European system did not.
    (B) European knights had no code of conduct similar to the Japanese ethos of Bushido.
    (C) Gunpowder was restricted in Japan and affected samurai less than it did knights in Europe.
    (D) Gunpowder weapons quickly ended the dominance of Japan's samurai, while European knights were not affected by such weapons.
    (E) Japanese feudalism was more repressive than European feudalism.

54. Which of the countries below was the last to grant suffrage to women?

    (A) United States
    (B) Canada
    (C) Great Britain
    (D) Italy
    (E) the USSR

55. What was the purpose of the Indian National Congress?

    (A) It served as the new legislature after India gained freedom.
    (B) It advanced the cause of national liberation in India.
    (C) It was a transitional body meant to share power with the British until full independence.
    (D) It lobbied to remain under British authority, but as a dominion, like Canada or Australia.
    (E) It made plans to launch a guerrilla war against the British colonizers.

56. What Asian religion was founded by Siddhartha Gautama?

    (A) Confucianism
    (B) Jainism
    (C) Hinduism
    (D) Eastern Orthodoxy
    (E) Buddhism

57. Which of the following accurately describes India's religious composition in the 1300s?

    (A) Islam had been forcibly introduced to much of India, especially in the north.
    (B) Buddhism enjoyed a major revival and became the second most popular faith after Hinduism.
    (C) Islam became especially prominent in the southern and eastern parts of the country.
    (D) Hinduism was nearly eradicated in fourteenth-century India.
    (E) Hinduism remained unchallenged as India's dominant faith.

58. The movable-type printing press:

    (A) appeared first in China.
    (B) helped spread Renaissance ideals and the religious debates that prompted the Reformation.
    (C) made it difficult for vernacular languages to gain literary importance.
    (D) was outlawed by the Catholic Church.
    (E) sparked the first wave of Islamic expansion by making the Qur'an more readily available.

59. Temples constructed in Southeast Asian nations such as Cambodia and Thailand are most likely to reflect the influence of

    (A) Christianity and Hinduism.
    (B) Islam and Confucianism.
    (C) Taoism and Buddhism.
    (D) Hinduism and Buddhism.
    (E) Shinto and Buddhism.

60. In what ways were the civilizations in Mesoamerica before 1000 C.E. more sophisticated than those in North America?

    (A) In Mesoamerica, astronomical knowledge and architectural skills were greater.
    (B) Mesoamerican societies had already adopted sophisticated systems of monotheistic worship.
    (C) Unlike North American tribes, Mesoamerican civilizations avoided human sacrifice.
    (D) Mesoamerican city-states were experimenting with participatory forms of government similar to Athenian democracy.
    (E) In no ways, because the North Americans had more advanced social structures.

61. In what way were the student demonstrations on Tiananmen Square in May 1919 similar to those in May 1989?

    (A) The students called for democracy.
    (B) The students called for an end to the communist regime.
    (C) The students called for violent overthrow of the government.
    (D) The students called for the radical transformation of culture and the arts.
    (E) The students called for capitalist reform of the economy.

62. The Hindu concept of samsara is BEST described as

    (A) a belief that the wicked are punished by everlasting torment after death.
    (B) a belief that one's soul lives, dies, and is reborn many times until it is pure enough to escape the cycle of rebirth.
    (C) a doctrine that justifies the caste system of India.
    (D) a declaration of nonbelief in the old Vedic gods and goddesses.
    (E) a belief that all actions, good and evil, have consequences in future lives to come.

63. Why are the 1600s and early 1700s in Europe considered a period of Scientific Revolution?

    (A) Isaac Newton and other scientists developed a unified system of physics and mathematics.
    (B) The scientific method was revived and used widely.
    (C) Scientists discovered that living things are made of cells.
    (D) The telescope and other scientific instruments were invented.
    (E) all of the above

64. One of the long-term effects of Mongol conquest was

    (A) to eliminate Buddhism in China.
    (B) to overthrow the fledgling Ottoman state.
    (C) to bring Islam to parts of Hungary and Poland.
    (D) to isolate Russia from Europe as the Renaissance got under way.
    (E) to disrupt Silk Road commerce in Central Asia.

65. How do most historians characterize the motives of the United States in its annexation of the Philippines?

    (A) The United States took the Philippines purely for economic reasons.
    (B) The United States annexed the Philippines for strategic purposes and because it felt American rule there would benefit the natives.
    (C) The United States wished to keep the Russians from gaining control of the islands.
    (D) The Filipinos requested that the United States take control of the islands, so annexation was not truly an imperial action in this case.
    (E) The United States took the Philippines in order to encourage the spread of Christianity.

66. Which of the following BEST encapsulates Confucian thought?

    (A) Political power is given to rulers by the gods; therefore, rulers may treat their people as they please.
    (B) Husbands and wives should share the responsibility for family leadership equally.
    (C) Social harmony is attained when superiors treat those below them with kindness, while inferiors respect those above them.
    (D) Only members of the aristocracy are capable of cultivating the qualities of etiquette and grace.
    (E) Society functions best when people are free to realize their individuality.

67. Which of the following sites in Africa experienced the greatest fusion of Arab, African, and Indian cultures in the nineteenth century?

(A) Alexandria
(B) Basutoland
(C) Madagascar
(D) Zanzibar
(E) the Gold Coast

68. Arab merchants

I. did much to spread Islam in places like Africa.
II. maintained caravan routes throughout the Sahara.
III. played a vital role in the Indian Ocean trade network.
IV. dominated the East African slave trade.

(A) I only
(B) III only
(C) II and IV
(D) I, III, and IV
(E) all of the above

69. How did the adoption of parliamentary monarchies change how ordinary Europeans lived in the 1700s?

(A) They were given fewer freedoms.
(B) They enjoyed more social mobility and greater freedom of religion.
(C) They were given the right to vote.
(D) Their average rate of literacy dropped.
(E) Social welfare systems protected them from poverty.

70. At the Berlin Conference (1884–1885)

I. Otto von Bismarck presided over the proceedings.
II. European leaders set parameters for intervening in Eastern Europe.
III. European powers established rules for making new claims in Africa.
IV. Socialist parties adopted an international manifesto.

(A) I, II, and III
(B) II, III, and IV
(C) I and III only
(D) II and IV only
(E) I and IV only

END OF SECTION I

SECTION II: FREE-RESPONSE QUESTIONS

Part A: Document-Based Question

TIME: 10 MINUTES TO READ DOCUMENTS; 40 MINUTES
TO COMPLETE ESSAY (RECOMMENDED, NOT OFFICIAL)

Directions: The following question is based on the accompanying documents. This question is designed to test your ability to work with historical documents. As you analyze the documents, take into account both the sources of the documents and the authors' points of view. Write an essay on the following topic that integrates your analysis of the documents. DO NOT SIMPLY SUMMARIZE THE DOCUMENTS INDIVIDUALLY. You may refer to relevant historical facts and developments not mentioned in the documents. Some documents have been edited. (Write your answer on a separate sheet of paper.)

1. The appearance of new inventions and new forms of science and technology often generates strong feelings within societies at large. The documents that follow speak to some of those feelings. How do various societies adapt to scientific and technological change? Be sure to identify the need for at least one additional type of document.

DOCUMENT 1

Source: Charlotte Brontë, English novelist, upon viewing the Crystal Palace at London's Great Exhibition (1851).

Yesterday I went for the second time to the Crystal Palace. . . . I must say I was more struck with it on this occasion than at my first visit. It is a wonderful place— vast, strange, new, and impossible to describe. . . . Whatever human industry has created you find there, from the great compartments filled with railway engines and boilers, with mill machinery in full work, with splendid carriages of all kinds, with harness of every description, to the glass-covered and velvet-spread stands loaded with the most gorgeous work of the goldsmith and silversmith. . . . It may be called a bazaar or a fair, but it is such a bazaar or fair as Eastern genii might have created. It seems as if only magic could have gathered this mass of wealth from all the ends of the earth.

DOCUMENT 2

Source: Victor Hugo, "This Will Kill That," *The Hunchback of Notre Dame* (1830).

Our readers must excuse us if we stop a moment to investigate the enigmatic words of the archdeacon: "This will kill that. The book will kill the edifice."

First of all, it was the view of a priest. It was the fear of an ecclesiastic before a new force, the printing press. It was the frightened yet dazzled man of the sanctuary confronting the illuminating Gutenberg press. . . . It signified that one great power was following upon the heels of another great power. It meant: The printing press will destroy the Church.

But besides this first thought, there was a second . . . but it no longer belongs to the priest alone, but to the scholar and to the artist as well. Here was a premonition that human thought had advanced, and, in changing, was about to change its mode of expression, that the important ideas of each new generation would be recorded in a new way, that the book of stone, [in which carvings and sculptures had provided the illiterate with a language of images and symbols], so solid and enduring, was about to be supplanted by the paper book, which would become more enduring still. In this respect, the vague formula of the archdeacon had a second meaning: That one art would dethrone another art. It meant: Printing will destroy architecture.

DOCUMENT 3

Source: Ito Hirobumi, young samurai from Japan, in letter to British official (1866).

Hitherto there have been a great number of stupid and ignorant persons in our provinces, who still adhered to the foolish old learning. They were unaware of the daily scientific progress of the Western nations, being like the frog at the bottom of a well. But lately they have learned. The eyes and ears of the stupid having thus been opened, the desirability of opening our country to foreign knowledge has become clear.

DOCUMENT 4

Source: Mohandas K. Gandhi, leader of Indian independence movement, *Gandhi: His Life and Message* (1954).

The incessant search for material comforts and their multiplication is such an evil, and I make bold to say that the Europeans themselves will have to remodel their outlook if they are not to perish under the weight of the comfort to which they are becoming slaves.

DOCUMENT 5

Source: Matteo Ricci, sixteenth-century Jesuit priest, showing a map of the world to the people of Canton during his visit to China (1578).

Of all the great nations, the Chinese have had the least commerce, indeed, one might say that they have had practically no contact whatever with outside nations, and consequently they are grossly ignorant of what the world in general is like. True, they had charts somewhat similar to this one, that were supposed to represent the whole world, but their universe was limited to their own fifteen provinces, and in the sea painted around it, they had placed a few islands to which they gave the names of different kingdoms they had heard of. . . . When they learned that China was only a part of the great east, they considered such an idea, so unlike their own, to be something utterly impossible. . . .

To them the heavens are round but the earth is flat and square, and they firmly believe that their empire is right in the middle of it. They do not like the idea of our geographies pushing their China into one corner of the Orient. They could not comprehend the demonstrations proving that the earth is a globe, made up of land and water, and that a globe of its nature has neither beginning nor end.

DOCUMENT 6

Source: Swiss author Henri Frédéric Amiel, on European industrialization, as seen at London's Great Exhibition (1851).

The useful will take the place of the beautiful, industry will take the place of art, political economy of religion, and arithmetic of poetry.

DOCUMENT 7

Source: Ali Akbar Davar, journalist and Iran's Minister of Public Works, editorial in *The Free Man* (1923).

Until we dedicate ourselves to an economic and technological revolution, nothing will move or change. We shall remain a nation of beggars, hungry and in ragged clothing, and we shall continue to suffer. We have six thousand years of history, but that will not translate into factories, railroads, hospitals, or schools. Schools alone without economic reforms will change nothing, as long as the environment outside the schools continues to reek of poverty. . . . When we have at least 5,000 kilometers of railways, 50 factories, 50 roads linking east and west, dams on the Karun River, and have eradicated locusts, we can then attend to the graduation of 1,000 students from institutions of higher learning.

DOCUMENT 8

Source: William Blake (1757–1827), English romantic poet, *Milton.*

And did those feet in ancient time
Walk upon England's mountains green?
And was the Holy Lamb of God
On England's pleasant pastures seen?

And did the Countenance Divine
Shine forth upon our clouded hills?
And was Jerusalem builded here
Among these dark Satanic Mills?

Bring me my Bow of burning gold:
Bring me my Arrows of desire:
Bring me my Spear: O clouds unfold!
Bring me my Chariot of fire.

I will not cease from Mental Fight,
Nor shall my Sword sleep in my hand
Till we have built Jerusalem
In England's green and pleasant Land.

Part B: Change-Over-Time Question

TIME: 40 MINUTES TO COMPLETE ESSAY
(RECOMMENDED, NOT OFFICIAL)

Directions: You are to answer the following question. In writing your essay, use specific examples to support your answer. (Write your essay on separate sheets of paper.)

2. Choose one of the following systems of labor. Discuss how it changed and/or did not change between the middle of the 1400s and the late 1800s.

   the Arab slave trade
   serfdom in Russia
   the Atlantic slave trade
   plantation agriculture in Latin America

Part C: Comparative Essay

TIME: 40 MINUTES TO COMPLETE ESSAY
(RECOMMENDED, NOT OFFICIAL)

Directions: You are to answer the following question. In writing your essay, use specific examples to support your answer. (Write your essay on separate sheets of paper.)

3. Compare TWO of the following revolutions. What do they have in common? How are they different?

   the Russian Revolution
   the Chinese Revolution
   the Cuban Revolution
   the Iranian Revolution

END OF SECTION II

Model Test 1

Answer Key

MODEL TEST 1

Section I

1. A	21. C	41. C	61. A
2. B	22. B	42. C	62. B
3. D	23. A	43. D	63. E
4. B	24. D	44. E	64. D
5. A	25. E	45. A	65. B
6. A	26. B	46. C	66. C
7. A	27. C	47. A	67. D
8. B	28. C	48. B	68. E
9. D	29. B	49. D	69. B
10. B	30. D	50. E	70. E
11. C	31. B	51. E	
12. E	32. D	52. D	
13. D	33. B	53. C	
14. C	34. C	54. D	
15. C	35. C	55. B	
16. D	36. A	56. E	
17. C	37. E	57. A	
18. C	38. D	58. B	
19. E	39. C	59. D	
20. D	40. E	60. A	

ANSWERS EXPLAINED

1. **(A)** Most African religions were animistic faiths that were based on the worship of spirits of animals and ancestors. Central and South American societies also worshipped many gods, and even shared some of the same gods.

2. **(B)** Western nations have developed postindustrial economies that emphasize services, consumerism, and cutting-edge technology. In turn, a greater part of the workforce in these countries has been employed in the services, including the biotech and computer industries, and there is a smaller proportion of unionized, blue-collar factory workers.

3. **(D)** During this period, Europe's economic dependence on the Atlantic slave trade actually increased. Not coincidentally, Europe's global power skyrocketed during the early modern period. Europe, unlike any other civilization, explored most of the globe, then conquered and colonized a vast portion of it. Europeans exploited human resources in Africa by capturing and enslaving people over hundreds of years.

4. **B.** Much of the population growth during the eighteenth century concerned the Agricultural Revolution, which amounted to a vast array of improvements in agricultural technology and technique. As a result, the number and severity of famines declined.

5. **A.** For decades, many regimes in Latin America were dictatorial and brutally repressive to their populations. However, the 1980s and 1990s witnessed a wave of democratization in such countries as Argentina, Brazil, Chile, and Nicaragua. One of the few exceptions to this trend was Cuba, which remained under the control of Fidel Castro.

6. **(A)** In 1231, the Holy Inquisition was established. It was essentially a set of special courts with wide-ranging powers. Its goal was to hunt out and harshly punish heresy and religious nonconformity.

7. **(A)** Methods for maintaining control over African colonies were particularly inhumane under the Belgians and Portuguese.

8. **(B)** By the 1800s, the Ottoman Empire was already in decline. This decline presented the European powers with a great geopolitical challenge, including how to prevent a power hostile to Europe from rising up in the area. However, Great Britain and France were not forced to support the Eastern European powers against the Turks.

9. **(D)** Powerful steam engines were developed near the end of the 1700s, when industrialization was just getting under way in England and other parts of Europe. Steam engines provided energy to machines that were key to producing manufactured goods in factories.

10. **(B)** Both the Spanish and Portuguese extracted natural resources from their colonies in the New World by exploited slave labor from Africa. Although they ceased to enslave indigenous peoples, they decimated large numbers of them owing to the fact that they brought diseases and had the advantage of more advanced military technology.

11. **(C)** Spanish flu was a major pandemic in the twentieth century. It struck during the end of World War I and killed nearly 20 million people worldwide. This number represented twice as many people as died fighting in World War I.

12. **(E)** Oceans have both separated human societies and brought them closer together, through trade. With the invention of instruments of navigation, oceans and seas offered societies with access to them an effective means by which to communicate, fight, and interact with each other.

13. **(D)** Between approximately 1250 and 1460, Mali was the biggest and most powerful Islamic state in western sub-Saharan Africa. It had large deposits of gold and metal ore and, as a result, became a key center for trade in eastern and northern Africa.

14. **(C)** The Europeans' primary motivation for exploration was economic. During the Middle Ages, Europeans had become aware of the fabulous wealth of other parts of the world, particularly in the east. They planned to acquire this wealth by seeking out direct trade routes to China and the East Indies.

15. **(C)** Under Mughal rule, the economy thrived thanks largely to a boom in the Indian cotton trade. However, as the Europeans gradually gained the upper hand in India during the 1700s, they defeated the Mughal state and established their own control over cotton production.

16. **(D)** In 1947, India gained independence from Britain and established a democratic government led by Nehru. Its present population is over one billion.

17. **(C)** During this period in Europe, a large number of relatively centralized states had emerged and were led by monarchs. In China, centralization was achieved first by Mongol rule beginning in the 1200s. Later, after the mid-1300s, China underwent even greater centralization under the Ming dynasty.

18. **(C)** The Muslim League paralleled the Congress Party's independence efforts, but both had different aims. The Muslim League advocated a separate Muslim state called Pakistan. The failure of the Muslim League and Congress Party to resolve their differences peacefully led to great bloodshed after Indian independence occurred in 1947. India and Pakistan were partitioned, but they continued to fight over Kashmir, a province of India that is heavily Muslim.

19. **(E)** The Boers possessed a very strong sense of racial superiority and enslaved the Xhosa people, who were indigenous to South Africa. In the mid-twentieth century, the Afrikaners, the Boers' descendants, created a system of apartheid (legal segregation of the races).

20. **(D)** The first Opium War, between China and Britain from 1839 to 1842, ended in a humiliating defeat for the Chinese. The Qing government was forced to allow all these measures, which the British had imposed in the Treaty of Nanking.

21. **(C)** Before World War I, Europeans were already beginning to lose faith in the notion of human progress. However, the destruction and despair caused by the war, not to mention the gloom surrounding Europe's clear loss of political and economic power, only worsened this sense of uncertainty and anxiety.

22. **(B)** Although generalizing about Paleolithic humanity is difficult, there is evidence that early humans domesticated dogs, painted and created music, constructed dwellings out of wood and stone, and buried their dead. However, concerning religious practices, early humans were polytheistic, meaning they worshipped more than one god.

23. **(A)** There is no evidence that imperialism leads to industrialization. Instead, industrialization came about in England in the late eighteenth century because it had a well-developed transportation system for the time and was already heavily urbanized. It also had a large pool of industrial labor compared with that in other European countries.

24. **(D)** The late Middle Ages lasted from approximately 1300 to 1500 C.E. These were years of great social stress in Europe, and all four answers are examples of some of these major problems.

25. **(E)** In the early nineteenth century, the British government began to give in to demands by the lower classes for greater political rights, including stronger economic protections. The three major Reform Acts would change Britain's electoral laws gradually.

26. **(B)** Japan's exports fell more than 50 percent, and farmers and factory workers were badly hurt. Nationalist sentiment increased markedly, and anti-Western feelings sharpened. By 1941, the Japanese military had gained control over the parliamentary government.

27. **(C)** The Dutch founded New Netherlands in the early 1600s. A Dutch settler, Peter Minuit, bought the island of Manhattan from a local Native American tribe in 1624.

28. **(C)** In Russia, the moderate Provisional Government attempted to establish a democratic government. It lasted only until the fall of 1917, and was relatively liberal. The first stage of the French Revolution lasted from 1789 to 1791, and the goal of the National Assembly was to create a constitutional monarchy.

29. **(B)** In 1944, the United States and its allies met in Bretton Woods, New Hampshire, to create new economic institutions that would promote free trade and a stable monetary system. The new institutions included the World Bank and the International Monetary Fund.

30. **(D)** Under the Tokugawa Shogunate, the government was centralized and dictatorial. There also was social stratification, with the samurai class becoming the new aristocracy.

31. **(B)** During this period, the Portuguese were the most prevalent group of Europeans in the region. They conquered a chain of cities along the East African coast, turning them into colonies and garrisons.

32. **(D)** Akbar was known for his religious tolerance when he ruled the Mughal Empire from 1556 to 1605. The Taj Mahal was built in 1648 by Shah Jahan in memory of his wife.

33. **(B)** None of these countries was democratic at the time. As in many parts of Europe, the economic pain brought about by the Depression had a negative effect on politics. It helped to incline Latin American politics toward extremism and dictatorship.

34. **(C)** The Seven Years' War was fought from 1756 to 1753. It was waged not only in Europe but also in North America and India. European colonization spurred a worldwide military competition among European powers for global dominance.

35. **(C)** The so-called Great Game was an intense competition between Russia and Britain for influence over Central Asia. It involved espionage and diplomatic intrigue. Tensions over Central Asia never resulted in outright war, although this rivalry lasted until shortly before World War I.

36. **(A)** This cooperation and efficiency gave rise to a number of major South American cultures, both before and after 1000 C.E. They included the Nazca, the Moche, the Huari, the Tiahuanaco, and the Chimu.

37. **(E)** The development of agriculture benefited early societies in several ways, including the four listed here. After agriculture emerged in separate parts of the world, cultural diffusion entered more often into the process. As more societies began to domesticate plants, certain techniques were borrowed and handed on.

38. **(D)** All these answers accurately describe the impact the Europeans had on West and Central Africa during this period. The Portuguese continued to expand along Africa's western shore until 1488. Later, the Dutch, English, and French landed there, began trading, and built permanent outposts.

39. **(C)** The Russo-Japanese War of 1904–1905 was a great victory for Japan. As a result of the war, it annexed new territories and compelled Russia to agree to recognize its sphere of influence in southern Manchuria.

40. **(E)** At the beginning of the twentieth century, the world's population was 1.6 billion. At the century's end, that number had risen to 6 billion.

41. **(C)** Many governments of Third World countries, including those of Indonesia and India, did not want to remain aligned exclusively with either side during the Cold War. Instead, they thought it was in their best interests to remain neutral or at least switch sides every few years, depending on who was willing to grant them economic and military assistance.

42. **(C)** Many English settlers during the 1600s were likely indentured servants. They agreed to work for their masters for a set number of years to pay for their passage across the Atlantic. On the other hand, slaves were forced to live in servitude.

43. **(D)** The Congress of Vienna, which met from 1814 to 1815, was dominated by representatives of Austria, Russia, Prussia, and Great Britain. They redrew the map of Europe, seeking to achieve a balance of power and prevent large-scale, long-lasting, and costly wars. Note that neither Germany nor Italy is united, a clue that the map predates the 1860s.

44. **(E)** All these innovations were made during World War II. The necessity to develop better and more effective military technology at this time had a huge effect on civilian technology long after the war ended.

45. **(A)** Rice-paddy farming probably originated in the Vietnamese states around 500 B.C.E. By the 1400s, this method had spread to other parts of Asia, including China and Japan.

46. **(C)** A Turkish colonel, Mustafa Kemal, later named Ataturk, formed a new government in Ankara, drove the Greeks from Turkey, and negotiated a new treaty with the Allies. In 1923, once the Ottoman Empire had fallen, Kemal established the Turkish Republic and became its first president.

47. **(A)** Bronze tools were greatly superior to stone implements in terms of quality and adaptability. Metal devices eventually replaced those of stone, ushering in the Bronze Age (ca. 3500–1200 B.C.E.).

48. **(B)** The Ottoman leaders implemented these measures from 1839 through 1876. They emphasized greater religious tolerance, legal reform, and improvements to public education.

49. **(D)** Waves of Asiatic and Germanic barbarians attacked Roman lands from the east and the north for more than four centuries, finally wearing it down to a final collapse in 476 C.E. In Han China, outside invaders, bandits, and rebels on the frontiers prevented them from effectively guarding their borders. In 200 C.E., the Han dynasty collapsed.

50. **(E)** Neo-Confucianism, along with Chinese tradition, was used to justify the greater subordination of women. Upper-class women, whose families were most likely to follow Confucian dictates, were particularly subject to restrictions.

51. **(E)** None of these answers is an accurate description of the Tokugawa Shogunate. Instead, the regime was authoritarian and isolationist. In addition, it experienced considerable economic growth and was very hierarchical.

52. **(D)** During the 1500s, Portuguese and Spanish colonies in Brazil and the Caribbean became major centers of sugar production. Massive profits from the sugar industry were built on the backs of African slaves.

53. **(C)** The Tokugawa rulers maintained a monopoly on gunpowder technology and kept the number of guns in Japan to a minimum.

54. **(D)** During the interwar period, Fascist Italy was extremely hostile to the notion of gender equality. Italy finally granted women suffrage in 1945, the year Mussolini was executed.

55. **(B)** The Indian National Congress was founded in 1885. Most of its members were English-speaking, educated members of the native upper classes.

56. **(E)** Siddhartha Gautama, who later took the name Buddha, founded Buddhism. His goal in founding this religion was to correct what he saw as the worst features of Vedism and Hinduism, as well as to modify some basic aspects of Vedic-Hindu doctrine.

57. **(A)** By 1206, the Muslims had captured Delhi, and most of northern India was in their hands. The major effect of the Muslim invasions and the establishment of the Delhi Sultanate was to introduce Islam into India.

58. **(B)** Johannes Gutenberg created the moving-type printing press. It was instrumental in raising literacy rates, spreading information, increasing the impact of new ideas and scientific theories, and encouraging the expansion of libraries and universities. (China, perhaps Korea, originated the less advanced technique of block printing.)

59. **(D)** Southeast Asian peoples adopted both Hinduism and Buddhism, and they built tens of thousands of temples reflecting the influence of both religions. The most famous example of Khmer architecture is Angkor Wat and Angkor Thom, former cities that consist of forty square miles of ornate palaces and pagodas.

60. **(A)** The Maya were accomplished astronomers and mathematicians. Their unusual calendar system was extremely intricate and accurate. They were also able architects, as shown by their pyramids and other buildings.

61. **(A)** On May 4, 1919, thousands of students gathered to protest against China's military government. They desired political and social reform. In May 1989, student protesters chose to demonstrate at this time because it marked the seventieth anniversary of the May Fourth Movement, and they felt inspired by that event.

62. **(B)** Samsara is also known as the wheel of life, a cycle of life, death, and rebirth. According to Hindu doctrine, union with the Brahman is achieved by experiencing this cycle.

63. **(E)** The Scientific Revolution ushered in a renewed interest in the ancient concept of the scientific method, as opposed to decision-making approaches based on superstition or narrow religious doctrines. Sir Isaac Newton, who introduced the laws of thermodynamics, is another important figure of this age.

64. **(D)** From 1237 to 1240, the Mongols of the Golden Horde conquered most of Russia and Ukraine. They maintained control over Russia until the mid-1400s.

65. **(B)** The United States wanted to keep the Philippines from falling into the hands of the Japanese. Possession of the Philippines also provided the United States with a strategic naval base in the Pacific and a way station for trade with China.

66. **(C)** Confucianism grew out of the teachings of a Chinese sage who lived during the 500s B.C.E. This belief system proposes that a happy, harmonious society can be created by a combination of benevolent rulership from above and good behavior from below.

67. **(D)** In the early 1800s, Zanzibar was the most important port in East Africa and controlled by Omani Arabs. Its primary trading partner was Bombay, India.

68. **(E)** Arab merchants achieved much more than amassing wealth for themselves. Their activities also helped spur the golden age of Islamic culture from the 700s through the 1200s.

69. **(B)** In parliamentary democracies in the 1700s, rulers became less powerful because they governed in conjunction with some kind of lawmaking body. Although poverty and inequality existed in parliamentary monarchies during this era, society was more flexible and social advancement was more feasible than in absolute monarchies.

70. **(C)** In 1884 and 1885, representatives of European nations met at the Berlin Conference to set down rules for expanding farther into Africa. They decided that no European state could make new claims there without demonstrating "effective occupation."

Answer Sheet

MODEL TEST 2

Section I

1 Ⓐ Ⓑ Ⓒ Ⓓ Ⓔ	21 Ⓐ Ⓑ Ⓒ Ⓓ Ⓔ	41 Ⓐ Ⓑ Ⓒ Ⓓ Ⓔ	61 Ⓐ Ⓑ Ⓒ Ⓓ Ⓔ
2 Ⓐ Ⓑ Ⓒ Ⓓ Ⓔ	22 Ⓐ Ⓑ Ⓒ Ⓓ Ⓔ	42 Ⓐ Ⓑ Ⓒ Ⓓ Ⓔ	62 Ⓐ Ⓑ Ⓒ Ⓓ Ⓔ
3 Ⓐ Ⓑ Ⓒ Ⓓ Ⓔ	23 Ⓐ Ⓑ Ⓒ Ⓓ Ⓔ	43 Ⓐ Ⓑ Ⓒ Ⓓ Ⓔ	63 Ⓐ Ⓑ Ⓒ Ⓓ Ⓔ
4 Ⓐ Ⓑ Ⓒ Ⓓ Ⓔ	24 Ⓐ Ⓑ Ⓒ Ⓓ Ⓔ	44 Ⓐ Ⓑ Ⓒ Ⓓ Ⓔ	64 Ⓐ Ⓑ Ⓒ Ⓓ Ⓔ
5 Ⓐ Ⓑ Ⓒ Ⓓ Ⓔ	25 Ⓐ Ⓑ Ⓒ Ⓓ Ⓔ	45 Ⓐ Ⓑ Ⓒ Ⓓ Ⓔ	65 Ⓐ Ⓑ Ⓒ Ⓓ Ⓔ
6 Ⓐ Ⓑ Ⓒ Ⓓ Ⓔ	26 Ⓐ Ⓑ Ⓒ Ⓓ Ⓔ	46 Ⓐ Ⓑ Ⓒ Ⓓ Ⓔ	66 Ⓐ Ⓑ Ⓒ Ⓓ Ⓔ
7 Ⓐ Ⓑ Ⓒ Ⓓ Ⓔ	27 Ⓐ Ⓑ Ⓒ Ⓓ Ⓔ	47 Ⓐ Ⓑ Ⓒ Ⓓ Ⓔ	67 Ⓐ Ⓑ Ⓒ Ⓓ Ⓔ
8 Ⓐ Ⓑ Ⓒ Ⓓ Ⓔ	28 Ⓐ Ⓑ Ⓒ Ⓓ Ⓔ	48 Ⓐ Ⓑ Ⓒ Ⓓ Ⓔ	68 Ⓐ Ⓑ Ⓒ Ⓓ Ⓔ
9 Ⓐ Ⓑ Ⓒ Ⓓ Ⓔ	29 Ⓐ Ⓑ Ⓒ Ⓓ Ⓔ	49 Ⓐ Ⓑ Ⓒ Ⓓ Ⓔ	69 Ⓐ Ⓑ Ⓒ Ⓓ Ⓔ
10 Ⓐ Ⓑ Ⓒ Ⓓ Ⓔ	30 Ⓐ Ⓑ Ⓒ Ⓓ Ⓔ	50 Ⓐ Ⓑ Ⓒ Ⓓ Ⓔ	70 Ⓐ Ⓑ Ⓒ Ⓓ Ⓔ
11 Ⓐ Ⓑ Ⓒ Ⓓ Ⓔ	31 Ⓐ Ⓑ Ⓒ Ⓓ Ⓔ	51 Ⓐ Ⓑ Ⓒ Ⓓ Ⓔ	
12 Ⓐ Ⓑ Ⓒ Ⓓ Ⓔ	32 Ⓐ Ⓑ Ⓒ Ⓓ Ⓔ	52 Ⓐ Ⓑ Ⓒ Ⓓ Ⓔ	
13 Ⓐ Ⓑ Ⓒ Ⓓ Ⓔ	33 Ⓐ Ⓑ Ⓒ Ⓓ Ⓔ	53 Ⓐ Ⓑ Ⓒ Ⓓ Ⓔ	
14 Ⓐ Ⓑ Ⓒ Ⓓ Ⓔ	34 Ⓐ Ⓑ Ⓒ Ⓓ Ⓔ	54 Ⓐ Ⓑ Ⓒ Ⓓ Ⓔ	
15 Ⓐ Ⓑ Ⓒ Ⓓ Ⓔ	35 Ⓐ Ⓑ Ⓒ Ⓓ Ⓔ	55 Ⓐ Ⓑ Ⓒ Ⓓ Ⓔ	
16 Ⓐ Ⓑ Ⓒ Ⓓ Ⓔ	36 Ⓐ Ⓑ Ⓒ Ⓓ Ⓔ	56 Ⓐ Ⓑ Ⓒ Ⓓ Ⓔ	
17 Ⓐ Ⓑ Ⓒ Ⓓ Ⓔ	37 Ⓐ Ⓑ Ⓒ Ⓓ Ⓔ	57 Ⓐ Ⓑ Ⓒ Ⓓ Ⓔ	
18 Ⓐ Ⓑ Ⓒ Ⓓ Ⓔ	38 Ⓐ Ⓑ Ⓒ Ⓓ Ⓔ	58 Ⓐ Ⓑ Ⓒ Ⓓ Ⓔ	
19 Ⓐ Ⓑ Ⓒ Ⓓ Ⓔ	39 Ⓐ Ⓑ Ⓒ Ⓓ Ⓔ	59 Ⓐ Ⓑ Ⓒ Ⓓ Ⓔ	
20 Ⓐ Ⓑ Ⓒ Ⓓ Ⓔ	40 Ⓐ Ⓑ Ⓒ Ⓓ Ⓔ	60 Ⓐ Ⓑ Ⓒ Ⓓ Ⓔ	

Model Test 2

SECTION I: MULTIPLE-CHOICE QUESTIONS

TIME: 55 MINUTES FOR 70 QUESTIONS

Directions: Each of the following questions has five suggested answers. Choose the one that is best in each case.

1. The Marshall Plan

   (A) dedicated funds to the subversion of Soviet rule in Eastern Europe.
   (B) ended the Cold War.
   (C) granted the British control over Palestine after World War I.
   (D) was meant to end the Vietnam War.
   (E) gave Western Europe billions of dollars to rebuild after World War II.

2. How did the German experience in colonizing Africa differ from that of the British and French?

   (A) The Germans never colonized Africa.
   (B) The British and French were more brutal in their treatment of the natives than the Germans were.
   (C) German colonies were less desirable, lost money, and involved the Germans in brutal wars against the natives.
   (D) The Germans colonized the northern coast of Africa, while the French and British took the eastern coast.
   (E) The German colonies were the most politically and economically successful in Africa.

3. The political and social effect of Neo-Confucianism in China was

   (A) to diminish public respect for China's emperor.
   (B) to reinforce the hierarchical organization of Chinese society.
   (C) to elevate the status of Chinese women.
   (D) to foster greater individualism among the Chinese.
   (E) to break down intergenerational relationships in Chinese families.

4. Which of the following is NOT true about the status of women in the twentieth century?

(A) Fascist Italy, Nazi Germany, and militarist Japan actively encouraged the equal treatment of women.
(B) During World War II, more women worked outside the home than during World War I.
(C) At least in theory, Soviet ideology was committed to the ideal of gender equality.
(D) Major goals of women's movements have been the achievement of legal equality and the elimination of culturally stereotyped gender roles.
(E) Achievements of women's movements include equal access to higher education and a greater role in political life.

5. Which of the following is NOT a trend associated with Europe's Industrial Revolution?

(A) urbanization
(B) population growth
(C) a general decline in prosperity
(D) a general increase in prosperity, especially after the 1840s
(E) the rapid expansion of the middle class

6. In the early 1900s, what kinds of changes did the Young Turks wish to bring to the Ottoman Empire?

(A) modernization and secularization
(B) a return to Islamic fundamentalism
(C) the revival of the janissary corps
(D) a strengthening of the sultan's powers
(E) closer diplomatic ties with the United States

7. The French colony of Louisiana consisted of

(A) what is now the state of Louisiana.
(B) what is now the province of Quebec.
(C) the mid-Atlantic coast of North America.
(D) the Great Lakes region and the Mississippi River valley.
(E) the coast of the Gulf of Mexico from what is now Texas to Florida.

8. Existentialists believe that

(A) a single God exists for the benefit of all humanity, and organized religion helps point the way to true morality.
(B) every religion is valid and that religion helps people to reach true divinity.
(C) the individual must learn to create his or her own ethical existence without the hope of an afterlife or the guidance of organized religion.
(D) the universe is uncaring and amoral, and therefore all life is meaningless.
(E) in the absence of a higher spiritual authority, might makes right, and everything is permissible.

9. Most historians consider that, during the Neolithic period, agriculture

   (A) was developed by all African and Eurasian cultures simultaneously.
   (B) was developed in many places independently but also was passed on or influenced by a process of cultural diffusion.
   (C) arose in one place, then was passed on to other cultures by means of cultural diffusion.
   (D) was brought to Eurasia by settlers migrating from the Americas.
   (E) did not develop at all but emerged much later.

10. The unification of Japan

   (A) created a regime that embraced open relations with the West.
   (B) was completed by the Tokugawa shoguns, who established a stable but dictatorial government.
   (C) was brought about from below by a popular mass movement.
   (D) was achieved relatively bloodlessly.
   (E) did not involve the use of gunpowder weaponry.

11. Why did the Russians conquer Central Asia in the 1800s?

   (A) feelings of nationalism
   (B) for its bounty of natural resources
   (C) a desire to establish warm-water ports on the Indian Ocean
   (D) to protect its long southern frontier
   (E) all of the above

12. What factors encouraged the wave of democratization in Latin America in the 1990s?

   I. cooperation among members of the Organization of American States
   II. economic improvements
   III. further decolonization
   IV. the end of the Cold War

   (A) I, II, and III
   (B) II, III, and IV
   (C) I, II, and IV
   (D) I and III only
   (E) II and IV only

13. For what reasons did medieval popes launch crusades?

   (A) to spread Christianity to Ireland
   (B) to fight Muslims, convert non-Catholics, and wipe out heresy
   (C) to enable England to conquer French lands
   (D) to grasp control of trade along the Silk Road
   (E) to conquer territory in sub-Saharan Africa

14. The travels of Ibn Battuta and Zheng He have what in common?

(A) They both demonstrate that the West did not have a monopoly on campaigns of exploration.
(B) They were both quite limited in their geographical scope.
(C) They were both motivated principally by the desire to gain religious converts.
(D) Both men compelled many of the places they visited to pay tribute to their home countries.
(E) They both involved the projection of military force.

15. Why did the Spanish abolish the *encomienda* system in the mid-1500s?

(A) Because Spain abolished slavery in all its colonial territories.
(B) Because the system was allowing Native Americans to regain control of their former lands.
(C) Because other countries agitated against its use.
(D) Because there was no longer any use for it.
(E) Because Catholic priests effectively and movingly protested against the system's abuses.

16. The Lend-Lease program

(A) offered U.S. and British economic assistance to recently decolonized states in the 1950s and 1960s.
(B) brought Eastern European economies under tight Soviet control during the early years of the Cold War.
(C) committed the United States to the economic support of Great Britain and the Soviet Union during World War II.
(D) created the foundations for greater economic union in Europe.
(E) established a regional trade network in East and Southeast Asia.

17. By the 1750s, which European power had defeated the Mughals?

(A) France
(B) Great Britain
(C) Holland
(D) Spain
(E) Italy

18. Which of the following best characterizes the ethnic development of Europe during the early medieval period?

    (A) The entire continent's racial composition was a direct legacy of Latin Romans, from whom all Europeans descended.
    (B) A mix of Celts, Latins, the many peoples the Romans had conquered, and Germanic and Asiatic tribes migrating from north and east contributed to Europe's ethnic composition.
    (C) Most remnants of the Roman legacy, racial and cultural, disappeared, to be replaced by an exclusively Germanic presence.
    (D) The Huns took over Europe, making the racial mix there heavily Asiatic.
    (E) The ancient Celts had the greatest influence on the racial composition of the European continent.

19. Which of the following does NOT belong to a list of common Enlightenment tenets?

    (A) Organized religions are conglomerations of superstitious beliefs.
    (B) Rational thought is capable of gaining a full understanding of the universe and its workings.
    (C) Logic and proper planning can alleviate most of society's problems.
    (D) Human beings should be guided as much by instinct and emotion as by the intellect.
    (E) Freedom of expression and freedom from arbitrary rule are political goals worth striving for.

20. Qing China's principal commodities for foreign trade were

    (A) cotton, silk, and gunpowder
    (B) spices, porcelain, and cotton
    (C) tea, gunpowder, and cloves
    (D) gunpowder, silk, and glassware
    (E) tea, silk, and porcelain

21. What was the Spanish conquistadores' PRIMARY motivation in gaining new territories in the Americas?

    (A) They were mainly concerned with making great profits.
    (B) Above all, they wanted to bring Catholicism to the Native Americans.
    (C) They planned to use the land to build prisons for Spanish felons.
    (D) They hoped to find a "fountain of youth."
    (E) They were dedicated to scientific research and geographical knowledge.

22. Which of the following statements accurately describes human tool use during the Stone Age?

    I. Humanity made use of axes, knives, and bows and arrows.
    II. Only stone tools were used.
    III. Humans lived not only in caves but in more advanced dwellings.
    IV. The greatest priority in tool use and design was insuring a supply of food.

    (A) I and III
    (B) I and II
    (C) II and III
    (D) I, III, and IV
    (E) all of the above

23. Of the statements below, which is the BEST assessment of the Renaissance?

    (A) It strengthened the papacy by emphasizing Catholic orthodoxy.
    (B) It boldly experimented with nonrealistic forms of artistic expression.
    (C) It combined a revival of Greco-Latin learning with a conviction that worldly human existence was worthwhile.
    (D) Its primary emphasis was on painting and sculpture, and therefore there were few Renaissance writers or poets.
    (E) Rigidly secular in its outlook, it ignored religious subject matter almost completely.

24. Which of the following factors helped to prompt and/or enable the European powers' campaigns of imperialism during the nineteenth century?

    I. economic factors, such as the need for more raw materials and new markets
    II. military issues, such as modern weapons and the need for naval bases
    III. a sense of cultural and racial superiority
    IV. greater scientific knowledge

    (A) I, II, and III
    (B) II, III, and IV
    (C) I and III only
    (D) III and IV
    (E) all of the above

25. Which of the following is an accurate statement about slavery in the Americas?

    (A) The Portuguese were the first to abolish it.
    (B) More slaves were brought to the United States than to Latin America and the Caribbean.
    (C) More slaves were brought to Latin America and the Caribbean than to the United States.
    (D) The French enslaved entire Native American tribes.
    (E) The outlawing of slavery by European powers in the early 1800s ended slavery in the Americas as well.

26. Which of the following correctly describes the emergence of the first cities?

    (A) No cities appeared before the Bronze Age.
    (B) Urban populations were less diverse than rural populations.
    (C) Cities allowed for the specialization of labor.
    (D) The first cities appeared in China.
    (E) Only peoples who had developed a system of writing built cities.

27. What is the central focus of the map above?

    (A) the Mongol Empire at its peak
    (B) the expansion of Muscovite Russia into Mongol territory
    (C) the breakdown of the Mongol Empire into smaller units
    (D) the decline and fall of the Delhi Sultanate
    (E) the rise of the Khmer Empire

28. Absolutism in seventeeth- and eighteenth-century Europe

    (A) was justified by political theories associated with the Enlightenment.
    (B) created systems in which there were no meaningful legal or theoretical checks on the power of the monarch.
    (C) generally involved the expansion of the aristocracy's power at the expense of the monarch's authority.
    (D) typically led to increased social mobility.
    (E) tended to encourage religious toleration.

29. What best describes the relationship between Islamic culture and medieval European culture and the Renaissance?

   (A) Muslim orthodoxy in Spain prevented the emergence of the Renaissance there.
   (B) Muslim scholars and philosophers borrowed heavily from English and French thinkers and scientists.
   (C) Muslim science, as well as Muslim translations of ancient Greek writings, were indispensable to the cultural growth of Europe.
   (D) The Crusades brought European architectural and artistic forms to the Middle East, where they were eagerly absorbed into the local style.
   (E) There was very little interaction between the two cultures owing to intense religious hostility.

30. Zimbabwe and Timbuktu were MOST alike in what respect?

   (A) They were both renowned centers of Islamic scholarship.
   (B) They were both key points in trade networks that extended beyond Africa's borders.
   (C) They were both great repositories of Swahili culture and learning.
   (D) They were both successful military powers and built powerful empires.
   (E) They were both largely cut off from all but their immediate surroundings.

31. Which of the following is NOT true of the Ottoman Turks' military campaigns between the late 1300s and late 1600s?

   (A) They succeeded in capturing Constantinople and Vienna.
   (B) They remained at or near the technological forefront with respect to weaponry.
   (C) They attained naval mastery over the eastern Mediterranean.
   (D) They conquered most of the Balkans and much of Hungary.
   (E) All of the above are true.

32. How have political developments changed in South Korea and Taiwan since the 1980s?

   (A) Both countries have become more authoritarian.
   (B) Taiwan has become more authoritarian than South Korea.
   (C) Leaders in both countries would now prefer to unite with their communist counterparts.
   (D) Both countries have democratized.
   (E) Both countries have become allies of the People's Republic of China.

33. How did Great Britain gain control over the Suez Canal in the late nineteenth century?

    (A) It colonized Egypt in the same way it had colonized India.

    (B) It built the canal itself and established a zone of influence in the canal's immediate vicinity.

    (C) It seized the canal from Egypt in a short but bloody war.

    (D) It bought up shares in the company that owned the canal, then used its economic interest as a pretext to install a pro-British regime in Egypt.

    (E) It threatened to bombard the canal with gunships if the Egyptians did not hand over custody of it.

World's Major Consumers of Primary Energy (1998) Measured in quadrillions of British thermal units (Btu)	
United States	94.57 quadrillion Btu
China	33.93 quadrillion Btu
Russia	25.99 quadrillion Btu
Japan	21.21 quadrillion Btu
Germany	13.83 quadrillion Btu
India	12.51 quadrillion Btu
Canada	11.85 quadrillion Btu
France	10.00 quadrillion Btu
United Kingdom	9.75 quadrillion Btu
Brazil	8.08 quadrillion Btu

34. On the basis of the data presented in the above table, which of the following conclusions might one safely make?

    (A) Brazil has a smaller population than Canada does.

    (B) The top energy-consuming nations are to be found mainly in the developed world.

    (C) Russia is a more efficient consumer of energy than China is.

    (D) Japan has a larger population than India does.

    (E) Per capita, the people of France are less wasteful of energy than those in the United States.

35. Angkor Wat is part of the architectural legacy of what country?

    (A) Japan

    (B) Indonesia

    (C) Cambodia

    (D) Singapore

    (E) Thailand

36. How did the demise of the communist regimes in Eastern Europe tend to differ from the collapse of the USSR?

    (A) In most East European countries, revolutions were sparked by popular protest, whereas in the USSR, political elites largely caused the collapse.
    (B) In the USSR, popular uprisings instigated the ultimate collapse, while in Eastern Europe, political leaders decided to change the form of government.
    (C) The USSR collapsed purely for economic reasons, whereas in Eastern Europe, communist regimes collapsed mainly because of ethnic conflict.
    (D) East European regimes collapsed owing to economic exhaustion, whereas the USSR's breakdown was caused by ethnic warfare.
    (E) The reasons for Soviet and East European collapse differed very little.

37. The *millet* system was

    (A) A technique for improving agricultural production in Japan.
    (B) The Ottoman Empire's method for grouping and governing peoples of various faiths.
    (C) The Aztec government's system for gathering tribute from neighboring tribes.
    (D) Tang China's method for keeping trade records.
    (E) A Zulu form of tactical organization.

38. The ancient Athenians used the above structure for what purpose?

    (A) a marketplace
    (B) a government meeting place
    (C) a temple
    (D) a public bathhouse
    (E) a museum

39. Which of the following is an incorrect description of agricultural societies?

    (A) Agriculture allowed humans to manipulate their environment like never before.
    (B) Women probably played a key role in promoting the transition from hunting and gathering to agricultural societies.
    (C) Agriculture promoted permanent settlements.
    (D) People began producing their own food nearly 12,000 years ago.
    (E) Agricultural societies were less organized than hunter-gatherer societies.

40. Russian domestic policy during the mid-to-late 1800s included which of the following?

    (A) the granting of a constitution
    (B) the improved treatment of Jews living in the Russian Empire
    (C) the emancipation of the serfs
    (D) the creation of a semiparliamentary legislative body
    (E) all of the above

41. Which of the following accurately describes patterns of trade in the Indian Ocean during the 1200s through the early 1400s?

    (A) ivory and gold from Africa; salt and cotton from India; porcelain and silk from China
    (B) gold and ivory from Africa; cotton from China; silk from India
    (C) spices from Africa; slaves from India; gold from China
    (D) ivory from India; porcelain and silk from China; tea from Africa
    (E) slaves and silk from China; gold and ivory from Africa; cotton from India

42. Who was the great voyager and explorer of early Ming China?

    (A) Yongle
    (B) Zheng He
    (C) Sun Tzu
    (D) Marco Polo
    (E) Zhu Yuan-chang

43. What best describes the Mississippian culture?

    (A) It erected large mounds for ritual purposes and built at least one large city.
    (B) It was the earliest civilization to appear in North America.
    (C) It was a highly warlike culture, attaining hegemony over most of North America.
    (D) It was one of the few monotheistic civilizations in the Americas during the pre-Columbian period.
    (E) It is known for having built complex cliff dwellings in the walls of canyons.

44. Which of the following statements would LEAST likely fit in with the ORIGINAL teachings of the Buddha?

    (A) All human suffering is caused by desire.
    (B) Enlightenment can most effectively be attained by coming to realize the Four Noble Truths and practicing the Eightfold Path.
    (C) Enlightenment leads to a moment of awakening and transcendent consciousness known as nirvana.
    (D) Enlightenment can most effectively be attained by venerating many gods and bodhisattvas.
    (E) none of the above

45. The rulers of Ethiopia and Asante had what in common?

    (A) They both used Western military technology to put up stiff resistance to external pressure from the West.
    (B) They were both devoutly Christian.
    (C) They both carried on the traditions of their Bantu ancestors.
    (D) They both took an active part in and profited from the Atlantic slave trade.
    (E) They both involved their countries heavily in the Indian Ocean trade network.

46. Which of the following statements about European settlements in North America is NOT true?

    (A) The French, more so than the English or Spanish, dominated the fur trade.
    (B) France's principal rival in the New World was England.
    (C) The Spanish once controlled Louisiana.
    (D) The Russians settled along the Pacific coast.
    (E) The French drove the Acadians out of their settlement in Nova Scotia to southern North America.

47. Nicolaus Copernicus is best known for which scientific accomplishment?

    (A) for describing the chemical states of matter
    (B) elaborating the theory of elliptical orbits
    (C) devising the first workable microscope
    (D) mathematically proving the heliocentric theory
    (E) inventing the telescope

48. Why did the United States support the Marcos regime in the Philippines?

    (A) because Marcos was strongly committed to democratic principles
    (B) because Marcos was strongly anticommunist
    (C) because Marcos was trying to prevent takeover by a right-wing dictator
    (D) to reward Marcos for observing international human rights standards
    (E) because of popular pressure from Filipino-American voters living in the United States

49. Which of the following statements can be said to apply to the French and American revolutions?

    I. The American war of independence was inspired by the initial success of the French Revolution.
    II. The cost of military support for the American Revolution was one of the factors that caused the financial crisis that led to the French Revolution.
    III. The Declaration of the Rights of Man and the Citizen was based largely on the ideals of the Declaration of Independence.
    IV. Both revolutions were influenced by the philosophical movement known as the Enlightenment.

    (A) I only
    (B) I and II
    (C) I, II, and III
    (D) II and III
    (E) II, III, and IV

50. In the early twentieth century, what type of people tended to lead independence movements in the Middle East, Africa, and Asia?

    (A) peasants
    (B) communists
    (C) members of the nobility
    (D) members of the educated elite
    (E) trade-union activists

51. In what key way did early Egyptian civilization resemble that in Mesopotamia?

    (A) They both buried their leaders in pyramids.
    (B) They both used cuneiform in preserving their important documents.
    (C) They both developed a centralized society ruled by a monarchy and a small caste of priests.
    (D) They both created law codes that protected the poor.
    (E) They both allowed women to act as priests.

52. What made the Silk Road unusual among premodern trade routes?

    (A) In an age when water transport was easier and cheaper, it allowed over-land trade over great distances.
    (B) It was the only means by which the Mediterranean world could trade with East Asia.
    (C) It was the only major trade route the Mongols allowed to function after their campaigns of conquest.
    (D) Only along the Silk Road could large animals, such as oxen, elephants, and horses, be transported.
    (E) It allowed the influence of Hinduism and Buddhism to spread westward.

53. Which of the following statements about East Africa in the 1800s is inaccurate?

    (A) From the late 1700s to the mid-1800s, most of coastal East Africa experienced freedom from external control.
    (B) Ethiopia's leaders were Christian.
    (C) No major slave markets operated in East Africa.
    (D) At one point, over 40 percent of the population was made up of slaves.
    (E) Arabs had gained a great deal of political influence.

54. When the Portuguese arrived in India and Southeast Asia, they

    (A) agreed with local powers not to allow Catholic priests to proselytize.
    (B) quickly conquered India and China thanks to their naval superiority.
    (C) were unable to gain control over any parts of Southeast Asia, in great contrast to their colonial successes on the African coast.
    (D) established control over certain port cities and small islands but not larger nations.
    (E) found that the difficulty of voyaging so far made trade with these regions unprofitable.

55. Which of the following statements does NOT accurately describe the economic instability Western democratic countries experienced in the 1970s?

(A) Western democracies suffered high levels of unemployment.
(B) Western democracies suffered from inflation.
(C) Western democracies suffered from severe economic depressions.
(D) Western democracies were adversely affected by an oil embargo.
(E) Western democracies were hurt by the devaluing of the U.S. dollar.

56. Which of the following accurately describes both the Han and Roman empires?

(A) Their leaders persecuted Christians up until the collapse of their empires.
(B) Their economic and political instability was largely caused by imperial overreach.
(C) Their leaders were satisfied to maintain their lands and expand as little as possible.
(D) They both tried to conquer most of the Eurasian interior.
(E) They both allowed women a high degree of social equality.

57. Which of the following was NOT a major characteristic of Middle Eastern political life after World War II?

(A) widespread democratization
(B) independence of former colonies and mandates
(C) tensions between religious fundamentalism and Westernization
(D) the Arab-Israeli conflict
(E) the persistence of human rights abuses

58. To deter workers from embracing radical ideologies in Germany in the late 1800s, what measures did Otto von Bismarck take?

(A) He outlawed the sale of all books by Karl Marx.
(B) He stirred up anti-Semitic resentment among German workers.
(C) He imprisoned anyone who joined the Communist Party.
(D) He granted universal male suffrage and gave workers many social benefits.
(E) He gave women the vote.

59. The innovation most associated with the ancient Hebrews is

(A) monotheistic worship.
(B) metal coinage.
(C) the chariot.
(D) hieroglyphics.
(E) aqueducts.

60. Which of the following did the communist dictatorship of the USSR and the Nazi regime in Germany NOT have in common?

    (A) Both controlled society partly by means of a feared and powerful secret police force.
    (B) Both made use of propaganda to indoctrinate their populations and glorify the leaders.
    (C) Both subscribed to ideologies that viewed women primarily as homemakers and mothers.
    (D) Both promoted industrial buildup and the creation of large armed forces.
    (E) Both created an elaborate network of camps for purposes of concentration and forced labor.

61. The leaders of the Mexican Revolution are best compared with those of the Latin American wars of independence as follows:

    (A) The original leaders of the Mexican Revolution were liberalizing aristocrats, whereas the commanders of the Latin American wars of independence rose up from the peasantry.
    (B) Both began as slave revolts, with leaders who imitated Toussaint L'Ouverture of Haiti.
    (C) The Mexican Revolution began as a revolt on behalf of the lower classes; by contrast, the commanders of the Latin American wars of independence were strictly concerned about the interests of the upper classes.
    (D) The commanders of the Latin American wars of independence were more accommodating to the possibility of sharing power with Spanish colonial authorities.
    (E) The original leaders of the Mexican Revolution were concerned mainly with the welfare of the lower classes; the commanders of the Latin American wars of independence were from the aristocracy, but they appealed at least partly to slaves and the lower classes.

62. What factor caused Southeast Asia to experience major political change between 1200 and 1400?

    (A) The Chinese and Mongols conquered parts of Southeast Asia at this time.
    (B) The countries of Southeast Asia adopted Confucianism.
    (C) The peoples of Southeast Asia began to adopt Christian ways.
    (D) Democracy became a leading force in political change.
    (E) Invading forces crossed the Indian Ocean from East Africa and raided coastal communities.

63. Which of the following best describes the effects of the "agricultural revolution" of the 1700s in Europe?

    (A) Less organic food was grown.
    (B) There were fewer famines and better crop yields.
    (C) Serfdom was abolished.
    (D) Peasants revolted and took control of manors.
    (E) Poverty was eliminated.

64. Why did the European Economic Community form?

(A) to prepare for economic mobilization in case of war
(B) to coordinate economic production during World War II
(C) to oppose U.S. exports
(D) to encourage the free movement of goods, services, money, and labor inside Europe
(E) to increase the number of internal tariffs within Europe

65. Which country lost the Spanish-American War, and what happened to it?

(A) the United States, which was forced to relinquish Cuba
(B) the United States, which was forced to hand over the Philippines
(C) Spain, which was stripped of its colonial possessions
(D) Spain, which lost only Cuba to the United States
(E) the war ended in stalemate

66. How were the decolonization processes in Rhodesia and South Africa similar?

(A) The African population in both countries was treated equitably.
(B) There was an intense conflict between black and white citizens in both countries.
(C) In both cases, decolonization resulted in mass genocide.
(D) French peacekeepers had to be brought in to maintain order.
(E) Decolonization in both countries required the intervention of United Nations peacekeeping forces.

67. In what way was the Chinese response to the growing presence of Western powers in East Asia during the 1800s different from the Japanese response?

(A) Japan was forced to grant outside powers economic concessions, while China was not.
(B) The Chinese modernized and industrialized, whereas the Japanese did not.
(C) The Japanese modernized and industrialized, whereas the Chinese did not.
(D) China defeated the Western powers in battle, while Japan tended to lose.
(E) China and Japan reacted to Western powers in nearly identical fashion.

68. The Declaration of the Rights of Man and the Citizen

(A) was adopted by the Constitutional Convention in Philadelphia.
(B) guaranteed basic civil rights and liberties for male citizens in France.
(C) included only people who were property owners.
(D) created a monarchy in Britain.
(E) influenced the Bolshevik Revolution.

69. Other than Jews and homosexuals, which groups did the German Nazis target for persecution?

   I. certain ethnic groups, such as Gypsies and Slavs
  II. political dissidents
 III. ethnically pure Germans
 IV. the mentally and physically disabled

  (A) I, II, and III
  (B) I, II, and IV
  (C) II, III, and IV
  (D) I and III only
  (E) all of the above

70. Which of the following is NOT true of gunpowder?

  (A) Several African states greatly boosted their regional power by acquiring firearms in the 1600s and 1700s.
  (B) Fearful of having its mastery of traditional weapons made obsolete, Japan's samurai class carefully controlled access to and ownership of guns.
  (C) The Ottoman Empire and Mughal India both proved adept at making use of gunpowder weaponry in the 1500s and 1600s.
  (D) The appearance of gunpowder led immediately to Western domination of the world's other major civilizations.
  (E) It is generally considered to have been invented in China.

END OF SECTION I

SECTION II: FREE-RESPONSE QUESTIONS

Part A: Document-Based Question

TIME: 10 MINUTES TO READ DOCUMENTS; 40 MINUTES
TO COMPLETE ESSAY (RECOMMENDED, NOT OFFICIAL)

Directions: The following question is based on the accompanying documents. This question is designed to test your ability to work with historical documents. As you analyze the documents, take into account both the sources of the documents and the authors' points of view. Write an essay on the following topic that integrates your analysis of the documents. DO NOT SIMPLY SUMMARIZE THE DOCUMENTS INDIVIDU-ALLY. You may refer to relevant historical facts and developments not mentioned in the documents. Some documents have been edited. (Write your answer on a separate sheet of paper.)

1. One of the most common forms of cultural interchange is the transfer of religious beliefs. As new faiths and spiritual ideas appear in a nation or among a community, reactions to them vary. How have various religions, missions, and proselytizing efforts have been received in different places at different times? Be sure to explain the need for at least one additional type of document.

DOCUMENT 1

Source: Thomas Coryate, English traveler in Turkey, on witnessing Sufi dervishes (1613).

> There is a College of Turkish Monks in Galata, that are called [Dervishes], . . . who every Tuesday and Friday do perform the strangest exercise of Devotion that ever I saw or heard of. . . .
>
> A little after I came into the room, the Dervishes repaired into the middle void space, sitting Cross-legged, bending their Bodies low toward the floor for Religion['s] sake, even almost flat upon their Faces . . . the whole company of them were about two and fifty. . . .
>
> [A] certain Singing-man sitting apart in an upper room began to sing certain Hymns, but with the most unpleasant and harsh notes that ever I heard, exceedingly differing from our Christian Church singing, for the yelling and disorderly squeaking did even grate mine ears. . . . [T]hree Pipers sitting in the room with the Singer began to play upon certain long Pipes not unlike Tabors, which yielded a very ridiculous and foolish Music . . . whereupon some five and twenty of the two and fifty Dervishes suddenly rose up bare-legged and bare-footed, and casting aside their upper Garments, some of them having their breasts all uncovered, they began by little and little to turn about the Interpreter of the Law. Afterward they redoubled their force and turned with such incredible swiftness, that I could not choose but admire it.

Model Test 2

DOCUMENT 2

Source: Fa-hsien, a traveling monk from China, on his reception by Indian Buddhists (399).

When they saw pilgrims from China arrive, they were much affected and spoke thus, "How is it that men from the frontiers are able to know the religion of family-renunciation and come from far to seek the law of the Buddha?" They liberally provided necessary entertainment according to the rules of religion.

[As we reached the Ganges, the local priests exclaimed,] "Wonderful! to think that men from the frontiers of the earth should come so far as this from a desire to search for the law. . . . Our various superiors and brethren, who have succeeded one another in this place from the earliest time till now, have none of them seen men of Han come so far as this before."

DOCUMENT 3

Source: Council of the Aztec city of Huejotzingo, letter to the king of Spain (1560).

Catholic Royal Majesty!

When your servants the Spaniards reached us and your captain general Don Hernando Cortés arrived, not a single town surpassed us here in New Spain, in that first and earliest we threw ourselves toward you.

. . . we also say and declare before you that [when] your padres, the sons of St. Francis, entered the city of Huejotzingo, of our own free will we honored them and showed them esteem. When they [told us to] abandon the wicked belief in many gods, we did it. Very willingly we destroyed, demolished, and burned the temples. . . .

But now we are taken aback and very afraid, and we ask, have we done something wrong, have we somehow behaved badly, or have we committed some sin against almighty God?

DOCUMENT 4

Source: Jean Bodin, French philosopher (1530–1596), on Ottoman religious policy.

The King of the Turks, who rules over a great part of Europe, safeguards the rites of religion as well as any prince in this world. He constrains no one, but on the contrary permits everyone to live as his conscience dictates. What is more, even in his seraglio at Pera he permits the practice of four diverse religions, that of the Jews, the Christian according to the Roman rite, and according to the Greek rite, and that of Islam.

DOCUMENT 5

Source: Ashoka, Mauryan emperor of India, *Edicts* (260s B.C.E.).

Whoever honors only his own religion and disparages another man's, whether from blind loyalty or with the intention of showing his own religion in a favorable light, does his own religion the greatest possible harm. Concord is best, with each hearing and respecting the other's teachings. It is the wish of the king that members of all religions should be learned and should teach virtue.

DOCUMENT 6

Source: Dante Alighieri, Florentine poet, *The Inferno,* Canto XXVIII, 28–36 (ca. 1307).

I stood and stared at him from the stone shelf;
    he noticed me and opening his own breast
    with both hands cried: "See how I rip myself!

See how Mahomet's mangled and split open!
    Ahead of me walks Ali in his tears
    his head cleft from the top-knot to the chin.

All the other souls that bleed and mourn
    along this ditch were sowers of scandal and schism:
    as they tore others apart, so are they torn."

DOCUMENT 7

Source: The Regulations of the City of Avignon (1243).

Likewise, we declare that Jews or whores shall not dare to touch with their hands either bread or fruit put out for sale, and that if they should do this they must buy what they have touched.

DOCUMENT 8

Source: Albert Schweitzer, German missionary, doctor, and humanitarian, letter to his sister (April 1913).

Medical knowledge made it possible for me to carry out my intention [of bringing Christ to Africa] in the best and most complete way, wherever the path of service might lead me. . . .

I'm really happy. I feel I've done the right thing in coming here, for the misery is greater than anyone can describe. . . . [T]here are all stages of leprosy. . . . I see a great deal of sleeping sickness. It is very painful for these poor souls. . . . And elephantiasis, that constantly increasing swelling of the limbs. It is dreadful; eventually the legs are so thick that the people can no longer drag them about.

Many heart cases; the people are suffocating. And then the joy when the digitalin works! Evenings I go to bed dead-tired, but in my heart I am profoundly happy that *I am serving at the outpost of the Kingdom of God!*

Part B: Change-Over-Time Question

TIME: 40 MINUTES TO COMPLETE ESSAY
(RECOMMENDED, NOT OFFICIAL)

Directions: You are to answer the following question. In writing your essay, use specific examples to support your answer. (Write your essay on separate sheets of paper.)

2. Choose ONE of the following trade routes. Discuss its global importance, as well as how patterns of economic exchange shifted and altered during the periods designated for each.

the Indian Ocean trade network (1000–1500)
the gold trade in West and Equatorial Africa (500–1300)
the Silk Road (100 B.C.E.–500 C.E.)
the eastern Mediterranean (500–1300)

Part C: Comparative Essay

TIME: 40 MINUTES TO COMPLETE ESSAY
(RECOMMENDED, NOT OFFICIAL)

Directions: You are to answer the following question. In writing your essay, use specific examples to support your answer. (Write your essay on separate sheets of paper.)

3. In most parts of the world, religious beliefs have been used to provide justification for various political systems and practices. Compare and contrast the political uses of Confucianism (and Neo-Confucianism) in East Asia with those of Roman Catholicism in Europe.

END OF SECTION II

Answer Key
MODEL TEST 2

Section I

1. E	21. A	41. A	61. E
2. C	22. D	42. B	62. A
3. B	23. C	43. A	63. B
4. A	24. E	44. D	64. D
5. C	25. C	45. A	65. C
6. A	26. C	46. E	66. B
7. D	27. C	47. D	67. C
8. C	28. B	48. B	68. B
9. B	29. C	49. E	69. B
10. B	30. B	50. D	70. D
11. E	31. A	51. C	
12. C	32. D	52. A	
13. B	33. D	53. C	
14. A	34. B	54. D	
15. E	35. C	55. C	
16. C	36. A	56. B	
17. B	37. B	57. A	
18. B	38. C	58. D	
19. D	39. E	59. A	
20. E	40. C	60. C	

ANSWERS EXPLAINED

1. **(E)** Fearing a repetition of the interwar period, when economic desperation had driven many regimes in Europe to political extremism, Secretary of State George Marshall proposed a large infusion of U.S. funds into the shattered economies of postwar Europe, in order to avoid having them become attracted to communism.

2. **(C)** Coming comparatively late to the empire-building competition, Germany tended to be left with less desirable colonies in Africa. Inexperience in colonial administration and a harsh approach embroiled Germany in several bloody wars of suppression, especially against the Herero.

3. **(B)** A revival of Confucian beliefs during the Song dynasty reaffirmed China's cultural commitment to traditional patriarchal values and social and political hierarchy. It also led to a decline in the status of women.

4. **(A)** In the Western democracies, women made all the advances listed in this question. Marxist ideology committed the Soviet Union in principle (not always in reality) to gender equality. By contrast, the dictatorships in Germany, Italy, and Japan actively opposed the principle of gender equality.

5. **(C)** Even during its early stage, when conditions for the lower classes were at their hardest, the Industrial Revolution generated great wealth. Levels of overall prosperity in Europe rose. That prosperity slowly began to become more evenly distributed after the 1840s.

6. **(A)** The Young Turks were westernizing modernizers who were impatient with the sultans' cautious, gradual approach to reform and dissatisfied with the influence of Islamic traditionalism in political life.

7. **(D)** The French colony of Louisiana encompassed much of the central portion of the present-day United States. It was resource-rich, and the Mississippi valley was economically and strategically crucial. Napoleon Bonaparte sold this territory to the United States in 1803, vastly expanding the size and potential power of the young country.

8. **(C)** Made famous after World War II by philosophers and authors such as Albert Camus, Jean-Paul Sartre, and Samuel Beckett, existentialism continued an intellectual trend begun earlier in the century by denying that there are any objective moral or religious truths to guide humanity. On their own, people must come to their own understanding of what is right and then do it for its own sake.

9. **(B)** Agriculture arose partly as a result of independent innovation, partly as a result of cultural diffusion. Cultivation of crops is thought to have begun in the ancient Middle East around 8000 B.C.E., then spread to nearby areas, as well as Europe. It probably began independently in India (around 7000 B.C.E.) and China (perhaps 6000 B.C.E.).

10. **(B)** After more than a century of civil war, Oda Nobunaga, Toyotomi Hideyoshi, and Tokugawa Ieyasu accomplished the reunification of Japan in the late 1500s and early 1600s. The Tokugawa Shogunate was dictatorial, socially stratified, and made a point of shielding itself from outside influences.

11. **(E)** All these factors motivated Russian imperialism in Central Asia. Russia has no natural, easily defended borders in the south. It desired for years to have more warm-water ports, and the cotton fields of Central Asia were an economic inducement. As in the rest of Europe, patriotic feelings spurred imperial tendencies in Russia.

12. **(C)** Having been free from colonialism for more than a century and a half, Latin America had no need to decolonize in order to democratize in the 1990s. Greater prosperity eased the transition from dictatorship to democracy, as did regional cooperation assisted by the Organization of American States. The end of the Cold War not only provided an example of successful democratization elsewhere but also enabled it in Latin America, by lessening superpower rivalry and interventionism there.

13. **(B)** Although the most famous crusades are those fought against the Middle East between 1096 and 1291, the popes launched crusades to combat heresy in Europe itself (especially in southern France) and to convert non-Catholic regions of Europe (such as parts of eastern Europe) by force.

14. **(A)** Although they resemble each other in that they feature non-Westerners engaged in wide-ranging campaigns of exploration, the travels of Ibn Battuta and Zheng He are in fact quite different. They both traveled great distances, but Ibn Battuta's journey was a private venture, with no military purpose or results. Neither man was interested in religious conversion.

15. **(E)** By the early-to-mid 1500s, Spanish priests had converted many Native Americans to Christianity. They had also become appalled by the treatment of Native Americans by the conquistadores, who forced them to labor under horrendous conditions. They petitioned the authorities in Spain to end the *encomienda* system that allowed such abuses. The appeal of Bartolomé de las Casas in *The Tears of the Indians* was particularly persuasive. Slaves from Africa replaced Native Americans as the principal source of manual labor in Spanish America.

16. **(C)** Even before the United States became directly involved in World War II, it had started to support Great Britain economically, especially once Britain faced the Axis alone. After Germany invaded the USSR in the summer of 1941, the United States extended economic aid to the Soviets as well. U.S. assistance amounted to billions of dollars worth of weapons, supplies, and raw materials. It was crucial in keeping the British and Soviet war efforts functioning during the most dangerous months of late 1941 and 1942.

17. **(B)** Although their presence was still restricted mainly to the coasts and the Ganges valley before the early-to-mid 1800s, the British, in 1757, handed the Mughals a decisive defeat at Plassey. This enabled the British to consolidate military power in India and gain great political influence over remaining Mughal rulers, most of whom the British controlled and used as pliable clients to govern on their behalf.

18. **(B)** The great wave of migrations that helped to bring an end to the Roman Empire also affected the ethnic composition of Europe during the early medieval period. Already present were Celts, Latins, and many others; Germanic and Asiatic tribes were added to the mix over the centuries. Although many of the

newcomers came as barbarians and invaders, they remained, intermarried, and became part of the cultures they had conquered or fought.

19. **(D)** Largely as a backlash against the Enlightenment, it was the romantic movement that stressed instinct and the emotions. All the other answers correctly reflect the ideals of the Enlightenment.

20. **(E)** The Chinese had traded silk and porcelain for centuries. In the 1700s and 1800s, tea joined—and eventually surpassed—them as a commodity for export. In particular, the sale of tea to Great Britain caused such a trade imbalance that the British responded by shipping opium illegally and by force to China.

21. **(A)** Religious conversion was important to the Spanish as they moved into the New World, and at least one conquistador, Ponce de León, was interested in finding a fountain of youth in Florida. However, the profit motive was paramount. Scientific knowledge for its own sake was not seen as that important, and it was Great Britain that made a practice of exiling, or "transporting," criminals to its colonies—first America, then Australia.

22. **(D)** All of these apply except for the assertion that Stone Age humans only made stone tools. Some of the most important tools were made of stone, and of course, it is the stone tools that have survived the longest and are thus available to archaeologists and paleontologists to study.

23. **(C)** Combining the classical tradition of the Greco-Latin era with Christianity, the culture of the Renaissance was more secular in its outlook than the culture of the medieval period, but it did not (and, practically speaking, could not) reject Christian belief altogether.

24. **(E)** A combination of factors, including all the ones listed in this question, prompted the Europeans to embark on the so-called new imperialism of the late 1800s.

25. **(C)** The Atlantic slave trade began largely to meet the desire of the Portuguese and Spanish for an exploitable labor force to use for sugarcane cultivation, silver mining, and plantation agriculture in the Caribbean, Brazil, and Central and South America. More slaves went to those regions than to the United States. Although Britain and most other European nations outlawed slavery and the slave trade in 1814 and 1815, slavery itself did not end in the New World. The United States ended slavery after the U.S. Civil War, and Brazil and Cuba practiced slavery until the 1880s.

26. **(C)** Urbanization led to labor specialization by creating food surpluses, which allowed some citizens to make a living in other ways besides food production. Cities were built long before the Bronze Age and in some cases by civilizations that did not have a system of writing.

27. **(C)** After 1260, the Mongol Empire began to split apart into the khanates depicted on the map. The map thus represents the empire after the peak of its power.

28. **(B)** The tendency in absolute monarchies is toward greater centralization and increased monarchal power. Generally, there are no meaningful legal or theoretical restrictions on the monarch's power (although informal factors or specific

circumstances may limit the power of a particular monarch). Most Enlightenment philosophers disapproved of what they saw as absolutism's tyrannical nature. Religious toleration and social mobility were associated more with parliamentary monarchy.

29. **(C)** The European debt to Muslim and Jewish scholars (many of whom lived in Moorish Spain), especially where the recovery of knowledge about the ancient Greeks is concerned, was immense.

30. **(B)** The people of Mali were not descended from the Bantu, and Zimbabwe at its peak was not Muslim. Neither city was part of the Swahili cultural group, and neither took direct part in the Atlantic slave trade. Both were vital trading centers.

31. **(A)** The Ottomans did everything listed except capture the Habsburg capital of Vienna. They besieged the city twice, in 1529 and 1683, but never took it. Failure to capture Vienna in 1683 led to a massive Christian counterattack that permanently ended the Ottomans as a serious threat to central and western Europe.

32. **(D)** Until comparatively recently, South Korea and Taiwan, although allies of the United States, were ruled by mildly authoritarian governments. Political changes in the 1980s and 1990s brought about greater democratization. For the moment, Taiwan maintains an awkward relationship of undeclared independence from the People's Republic of China, which considers the island a renegade province. South Korea has remained divided from North Korea for more than half a century.

33. **(D)** The French, not the British, built the Suez Canal. It was America, in Panama, that employed the strategy of building a canal and then claiming military jurisdiction over the surrounding area. The British bought up a majority of the shares in the company that owned the canal. It then used its ownership as an excuse to intervene in a local political crisis and install a ruler, the khedive, who was pro-British and easily pliable.

34. **(B)** Without knowing the population of the countries listed on the chart, any precise conclusions about population or per capita comparisons are impossible. What can be determined for certain from general knowledge is that most of the countries included on the chart are from the developed world.

35. **(C)** Angkor Wat was the capital and religious center of the Khmer civilization, which ruled Cambodia for almost a thousand years.

36. **(A)** Mass movements, such as Polish trade union Solidarity and the dissident group led by Vaclav Havel in Czechoslovakia, played the decisive role in ending communist rule in Eastern Europe. While popular discontent and breakaway tendencies on the part of non-Russian populations in the Soviet Union weakened the country, the final collapse came after the attempted coup against Gorbachev in August 1991 and then the decision later that year by the leaders of key Soviet republics—Russia, Ukraine, and Belarus—to form the Commonwealth of Independent States.

37. **(B)** The Ottoman Empire organized its population into administrative groups based on religion. These were called *millets*, meaning "nations." For the most part,

the Ottomans practiced religious tolerance, although non-Muslims had to pay special taxes and had certain rights restricted.

38. **(C)** The Athenian Parthenon, located on the Acropolis ("high city"), served as the temple of Athena, the city's patron deity. It remains one of the best-known landmarks in Greece.

39. **(E)** Agricultural production required a great deal of organization and planning. It required manipulation of the environment, management of property, and often a high degree of social cooperation.

40. **(C)** During the reign of Alexander II (1855–1881), Russia experienced a brief period of relatively liberal rule. Alexander's series of "Great Reforms" included the emancipation of serfdom, which ended centuries of peasant bondage in Russia. Tsarist Russia never had a constitution, and only after the 1905 Revolution that nearly toppled Nicholas II from the throne was the Duma, Russia's semiparliamentary legislature, created. Anti-Semitic activity steadily worsened between the death of Alexander II and the Russian Revolution of 1917.

41. **(A)** Africa contributed gold and ivory to the Indian Ocean trade network. India was a source of salt and cotton (and also elephants). China traded porcelain and silk, among other goods. Southeast Asia took part as well, adding cinnamon and other spices; Japan was a source of silver.

42. **(B)** Following the successful reign of Kublai Khan, who adopted Chinese ways and transformed his portion of the Mongol Empire into the Yuan Empire, China was struck by the bubonic plague (which then went on to ravage the Middle East and especially Europe). The resulting economic decline led to peasant unrest. The Mongol invasions had taken place some time ago (and had, in fact, resulted in the reunification of China under Kublai Khan), and the Taiping Rebellion would not trouble China until the 1800s. The Manchus defeated the Ming in the mid-1600s; they did not lay the foundation for their takeover of China.

43. **(A)** Neither the first nor the most warlike civilization in North America, the Mississippian culture is best known for building large earth mounds. Cahokia, in what is now western Illinois, was a sizable city. No Native American tribes are known to have practiced monotheism in the pre-Columbian era. The Anasazi and other peoples of the U.S. Southwest, not the Mississippians, are famed for their cliff dwellings.

44. **(D)** The original teachings of the Buddha mainly concerned meditation, self-knowledge, and the extinguishing of human desire. They had little to say about gods, rituals, or an afterlife. The school of Buddhism that developed later, Mahayana Buddhism, popular in parts of Asia north of the religion's birthplace of India, placed a much greater emphasis on such things.

45. **(A)** The Asante, also known as the Ashanti, took an active part in the Atlantic slave trade, capturing neighboring Africans and exchanging them for gold and guns. Their military power allowed them to resist Western attacks until very late in the 1800s. The kings of Ethiopia, especially Theodore II and Menelik II, modernized and equipped their armies in the modern style. This policy paid off in 1896, when Ethiopian troops humiliated an Italian invasion force at the battle of Adowa.

46. **(E)** The Acadians, French-speaking colonists in Canada, were driven away from their homes by the British, who took over Quebec after the pivotal battle of Abraham Fields in 1759. The Acadians migrated south, many of them settling in the state of Louisiana, where their name evolved into the popular term *Cajuns*.

47. **(D)** By proving mathematically that the earth and other planets revolve around the sun, Polish astronomer Nicolaus Copernicus set into motion an intellectual earthquake. During the Scientific Revolution of the 1600s, his conclusions were confirmed by the observations of Tycho Brahe (who nonetheless did not believe in the heliocentric theory), Johannes Kepler, and Galileo. Because scientific orthodoxy and, more important, Catholic doctrine held that the sun revolved around the earth, home to humanity, God's favored creation, to support the heliocentric theory was not only controversial, it was, until the 1700s, dangerous.

48. **(B)** During the Cold War, the United States pursued a geopolitical strategy of attempting to contain Soviet expansion wherever it seemed to threaten American interests. When choosing allies and regimes to support in various parts of the world, the United States tended to focus more on whether they were anticommunist rather than on whether they ran democratic governments, allowed civil liberties, or observed human rights. Marcos was one of many authoritarian leaders who received U.S. backing during the Cold War.

49. **(E)** Both revolutions were inspired by Enlightenment ideals and political theories. The American Revolution preceded the French Revolution by more than a decade. Not only did French assistance to the American rebels worsen the financial crisis that helped bring about revolution in France, but the successful example of Americans putting Enlightenment ideals into practice helped to inspire the French Revolution. The Declaration of the Rights of Man and the Citizen drew directly upon the U.S. Declaration of Independence; the author of the latter, Thomas Jefferson, was present in Paris during the early stages of the French Revolution and helped write the French declaration.

50. **(D)** Revolutionary movements of all types, whether nationalist, communist, or anticolonial, have frequently been led by intellectuals and educated elites.

51. **(C)** Neither ancient Egypt nor the civilizations of Mesopotamia gave equal rights to the poor, and in both, males dominated the clergy. Only the Egyptians built pyramids; the Mesopotamians built ziggurats, which they used as temples, not tombs. Cuneiform was the Sumerians' system of writing; the Egyptians used hieroglyphics. They both had roughly the same system of social organization.

52. **(A)** Before industrial-era forms of transport such as railroads and highways made overland transport easy and cost-effective, it was much cheaper and more efficient to move goods and passengers by water. Therefore, most major trade routes grew up along rivers or coastlines. The Silk Road, which stretched for more than 5,000 miles between the Mediterranean and China, was remarkable in its ability to allow the transfer of goods, travelers, ideas, and new technologies over such great distances by land.

53. **(C)** Although the Atlantic slave trade was larger and remains more famous, the East African slave trade, largely run by Arab traders, played a signficant role in the life of the region and lasted until the 1800s.

54. **(D)** In the late 1400s and 1500s, countries such as China, Japan, and India were strong enough to resist Western colonial pressures. The Portuguese gained some footholds in South and Southeast Asia but, like the other Europeans who followed them, could not conquer or intimidate the larger nations of Asia. Europe did not gain that ability until the 1700s and 1800s.

55. **(C)** While the 1970s were an economically painful time for Western Europe and North America, they cannot be considered a time of severe economic depression. Unemployment and inflation rose, and the U.S. dollar was uncoupled from the gold standard, sending shock waves through the economies of the West. The oil embargo imposed by the OPEC nations caused great stress as well.

56. **(B)** Existing roughly at the same time, governing large, multiethnic empires, Han China and ancient Rome have much in common—but not the persecution of Christians or an interest in conquering the inner parts of Asia. Neither treated women as equals to men. Both were expansionist. The most obvious commonality is the way that imperial overreach—expanding their territory beyond their ability to administer and defend it—brought about an end to both empires.

57. **(A)** Middle Eastern regimes in the postwar era have tended to be authoritarian to one degree or another, ranging from mild authoritarianism to severe dictatorship. Civil liberties and human rights have not been widely observed. An economic consequence has been a general failure to distribute wealth fairly, even in the region's oil-rich states.

58. **(D)** Although Bismarck sometimes governed Germany with an iron hand, he also knew when to use positive inducements instead of outright repression. He put into effect labor laws and a social welfare system appealing enough to keep most workers from feeling that they had to join trade unions or socialist parties to improve their lot. All German males could vote, but this inducement was less significant, because the electoral system was organized in such a way as to make the vote of someone from the upper classes count for more.

59. **(A)** The great contribution of the ancient Hebrews is monotheistic worship, the veneration of only one deity. This gave birth to the Judeo-Christian tradition, still a bedrock of Western culture. Zoroastrianism, a dualistic faith, can also be said to have embraced monotheism but not as deeply as Judaism did.

60. **(C)** Despite the fact that fascism and communism are polar opposites on the ideological spectrum, many of the regimes based on them share similar features: dictatorship, rule by terror, intense propaganda, state control over the economy, and more. One noteworthy exception is their attitude toward women. Fascism tends to be opposed to gender equality, while communism embraces it. Furthermore, the superindustrialization campaigns of Soviet Russia required a large workforce, and female workers were needed just as much as male workers.

61. **(E)** The Mexican Revolution began as a people's movement, led by priests who were concerned about the lower classes. (It was completed by aristocrats with a very different view of what the new regime should look like.) Simón Bolívar, leader of the wars of independence in Spanish South America, was a liberal, constitutionally-minded member of the privileged classes. However, on principle and because he knew it was good strategy, he appealed to slaves and the lower classes as well.

62. **(A)** Mongol conquest extended to Southeast Asia during the 1200s, changing political systems and patterns of economic activity.

63. **(B)** By encouraging the use of better technology and more scientific methods of crop production, the agricultural revolution of eighteenth-century Europe increased yields, made crop failures rarer, and caused the rate of population growth to increase. It did not eliminate poverty or by itself cause political or social upheaval.

64. **(D)** Economic cooperation and the removal of obstacles to free trade were seen as ways to boost European prosperity and economic clout after World War II, which had badly damaged all European economies, even those of the victorious nations.

65. **(C)** Spain lost the Spanish-American War decisively, and its status as a colonial power steeply declined as a result. The United States took Puerto Rico, Cuba, the Philippines, and other colonial possessions from it—in effect, becoming an imperial power itself.

66. **(B)** Both in Rhodesia and South Africa, the population that won independence from Britain was governed not by blacks but by whites. In each case, racial tensions between the white governments and the native black populations led to political turmoil: violence and civil war in the case of Rhodesia (which became Zimbabwe after the overthrow of the white regime) and the prolongation of the apartheid system in South Africa until the 1990s.

67. **(C)** Until far too late, the Qing regime in China remained oblivious to the need to Westernize and modernize if it wanted to stay free of foreign domination. Although it was never technically colonized, China lost territory to the Western powers and was forced to grant them tremendous concessions. Upon the accession of the Emperor Meiji in 1868, Japan pursued a course of active Westernization, focusing especially on industrial buildup and military modernization.

68. **(B)** The Declaration of the Rights of Man and the Citizen was a statement of the core beliefs of the French Revolution, as well as the instrument that put them into political effect. It was a product of Enlightenment philosophy, political action, and influence from American revolutionaries.

69. **(B)** All three of these groups were considered by the Nazis to be "subhuman" and therefore "undesirable."

70. **(D)** Although Europe eventually came to use gunpowder weaponry more efficiently and more systematically than any other civilization, it took a number of years to achieve domination. In the meantime, other cultures—the Ottomans and the Mughal Indians among them—used gunpowder weapons effectively as well.

Appendix: Map of Selected World Regions

Selected World Regions

Caribbean islands

North Africa

West Africa

East Africa

Central Africa

Southern Africa

Middle East

East Asia

Southeast Asia

South Asia

Latin America, including regions
of Mesoamerica and the Caribbean

Index

NOTES

NOTES

NOTES

NOTES

NOTES